Speech-hearing Tests
and the Spoken Language
of Hearing-impaired Children

Dedication

For Pierre Gorman: to acknowledge his
encouragement and his suggestion that
the spoken language of the hearing-
impaired child would repay
investigation.

Speech-hearing Tests and the Spoken Language of Hearing-impaired Children

Edited by

JOHN BENCH

School of Communication Disorders,
Lincoln Institute,
Carlton, Victoria, Australia

and

JOHN BAMFORD

Audiology Unit,
Royal Berkshire Hospital,
Reading, England

1979

ACADEMIC PRESS
London · New York · San Francisco

A Subsidiary of Harcourt Brace Jovanovich, Publishers

ACADEMIC PRESS INC. (LONDON) LTD.
24/28 Oval Road
London NW1

United States Edition published by
ACADEMIC PRESS INC.
111 Fifth Avenue
New York, New York 10003

British Library Cataloguing in Publication Data
Speech-hearing tests and the spoken language of hearing-impaired children.
  1. Children, Deaf – Language
  2. English language – Spoken English
  I. Bench, John   II. Bamford, John
  428′.3   HV2471   78-75277
  ISBN 0-12-088450-X

Printed in Great Britain by
Butler & Tanner Ltd, Frome and London

List of Contributors

J. M. BAMFORD, *Audiology Unit, Royal Berkshire Hospital, Reading, Berkshire, RG1 5AN, England*

R. J. BENCH*, *School of Communication Disorders, Lincoln Institute, 625 Swanston Street, Carlton, Victoria 3053, Australia*

Å. KOWAL, *Audiology Unit, Royal Berkshire Hospital, Reading, Berkshire, RG1 5AN, England*

D. L. MENTZ*, *The Arts Support Research Unit, Arts E, University of Sussex, Falmer, Brighton, Sussex, BN1 9RH, England*

I. M. WILSON, *Department of Applied Statistics, University of Reading, Whiteknights, Reading, Berkshire, RG6 2AH, England*

* Formerly at: Audiology Unit, Royal Berkshire Hospital, Reading, Berkshire, England.

Foreword

When I first began work with deaf children my researches were concerned
with the relationship between auditory state, intelligence and various academic skills. The work involved visiting most of the schools for deaf children
in England, Wales and Ireland and, in practically every school I visited, concern was expressed by teachers about the then current audiometric procedures. During the intervening years, pressure has grown for the development of a test which will identify speech discrimination skills in language
structures which do not of themselves militate against success. Sentence and
word lists for speech audiometry have been in existence for some years, but
it was widely felt that their semantic and syntactic content tended to depress
scores independent of factors concerned directly with hearing ability.

After considerable discussion in the department, we began to examine the
feasibility of recording partially-hearing children's own utterances. These
utterances would be analysed for linguistic function and, based upon the information derived, a series of audiometric test sentences would be constructed which could then be standardized.

John Bench and his colleagues, supported by a grant we had obtained from
the Medical Research Council, worked for three years and amassed a huge
amount of material. Hearing-impaired children were visited in schools and
asked to describe the activities in a series of specially-chosen coloured
pictures. These verbal descriptions were tape-recorded and subsequently
transcribed for analysis.

This book describes and discusses in detail the subjects, procedures,
analyses, and results of the research. The primary outcome—balanced lists
of sentences for speech audiometry with children—is presented in written
form in Appendixes 1 and 2, while Part I of the book describes the procedures
and analyses directly concerned with this outcome. In Part II, the data on

the grammar and vocabulary of the children studied are presented in detail in their own right. As such, they help to fulfil a series of secondary aims of the research, which were concerned with expanding our rather scant knowledge of the effects of hearing-impairment on certain aspects of language development.

Readers of this book will obviously make their own selections from it. The researcher will want to read it all and may use much of the immaculately presented information as a basis for other work. The teacher, audiologist or speech therapist interested in partially-hearing children will find the first section valuable and fascinating reading.

I am probably biased because of my early association with the preliminary planning of the research, but I must express my admiration for the rest of the work, with which I was minimally involved. It is a considerable piece of scholarship, meticulously planned and executed, clearly set out, well organized and put together. The authors are to be congratulated.

February 1979   K. P. MURPHY

Preface

It is often argued that if hearing-impaired children are given adequate help with hearing aids and are also given continuous and guided exposure to natural language, then most of them will be able to acquire normal linguistic skills and reasonably normal speech. However, it is also widely agreed that by no means all hearing-impaired children do reach such a level of achievement, even when their hearing loss is less than profound. The reasons for this situation are a continuing topic for discussion, not least because there are insufficient tests for assessing how much of "natural" language can be perceived by a hearing-impaired child.

This book reports on the work of a group of researchers based at the Royal Berkshire Hospital, Reading, whose members set out to devise tests for assessing aspects of the partially-hearing child's ability to perceive "natural" language. Some profoundly deaf children were assessed as a small part of this work, hence the use of "Hearing-impaired" in the title of the book instead of "Partially-hearing".

We were especially concerned to devise tests of hearing for connected-speech, which would largely be free from artefacts arising from different levels of familiarity on the part of hearing-impaired child listeners with such linguistic factors as grammar and vocabulary. To this end, we recorded the spoken language of a large number of such children, analysed its linguistic content, and used the results of this analysis as a basis for test construction. Thus the tests were devised from the spoken language of the kind of children for whom the tests were intended. However they are essentially tests of hearing rather than of linguistic ability.

The goal of our research was, therefore, rather specific, and was attained by the production of lists of short sentences (the BKB—Bamford–Kowal–Bench—Sentence Lists for children) which we feel come close to meeting the need for tests of the partially-hearing child's ability to perceive connected-speech, while obviating difficulties associated with the familiarity of the test materials. The sentence lists are given in appendices at the end of this book.

They are of two types: the Standard Test, consisting of 21 lists, each containing 16 sentences and 50 key words; and the Picture-related Test, consisting of 11 lists, each also containing 16 sentences and 50 key words, but designed to be administered in conjunction with a set of coloured pictures, to which the sentences closely relate. Both the Standard and the Picture-related Tests are available, recorded by a female speaker, on magnetic tape (see below).

The book has been written in two parts. In Part I, the audiological and audiometric background is discussed first, followed by chapters which review existing studies of the spoken language of partially-hearing children, describe the design of our field studies whereby we collected our own spoken language material, explain how we used this material to construct our lists of sentences, and discuss the pilot testing, modification and reliability of our sentence lists. In Part II, the spoken language samples of our hearing-impaired children are analysed in greater detail than was necessary for the construction of the sentence lists described in Part I. This detailed analysis, which consists of a description of the hearing-impaired child's vocabulary and grammatical abilities (but not semantic skills), has been included because the information obtained does not exist elsewhere, and is likely to be of use to a great many clinicians, educators and others who work with hearing-impaired children, and who require a compendium of linguistic data on which to draw in preparing, for example, teaching materials.

Besides teachers and such clinicians as otologists, audiologists and speech pathologists, the book contains material which we hope will be of interest to the applied psychologist and the applied linguist, especially as regards Part II.

On a cautionary note, the reader should remember that language tends in part to reflect educational approaches, perhaps especially where the hearing-impaired child is concerned. Such approaches will change over the years with developments in education, and hence aspects of child language may be affected concomitantly. This means that the younger children in our study sample may not necessarily be taken as an age control for the older children;

As the study was nearing completion, J. Bench left the UK to take up a position at the Lincoln Institute, Victoria, Australia, whence part of his editorial function has been conducted. Naturally, readers in Australia will be interested to learn how the material reported in this book relates to the Australian scene. It would appear that generally this material has a high validity for Australia: the standard form of English used in Australia seems for many aspects to lie somewhere between the standard English of the UK and the standard English of the USA, but closer to the former than the latter. The Australian reader will also be interested to learn that an Australian version (BKB/A) of the Standard BKB Sentence Lists has been prepared by J. Bench with the help of a research grant from Lincoln Institute. This Australian version contains some changes to the original vocabulary and hence to the semantics. Printed copies of the BKB/A Sentence Lists may be obtained on application to him at Lincoln Institute.

i.e. the performance of the younger children should not be assumed to be a "younger" version of the performance of the older children.

Tape recordings of the Sentence Lists may be obtained from:

> The Audiology Unit (Tape recordings),
> Royal Berkshire Hospital,
> Reading,
> Berkshire,
> RG1 5AN,
> England

February 1979   JOHN BENCH

                                                     JOHN BAMFORD

Acknowledgements

Our grateful thanks are due to a large number of people who helped and advised us when we were carrying out the work on which this book is based. It is not possible to mention them all by name, and therefore we have had to limit these acknowledgements to those who particularly went out of their way in assisting us, or to groups and institutions. Thus we are grateful to the Berkshire Area Health Authority (West District) for accommodating and administering the project staff, and especially to Mr T. Heyworth, Consultant Otologist, Mr R. J. Childs of the Area Transport Department and Mr A. Taylor of the Finance Department. Most of the supporting funds were provided by the UK Medical Research Council under Project Grant G.975/245/N. Access to hearing-impaired children at a variety of schools was kindly approved by the Departments of Education/County Education Officers and the Organizing Teachers of the Deaf of Berkshire, Hampshire, Buckinghamshire, Hertfordshire, Surrey and Oxfordshire, the Surrey Area Health Authority (South-west Surrey District), the Research Group of the Inner London Education Authority, and the Headmasters of some independent schools. The Principals and staff at all the schools we visited were unfailingly helpful, as were the pupils. A list of schools visited is given in Appendix 4.

We received much help and advice from Professor D. Crystal, Dr P. Fletcher and Dr M. Garman, Department of Linguistic Science, University of Reading; Dr Sarah Cotter, Department of Applied Statistics, University of Reading; Mrs Betty Root of the Reading Centre; the staff of the Reading University Computer Unit; and Professor A. Fourcin, Dr Evelyn Abberton, Suzanna Evershed and Ann Parker, Department of Phonetics and Linguistics, University College, London.

Vivien Keith, Kate Kingsley-Hall, Anne Kingston and Angela Morrison spent many tedious hours transcribing speech material from electromagnetic tapes, and Carolyn Webb subsequently analysed the transcripts according to LARSP.

Having prepared our lists of sentences in draft, comments were sought and gratefully received from Mary Auckland, Professor D. B. Fry, Mr T. Heyworth, Dr K. P. Murphy, Mr F. Priddle, Mr J. P. Simpson, Dr T. J. Watson and Jane Welsh. The revised sentence lists and other material were recorded with the voice of Carolyn Webb and the technical assistance of Mr T. Dowding and Mr T. Watson.

Joan Slater put in many hours of hard work in typing the research protocols and data sheets, and cheerfully undertook the typing of the manuscript for this book. Mr L. Williams of the Royal Berkshire Hospital Department of Medical Photography assisted with the illustrations.

Of the many people who assisted with data collection and analysis we would like to thank particularly Liz Edmunds and Lynn Weatherby.

Permission to reproduce the pictures used for eliciting speech was kindly granted by CUES/Learning Materials Service, ILEA, MacDonald Educational Ltd, and Developmental Learning Materials, Niles, Illinois (sole UK distributors are Taskmaster Ltd, Morris Road, Clarendon Park, Leicester). Figures 1 and 2 (Chapter 7) are the copyright of Edward Arnold Ltd, and are reproduced with their permission.

Contents

Part I
The Design and Construction of Sentences for Speech-hearing Assessment

Part I

The Design and Construction of Sentences for Speech-hearing Assessment

1

Background to the Study

JOHN BENCH AND JOHN BAMFORD

I. Introduction

Since most publications relating to the audiological, otological, psychological and educational assessment and remediation of the hearing-impaired
child contain references to expressive and receptive language problems

(e.g. Myklebust, 1960), the professional worker needs no reminder of the importance of such problems. However, in writing this account of our own approach to these problems we have felt a need for a modest summary, and we hope that it will prove useful to the reader who does not work with such children.

This chapter falls into three main sections. These are:

II. a short review of the language problems of the hearing-impaired child;

III. a discussion of the need, design and use of tests for the assessment of hearing for speech; and

IV. a guide to the organization of the remainder of this book.

The first of these describes the background to the problems to which this book is addressed. The second outlines the need for speech audiometric tests and the problems associated with their design and use, with special reference to sentence tests and the assessment of children. The third section is intended as a guide to help the reader to follow the rationale adopted in presenting the material in the rest of the book.

II. The language problems of the hearing-impaired child

A language may be briefly defined as a socially recognizable code for conveying messages and consists of a rule-governed system of symbols (Lewis, 1968), in which each symbol has a systematic relation to each other symbol. These interlocking symbols permit the generation of messages (Carroll, 1964). Moreover, a language allows the production of an infinite number of novel sentences which, though not previously generated, will still be understood by another user of the same language, and requires a distinction between a surface structure which describes its (spoken or written) form and a deep structure which decides its meaning (Chomsky, 1971). Language is usually taken to refer to verbal language (i.e. language which is spoken, written, heard or read), but other kinds of languages are also employed, notably by handicapped persons. Thus tactile devices (Gault, 1936) have been investigated with a view to use by the hearing-impaired, who may also employ a number of gesture or sign languages. We are aware that the status of sign languages as "full languages" may be questioned, because although sign languages conform to the first parts of the brief definition of a language which we have given above, and can cope with syntactical arrangements, transformational rules and many semantic aspects (Stokoe, 1958), there may be some doubt as to whether they are fully as productive as the verbal languages, and as sophisticated in requiring so many distinctions between surface and deep structure. An up-to-date and very readable assessment of attempts to answer the question of "What is language?" will be found in Cohen (1977).

Normally-hearing children acquire verbal language by continual auditory/vocal interaction with other people around them. They do this by listening and replying to the speech of their parents and their peers, and the resulting language acquisition is apparently effortless. In view of the enormous task of assimilating such aspects of language as grammar, prosody, vocabulary and semantics, not to mention the acquisition of phonetic and other skills, into a consistent and coherent body of language, the child's achievement is astonishing, as many have pointed out. Moreover, normal language acquisition appears to progress smoothly, without any obvious differentiation of its separate aspects (Herriot, 1970) which develop in close association, though there is some controversy about both the nature of the interactions between the aspects and their relative importance (Chomsky, 1971; Morton, 1971), and about the treatment of such conditions as memory limitation, errors, distractions and shifts of interest (Wold, 1978). It is thus only in cases of abnormal language development that various aspects may appear out of phase (Suci, 1969).

With the exceptions of intonation (Cruttendon, 1974), the combination of sentences into continuous discourse (Lenneberg, 1967) and vocabulary, whose acquisition takes many years, much of language acquisition is essentially complete well before the child begins school (McNeill, 1966; Menyuk, 1971; Dale, 1972; Brown, 1973). Sentences with complete internal clause structure are formed by the child of three years of age who thus possesses sufficient syntactic ability to communicate his everyday needs. It has been argued that deprivation of auditory experiences early in life because of impaired hearing or other cause has long-lasting, deleterious and possibly irreversible effects on the development of speech and language (Tervoort, 1965; Lenneberg, 1967, pp. 175–178; Northern and Downs, 1974, pp. 71–74), and hence the early years are critical linguistically. The usefulness of the critical period concept has been criticized, however (Bench, 1971), and remains controversial (Northern and Downs, 1974; Bench, 1978). We shall not discuss it further here.

Since language is usually acquired by listening to and speaking with other language users, i.e. through aural and oral mediation, it follows that hearing and speech defects are likely to interfere with the normal acquisition of language, and the greater the defect, the greater will be the impairment in the development of language. In the case of hearing impairment, most severely deaf children are markedly handicapped in both language reception and expression. In the case of the latter, they incur a double disadvantage because they are handicapped not only by their poor development of "inner" or mediational language (Vigotsky, 1939; Conrad, 1970), but also by poor control of the intonation of their speech, occasioned largely by their reduced ability to monitor properly the sounds of their voices. This poor control of intonation then impairs the social interaction necessary for language to develop further. Although the linguistic potential of a hearing-impaired child is equivalent at birth (in the absence of other pathology) to that of normally-hearing children, without special teaching his language performance tends to fall progressively with age behind that of the normal child, because language development is dependent on experience as well as biological potential. This holds even where the child achieves considerable skills in acquiring a sign language, because sign languages are much more limited in scope than spoken languages (Rutter, 1972), although recent attempts have been made to increase their scope and flexibility (Bornstein, 1974).

If linguistic abilities do not come naturally to the hearing-impaired child by the relatively effortless acquisition or latent learning through social interaction mentioned above, it follows that they must be taught, and that such a child must be active in learning rather than passive in acquiring them. This distinction could prepare the way for a discussion of teaching methods, but since the topic of teaching methods is not relevant to this book (all the children whom we investigated were taught formally by oral methods), and since in any case teaching methods have been discussed widely elsewhere (e.g. Wolff, 1973), we are content to forgo the opportunity to indulge in the continuing "oral vs. manual" debate.

We have now briefly outlined the nature of language for the normally-hearing individual and have discussed some of the reasons why the hearing-impaired child is confronted with a language problem. We could end this Section here, especially as this book is concerned with the partially-hearing child, whose language development, though characterized by retardation and possibly other factors as discussed in later chapters, roughly approximates to that of the normally-hearing child. However, we have written almost nothing which relates to the child who is profoundly deaf from a very early age and who has not been taught verbal or any other language. Such a child represents, of course, a limiting case, antithetical to the normally-hearing child, on the dimension of language ability. It may be useful to consider such a deaf child because, firstly, his case illustrates some of the general issues which occur in a discussion of language difficulties; secondly, because he provides an extreme example when considering how communication may develop in the absence of the normal acquisition of language; thirdly, because he provides a yardstick against which success in learning verbal language as a means of communication may be assessed; and, fourthly, because his case provides evidence on the question of whether the language problem for a hearing-impaired child is a problem of verbal language in particular or of language in general.

A convenient reference illustrating some of these points is to be found in the work of Heider and Heider (1941). The Heiders' work was unique in the systematic way in which they assessed aspects of communicative behaviour and in the implications of their findings. The Heiders studied 14 deaf (effectively profoundly deaf) children at the Clarke School for the Deaf as two groups of seven children with average ages of four years nine months and five years eleven months; and 34 hearing children as two groups of 18 and 16 children with mean ages of four years three months and three years ten months. The different groups arose from different lengths of schooling or different home backgrounds. The technique was to observe each child in free play in his group, recording by the minute what he did and said, after the children had been members of their groups for several weeks. Hence deaf children were recorded in interaction with other deaf children and hearing adults, while the hearing children were recorded in interaction with other hearing children and hearing adults. In addition to the observers' written record, short motion pictures were made of pairs of the deaf children, because the meaning associated with the deaf child's activity was often inferred from gestures and facial expression, which required motion picture analysis for its detailed record.

Early in their account, the Heiders list and describe the tools or means by which their deaf children communicated, which were rather different from conventional signs and symbolic gestures, and whose meaning was ascertained with reference to the social context in which they were produced. The tools seem to have been spontaneously acquired rather than deliberately learned.

The Heiders argued from observations of the use of linguistic tools, mainly of the gestural type, that while some of the tools served genuine symbolic functions, the more usual means of communication by their young deaf children were pointing and expressive movements. Communication relied on the context, and especially on the social context, to a far greater degree than would be found in normally-hearing children and presumably in partially-hearing children, except for those severe partials who fail to develop adequate verbal language. Some of the gestures were used globally in the sense that their meaning could not be analysed into the equivalents of single words, but in other instances gestures were combined "syntactically" to give a phrase or sentence structure, at a stage of linguistic development formed in normally-hearing children aged two to two and a half years of age. The language functions differentiated from their observational records by the Heiders were expression, evocation and representation. In the light of the foregoing remarks, it is clear that expression and evocation were used the most commonly, and representation was used less frequently, but was within the children's linguistic performance.

If we can assume that the gestural language of the Heiders' deaf children had largely been acquired passively, rather than deliberately taught and learned, as seems fairly likely, then the Heiders' report is reassuring in the sense that deaf children, with apparently little or no useful hearing (i.e. profoundly deaf), would seem naturally able to perform at a linguistic level equivalent to that observed for the two-and-a-half-year-old normally-hearing child, and, although it is only proper to emphasize the importance of the acquisition of verbal language, it is as well to recognize that non-verbal gestural language can apparently progress to the level of elementary syntax without specific direction. In other words, although it is important to stress that the hearing-impaired child has a severe problem in the acquisition of language, this problem seems specific to verbal language, and not to language in general.

Surprisingly, this point seems to have become widely appreciated only fairly recently. Thus, even as late as the mid 1960s, researchers working on the relationship between language and cognition (Myklebust, 1964; Furth, 1966) were tending to argue that prelingually profoundly deaf children could act as a language-less group. Specifically they developed the theme that if the deaf were lacking in language, they should perform poorly in problem solving, thinking and other cognitive tasks. As work based on this hypothesis produced data showing, by and large, that the prelingually profoundly deaf performed at similar levels to normally-hearing persons in cognitive tasks which were not particularly influenced by verbal language (e.g. Furth, 1971; Youniss *et al.*, 1971; Furth and Youniss, 1975), it became apparent that cognitive functioning was possible in the seemingly "language-less" deaf.

Hence, despite the indications from the early work of the Heiders (1941), it is only fairly recently (Bellugi, 1970; Stokoe, 1972; Woodward, 1973; Cohen, 1977) that gestural and signing methods of communication have been proposed as valid languages with their own vocabulary, syntax and semantics. We have already concluded that groups of deaf children will develop gestural languages of their own, and Charrow (1975) has stated that every deaf child has some means of communication, which does not have to be the accepted (verbal) language of his society nor an accepted standard sign language, though it has to be recognized that a "means of communication" may not deserve the designation of a "language" (see above).

Charrow (1975) has also argued that standard English is not the deaf person's native language. Because the prelingually profoundly deaf cannot hear the natural language of their society, they cannot acquire it spontaneously, but have to learn it with protracted effort in schooling; they make syntactical errors which the normally-hearing do not make; they produce the quaint expressions commonly referred to as "deafisms"; and their ultimate performance in reading and writing is poor. The result is "Deaf English", a variant of standard English which tends to crystallize in the same way as do pidgin languages in the teen years. On the basis of published work we do not know whether partially-hearing children also use "Deaf English" to an appreciable degree, but the later chapters in this book may go some way to answering this question. Charrow referred to "Deaf English" as a dialect of English, but this view has been queried by Russell *et al.* (1976, pp. 200–201) on the grounds that the language problem of deaf children is much more complex than one of a simple dialect. Moreover, it should be noted that Charrow's views are concerned with the deaf who have been taught sign language as a first language, and thus standard verbal English is for such persons a *de facto* second language, unless perhaps the sign language is linguistically isomorphic with standard English.

We have chosen to make special mention of the work of Heider and Heider (1941) and of Charrow (1975) because of the illuminating insights which their studies offer on the nature of language and communication. Thus, the Heiders showed some years ago that in the virtual absence of verbal language, profoundly deaf children are nonetheless able to develop a symbolic communication system which, as it contains, even if only at an elementary level, such aspects as vocabulary, syntax and semantics, deserves to be called a "language". The importance of this finding is that it shows that the need for language is very strong indeed, and hence the motivation to develop language, even in the absence of useful hearing, is very powerful. The problem for the educator or therapist is not therefore how to instill in the hearing-impaired child a desire to acquire language, but how to teach that particular language which has the greatest social utility, namely verbal language.

For children with chronic hearing loss of greater than, say, 40 dB, who are suitable cases for aural rehabilitation, it is often the case that their hearing impairment will not receive a reasonable degree of rehabilitation until the age of two to five years, and even then the aural rehabilitation is unlikely to equate to normal hearing. Thus most partially-hearing and all profoundly deaf children will be deficient in hearing for language at the time when normally-hearing children are rapidly acquiring it. Because they still have a need to communicate, they are likely to rely more on gestures than the normally-hearing child, and these gestures will have a linguistic function. The report of Heider and Heider (1941) who referred to the profoundly deaf child, may thus have some direct bearing on the language development of partially-hearing children, though it will be a task for future research to indicate just how important is the role of gesture for such children, and whether it is of the same type as that described for the profoundly deaf child.

III. The assessment of hearing

A. The function of audiometric tests

Since impairment of hearing has such a deleterious effect on the verbal language performance of children, particularly if the onset of the impairment is in the child's first few years, it is frequently necessary for clinical and educational reasons, to assess the nature and the degree of the impairment. Audiometric tests have been designed to provide such assessments. The audiologist has at his disposal a battery of tests, each with its own advantages and disadvantages, with which to test a patient. Some tests relate to an overall assessment of hearing performance, while others offer a prospect for differential diagnosis, namely the diagnosis of dysfunctions in different parts of the auditory system. Some tests, such as the widely-used pure tone test, require that the listener "understands" and actively participates in the task while others, impedance audiometry for example, do not. The results of audiometric tests are used not only to assess hearing level and to aid differential diagnosis, but to suggest possible methods of treatment, to monitor the rehabilitation of the patient, to guide correct educational placement if the patient is of school age, and so on.

B. The assessment of hearing for speech

When assessing the hearing level and its effect upon speech perception, it is not enough to use tests which reflect principally the functioning of the end organ and the peripheral-neural parts of the system in response to simple stimuli such as pure tones and clicks. Such tests are not necessarily good predictors of the patient's ability to hear speech, for this ability may not only be differentially affected by the anatomical site of the lesion, but perhaps more importantly, it will depend upon a whole series of variables—age at onset of the hearing loss, age at diagnosis, degree of linguistic attainment, amount of auditory training, and so on—which reflect the degree of exposure to normal language and are different in quality from those variables concerned simply with the input side of the system. Given a degree of impairment of the end organ and peripheral auditory tract, the use that is made of the resulting reduced and/or distorted input by the higher cognitive processes will vary from patient to patient. It is therefore not surprising that, for example, Harris *et al.* (1956) examined several methods of relating pure tone hearing loss to the speech-hearing threshold for lists of words, and concluded that no one system completely predicted speech-hearing ability.

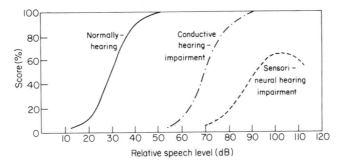

Fig. 1   Schematic speech audiograms according to type of hearing loss.

To satisfy the need for assessments of speech-hearing ability, the audiologist has turned to the so-called speech audiometry tests, in which the stimuli are lists of spoken words or (less usually) sentences. The patient is required to repeat back each item (i.e. word or sentence) immediately following its presentation. Functions can be derived under specified stimulus conditions relating the percentage of correct responses (scored in terms of whole sentences, key words, phonemes, or whatever) to the relative intensity of the speech signal. Changes in the shape and/or position of the functions may occur with different stimulus conditions (e.g. signal/noise ratio, hearing aided/unaided, and so on) and these changes may be useful in both diagnosis and remediation.

Figure 1 illustrates schematically a function for a normally-hearing person assessed in the quiet and compares it with the function for a patient with a purely conductive loss, in which the input signal is linearly attenuated by the middle ear (i.e. equally attenuated across all audio-frequencies), the effect being to shift the curve uniformly to the right; and with the function for a patient with a sensori-neural hearing loss, in which the input signal is attenuated in a non-linear fashion (i.e. distorted), altering the basic sigmoidal shape of the curve, as well as displacing it to the right.

These functions relating the percentage reported correctly, or the intelligibility score, to the speech level are known as speech audiograms. Other common or fairly common names are speech intelligibility curves, discrimination curves, articulation functions, and performance–intensity functions. The speech level itself is usually referred to as the *relative* speech level for reasons that are discussed in Chapter 5 (particularly Section IV: Electro-acoustic and Subjective Calibration). The speech intelligibility threshold (SIT) is that speech level at which a specified proportion of the speech is correctly reported according to a chosen scoring method. Fifty per cent is the proportion in most frequent use. Coles *et al.* (1973) suggest instead the use of the Half Peak Level (HPL)—half the maximum score, which recognizes that the maximum score may be less than 100%. The maximum score obtained at the peak performance level is itself called the optimum intelligibility score (OIS). For the "normally-hearing curve" and the "conductive loss curve" in Fig. 1 the OIS would in both cases be 100% or thereabouts, but the OIS for the "sensorineural curve" is only 64%. The HPLs would be taken at 50%, 50% and 32% intelligibility scores respectively. The difference between OIS and the maximum possible (100%) is often referred to as the intelligibility (discrimination) loss.

Despite certain limitations (Coles *et al.*, 1973) speech audiometry tests have a measurable and generally acceptable reliability, and a generally acceptable face validity. Perhaps their greatest potential is in the rehabilitation field—in monitoring progress on an auditory training scheme, helping to select the most appropriate hearing aid, and so on—but a recent statement (personal communication) by a consultant otologist illustrates that speech tests can also be useful at earlier stages: "As a clinician, I treat hearing-impaired children thus: firstly, what is the diagnosis? Secondly, what is the hearing level and how does this affect the patient's ability to understand and reproduce language? Thirdly, having taken these two factors into account, what is the best method of treatment (surgery, hearing aid, etc., and if a hearing aid is to be chosen, what type, power, etc.)? Finally, how can I advise on the best educational placement?" Taking each point in turn, speech tests are useful in diagnosis—helping to distinguish between VIIIth nerve and cochlear patterns of dysfunction, for example (Jerger and Jerger, 1967), in obtaining a reliable indication of a patient's ability to understand and reproduce aspects of language, in deciding on the appropriate treatment, particularly in helping to choose between possible hearing aids, though this is a controversial area, and in educational placement, where the aim may be to arrive at homogeneous groups or "balanced mixes" of pupils, at least as far as the underlying hearing handicap is concerned.

We have noted that two sorts of speech tests are used in conventional speech audiometry: lists of words (spondees, monosyllabic CVCs, etc.), and, less commonly, lists of sentences. Very recently, developments in acoustic phonetics have permitted the use of computer-synthesized material with an emphasis on distinctive features (Fourcin, 1978). In all three cases, a test will usually consist of several lists, and each list will consist of several items, be they words or sentences. Different lists are presented at different relative hearing levels and the score obtained on each list establishes one point on the percentage correct/relative hearing level function (the speech audiogram, see Fig. 1). Word lists are often "phonemically balanced", that is, the test material is selected to reflect the phonemic composition of everyday speech, such that the different phonemes appear in the test lists in the same proportions as in everyday speech. It is argued that this type of balancing is necessary for test validity, since if a listener were totally unable to perceive a particular phoneme which in natural language occurs only infrequently, his handicap (which the score on a test is supposed to indicate) is less than if the phoneme had been a more common one. The very marked grammatical and semantic constraints inherent in sentences lessen the relevance of this type of balancing in sentence lists. In any case, the value of phonemic balancing has been called into question (Lyregaard *et al.*, 1976). Undoubtedly more important in speech audiometry, where lists need to be interchangeable, is what Lyregaard *et al.* call phonemic equalization, although this is sometimes confused with phonemic balance. Phonemic equalization implies that the relative occurrence of phonemes in each list should be balanced with those in every other list. This equalization is a feature of word lists, though again the linguistic and sequential factors occurring in sentences diminish its importance in sentence lists. The goal, list interchangeability, remains crucial for both word and sentence lists, but for sentences this will depend more upon equalization across lists of such factors as sentence length and structure, and word-frequency effects, than on phoneme equalization.

C. Existing speech audiometric tests

Table I shows the principal speech audiometry tests available in the UK. For a discussion of the development of these tests, the reader is referred to Lyregaard *et al.* (1976).

Table I.	The principal speech audiometry tests available in the UK prior to the current project. (From Lyregaard et al., 1976)

Name of test	Type of material	Reference	No. of items per list	No. of lists
MRC Word Lists	Phonemically balanced monosyllables	MRC (1947)	25 mono-syllables	40
Fry Word Lists	Phonemically balanced monosyllables	Fry (1961)	30 CVCs+ 5 CV/VCs= 100 phonemes	10
Fry Sentence Lists	Sentences	Fry (1961)	25 sentences (100 key words)	10
Boothroyd Word Lists	Iso-phonemic monosyllables	Boothroyd (1968)	10 CVCs (30 phonemes)	15
Manchester Sentence Test	(Simple) sentences	Univ. of Manchester	10 sentences (+1 practice)	5
Manchester Sentence Test	Sentences	Univ. of Manchester	10 sentences	5

The two Manchester sentence tests, one containing short, simple sentences, the other longer, complex and often obscure sentences, have not been recorded and are presumably intended for live-voice presentation. Live-voice presentation, although perhaps more suitable for young children or children who are difficult to test, is not very satisfactory since even with practised speakers some measure of control over the expression of the material is lost, and reliability becomes doubtful and difficult to measure. Furthermore, the Manchester tests are not readily available in print.

Pioneering work on speech tests was carried out in the USA chiefly at the Bell Telephone Laboratories and later at the Psychoacoustic Laboratory, Harvard University. The main impetus for this work was the need to rate the quality of communication systems, but after the Second World War some of the tests developed were found to be particularly suited to determining the threshold of hearing for speech. The Harvard PB-50 word lists in particular were later modified and improved at the Central Institute for the Deaf (Hirsh et al., 1952). The resulting test, labelled W-22, consists of monosyllabic

Table II. Speech audiometry tests from the USA. The earlier tests are no longer widely used

Year	Name of test	Reference	Type of material	No. of items per list	No. of lists
1962	Western Electric 4A, 4B and 4C	Fletcher and Steinberg (1929), Hudgins *et al.* (1947)	Digits in groups of 2 or 3	36	1
1944	PB-50	Egan (1944)	Monosyllabic words in carrier sentence	50	20
1944	Auditory Test No. 9	Egan (1944), Hudgins *et al.* (1947)	Spondees in carrier sentence	42	2
1944	Auditory Test No. 14	Egan (1944), Hudgins *et al.* (1947)	Spondees in carrier sentence	42	2
1952	CID-W1	Hirsh *et al.* (1952)	Spondees in carrier sentence	36	1
1952	CID-W2	Hirsh *et al.* (1952)	Spondees in carrier sentence	36	1
1952	CID-W22	Hirsh *et al.* (1952)	Monosyllabic words	50	4
1958	Rhyme Test	Fairbanks (1958), Kreul *et al.* (1968)	Monosyllabic words (forced choice test)	50	5
1962	Staggered Spondaic Word Test (SSW)	Katz (1962)	Spondees	40	1
1963	NU No. 4	Tillman *et al.* (1963)	CNC words	50	2
1965	Synthetic Sentence Identific-ation Test (SSI)	Speaks and Jerger (1965)	Controlled-redundancy sentences	10	24
1966	NU No. 6	Tillman *et al.* (1966)	CNC words	50	4
1969	—	Davis and Silverman (1970)	Everyday speech sentences vary-ing in length	10 (50 key words)	10

words and is widely used in the USA. Hirsh *et al.* also developed the W1 and W2 tests from earlier Harvard tests; these consist of spondee words (i.e. bisyllabic words, with equal stress given to both syllables) conveyed in a carrier sentence. Table II, adapted from Lyregaard *et al.* (1976), shows the more important speech audiometry tests from the USA. It will be noticed that only two of the tests use sentences for stimulus items.

Our primary concern in this book is with valid and reliable speech audiometric tests for clinical and educational use. There are, however, some areas of study, particularly research, in which speech stimuli are used extensively, but in these areas it is often the case that the investigator will construct his own speech material or adapt existing material to his own specific needs. Jerger *et al.* (1966), for example, constructed their own sentence intelligibility material to examine the assumptions upon which hearing-aid selection is based. Such one-off tests have not been included in Tables I or II, since they have not been designed or published for general use. Occasionally material originally designed for a specific piece of research does come into wider use, if only for other specialized work. Such is the case with the Synthetic Sentence Identification Test (SSI) and the Staggered Spondaic Word Test (SSW), both of which are listed in Table II. However, neither test is used in the clinic for threshold testing; they tend instead to be used in audiological research, particularly in the investigation of central auditory dysfunction. This is a fast-growing research area, where speech stimuli play a crucial role precisely because central dysfunctions tend to have their greatest effects on speech. The needs of the investigators in this work are rather specialized, since they are interested not in thresholds *per se* but in the effect upon supra-threshold speech perception of such manipulations as time-compression, filtering, alternate binaural presentation, etc., and existing speech tests are rarely suitable. For an up-to-date evaluation of the use of speech stimuli in the investigation of central auditory dysfunctions the reader is referred to Keith (1977).

D. A comparison of word lists and sentence lists

The great advantage of word tests over sentence tests is that of speed of administration. If we need, say, five data points in order to be able to draw a speech audiogram with reasonable accuracy and reliability, it might take only 10 minutes to do so using, say, Boothroyd's word lists, but half an hour or so to do the same using Fry's sentence lists. In the latter case we have to guard against fatigue effects which may contaminate the patient's scores (of all the tests listed in Tables I and II, Fry's sentences are particularly vulnerable to this criticism because there are 25 sentences per list). When children are being tested, fatigue effects become a serious problem, necessitating frequent rest periods.

Nonetheless, despite the advantage of having a large number of items per list, which for statistical reasons has the effect of reducing the variability of the list score, and therefore making it more reliable, a list need not be as long as Fry's sentence lists, and the time factor associated with sentence tests need not therefore be a disqualifying property. This is particularly so when we consider the advantages of sentences over words. Simply stated, it rests on the fact that because sentences are more than mere strings of words, perception of words in isolation is not necessarily a good predictor of the perception of sentences, which constitute the material of everyday speech. This is largely due to the redundancy provided by the "rules" of context, both gram-

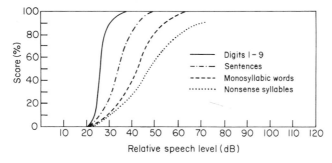

Fig. 2 *Schematic speech audiograms showing the effects of different speech material.*

matical and semantic—rules which are a feature of words in sentences but not words in isolation. A related advantage of sentences over words, pointed out by Speaks and Jerger (1965), is that they allow systematic investigation of the time domain, since they are of sufficient duration to permit alteration of the temporal characteristics of speech.

Increasing redundancy means decreasing uncertainty, and in the context of the speech audiogram the effect of increased redundancy is in general to steepen the slope of the audiogram, thus reducing variability and making estimates of SIT and HPL more reliable. Thus in Fig. 2, which shows schematically the effects of different kinds of speech material, the redundancy associated with the speech material decreases from digits, through sentences, then words, to nonsense words. To put it the other way round, the amount of uncertainty for the listener increases from digits to nonsense words. Figure 2 illustrates the resultant effect on the slopes of the audiograms for normally-hearing listeners. Some effects for hearing-impaired adults have been discussed by Niemeyer (1970). The degree to which the slope increases with increased redundancy will also be affected by subject variables, and in particular, the listener with adequate linguistic skills and a hearing impairment may rely more on these statistical properties of connected-speech than his normally-hearing counterpart (Fry, 1964). When time permits, then, and where the difference between word tests and sentence tests could be important (as in hearing-aid selection, assessment of the degree of handicap, monitoring rehabilitation, educational placement, assessment of the effect of hearing level upon speech reception, and sometimes in diagnosis), the audiologist would seem obliged to accept the face-validity argument and use sentences rather than words.

E. The linguistic content of sentence tests

Although we recognize that it is not possible in a speech (sentence) test to separate hearing, linguistic and cognitive abilities completely we must nonetheless emphasize that the speech tests under consideration are primarily tests of *hearing*. Thus the basic requirements of the speech test material are that they should be within the "linguistic ability" of the person whose hearing is being tested. That is, the words that make up the sentences should be within his vocabulary, and furthermore they should be commonly occurring, in order to minimize the effect of word frequency on intelligibility (Howes, 1957); the grammar of the sentences should not exceed his grammatical ability; and the length of each sentence should not exceed his memory span. If any or all of these criteria are not met, then the test results are confounded: the listener's score on a sentence list presented at a given intensity will be depressed for reasons other than those associated primarily with hearing.

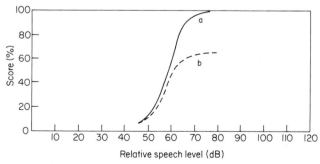

Fig. 3   Schematic speech audiogram for a listener with a conductive hearing loss (curve a), and a possible audiogram for the same listener using test material which is beyond his linguistic ability (curve b).

In other words, the listener will be penalized unfairly. The effect on the speech audiogram will be to alter the slope, the SIT and the OIS. For example, the unbroken line (curve a) in Fig. 3 represents a speech audiogram that might be obtained from a patient with a conductive hearing loss, using test material which is well within the patient's linguistic ability. The broken line (curve b) shows what might be expected if the speech test material is not within the patient's linguistic ability. The latter graph thus gives an ambiguous assessment of the patient's hearing for speech. Indeed, such a curve might be confused with that typical of patients with a sensori-neural impairment, in whom the OIS tends to be depressed, either moderately (cochlear lesions) or markedly (VIIIth nerve lesions).

F. Sentence tests for children

Unfortunately, it is not certain that Fry's sentence lists are linguistically simple enough for the less able, normally-hearing adult listener, containing as they do some words which have a low frequency of occurrence and long sentences, not to mention references to a bygone age of housekeepers and servants. When the linguistic ability of children is considered, the situation becomes even more problematical. For children with hearing-impairments which may have been present since birth and which themselves retard language development, the Fry sentence test is clearly inappropriate. The Davis and Silverman CID sentence lists (see Table II) had in 1970 been recorded but "not yet released for general use until the properties of the speech sample have been thoroughly studied" (Davis and Silverman, 1970, p. 492). The sentences were constructed to fairly rigorous specifications, but are in any case unsuitable for the purposes of testing children since the vocabulary is described as being "appropriate to adults", and several of the sentences contain too many words for young children. The Synthetic Sentence Identification Test (see Table II) was designed for research purposes to contain sentences with controlled informational content. That is, the degree of redundancy in the sentences is controlled, using the method of Miller and Selfridge (1950). More important from our point of view, however, is the fact that the redundancy in the sentences is limited, in no case being greater than third-order approximation to English. Since we are particularly concerned with the perception of naturally-occurring speech material, for reasons of its face-validity in clinical and educational use, the SSI test is therefore inappropriate.

There is, then, no recorded sentence test available for use with partially-hearing children, despite the evident need for one. The primary aim of our work was to design and standardize such a test. If any of the tests that are available in print were linguistically suitable for partially-hearing children, then our task would be rendered considerably simpler: we could take such a test, record it, and go straight into a full-scale standardization. However, none of the printed tests are suitable. One of the Manchester Tests (see Table I) contains sentences which are too complex for children, both in terms of grammar and vocabulary. The other contains sentences which are linguistically more appropriate, but there are too few sentences and too few lists. Magner (1972) has presented a list of 600 sentences which were designed at the Clarke School for the Deaf, Massachusetts, USA: these are used to assess the intelligibility of the speech of deaf pupils, but they might have served our purpose since apparently they were designed with the linguistic ability of deaf children in mind. Nevertheless, we feel that the sentences are too long and grammatically too complex, often containing more than one clause. Furthermore, although the vocabulary is simple, some of it is not appropriate for use in the UK. Thus it was necessary for us to design our own sentences and balanced sentence lists. The sentence test which we intended to design and standardize was to be suitable for use with (at least) partially-hearing children aged from 8–15 years. This age range was chosen as that whose need was the greatest: below 8 years the number of such children who are able to cope with sentences presented from a tape-recorder, without lip-reading cues, falls off fairly rapidly, and above 15 the more important years for re-habilitation have passed. However, it is less important to delineate precisely the upper age limit, since if the sentences are simple enough for most partially-hearing 8-year-olds, then they will surely be suitable for older children (and for some younger children who have minor impairments).

IV. A guide to the further organization of this book

We would now like to give some information about the organization of the book to help the reader on his way. In Part I, Chapter 2, the lack of basic information about the linguistic ability (in terms of vocabulary and grammar) of partially-hearing children is pointed out, and the need for such information is established before we begin the account of our attempts to construct new test sentences. The methodology for obtaining this information from a sample of hearing-impaired children is described in Chapter 3, and in Chapter 4 the use of the data to construct the sentences and balanced sentence lists is described. In Chapter 5 we consider practical aspects of the new tests—list equalization, test–retest variability, calibration, and scoring methods. Then, in Part II, Chapters 6 and 7 describe in greater detail the data which provided the linguistic guide-lines for the construction of our tests. This detail results from the realization, early in our work, that much more linguistic data would be available for analysis than that which would be needed simply to draw up rules for sentence construction, and that this abundance of data would furnish a great deal of new and useful information about the spoken language of partially-hearing children. These two chapters are followed in Chapter 8 by a consideration of the need for future work in the area. The Sentence Lists themselves are presented in the Appendixes.

References

BELLUGI, U. (1970). The signs of language and the language of signs. Paper presented at Stanford University Colloquium.

BENCH, R. J. (1971). The rise and demise of the critical period concept. *Sound (Brit. J. Audiol.)* **5,** 21–23.

BENCH, J. (1978). The basics of infant hearing screening: why early diagnosis. *In* "Early Diagnosis of Hearing Loss" (S. E. Gerber and G. T. Mencher, eds), pp. 155–175. Grune and Stratton, New York, USA.

BOCCA, E., CALEARO, C. and CASSINARI, V. (1954). A new method for testing hearing in temporal lobe tumours: a preliminary report. *Acta Otolaryng.* **44,** 219–221.

BOOTHROYD, A. (1968). Developments in speech audiometry. *Sound (Brit. J. Audiol.)* **2,** 3–11.

BORNSTEIN, H. (1974). Signed English, a manual approach. *J. Speech Hear. Disord.* **39,** 330–343.

BROWN, R. (1973). "A First Language". Harvard University Press, Cambridge, Mass., USA.

CARROLL, J. B. (1964). "Language and Thought". Prentice Hall, Englewood Cliffs, NJ, USA.

CHARROW, V. (1975). A psycholinguistic analysis of "deaf English". *Sign Lang. Studies* **7,** 139–150.

CHOMSKY, N. (1971). Deep structure, surface structure and semantic interpretation. *In* "Semantics" (D. Steinberg and L. Jakobovits, eds), pp. 183–216. Cambridge University Press, Cambridge, UK.

COHEN, G. (1977). "The Psychology of Cognition". Academic Press, London and New York.

COLES, R. R. A., MARKIDES, A. and PRIEDE, V. (1973). Uses and abuses of speech audiometry. *In* "Disorders of Auditory Function" (W. Taylor, ed.), pp. 181–202. Academic Press, London and New York.

CONRAD, R. (1970). Profound deafness as a psycholinguistic problem. *In* "Speech Communication Ability and Profound Deafness" (G. Fant, ed.), pp. 147–155. Alexander Graham Bell, Washington, USA.

CRUTTENDON, A. (1974). An experiment involving comprehension of intonation in children from 7–10. *J. Child. Lang.* **1,** 221–231.

CRYSTAL, D., FLETCHER, P. and GARMAN, M. (1976). "The Grammatical Analysis of Language Disability". Edward Arnold, London, UK.

DALE, P. S. (1972). "Language Development: Structure and Function". Dryden Press, Hinsdale, Illinois, USA.

DAVIS, H. and SILVERMAN, S. R. (1970). "Hearing and Deafness". Holt, Rinehart and Winston, New York, USA.

EGAN, J. P. (1944). Articulation testing methods II. O.S.R.D. Report No. 3802, Psychoacoustic Laboratory, Harvard University, Cambridge, Mass., USA.

FAIRBANKS, G. (1958). Test of phonetic differentiation: The Rhyme Test. *J. Acoust. Soc. Amer.* **30**, 596–600.

FLETCHER, H. and STEINBERG, J. C. (1929). Articulation testing methods. *Bell Syst. Tech. J.* **8**, 806–854.

FOURCIN, A. J. (1978). Speech pattern audiometry. Paper presented to Brit. Soc. Audiol. meeting on Speech Audiometry, London.

FRY, D. B. (1961). Word and sentence tests for use in speech audiometry. *Lancet* July 22, 197–199.

FRY, D. B. (1964). Modifications to speech audiometry. *Int. Audiol.*, **3**, 226–236.

FURTH, H. G. (1966). "Thinking Without Language: Psychological Implications of Deafness". Free Press, New York, USA.

FURTH, H. G. (1971). Linguistic deficiency and thinking; research with deaf subjects 1964–1969. *Psychol. Bull.* **74**, 58–72.

FURTH, H. and YOUNISS, J. (1975). Congenital deafness and the development of thinking. *In* "Foundations of Language Development" (E. H. Lenneberg and E. Lenneberg, eds), pp. 167–176. Academic Press, London and New York.

GAULT, R. H. (1936). Recent developments in vibro-tactile research. *J. Franklin Inst.* **221**, 703–719.

HARRIS, J. D., HAINES, H. L. and MYERS, C. K. (1956). A new formula for using the audiogram to predict speech hearing loss. *Arch. Otolaryng.* **63**, 158–176.

HEIDER, F. and HEIDER, G. M. (1941). Studies in the psychology of the deaf. *Psychol. Monogr.* **53**, 1–56.

HERRIOT, P. (1970). "An Introduction to the Psychology of Language". Methuen, London, UK.

HIRSCH, I. J., DAVIS, H., SILVERMAN, S. R., REYNOLDS, E. G., ELDERT, E. and BENSON, R. W. (1952). Development of materials for speech audiometry. *J. Speech Hear. Disord.* **17**, 321–337.

HOWES, D. (1957). On the relation between the intelligibility and frequency of occurrence of English words. *J. Acoust. Soc. Amer.* **29**, 296–305.

HUDGINS, C. V., HAWKINS, J. E., KARLIN, J. E. and STEVENS, S. S. (1947). The development of recorded auditory tests for measuring hearing loss for speech. *Laryngoscope* **57**, 57–89.

JERGER, J. and JERGER, S. (1967). Psychoacoustic comparison of cochlear and VIIIth nerve disorders. *J. Speech Hear. Res.* **10**, 659–688.

JERGER, J., SPEAKS, C. and MALMQUIST, C. (1966). Hearing-aid performance and hearing-aid selection. *J. Speech Hear. Res.* **9**, 136–149.

KATZ, J. (1962). The use of staggered spondaic words for assessing the integrity of the central auditory nervous system. *J. Aud. Res.* **2**, 327–337.

KEITH, R. W. (1977). "Central Auditory Dysfunction". Grune and Stratton, New York, USA.

KRUEL, E. J., NIXON, J. C., KRYTER, K. D., BELL, D. W., LANG, J. S. and SCHUBERT, E. D. (1968). A proposed clinical test of speech discrimination. *J. Speech Hear. Res.* **11**, 536–552.

LENNEBERG, E. H. (1967). "Biological Foundations of Language". Wiley, New York and London.

LEWIS, M. M. (1968). Language and mental development. *In* "Developments in Human Learning, II" (E. A. Lunzer and J. F. Morris, eds), pp. 144–169. Staples Press, London, UK.

LYREGAARD, P. E., ROBINSON, D. W. and HINCHLIFFE, R. (1976). A feasibility study of diagnostic speech audiometry. NPL Acoustics Report Ac 73, National Physical Laboratory, Teddington, Middlesex, UK.

MAGNER, M. E. (1972). A Speech Intelligibility Test for Deaf Children. Clarke School for the Deaf, Northampton, Mass., USA.

McNEILL, D. (1966). Developmental psycholinguistics. *In* "The Genesis of Language" (F. Smith and G. A. Miller, eds), pp. 15–84. MIT Press, Cambridge, Mass., USA.

MENYUK, P. (1971). "The Acquisition and Development of Language". Prentice Hall, Englewood Cliffs, NJ, USA.

MILLER, G. A. and SELFRIDGE, J. A. (1950). Verbal context and the recall of meaningful material. *Amer. J. Psychol.* **53**, 176–185.

MORTON, J. (1971). Psycholinguistics. *Brit. Med. Bull.* **27**, 195–199.

MRC Special Report No. 261 (1947). Hearing aids and audiometers.

MYKLEBUST, H. R. (1960). The psychological effects of deafness. *Amer. Ann. Deaf* **105**, 372–385.

MYKLEBUST, H. R. (1964). "The Psychology of Deafness". Grune and Stratton, New York, USA.

NIEMEYER, W. (1970). Studies on speech perception in dissociated hearing loss. *In* "Speech Communication Ability and Profound Deafness" (G. Fant, ed.), pp. 107–139. Alexander Graham Bell, Washington, USA.

NORTHERN, J. L. and DOWNS, M. P. (1974). "Hearing in Children", Williams and Wilkins, Baltimore, USA.

RUSSELL, W. K., QUIGLEY, S. P. and POWER, D. J. (1976). "Linguistics and Deaf Children". Alexander Graham Bell, Washington, USA.

RUTTER, M. (1972). The effects of language delay on development. *In* "The Child with Delayed Speech" (M. Rutter and J. A. M. Martin, eds), p. 177. Heinemann, London, UK.

SPEAKS, C. and JERGER, J. (1965). Method for measurement of speech identification. *J. Speech Hear. Res.* **8**, 185–194.

STOKOE, W. (1958). Sign language structure. *In* "Studies in Linguistics". Occasional Paper No. 8, University of Buffalo, Buffalo, USA.

STOKOE, W. C. (1972). "Semiotics and Human Sign Language". Mouton, The Hague, Netherlands.

SUCI, G. J. (1969). Relations between semantic and syntactic factors in the structuring of language. *Lang. Speech* **12**, 69–79.

TERVOORT, B. (1965). Development of language and the "critical period". *Acta Otolaryng. Suppl.* **206**, 247–250.

TILLMAN, T. W. and CARHART, R. (1966). An expanded test for speech discrimination utilizing CNC monosyllabic words (NU auditory test No. 6). Technical Report No. SAM-TR-66-55, USAF School of Aerospace Medicine.

TILLMAN, T. W., CARHART, R. and WILBER, L. (1963). A test for speech discrimination composed of CNC monosyllabic words (NU auditory test No. 4). Technical Report No. SAM-TDR-62-135, USAF School of Aerospace Medicine.

VIGOTSKY, L. S. (1939). Thought and speech. *Psychiatry* **2**, 29–54.

WOLD, A. H. (1978). "Decoding Oral Language". Academic Press, London and New York.

WOLFF, J. G. (1973). "Language, Brain and Hearing". Methuen, London, UK.

WOODWARD, J. C. (1973). Some characteristics of pidgin sign English. *Sign Lang. Studies* **3**, 39–46.

YOUNISS, J., FURTH, H. G. and ROSS, B. (1971). Logical symbol use in deaf and hearing children and adolescents. *Develop. Psychol.* **5**, 511–517.

2

Introductory Review

JOHN BENCH

I. Introduction

This Chapter is concerned with a review of what is known of language production and reception by the hearing-impaired child, considered in terms of spoken language and hearing for connected-speech. The contribution of such related topics as lip-reading (Oyer and Frankmann, 1975; Erber and McMahan, 1976; Ivimey, 1977), finger-spelling (Birch and Stuckless, 1964), cued speech (Cornett, 1970) and reading and writing (Russell *et al.*, 1976) have been reviewed elsewhere, and will not be further mentioned, except where they offer information particularly relevant to the language spoken and heard by the hearing-impaired child. The reader who is interested in an overall review of the language performance of hearing-impaired persons is referred to Swisher (1976), who discussed their spoken language, reading levels, written language and other aspects. Swisher cited departmental reports and unpublished material which we do not include in the present review. Also, Simmons (1962) has reported a comparison of the type/token ratio in the spoken and written language of deaf and hearing children. Besides dealing with the language, spoken and heard by the hearing-handicapped child, the present Chapter is also concerned with the production and knowledge of vocabulary, which is conveniently treated separately from other linguistic aspects. In both Sections the topics will be treated at the level necessary to introduce the previous work, not only to the following chapters of Part I (the design and construction of sentence tests) but also to the more detailed chapters of Part II (the analyses of the spoken language of our own sample of hearing-impaired children).

II. Language production and reception

A. General remarks

In 1941, Heider and Heider remarked (p. 1) that the literature on the psychology of the deaf pre-school child was very meagre. There existed reports of curriculum studies and play materials and there were publications describing sensory training, speech and speech reading (lip-reading), but there were no systematic observations of the means of communication and other social phenomena relating to the young deaf child. At that time, it would probably have been appropriate for the Heiders to have made their remark more general, because until they produced their report, it would have been fair to say that there were few published analyses of the language of profoundly deaf or partially-hearing children of any age. Since Heider and Heider published their work, there has been a gradual increase of interest in aspects of language development in hearing-impaired children, accompanied by the publication of several papers and a few books. The publications describing spoken language and speech reception are however not so many that it is not feasible to review most of them in the present Chapter. In such a review, and therefore in what follows, we seek to give the reader an account of the findings for most of the publications in the field, as a preliminary to discussing our own work.

On surveying the published literature, it is apparent that most of the work has been conducted on the profoundly deaf child; there are relatively few reported studies of partially-hearing children. This is probably partly because some of the workers in the field have been interested in the language of profoundly deaf children for theoretical reasons, because congenital profound deafness naturally precludes the normal development of verbal language, and hence the congenitally profoundly deaf child presents a kind of natural experiment for those who wish to study language development in the absence of verbal inputs. This reason is especially valid for some of the earlier work when the provision of hearing aids and deaf education was generally less effective than it has been more recently.

In some of the work to be reviewed here, however, although the children described as deaf are probably mostly profoundly deaf, the samples may include some partially-hearing children, with consequently generally more advanced language. Clearly, this contamination of the profoundly deaf with partially-hearing children can only be resolved where audiometric or other data are quoted. Where they have not been given, and where no distinction is made even between rough categorizations such as profound and partial hearing loss, the reader should bear in mind that the language data which purport to describe the profoundly deaf may be rather optimistic.. But even where audiometric information has been given, it is sometimes not clear whether the hearing losses have been expressed in terms of dB ASA, ANSI, BS or ISO, which differ by up to about 15 dB. Hence the reader is cautioned against taking all the hearing losses quoted in the descriptions of subject samples as referring to the same audiometric zero; where an author has given an audiometric reference, we have quoted it. The reader is also reminded that hearing-impaired children with usable residual hearing (hearing losses < 90–95 dB ISO) are referred to as hard of hearing in North America, and as partially-hearing in Britain. We use the latter term throughout this book. Children with losses greater than 90–95 dB ISO are referred to as deaf or profoundly deaf.

Similar methodological problems are encountered with the description of the children's I.Q.s. Most, but not all workers, have recorded performance I.Q. levels or ranges, but often the test instruments used to determine the quotients were not recorded, partly because different instruments were used for different subjects or schools and the authors did not themselves redetermine the quotients with a named test instrument.

In this Chapter we shall review most of the published work relating to the produced (spoken) language and the received language (i.e. the hearing for connected-speech) in the hearing-impaired child. But we shall not discuss publications which are "philosophical" in nature, which consist mainly of brief examples, or which are seriously deficient in important ancillary information, which may affect the generality of the conclusions (e.g. Ewing, 1963; Simmons, 1966), even though such papers may have value in posing questions of general concern. Moreover, we shall not deal with the quality of the children's speech from the phonetic viewpoint which relates to what Brannon (1966) has referred to in his review paper as speech production, nor shall we deal with the intelligibility of "deaf speech" to listeners. Further, we shall not deal with the child's hearing for speech as assessed by word list audiometry, nor his hearing in regard to distinctive phonetic features. Ideally it would have been helpful if we could have considered separately such aspects as prelingual/postlingual language, morphological/syntactical/semantic issues, profound/partial hearing loss, production/reception, pre-school/ school age language, and so on. Unfortunately, this would be very difficult, and in part impossible, because the information necessary to subdivide the "deaf" into different sub-groups is sometimes omitted from published reports, and because although several papers have covered many of these aspects few if any have covered all.

On reading the literature published in the English language, a general distinction becomes apparent between the approaches of workers on different sides of the Atlantic. By and large, the researchers in the United Kingdom have been Owrid and his colleagues, working in north-west England. They have studied verbal language in children of pre-school and primary school age; they have been concerned to develop tests of linguistic ability, or have studied the use of existing tests relevant to the area; and their approach has thus been psychometric and linguistically rather molar. Also, they have tended to relate at least some of their work to educational assessment. In North America, on the other hand, studies have generally been made of rather older and adolescent children. The work has tended to be experimental in nature and has been more concerned with details of linguistic constructions. For want of a better rationale, we shall review the literature under the headings of "British Studies" and "North American Studies", and under each heading we shall review the published material in the chronological order of its publication.

B. British studies

We begin this section with Owrid (1960a, b) who summarized his research designed to provide measures for the assessment of spoken language in young hearing-impaired children aged 18 months to 8 years. As can be seen from the age range, Owrid's aim was to design tests of language ability for very young children, even those whose performance was very immature. Two research tools were constructed. The first consisted of schedules for defining and tabulating developmental stages in the comprehension and use of speech. The second, which is to be discussed here, consisted of three specially constructed tests for children aged 5–8 years inclusive: the Toy Vocabulary test, in which the child had to name 25 toys and objects; the Comprehension test, which consisted of 70 spoken directions, for which the children were required to respond by pointing to, or arranging, objects for play material in certain ways; and the test of the Use of Speech, in which the children were asked to describe a series of pictures. Data were obtained from more than 300 children, all with pure tone average hearing losses of $> 30\,dB$, of whom about two-thirds were in residential, and the remainder in day schools. Children with a severe mental handicap in addition to deafness were excluded. Ratings of intelligence by the children's teachers were made for nearly 200 children, and appeared to show a satisfactory distribution though the teachers seemed to be cautious in attributing very good or very poor intelligence. The sample included rather more boys than girls, reflecting the sex ratio of the special schools which were attended by the great majority of the sample. For analysis, Owrid divided the children into two groups according to the severity of their hearing losses, with the divide at 75 dB (pure tone average), and thence into four groups according to age in years, to give eight sub-groups in all.

The correlations between the children's test scores were high: between Toy Vocabulary and Comprehension, $r = 0.91$; between Toy Vocabulary and Use of Speech, $r = 0.72$; and between Comprehension and Use of Speech, $r = 0.85$. Performance on the tests correlated positively, though not very highly, with teachers' ratings of intelligence: between Intelligence and Toy Vocabulary, $r = 0.35$; between Intelligence and Comprehension, $r = 0.41$; and between Intelligence and Use of Speech, $r = 0.31$. The tests were validated by comparing the children's performances on the tests with teachers' estimates of the children's levels of attainment in the use and comprehension of speech, giving for Toy Vocabulary, $r = 0.59$; for Comprehension, $r = 0.62$; and for Use of Speech, $r = 0.63$: all of these were thought to be reasonably satisfactory. Owrid also administered the tests to a number of normally-hearing children from nursery schools aged 2–5 years. The results gave additional validating information, since the patterns of response of these hearing children resembled in many ways the response patterns of the hearing-impaired children. Those items with which the hearing-handicapped children had difficulty also tended to cause difficulty for the normally-hearing children. Exceptions were the responses to some items involving the names of colours, where for certain colours the hearing-impaired children performed markedly better than the hearing nursery school children, which was perhaps only to be expected.

Having completed a standardization of his tests, Owrid further studied his data to analyse the effect of certain variables on the hearing-impaired children's linguistic performance as measured by the tests. He found big differences in the mean scores of sub-groups of the same age, but from different hearing loss categories, for all three tests. He went on to analyse more closely the effect of hearing loss by combining the age groups and dividing hearing losses into the ranges 30–50, 51–60, 61–70, 71–75 for the hearing loss category 30–75 dB, and 76–85, 86–95 and > 95 for the category > 75 dB, using scaled scores. He found that for all three tests the resulting pattern of scores was favourable, and generally statistically significantly so, to the groups with better hearing within the 30–75 dB category, and that although the same tendency persisted in the > 75 dB category, it was not so pronounced.

In assessing the effects of age, Owrid noted that some of the increases in the test scores which increased with age were not very large, and that not all the differences (between whole years of age) reached statistical significance. He therefore made an alternative classification of age by reclassifying the children according to whether their birthdays fell into the first, second, third or fourth quarters of the year, and combined the year groups. Scaled scores for the first and fourth quarters of the years were not significantly in favour of the older children for the Comprehension Test, for either hearing loss category, though there was a tendency in this direction for the 75 dB category, but were significantly in favour of the older children for Toy Vocabulary and Use of Speech. Thus the improvement in Toy Vocabulary and in Use of Speech was significant within the period of one year. The effects of sex, schooling and home training on test scores were also assessed. On none of the tests were consistent sex differences found. As regards schooling, there were differences for each test in favour of the day pupils over the residential pupils in both hearing loss categories, which were more pronounced for the 30–75 dB category. When the effects of home training were investigated, it was found that children whose parents had received guidance on the home training of their children before these attended school performed significantly better on all three tests than a sample of those who had not received such training, though the former children proved to have significantly higher intelligence as rated by teachers, and hence the interpretation of the finding is somewhat equivocal.

Owrid's results show clearly that the degree of hearing loss, and to a lesser extent, age, had marked and statistically significant effects on certain aspects of the linguistic development of his large sample. Our main comments are firstly that the level of the linguistic analysis was rather global and not very deep, though this could be remedied by further analysing some of the large pool of collected language data, especially on the Use of Speech, and secondly that the degree of statistical analysis was not very extensive. As in the case of Hardy *et al.* (1958), most readers are as interested in the nature of the relationships between the variables as in seeking significant differences in linguistic performance as a function of somewhat arbitrary groupings of the variables reflecting the antecedent conditions. Hearing loss, intelligence and age, for example, are generally regarded as affecting linguistic performance in a continuous and additive way. Therefore correlation or regression techniques, and particularly multiple correlation or regression, might have made the presentation less subject to criticisms of rather arbitrary delineation into sub-groups.

Owrid (1970) studied a group of primary school children who visited a clinic for school-children, were aged 5–11 years, and who had conductive, "perceptive" (inner-ear disorder) or mixed hearing losses. (No quantitative audiometric data were given, but it is likely that the children would be classed by us as partially-hearing.) The children were in three groups: Group I contained 12 children with hearing within normal limits at the time of testing, but who had a history of conductive fluctuating hearing levels; Group II was composed of 14 children with basically monaural losses (two conductive, seven perceptive, five mixed); and Group III contained 33 children with significant impairment (6 conductive, 19 perceptive, 8 mixed) in both ears. The results for these children are given by Owrid from the following four tests:

(1) Comprehension Vocabulary, a test of understanding the meanings of spoken words without requiring a spoken response (the Peabody Picture Vocabulary Test).
(2) Expressive (Spoken) Vocabulary, using Raven's Vocabulary Scales.
(3) Expression in Conventional Structures of English, used to group the children into three classes from their spoken descriptions of 10 illustrations according to whether their expression showed no deviations, some deviations, or marked deviations from conventional English structures.
(4) Reading, using the Schonell Graded Word Reading Test.

Owrid found considerable variation in performances on the verbal measures, and few children attained high levels. Many indeed were linguistically immature, producing data which was sometimes difficult to treat statistically. The fullest data came from the Comprehension Vocabulary test, showing a clear variation in performance between the groups. The mean score for Group I (variable or slight impairment) was at 96·50 below the test mean, and that for Group II (monaural impairment) was at 108·57 noticeably above the mean, but neither difference was statistically significant. However, the mean score for Group III (binaural impairment) was at 79·82 well below the test mean, and significantly so. The Comprehension Vocabulary scores for Group III were further analysed by correlating the scores with pure tone threshold indices (not specified) giving $r = 0·32$, $N = 33$, P just greater than 0·05. When the scores were correlated with indices of hearing for speech (not specified) the negative correlation was more marked: $r = -0·46$, $N = 28$, $P < 0·05$.

This paper by Owrid is an interesting departure from most of the material in the field, inasmuch as it is particularly concerned with different diagnostic categories and the monaural and binaural aspects. It is thus rather a pity that the children were not more fully described and that the statistical analyses were not more thorough.

Owrid concludes his paper with some interesting and important observations of a mainly qualitative type which are noteworthy as a spur to encourage further research. He remarks that Group I children may appear to have no handicap, but this apparent lack of handicap could be misleading. The fluctuating hearing loss may be associated with the child's general health with a consequent absence from school, with a lack of receptivity to teaching, and with variations in attention. As regards Group II, while hearing in the quiet may be good, hearing in noise is relatively poorer than is the case for those with good binaural hearing, though the experience of spoken language over a period for Group II children may well be better than for those in Group I. For Group III, Owrid felt that they were best placed educationally in ordinary school classes i.e. where most had stayed, rather than being taught in special schools or units. Even though many had poor reading abilities, others were mastering the process of reading, and hence might increase their vocabularies and other linguistic attainments in a way not possible through spoken language.

Hine (1970) studied partially-hearing children using both the verbal and the performance scales of the Wechsler Intelligence Scale for Children (WISC), on the grounds that a study was needed in which WISC I.Q. measures could be related to well-documented audiological data. He hypothesized that firstly, the verbal quotients would be negatively correlated with pure tone average hearing losses, secondly, the verbal quotients would be positively correlated with performance quotients (since both to some degree tap a common general ability), and thirdly, the influence of hearing loss and performance quotients on verbal quotients would be independent of each other. Of Hine's 100 subjects, all but a few were enrolled at a school for the partially-hearing. Their ages ranged from 8–16 (mean 12·1) years. They communicated by speech and lip-reading both in and out of the classroom, and were unusual in that they had for hearing-impaired children particularly natural language—a matter of obvious importance with reference to the WISC verbal scale, for which very little modification of items was needed. The pure tone average hearing losses ranged from about 35–90 dB, with a few children at about 105 dB (abstracted from the published frequency distribution). The mean WISC performance quotient was 97·9 and the mean verbal quotient was 81·1, with standard deviations of 12·7 and 11·6 respectively. The correlation coefficients of interest were: between verbal and performance quotients, $r=0·38$; between hearing losses and verbal quotients, $r= -0·31$; and between hearing losses and performance quotients, $r=0·08$, the latter not being significant. The multiple correlation between verbal quotients and performance quotients with hearing losses was $R=0·51$. Performance and verbal quotients were distributed relatively normally, but both showed less variance than that of the WISC standardization data. All three hypotheses were confirmed, since verbal quotients tended to decrease with hearing loss, performance quotients were not related to hearing loss, and verbal and performance quotients were related, but less so than would be expected on reference to the original WISC standardization. In part the latter outcome is probably due to variability in the amount of hearing impairment between different children, as confirmed by adding hearing loss into the regression to give a multiple R of 0·51—much closer to Wechsler's standardization figures. This work of Hine's is a useful piece of research, which helps to fill a gap not covered elsewhere, in view of the fact that performance quotients are frequently used to describe the intelligence of samples of hearing-handicapped children.

Hamilton and Owrid (1974) described two studies which in part relate to Owrid (1970) reviewed above. The first of these studies was a short report concerned with the verbal attainments of partially-hearing children (not defined audiometrically) attending special schools or classes as compared with two groups of normally-hearing children, one group from a school whose pupils were of "average" ability and the other group from a priority school in an educational priority area. There were 15 children in each group who were studied in the final year of infant schooling, and the main chronological ages were six years six months for the normally-hearing children and seven years three months for the partially-hearing. The children were assessed individually on six measures, of which five were reported. These were:

(1) Raven's Coloured Progressive Matrices, block board version, for estimating non-verbal ability.
(2) English Picture Vocabulary, pre-school version and Test 1 (Brimer and Dunn, 1962), for estimating comprehension of spoken vocabulary.
(3) Crichton Vocabulary Scale, measuring the ability to give spoken definitions of words.
(4) Understanding of the Spoken Word (Richards, 1967), for measuring the ability to comprehend spoken directions, and consisting of seven directions of differing length and complexity.
(5) Sentence Repetition, comprising six sentences of increasing length.

Hamilton and Owrid reported large differences in all the verbal tests between the mean scores of the partially-hearing children and those of the two normally-hearing groups. For the educational priority children, the mean scores were significantly below those of the "average" group but far ahead of the partially-hearing children, even though the latter were of greater mean age than the other two groups. On the other hand, there were no significant differences between the groups on (1), the non-verbal test, where mean scores were in fact very close. Hence although the educational priority children were at a significant disadvantage with regard to the "average" children, this disadvantage was relatively slight when compared with that of the hearing-impaired group.

The second study reported by Hamilton and Owrid examined in more detail than Owrid (1970) the effects of slight degrees of hearing loss on linguistic abilities, including spoken language, and reading (which will not be reviewed here) in groups of children with different degrees of hearing loss and different socio-economic backgrounds (General Register Office classification) attending ordinary schools. The findings were compared with the linguistic attainments of normally-hearing children attending the same schools. The hearing-impaired children formed two groups. One group ($N=30$), with a mean pure tone hearing loss of 38 dB, was characterized by inner-ear hearing loss, while the other ($N=30$) with a mean loss of 32 dB consisted of children with conductive losses. The normally-hearing children ($N=58$) were selected by teachers from the same school year as their hearing-handicapped peers as having average language levels in their class year. They came from similar socio-economic backgrounds to the hearing-impaired children and were of average ability as measured by the Coloured Progressive Matrices test. Although children of less than average non-verbal ability were excluded, the groups of hearing-impaired children included some with above average non-verbal skills, such that differences between the hearing-impaired and the normally-hearing children on the Matrices test, though small, were significantly in favour of the hearing-impaired. This was not true for the verbal measures, where on both the English Picture Vocabulary Test and the Crichton Vocabulary Scale, the normally-hearing children were markedly superior to the partially-hearing groups, whose performances were very similar to one another. When test results for the hearing-impaired children (conductive and inner-ear disorders combined i.e. N = 60) were assessed according to parental occupation (social classes I–III vs. IV–V) the differences were statistically significant and in favour of classes I–III. However, although the children from the higher parental occupational classes scored well above the children from the lower classes, their scores were still well below the mean scores for normally-hearing children.

Hamilton and Owrid also found that hearing-impaired children living in owner-occupied and privately rented property had better linguistic abilities than those living in houses owned by the local authority, but again the highest verbal scores were well below those of the normally-hearing child. Other home background features which affected the hearing-impaired children were: the reading habits of the parents, the availability of the mother during pre-school years and the size of the family. The first of these, parental reading habits (assessed from the amount of reading by parents, the numbers of books in the home, and membership of libraries), significantly affected English Picture Vocabulary Test Scores in the expected direction. The effects of the mother's availability and the size of the family were not significant.

This report by Hamilton and Owrid on their second study is interesting and innovative. Although we might have wished to see fuller information concerning details of the statistical analyses and the audiometric descriptions of the children, this study was well designed, and possible bias (e.g. the superiority of the hearing-impaired groups over the normally-hearing children on the Matrices test) was clearly stated. Also, Hamilton and Owrid provided clear information, which is badly needed, on the importance of the otological diagnosis to the linguistic attainments of their children whose actual hearing losses were similar (the diagnosis did not seem to matter very much). The additional information on the effects of social class and home background is rather novel for the area and of considerable interest. One major point of concern which relates to most of the papers of Owrid and his colleagues which we have reviewed, is that there may be some common linguistic factor or factors underlying most or all of the language tests which they use. Indeed, it would be rather surprising if such tests were not related in some way, though Owrid makes little mention of this.

Solly (1975) was concerned to develop tests of comprehension of spoken language which could be used with young hearing-impaired children in situations in which Owrid's Comprehension Test (1960a, b), though apparently suitable, was in practice too lengthy. Although other tests were available which might have been appropriate, she argued that there is a place for tests which would be cheap to produce and relatively simple to administer, yet would give useful information about the progress of individual children. She saw a particular need for tests of receptive language suitable for use during the pre-school years.

Solly developed four short tests, two for children about to start school at five years and two for children aged seven or eight years. The tests were:

(1) Sentence Comprehension Test I.
(2) Directions I.
(3) Sentence Comprehension II.
(4) Directions II.

The items making up (1) and (3) were chosen from the comprehension section of the Gates MacGinitie Reading Test (1965), with some slight modifications. The children first had to look at four pictures, and then listen to and lip-read the stimulus sentence before pointing to the most appropriate picture. Many of the items of (1) were made up of short sentences, while the material for (3) contained more complex sentences, and tested skills in verbal memory, in extracting information and in understanding a progression of ideas. The most difficult seemed to be those items in which attention to a whole passage with a developing argument was required for a correct response. Normally-hearing children coped fairly well with these tests at five and six years of age, the design ages, but a number of partially-hearing children could not grasp sentences as whole units, and made guesses based on the recognition of single words. Hence Solly designed the Directions Test, since the use of spoken directions requiring more active participation and reducing guessing seemed a possible solution. Directions Test I was constructed for the younger children aged 5–6 years, and involved the manipulation of small objects and toys in response to ten spoken instructions (e.g. "Show me a car and a chair") which increased in length and complexity as the test progressed.

All four tests were evaluated in conjunction with the English Picture Vocabulary Test I (E.P.V.T. I) used as a validating measure on four groups of children, with each child taking the Sentence Comprehension and Directions Tests appropriate to his age group: 25 normally-hearing children aged between 5·0 and 5·11 (mean 5·5) years; 20 hearing-impaired children aged between 5·3 and 6·11 (mean 6·4) years; 23 normally-hearing children aged between 7·0 and 7·9 (mean 7·4) years; and 20 hearing-impaired children aged between 7·0 and 8·5 (mean 7·10) years.

The normally-hearing children were selected for homogeneity in age, verbal ability (within standardized scores of 90–110 on E.P.V.T. I) and normal school placement. The hearing-impaired children had partial losses, and were heterogeneous apart from their hearing losses. A wide range of hearing loss and verbal ability existed at both age levels, and children were included from special schools, units, and ordinary schools. The cause and degree of hearing loss, the age at which the handicap had been diagnosed, and the type and amount of early help varied from child to child, but Solly gave no details, nor was information given about the scoring procedures for Sentence Comprehension Tests I and II.

The differences between the mean scores of the normally-hearing and the mean scores of the partially-hearing for E.P.V.T. I, Directions Test I and Sentence Comprehension Test I were all statistically significant beyond the 1% level for both the younger and the older children, in favour of the normally-hearing, even though the hearing-impaired children were rather older than the corresponding normally-hearing children. The standard deviations for all three tests were greater for the normally-hearing than the partially-hearing children, especially in the case of the Directions Tests for both age groups. Correlation coefficients were computed for all three test scores of the partially-hearing children to assess inter-test comparisons. The results showed moderate to high agreement between the tests: for E.P.V.T. I vs. Directions I, $r = 0·60$; and for E.P.V.T. I and Directions II, $r = 0·82$, giving fair to high validating support to the Directions Tests. For E.P.V.T. I vs. Sentence Comprehension I, $r = 0·55$, and for E.P.V.T. I vs. Sentence Comprehension II, $r = 0·59$, giving moderate validating support to the Sentence Comprehension Tests. For Directions I vs. Sentence Comprehension I, $r = 0·62$, and for Directions II vs. Sentence Comprehension II, $r = 0·80$, giving moderate to good correspondence. The degree of internal reliability of the new tests was computed by the split-half correlation, the results ranging from $r = 0·95$ to $r = 0·98$, i.e. very satisfactory. Correlation coefficients were also computed for each test with the average pure tone hearing loss. As expected, the coefficients were all negative, and ranged from low to moderately high values. Thus for E.P.V.T. I, $r = -0·22$; for Directions I, $r = -0·43$; for Sentence

Comprehension I, $r = -0.10$; for the younger hearing-impaired children. For the older partially-hearing children, the coefficients were for E.P.V.T. I, $r = -0.41$; for Directions II, $r = -0.55$; and for Sentence Comprehension II, $r = -0.63$, which generally compared moderately well with Hine's (1970) correlation coefficient of -0.31 between WISC verbal quotients and pure tone average loss. The difference between the coefficients for the two Sentence Comprehension Tests was rather large, but Solly did not remark on it.

Of the four new tests designed by Solly, the two Directions Tests appeared to be the most useful in distinguishing between groups of normally- and partially-hearing children as far as mean scores were concerned, and they received better validating support than the Sentence Comprehension Tests. However, if the difference between the means for the groups is assessed in conjunction with the standard deviations of group scores on the tests, this advantage for the Directions Tests seems less remarkable, since besides yielding larger differences between group mean scores, the Directions Tests were associated with higher standard deviations for the scores than the Sentence Comprehension Tests. Also, considering the fact that the normally-hearing group was a selected group (according to a restricted range of E.P.V.T. I scores), the variability of scores obtained via the new tests is likely to underestimate the normal population variability. Hence Solly's statement that each test discriminated well (especially the Directions Test) between the children may be rather optimistic, especially if referred to a comparison with the normal population. Within the hearing-impaired groups, for whom the tests were designed, the low to moderate correlations with hearing loss support our caution. However, it is only fair to point out that the capacity of the new tests to discriminate between children, and the estimated levels of validity and reliability, seem generally comparable to those observed with other tests of this kind.

Bench and Cotter (1979) have recently studied the performance of a well-defined group of 20 partially-hearing children on the Auditory-Vocal Tests only of the Illinois Test of Psycholinguistic Abilities (ITPA), with a view to finding, *inter alia*, whether the children would perform differently on different sub-tests. The authors were thus, in part, interested to see whether the ITPA sub-test data would show linguistic retardation in general, or whether there were specific areas of language disability. The children, who had WISC performance quotients in the range of 90–110, were 9·11–18·2 (mean 13·1) years old, with pure tone average hearing losses of 25–92 (mean 51) dB (ISO). All had been issued with one post-aural hearing aid, replacing a body-worn aid, not less than one year previously and all could hear the stimulus material to a given criterion. Bench and Cotter found that performances of their group of partially-hearing children on the different sub-tests were moderately to highly and significantly correlated with a range of product moment correlation coefficients of $r = 0.58$ to $r = 0.94$. In other words, a child who tended to score low on, say, the Auditory Reception sub-test, also tended to score low on Auditory Association, Auditory Sequential Memory, Verbal Expression, Grammatic Closure, Auditory Closure, and Sound Blending. Besides the correlation analysis, the data from the ITPA sub-tests were also subjected to a principal components analysis, whence the first principal component, hypothesized as reflecting linguistic advancement, accounted for 83.7% of the variance. The second and third principal components accounted for only 8.3% and 3.2% of the variance respectively. These findings supported a general rather than a specific pattern of linguistic retardation, though it is possible, of course, for partially-hearing children to show specific linguistic deficiencies in aspects of language not measured by ITPA (e.g. verbal forms as noted by Pressnell (1973) and Wilcox and Tobin (1974)—see below). Such aspects will be discussed in Chapter 7.

To summarize this review of the British studies, most of the work generally shows that hearing loss and probably to a lesser extent intelligence and age (above five years) have considerable effects on a variety of linguistic skills, assessed psychometrically and covering spoken language and the perception and comprehension of speech. The findings support a generalized retardation in linguistic ability with hearing loss, rather than specific problems or "deviances", but caution is necessary since most of the psychometric measures used were rather blunt instruments for investigations in this particular area. It is interesting that over the ranges of values commonly assessed pure tone average hearing loss was clearly the most important variable, outweighing not only intelligence and age, but also otologic diagnosis, the effects of parental occupation, home environment, and other socio-economic factors. However, apart from the study reviewed last (which admittedly was designed in recognition of the shortcomings of some of the other publications), the description of the subjects and the general level of statistical analysis in this review area were limited. Thus, on the one hand, it will be difficult for other workers to reproduce the studies described, though we would not go quite so far as Montgomery (1968) who remarked that "any presentation of the results of cognitive tasks . . . which does not allow for, or at least record, the age of onset, type and degree of deafness scarcely deserves to be taken seriously". On the other hand, the data of the studies reviewed have mostly been analysed only in part, or at least the analyses have been only partly reported. The outcome of both criticisms is that the potential yield of most of the studies has been reduced by the form of their publication.

C. North American studies

We begin here with a review of Hardy *et al.* (1958), who studied two groups each of 20 children, one normally- and the other partially-hearing. In the latter case the sample was taken from the patients attending the Johns Hopkins Hospital with a range of pure tone losses (better ear) of 26·6–50·0 (mean 42) dB, and generally with hearing losses increasing with increasing audio-frequency. The two groups were matched for age (in the range 6–15 years) and for socio-economic environment. Eighteen of the partially-hearing group regularly wore hearing aids, though the age at which the aid had been issued and the length of time for which it was worn varied considerably. Seven of the children could not perform an unaided/aided speech discrimination test, and of the remainder three performed worse with their aids than without them, while four obtained the same scores under both conditions (cf. Bench *et al.*, 1976). The mean Binet I.Q.s were 121·0 and 101·25 for the normally- and partially-hearing groups respectively, and higher than would be expected for both groups on a random sampling basis. One of the partially-hearing children had a conductive loss, while the remainder had inner-ear pathologies.

Three aspects of the methodology of Hardy *et al.* (1958) require comment. Firstly, although the presentation of the material in the main body of the paper was rather brief, individual case histories for the partially-hearing children were given in an appendix. Thus the child sample was particularly well defined, especially in view of the relatively early date of the study, but this is perhaps only to be expected since the work was designed to assess closely some relationships between hearing-impairment and aspects of language development. Secondly, the main procedure used to assess the relationship between hearing-impairment and linguistic ability was to compare the groups by means of *t*-tests. A more efficient use of the data would have been, in addition, to use correlation techniques between the variables describing hearing loss and the measures of linguistic ability, as was done in the assessment of language skills (see below). Thirdly, four hypotheses have been advanced concerning the importance of inner-ear and cortical function and verbal language development, the reflection of these functions in details of speech patterns, the learning of the sensory-motor aspects of speech, and the delineation of significant differences between normal and partially-hearing children for hearing, speech and language. These hypotheses, however, were expressed in such a general way as to restrict the relevance of the study. However, to concentrate on those features of the work which reflect our immediate interest, we shall consider some of the findings related to language skills, particularly from the analyses of tape-recorded speech elicited by pictures and a request to tell a story.

Hardy *et al.* found a significant difference between their groups in vocabularly quotient, but not in reading quotient (Metropolitan test series). The correlation between vocabulary quotient and reading quotient for their hearing-impaired group was $r = 0.91$ and for their normally-hearing group was $r = 0.75$, which was attributed to the hypothesis that reading was a relatively more important resource of vocabulary for the hearing-impaired than for the normally-hearing child. Hardy *et al.* found no basic difference between their two groups in the ratios of four syntactical categories (actor, action, connective and modifier) to the total number of different words (types) and to the total number of words (tokens), a fact which they considered as rather startling, considering the differences in Binet I.Q.s and hearing abilities. However, granted that both groups were of relatively high mean I.Q., that the hearing-impaired group did not have a very marked degree of mean hearing loss, and that only four syntactical categories were used among which to apportion the data, perhaps this finding is not too surprising. As the authors say elsewhere in their paper, the partially-hearing group scored higher than predicted, which suggests that this group was atypical of partially-hearing children. It is supported by the authors' statement that the partially-hearing group's comprehension (of what in particular is not explained) was excellent, without exception.

Olson (1963) described the use of the Illinois Test of Psycholinguistic Abilities (ITPA) in assessing deaf, receptive aphasic and expressive aphasic children, with a view to collecting data on the differential diagnostic potential of ITPA. The deaf ($N = 25$) and receptive aphasic ($N = 27$) groups came from the Central Institute for the Deaf, St Louis, Missouri. The expressive aphasic group ($N = 24$) came from the Institute of Logopedics, Wichita, Kansas. The deaf group contained mainly children with extreme hearing losses such that their language ability depended on special training, but no further audiometric description was given. The chronological ages and performance I.Q.s from various scales were: 99·40 (SD 13·01) months and 114·12 (SD 14·65) points for the deaf; 92·44 (SD 12·49) months and 111·52 (SD 12·73) points for the receptive aphasics; and 92·36 (SD 16·75) months and 83·07 (SD 11·94) points for the expressive aphasics.

By analysis of covariance controlling for age differences, F-ratios significant at $P < 0.01$ were obtained between the groups for all tests apart from the Auditory Vocal Sequential, indicating the ITPA discriminated between the linguistic abilities of the three groups studied. Olson remarked that the deaf and receptive aphasic groups had relatively stable linguistic handicaps with the major deficiency in the auditory decoding channel, and thus their psycholinguistic profiles were predictable at above chance level, whereas the profiles of the expressive aphasics were difficult to predict. As regards Olson's deaf group, we wonder to what degree the performance on the Auditory-Vocal Tests was handicapped by registration difficulties (cf. Bench and Cotter, 1979). In other words, was the observed poor performance on the Auditory-Vocal Tests (which was much poorer than on the Visual-Motor Tests) due to failure to hear the auditory stimulus material, rather than to having insufficient linguistic aptitude to comprehend it (cf. Wilcox and Tobin, 1974)?

We consider next the work of Goda (1964), who studied syntactical structures in the speech of normal, deaf, and retarded adolescents. Goda collected speech samples from 28 normal adolescents aged from 12–18 years inclusive attending a regular secondary school in New Jersey, from 42 mentally retarded adolescents (I.Q. 55–85, mean 65) attending a New Jersey residential school, and from 56 deaf (pure tone average hearing loss 75 dB) adolescents of normal intelligence attending a residential school in Michigan, by requiring each child to utter a sentence in response to each of 16 pictures, depicting everyday scenes (cf. Goda, 1959). The sentences were recorded in writing by E immediately after they had been uttered. To deal with the problem of understanding deaf speech, Goda asked the deaf adolescents to speak their responses three times. If the child was still not understood the child wrote his own responses. The number of words for each group was totalled into continuous different word samples, each of 100 different words, when it was found that the normal and retarded adolescents each yielded 20 continuous 100-different-word samples, while the responses of the deaf adolescents yielded only 13. Goda also made use of Fries' (1952) "parts of speech" classification, in which a sentence is analysed by means of the positions or structural arrangements of its constituent words into word classes. Goda found that Class 1 words (roughly corresponding to "nouns") were used more than any other class of words by all three adolescent groups, followed for the normal adolescents by function words and for the two other groups by Class 2 words (corresponding to "verbs"). Three-quarters of the speech of the deaf group consisted of Class 1 and Class 2 words. An analysis of variance of the 53 100-different-word samples for the three adolescent groups gave statistically significant differences ($P < 0.01$) for Class 2, for Class 3 (corresponding to "adjectives") and for function words. Significantly, both the deaf and retarded groups used more Class 2 and fewer Class 3 and function words than the normals, and the deaf used more Class 2 and Class 3 and fewer function words (auxiliary verbs, prepositions, conjunctions, particles, articles, and so on) than the retarded. Goda also found that of the three adolescent groups, the normals more closely approached the adult performance indicated by Fries in the ratio of the four main classes of words and function words as would be expected. Goda's results indicated that the limited language skills of his deaf adolescents were clear from their use of relatively few different words, and that the greater use of Class 2 words by the deaf as opposed to both the retarded and the normal group seemed to reflect in part differences in teaching methods, because the teaching of language to deaf children had to be illustrated, and needed to be concrete and specific. He commented that the children were taught about physical activities ("walk", "sit", "stand", etc.) among their first verbal symbols. They also learnt the names of persons who perform these activities, and were frequently taught with the aid of pictures, showing these persons and activities in a concrete way, with the persons symbolized as Class 1 words performing the actions symbolized by Class 2 words. Hence the verbal language of the deaf tended to become stereotyped.

Goda's paper was one of the first to raise some new aspects concerning the linguistic performance of hearing-impaired children, of which perhaps the most interesting is derived from the preceding paragraph. Thus Goda's work had the interesting implication that, at the time of his study, the language teaching of some deaf adolescents was linguistically unbalanced, in that concrete events were overemphasized, with a resulting high ratio of Class 1 and Class 2 words in their speech. This emphasis is, of course, perfectly understandable, for reasons given by Goda, especially in the teaching of verbal language to younger deaf children, but it raised a challenge for deaf education. It would be interesting to discover how far this challenge has subsequently been met.

In a similar study to that of Goda (1964), Brannon and Murry (1966) elicited three or four spoken sentences to each of 14 coloured pictures depicting children and adults engaged in daily activities from 30 normally-hearing and 30 hearing-impaired children. The normally-hearing group had an age range of 12·0–13·5 (mean 12·6) years and a mean verbal I.Q. of 102. The hearing-impaired children, who were not institutionalized, averaged 12·6 years of age with a range of 8·7–18·5 years, and had a mean performance I.Q. (Leiter International Scale) of 100. They were divided into two groups (each of N = 15) with pure tone average losses (better ear) of 27–66 dB and > 75 dB (ASA, 1951). The children's utterances were tape-recorded and then evaluated according to Myklebust's (1964) error classification system, with categories for word additions, omissions, and substitutions and word order errors. The hearing-impaired children considered as one large group (N = 30), when compared with the normally-hearing, produced a lower total word count, fewer words per sentence, and more total errors at statistically significant levels. Their most common syntactical error was substitution, followed by addition, omission and word order errors. Within the larger group of hearing-impaired children, the deafer sub-group performed significantly worse on all the language measures.

Brannon and Murry pointed out that, although there were exceptions which might have been important, their results suggested a generalized retardation in spoken language for their hearing-handicapped children in that the children who were superior in one aspect were generally superior in the others (cf. our review of the British studies). In confirmation of Goda (1964), Brannon and Murry also noted that most of the sentences spoken by their hearing-impaired children were of the simple, active, declarative type in the form of subject, verb, object, and that words used to expand utterances (auxiliary verbs, etc.) were under poor control. As a concluding remark, we may note that some readers may object to "error" analyses of hearing-impaired children's utterances (cf. Charrow, 1975), in so far as present debate seems to be increasing as to whether "deaf language" is "deviant", or is a dialect of standard English, or is a different but valid language *sui generis* (Ivimey, 1976), whether as a result of teaching (Goda, 1964) or other factors.

Elliot *et al.* (1967) also used picture-description to study the spoken language of normally-hearing and hearing-impaired children, but their analyses of the utterances, which were tape-recorded and transcribed by an experienced listener, were rather different in some respects from the foregoing. The hearing-impaired children consisted of two groups. That group which was from a partially-hearing division (N = 30) ranged in age from 4·1–9·9 years and had hearing losses at 250 and 500 Hz from 29–92 dB ISO. All these children wore hearing aids. A second group from a profoundly deaf division (N = 25) ranged in age from 5·6–9 years with a mean hearing loss at 250 and 500 Hz of 90 dB. These children also wore hearing aids. A third small group (N = 19) was presumed normal hearing and ranging in age from 2·1–8·2 years was also studied. Intelligence measures were not included, though other studies conducted at the investigation centre (the Central Institute for the Deaf at St Louis) showed that the children there were of average or above average abilities. The transcriptions were analysed according to operationally specified rules (the objective measures) and to ratings (qualitative judgments). The objective measures were the total number of understandable words, frequency of word usage, and word classification according to Fries (1952), where separate counts were made of infinitives and five categories of function types: auxiliaries, conjunctions, determiners, prepositions and intensifiers. Both types (the number of different words) and tokens (the total number of words) were counted. Word frequency was determined with reference to the Thorndike (1927) Word-Frequency List, a somewhat questionable procedure, in view of the possibility that words frequently uttered by the hearing-impaired child may not accord with frequently written words from normally-hearing adult authors. Ratings were made for the transcriptions obtained from two of the pictures for structural sophistication, grammatical accuracy, content and creativity, according to seven-point scales. The ratings were conducted in two categories: for rating 1, ten teachers of the deaf rated 30 pairs of responses (to the two pictures) from the partially- and normally-hearing children, and for rating 2, 32 college women judged 118 pairs of responses from the partially-hearing group together with material from the normally-hearing and profoundly deaf children. The results showed that the ratings made by the teachers (rating 1) were reliable ($P < 0.01$) as assessed by correlations of mean ratings of the two pictures, and were similar across all four scales. The ratings made by the college women (rating 2) were also reliable ($P < 0.01$), especially for the partially-hearing children, though there was an unexplained difference in reliability between the structural sophistication and grammatical accuracy scales (very high reliability) and the creativity and content scales (moderately high) for the profoundly deaf material. Since all the correlation coefficients were reasonably high, especially when structure was one of the pair, the structural sophistication scale was chosen as the index of judges' evaluations of language "goodness". A multiple regression model was then used to predict scaled scores on the first picture material for the partially-hearing group on ten objective measures, giving multiple $R = 0.85$. Some objective measures were then discarded until four remained, all with t-values for the beta coefficient > 2.8, giving multiple $R = 0.84$. These four were: measures of speaking time, total word output, word frequency, and classification of words by usage. When applied to data from a second picture, the derived multiple regression equation showed a slightly better fit, and predicted structure scores correlated with judges' mean structure scores at $r = 0.91$. When the equation was applied to the normally-hearing and profoundly deaf data, the fit was also good.

Repetitions by the children of Brown and Fraser sentences (1964) were scored for the number of sentences repeated correctly and for omission, substitution, addition and alteration errors. Performances varied widely for the partially-hearing children. The correlation between structure score and the number of sentences correct was $r = 0.57$, and between structure score and number of errors was $r = -0.69$. On second and third administrations of the sentence repetition task, these correlation coefficients (for the combined data) became $r = 0.75$ and $r = -0.75$ respectively. When the data of partially-hearing and profoundly deaf children were combined, the coefficients became $r = 0.76$ and $r = -0.79$. Hence there was a fairly strong relationship between the spoken repetition of sentences and free spoken production of new utterances. The total mean errors for the profoundly deaf group were about three times as high as for the partially-hearing children, a ratio which confirms some of the findings of Goda (1964), as far as comparison of different children with differently-categorized hearing losses and ages will allow.

Elliot *et al.* also presented other data to show that for some children considerable improvement in their indices of language ability was apparent over fairly short intervals of time. Thus for one five-year-old partially-hearing child with a pure tone average loss of *c.* 87 dB the ratings for the second and third testings, which were separated by five months, were: structure, 2·47 and 4·66; grammar, 2·87 and 5·32; creativity, 3·09 and 4·55; and content, 2·06 and 4·94. This and other cases described seemed to show that severely impaired children can achieve reasonable improvements in spoken language over a period of a few months, at least for the early stages, given suitable training and amplification.

Elliot *et al.* pointed out that their finding of an essentially unitary dimension of "language goodness", and the fact that this could be predicted well from counts of specific features of spoken language, were not immediately easy to reconcile with the idea that some aspects of language use at least should transcend mere counts. They cited Carroll's (1958) study of written language, which did not produce similar findings. However, as Elliott *et al.* suggested, Carroll's material was linguistically more sophisticated, and in any case was written and not spoken. They also suggested and adduced from supporting data that the prediction of a unitary dimension of language ability from objective counts may apply most strongly to the early stages of language development.

Brannon (1968) used the fourteen-word classification system of Jones *et al.* (1963) to study the word classes in the spoken language of normal, partially-hearing and deaf children from public schools. Brannon thus took 30 normally-hearing children with a mean age of 12·6 years; 15 partially-hearing children, with pure tone average hearing losses of from 27–66 (mean 52·1) dB (ASA) in the better ear; and 15 deaf children with pure tone average losses of 75–100 (mean 82·0) dB in the better ear. The two hearing-impaired groups ranged in age from 8·7–18·5 (mean 12·6) years. The mean I.Q. for the normally-hearing children was 102, and the mean (non-verbal) I.Q. for the hearing-impaired children was 100. Fifty spoken sentences were elicited from each child in response to 14 coloured pictures depicting children and adults engaged in everyday activities. The sentences were tape-recorded, and also the hearing-impaired children wrote down each sentence after speaking it to assist in the transcription. Then every intelligible word was sorted into one of the 14 categories.

The total numbers of words sorted were 11 400 for the normally-hearing, 5149 for the partially-hearing, and 4385 for the deaf children, including 84 unintelligible words for the partially-hearing and 665 unintelligible words for the deaf. The total number of types of words (excluding unclassified and unintelligible words) were 828 for the normally-hearing, 569 for the partially-hearing and 298 for the deaf. Words used six times or more were defined as constituting a basic vocabulary giving, for tokens, 10 974 for the normal, 4440 for the partially-hearing, and 3256 for the deaf children, and for types, 243 for the normal, 144 for the partially-hearing, and 87 for the deaf children. Thus it is very clear that, for his samples, Brannon found a marked diminution in the number of words used with increasing hearing impairment. In a more detailed analysis he found that whereas the deaf differed for tokens from the normally-hearing in all the 14 word classes except conjunctions, the partially-hearing were not significantly different from the normally-hearing for most of the classes, and deviated notably only in using adverbs, pronouns and auxiliaries, in which the deaf children were also the most deficient. When the number of words used by each group in each class was converted into a percentage, both the hearing-impaired groups showed a reduced output of adverbs, pronouns and auxiliaries, and tended relatively to over-use nouns and articles. Additionally, the deaf group alone underused prepositions, quantifiers and indefinites.

As regards the analysis of the types of words, an analysis by percentages showed that about 45% of the vocabularies of all groups equally were nouns, about 20% of all groups equally were verbs, etc. This method of analysis, noted Brannon, thus made the groups look more equal. However, despite the apparent equality for the more common words, the deaf children in particular were relatively lacking in adverbs, prepositions, quantifiers, and indefinites. Even so, we feel that it could be argued that these differences were not too reliable because as percentages they became very small quantities, and in any case the pattern appeared to reverse, e.g. comparison of groups for percentages of types showed the use of auxiliaries was higher for the deaf by about 2% than for the other groups. Thus the percentage analyses seemed to argue that the deaf group data contained *more* different auxiliaries than for the other groups, but the deaf used them less often. This paper by Brannon closely resembled in its subjects and methodology that of Brannon and Murry (1966), though Brannon strangely did not refer to the latter, perhaps because the analysis of the data was rather different. Brannon (1968) confirmed Goda (1964) in that the uttered speech of the deafer children seemed to be "telegraphic" in the sense of restricted use of auxiliaries (as tokens) and other function words, and was inferior in that it included relatively fewer different words. One possible difference between Brannon (1968) and Goda (1964) was in the relative use of verbs (including auxiliaries). For Brannon (1968) verbs appeared somewhat less used than, say, nouns, whereas for Goda (1964), verbs (equated here with Class 2 words) were almost as commonly used as nouns. Brannon and Murry (1966) remarked that a general retardation in spoken language was found for their subjects, suggesting that children who were superior in one aspect of spoken language would tend to be superior in others. Brannon (1968) offered some support for this view, but his findings also seemed to imply that while being a valid general conclusion, it possibly might not hold true for some particulars (e.g. indefinites, though the numbers of indefinites used by all groups was low).

Pressnell (1973) reported a study of the comprehension and production of syntax in the spoken language of 47 hearing-impaired children. The children were attending either private or public schooling for the hearing-impaired. They were taught orally, and ranged in age from 5–13·25 years. Twenty-four of the children were profoundly deaf or nearly so with pure tone average losses of 93 dB (ISO) or more (mean 99·1 dB). The remaining 23 were partially-hearing, with losses ranging from 50–92 (mean 79·2) dB. All the children wore individual aids outside the classroom and "were provided with amplification" (not further specified) inside the classroom. All were identified as hearing-impaired before the age of two years, and all were linguistically beyond the "naming" stage, i.e. they were able to use at least two-word constructions. The Northwestern Syntax Screening Test (NSST, from Lee, 1969) was administered to each subject individually, and a "spontaneous" language sample of 50 sentences was elicited with toys and pictures (Lee and Canter, 1971) and recorded for later analysis. The NSST receptive and expressive parts, consisting of 20 sentence pairs each, were presented orally together with pictures. The NSST has a maximum of 40 points for each section, with one point awarded for each correct response to each item, such as "Point to : 'the boy is not sitting'". Additionally, a second (raw) score is derived for the expressive part of the NSST, in which a response is scored as correct if the child responds with the appropriate grammatical construct being tested, but does not produce a grammatically correct sentence. The 50 spontaneous sentences were scored following Lee and Canter (1971) with points for parts of speech. A developmental sentence score (DSS) was derived for the spontaneous language by summing the obtained points and dividing by 50. Error scores for omission, substitution, incorrect form or partial construction were also computed.

Pressnell's analysis of the results for the receptive NSST showed that the older children scored better than the younger, but the rate of increase in score with age was significantly ($P < 0.001$) less than that previously obtained by Lee for normal children. Despite the test by Pressnell for differences in linear regression, the scattergram shown in her Fig. 1 appears on inspection to suggest curvilinearity, with receptive NSST scores reaching an asymptote at about nine years of age, with no subsequent change. For the age group of 5–9 years, the increase in scores with age seems to have nearly the same slope as the line for normals, but is displaced downwards (lower scores). However, the hearing-impaired children showed significantly ($P < 0.001$) more variability about the regression line than did the normal children, so the situation is rather unclear. The receptive test scores for the hearing-impaired children ranged from 9–33 (mean 24·02).

The analysis of the results for the expressive NSST also showed that the performance of the older hearing-handicapped children was superior to that of the younger children. The increase in expressive scores was greater for children aged between five and nine years than for children aged between nine and thirteen years. In the case of the latter it seems arguable from Pressnell's scattergram (Fig. 2, p. 17) that there was any increase and there is a suggestion of a decrease in scores after the age of about nine years. Hence, by inspection, the slope of the relationship between expressive score and age could have been curvilinear or quadratic, but Lee again used a comparison of linear regressions in comparing this data with her normals, finding a significantly ($P < 0.001$) less steep curve for the hearing-impaired children. Once more, inspection of the scattergram suggests to us that, for the rate of increase in scores over the age range 5–9 years, the slope was very similar to that shown for Lee's normals, but, again, is displaced downwards in the direction of lower scores. As in the case of the receptive scores, Pressnell noted considerable variability for the expressive scores, which ranged from 0–33 with a mean score of 16·79.

The data from the 50 token sentences analysed into Developmental Sentence Scores (DSS) showed considerable variability, with no significant increase with age for the whole group, though inspection of Pressnell's Fig. 3 (p. 18) once again suggests a possible increase in DSS scores over the age range from 5–9 years.

The language constructions used in the spontaneous language of the hearing-impaired children, and scored according to Lee and Canter (1971), showed that of the parts of speech listed, the children had the greatest difficulty (not apparently tested statistically) with main verbs, especially: *is* + verb + *ing*; *must*, *shall* + verb; *have* + verb + *en*; *have('ve) got*; and to a lesser extent with *-s* and *-ed*. There was relatively little difficulty with the un-inflected verbs and the copula. These results were not surprising, as we would have expected hearing-impaired children to have difficulties with auxiliary verbs and the morphological aspects of language, such as inflexions.

Correlational techniques were used to assess the relationship of receptive NSST, expressive NSST and DSS with age, degree of hearing loss, age at identification of hearing loss, age of first use of amplification, age of first training, and years of training. Using canonical correlation, only one signifi-cant correlation was obtained: $r = 0.721$ ($P < 0.0028$), and this was thought to relate age and degree of hearing loss with linguistic performance.

In commenting on Pressnell's paper, we wonder what effect the combina-tion of what we would see as two rather different groups—the 24 profoundly deaf and the 23 moderately hearing-impaired—has had on the results. We also wonder whether the differences in I.Q. of Pressnell's subjects, which were not given, could have accounted for some of the variability in NSST and DSS scores. However, our main criticisms of the paper as presented are con-cerned with the adequacy of the statistical analyses. We have raised specific queries of a statistical nature above. Most of these queries could have been answered had Pressnell applied tests for goodness-of-fit of various regression models to her data. Until this is done, some of the main findings seem to be equivocal. Also, it is rather difficult to interpret the age trends of the nor-mally-hearing subjects, when the age ranges shown were markedly unequal. Thus we have some reservations about Pressnell's comparison of age trends for hearing-impaired subjects for whom data was taken from Lee (1969) and Lee and Canter (1971). None of the latter were aged more than seven years, and the regression line relating their test scores to age might have departed from the presumed linear fit if the age range had been increased.

West and Weber (1974) studied in some depth the speech of one binaurally-aided, hearing-impaired four-year-old girl with apparently a mixed (con-ductive and inner-ear) disorder, and average pure tone threshold of 58 dB ISO in the right ear and 68 dB in the left ear. They analysed tape-recordings made while the child was engaged in various activities, such as looking at pictures, playing, etc. in a nursery school for the deaf, to investigate what a hearing-impaired child actually knows about language. To this end, West and Weber made a narrow phonetic transcription of all the audible utterances. Following a further orthographic transcription they then used a morphemic inventory and syntactic analysis of those of the child's utterances which corresponded to English words. Unfortunately, what they considered to constitute an utterance was not made very clear, even though this aspect would appear to be of importance. However, West and Weber reported that the results gave a large number of single-morpheme words identical in structure to adult English, though a number of non-standard forms were also produced. For example, several adult words had not attained whole word status but were used as bound morphemes (e.g. "badboy"). Syntactically, six word-classes were identified, with seven main rules combining words into two- and three-word syntactic structures. The word-classes were devised via the syntactic slot technique, namely by studying each word for instances in which it was found in a position similar to that in which another word was used. This method is of interest, but if it is the only method used in the analysis of immature speech, as in this report, it can lead to seemingly peculiar classification (e.g. "where" was classed with "Tina" and "Barry", because it filled the slot "— ball", as a noun-like word).

A single-case study like this report by West and Weber is of limited value in that it gives no indication of how the child's language compares with that of normal children, nor of the applicability of the findings to other hearing-impaired children. Also, though their method of analysis at this relatively early stage of language development does provide some insight into the language behaviour of the child reported, it would appear to be very laborious in the case of children using much longer utterances and with a much wider vocabulary.

In spite of the limited data at their disposal, the authors proceeded to give suggestions for language education. These suggestions would appear to be rather speculative and not necessarily prescribed by the data they have produced. Indeed their remark that the child should be provided with "language models which are either no more, or only minimally more, differentiated than her own" has a weak psycholinguistic basis and might be counter-productive in terms of language development.

Wilcox and Tobin (1974) used a sentence repetition task to study the spoken language of 11 hearing-impaired children. A repetition task was chosen because the authors were in part concerned to obtain material on the children's receptive ability for the more complex linguistic constructions, and because the absence of a given construction in a spontaneous utterance does not necessarily mean that the child does not know that construction. Special attention was paid to verb constructions, and the verb forms selected for study were: present tense, auxiliary (*be + ing*), auxiliary (*have + en*), auxiliary (*will*), passive, and negative passive (preliminary work by Wilcox and Tobin had shown that simpler forms, such as question, negative and past tense, had been mastered by a similar group of children to that described in the present sample). A set of six sentences containing each of the selected verb constructions was designed, and a second set was prepared by interchanging the verb forms. The subject was the same in each of the sentences, which consisted of seven syllables, plus or minus one, e.g. "Mary has washed the dishes". Only weak verbs were used.

Wilcox and Tobin used three experimental conditions:

(1) Repetition with visual stimuli, for which the subject was required to repeat a sentence after listening to it and seeing a picture related to it.

(2) Recall from pictures, for which the order of the pictures was randomized, and the subject was asked to recall the appropriate sentence on the presentation of each picture.

(3) Repetition without visual stimuli, when the subject was asked to repeat the second set of sentences after listening—this task was similar to (1), but no pictures were used.

The sentence stimuli were presented in free-field via a tape-recorder to the subjects who wore ear-level hearing aids set at 39 dB above the subjects' speech awareness threshold, sufficient to achieve the best sentence intelligibility. Also, a speech discrimination test was given in case intelligibility *per se* was a factor influencing the subjects' performance. The sentences were recorded by a speaker with a "general American" dialect at a monitored intensity level and using normal speech rhythms and pauses. The children's responses were tape-recorded, and the recordings were transcribed by each of five persons. A valid response required the agreement of at least three of the five transcribers which was obtained for 95% of the material. The presence or absence of a correct response was noted for each of the language constructions for each experimental condition. A grammatically correct substitution was regarded as an error for that tested construction, though it received a credit for the construction substituted.

The 11 congenitally deaf subjects, from public schools, had an age range of 8·10–11·8 (mean 10·4) years, a performance I.Q. range (on various tests) of 87–147 (mean 106), and unaided pure tone average hearing losses of 47–88 (mean 61) dB (ANSI). All had worn hearing aids during all their school training, both at home and at school, and the aids were functioning correctly before testing. Eleven normally-hearing subjects of the same grade level as the hearing-impaired children were also studied. They had an age range of 8·7–11·11 (mean 10·11) years, and were regarded by school authorities as having normal I.Q., although this was not formally assessed.

Analysis of the data showed that the linguistic performance on the verbal constructions was significantly ($P < 0.001$) poorer for the partially- than for the normally-hearing group. Also, a significant ($P < 0.001$) difference occurred among the three experimental conditions, showing that both groups scored lower on the recall task than on the other two conditions. This poorer performance on recall reflected a tendency to substitute verb forms which were grammatical but not appropriate. Thus both groups tended to give verb substitutions on the recall task, for which the normally-hearing children usually substituted (*be* + *ing*), while the hearing-impaired children did not show such a preference for substituting with just one verb form. This suggested, according to Wilcox and Tobin, difficulty with the original form, which the normally-hearing children, with their "universal" substitution, did not have, though this argument seems to us to be none too clear. The differences between individual verb constructions and all interactions were not significant, though for all the constructions the partially-hearing performed at a poorer level and showed a wider range of scores than the normally-hearing children. Wilcox and Tobin concluded from the data that the performance differences across verb forms were distinguished in quantity rather than in quality, since the patterns of scores were similar for both groups, with the difference being in degree and not in kind, apart from (*have* + *en*), and more especially negative passive. An explanation given by the authors is that (*have* + *en*) could be interpreted as a simple past construction, which would still result in a grammatical form on repetition. The same interpretation could have occurred for negative passive forms, but not for any other verb constructions. The test sentences were recorded in the uncontracted form, from which it might have been predicted that the hearing-impaired group would have had greater registration difficulties (i.e. difficulties directly attributable to the hearing loss especially for high frequencies) with the future auxiliary (*will*) than with the passive or negative passive. Such, however, was not the case, so that registration difficulties do not seem to have been of major importance in explaining the difficulties with (*have* + *en*) and negative passive.

Although it was reported that there were no significant differences between individual verb constructions, nor interactions, Wilcox and Tobin remarked that there was a marked divergence in performance for (*have* + *en*) and negative passive. These divergences are clearly seen in their table on p. 290 of their paper. The question is, were separate statistical tests applied to analyse the differences? It is an important question because, particularly in the case of the negative passive, the difference in the figures is very considerable (0·083 and 0·911 for the partially- and normally-hearing children respectively, as mean proportions of correct response), and because it suggests a difference in quality rather than quantity of responding, the opposite of what the authors maintain. It is also important because a reliable difference would receive support from Pressnell (1973), who presented data suggesting that hearing-impaired children have difficulty with some or all of: *must, shall +* verb, *have* + verb + *en, have('ve) got,* although she did not assess the importance of individual forms among these. Pressnell (1973) can provide no usable information on negative passive, since the data she presented on the use of the passive was derived from only one instance. However, in the case of *is +* verb + *ing* her subjects had rather greater difficulty than the children of Wilcox and Tobin on auxiliary *be + ing,* for which it is difficult to account in specific terms, though the samples of children and the types of task were rather different.

The American studies which we have discussed so far would support Davis (1977), who remarked that few published studies involved the use of standardized language tests with hearing-impaired children, whereas many studies have used the experimental approach. She argued that a standardized language test was needed, and further argued that the Test of Auditory Comprehension of Language (TACL) (Carrow, 1973) was appropriate for the purpose. This argument does not concern us here, but we are interested to discover how the use of TACL may illustrate the problems of hearing-impaired children in receiving auditory language.

Davis studied two groups of hearing-impaired children. One group consisted of 10 children, aged from 8·2–10·6 (mean 9·2) years, with pure tone average hearing losses of 40–66 (mean 47) dB (ANSI, 1969), who were being taught by oral-aural (presumably what is referred to in the UK as oral) methods. The second group consisted of eight children aged 8·5–10·4 (mean 9·8) years, with pure tone average hearing losses of 77–106 (mean 89) dB, educated by the total-communication (i.e. oral and gestural) method. These children were judged as "typical of those hearing-impaired children in schools or clinics for whom such testing" (i.e. language testing) "is usually appropriate for purposes of follow-up and educational planning". The TACL was administered to both groups of children on two occasions, separated by one to two weeks. The oral-aural group of children were tested in a face-to-face situation in which the child was encouraged to both look and listen. The total-communication group received test stimuli which were both spoken and signed, also with encouragement to both look and listen. Since the pairs of scores resulting from the two-fold administration of the test were very similar ($r = 0·96$ for the oral-aural group and $0·90$ for the total-communication group), Davis chose to further analyse her data from the first test administration only. The difference between the mean performance of the two groups (on 101 test items) was not significant. Errors were made on 51 of the 101 items between the two groups: 20 items accounted for 78% of the errors of the oral-aural, and 85% of the errors of the total-communication, group, with seven items accounting for 45% of the errors of the oral-aural, and 39% of the total-communication, group. The performance of the two groups was thus generally very similar. The seven items of greatest linguistic difficulty were linguistically relatively advanced: noun derivational *-ist*, future tense, present perfect (*has* verb), passive voice, neither/nor, and third person present tense. Failure on some of these items clearly involves difficulties in coping with inflexions, though Davis did not give enough information to assess such specific linguistic aspects in detail. Her findings thus at least in part confirm Brannon and Murry (1966), Pressnell (1973), and Wilcox and Tobin (1974). Further, since her findings also suggest that hearing-impaired children have difficulties with items which are linguistically advanced (e.g. neither/nor), they seem to support the case that hearing-impaired children show linguistic retardation.

We would now like to summarize the American studies, in comparison with the British work reviewed previously. Firstly, it will be obvious that much of the American work relies on grammar ("parts of speech" e.g. Fries, 1952) and most of the British work has been concerned with global types of approach (assessments of sentence length and comprehension), rather than grammatical analysis such as Crystal *et al.* (1976) or linguistic analyses such as Chomsky's (1957, 1971) transformational generative grammar. Secondly, it is clear that on the interesting question of whether or not the spoken language of hearing-impaired children is deviant (in the narrow sense of using different rules) or merely retarded, the generally more specific and "controlled" experimental approaches of most of the American workers has still for the most part left the question unanswered (cf. Swisher, 1976, p. 88), although at the syntactical level (Pressnell, 1973; Wilcox and Tobin, 1974) it appears that the poor linguistic performance may be explained on the basis of general retardation, rather than deviancy, since evidence for deviant syntax of verb forms was rather slight and questionable. Thirdly, the American studies are in agreement with the British work in that hearing loss, especially when severe, has marked and significant effects on several measures of spoken language. They amplify the British work in such particulars as information on word types and tokens, words used per sentence, errors of various kinds and aspects of syntax, though in some studies the results were obscured by an inadequate or unrealistic separation of the partially-hearing subjects from the profoundly deaf children with no useful hearing for speech and consequently poor speech ability (Montgomery, 1967, 1968). Fourthly, the American studies with their experimental emphasis, contained rather more adequate descriptions of their subjects. On the other hand, the frequent demarcation of hearing-impaired "experimental" groups and normally-hearing "control" groups is open to criticism. Thus none of the authors described the rationale behind their use of controls, and sometimes it is not clear as to just what was being controlled. Controls for age and I.Q. (usually performance I.Q., though the name of the test was often omitted) were usual in what we have reviewed, with degree of hearing loss as the experimental variable allowed to vary over selected ranges, but other variables which might reasonably have been thought to affect the results, such as the diagnosis and age at onset of the hearing loss, type of schooling, socio-economic status and so on, were rarely controlled, and sometimes not even described. This topic of controls has been frequently discussed elsewhere, and we shall not dwell on it. However, we feel obliged to comment on certain aspects. Thus some of the controls used seem inappropriate e.g. the use of performance I.Q.s for hearing-impaired children matched with verbal I.Q.s for normally-hearing controls. Also, what were designated as "control" groups would have better been described as comparison groups, because complete control of all known intervening variables is impossible at a practical level. Taken to an extreme this view argues that the experimental approach, i.e. the contrasting of experimental hearing-impaired with normally-hearing control groups, is invalid because the controls are inadequate, though all workers seem content to make do without this degree of rigour. Lastly, a more important practical objection to the use of "controls" is that they tend to limit the general reference of the findings, because controls imply the pre-selection of set levels for intervening variables. Thus the experimental approach, using controls, is suited to the study of specific questions, and may be conducted on a relatively small scale, whereas more general questions, involving the general relationships between groups of variables associated with hearing impairment, are better solved by large-scale correlational studies.

With our goal of devising connected-speech tests of hearing in mind, we need to ask how far the material which we have reviewed will be of direct use to us linguistically (Bamford and Bench, 1979). As the reader will have surmised, the published material is mainly of only peripheral utility. Thus the reports of the British studies are too wide ranging and of too general a nature, lacking sufficient detail as regards syntactic content. Some of the American studies offer more directly useful information. They provide data on parts of speech (Hardy *et al.*, 1958; Goda, 1964; Brannon, 1968), sentence length (Brannon and Murry, 1966), sentence type (Brannon and Murry, 1966) and constructions with which hearing-impaired children may have particular difficulty (e.g. verb forms, Pressnell, 1973; Wilcox and Tobin, 1974). Yet this information is narrowly based on relatively small samples of hearing-impaired children and does not provide sufficient detail for our purpose at the grammatical level of analysis, which is so important for sentence construction. Thus it does not offer directly useful guide-lines on the frequency of expression of clause structures in terms of clause elements, for example, nor of phrase structures, nor of the ratio of phrases to clauses, nor of the frequency of use of word structures, and so on. Also the studies which we have just reviewed do not give much information on the way in which detailed linguistic structures may vary with various levels or ranges of hearing loss and I.Q. Clearly, for our purpose, we would have to assess the usage of grammatical structures by collecting and analysing speech samples of our own, as described in Chapters 3 and 4.

III. Vocabulary

A. General remarks

"If it cannot truthfully be averred," wrote Zipf (1936) "as is sometimes felt that the stream of speech is primarily a stream of words rather than a stream of, say, phonemes or sentences, the word does seem, nevertheless, to occupy a middle terrain between the smaller elements which are its components, and the larger phrasal, clausal and sentence elements of which the word is in turn but a part." Thus strictly speaking, it may not be valid to analyse streams of speech into words, as the study of acoustic phonetics has recently tended to show (e.g. Liberman *et al.*, 1967). However, the usefulness of so doing is at the practical level a convenience of such proportions that we propose to adopt it without further discussion.

For our present purpose (see Chapters 3 and 6) we are interested in compiling a lexicon of words spoken by a sample of partially-hearing children. This lexicon should be sufficiently large to permit us to design some 500 simple declarative sentences with which to test children's hearing for aspects of connected-speech, in the knowledge that the words used in the sentences will be within the children's vocabulary. We shall be interested, not only in compiling a "dictionary" as such, but in making a word count to be ordered alphabetically and in terms of parts of speech in a form useful for quick and easy reference. However, before embarking on the particular description of this exercise which is detailed in Chapter 3, we shall review some of the large body of literature devoted to this kind of work, though only the more recent literature has very much to say about the vocabulary counts derived from spoken as opposed to written or printed words, and from large groups of children, as opposed to the individual child or small groups of children. We shall begin with a brief discussion of some methodological points, and will then discuss separately some studies based on material from written sources and some studies based on material from spoken sources. We shall conclude with comments on a study of the vocabulary of deaf children.

B. Methodology

In this review, we shall be concerned largely with the methodology of making vocabulary counts, and for each published paper which we cite, we shall give a brief description followed by a comment or criticism. Our main interest will be in those publications which relate not to adults (e.g. Howes, 1966) but to children—we would like to have referred to work on hearing-impaired children, but there is to our knowledge only one such publication available which is of sufficient substance to merit a review.

Templin (1957) has presented a convenient and succinct account of assessments of the vocabulary of children. She remarked that great discrepancies appear in the literature in the estimated size of children's vocabularies. The differences are due to such factors as the kind of vocabulary being measured, the definition of a "word", the criterion accepted for knowledge of a word, the type of vocabulary test used, and so on. By "kind of vocabulary" is meant principally the issue of whether the researcher is concerned with the vocabulary of use or the vocabulary of understanding. The vocabulary of use consists of words which are spoken or written: the vocabulary of understanding is made up of words which are comprehended when heard or read. There is of course a very considerable overlap of these two vocabularies, but they are not identical: it is generally agreed that the vocabulary of understanding is greater than the vocabulary of use (Bellugi, 1973). The operational definition of what is to be regarded as a "word" also affects the measured vocabulary size, and these definitions may vary considerably. Commonly, the problem is solved by regarding as a "word" any bold-type word entry in a standard dictionary. Knowledge of a word may be regarded as recognizing the word as part of a picture, or as an object from a description, or by using the word in a sentence. Generally, in assessing the size of a person's vocabulary, the estimated size of the vocabulary depends on the number of test words used. To economize on effort, the test sample needs to be as small as possible. However, the smaller the test sample, the less likely it is to reflect accurately total word knowledge.

C. Studies based on material from written sources

For obvious reasons, such as the ready availability of the raw material which is to be counted, the most extensive word counts have been derived from written sources. The best known and the most widely-used counts of this type, although rather dated, are recorded in the work of Thorndike (1921, 1932), improved and extended in Thorndike and Lorge (1944). Thorndike (1932) consisted of word counts, arranged in alphabetical order and annotated in terms of frequency of occurrence in lots of 500s and thousands, of the twenty thousand words found most frequently and widely in general reading for children and young people. The sources included classical novels familiar to children, school readers, the Bible, Shakespeare, poetical works, official US regulations, newspapers and correspondence. Thorndike pointed out that he had much greater difficulty in accurately placing the twentieth thousand than the first thousand words, and that even his 279 sources with ten million words were not enough for this purpose. Nevertheless he felt that the twenty-thousand-word list came very close to the actual twenty thousand words of most frequent and wide use in general reading. Thorndike and Lorge (1944) added to Thorndike (1932) by including data from three other counts of over four and a half million words each. The presentation of the 1944 data was arranged according to frequency of occurrence in the Thorndike (1932) work, a Lorge magazine count, a Thorndike count of 120 juvenile books, and a Lorge–Thorndike semantic count. However, as Thorndike himself pointed out, although the work was very comprehensive, it has become increasingly less reliable (apart perhaps for words counted from the classics), because words from modern fiction, scientific terms, and so on, become increasingly common with the passage of time.

It has often been pointed out that word counts of the above type may not be representative of the vocabulary of usage and the vocabulary of understanding or knowledge. Thus while word counts based on written material may serve well as a basis or starting point for testing the knowledge of words in particular, the results of such tests may show that the frequency of occurrence of known words may be at a considerable remove from the frequencies listed in the original word counts. For example Dolch (1951) described a comparison of the results of an interview vocabulary study and a word count report in four areas of children's experience: house and home, clothing, recreation, and animals. The description of the child sample was sparse, but the findings were generally quite clear. The children were asked to name physical objects and items in pictures, or were asked for explanations. A word was regarded as "known" if 75 out of 100 children could perform these tasks for any given word. When such "known" words were compared with tables of frequencies of occurrence in Rinsland's (1945) count, some of the "known" words did not occur at all in Rinsland while others occurred up to 1217 times (e.g. "make"), and within this range there was very considerable variation in frequency between different words.

Fullmer and Kolson (1961) have commented on the further aspect that vocabularies may need to be refined from word counts for applicability to a narrow area, because the primary word counts may be too long and cumbersome for the teacher or practitioner to work with effectively. Fullmer and Kolson sought to derive from 45 reading books and primers lists of words which were then compared with such word counts as the International Kindergarten Union List (1928) and the Dolch Basic Sight Vocabulary (Dolch, 1945). Their aims were to produce a small vocabulary containing words frequently used by children of a particular grade or educational level, which was relatively easy to manage, had numerous applications in teaching reading, reflected current word usage, was established by known research techniques, was derived from a number of recognized sources, and correlated with the findings of similar approaches by other workers. Only outline data was reported by Fullmer and Kolson but, within broad limits, their vocabulary seems to have met their aims.

The main problems involved in estimating vocabulary size of children and adults have been reviewed by Lorge and Chall (1963). Following Templin (1957), they remarked that vocabulary estimates for groups of the same age varied considerably, with some studies reporting ten times the vocabulary size quoted in other work. The discrepancies occurred across a wide range of age—for first graders, third graders, and University students. Lorge and Chall pointed out that the incidence of cultural changes (e.g. the advent of television) could explain, at least in part, discrepancies found between vocabularies measured at widely separated times, but their main interest was in the method of assessing the compilation of the vocabulary as an explanation of discrepancy.

Taking up some of the points mentioned above, Lorge and Chall noted that vocabulary size tends to be estimated in two main ways, both of which depend on word knowledge. Firstly, it may be estimated by the dictionary-sampling method in which a sample of words is selected from a standard dictionary, assumed to be the universe of English words, and a person's vocabulary size is computed by multiplying the number of sample words known by the person by the ratio that the sample bears to the total number of words in the dictionary. This method is limited by size of the dictionary, the dictionary's definitions of words, and by the validity of the sample as a representation of the dictionary. Secondly, vocabularies may be assessed by the frequency-sampling method, in which a person is tested on samples of words from standard word frequency counts e.g. Thorndike (1921, 1932). The obvious limitation to this method is the number of words listed in the standard frequency count—in the case of Thorndike (1921) it is 10 000, and in the case of Thorndike (1932) it is 20 000.

Estimates of vocabulary size based on use, namely from speech or writing, tend to be lower than those based on word knowledge. Thus recognition vocabularies are larger than expressed vocabularies. Also, the measurement of spoken vocabularies is limited by difficulties in recording, transcription, and the restricted sampling of social occasions in which speech is used. Written vocabularies suffer additionally from restrictions of topic or subject matter, and from a major consideration for the reader's interests.

Buckingham and Dolch (1936) used a free-response method, asking children to write down any words which came into their minds during a 15 minute period. This method suffers from limitations given above regarding written vocabularies. It suffers also from the time constraint, and tends to lack words which would arise through syntactical considerations, e.g. words which would normally be produced in writing connected grammatical material.

As remarked by Lorge and Chall (1963), an adequate determination of a vocabulary can best be obtained by the exhaustive (and exhausting) method of counting all the words in the English language, and measuring the proportion of them which is known. The dictionary-sampling method is, of the methods described, the closest approximation to this technique, and it is the method which has most commonly been used. It is, however, limited to the estimation of vocabulary size, and the raw data which it provides will incidentally be of little use in the determination of the grammatical knowledge of the subject—a limitation largely overcome by the use of written or spoken materials.

However, since written or published material as a source for estimates of vocabulary size is not of major interest in the present book, and since comprehensive information and comment on vocabularies derived from such sources is available elsewhere (e.g. Kucera and Francis, 1967), we will turn now to a brief review of some studies of vocabularies based on spoken material.

D. Studies based on material from spoken sources

As in the case of work based on written or printed sources, studies of vocabularies based on spoken material have a relatively long history, and noteworthy publications are available at least from the 1920s and 1930s. For example, French *et al.* (1930) described in some detail the vocabulary and the relative frequencies of occurrence of speech sounds used in telephone conversations. They remarked that the sentences of speech conversation were likely to be shorter than written sentences. Also, spoken sentences were often relatively incomplete, repeated, lacking in synonyms, and contained relatively fewer dependent clauses, so that those connective words used in writing to produce the more involved grammatical constructions were less often used in speech, whereas auxiliary verbs and pronouns tended to be used more. As a result, the more common words tended to be used more frequently in spoken than written material. Notable studies of children's spoken vocabularies began to be published at about the same time, though they are in part now out of date (Horn, 1925; McCarthy, 1930; Davis, 1938). These studies showed a concern for developmental aspects, though longitudinal studies of individual children, which are now even more dated, had been made much earlier (cf. Doran, 1907; Nice, 1915).

One of the more detailed and comprehensive British studies was published by Burroughs (1957). He remarked that at the time of his work some reports were, as we have seen, obtained from the study of one or a few children; others which were cross-sectional had been pursued in North America, and had been used in Britain with little evidence that they were valid for the United Kingdom, and most had been derived from rather young children of higher intelligence than average. Burroughs wished to obtain a vocabulary which had been learnt orally and not from books. He thus took the age of $6\frac{1}{2}$ years as the upper age limit for his work, and in fact studied three age ranges: $5-5\frac{1}{2}$, $5\frac{1}{2}-6$ and $6-6\frac{1}{2}$ years, with 55 boys and 55 girls in each age range. The children were obtained from both urban and rural schools in the Midlands. Sampling within the schools was random. Student teachers employed on the vocabulary collection encouraged each child to converse freely on a range of topics, assisted by pictures of scenes and by scrapbooks, in 10 periods of 10 minutes each. Every fresh word used by a child was noted, and if it occurred again was ignored. This method was used because there was little recourse to recording apparatus. One result was that instead of providing word frequency tables for each child, the data analysis showed the number of children using a given word. The total number of words used by the children was 90 040, with 3504 being different words (types). The latter were listed in alphabetical order in one list which gave the first 1909 words used by five or more of the 330 children, and in a second list which gave the remaining 1595 words used by four or fewer children.

Burroughs checked the reliability of his lists by repeating the study at Weymouth in south-west England on a sample of 42 children, finding that about

440–445 of the first 500 words in the first Birmingham list were reproduced in the Weymouth list. This was a reasonably encouraging finding because, in addition to the experimental variability of the study, there was a geographical variation in the use of certain words. Burroughs also compared his findings with other work, finding good or reasonably good agreement, in view of the different methods of data collection, geographical area, etc., with a Scottish study (1948), and the lists of Thorndike (1921), Dolch (1927), Rinsland (1945), Gates (1926) and others. Sex and age differences in the Burroughs study were rather small.

The remaining studies which we shall review here not only compiled vocabularies from the spoken language of children, but attempted to analyse or to classify each word usage in terms of parts of speech, namely the grammatical function of each word, as noun, verb, adjective, etc. Reference has been made above to such classifications in work with hearing-impaired children, but here we are concerned with subjects other than the hearing-impaired.

Mein (1961) described two studies of the speech of severely subnormal patients aged 10–30 years using conversational interviews and pictures to elicit the speech. In these two studies, the words uttered were analysed into separate counts of verbs, nouns, adjectives, adverbs, prepositions, pronouns, articles, conjunctions and miscellaneous. The first study, comparing the grammatical structure of normal and severely subnormal cases, found a progressive decrease in the percentage of nouns with increasing mental age, reflecting aspects of language maturation in normal children. The second showed statistically significant differences in the usages of nouns and articles between pairs of mongol and non-mongol patients matched for sex, mental age and chronological age, when mongols used a higher percentage of nouns than non-mongols. Mein argued a case for regarding a decrease in the spoken use of nouns as an index of language advancement which might be applied to pathological as well as normal groups of children, following the earlier work of McCarthy (1930), who commented that a large percentage use of nouns was characteristic of less mentally mature children. Mein also found a difference between conversational and picture-elicited word samples—an effect previously noted by Little *et al.* (1937), in that picture-elicited material tended to contain more nouns, articles and conjunctions, while conversation elicited more verbs, prepositions and pronouns.

A similar approach to that of Mein was adopted by Jones *et al.* (1963), in classifying the parts of speech for the characterization of aphasia. We shall describe it in some detail, as it raises questions related to our own approach in Chapters 3 and 6. The method of Jones *et al.* was a development of Fillenbaum *et al.* (1961), in which spoken words were classified into noun, verb, adjective, adverb, pronoun, other (prepositions, conjunctions, articles), gesture (including interjections), and unclassifed, according to the designations in the American College Dictionary. Jones *et al.* argued that the major faults of this system were the faults of the rather capricious classification of the dictionary, which did not specify its criteria or acknowledge their source, and produced apparent inconsistencies in classification. They remarked that, for example, *where* and *when* were classed as adverbs when used interrogatively and as conjunctions when introducing subordination, whereas *why* was classed as an adverb in both uses. Jones *et al.* sought to devise a classification system in which the various uses of *where, why, when* and *how*, for example, could be grouped within a single part of speech, arguing that this would be particularly suitable for the study of aphasic speech, where context was a poor guide to classification. This approach obviously gave some rather different classifications to the customary "traditional grammar" approach. Among the more important differences were the following. For verbs, auxiliaries were classified separately; participles were classed as adjectives if they could be preceded by *very* (e.g. *very excited*), but otherwise as verbs (e.g. *eating*); gerunds were classed as nouns or verbs, depending on whether they could be accompanied by an adjective (e.g. the public *reading* of newspapers) in the case of noun classification, or by an object and/or adverb (e.g. *reading* newspapers publicly) in the case of verb classification. The demonstratives *this, that,* etc., and the possessive pronouns (*his, hers*) were classed with pronouns, not with adjectives. Such modifying words as *some, all, much, less,* etc. were classed in a new category termed quantifiers. For adjectives, the major addition was to include adverbs derived from adjectives by the suffix *-ly* (e.g. *quickly*) but with exceptions (*surely, possibly, really, truly, certainly, probably*) which were retained in the adverb class, because of frequency of use, use in isolation, modification of the whole sentence in which they appeared rather than modification of a verb or adjective in the sentence, and uniqueness in appearing before and after the subject in sentences such as "*certainly* I *really* can come". Thus with the system of Jones *et al.* the maximum number of possible entries in the adjective class would increase relative to a standard dictionary classification, and the number of possible entries in the adverb class, a very heterogeneous class, would decrease so that the class would become more homogeneous, though Jones *et al.* did not trouble to reduce the heterogeneity further, apart from classifying adverbially-used prepositions (e.g. put *up with*) as prepositions. In the class of relatives were included all forms which might introduce subordinate and interrogative forms (e.g. *who, what, why,* etc.), and *that* when used for subordination rather than as a demonstrative (e.g. "I know *that* is the reason").

Uses of *some, no, every,* or *any* together with *one, body, thing, where* or *place,* were classed as indefinites, whereas *somehow, anyhow,* etc., which could not be followed by *else,* were classed as adverbs. Contractions were transformed into a two-word form prior to part of speech classification (e.g. *didn't = did not*). Compound forms, such as *kind of* and *sort of,* when preceding an adjective, were classed as single-word adverbs. Inflexions (plurals, third person singular *s* or *es,* etc.) were collapsed into their uninflected base forms.

Much of this classification system seems to be fairly logical, though it appears to be a compromise for certain classes (e.g. adverbs) between the "traditional grammar" approach, and the more refined kind of analysis proposed by Chomsky (1957). Some of the reasons indeed seem more a matter of convenience (e.g. frequency of use) than of linguistic propriety. Our main comment therefore is that the rationale, while apparently reasonable, appears on inspection rather as a collation of reasons which are variously linguistic and practical. However, it is only fair to recall that Jones *et al.* originally devised their system with a main regard to the study of aphasia, a matter beyond our present competence, and therefore we will not comment further on the system's suitability for that task.

Jones and Wepman (1966) have used their approach to classify the speech of normal adults, and Wepman and Hass (1969) have used it in a spoken word count derived from normal children aged five, six and seven years. By implication, this further work, and the inclusion of an analysis of the speech of normal speakers in Jones *et al.* (1963), argues for the general applicability of their system of classification. Moreover, Jones *et al.* (1963) submit their system for adoption as *the* common word-classification system, to facilitate direct comparability of research findings. We therefore need to consider the system rather more deeply, and in particular, to discuss its suitability for our own work.

At first sight, and in view of examples of the spoken language of partially-hearing children which we have previously reported (Bamford and Bench, 1979), the approach of Jones *et al.* may have some attraction. Thus, we have found that several partially-hearing children produce one-word "sentences" in their spoken language, which are difficult to analyse as they are deficient in both syntactic and semantic context. This kind of material is similar to that produced by some aphasics, and is the kind of utterance which led Jones *et al.* to attempt to devise a classification system based on parts of speech. However, a crucial point put forward by Jones *et al.* is that, of the most common 400 words of spontaneous speech, almost all can be classified automatically, since each word has a dominant part of speech usage, even though more than one grammatical use is possible (e.g. "act" can be either verb or noun). In short, any occurrence of a word which is found among the more commonly-used words, can automatically be treated as the use of the most common class with only a small probability of error. But we felt that without supporting evidence it would be unsafe to assume, in our own work, that the words of the speech of partially-hearing children could be classified automatically. Also, the method which we used in our own work (see below, Chapter 3) to collect a corpus of spoken material was not that of spontaneous utterance, guided as in the case of Jones *et al.* by use of the rather nebulous pictures of the Thematic Apperception Test (Murry, 1943), but that of a more constrained range of utterances guided by fairly simple and straightforward pictures in which objects and actions were clearly shown. We have already remarked in our discussion of Mein (1961), that there seem to be considerable differences between conversational and picture-elicited utterances as analysed by a parts of speech approach. If the spontaneous speech of Jones *et al.* is assumed to give similar results to conversation, then there are reasonable grounds for suspecting that the system of Jones *et al.* could not be applied to give such categorical results for the picture-elicitation technique which we decided to adopt. We therefore adopted a more conventional parts of speech analysis in our own work.

Hart and his colleagues at Mount Gravatt, Brisbane (1977), have recently explored aspects of the spontaneous spoken language of normal children aged $2\frac{1}{2}$–$6\frac{1}{2}$ years in home and school. The children's utterances were computer-processed to bring identical words and strings of words together in alphabetical order. Together with an index of frequency of use, a "communication index" was devised to reflect the generality of usage, and some parts of speech analyses of individual words were conducted according to age. This work is noteworthy in that, despite different sampling techniques, the child language data obtained in Australia was very similar to that obtained from samples of Canadian and English children, and in that the listing of strings of words is innovative, and of obvious utility to educators who seek to devise reading and other linguistic material for young children. On the other hand, it could reasonably be argued (Wells, personal communication) that frequency counts of single words, and pairs and triplets of words, do not of themselves explain a child's linguistic knowledge, the understanding of which requires a closer analysis in terms of accepted linguistic categories. This is, of course, not necessarily a criticism of the listings, but of the arguments developed therefrom in accounting for language behaviour. In other words, the Mount Gravatt approach detects and partially describes growth in language performance, but does relatively little to explain it.

E. Studies based on material from deaf children

Lastly, in this section, we consider the report of vocabulary norms for deaf children published by Silverman-Dresner and Guilfoyle (1972). This report is based on a typewritten vocabulary test in which the child was required to select from a range of four definitions the definition which was most appropriate to a given test word. The study was thus a visual recognition test of printed material rather than a study of the spoken vocabulary, but it is the only vocabulary study of deaf children of which we know which was conducted on a comprehensive and large scale. The sources of the words were the "Dale 3000 Word List" (Dale and Chall, 1948) and "Children's Knowledge of Words" (Dale and Eichholtz, 1960), from which a vocabulary of 7300 words was selected. These words were sampled to produce 73 sets of 100 randomly selected words each (thus giving a range of difficulty) which were then converted into vocabulary tests and administered to 13 207 children aged from 8–17 years attending 89 residential schools for the deaf in the United States. Unfortunately, audiometric and performance I.Q. data were not reported, but information was obtained on age and sex. All children were asked to respond to two vocabulary sets (i.e. 200 words).

For mean correct responses, girls scored significantly higher than boys, confirming McCarthy (1946), and there was an almost perfect overall linear relationship with age, with successive years combined into pairs, e.g. 8–9 years, 10–11 years, and so on, up to 16–17 years. When the responses to words classified as parts of speech were assessed, there was an overall geometric increase with age for all classes, i.e. for nouns, adjectives, verbs, adverbs, noun-related words (i.e. pronouns, determiners and function nouns, e.g. "all") and function words. The relative gains were greatest in the early years, as expected. At the age of 16 or 17 years 48% of the function words and 71% of the noun-related words were correctly identified. The total number of words which could be considered as known by the children at a criterion of 50% correct identification, when corrected for guessing, was 18 words at age 8–9, 157 at age 10–11, 660 at age 12–13, 1560 at age 14–15 and 2545 at age 16–17. The main part of Silverman-Dresner and Guilfoyle (1972) follows this information in the form of four lists of words known to the above criterion in the five age groups: Words by Age and Percent Correct; Words by Part of Speech and Earliest Age Known; Words by Topical Classification, Part of Speech, and Earliest Age Known; and Words by Definition and Topical Classification.

The increase in number of words in the known vocabularies in this study of deaf children was notable for the marked rate of increase from the age of 8–9 years, which was presumably due in large part to an increase in reading ability, though increased social interaction giving increased exposure to speech will have played a part also. Thus Silverman-Dresner and Guilfoyle have shown that as far as vocabulary is concerned, the understanding of the hearing-impaired child improves rapidly from the age of eight years, but this does not imply that the expressive aspect, namely the use of vocabulary in his spoken language, improves at the same rate also. The finding that the relative knowledge of words increases at roughly the same rate with age, irrespective of their classification as parts of speech, would not be expected to hold true for uttered words, where, as we have mentioned, the proportion of e.g. nouns would be expected to fall with increasing linguistic maturation, and the sex difference in known words may also not apply to spoken language, or at least not so prominently (Burroughs, 1957). We have already remarked that intelligence quotients and audiometric data were not given by Silverman-Dresner and Guilfoyle, and this is a pity in view of the large scale on which the work was conducted and the heterogeneity of linguistic ability in hearing-impaired children. Had the data been analysed for such effects, a more interesting and useful outcome should have been possible.

Can we make use of the work of Silverman-Dresner and Guilfoyle in devising tests of hearing for connected-speech? Certainly, their lists of recognition vocabularies with age look potentially useful. However, we would have reservations in using North American data as a base for tests intended for use mainly with British children. Also Silverman-Dresner and Guilfoyle collected material from schools for the deaf, whose pupils would have been severely or profoundly deaf, and would have contained relatively few mildly or moderately hearing-impaired, so that the children with milder partial hearing would have been markedly under-represented. Also, we required not only vocabulary, but a reliable indication of the part of speech for each word entry in order to construct our tests, and this information was, by design, not part of the Silverman-Dresner and Guilfoyle study. Thus, as we concluded following our review in Section III, we decided that we would have to collect and analyse our own sample of speech from partially-hearing children. From this sample we would compile vocabulary lists according to age, non-verbal I.Q. and hearing loss, and record the part of speech usage for each count of each word. Details of this approach are given in the following chapters of this book.

Since this chapter went to press, an evocative and practically-oriented book by Clezy (1979) has appeared, to which the reader who is actively concerned with language therapy is referred. The author discusses the importance of the mother–child interchange in the development of receptive and expressive language in children with impaired hearing and in children with other handicaps.

References

ANSI (1969). American National Standards Institute. Specifications for Audiometers. ANSI s3.6—1969, New York, USA.

ASA (1951). American Standards Association. Audiometers for Diagnostic Purposes. ASA 224.5—1951, New York, USA.

BAMFORD, J. M. and BENCH, J. (1979). A grammatical analysis of the speech of partially-hearing children. *In* "Working with LARSP: Methods and Applications" (D. Crystal, ed.). Edward Arnold, London, UK. (In press.)

BELLUGI, U. (1973). Development of language in the normal child. *In* "Language Intervention with the Retarded. Developing Strategies" (J. E. McLean, D. E. Yoder and R. Schiefelbusch, eds), pp. 33–51, Univ. Park Press, Baltimore, USA.

BENCH, J. and COTTER, S. (1979). Psycholinguistic abilities and audiometric performance in partially-hearing children. *Brit. J. Disord. Comm.* (In press.)

BENCH, J., WATSON, T. and DOWDING, T. (1976). Children's use of hearing aids. *Lancet* **1**, 1192.

BIRCH, J. W. and STUCKLESS, E. R. (1964). "The Relationship between Early Manual Communication and Later Achievement of the Deaf". Univ. of Pittsburgh, Pittsburgh, USA.

BRANNON, J. B. (1966). The speech production and spoken language of the deaf. *Lang. Speech* **9**, 127–136.

BRANNON, J. B. (1968). Linguistic word classes in the spoken language of normal, hard-of-hearing, and deaf children. *J. Speech Hear. Res.* **11**, 279–287.

BRANNON, . J. B. and MURRY, T. (1966). The spoken syntax of normal, hard-of-hearing and deaf children. *J. Speech Hear. Res.* **9**, 604–610.

BRIMER, M. A. and DUNN, L. M. (1962). *The English Picture Vocabulary Tests*. Education Evaluation Enterprises, Bristol, UK.

BROWN, R. and FRASER, C. (1964). The acquisition of syntax. *Child Devel. Monogr.* **29**, 43–79.

BUCKINGHAM, R. B. and DOLCH, E. W. (1936). "A Combined Word List". Ginn & Co., Boston, USA.

BURROUGHS, G. E. R. (1957). "A Study of the Vocabulary of Young Children". Oliver and Boyd, Edinburgh and London, UK.

CARROLL, J. B. (1958). Vectors of prose style. *In* "Style in Language" (T. A. Sebeok, ed.), pp. 283–292. M.I.T. Press, Cambridge, Mass., USA.

CARROW, E. (1973). "The Test for Auditory Comprehension of Language". Learning Concepts, Austin, Texas, USA.

CHARROW, V. (1975). A psycholinguistic analysis of "deaf English". *Sign Lang. Studies* **7**, 139–150.

CHOMSKY, N. (1957). "Syntactic Structures". Mouton, The Hague, Netherlands.

CHOMSKY, N. (1971). Deep structure, surface structure and semantic interpretation. *In* "Semantics" (D. Steinberg and L. Jakobvits, eds), pp. 183–216. Cambridge Univ. Press, Cambridge, UK.

CLEZY, G. (1979). "Modification of the Mother–Child Interchange in Language, Speech and Hearing". Univ. Park Press, Baltimore, USA.

CORNETT, R. O. (1970). Cued speech. *In* "Speech Communication Ability and Profound Deafness" (G. Fant, ed.), pp. 213–222. Alexander Graham Bell, Washington, USA.

CRYSTAL, D., FLETCHER, P. and GARMAN, M. (1976). "The Grammatical Analysis of Language Disability". Edward Arnold, London, UK.

DALE, E. and CHALL, J. S. (1948). A formula for predicting readability. *Educ. Res. Bull.* **27,** 11–20 and 37–44.

DALE, E. and EICHHOLTZ, G. (1960). "Children's Knowledge of Words". Bureau of Educ. Res., Ohio State Univ., Columbus, Ohio, USA.

DAVIS, E. A. (1938). Developmental changes in the distribution of parts of speech. *Child Develop.* **9,** 309–317.

DAVIS, J. M. (1977). Reliability of hearing-impaired children's responses to oral and total presentations of the Test of Auditory Comprehension of Language. *J. Speech Hear. Disord.* **52,** 520–527.

DOLCH, E. W. (1927). Grade vocabularies. *J. Educ. Res.* **16,** 16–26.

DOLCH, E. W. (1945). "Manual for Remedial Reading". Garrard, Champaign, Illinois, USA.

DOLCH, E. W. (1951). Tested word knowledge vs. frequency counts. *J. Educ. Res.* **44,** 457–470.

DORAN, E. W. (1907). A study of vocabularies. *Pedagog. Semin.* **14,** 401–438.

ELLIOT, L. L., HIRSH, I. J. and SIMMONS, A. A. (1967). Language of young hearing-impaired children. *Lang. Speech* **10,** 141–158.

ERBER, N. P. and McMAHAN, De.A. (1976). Effects of sentence context on recognition of words through lipreading by deaf children. *J. Speech Hear. Res.* **10,** 112–119.

EWING, Sir Alexander W. G. (1963). Linguistic development and mental growth in hearing-impaired children. *Volta Rev.* **65,** 180–187.

FILLENBAUM, S., JONES, L. V. and WEPMAN, J. M. (1961). Some linguistic features of speech from aphasic patients. *Lang. Speech* **4,** 91–108.

FRENCH, N. R., CARTER, C. W. and KOENIG, W. (1930). The words and sounds of telephone conversations. *Bell Syst. Teleph. J.* **9,** 290–324.

FRIES, C. C. (1952). "The Structure of English". Longman, London, UK.

FULLMER, D. W. and KOLSON, C. J. (1961). A beginning reading vocabulary. *J. Educ. Res.* **54,** 270–272.

GATES, A. I. (1926). "A Reading Vocabulary for the Primary Grades". Columbia University Press, New York, USA.

GATES, A. I. and MACGINITIE, W. H. (1965). Gates MacGinitie Reading Test, Teachers' Manual. Teacher's College, Columbia, New York, USA.

GODA, S. (1959). Language skills of profoundly deaf adolescent children. *J. Speech Hear. Res.* **2,** 369–376.

GODA, S. (1964). Spoken syntax of normal, deaf and retarded adolescents. *J. Verb. Learn. Verb. Behav.* **3,** 401–405.

HAMILTON, P. and OWRID, H. L. (1974). Comparisons of hearing impairment and socio-cultural disadvantage in relation to verbal retardation. *Brit. J. Audiol.* **8,** 27–32.

HARDY, W. G., PAULS, M. D. and HASKINS, H. L. (1958). An analysis of language development in children with impaired hearing. *Acta Otolaryng. Suppl.* **141.**

HART, N. W. M., WALKER, R. F. and GRAY, B. (1977). "The Language of Children—a Key to Literacy". Addison-Wesley, London, UK.

HEIDER, F. and HEIDER, G. M. (1941). Studies in the psychology of the deaf. *Psychol. Monogr.* **53,** 1–56.

HINE, W. D. (1970). Verbal ability and partial hearing loss. *Teacher of the Deaf* **75,** 450–459.

HORN, E. (1925). The commonest words in the spoken vocabulary of children up to and including six years of age. *Nat. Soc. Study Educ. Yearbook* **24,** 185–198.

HOWES, D. (1966). A word count of spoken English. *J. Verb. Learn. Verb. Behav.* **5,** 572–604.

INTERNATIONAL KINDERGARTEN UNION (1928). "A study of the vocabulary of children before entering first grade". I.K.U., Baltimore, USA.

IVIMEY, G. P. (1976). The written syntax of an English deaf child: an explanation in method. *Brit. J. Disord. Comm.* **11**, 103–120.

IVIMEY, G. P. (1977). The perception of speech: an information-processing approach. Part 3—lipreading and the deaf. *Teacher of the Deaf* **75**, 90–100.

JONES, L. V. and WEPMAN, J. M. (1966). "A Spoken Word Count". Language Research Associates, Chicago, Illinois, USA.

JONES, L. V., GOODMAN, M. F. and WEPMAN, J. M. (1963). The classification of parts of speech for the characterisation of aphasia. *Lang. Speech* **6**, 94–107.

KUCERA, H. and FRANCIS, W. N. (1967). "Computational Analysis of Present-day American English". Brown University Press, Providence, R.I., USA.

LEE, L. L. (1969). "The Northwestern Syntax Screening Test". Northwestern Univ. Press, Evanston, Illinois, USA.

LEE, L. L. and CANTER, S. M. (1971). Developmental sentence scoring: A clinical procedure for estimating syntax development in children's spontaneous speech. *J. Speech Hear. Disord.* **36**, 315–340.

LIBERMAN, A. M., COOPER, F. S., SHANKWEILER, D. P. and STUDDERT-KENNEDY, M. (1967). Perception of the speech code. *Psychol. Rev.* **74**, 431–461.

LITTLE, M. F., McFARLAND, M. L. and WILLIAMS, H. M. (1937). Development of language and vocabulary in young children. *Univ. Iowa Studies in Child Welfare* **13**, No. 2.

LORGE, I. and CHALL, J. (1963). Estimating the size of vocabularies of children and adults: an analysis of methodological issues. *J. Exp. Educ.* **32**, 147–157.

McCARTHY, D. A. (1930). The language development of the preschool child. *Inst. Child Welf. Monogr. Ser.* **4**. Univ. Minnesota Press, Minneapolis, USA.

McCARTHY, D. (1946). Language development in children. *In* "Manual of Child Psychology" (L. Carmichael, ed.), pp. 476–581. Wiley, London and New York.

MEIN, R. (1961). A study of the oral vocabularies of severely subnormal patients, II. Grammatical analysis of speech samples. *J. Ment. Defic. Res.* **5**, 52–59.

MONTGOMERY, G. W. G. (1967). Analysis of pure tone audiometric responses in relation to speech development in the profoundly deaf. *J. Acoust. Soc. Amer.* **41**, 53–59.

MONTGOMERY, G. W. G. (1968). A factorial study of communication and ability in deaf school leavers. *Brit. J. Educ. Psychol.* **38**, 27–37.

MURRY, H. A. (1943). "Thematic Apperception Test". Harvard Univ. Press, Cambridge, Mass., USA.

MYKLEBUST, H. R. (1964). "The Psychology of Deafness". Grune and Stratton, New York, USA.

NICE, M. M. (1915). The development of a child's vocabulary in relation to environment. *Pedagog. Semin.* **22**, 36–64.

OLSON, J. L. (1963). A comparison of receptive aphasic, expressive aphasic, and deaf children on the Illinois Test of Psycholinguistic Abilities. *In* "Selected Studies on the Illinois Test of Psycholinguistic Abilities" (J. McCarthy, ed.), pp. 46–69. University of Illinois, USA.

OWRID, H. L. (1960a). Measuring spoken language in young deaf children, Part 1. *Teacher of the Deaf* **58**, 24–34.

OWRID, H. L. (1960b). Measuring spoken language in young deaf children, Part 2. *Teacher of the Deaf* **58**, 124–128.

OWRID, H. L. (1970). Hearing impairment and verbal attainments in primary school children. *Educ. Res.* **12**, 209–214.

OYER, H. J. and FRANKMAN, J. P. (1975). "The Aural Rehabilitation Process". Holt, Rinehart and Winston, New York, USA.

PRESSNELL, L. McK. (1973). Hearing-impaired children's comprehension and production of syntax in oral language. *J. Speech Hear. Res.* **16**, 12–21.

RAVEN, J. C. (1948). "Mill Hill Vocabulary Scale". H. K. Lewis, London, UK.

RICHARDS, C. M. (1967). A test of understanding the spoken word. *Brit. J. Disord. Comm.* **2**, 124–133.

RINSLAND, H. D. (1945). "A Basic Vocabulary of Elemental Schoolchildren". MacMillan, London, UK.

RUSSELL, W. K., QUIGLEY, S. P. and POWER, D. J. (1976). "Linguistics and Deaf Children". Alexander Graham Bell, Washington, USA.

SCHONELL, F. J. and SCHONELL, F. E. (1956). Graded word reading test. *In* "Diagnostic and Attainment Testing" (F. J. Schonell, ed.), pp. 38–42. Oliver and Boyd, London, UK.

SILVERMAN-DRESNER, T. and GUILFOYLE, G. R. (1972). "Vocabulary Norms for Deaf Children". Alexander Graham Bell, Washington, USA.

SIMMONS, A. A. (1962). A comparison of the type-token ratio of spoken and written language of deaf and hearing children. *Volta Rev.* **64**, 417–421.

SIMMONS, A. A. (1966). Language growth for the pre-nursery deaf child. *Volta Rev.* **68**, 201–205.

SOLLY, G. M. (1975). Tests of comprehension of spoken language for use with hearing impaired children. *Teacher of the Deaf* **73**, 74–85.

SWISHER, L. (1976). The language performance of the oral deaf. *In* "Studies in Neurolinguistics" (H. Whitaker and H. A. Whitaker, eds), Vol. II, pp. 59–94. Academic Press, London and New York.

TEMPLIN, M. C. (1957). "Certain Language Skills in Children". University of Minnesota Press, Minneapolis, USA.

THORNDIKE, E. L. (1921). "Teachers' Word Book". Columbia University Press, New York, USA.

THORNDIKE, E. L. (1927). "Teacher's Word Book", 2nd edition. Teacher's Coll., Columbia Univ., New York, USA.

THORNDIKE, E. L. (1932). "A teachers' word book of the twenty thousand words found most frequently and widely in general reading for children and young people". Gale Research Co., Detroit, USA. (Reissued 1975.)

THORNDIKE, E. L. and LORGE, I. (1944). "The Teacher's Word Book of 30,000 words". Teacher's Coll., Columbia University Press, New York, USA.

WECHSLER, D. (1949). "Wechsler Intelligence Scale for Children: Manual". Psychol. Corp., New York, USA.

WEPMAN, J. M. and HASS, W. (1969). "A Spoken Word Count (Children—Ages 5, 6 and 7)". Language Research Associates, Chicago, Illinois, USA.

WEST, J. J. and WEBER, J. L. (1974). A linguistic analysis of the morphemic and syntactic structures of a hard-of-hearing child. *Lang. Speech* **17**, 68–79.

WILCOX, J. and TOBIN, H. (1974). Linguistic performance of hard-of-hearing and normal-hearing children. *J. Speech Hear. Res.* **17**, 288–293.

ZIPF, G. K. (1936). "The Psycho-biology of Language". Routledge, London, UK.

3

The Design of the Study

JOHN BAMFORD

I. Introduction

In speech audiometry, use is made of balanced lists of linguistic items, usually words or sentences, which the listener is required to repeat back. His hearing is then assessed in terms of the speech audiogram, which relates the percentage reported back correctly as a function of the intensity of the speech. Since speech audiometry tests are designed to assess hearing ability, and not language ability, it is essential that the test material for any such test be within the linguistic ability of the listener (see Chapter 1). Graham (1968), for example, working with educationally subnormal (ESN) children and using sentences containing familiar vocabulary, found that sentence repetition is related to both sentence length and grammatical structure. For speech audiometric tests using sentences as the test items the words used should be common words which are within the listener's vocabulary; the length of each sentence should be well within the listener's capabilities; and the grammar used should be uncomplicated and familiar to the listener.* In addition to these structural criteria the final sentences should all, of course, be semantically "reasonable".

The first stage in the development of a new sentence test, then, is to obtain information about the linguistic ability of those listeners for whom the test is to be designed. The restricted auditory input of partially-hearing children is known to retard aspects of their ability with reference to the language of normally-hearing children (e.g. Owrid, 1960; Brannon and Murry, 1966; Hine, 1970; Solly, 1975). Precisely what these aspects are, and to what extent they are not only different in degree (i.e. retarded) but different in kind from the language of the normally-hearing remains, however, an open question. Information about the linguistic ability of hearing-impaired children, and in particular the partially-hearing, is hard to come by, and what little there is has often been obtained with methodologically questionable techniques or with inadequately defined groups of subjects (see Chapter 2). It became apparent to us, therefore, that the required information would have to be derived from direct observation by ourselves of a large sample of partially-hearing children. This Chapter describes the background (Section I), the subjects (Section II), the procedure for data collection (Section III) and the procedure for data analysis (Section IV) of this exercise. The use of these data to provide the linguistic guide-lines for the construction of the test sentences is described in Chapter 4, while the results and further analyses in detail are presented and discussed in Chapters 6 and 7.

Templin (1957) has pointed out the distinction between vocabularies of word use (spoken or written), and vocabularies of word understanding (comprehension of the spoken or written word), and it is generally agreed that for normally-hearing children at least, vocabularies of understanding, or

---

* Following Crystal *et al.* (1976), the term "grammar" is used "to refer to all matters of structural organization exclusive of pronunciation and semantics". In this, the use differs from its use in generative linguistics, where the term covers all three notions. There are two aspects of grammar: morphology and syntax. The former is concerned with word structure (prefixes, compounds, word endings, etc.), the latter with the ways in which sequences of words constitute larger patterns (phrases, clauses and sentences). In this study, for various reasons, rather more emphasis is placed on syntax, although some of the analysis takes place at the morphological level.

recognition vocabularies, are larger than vocabularies of use, or expressed vocabularies (e.g. Bellugi, 1972). Furthermore, in its grammatical aspects comprehension tends to precede expressed language (e.g. McCarthy, 1954; Fraser *et al.*, 1963). Lackner (1968) investigated the spoken language and sentence repetition of a small group of mentally-retarded children and a small group of normal children, and showed that both groups were able to repeat back those sentences constructed from vocabulary items and syntactic types found in their own spoken repertoire. With sentences involving familiar vocabulary but more complex syntax, the children either did not understand a sentence and failed to repeat it back correctly; or they understood the sentence and repeated it back telegraphically, with a simpler syntax. Bearing in mind the distinction between expressed and comprehended language, it was decided to "play safe", by deriving the required linguistic information from the *expressed* language of our sample of partially-hearing children. We further decided to use the spoken language rather than the written language of our children as the source of the linguistic data; since we are concerned here with the design of a test for the hearing of *speech*, it makes good sense to derive our information from spoken language, for by so doing one can avoid assumptions about the equivalence of speech and writing. Apart from the relative informality, incompleteness and unsophistication of speech in comparison with writing, it has been argued (French *et al.*, 1930) that the more common words tend to be used more frequently in spoken than written material. This is an important point if one is primarily interested, as we are, in compiling lists of frequently-used words, these words to provide the vocabulary for our sentences.

Thus, given that the sample of partially-hearing children is representative, if the test sentences contain only those words and those grammatical structures spoken by the children themselves, then they ought to be within the linguistic ability of the proposed listeners. Of course, in the end a test for the hearing of connected-speech is an individual test and not a statistical approximation, and so ultimately the tester will have to satisfy himself that the particular person he is testing is indeed linguistically able enough for the test. Provided, however, that the initial study of the spoken language of partially-hearing children shows that all but the poorest of them do string words together in the form of sentences, albeit simple, and provided that sentence lists are constructed with criteria (*vis-à-vis* vocabulary, grammar and sentence length) derived from the less advanced children in the sample (not including those whose "sentences" consist of single words, and who would be unable to cope with a sentence repetition task however simple the sentences were made), then the test will be appropriate in most cases.

Dolch (1951) is another who has discussed the word use/word comprehension distinction. Different rates of linguistic development aside, he felt that there were two obvious reasons why word use and word comprehension are not identical: one is opportunity (there is more chance to talk about some things than others), and the second reason is interest or "set" (some topics, ideas or words are more agreeable than others). The effect of these two variables gradually diminishes as one increases the size of the spoken language sample from each subject, but the time expended on data collection and data analysis is increased without ever completely removing the effect. If one uses picture-description speech rather than conversational speech as the source of the spoken language samples, the effect of the two biasing factors in word counts can be controlled. However, where the aim of the research is in some way to define the unrestricted vocabulary knowledge of a group of subjects, then picture-description, with its highly restricted opportunities for vocabulary, is no substitute for conversational speech, and the effects of Dolch's two biasing variables have to be minimized in other ways: for example, by following word counts with interview tests, as he suggests. In the present study the aim is not to investigate the full range of vocabulary knowledge of our partially-hearing children, but simply to identify a certain number of words with which they are familiar, and which can be used, therefore, to make up the sentences for the speech test. For such an aim picture-description is quite satisfactory, given a sensible selection of pictures; furthermore, time is saved, since with the restricted subject matter reasonably stable frequencies will be achieved more quickly. There is, anyway, a problem with exactly how to elicit or record conversational speech: should the speech be obtained in the class, at home, or in the laboratory, should it be elicited by an experimenter, or what? Finally, it is the case that the speech of some hearing-impaired children is difficult to understand, but where the subject matter is clear, as in picture-description, this problem is considerably reduced.

The question of whether to use picture-description or conversational speech of one sort or another to furnish the material for linguistic analysis depends upon whom we are studying and what we are hoping to achieve. If the aim is to assess the grammatical structure of speech, then clearly it is best to use spontaneous speech itself as the source material, since unnecessary assumptions are thereby avoided. Thus Nice (1932) used the conversational speech of members of her own family in a study of the variation of children's parts of speech with age. Similarly, Harwood (1959) used spontaneous conversational speech for an analysis of the spoken syntax of a group of Australian children. Goda (1964), apparently because of the difficulty in understanding the speech of deaf children, used a highly constrained procedure for comparing the spoken syntax of normal, deaf and retarded adolescents, in which each subject uttered one sentence only in response to each of 16 different pictures. The analysis was largely in terms of Fries' (1952) parts of speech system (see Chapter 2), and indicated that 75% of deaf adolescent language consisted of Class 1 and Class 2 words, with few Class 3 words and very few "function" words (prepositions, conjunctions, auxiliaries, etc.). A similar study by Brannon and Murry (1966) compared the spoken syntax (in terms of sentence length, clause structure and parts of speech) of normally-hearing, partially-hearing and deaf children aged about 12 years. Like Goda, they chose to elicit speech in response to pictures: each child uttered three or four sentences in response to each of 14 coloured pictures, and "each child was instructed to say one sentence and stop; also, each hearing-impaired child wrote his response after saying it". A rather less formal and constrained picture-description method was used by Elliot *et al.* (1967), in which young hearing-impaired children were shown pictures and instructed simply "Tell me about this picture". The authors used several measures—total number of words, total number of different words, frequency of different classes of function words, etc.—in an attempt to arrive at an assessment of the advancement of their subjects' spoken language.

An examination of these and other studies indicates that as a source material for studies of grammar, picture-description speech does have two disadvantages. Firstly, it elicits mainly statements, with very few examples of exclamations, commands and questions. Secondly, and partly as a consequence of this, the proportion of nouns in picture-description speech is unnaturally high. Mein (1961), for example, in a study of severely subnormal patients, found that the proportion of nouns rose from 21–31% in their conversational speech (derived from the second of two fairly unstructured interviews with a familiar experimenter) to 42–56% in their picture-description speech. In the present study, however, these disadvantages are not critical. As far as the first is concerned, it was decided in any case to restrict the sentences in the proposed speech audiometric test to statements, and not to use questions or commands, since such items can cause difficulties in a test where the task is to repeat the sentence (and not to answer the question or to obey the command). For this reason, information on the grammatical ability of the partially-hearing children with which to guide sentence construction was required only for statements. Again, for the primary task of sentence construction the second disadvantage of picture-description speech is not important, provided the ensembles of parts of speech other than nouns are large enough to furnish an adequate selection of words.

Thus, bearing in mind the aims of the present project, we decided to use picture-description to elicit the speech samples from the partially-hearing children. Where the vocabulary data and the grammatical data are presented in detail as research findings in their own right, however (Chapters 6 and 7 respectively), the limitations to the data as a result of the methodological considerations discussed above must be remembered.

The pictures that were finally chosen for the task are shown in Figs 1–5 (see pp. 87–91). They were selected from speech therapy materials, reading materials, and so on. Although reproduced here in black and white, the pictures shown to the children were coloured originals.

II. Subjects

The total number of subjects seen was 263. These were children aged from 8–15 years inclusive, with non-verbal I.Q.s (WISC performance scales) of between 64 and 150, and a pure tone hearing loss in the better ear of not less than 40 dB ISO (averaged threshold at 500, 1000 and 2000 Hz). The children attended ordinary schools, partial-hearing units, partial-hearing schools, schools for the deaf and other special schools in Berkshire, Hampshire, Surrey, Sussex, London, Hertfordshire, Buckinghamshire and Oxfordshire. A list of the schools visited is given in Appendix IV. All the children were receiving an oral education; this was not a consideration in the selection of subjects, but is simply a reflection of the educational approach in use in our area.

There were 140 male and 123 female children. The mean age was 11·6 years, and the distribution of ages is shown in Table I.

Table I. The distribution of ages of the subjects

Age in years	8	9	10	11	12	13	14	15
Number of subjects	28	22	42	30	37	39	35	30

The mean non-verbal I.Q. score was 103·4 (standard deviation = 16·6). The distribution of these I.Q. scores is shown in Table II. (The rather unusual choice of intervals in Tables II, III and V is a by-product of the computer programme used to sort the data.)

The mean pure tone average hearing loss in the better ear across all subjects was 73·3 dB ISO (standard deviation = 15·6). The distribution of hearing losses is shown in Table III.

Risberg and Martony (1970) have devised a method for describing the

Table II. The distribution of WISC non-verbal I.Q. scores

Performance I.Q.										
From	64	73	82	90	99	108	116	125	133	142
To	72	81	89	98	107	115	124	132	141	150
Number of subjects	10	12	36	38	56	49	32	21	8	1

Table III. The distribution of average pure tone hearing losses in the better ear (averaged at 500, 1000, 2000 Hz)

Average pure tone hearing loss										
From (dB)	40	47	53	59	66	72	78	85	91	97	102
To (dB)	46	52	58	65	71	77	84	90	96	102	+
Number of subjects	13	16	27	30	34	29	38	31	25	15	5

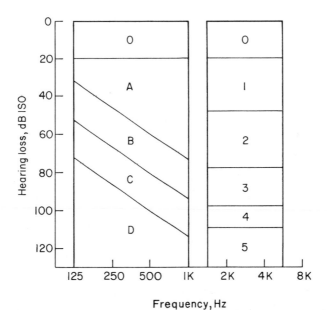

Fig. 6   The Risberg and Martony (1970) system for classifying pure tone audiograms. (By kind permission of the Alexander Graham Bell Association for the Deaf, Inc.)

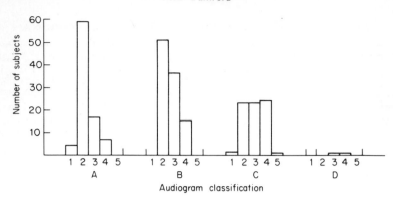

Fig. 7   The number of subjects in each of Risberg and Martony's (1970) pure tone audiogram classifications.

shape of the pure tone audiogram. Such a procedure is rather more informative than simply averaging the thresholds at 500, 1000 and 2000 Hz. Stated briefly, they divide the low-frequency part of the audiogram, below 1000 Hz, into four areas labelled A, B, C and D (see Fig. 6), and the high-frequency part of the audiogram, above 1500 Hz, into five areas labelled 1, 2, 3, 4 and 5. Any pure tone audiogram can be classified according to the areas in which the low and high parts of the audiogram mainly lie. Thus a flat audiogram of uniform 30 dB loss would be classified A1, while a steeply descending "ski slope" audiogram with fairly good low-frequency response might be classified A3. The frequency of occurrence of the different classifications among the subject sample is shown in Fig. 7.

When available, certain background information about the subjects was collected. This information is presented below.

Details of the cause of the hearing-impairment were available for 172 subjects. There are five categories of cause of impairment, and the number of subjects falling into each category is shown in Table IV.

Details of the age at onset of the hearing-impairment were obtained for 188 subjects. The distribution of these onset ages is shown in Table V, and it will be seen that the hearing of the clear majority of the sample had been impaired at birth or within a few months thereafter.

Details of the age at which the hearing-impairment was diagnosed were obtained for 216 subjects. The distribution of these diagnosis ages is shown in Table VI, and it will be noticed that many of the diagnoses were made somewhat later than one might expect, given the large number of children with early onset ages.

All the subjects had been issued with hearing aids. It was decided to note

Table IV. The categories of causes of hearing-impairment and the number of subjects in each category

Cause of hearing-impairment	Number of subjects
1. Hereditary/genetic/familial	29
2. Other congenital	
(a) Pre-natal (e.g. rubella)	57
(b) Peri-natal complications (e.g. anoxia)	52
3. Post-natal accidental (e.g. bang on head)	4
4. Post-natal clinical (e.g. measles; otitis media)	25
5. Multiple (i.e. combinations of categories 1–4)	5
Total for whom information available	172

Table V. The distribution of ages at onset of hearing-impairment, in months from birth

Age at onset of hearing-impairment in months	From	0	8	16	24	32	40	48	56	64	72	80
	To	7	15	23	31	39	47 ⁹	55	63	71	79	87
Number of subjects		158	11	2	6	1	1	2	1	4	0	2

Table VI. The distribution of ages at diagnosis of hearing-impairment, in years since birth

Age at which hearing-impairment was first diagnosed, in years.	From	0	1	2	3	4	5	6	7	8	9	10
	To	1	2	3	4	5	6	7	8	9	10	11
Number of subjects		52	42	32	26	27	26	4	2	1	3	1

the type of aid (body-worn or post-aural) and the number of aids (one or two) some time after testing had begun, so the data are available for only 186 subjects. The number of subjects wearing each type of aid is shown in Table VII.

The numbers of subjects who, at the time of testing, were attending residential schools for the hearing-impaired, partial-hearing units attached to schools for the normally-hearing, schools for the normally-hearing (i.e. fully integrated), or other special schools are shown in Table VIII.

Finally, details of the occupations of the children's parents were obtained

Table VII. The number of subjects issued with each type of hearing aid

Aid	N
Bone conduction	1
1 post-aural	52
2 post-aural	21
1 body-worn	51
2 body-worn	57
Body-worn Y-lead	4
Total for whom information available	186

Table VIII. Number of subjects according to type of school

Type of school or class	Number of subjects
Residential (deaf or partially-hearing)	145
Partial Hearing Unit attached to an ordinary school (with or without some integration into normally-hearing classes)	101
Fully integrated into normally-hearing classes	15
Other special schools	2

for most of the sample. The occupation of the family "bread-winner" was classified according to the scheme of the Office of Population Censuses and Surveys (Classification of Occupations, 1970), which distinguishes five "Social Classes" and 16 "socio-economic groups". The Social Classes are "selected so as to ensure that, so far as is possible, each category is homogeneous in relation to the basic criterion of the general standing within the community of the occupations concerned". Table IX shows the children classified according to the Social Class of the "bread-winning parent".

Classification by socio-economic group is designed such that "each socio-economic group should contain people whose social, cultural and recreational standards and behaviour are similar". The group headings and the number of children with "bread-winning parents" in each group is shown in Table X.

Since the aim of the project was to produce sentence lists for partially-hearing children in particular, the 22 subjects with an average pure tone hear-

Table IX. Parental occupations classified according to social class

Social class	Number of subjects
I Professional occupations	29
II Intermediate occupations	35
III Skilled occupations	71
IV Partly-skilled occupations	43
V Unskilled occupations	7
Members of armed forces (not given a S.C. classification)	10
Deceased, retired or unemployed	28
Total for whom information available	223

Table X. Parental occupations classified according to socio-economic group

Socio-economic group	Number of subjects
1. Employers and managers in large establishments	11
2. Employers and managers in small establishments	7
3. Professional workers—self-employed	0
4. Professional workers—employees	29
5. Intermediate non-manual workers	14
6. Junior non-manual workers	21
7. Personal service workers	16
8. Foremen and supervisors—manual	1
9. Skilled manual workers	44
10. Semi-skilled manual workers	29
11. Unskilled manual workers	11
12. Own account workers (other than professional)	1
13. Farmers—employers and managers	0
14. Farmers—own account	1
15. Agricultural workers	0
16. Members of armed forces	10
Occupation inadequately described	0
Deceased, retired or unemployed	28
Total for whom information available	223

ing loss in the better ear of 96 dB or more were dropped from the sentence construction exercise (Chapter 4) and from the vocabulary analysis (Chapter 6). Of course, there is no complete agreement on a definition of "partially-hearing". Some use it in an educational context (i.e. the extent to which the child will benefit from an essentially oral education), while others are satisfied to define it in terms of pure tone hearing loss. If the latter, there is some discussion as to what hearing loss is to be considered "profound" rather than "severely partial" in its effect. Newby (1972), Vernon (1976) and Kyle (1977), assessing the effect of pure tone loss on either speech production (articulation, etc.) or spoken language (grammar, vocabulary, etc.), agree that a loss equivalent to 85 dB ISO tends to divide the "profounds" from the "severes". O'Neill and Oyer (1973) suggest a figure of 90 dB. Any solution will be to some extent arbitrary, and with this in mind as well as wishing to throw the net too widely rather than too narrowly, it was decided to include all subjects with an average loss up to and including 95 dB for the purposes of sentence construction and vocabulary analysis. The grammatical analysis included not only these but also the 22 subjects with hearing losses above 95 dB.

In order to obtain the fullest range of subjects possible (within the limits of Berkshire and surrounding counties), a deliberate policy of quota sampling was adopted. That is, a 27-cell matrix was drawn up of age vs. non-verbal I.Q. vs. average pure tone hearing loss, each at three levels: ages 8–10, 11–13 and 14–15 years; non-verbal I.Q. scores 64–90, 91–110 and 111 or above; and average pure tone hearing losses in the better ear of 40–60, 61–80 and 81 dB or above. Each of the 27 cells in the matrix is designated with a letter (see Fig. 8), the Scandinavian letter Å providing the twenty-seventh character. The aim of the sampling procedure was to obtain a reasonable number of subjects per cell (say, 10 in each cell). Largely because I.Q. is distributed normally, but also because the members of cell Y, for example, are likely to be fully integrated into normally-hearing secondary schools and will therefore be difficult to locate, this aim was not entirely fulfilled. Nonetheless, a generally reasonable spread across the three major variables of age, non-verbal I.Q. and hearing loss was obtained.

Unforseen circumstances resulted in the loss of some parts of the data from a small number of subjects. The effects of these losses are negligible, but for the sake of clarity the numbers of subjects in each cell for each part of the analysis of the data are shown in Table XI.

Non-verbal I.Q.	Age: 8, 9, 10 years			Age: 11, 12, 13 years			Age: 14, 15 years		
Hearing loss	64 – 90	91 – 110	III +	64 – 90	91 – 110	III +	64 – 90	91 – 110	III +
40 – 60 dB	A	D	G	J	M	P	S	V	Y
61 – 80 dB	B	E	H	K	N	Q	T	W	Z
81 dB and above	C	F	I	L	O	R	U	X	Å

Fig. 8   The 27 cells of the subject classification matrix, whereby subjects are classified according to age, non-verbal I.Q., and average pure tone hearing loss in the better ear. Each cell is designated by a letter.

Table XI. The number of subjects used in each cell for the vocabulary analysis (Chapter 6), the sentence construction procedure (Chapter 4) and the grammatical analysis (Chapter 7). Note that only the latter includes those 22 subjects with an average pure tone hearing loss of greater than 95 dB

Cell	N for vocabulary analysis	N for sentence construction	N for grammatical analysis
A	6	6	6
B	7	9	9
C	3	3	9
D	9	13	13
E	13	13	13
F	16	14	19
G	3	3	3
H	6	6	6
I	11	9	14
J	7	7	7
K	14	14	14
L	7	6	7
M	10	10	10
N	14	14	14
O	9	11	12
P	6	6	6
Q	17	17	17
R	14	16	19
S	3	3	3
T	9	9	9
U	4	4	4
V	9	9	9
W	9	10	10
X	6	6	6
Y	2	2	2
Z	11	11	11
Å	10	10	11
Total	235	241	263

Fig. 1　The "Ice" picture. Copyright: CUES/Learning Materials Service, ILEA.

Fig. 2   The "Crash" picture. Copyright: CUES/Learning Materials Service, ILEA.

Fig. 3   The "Football" picture. Copyright: CUES/Learning Materials Service, ILEA.

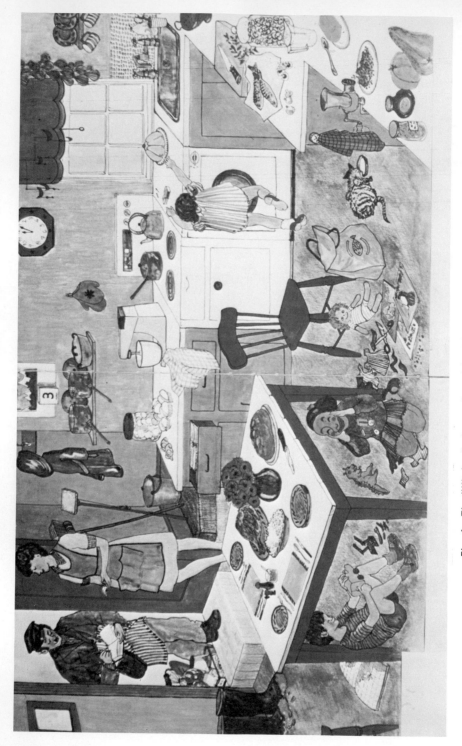

Fig. 4   The "Kitchen" picture. Copyright: Macdonald Educational Limited.

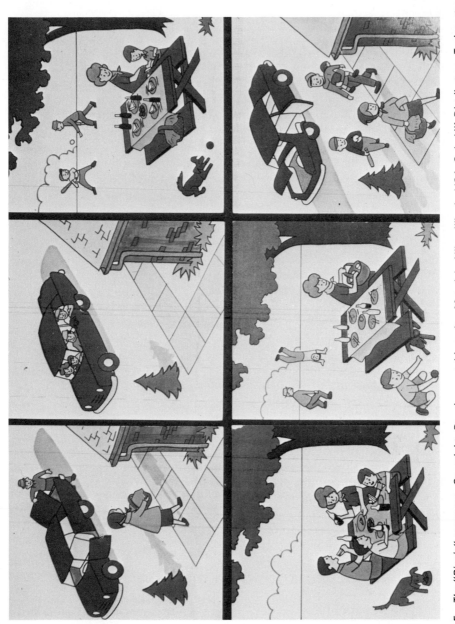

Fig. 5   The "Picnic" sequence. Copyright: Developmental Learning Materials, Niles, Illinois, USA. Sole UK Distributors: Taskmaster Limited, Morris Road, Clarendon Park, Leicester.

III. The procedure for data collection

The children were seen individually during school hours at their school. Each subject was tested for about an hour and a quarter, divided if necessary into two or more sessions to avoid fatigue. During this time, for anything up to 25 minutes, the child described and talked about the pictures (Figs 1–5), which were shown to him one at a time. The pictures belonging to the Picnic sequence (Fig. 5) were shown to the subject one at a time, in order. The "interview" (a rather formal title for what was intended to be as relaxed as possible) was conducted in an informal manner in order to elicit more "natural" utterances. Generally, questions (which tend to elicit elliptical replies) were avoided, and unspecific prompts were given, such as "Tell me what's happening here" and "Tell me some more". Occasionally, however, it was expedient to encourage a hesitant subject by asking him a direct question (e.g. "Who is in the car?"), to which the reply would often be elliptical (e.g. "Daddy, mummy and the dog"). The interview was tape-recorded on a portable cassette recorder. The poor articulation of some of the more severely impaired was not a serious problem, since by actually seeing the child and his articulatory movements, and knowing the picture material to which he was responding, and with the aid of repetition by the interviewer if necessary, the interviewer could record the child's utterances correctly as the interview proceeded. Any doubtful utterances, either at the interviewing stage or at the later transcription stage (see below), were dropped, but these were very infrequent.

The remainder of the testing time was taken up with assessing the child's pure tone hearing, and his or her non-verbal I.Q. using the WISC performance scales. In addition, when the information was available the other variables thought to be relevant to language development were noted: previous schooling, parental occupation, type of hearing aid (body-worn or post-aural, one ear or two), age at onset of hearing-impairment, age at diagnosis of hearing-impairment, the diagnosis and the cause. In general, the hearing and I.Q. testing was done first, and the interview with those children who did not satisfy the sampling needs was terminated without asking them to perform the picture-description task.

IV. The procedure for data analysis

The tape-recording of each subject's picture-description was later transcribed by one of six paid transcribers. They were given copies of the pictures and the following instructions:

"Notes to transcribers

1. The task is to write down everything said by the child interviewed. If, after listening to a word, phrase or sentence twice, you still can't be sure what was said, then leave it. When necessary, the interviewer repeats some of the child's statements and this will help. Indeed, with some children, this will be your only source of information. Please omit all the interviewer's questions, etc. All we need is what the child actually said, errors and all. Sometimes the interviewer prompts the child with a word or phrase, and the child repeats it back. In such cases, the word or phrase was not spontaneously supplied by the child, and it should *not* be recorded. Similarly, a child may sometimes *read* from a picture (e.g. "Danger thin ice"), and such utterances should not be recorded (the interviewer will note on the tape when this happens).

2. Do not expand contractions (won't, she'll, there's, man's (=man is), etc.), but record as said. Also, vice versa: do not record, e.g. *there's* when the child clearly said "There is". Rely on the interviewer's repeats when in doubt.

3. This is most important: leave *four* blank lines (for later grammatical analysis) in between each line for writing. In addition, leave a wide margin (about one inch), and begin new paragraphs liberally.

4. Each taped interview should be preceded by the child's name and school. If by any chance the interviewer has omitted this information, make a note of the children and their schools who were immediately before and after the unidentified interview. This will help us to identify it.

5. Occasionally, due to the frequent stopping and starting which will be necessary, a tape may stretch or twist. If this happens, stop transcribing and return the cassette to us.

6. Tape-recorders are not supplied but will be repaired, if necessary, free of charge.

7. Keep an accurate account of time taken.

   Many thanks. This is a crucial part of a three-year project to design and standardize a speech-hearing test for hearing-impaired children. This part is concerned with finding out what stage of language development certain children have reached."

Transcription was alphabetic, therefore, rather than phonetic. The transcription task was to some extent interpretive and hence errors could intrude, but not to any significant degree. For example, the presence or absence of ellisions such as "there's" is often difficult to determine and must to some extent be a source of transcriber variance. As a check, some of the tapes were retranscribed by another member of our team. The number of discrepancies between the two transcriptions was extremely small. After considerable discussion, it was decided not to mention punctuation of the transcription in the instructions. The result was that the transcribers tended to fall into a system where they simply marked the major pauses and natural breaks with commas or full-stops. The important decision for grammatical analysis as to what is a "sentence" was made at the later grammatical analysis stage, when due consideration was given to the transcribers' "natural" or unelicited punctuation.

Each transcription was then analysed for vocabulary and grammatical content.

A. Vocabulary content

The aim of the vocabulary analysis was to derive lists of the words used by the children, with an indication of how many times each word had been used. There was to be one list for each of the 27 groups of subjects (see Fig. 8). These lists would then be used to guide the selection of vocabulary for the construction of the test sentences, such that only the more frequently-used words would be selected (see Chapter 4). The problem with simple uncategorized alphabetical lists of words is that the user is unable to distinguish between quite different uses of the "same" word: *cooks*, for example, as in "she cooks" and "the cooks". The traditional solution to this problem is to categorize the words into "parts of speech" such as verbs, nouns, adverbs and so on, in which case "cooks" can be listed either as a noun, or a verb, or both, depending upon the grammatical and semantic contexts in which it appears. Such a method of arranging the word lists also has the advantage from our point of view of ease of entry: if one is searching for an acceptable high-frequency verb to use in a sentence, considerable savings in time are made by being able to go straight to the verb category within the list. Mein (1961) used the following categories: nouns, verbs, adjectives, adverbs, prepositions, pronouns, articles, conjunctions and miscellaneous. Fillenbaum *et al.* (1961) used nouns, verbs, adjectives, adverbs, pronouns, others (prepositions, conjunctions and articles) and gestures (including interjections). The problem with these traditional parsing categories is that for many common words the distinctions between the categories are unclear—because of the very nature of language and word use, which is essentially fluid, dynamic and often ambiguous—and for many such words the category selected will depend upon nothing more absolute than which dictionary one chooses as one's source. Words like *where, when* and *to* can be especially difficult to categorize reliably. The grammatical and semantic contexts in adult language tend to reduce the size of this problem such that it is of interest only to the theorist, and for most practical purposes the traditional word categories will suffice. In the speech of children with hearing-impairment, however, context can be sparse or misleading, and may be a poor guide to word-usage. In order to classify word-usage in aphasic speech, which suffers from similar problems of lack of contextual cues, Jones *et al.* (1963) claimed to have defined the word categories rather more reliably by simply placing each word into its "most-commonly used" class, given the classes: nouns, verbs, pronouns, adjectives, quantifiers, adverbs, prepositions, relatives, indefinites. Bench (Chapter 2) has discussed this method in some detail, and it will suffice to say here that for our purpose, the analysis of *picture-description* speech, it is not strictly applicable.

It was decided in the end that despite the inherent limitations in a classical parts of speech analysis such an approach would be suitable enough for the present project. We are not attempting an exhaustive description of partially-hearing language in terms of parts of speech; we simply need lists of words used by the children, which we ourselves can use, and it can be safely assumed that for this purpose the proportion of entries which are not correct categorizations or good approximations to such, given the large number of uttered words to be analysed, will be acceptably small. Each word in each transcription was classified into its part of speech according to the following instructions:

"Notes for Parsing the Transcriptions

1. Parse every word into one of the ten categories (below). Categorize all the words in a transcription by writing one of the ten numerals above each word:

    1. Nouns
    2. Verbs
    3. Adjectives
    4. Adverbs
    5. Pronouns
    6. Prepositions
    7. Conjunctions
    8. Contractions (e.g. He'll; don't; man's (=man is))
    9. Interjections (e.g. "Well, ..." "Oh!")
    0. Other, including "yes", "no", and articles (the, a, an).

2. Word order can be an important indicator of part of speech. Thus "broken eggs" is to be taken as Adjective-Noun, while "eggs broken" is to be taken as Noun-Verb.
3. Possessive pronouns (his, her, their, my, our, your) are marked as pronouns.
4. Nouns used as adjectives, (e.g. *picnic* basket, *garden* shed) are recorded as nouns. Similarly, genitive nouns are recorded as nouns (e.g. *mummy's* bag).
5. Infinitives: "to" is a preposition, "go" is a verb.
6. Context is an important indicator of part of speech, particularly in distinguishing between verb particles and prepositions. Thus in "He looked over (=examined) the room", "over" is v. particle and is recorded as an adverb. In "He looked over (=gazed across) the river", "over" is marked as a preposition.
7. Where the part of speech is not clear refer to the Concise Oxford Dictionary, 5th edition, 1963."

The reader should note that at a later date an eleventh category was created by separating the articles from category 0.

The words and their category numbers from each transcription were then punched onto 80 column cards for a computer-run vocabulary count, the details of which are as follows.

The category number of each word was punched as the final character of that word. Words were separated by spaces. Each subject's block of speech began with two codes, identifying the subject's group (A–Z, plus Å) and his position in the group, and ended with a terminating character !. Errors during punching were indicated by a "<" symbol, which caused the immediately preceding word to be ignored by the programme. The ease with which

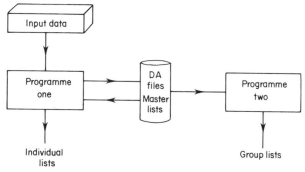

Fig. 9   *The analysis system for the vocabulary count.*

the speech could be punched onto cards was a major consideration in designing the data format, since a large proportion of the effort of the whole analysis lay in this process.

The processing (see Fig. 9) was carried out using the ICL 1906S computer of the University of Reading Computer Centre, with two programmes written in ALGOL 68-R (Woodward and Bond, 1974).

The first programme accepted as input a complete block of speech, and assembled in one pass a complete list of the words used with their parsing categories. With this list stored in core, a second pass was made, reducing the list to one in which all the *different* words with their frequencies and categories were stored. This list was then output. In the next stage of analysis, the master word list for the subject's group, which was held on a direct access file, was amended by the addition of the subject's word list. Thus as individual subjects were dealt with, the word lists for the groups were updated until all the subjects in a group had been processed. When this had been done, the group word list was passed on to the second system programme and then to the line printer.

In the design of the system the constraints of time taken had to be balanced against that of core usage, the one increasing as the other decreased. Storing the large lists in core had the advantage of increasing the speed with which they could be processed, but necessarily imposed size restrictions. These were, that a maximum of 2000 words could be accepted as input for each subject, and that words could be up to 12 characters long. These constraints were not restrictive and only came into effect in a small number of cases.

The time taken to process an individual subject varied between 100 and 400 seconds of mill-time, with a mean of about 250 seconds, and the total time taken was some 65 000 seconds of mill-time, distributed over about five months of fairly constant processing.

Thus, after sorting, the grouped vocabulary data took the form of 27 print-outs, one for each cell of the subject classification matrix. Each print-out showed the number of occurrences of each word spoken by the members of that group, sorted alphabetically within parsing categories. Also shown was the total number of words in each parsing category (tokens), and the total number of *different* words (types) in each parsing category. These data are discussed and analysed in Chapter 6.

B. Grammatical content

The aim of the grammatical analysis was to determine those syntactic and morphological structures that all or most of the children knew, as shown by their frequent use. These structures would then be used to guide the construction of test sentences. It was hoped, both for the vocabulary and the grammatical analysis, that in fulfilling the primary aims of the study we would at the same time amass a considerable amount of data of general theoretical and practical interest on the spoken language of partially-hearing children, data that are not available in any detail in the literature. As for the vocabulary analysis, it seemed the best course, bearing in mind our primary aims, to adopt a traditional description of grammatical structure. It has been fahionable for some time now, however, to describe grammar not in the general tradition of structuralist linguistics but using the transformational-generative approach of Chomsky (e.g. 1965) and others. It should be pointed out that for our purposes this approach would not be satisfactory. The sentences we wish to construct for the hearing test will all be of the active declarative type, of similar base structure, and what we need to know are the sentence-level units that we can use in the sentences. In any case, several studies have shown that transformational-generative grammar is not a good discriminator between the language of pathological and normal groups: Morehead (1972) states that "the deviant child's deficit lies not in his ability to develop base aspects of grammar but rather in his ability to develop additional terms and the relations in which to use those terms". Morehead and Ingram (1973) found little difference between a group of normal and a group of deviant children in terms of the transformational features of their language; but they did find important differences in terms of constructional types. Russell *et al.* (1976) have summarized the transformational-generative approach and its use in the analysis of the written language of deaf children by themselves and others. However, many of their findings relate primarily to surface structure, and the authors note that as regards phrase structure "deaf children appear to have relatively little difficulty in learning the more general phrase structure rules of English, but very great difficulty indeed in learning their more subtle manifestations in surface structure ..." (p. 67).

Thus we have adopted a structuralist approach to the grammatical analysis of the speech samples, although it might be better described as an orientation rather than an approach, since it does not preclude the use of transformational notions where useful. The particular method of analysis which we decided to adopt is that of Crystal *et al.* (1976), using a slightly modified version of their Language Assessment, Remediation and Screening Procedure (LARSP) profile. The profile is essentially a check list of syntactic and morphological items, and is shown in Fig. 10 (this particular profile has been used to analyse the speech sample from one of our subjects).

The analyser works through a transcription, recording the occurrence of each grammatical item onto the profile as it occurs. The first task is to divide the transcription into consecutive sentences. This is probably the most difficult part of the analysis, and the largest source of analyser "error". However, it should be noted that the transfer of data from transcripts to profiles was performed entirely by one trained analyser, keeping such error variance to a minimum. Unelicited transcriber punctuations, semantic "flow" and syntactic structure all served as clues to the delineation of sentences. The minimum length of a sentence is one word (e.g. "Yes", "Hello", "Car", etc.), but theoretically there is no upper limit since there is no grammatical constraint on the endless use of conjunctions. Lee and Canter (1971) introduced their own constraint to get over this "problem" (only one *and* per sentence at clause level was allowed), but the analysis used in the present study acknowledges the importance and the reality of clause-linking conjunctions at certain ages, and does not impose such arbitrary restrictions. With certain children, then, 20- and 30-word sentences were not uncommon.

UNANALYSED:

Deviant	Ambiguous
1	1

Analyser's Comments:

ANALYSED

		Minor "Sentences": Social		Stereotypes			Problems	

				Major	"Sentences"			

| | | Excl. | Comm. | Quest. | | Statement | | |

STAGE 1 (0.9 – 1.6)

			'V'	'Q'	'V' **4**	'N' **28**	Other **1**	Problems

				Conn.	Clause		Phrase		Word

STAGE 2 (1.6 – 2.0)

	VX	QX	SV **5**	VC/O **4**	DN **22**	vv	Inf.
			S C/O **1**	AX **1**	Adj N **1**	v part **2**	-ing **12**
					NN **1**	int x	pl. **4**
			Neg X	Other	Pr N **3**	other	
							fut.

STAGE 3 (2.0 – 2.6)

	VXY	QXY	X+S:NP **2**	X+V:VP **3**	X+C/O :NP **2**	X+A:AP	-ed
	let XY	VS	SVC/O **12**	VC/O A	D Adj N	Cop **2** / Aux **8**	-en
	doXY		SVA **6**	V O_d O_i	Adj Adj N	Pron **2**	3s
					Pr DN **4**	Pr Pron	
			Neg XY	Other	N Adj N	Other	

STAGE 4 (2.6 – 3.0)

		QXYZ	XY+S:NP **5**	XY+V:VP **4**	XY+ C/O:NP **5**	XY+A:AP **3**	gen
	+S	QVS	SVC/OA **1**	AAXY	N Pr NP	Neg V	n't
			SVO_dO_i	Other	Pr D Adj N **1**	Neg X	'cop
					c X	2 aux	
					X c X	Other	'aux

STAGE 5 (3 – 3.6)

how		and	Coord. 1 1+		Postmod. 1 1+ clause	-est
	tag	c	Subord. 1 1+			
			Clause: S		Postmod. 1+ phrase	-er
what		s	Clause: C/O	Comparative		-ly
		other	Clause: A			

STAGE 6 (3.6 – 4.6)

	+			–		
	NP	VP	Clause	NP	VP	Clause
Initiator	Complex		Passive	Pron. Adj. Seq.	Modal	Concord
					Tense	A Position
Coord.			Complement	Det. N irreg.	V irreg.	W Order

| Other: | | | | Other: | | |

STAGE 7 (4.6+)

A connectivity:	Emphatic order:	it:
Comment clause:	Other:	there:

NUMBER OF WORDS IN EACH SENTENCE*   **MEAN NO. WORDS PER SENTENCE = 4.06.**

Here sentence means: Any utterance which is neither deviant nor ambiguous, but excluding all Stage 1 utterances.

Fig. 10   The LARSP profile (after Crystal et al., 1976). The speech sample from an eleven-year-old girl of below average non-verbal I.Q., and with a pure tone hearing loss (averaged in the better ear) of 92 dB, has been analysed onto this profile.

Having delineated the subject's sentences, the next problem for the analyser is to decide whether each sentence is deviant, ambiguous or acceptable.
A "deviant" sentence (see Chapter 7, section II) is one which is both structur-
ally inadmissible in the adult grammar, and which is not part of the expected
grammatical development of normal children (as far as this can be established
by reference to the literature). An "ambiguous" sentence is one which could
have two or more equally plausible syntactic interpretations, and it is unclear
from all available information (structural or situational) which is correct.
If the sentence is deemed either deviant or ambiguous, an entry is made in
the appropriate box at the top of the profile (Fig. 10), and no further analysis
of that sentence is undertaken. If, on the other hand, the sentence is acceptable, its grammatical analysis onto the main body of the profile takes place.

No attempt will be made here to describe and discuss the profile in its
entirety. For this, the reader is referred to the original source (Crystal *et al.*,
1976, especially Chapters 3 and 4). Nevertheless, it is important to understand
the basic principles of its organization, and the meaning of the grammatical
symbols within it. To this end, the remainder of this Chapter is given over
to a shortened description of the main body of the profile. Any reader who
is already familiar with this, or who feels that he is labouring unnecessarily,
may wish to omit the rest of the Chapter.

Given an acceptable sentence (i.e. one that is neither deviant nor ambiguous) the analyser decides whether it is a Minor Sentence or a Major Sentence. Examples of the former are: "Yes." "Oh!" "First come, first served."
"I don't know." Such sentences are noted in the appropriate place on the
profile, and analysed no further. If it is a Major Sentence, the analyser must
decide whether it is an exclamation (Excl.), a command (Comm.), a question
(Quest.) or a statement. As we have already noted, the picture-description
task tends to elicit very little other than statements, so Excl., Comm. and
Quest. will not be discussed further.

The grammatical analysis of Major Sentence Statements forms the main
part of the exercise. Crystal *et al.* have identified a set of syntactic stages
through which normal children pass in their progress towards adult languages, and these Stages are labelled 1–7 in order of advancement. The
arrangement of the profile is such that as one goes down it from top to
bottom, the Stages and structures become more advanced. It must be
stressed, however, that Stages are not "discrete entities, periods of ability
which switch off and on, like a sequence of relays. Syntactic development
is a continuous process, and our Stages are arbitrary divisions along it" (Crystal *et al.*, p. 61). They are, however, divisions which have theoretical validity,
since each Stage corresponds to some general linguistic process which it is

possible to identify in formal terms. The figures associated with each Stage, on the left-hand side of the profile, refer to the age range, in years, in which those structures associated with that Stage *tend to first appear* in normal children. Figure 11 shows the model of Stages, and illustrates that normal adult language contains many Stage 2 and 3 structures, for example, along with Stage 4 structures.

Stage 1 statements consist simply of one element, verb-like ("V") or noun-like ("N") utterances. Utterances like "Daddy", "Car", "Eating" would be recorded as Stage 1 entries. The inverted commas around the symbols "V" and "N" serve to emphasize the especially tentative nature of word-classes at this stage of development. From Stage 2 to Stage 5 on the profile, Statements are analysed at three distinct levels: clause level, concerned with the number and arrangement of subject, verb, object, adverbial and complement

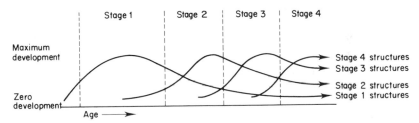

Fig. 11 A diagrammatic illustration of the emergence and development of the linguistic Stages on the LARSP profile (reproduced by kind permission of Crystal et al., 1976).

elements; phrase level, concerned with the occurrence and development of phrase structures within clause elements; and word level, concerned mainly with the occurrence of particular word endings. Note that according to our earlier definitions the latter provides morphological data, while the remainder of the profile provides syntactical data. Furthermore, it should be noted that information in the literature about the order of emergence of morphological structures is somewhat scant and Crystal *et al.* have not attempted, therefore, to divide the word structures into Stages of development, although the order in which they appear on the profile (top to bottom) is thought to be a reasonable guess at the order of emergence.

A brief description of Stages 2–5 is now given, at the three levels of clause, phrase and word. Stage 2 clauses contain two elements: subject-verb (SV), subject with complement or object (SC/O), verb with complement or object (VC/O), an adverbial and one other element (AX), or a negative and one other element (Neg X). Examples would be: "He cried" (SV), "Eat biscuit"

(VC/O). Stage 2 phrases are: determiner-noun (DN), adjective-noun (AdjN), noun-noun (NN), preposition-noun (PrN), verb–verb (vv), verb particle (v part), and intensifier with any other phrase element (int x). Examples would be: "Very hard" (int x), "The ball" (DN), "In garden" (PrN), "Put off" (v part).

Stage 3 clauses contain three elements: subject-verb-(complement or object) (SVC/O), subject-verb-adverbial (SVA), verb-(complement or object)-adverbial (VC/OA), verb-(direct object)-(indirect object) (VO_dO_i), or a negative with any two elements (Neg XY). Examples would be: "Daddy drives fast" (SVA), "Man throwing ball" (SVC/O). Stage 3 phrase structures are: determiner-adjective-noun (DAdjN), adjective-adjective-noun (AdjAdjN), preposition-determiner-noun (PrDN), noun-adjective-noun (NAdjN), copula (Cop), auxiliary verb (Aux), pronoun (Pron), and preposition-pronoun (Pr Pron). Examples would be: "The red ball" (DAdjN), "In the garden" (PrDN), "He *is* big" (Cop), "He *is* running" (Aux), "*He* fell" (Pron), "in it" (Pr Pron).

An important distinction is made between those two and three element clauses in which the elements are expanded into verb, noun or adverbial phrases, and those two or three element clauses where the elements remain as single words, not so expanded. When none of the two or three elements in the clauses are expanded, the clauses are examples of Stage 2 and Stage 3 clause structures respectively. When, however, one or more of the elements is expanded (subject to noun phrase (NP), verb to verb phrase (VP), object to noun phrase, or adverb to adverbial phrase (AP)), then not only does the clause give a clause-level entry in Stage 2 or Stage 3, but it gives additional entries in the appropriate "expansion" boxes in Stages 3 and 4 respectively. Thus, for example, the sentences "Man digging" and "Man digging hole" get entries at SV and SVO respectively. But if the sentences had been "The man digging" and "The man is digging a hole" there would not only have been entries at SV and SVO, but additional entries in the "expansion" box labelled X + S: NP (because "man" is expanded into the noun phrase "the man") for the first sentence; and for the second sentence, there would have been an additional entry in the expansion box labelled XY + S: NP (because "man" is expanded into the NP "the man"), an additional entry in the expansion box labelled XY + V: VP (because "digging" is expanded into the verb phrase "is digging"), and an additional entry in the expansion box labelled XY + C/O: NP (because "hole" is expanded into the NP "a hole").

Stage 4 clauses (other than Stage 3 expansions) contain four elements: for example, "(the boys) (are throwing) (stones) (at the dog)" (SVC/OA); "(she) (gave) (him) (a kiss)" (SVO_dO_i); "(they) (ran) (up the hill) (quickly)"

(AAXY). Stage 4 phrases are: noun-preposition-noun phrase (N Pr NP), pre-position-determiner-adjective-noun (Pr DAdj N), connector and a phrase element (cX), a connector between two phrase elements (X c X), a negated verb (Neg V), any other negated phrase element (Neg X), and two auxiliary verbs together (2 aux). Examples would be: "In the big garden" (Pr DAdj N), "bread and butter" (X c X), "They *have been* running" (2 aux).

The maximum number of clause elements that it is possible to have within a single clause is four, and therefore Stage 5 sees the emergence of multiple sentences, which consist of more than one clause. Such sentences can be long (in theory, there is no structural limit to length) and complex. Each clause will, in addition to giving an entry (or entries—see below) at Stage 5, have its basic pattern analysed into a clause-level entry within Stages 2–4. There are two types of multiple sentences. Firstly, there are those in which the clauses are strung together and linked with co-ordinating devices (*and, c*): "*He went to bed* and *fell asleep*". These co-ordinated clauses give profile entries at co-ord. 1 (two clauses co-ordinated) or at co-ord. 1+ (more than two clauses co-ordinated). In addition, the use of the co-ordinating devices (e.g. and, but, then) is noted in the Conn. (connector) column, with a distinction between the commonly-used "and" and all other co-ordinating devices (c). Secondly, there are the multiple sentences in which all the clauses except one are subordinate; that is, they depend upon or form part of a main clause. They will often be linked to the main clause by a subordinating device, and this is noted (s) in the connector column. Again, each subordinate clause will give an entry within Stages 2–4 (as will the main clause) in addition to any Stage 5 entries it may give. If there is one subordinate clause embedded in a main clause, then it is marked at Subord. 1, while the occurrence of two or more subordinate clauses within a main clause will be noted by an entry at Subord. 1+. A commonly-occurring multiple sentence containing a main and a subordinate clause is that in which the adverbial element in the main clause has been expanded into a clause in its own right, and is linked into the main clause by a subordinator: "She woke up *because she was hungry*". There is some ambiguity in Crystal *et al.* (1976) as to what exactly is meant by subordinate but in the present project the following scheme was adopted. Any clause element (S, C, O, A) except V can be itself a clause, and is marked as such in Stage 5 (Clause:S; Clause:C/O; Clause:A). Examples would be: "*What he said* was interesting" (Clause:S in an SVC sentence); "We saw *that the man was hitting the boy*" (Clause:O in an SVO sentence). Only if such clauses can be deleted from the main clause, leaving a grammatically acceptable sentence (in terms of adult grammar), are they also counted as subordinate and marked as such. Thus: "*That he missed the meeting* was unfortunate" is marked at Clause: S, but no entry is put at Subord. 1 since the deletion of the Subject clause would not leave an acceptable sentence. On the other hand, "He ran home *when he realized the time*" is marked not only at Clause: A, but at Subord. 1, since the deletion of the adverbial clause would still leave an acceptable sentence. There is, therefore, a degree of "double-marking" in Stage 5, and this should be remembered when the completed profiles are being examined and the relative numbers of clause-level entries at each Stage is being compared. Subordinate clauses need not be finite, as in the examples so far; they can be non-finite, in which case they are introduced by a participle or an infinitive (e.g. "*Having a headache* is terrible"; "He wanted *to run away*").

The Stage 5 phrase-level structures are also recursive, being concerned with those developments in noun phrases in which the dependent words which follow the "head" (i.e. the noun itself) of a noun phrase are expanded either into two or more phrases (Postmod. phrase 1 +) or into a clause (Postmod. clause 1) or clauses (Postmod. clause 1 +). Examples would be: "The man (*in the car*) (*with the hat*) . . ." (Postmod. phrase 1 +); "The man *who is wearing the hat* . . ." (Postmod. clause 1).

The word-level structures which emerge throughout Stages 2–5 are as follows: the infinitive (Inf.); -ing ending on verbs (-ing); plurals (pl.); future tense (fut.); past tense (-ed); past participle (-en); 3rd person singular (3s); genitive (gen); contracted negative (n't); contracted copula ('cop); contracted auxiliary ('aux); superlative (-est); comparative (-er); and adverbial suffix (-ly). As noted previously, these structures are arranged in a tentative order of emergence for normal children, but the research upon which the order is based is not plentiful.

Crystal *et al.* anticipated that some testers, depending upon their particular aims, might wish to add further items to the profile if, for example, their testees were using hitherto unmarked structures to a significant degree. For the purposes of the present project, four such items were added to the original profile: preposition-pronoun (PrPron) at Stage 3, phrase level; Clause: A at Stage 5, clause level (see above); and at the word level of analysis the "to" form of the infinitive (Inf.), and the future tense (fut.). The latter is usually indicated by the use of the special auxiliaries "will" or "shall", but any other construction which indicated a cognitive awareness of events in the future (e.g. "is going to . . .") also qualified for an entry under fut. Strictly speaking both Inf. and fut. would have been better placed at the phrase level on the profile, probably at Stage 3, since the word level is concerned with the analysis of inflectional endings on words: that is, with morphology rather than syntax.

By the time language structure has developed through to Stage 5, it is clear to the listener that the bulk of the language development has taken place, and that the spoken language is highly intelligible. Thus by Stage 5 "the child is doing so much *right* ... that it is not economical to any longer describe solely in terms of what he *can* do; it is more practical to describe what he *cannot* do, as evidenced by his residual syntactic mistakes. Stage 6, then, to a great extent, reverses the direction of the analysis hitherto, incorporating information which is, in effect, a kind of error analysis" (Crystal *et al.*, p. 78). Errors (denoted as minus (−) features) are classified as occurring in the noun phrase (NP), the verb phrase (VP), or as somehow affecting the overall clause structure (Clause). In addition, certain sophisticated features of language are still emerging in this Stage, and these are noted as plus (+) features, classified under the same headings.

Stage 7 notes the final emergence of five other linguistic features. They are: sentence-connecting devices, such as "however", "actually"; comment clauses, such as "you know"; word order patterns controlling emphasis, such as "hardly had I gone ..."; and clause sequences introduced by "it" and "there", such as "There's a party tonight" or "It's raining".

Finally, the analyser notes at the foot of the profile how many words there were in each "sentence", excluding all deviant, ambiguous, minor and Stage 1 entries from consideration. The minimum possible sentence length for this particular exercise, then, will be two (e.g. an unexpanded two-element clause such as "Daddy go").

The bulk of the objective quantitative grammatical analysis takes place in Stages 1–5. Stages 6 and 7 are based on piecemeal knowledge of the more sophisticated features of mature language. They are more difficult to score reliably, and it is expected that for our purposes they will turn out to be less important as good discriminators between subjects than the structures within the first five Stages. As a reflection of this point, it should be noted that we decided to omit from our profile three "boxes" which occur on the original profile in Stage 7, and which offer the analyser an opportunity to comment in a qualitative fashion on the "style", the "syntactic comprehension" and the "discourse" of the subject.

The only other major difference between our profile and the original is that in the latter there is provision to analyse "responses" as well as "spontaneous" sentences. Most of these responses would be elliptical replies to questions (for example, "Writing in the book" in reply to the question: "What's the milkman doing?"—see Fig. 4), and as we have noted already, the picture-description task and the purposely non-specific prompts given by the tester resulted in few elliptical sentences. Since "responses" constituted such a very small proportion of the utterances, this part of the original profile was discarded and what "responses" there were have simply been treated as if they were "spontaneous" utterances.

The following is an extract from the transcription of the eleven-year-old girl of below average non-verbal intelligence, and with a pure tone hearing loss in the better ear (average at 500, 1000, 2000 Hz) of 92 dB, whose completed profile is shown in Fig. 10.

"A car. A man. Open car. Mummy. Basket. Mummy is basket. House. In the car. Daddy. Mummy. Boy. Dog. Picnic. Ball. Dog is play the ball. Throw the ball. Boy. Book. Read the book. Mummy looking boy book. Bread. Drink. Drinking. They is drinking. Dog eat food. Boy throw the ball. In the basket. Food. To home. Sleeping. Snow. Boy is in the hole. Boy holding a stick. Dog. Dog looking boy. Slide. Boots. Van. Police. Boy fall. Ladder. The boy running with ball. Over. The boy is over. The boy is looking. The car is crashing apple. Banana. Cabbage. Money fall lady."

The entries in Fig. 10 will not be discussed in detail here, since Chapter 7 is concerned with the analysis of the grammatical data from all subjects. It should be noted in passing, however, that it is an illustration of a profile clearly less advanced than one would expect from an eleven-year-old: number of words per sentence is low, recursions are absent and Stage 4 structures are rare; pronouns, auxiliary verbs and most phrase structures appear infrequently; and word-level structures are even less advanced than the phrase and clause-level structures. There are as many one-element (Stage 1) entries as there are in all the other Stages (at the clause level) combined. Note, however, the small number of deviant and ambiguous sentences.

No definite limit was set on the number of sentences to be analysed onto the profile for each subject. This was left to the discretion of the analyser, given that enough sentences should be analysed to provide a stable profile picture. In a very few cases the elicited language sample was so short that all the sentences were analysed. In most cases this was not so, and the analyser transferred something in the region of 40 or 50 major sentences onto the profile. In all such cases, the analysis began at the beginning of the transcript and ended somewhere in the middle. As a quick check on the reliability of the analysis, and upon the homogeneity of the two halves of those transcripts which were not analysed in their entirety, the first and second halves of the transcripts of a small number of subjects ($n=9$), picked at random from the subject sample, were analysed onto separate profiles. In order to compare the two profiles, the entries on each profile were collapsed (i.e. summed) into 14 totals:

Stage 1: all entries
Stage 2: clauses

Stage 3: expansions
Stage 3: clauses
Stage 4: expansions
Stage 4: clauses
Stage 5: connectors
Stage 5: clauses
Stage 2: phrases
Stage 3: phrases
Stage 4: phrases
Stage 5: phrases
All "Word" entries
All Stage 7 entries

Thus for each subject there were 14 totals, twice over: the first from the first profile, the second from the second profile. The correlation coefficient (Spearman's Rho) between these two sets of totals was calculated for each subject. The results of these calculations are shown in Table XII.

Table XII. The correlation coefficients between two language analysis profiles for nine subjects. Also shown are the results of t-tests and the significance levels for each correlation coefficient

Subject	Correlation coefficient (Spearman's Rho)	t	P
1	0·93	8·59	$P < 0.001$
2	0·91	7·82	$P < 0.001$
3	0·89	6·76	$P < 0.001$
4	0·94	9·70	$P < 0.001$
5	0·89	6·97	$P < 0.001$
6	0·95	11·00	$P < 0.001$
7	0·94	9·80	$P < 0.001$
8	0·92	7·88	$P < 0.001$
9	0·96	12·72	$P < 0.001$

It will be seen that the correlations are satisfactorily high, and a t-test on each coefficient showed them all to be significant beyond the 0·1% level.

The data from each of the 263 profiles were punched onto 80-column cards for analysis. The number of occurrences of each item on each profile was entered. In addition, sentence-length means, minima, maxima and number of sentences analysed were punched.

References

BELLUGI, U. (1972). Development of language in the normal child. *In* "Language Intervention with the Retarded. Developing Strategies" (J. E. McLean, D. E. Yoder and R. Schiefelbusch, eds), pp. 33–51. Univ. Park Press, Baltimore, USA.

BRANNON, J. B. and MURRY, T. (1966). The spoken syntax of children. *J. Speech Hear. Res.* **9**, 604–610.

CHOMSKY, N. (1965). "Aspects of the Theory of Syntax". MIT Press, Cambridge, Mass., USA.

CRYSTAL, D., FLETCHER, P. and GARMAN, M. (1976). "The Grammatical Analysis of Language Disability". Edward Arnold, London, UK.

DOLCH, E. W. (1951). Tested word knowledge vs. frequency counts. *J. Educ. Res.* **44**, 457–470.

ELLIOT, L. L., HIRSH, I. J. and SIMMONS, A. A. (1967). The language of young hearing-impaired children. *Lang. Speech* **10**, 141–158.

FILLENBAUM, S., JONES, L. V. and WEPMAN, J. M. (1961). Some linguistic features of speech from aphasic patients. *Lang. Speech* **4**, 91–108.

FRASER, C., BELLUGI, U. and BROWN, R. (1963). Control of grammar in imitation, comprehension and production. *J. Verb. Learn. Verb. Behav.* **2**, 121–135.

FRENCH, N. R., CARTER, C. W. and KOENIG, W. (1930). The words and sounds of telephone conversations. *Bell Syst. Tech. J.* **9**, 290–324.

FRIES, C. C. (1952). "The Structure of English". Longman, London, UK.

GODA, S. (1964). Spoken syntax of normal, deaf and retarded adolescents. *J. Verb. Learn. Verb. Behav.* **3**, 401–405.

GRAHAM, N. C. (1968). Short-term memory and syntactic structure in educationally sub-normal children. *Lang. Speech* **11**, 209–219.

HARWOOD, F. W. (1959). Quantitative study of the speech of Australian children. *Lang. Speech* **2**, 236–271.

HINE, W. D. (1970). Verbal ability and partial hearing loss. *Teacher of the Deaf* **68**, 450–459.

JONES, L. V., GOODMAN, M. F. and WEPMAN, J. M. (1963). The classification of parts of speech for the characterization of aphasia. *Lang. Speech* **6**, 94–108.

KYLE, J. G. (1977). Audiometric analysis as a predictor of speech intelligibility. *Brit. J. Audiol.* **11**, 51–58.

LACKNER, J. R. (1968). A developmental study of language behaviour in retarded children. *Neuropsychologia* **6**, 301–320.

LEE, L. and CANTER, S. M. (1971). Developmental sentence scoring: a clinical procedure for estimating syntactic development in children's spontaneous speech. *J. Speech Hear. Disord.* **36**, 315–340.

McCARTHY, D. (1954). Language development in children. *In* "Manual of Child Psychology" (L. Carmichael, ed.), pp. 492–630. Wiley, New York and London.

MEIN, R. (1961). A study of the oral vocabularies of severely subnormal patients, II. Grammatical analysis of speech samples. *J. Ment. Defic. Res.*, **5**, 52–59.

MOREHEAD, D. M. (1972). Early grammatical and semantic relations: some implications for a general representational deficit in linguistically deviant children. *Pap. Rep. Child Lang. Develop.* **4**, 1–12.

MOREHEAD, D. M. and INGRAM, D. (1973). The development of base syntax in normal and lingustically deviant children. *J. Speech Hear. Res.* **16,** 330–352.

NEWBY, H. A. (1972). "Audiology". Appleton Century Crofts, New York, USA.

NICE, M. M. (1932). An analysis of the conversation of children and adults. *Child Develop.* **3,** 240–246.

O'NEILL, J. J. and OYER, H. J. (1973). Aural rehabilitation. *In* "Modern Developments in Audiology" (J. Jerger, ed.), pp. 212–247. Academic Press, New York and London.

OWRID, H. L. (1960). Measuring spoken language in young deaf children. *Teacher of the Deaf* **58,** 24–34 and 124–138.

RISBERG, A. and MARTONY, J. (1970). A method for the classification of audiograms. *In* "International Symposium on Speech Communication Ability and Profound Deafness" (G. Fant, ed.), pp. 135–139. Alexander Graham Bell, Washington, USA.

RUSSELL, W. K., QUIGLEY, S. P. and POWER, D. J. (1976). "Linguistics in Deaf Children". Alexander Graham Bell, Washington, USA.

SOLLY, G. (1975). Tests of comprehension of spoken language for use with hearing-impaired children. *Teacher of the Deaf* **73,** 74–85.

TEMPLIN, M. (1957). "Certain Language Skills in Children". Minneapolis, University of Minnesota Press, USA.

VERNON, M. (1976). Communication and education of deaf and hard of hearing children. *In* "Methods of Communication Currently Used in the Education of Deaf Children", pp. 99–109. RNID, London, UK.

WOODWARD, P. M. and BOND, S. G. (1974). "ALGOL 68-R. A User's Guide". Her Majesty's Stationery Office.

4

Sentence List Construction and Pilot Test

Åse Kowal

I. Introduction

In this Chapter we discuss how our new Sentence Tests for children—the two Bamford–Kowal–Bench (BKB) Tests—were constructed. They are speech audiometric sentence tests and are intended to measure aspects of the partially-hearing child's hearing for connected-speech. A speech audiometric sentence test consists of a number of lists of sentences. The sentences are usually played one at a time from a tape-recorder to the listener who is required to repeat each sentence back to the tester in turn. By varying the intensity level for each list, speech audiograms can be derived by plotting the percentage of, say, words correctly repeated for each list against the relative intensity of the speech signal. The function so derived will depict the child's range from poor to good hearing for speech. It is clear that, with the exception of the intensity of presentation, each list should be of the same level of difficulty for the listener as any one of the other lists. As the test is a hearing test and not a comprehension test, we would argue that the best way of achieving equal difficulty of lists is by ensuring that the sentences are within the linguistic ability of the majority of the children who are going to listen to them, and by balancing the sentence lists against each other through strict adherence to a comprehensive set of rules governing their construction. Consequently in this Chapter we shall indicate firstly how we have used the speech material which we had previously collected from a sample of 263 hearing-impaired children (described in Chapter 3) to keep the grammatical structure of the sentences within the boundaries of what most partially-hearing children can cope with; secondly, how a set of rules were devised for the construction of the sentences; and thirdly, how we selected the vocabulary items used in our tests. Furthermore, we shall discuss the subsequent pilot test which was designed to identify any obvious problems associated with the sentences. But first of all we shall explain why we chose to construct two sentence tests rather than one, and we shall briefly indicate in what respects they are different from and to what extent they resemble each other.

II. The two BKB sentence tests

A hearing-impaired child may be difficult to test for various reasons, especially when the test relies on auditory input only. For instance, it may be difficult to maintain the child's attention for the required length of time, especially in the case of the younger child, or he may be rather shy. To deal with this problem we decided to construct two separate tests:

(1) the ST (standard) test for which the child listens to each sentence and repeats back what he has heard;

(2) an alternative test, the PR (picture-related) test, where in addition

to the auditory presentation of the sentences the child is shown a series of pictures illustrating activities familiar to most children, and where each sentence directly relates to an aspect of the picture at which the child is looking.

The ST test will probably be suitable for most partially-hearing children from 8–15 years old, whereas the PR test may be preferable where the child proves to be difficult to test. In the case of the PR test, the intention is that when it is administered the child is first asked to look at each picture in turn, to familiarize himself with each one, and later asked to repeat back the sentences with the relevant picture displayed before him as he listens. While the tester should refrain from discussing the content of the pictures with the child, as this may prime parts of the pictures, the set of pictures are such that they are thought to be of sufficient interest to focus the attention of the child on the pictures rather than on the testing environment. This should help the restless as well as the shy child to concentrate on the task at hand. Thus, so far as content is concerned, the ST test sentences are tied to no particular theme but are intended to be familiar to most children, while the PR test sentences relate specifically to a set of pictures.

Initially, when designing the PR test we tried to make test administration easy by constructing each list so that all the sentences in the list would refer to one picture only, but this led to an over-use of some vocabulary items and in the end proved to be impossible because of the limited content of each picture. We were therefore forced to construct the lists so that each picture contributed a number of sentences to each list. The same event could then be referred to in different lists by using a different vocabulary. On the other hand, basing all the PR lists on the same pictorial material should tend to reduce the variability between the lists, namely the variability which might be produced by the different vocabulary of each picture and any variability which might be caused by differences in attention-holding properties between the various pictures.

The pictures used in the PR test were the same five as those which we had previously used to elicit speech from hearing-impaired children (see Chapter 3, Figs 1–5). This had the obvious advantage of providing us with an appropriate vocabulary, and the disadvantage of limiting the number of relevant sentences when the various constraints for sentence construction (outlined later in this Chapter) were applied. The effect of this was to limit the PR test to 11 sentence lists as compared with the 21 lists of our Standard Test.

We arrived at the latter number by considering how many lists the tester might need for sets of reasonably well-defined audiograms. In practice the child's performance and the time available will determine the number of lists administered, but clinical work using other sentence tests indicate that normally after one practice list has been used to familiarize the child with the task and to establish the likely intensity range needed, about five lists are sufficient to estimate the child's speech audiogram. There are, however, a variety of conditions under which the audiologist or the teacher may wish to test the child's performance; for instance he may wish to compare reception with earphones vs. free-field reception and with/without background noise or before/after a chosen rehabilitation programme has been implemented. Hence the tester ideally needs to have a large number of different, but comparable, lists at his disposal. Consequently for the BKB Standard Test we have constructed one list for practice and four lots of five lists to cover up to four different test conditions giving 21 lists in all, whereas our PR Test, as mentioned, consists of 11 lists, sufficient for two test conditions with one list as a practice list.

However, apart from the difference in the use of pictures and the consequent difference in availability of contextual cues, and apart from the different number of lists within each test, the Standard Test and the Picture-related Test are very similar, since the same rules and constraints were employed when the two tests were constructed. We shall now proceed to outline the features which the Standard and the Picture-related tests share. However, the reader may find it helpful first to have a look at the two tests. They are shown in Appendixes I and II.

III. How many sentences per list?

We now turn to the construction of the tests. Each test consists of a number of lists, and each list consists of a number of sentences. The first question to be resolved was how many sentences each list should contain. To answer this question at least three further questions need to be considered:

- (a) how are the sentences to be scored?
- (b) bearing in mind the limited time usually available to the tester, how short can each list be and still reliably measure what it sets out to measure?
- (c) how long can each sentence be without over-taxing a young hearing-impaired child of limited language ability?

The last of these questions is in fact associated with a number of other considerations concerning the complexity of the sentences which we shall discuss later on in this Chapter.

The method of scoring will be dealt with in detail in Chapter 5. However, a unit of scoring had to be decided on here as the length of each sentence list depended upon how many of these units, or items, each list should ideally contain. It is possible to score the sentences repeated by the child in a number of ways. For instance, one could score all the phonemes correctly reproduced. This has the advantage of providing detailed information about the child's perception, but in practice the accuracy of this measure can be seriously affected by the faulty speech production encountered in hearing-impaired patients, and previous experience of the child's speech defect might be necessary for the examiner to determine whether some of the faulty responses were due to the child's failure to hear the speech sounds or due to his incorrect reproduction of the sounds. The use of written responses might resolve this question with some of the children, but is too time-consuming a procedure for regular use and would also assume that the child can write all the words he is saying. Another, and perhaps the major, criticism of scoring by phonemes is that for connected-speech a high phoneme score is possible although the meaning of the original message has been lost, or is hopelessly distorted.

Alternatively, one could score every single word of the sentence, but as sentences often contain a number of words which are largely redundant to the meaning there is the difficulty, when the child fails to report these, of deciding whether he in fact has heard the redundant words but fails to repeat them because they seem unimportant to him, or whether he actually did not hear them. It might be that with some children this difficulty could be overcome through appropriate instructions to the child before he is tested with the sentences, but it is likely that there would still be an element of doubt in some cases. There are other disadvantages to scoring every word of each sentence; it is not necessary to give them in detail here. It suffices to say that a strenuous listening task is made even more strenuous if the child has to concentrate on repeating every single word of the sentence, and to point out that if the aim of a speech audiometric test is to establish how his hearing affects the child's ability to understand what is being said to him, then it would be more reasonable to concentrate on the basic meaning of the sentence rather than on the reception of each word. Consequently, when designing our tests, we chose to construct them with a view to scoring those words within each sentence which convey its essential meaning and not to scoring words which are relatively unimportant, such as articles, auxiliary verbs and some prepositions. For instance, in the sentence "The fruit lies on the ground" the meaning is conveyed mainly by the three words: fruit—lies— ground, and only these words need be scored to account for the meaning.

The words which carry most of the meaning of the sentence (underlined in the test sentences in the Appendix) will be referred to as *key words*. The number of sentences per list thus depended on the number of key words per sentence.

The higher the number of units to be measured per list, the more reliable the measurement will be, because, for statistical reasons, as the number of items increases so the variance decreases. On the other hand, the more items there are to be measured the longer the test duration. This trade-off between precision and the number of units per list has been described by Lyregaard *et al.* (1976), who have dealt with the question statistically. In practice it is important not to make each list too long, partly because the younger children especially may find it too tiring to repeat several long lists, and partly because the tester may not have the time to administer a lengthy test. He might, there-fore, be tempted to present only a proportion of each list. However, such an expediency would probably have a *more* detrimental effect on precision than would have been the case had the test been designed from the outset to contain the same, lesser, number of measured items. The reason for this is that while it is possible to design whole lists so that each list is of equal difficulty, it is in practice impossible to construct them so that an arbitrarily chosen proportion of one list is of matched difficulty with the same propor-tion of any other list. It is, therefore, extremely important that the tester does not arbitrarily curtail the lists as this will destroy their interchangeability. Only in their entirety are the lists interchangeable. Now, our previous clinical work using Fry's Sentence Lists (1961) indicated that the lists should be designed to take a shorter time to administer than Fry's lists. If Fry's lists are similarly analysed for key words, they will be found to contain 100 key words per list. However, following Lyregaard *et al.*, if 100 items give a score within 10% of the "true" score with 95% probability, then 50 items for the same probability level will yield a score within 14% of the true score. By choosing to include 50 key words per list rather than 100 we have thus lost only 4% in precision. (That, however, does not imply that Fry's test takes double the time to administer as there are factors involved other than number of key words.) A percentage score for our lists is obtained simply by multiply-ing the raw score by two.

The number of key words per sentence and thereby the number of sentences per list was determined in conjunction with considerations of sentence structure and sentence length. We will deal with these aspects in detail in a moment. However, an analysis of the speech collected from our sample of hearing-impaired children indicated that we would need to make up simple, short sentences if we wished to be certain that we would not exceed the children's language ability. Thus having considered various facets of the sampled speech we decided that each list should consist of 16 sentences of which 14 sentences were to have three key words, and two sentences four key words each.

Before proceeding to the question of which types of sentence we should use, it will be necessary first to indicate how we derived a set of criteria which were used as general guide-lines for the sentence construction.

IV. Setting criteria relative to linguistic development

A hearing test should primarily test hearing as opposed to language ability and should consequently be within the linguistic attainment of the listener. This means that the words used should be common words which should be within the child's own vocabulary, that the length of each sentence should not exceed his memory span for sentences, and that the grammar should be relatively simple so that the sentence construction and word-form present no difficulty to him. In addition to these criteria the sentences should, of course, be semantically "reasonable".

It is well known that a restricted auditory input has a general retarding effect on aspects of partially-hearing children's linguistic ability (e.g. Owrid, 1960; Brannon and Murry, 1966; Hine, 1970a, b). However, for our purposes the extent of this ability needed to be quantified. Consequently, having previously obtained samples of speech from 241 partially-hearing children, we used this material to supply us both with knowledge about their grammatical ability and to supply us with a pool of vocabulary on which we could draw (see Chapters 3, 6 and 7).

Characteristics of the children and of the procedures for collecting and analysing the speech samples are discussed in detail in Chapter 3, but in outline the speech was collected from children from 8–15 years of age with a non-verbal I.Q. of not less than 64 points and an average hearing loss in the better ear of between 40 and 95 dB ISO in the 500, 1000 and 2000 Hz range of frequencies. (In fact speech was sampled from another 22 children whose data were subsequently excluded from the sentence construction exercise, since their mean hearing loss exceeded 95 dB and they were considered deaf rather than partially-hearing.) The speech took the form of tape-recorded descriptions of a set of pictures which had been shown to each child.

The tape-recorded material was transcribed and the transcribed speech samples from each child were analysed by the use of a slightly modified

LARSP profile (Crystal *et al.*, 1976). From the profiles five measures which were thought to reflect the level of the children's grammatical ability were then considered. These were:

(1) the profile stages which contained the largest and second largest number of clause entries;
(2) the mean sentence length;
(3) the phrase to clause ratio, that is the total number of phrase entries in Stages 2, 3 and 4 of the LARSP profile divided by the total number of clause entries in Stages 2, 3 and 4;
(4) the number of different phrase structures used, irrespective of how often they were used; and
(5) the number of different word structures used, again irrespective of how often they were used.

Frequency distributions were drawn for the subjects' scores on each of these measures. On the basis of the distributions a criterion was set for each measure such that most of the sample was included, while allowing us to construct sentences which were not too restricted semantically.

There were 33 children whose speech fell below one or more of these criteria. Consequently, to decide which particular sentence-, phrase- and word-forms would be most suitable for our sentences these forms were subsequently selected from the grouped profile of the remaining 208 children (see Fig. 8). Thus, the particular syntactical forms which we used in designing our sentences were based on the speech of the partially-hearing children who met the criteria.

A. Test construction—clause level

The general approach to selecting criteria based on the children's own speech production was adopted firstly at the clause level; secondly at the level of phrases; and thirdly at the level of word structures.

Considerations of complexity and sentence length led us from the outset to limit each test sentence to only one clause, with no subordination or co-ordination of clauses. Thus the main questions at the clause level of analysis concerned how many and which elements should be used in the clauses.

1. Language advancement and clause type

Our first requirement was a general measure of the children's language ability with regard to the use of clauses. It was possible to derive such a measure in terms of the clause stages which recruited the largest and the next largest number of entries on the LARSP profile of each child. The clause stages are stages of syntactical development through which it is thought that the language of normal children proceeds (see Fig. 11, Chapter 3). Thus an infant whose LARSP profile shows that there are, say, a predominance of Stage 2 clause entries will have reached a level where most of his clauses have two elements (subject-verb, subject-object, etc.), though a few of his clauses may have reached Stage 3 and a large number of the remainder will still be at Stage 1. On the histograms depicted in Figs 1–7 the clause development of such a child would be given as 2/1 on the abscissa. The histograms of Figs 1–7 show the level of syntactical development in terms of the clause stages containing the largest and the next largest number of entries. Figure 1 is the most important figure from the point of view of the sentence construction task, as it shows the overall distribution, while the following histograms in the block give an indication of the spread of the data with respect to non-verbal I.Q. (Figs 2–4), and hearing loss (Figs 5–7) across age groups.

Figure 1 shows that in the total sample of 241 partially-hearing children just over 50% used Stage 3 clauses most often and that they used Stage 5 clauses next most frequently (shown as 3/5 on the abscissa). About 19% used Stage 3 clauses mostly and Stage 2 next most frequently, while about 16% had less well-developed clauses, and approximately 16% used more advanced clauses with a predominance of Stage 5 clause entries. The reason for the seemingly curious fact that none of the children used Stage 4 preferentially whereas about 16% of the children had a preference for Stage 5 clauses appears to be that often, instead of using the more advanced clause construction of Stage 4 (clauses containing four elements e.g. subject-verb-direct object-indirect object), the children would string syntactically simpler two- and three-element clauses together by using the connective "and" between statements to convey more complicated ideas.

Turning now to the construction of our sentence lists there is, when deciding on the structure and length of each sentence, a lower limit beyond which it is impossible to go if "natural language" is to be preserved. By the definition of connected-speech, Stage 1 utterances are excluded, and of the Stage 2 clauses only the subject-verb construction appears with any frequency in "natural language" statements, with the exception of commands (e.g. "look out" or "come here"), but commands are for obvious reasons not ideal items for an audiometric test which requires the child to repeat the item. We therefore concluded that from the naturalness viewpoint Stage 2 clauses were acceptable, but to a limited extent only. Referring back to Fig. 1, the data indicate that the majority of the partially-hearing children used clauses at the Stage 3 followed by Stage 2 level (the 3/2 combination in our notation) or

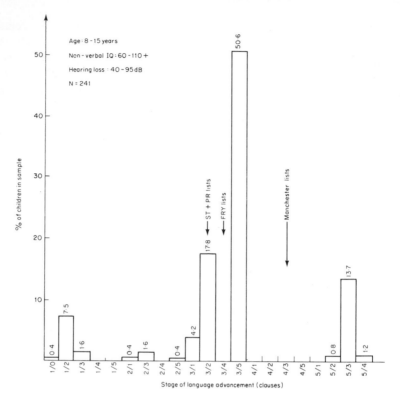

Fig. 1   Most and second most frequently occurring LARSP clause Stages in the speech of a group of 241 partially-hearing children.

Fig. 2   Most and second most frequently occurring LARSP clause Stages in the speech of a sub-group of 18 partially-hearing children, differentiated by age and I.Q. Youngest, least intelligent group.

Fig. 3   Most and second most frequently occurring LARSP clause Stages in the speech of a sub-group of 35 partially-hearing children, differentiated by age and I.Q. Medium age and I.Q. group.

Fig. 4   Most and second most frequently occurring LARSP clause Stages in the speech of a sub-group of 23 partially-hearing children, differentiated by age and I.Q. Oldest, most intelligent group.

Fig. 5   Most and second most frequently occurring LARSP clause Stages in the speech of a sub-group of 26 partially-hearing children, differentiated by age and hearing loss. Youngest, most impaired group.

Fig. 6   Most and second most frequently occurring LARSP clause Stages in the speech of a sub-group of 45 partially-hearing children, differentiated by age and hearing loss. Medium age and impairment group.

Fig. 7   Most and second most frequently occuring LARSP clause Stages in the speech of a sub-group of 14 partially-hearing children, differentiated by age and hearing loss. Oldest, least impaired group.

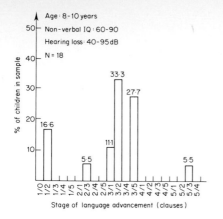

Fig. 2

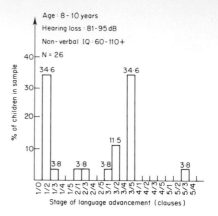

Fig. 5

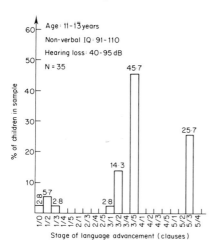

Fig. 3

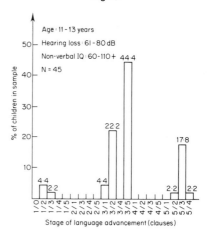

Fig. 6

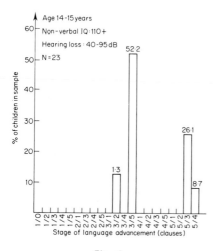

Fig. 4

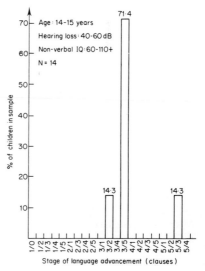

Fig. 7

more advanced clauses. Consequently, the BKB sentences consist mainly of Stage 3 clauses with some Stage 2 clauses.

Figure 1 shows that 16% of the total sample did not come up to this level of clause advancement. These children would possibly not be able to cope with our sentence tests until their language ability had reached a higher stage of development, and a word list might be more suitable for this minority. Although inspection of the individual subjects' LARSP profiles showed that these children did not form a homogeneous group as far as age, intelligence and hearing loss were concerned, we would expect nevertheless that those children who would have most difficulty in coping with a hearing test of any complexity would be predominantly the younger children of lower intelligence and with the greatest degree of hearing loss. Figures 2–7 show that this in fact is the trend in the children's own speech production. Figures 2, 3 and 4 indicate the effects of age and intelligence on the complexity of the language used without differentiation by hearing loss. Figure 2 shows the clause stages which were predominant in the speech of the youngest, least intelligent children; Fig. 3 the clause stages most often attained by the 11- to 13-year-old children of average intelligence; and Fig. 4 the clause stages most often found in the speech of the oldest children with above average intelligence: i.e. the figures illustrate the two extremes and the middle group. Figure 2 shows that 16% of the group comprising the youngest, least intelligent children have a strong tendency to produce only one-word utterances. This would still be the case for 11% of the children in the middle group (Fig. 3), but would be well superseded by more advanced language in all the oldest and brightest children (Fig. 4). Similarly, Figs 5, 6 and 7 show the results for the two extremes and the middle group on the age and hearing loss dimension without differentiation by I.Q. Overall, this set of figures is similar to the set of Figs 2, 3 and 4 respectively. However, Fig. 5 when compared with Fig. 2 shows that severe hearing loss evidently has a greater effect on language advancement in terms of clause usage than low intelligence with 38% (Fig. 5) as opposed to 16% (Fig. 2) of the young children having a preference for Stage 1 utterances.

It is interesting to compare the clause level chosen for our tests with those of other available speech audiometric tests. There are three other UK sentence tests which may be used for speech audiometry, namely the Manchester sentence lists for children (devised by Manchester University, Department of Audiology and Education of the Deaf), Fry's (1961) sentence lists and the Manchester sentence lists (Watson, 1967). Of these the Manchester test for children consists of very simple sentences (in fact not unlike the ones which we came to construct), but it is not available on tape and consequently, with live voice presentation, it is subject to unknown variability of presentation. Also, this test contains only a very small number of sentences, so we have not concerned ourselves with it. Of the two remaining tests neither seems particularly suitable for the general assessment of children. However, if for the sake of comparison, these two tests are analysed by the LARSP method, Fry's lists will be found to have a preponderance of Stage 3 clauses followed by Stage 4, while the Manchester lists contain mostly Stage 4 clauses and less frequently, Stage 3 clauses (see Fig. 1).

Having ascertained that the clause-level Stage should be at the Stage 3 and Stage 2 level the next step was to examine the grouped LARSP profile from the 208 children (see Fig. 8) to ascertain which particular type of clause the children themselves were most familiar with. As the profile shows, by far the largest number of clause entries at the Stage 3 level were subject-verb-object (SVO) and subject-verb-complement (SVC) clauses followed by subject-verb-adverb (SVA) clauses. At Stage 2 subject-verb (SV) clauses were used more frequently than all the others. On this basis we designed each sentence list to consist of seven SVO clauses, six SVA clauses, two SVC clauses, and one SV clause.

2. Sentence length

To repeat a sentence correctly it is obviously necessary to remember what has been heard. Our data indicate that the mean sentence length in the children's own speech is influenced by age, non-verbal intelligence and hearing loss. However, it is possible that so far as the actual number of words per sentence is concerned there is a difference in the length of sentence a child will produce when he is generating speech and how many words he can remember when repeating a sentence. In the absence of data relating to the children's memory in a repetition task closely relevant to speech audiometry with sentences, we used the information which we had obtained on the mean length of the children's own sentences as a guide when constructing our sentences. Figure 9 refers to sentence length in the whole sample, while Figs 10–15 refer to the previously mentioned sub-groups, selected to indicate the range across age + non-verbal I.Q. and age + hearing loss. On this basis, Fig. 9 shows that a criterion of mean sentence length of three words seems to suit the ability of almost all the children as 97% of them tended to speak in sentences of that length or longer. However, in practice it would be impossible to limit such a large number of test sentences to only three words. Instead we chose a criterion of five words per sentence on average with a maximum number of seven syllables. Figure 9 shows that 87% of the children produced sentences with a mean length of five words or more. The trend across the sample distribution is the same as in the case of the stage of clause development reached, i.e. the majority of the children who may have difficulties in managing sentences of this length will be found in the youngest, least intelligent group (Fig. 10) and among the youngest, most hearing-impaired children (Fig. 13).

When we came to record the BKB sentences (see Section VI), one minor modification was made in order to present the tape-recorded speech in as natural a way as possible. That is, words which would usually be contracted in everyday speech were recorded in their contracted form, e.g. "They're by the gate" rather than "They are by the gate". Counting each contraction as one word, the mean sentence length of our tests is 4·9 words, which compares favourably with the Fry sentences (Fry, 1961), which have a mean length of 5·6 words, and with the Manchester sentences (Watson, 1967), which have an average of 7·2 words per sentence (Fig. 9).

3. The first word of the sentences

For each list there should be the same chance that the child is ready to hear the first scoreable words in the sentences. We therefore adopted two strategies. Firstly, when the sentences were recorded we inserted a broad-band alerting noise immediately before each sentence (using a low-pass filter with a cut-off at 800 Hz, on the basis that most partially-hearing children have better low-frequency than high-frequency hearing). Secondly, we equalized the sentence starts across all the lists. Thus, for each list 11 of the sentences begin with a determiner, and, as the aim was to keep the sentences as close as possible to natural speech, each list contains one sentence beginning with a noun and four sentences beginning with a personal pronoun. The first and second person pronouns were avoided in order that the test should be impersonal to the children being tested, whereas the third person plural, "they", has been used twice and "he" and "she" once in each list—a particularly useful choice in the case of the Picture-related Test for which the pictures depict actions, but the variety of actors is limited.

As a further stabilizing device, since personal pronouns are usually unstressed in natural speech, and since we counted personal pronouns as key words, each pronoun is cued later on in the sentence by the corresponding genitive form, e.g. "He eats his cake".

B. Test construction—phrase level

Having dealt with aspects of sentence construction at the level of the sentences as a whole, we now turn to considerations relating to the number and type of phrases which were used in the sentences.

Fig. 8   LARSP profile for 208 partially-hearing children aged 8–15 years, excluding those children (N=33) who failed to reach one or more of the five language advancement criteria.

UNANALYSED:

Deviant	Ambiguous	Analyser's Comments:
	191	GRAND TOTAL (N = 208)

ANALYSED

		Minor "Sentences": Social 192			Stereotypes 43		Problems	

Major "Sentences"

<table>
<tr><td colspan="2"></td><td>Excl.</td><td>Comm.</td><td>Quest.</td><td colspan="4">Statement</td></tr>
<tr>
<td rowspan="2">STAGE 1</td><td rowspan="2">0.9 – 1.6</td>
<td rowspan="2">55</td>
<td>'V'</td><td>'Q'</td><td>'V'</td><td colspan="2">'N'</td><td>Other</td><td>Problems</td>
</tr>
<tr><td>136</td><td>11</td><td>99</td><td colspan="2">812</td><td>22</td><td></td></tr>
</table>

<table>
<tr>
<td rowspan="3">STAGE 2</td><td rowspan="3">1.6 – 2.0</td>
<td></td><td></td><td>Conn.</td><td colspan="2">Clause</td><td colspan="2">Phrase</td><td>Word</td>
</tr>
<tr>
<td>VX
41</td><td>QX
18</td><td></td>
<td>SV 1770</td><td>VC/O 743</td>
<td>DN 11 765</td><td>vv 913</td>
<td>Inf. 1052
-ing 4753</td>
</tr>
<tr>
<td></td><td></td><td></td>
<td>S C/O 140</td><td>AX 494</td>
<td>Adj N 876
NN 130
Pr N 584</td><td>v part 2 669
int x 282
other 11</td>
<td>pl. 2294

fut. 285</td>
</tr>
<tr>
<td></td><td></td><td></td>
<td>Neg X 20</td><td>Other 1</td>
<td></td><td></td><td></td>
</tr>
</table>

<table>
<tr>
<td rowspan="4">STAGE 3</td><td rowspan="4">2.0 – 2.6</td>
<td>VXY
7</td><td>QXY
11</td>
<td>X+S:NP
1 015</td><td>X+V:VP
1 541</td>
<td>X+C/O :NP
539</td><td>X+A:AP
325</td>
<td>-ed 2882</td>
</tr>
<tr>
<td>let XY
1
doXY
1</td><td>VS
16</td>
<td>SVC/O 5 445</td><td>VC/O A 286</td>
<td>D Adj N 1 277
Adj Adj N 77
Pr DN 2979</td><td>Cop 1 656
Aux 4 231
Pron 4 629
Pr Pron 337</td>
<td>-en 623
3s 1822</td>
</tr>
<tr>
<td></td><td></td>
<td>SVA 2 047</td><td>V O$_d$ O$_i$ 24</td>
<td></td><td></td>
<td></td>
</tr>
<tr>
<td></td><td></td>
<td>Neg XY 5</td><td>Other 51</td>
<td>N Adj N</td><td>Other 73</td>
<td>gen 1177</td>
</tr>
</table>

<table>
<tr>
<td rowspan="3">STAGE 4</td><td rowspan="3">2.6 – 3.0</td>
<td></td><td>QXYZ
15</td>
<td>XY+S:NP
3 668</td><td>XY+V:VP
3 595</td>
<td>XY+ C/O :NP
4 639</td><td>XY+A:AP
1 654</td>
<td>n't 299</td>
</tr>
<tr>
<td>+S
1</td><td>QVS
22</td>
<td>SVC/OA
1 447</td><td>AAXY
366</td>
<td>N Pr NP 23
Pr D Adj N 299</td><td>Neg V 340
Neg X 51</td>
<td>'cop 735</td>
</tr>
<tr>
<td></td><td></td>
<td>SVO$_d$O$_i$
108</td><td>Other
92</td>
<td>c X 95
X c X 1093</td><td>2 aux 128
Other 71</td>
<td>'aux 1343</td>
</tr>
</table>

<table>
<tr>
<td rowspan="4">STAGE 5</td><td rowspan="4">3 – 3.6</td>
<td>how</td><td></td><td>and
3332</td>
<td>Coord. 1 2419 1+ 527</td>
<td>Postmod. 1 271 1+ 3
clause</td>
<td>-est 74</td>
</tr>
<tr>
<td></td><td></td><td></td>
<td>Subord. 1 892 1+ 2</td>
<td></td><td></td>
</tr>
<tr>
<td></td><td>tag
4</td><td>c 288</td>
<td>Clause: S 10</td>
<td>Postmod. 1+
phrase 14</td>
<td>-er 55</td>
</tr>
<tr>
<td>what</td><td></td><td>s 864
other
3</td>
<td>Clause: C/O 757 Comparative
Clause: A 607</td>
<td></td>
<td>-ly 172</td>
</tr>
</table>

<table>
<tr>
<td rowspan="3">STAGE 6</td><td rowspan="3">3.6 – 4.6</td>
<td colspan="3" align="center">+</td><td colspan="3" align="center">—</td></tr>
<tr>
<td>NP</td><td>VP</td><td>Clause</td><td>NP</td><td>VP</td><td>Clause</td>
</tr>
<tr>
<td>Initiator 308
Coord. 30</td>
<td>Complex 16</td>
<td>Passive 2
Complement 2</td>
<td>Pron 52 Adj. Seq. 5
Det. 74 N irreg. 18</td>
<td>Modal 11
Tense 119
V irreg. 18</td>
<td>Concord 69
A Position 1
W Order 40</td>
</tr>
</table>

		Other:			Other: 2820		

<table>
<tr>
<td rowspan="2">STAGE 7</td><td rowspan="2">4.6+</td>
<td>A connectivity: 297</td>
<td>Emphatic order: 3</td>
<td>it: 330</td>
</tr>
<tr>
<td>Comment clause: 91</td>
<td>Other:</td>
<td>there: 628</td>
</tr>
</table>

NUMBER OF WORDS IN EACH SENTENCE*

$$\overline{X} = 8.33$$

*Here sentence means: Any utterance which is neither deviant nor ambiguous, but excluding all Stage 1 utterances.

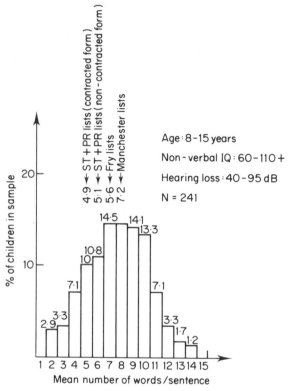

Fig. 9   Mean number of words per sentence in the speech of 241 partially-hearing children.

Fig. 10   Mean number of words per sentence in the speech of a sub-group of 18 partially-hearing children, differentiated by age and I.Q. Youngest, least intelligent group.

Fig. 11   Mean number of words per sentence in the speech of a sub-group of 35 partially-hearing children, differentiated by age and I.Q. Medium age and I.Q. group.

Fig. 12   Mean number of words per sentence in the speech of a sub-group of 23 partially-hearing children, differentiated by age and I.Q. Oldest, most intelligent group.

Fig. 13   Mean number of words per sentence in the speech of a sub-group of 26 partially-hearing children, differentiated by age and hearing loss. Youngest, most impaired group.

Fig. 14   Mean number of words per sentence in the speech of a sub-group of 45 partially-hearing children, differentiated by age and hearing loss. Medium age and impairment group.

Fig. 15   Mean number of words per sentence in the speech of a sub-group of 14 partially-hearing children, differentiated by age and hearing loss. Oldest, most intelligent group.

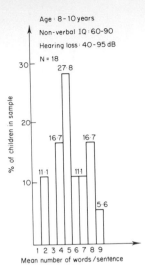

Age : 8 - 10 years

Non-verbal IQ : 60-90

Hearing loss : 40-95 dB

N = 18

Fig. 10

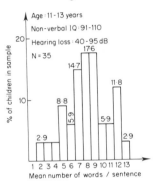

Age : 11-13 years

Non-verbal IQ : 91-110

Hearing loss : 40-95 dB

N = 35

Fig. 11

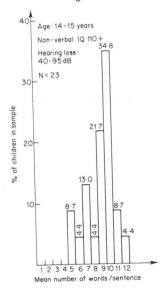

Age : 14 -15 years

Non-verbal IQ 110 +

Hearing loss : 40-95 dB

N = 23

Fig. 12

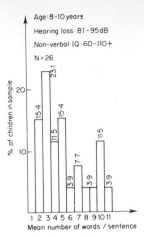

Age : 8-10 years

Hearing loss : 81-95dB

Non-verbal IQ : 60-110+

N = 26

Fig. 13

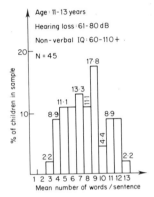

Age : 11-13 years

Hearing loss : 61-80 dB

Non-verbal IQ : 60-110+

N = 45

Fig. 14

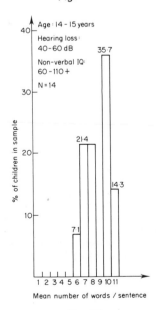

Age : 14 - 15 years

Hearing loss : 40-60 dB

Non-verbal IQ : 60-110+

N = 14

Fig. 15

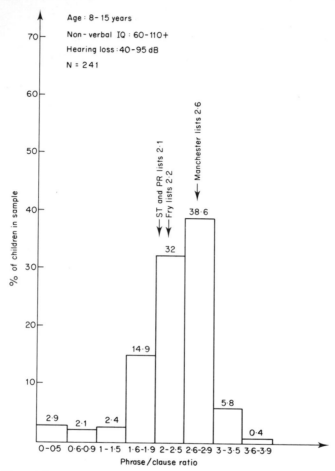

Fig. 16   Phrase/clause ratio in the speech of 241 partially-hearing children (Stage 1 utterances not included).

Fig. 17   Phrase/clause ratio in the speech of a sub-group of 18 partially-hearing children, differentiated by age and I.Q. Youngest, least intelligent group.
Fig. 18   Phrase/clause ratio in the speech of a sub-group of 35 partially-hearing children, differentiated by age and I.Q. Medium age and I.Q. group.
Fig. 19   Phrase/clause ratio in the speech of a sub-group of 23 partially-hearing children,, differentiated by age and I.Q. Oldest, most intelligent group.
Fig. 20   Phrase/clause ratio in the speech of a sub-group of 26 partially-hearing children, differentiated by age and hearing loss. Youngest, most impaired group.
Fig. 21   Phrase/clause ratio in the speech of a sub-group of 45 partially-hearing children, differentiated by age and hearing loss. Medium age and impairment group.
Fig. 22   Phrase/clause ratio in the speech of a sub-group of 14 partially-hearing children, differentiated by age and hearing loss. Oldest, least impaired group.

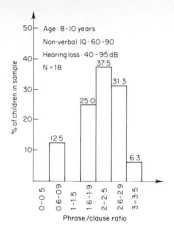

Fig. 17

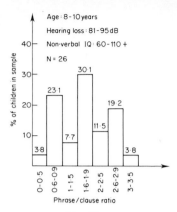

Fig. 20

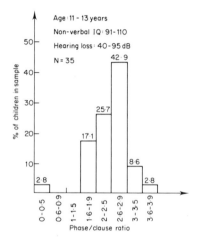

Fig. 18

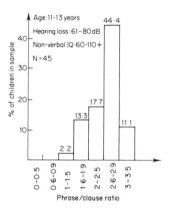

Fig. 21

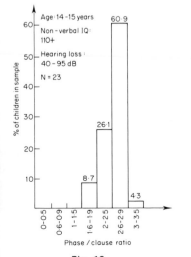

Fig. 19

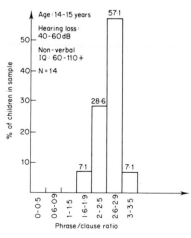

Fig. 22

1. Phrase/clause ratio

A characteristic feature of the speech of the more severely-impaired children is their relatively restricted use of whole phrases, often through the omission of a determiner or an auxiliary verb. The phrase/clause ratio for the speech produced by the children whom we had interviewed was calculated by taking the absolute number of phrase entries for LARSP Stages 2, 3 and 4 (excepting cX and XcX which are not mutually exclusive) and dividing this by the absolute number of clause entries for the same Stages. The phrase/clause ratio is shown for the whole sample in Fig. 16, while Figs 17–19 relate to the ratio for sub-groups along the age + intelligence dimension, and Figs 20–22 indicate the range of data on the age + hearing loss dimension.

Figure 16 indicates that if the cut-off was chosen at a mean phrase/clause ratio of 1·6/1 only 7·4% of the children would fail to reach the criterion, though the youngest, least bright children (Fig. 17), and especially the youngest, most hearing-impaired children (Fig. 20) may still have problems at that ratio. However, on practical grounds we found that this ideal could not be met for the very large number of sentences required, especially given the limited pool of spoken material with which the children had provided us. We had to be content with the aim of keeping the phrase/clause ratio as low as practically possible, which was a level of 2·1/1. When we compare the ratios for the speech produced by all the children with this ratio (Fig. 16), we see that some 22% of the children had a ratio of less than 2/1, though our sentence tests have a lower ratio than both Fry's sentences (Fry, 1961) and the Manchester sentences (Watson, 1967), the ratio of Fry's sentences being 2·2/1 and that of the Manchester sentences 2·6/1.

In the case of the youngest, least intelligent children (Fig. 17) up to 37·5% had a ratio of less than 2·1/1 in their own speech, and at the other end of the age and intelligence range (Fig. 19), just under 9% spoke at a phrase/clause ratio of less than 2/1. However, as Fig. 20 shows, the low ratios are tied up with young age and high hearing loss in particular, as the speech of as many as 64·7% does not reach this 2·1/1. As we would expect, from the youngest, most hearing-impaired group, through the intermediate group (Fig. 21), to the oldest, least impaired group (Fig. 22), there is marked improvement as the percentage of those who failed to produce a phrase/clause ratio of 2/1 falls to about 7%.

To some extent irregularities in the children's language may account for the discrepancy between what we found to be the practicable minimum number of phrases and what the children with a lower ratio had obviously used in their speech. This discrepancy is also, to some extent, related to the previously mentioned strategy of using the definite or indefinite article as the start to a large proportion of the sentences in our attempt to equate the initial words of the sentences across the lists. It may well be that at the end of the practice lists the child has become familiar with the determiner-noun sentence starts.

2. Type of phrase structures used

It could be argued that the phrase/clause ratio may be a lesser obstacle to a child's comprehension than phrase structures with which he is not familiar. Selecting suitable phrase structures involved firstly a decision on how many different phrase structures we could use in accordance with evidence from the children's own speech, and secondly singling out the constructions most widely used by them.

Figures 23–29 refer to the number of different phrase structures which the children used within Stages 2–4, excluding cX and XcX entries which were overlapping categories. (At Stage 1 there can, of course, be no phrases, while at Stages 5 and 6 of the LARSP analysis the phrases are not discrete in the same sense as at the earlier stages.) The maximum number of different phrase structures is 23.

As can be seen (Fig. 23) the vast majority of the children used seven or more different phrase structures, only $3\frac{1}{2}\%$ failing to produce this number. Hence, seven phrase structures were chosen as our criterion. Again, there may be a small number of the youngest and least intelligent children who may find this number exceeds their ability. Thus Fig. 24 shows that 11% of this group failed to reach the criterion, and again the children having the greatest difficulty would be found among the youngest and most hearing-impaired, as 27% in this group (Fig. 27) failed to reach the criterion. Of the remaining comparison groups (Figs 25, 26, 28 and 29), all the children produced at least seven phrases with the exception of one child (Fig. 25).

In comparison with our tests, both Fry's sentences (1961) and the Manchester sentences are considerably more demanding, as both of these tests employ 15 different phrase structures (see Fig. 23).

By referring to the grouped LARSP profile of Fig. 8, and bearing in mind our decision to use selected pronouns as the initial words of some sentences, we decided to use six pronouns in all for each list (that is, four sentence starts and two supporting genitives—see Section IV A3). We also decided to use three auxiliaries, and to employ DN, v part, DAdjN, PrDN, and Cop phrase structures, and, as the intensifier "very" accounts for a large proportion of the entries under int x on the collective profile, this intensifier was also used in our sentences.

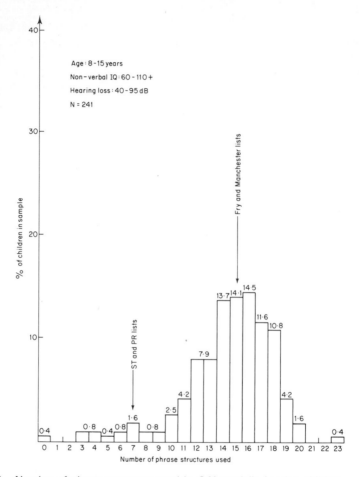

Fig. 23   Number of phrase structures used by 241 partially-hearing children.

Fig. 24   Number of phrase structures used by a sub-group of 18 partially-hearing children, differentiated by age and intelligence. Youngest, least intelligent group.

Fig. 25   Number of phrase structures used by a sub-group of 35 partially-hearing children, differentiated by age and intelligence. Medium age and intelligence group.

Fig. 26   Number of phrase structures used by a sub-group of 23 partially-hearing children, differentiated by age and intelligence. Oldest, most intelligent group.

Fig. 27   Number of phrase structures used by a sub-group of 26 partially-hearing children, differentiated by age and hearing loss. Youngest, most impaired group.

Fig. 28   Number of phrase structures used by a sub-group of 45 partially-hearing children, differentiated by age and hearing loss. Medium age and impairment group.

Fig. 29   Number of phrase structures used by a sub-group of 14 partially-hearing children, differentiated by age and hearing loss. Oldest, least impaired group.

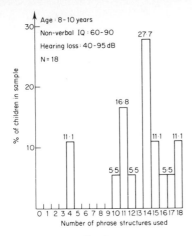

Fig. 24

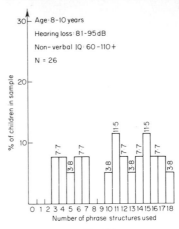

Fig. 27

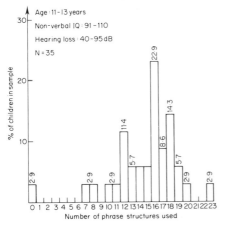

Fig. 25

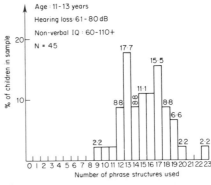

Fig. 28

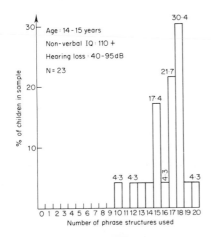

Fig. 26

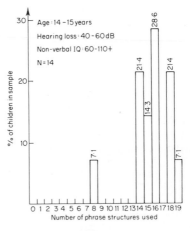

Fig. 29

C. Test construction—word structure level

Our approach to the selection of suitable word structures followed the same method as that applied for selection of phrases. First we established how many different word structures should be used and then, by examination of Fig. 8, we decided which word structures were preferable for inclusion in the test material.

1. Number of word structures used

Our modified version of the LARSP profile contains 14 different word structures (Fig. 8). For each child, we noted how many different word structures he or she used, and the results are given for the sample as a whole in Fig. 30 and for selected sub-groups in Figs 31–36.

Inspection of Fig. 30 reveals that if only six different word structures were employed in our sentences, this would not exceed the performance of 90% of our sample. This, then, was our initial criterion. The children did not generally contract auxiliaries and copulas with the noun or pronoun governing them (e.g. "She is brushing her hair"), but as this is a rather literary form, whereas often in natural spoken language the two words are contracted ("She's brushing her hair"), we subsequently decided to include the contracted forms, thereby allowing ourselves eight different word structures. Figure 30 shows that about 80% of the children used as many, or more, different word structures. Again, Figs 31 and 32 indicate that some of the younger and less intelligent children (22·4% and 14·5% respectively of the children in these groups) did not reach this level of language development. However, it was the youngest, most hearing-impaired children (Fig. 34) who produced the lowest number of different word structures with only 50% reaching eight different structures. Figures 35 and 36 show the expected improvement with increasing age and decreasing hearing loss in number of word structures used, but Fig. 34 also shows that for the youngest, most hearing-impaired children there is no clear cut-off point. Inspection of these children's individual LARSP profiles and their background data indicates that the reason for their rather infrequent use of different word structures may be a combination of hearing loss and educational background.

Again, the Fry and Manchester sentence tests are more demanding than ours with respect to the number of word structures employed. Fry's sentences (1961) include 10 different word structures, and the Manchester sentences include 12. The latter test possibly exceeds what we might expect the majority of partially-hearing children to cope with—see Fig. 30.

2. Type of word structures used

The word structures which we used were generally the word structures most frequently employed by our sample. Our children produced verbs ending in *-ing* more frequently than they used any other verb form, with or without the appropriate auxiliary verb accompanying the main verb, and consequently we were able to use the present progressive as well as the unexpanded present and past tenses. The present progressive was chosen in preference to the past progressive. The reason is that if, in the case of the Picture-related Test, both the simple present and the past progressive tenses were employed, the latter would not actually refer to the action in the pictures, but rather it would require the child to make inferences about what had happened prior to the depicted action, because the use of the present tense would have fixed the ongoing action in the immediate present.

We used plural as well as singular forms of nouns. The plural has usually been marked additionally either by employing nouns which have an irregular plural form, or by using the present tense of the verb, which therefore also changes, or by omitting the article, e.g. "Children (*irregular*) like (*present tense plural*) strawberries (*no article*)". The possessive form of nouns has not been employed in spite of the children's frequent use of it; the reason is that *'s* may easily be confused with the plural *s*, thereby introducing an unnecessary element of uncertainty which may not reflect the "live" situation where the context is likely to indicate which usage is meant.

As for adverbs, the children did not generally add *-ly* to adjectives to form adverbs, but a few particular *-ly* adverbs did seem to be used fairly frequently e.g. "quickly" and "suddenly". It therefore seemed reasonable to use these particular *-ly* adverbs.

D. Test construction—composite language advancement scores

So far we have considered the various aspects of sentence length, types of clause, phrase and word separately, but it is clear that in order to obtain some indication of the general level of difficulty, some assessment had to be made of all these aspects in conjunction. Consequently, a rating procedure was adopted whereby the dominant clause stage, mean sentence length, phrase/clause ratio, number of phrase structures used, and number of word structures used were each given a score on a 1–5 rating scale for each child, so that on each of these measures the more advanced the speech of the child the higher the score would be. For each child the ratings were then added together. The minimum score was thus five and the maximum 25. The

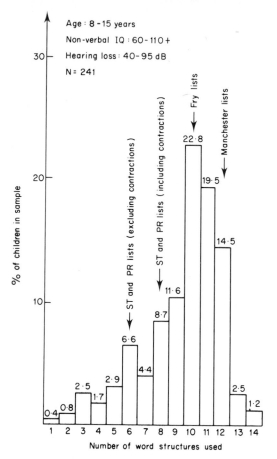

Fig. 30   Number of different word structures used by 241 partially-hearing children.

Fig. 31   Number of different word structures used by a sub-group of 18 partially-hearing children, differentiated by age and intelligence. Youngest, least intelligent group.
Fig. 32   Number of different word structures used by a sub-group of 35 partially-hearing children, differentiated by age and intelligence. Medium age and intelligence group.
Fig. 33   Number of different word structures used by a sub-group of 23 partially-hearing children, differentiated by age and intelligence. Oldest, most intelligent group'
Fig. 34   Number of different word structures used by a sub-group of 26 partially-hearing children, differentiated by age and hearing loss. Youngest, most impaired group.
Fig. 35   Number of different word structures used by a sub-group of 45 partially-hearing children, differentiated by age and hearing loss. Medium age and impairment group.
Fig. 36   Number of different word structures used by a sub-group of 14 partially-hearing children, differentiated by age and hearing loss. Oldest, least impaired group.

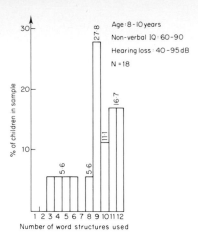

Fig. 31

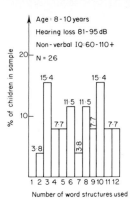

Fig. 34

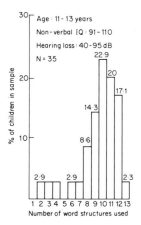

Fig. 32

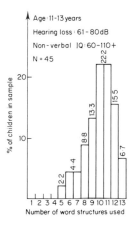

Fig. 35

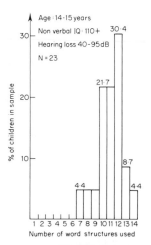

Fig. 33

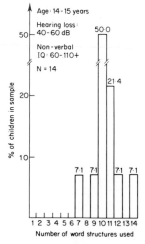

Fig. 36

distribution of the resulting totals is depicted in Fig. 37, from which it can be seen that 90% of the children produced speech to score 13 or more points. This is also the score for our two BKB tests if they are analysed in the same way. To try to cater for the remaining 10% by lowering our criteria further would have made the task of designing the required total of 512 sentences (21 lists each of 16 sentences for ST + 11 lists each of 16 sentences for PR) impossible, and it must be accepted that a small fraction of the younger more

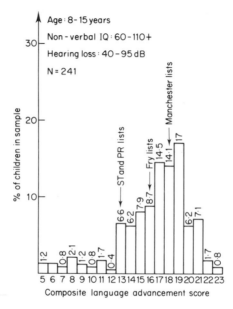

Fig. 37   *Composite language advancement score for 241 partially-hearing children, in-corporating their scores on LARSP Stage reached, number of words per sentence, phrase/ clause ratio, number of phrase and word structures used.*

impaired children do not yet have language which is sufficiently developed to cope with even the simplest sentence test.

If Fry's sentences and the Manchester sentences are rated on this 1–5 rating scale, Fry's sentences are found to have a complexity score of 16 and Manchester of 18. Only just under half of our sample produced language as complex as that of the Manchester sentence test, whereas 70% reached the level of Fry's sentences, so our tests are closer to the children's level as indicated by our study of their own speech than both of these alternatives.

V. Selecting the test vocabulary

Having discussed guide-lines with regard to the relevant grammatical aspects of our test sentences, we now turn to how we proceeded to select the vocabulary items used in the two tests.

The actual words used in our sentence tests were chosen from our samples of the hearing-impaired children's own speech. The texts of the transcribed tape-recordings were parsed into 11 different traditional parts of speech categories for each of 27 groups of children, the children having been allocated to these groups on the basis of their age, non-verbal I.Q. and hearing loss—see Chapter 3 for details. The data provided us with information about which nouns, adjectives, verbs, etc. had been used by each group of children and showed how frequently each word had been employed. When selecting the vocabulary for the sentences we made no attempt to replicate the overall distribution of the words produced by the children, but we did make an effort to include the words which had an overall high frequency of occurrence and to avoid words which did not appear to be commonly used. Also, when selecting from the group vocabulary data, extra consideration was given to the younger and more impaired children's production by selecting vocabulary preferentially from that part of the sample. The minimum requirement was that any word used had to appear at least twice in the collected data as a whole. Additionally we assumed that the children to be tested would know all the cardinal numbers up to 10 and all the primary colours even if not all of them had been elicited by the pictures.

As 50 key words were needed for each of the 32 lists of the ST and PR tests, and as the pool of vocabulary was limited by the content matter of the pictures to which it referred, it became necessary to use some of the words more than once. However, it can be demonstrated experimentally that the activation of a word seems to facilitate its reactivation: that is, there is a tendency for a word which has been seen or heard once to be more easily seen or heard again than another word similarly presented. This effect was described by Morton (1969), who postulated that under conditions of reading, for example, it would last only about one second, but that it could last much longer than that under experimental circumstances, though he did not specify how much longer. To minimize such facilitation no key word was allowed to occur more than once in each list unless it occurred in a phonetically as well as semantically different form, e.g. "The big fish *got* away" and "The grass is *getting* long". Moreover, on the rare occasions where a word does appear twice (even if the two uses are phonetically and semantically different), the two sentences never follow each other immediately.

Not only does a word previously presented make that same word relatively more discernible, but also one sentence may "prime" a later sentence. Meyer and Schvaneveldt (1971) have found that for visually presented material a word which has a well established semantic association with another word, e.g. nurse—doctor, or bread—butter, also has the effect of making that word readily available as opposed to a word which has no semantic connection, e.g. nurse—butter, or bread—doctor. If there is such a semantic association also for sentences presented one after another auditorily, then it should be controlled. In our Picture-related test the pictures may be said to constitute a control in that a picture provides a semantic anchor for each of the sentences. As regards the Standard lists, the sentences are so arranged that each is semantically independent of the immediately adjacent sentences. Also, in both tests any two key words can occur only once in conjunction within the test as a whole. For instance, given the sentence "The postman shut the gate" no other sentence in that test has been allowed to contain *both* the words *postman* and *shut*, nor *shut* and *gate*, nor *postman* and *gate*.

The reader will be able to judge how well we have succeeded in these respects by reviewing the test sentences in Appendixes I and II.

VI. Recording of test sentences

The two BKB tests were subsequently recorded on magnetic tape and pilot tested via speech audiometry on 45 hearing-impaired children. The remaining sections of this Chapter are concerned with the initial recording of the tests, pilot-testing, consequent amendments and the final recording.

In speech audiometric tests it is important to choose the speaker carefully. To select our speaker we asked 10 young adult female speakers to record a sample of speech (Fry's (1961) Sentence List A). These recordings were evaluated by staff of the Department of Phonetics and Linguistics, University College, London, who recommended a speaker from the submitted recordings on the grounds of appropriate accent (Southern English), good intonation, clear articulation and good voice quality. The chosen speaker was a trained speech therapist whose voice qualities were typical of the kind of standard Southern English well known from the media. As Lyregaard *et al.* (1976) have pointed out, the dialect of the listener may not be particularly important if the material is recorded in the manner typical of broadcasting speakers, as listeners will generally be familiar with this kind of speech. Reel-to-reel recordings were made of the two BKB tests using high-quality recording equipment (Ferrograph Super 7) in a sound-proofed, non-reverberant room.

A one-minute duration 1 kHz calibration tone was recorded at the beginning of each tape, and recording levels were set such that the speech peaks reached approximately the same level as the calibration tone. Also, a warning noise of two seconds duration was recorded before each sentence at the same level as the calibration tone, in order to alert the listener to the arrival of each stimulus sentence. There was an interval of approximately one second between the cessation of the warning signal and the start of the sentence. The signal was a broad spectrum noise consisting of frequencies mainly below 800 Hz, chosen because most hearing-impaired children tend to have better hearing at the lower frequencies. The interval between the end of each sentence and the onset of the next warning signal was approximately five seconds, generally allowing ample time for the child to respond.

VII. Pilot study and consequent amendments to sentence lists

Following recording, a pilot test was conducted. The aims of the pilot test were:

(a) to identify any unforeseen problems;
(b) to give some indication of the relative difficulty of each list;
(c) to pinpoint any atypical sentence items; and
(d) to find out if there was a difference in scores between the ST and the PR lists in favour of the PR lists.

Nineteen girls and 26 boys aged from 6–17 years (average 13·2 years) took part in the pilot study.

Their mean pure tone hearing loss in the better ear ranged from 30–105 dB (ISO), averaged over the speech frequencies of 500, 1000 and 2000 Hz. Their task was to listen to the sentences which were presented to their better ear through headphones and to repeat them back to the tester.

A balanced design was adopted whereby the 21 sentence lists of the ST test and the 11 PR sentence lists were divided into approximately equal blocks of five or six lists each, giving a total of six blocks as shown in Table I.

Blocks were combined in pairs to produce 15 test conditions (see Table I). Each child was randomly assigned to a condition. This procedure gave three children per condition and therefore 15 children per block. With this design comparisons could be made between the lists within each block, but not between lists across blocks. This design also allowed us to compare the

Table I. Diagram of pilot test design

			Blocks	Conditions
			1+2	1
	Lists	= Block	1+3	2
			1+4	3
	1– 5	1	1+5	4
21 ST Sentence	6–10	2	1+6	5
Lists	11–15	3	2+3	6
	16–21	4	2+4	7
			2+5	8
			2+6	9
			3+4	10
	Lists	= Block	3+5	11
11 PR Sentence			3+6	12
Lists	1– 5	5	4+5	13
	6–11	6	4+6	14
			5+6	15

ST test and the PR test, since 24 of the children were assessed with both tests (i.e. those tested in conditions, 4, 5, 8, 9 and 11–14).

The children were tested in two sessions each. Standard instructions were given and, prior to testing in the first session, two practice lists were administered to familiarize the child with the task and to allow us to find a suitable task level such that the child scored at the level where he or she would get about 50% correct—i.e. avoiding ceiling and floor effects. The presentation level was then maintained throughout both sessions. A further practice list was given at the start of the second session.

A detailed record was kept of all the responses spoken by the children so that the maximum amount of information about the test material was obtained. However, for scoring purposes we chose to count key words only, and to count the key word as correct provided that the child repeated the stem of the word. Morphological errors were thus disregarded. The reasoning was that to perceive the roots of the key words would be sufficient for the meaning to be understood and therefore enough for communication to take place. Counting the responses by key words then allowed us to obtain the child's percentage score for each list.

The data obtained from each block of lists were subjected to an analysis of variance to find out if lists within blocks were of equal difficulty. No significant differences were found between lists within blocks two, three and six, but there were significant differences within blocks one, four and five.

Within the latter blocks of lists, those lists whose means differed most from the block mean were identified. Further analyses of variance from which these suspected problem lists were excluded confirmed that ST Lists 3 and 4, 19 and 21 were the divergent ones together with PR List 2. When these lists were excluded there were no significant differences between the remaining lists within blocks.

In summary, the result as regards list interchangeability was quite good, indicating that of the PR lists only List 2 might be significantly easier than the others, and that of the ST lists, List 3 might be rather easier than the others and Lists 4, 19 and 21 somewhat more difficult than the rest. However, it should be noted that the absolute values of the differences between extreme lists within blocks were not great in terms of their ultimate use, namely the estimation of the Speech Intelligibility Threshold (at the 50% score) from the speech audiogram.

As for the relative difficulty of the ST and the PR tests, 16 children gave higher mean scores on PR than on the ST lists, the percentage difference between tests ranging from 0·9–34·4%, and seven subjects gave higher mean scores on the ST than on the PR lists, the percentage difference ranging from 0·7–16·0%. The results from one subject for whom the presentation levels were inadvertently altered between sessions were discarded. A Wilcoxon Signed Ranks Matched Pairs test showed that, as predicted, there was a significant tendency for the PR scores to be higher ($T = 80·5$, 23 d.f., $P < 0·05$, one-tailed). If, however, the test is regarded as two-tailed, the results failed to reach the 5% significance level.

On this evidence it cannot be claimed that there was a sizeable and reliable tendency across all subjects for the PR test to give higher scores, as predicted. However, some individual children did have a clear tendency to score higher on the PR test. Precisely why some children are able to use the picture context in the PR test to increase their score and some are not is uncertain. It may be due to the child's attentional strategy.

One might expect that the effect of the added contextual clues in the PR test would be to make the slope of the speech audiogram steeper rather than simply shift its position on the horizontal axis. The data from this pilot study, however, are insufficient to show the relationship between the slopes; such a comparison must wait until an ongoing large-scale standardization procedure provides more data. However, the fact remains that some children find the PR test easier, and therefore it seems to be a useful alternative test for those children who for some reason fail to give an adequate speech audiogram with the ST test.

In addition to the pilot test, copies of the tests were distributed, together with the pictures for the PR test, to several experienced persons working in the field of hearing-impairment, including teachers of the deaf, audiologists, speech therapists, phoneticians and otolaryngologists, for their comments. Taking their remarks in conjunction with the results from the pilot study, the following points emerged.

The lists contained no obvious flaws. However,

(a) certain sentence items were unsatisfactory. Furthermore, in a few cases, the rationale for selecting certain key words as key words was questioned;

(b) four of the ST lists were somewhat easier or harder than the remainder, and one of the PR lists was somewhat easier than the remainder;

(c) for some children, but not all, the PR test gave higher scores. It may be useful as an alternative test for some children.

The unsatisfactory sentences were amended. The suspect lists were not dropped, but an attempt was made to bring them more into line with the other lists, mainly by changing some words, by dropping others and by making some additional prepositions into key words.

Information on the interchangeability of the amended Standard Test was later obtained from a sample of normally-hearing children who listened to all its 21 lists. The results of this check on list equalization are presented and discussed in Chapter 5, and they indicate that (with certain limitations) the lists are reasonably interchangeable.

The BKB Sentence Lists given in Appendixes I and II are the revised versions.

VIII. Final recording

The amended sentence lists were recorded using the same speaker as before. Again, high-quality equipment was used in a sound-proofed and relatively anechoic room; a one-minute calibration tone of 1kHz was recorded at the start of each tape and the recording level was adjusted so that the maximum speech peaks just reached the level of the calibration tone (judged on a VU-meter); and warning signals (low-pass noise bands) were added prior to each sentence, at a level equal to the calibration tone.

Subsequent experience during the large-scale standardization work has shown that the intensity of the warning signal may need to be lowered, as some children found the signal uncomfortably loud when the tapes were played at a level of loudness where their hearing for sentences was at its best. A possible reason is that they suffered from recruitment, affecting their perception of the warning signal in particular because although consisting predominantly of low frequencies it was presented at the level of the speech peaks, but lasted longer. Moreover, a complete sound with a bandwidth as wide as 800 Hz is likely to produce loudness summation at least in listeners with normal hearing (Zwicker and Scharf, 1965).

References

BRANNON, J. B. and MURRY, T. (1966). The spoken syntax of normal, hard-of-hearing and deaf children. *J. Speech Hear. Res.* **9**, 604–610.

CRYSTAL, D., FLETCHER, P. and GARMAN, M. (1976). "The Grammatical Analysis of Language Disability". Edward Arnold, London, UK.

FRY, D. B. (1961). Word and sentence tests for use in speech audiometry. *Lancet* July 22, 197–199.

HINE, W. D. (1970a). The attainment of children with partial hearing. *Teacher of the Deaf* **68**, 129–135.

HINE, W. D. (1970b). Verbal ability and partial hearing loss. *Teacher of the Deaf* **68**, 450–459.

LYREGAARD, P. E., ROBINSON, D. W. and HINCHCLIFFE, R. (1976). A feasibility study of diagnostic speech audiometry. NPL Acoustics Report Ac73, National Physical Laboratory, Teddington, Middlesex, UK.

MEYER, D. E. and SCHVANEVELDT, R. W. (1971). Facilitation in recognizing pairs of words: evidence of a dependence between retrieval operations. *J. Exp. Psychol.* **90**, 227–234.

MORTON, J. (1969). Interaction of information in word recognition. *Psychol. Rev.* **76**, 165–178.

OWRID, H. L. (1960). Measuring spoken language in young deaf children. *Teacher of the Deaf* **58**, 24–34 and 124–138.

WATSON, T. J. (1967). "The Education of Hearing Handicapped Children". pp. 208–209. University of London Press, London, UK.

ZWICKER, E. and SHARF, B. (1965). A model of loudness summation. *Psychol. Rev.* **72**, 3–26.

5

Methodological Considerations and Practical Aspects of the BKB Sentence Lists

JOHN BAMFORD AND IAN WILSON

I. Introduction

It might be thought that the fundamental units of the BKB Sentence Tests are the sentence items themselves, but in order to derive a statistically reliable measure of the percentage reported correctly under given listening conditions (i.e. at a given relative intensity of the speech, with or without a hearing aid, with or without noise, and so on) it is obviously not enough to present the listener with only one sentence under each condition. For this reason the sentences are arranged into lists, each of which provides a convenient and reliable measure of the patient's hearing ability under specified conditions. By "convenient and reliable" we are referring to the problem of finding a suitable balance between list length and list variability: as list length is increased, the reliability of the scores obtained from that list increases, but at the cost of increased test duration. Increasing the list length beyond a certain point does not increase (and may even decrease) its reliability, since other factors such as fatigue begin to intrude. Lyregaard (1973) has expressed the relationship between precision and list length mathematically, but it is sufficient here to be aware of the general nature of the problem. In our experience, the Fry Sentence Lists (which contain 25 sentences per list) are too long, and fatigue effects do indeed tend to intrude, especially if they are used with children. Furthermore, from the clinician's point of view, the testing time is unacceptably long and both this and the fatigue problem may tempt him to use split-lists: that is, to divide each list into, say, two halves and use both halves as independent lists which establish separate points on the speech intelligibility curve. There is no reason why the tester should not give the listener a short rest in the middle of a particular list; but there are good reasons against dividing a single list into two separate lists, since by so doing the methodological requirement of list interchangeability (see below) is violated. The aim of test designers is, therefore, to decide on a list length which will give high reliability, without resulting in fatigue or loss of attention on the part of the proposed listeners, or in undue test duration leading to "list-splitting" on the part of the tester. We decided that 16 sentences per list achieved the right balance between list reliability and test duration.

It is useful to potential users of sentence lists if they are given an estimate of the list reliability. The standard method of obtaining such an estimate is to administer the sentence lists to the same listener on two different occasions, under identical conditions. If this is done with a representative sample of listeners, one can arrive at a measure of the so-called test–retest variability, and the greater this variability the less reliable is the test. The test–retest variability is a measure of that variability which is attributable to "random error" in the test or in the listeners. Such error is not truly random, but is in effect the variability which is not attributable to any known or measured factors: fluctuations in listener motivation and attention, for example. In Section III (Test–Retest Variability), we describe just such a procedure applied to the BKB Sentence Lists (ST version). However, before we can consider this aspect of the lists, we must deal with the separate problem of list interchangeability.

In a very real sense the fundamental units of the BKB Tests are not the sentences, but the sentence lists. By administering different lists at different intensity levels one can determine sufficient points to estimate the speech intelligibility curve, provided that the lists are interchangeable. That is, any listener giving a particular percentage correct score on one list under certain listening conditions should give the same score (within certain limits) on any other list if all else remains equal. To put it simply, for the reliable estimation of speech intelligibility curves (speech audiograms), it is important that no list is intrinsically any easier or harder than any other list.

There are two basic sources from which differences in list difficulty may arise: linguistic sources and recording sources. By linguistic sources, we mean that different lists may contain different vocabulary items, different syntactic structures, different morphological structures, or different phoneme frequencies, any or all of which may differentially affect a listener's ability to hear and report back the sentences. In Chapter 4 we described in detail the lengths to which we went to be reasonably certain that all the vocabulary in the BKB Lists is known to partially-hearing children and is of similar frequency of usage. We also described the lengths to which we went to balance the lists for syntactic and morphological structure. As far as phonemic imbalance between lists is concerned, the danger is that a particular listener might, because of the nature of his hearing loss, find particular phonemes easier or harder to perceive than others, and might therefore perform significantly differently on different lists despite identical testing conditions. However, we did not attempt to balance the lists for phonemic content since the grammatical and semantic constraints inherent in connected-speech, as well as the large number of phonemes in a sixteen-sentence list, make it unlikely that any given list is particularly deviant from any other list in its phonemic content. The necessity for phonemic balance across lists is more urgent when the items in a speech audiometric test are single words rather than sentences, because the burden of perception of such items is anchored firmly at the phonemic level without semantic or syntactic cues, and since word lists generally contain far fewer phonemes per list than is the case with sentence lists, the danger of imbalance is that much greater.

Even if, as in the BKB Sentence Lists, the test designers have gone to considerable trouble to balance the sentence lists for their linguistic content, differences in list difficulty may still intrude because of problems encountered in the recording of the material. In particular, it may be that the intensity level of the recorded speech varies across lists. Such variability may be due to changes in the level of the speaker's voice because of fatigue or an inability continuously to match the intensity of her voice to some invariant internal standard; thus Brandy (1966) found that the intelligibility of a list of 25 words recorded by the same speaker on three separate occasions differed significantly. More fundamentally, the very nature of the speech material itself, the physical parameters of which are extremely difficult to define fully, makes complete matching of lists an impossibility: "In its acoustic manifestation (or electric equivalent), the speech signal is a broad-band non-stationary signal, and the problem encountered in attempting to prescribe a method of determining the level of such a signal is precisely analogous to that of defining the level of an environmental noise signal. A popular misconception is that such a signal, regarded as a physical signal, has a uniquely defined level ... In fact any definition of speech level will be arbitrary, and no one of them will, physically speaking, be 'better' than any other" (Lyregaard *et al.*, 1976, p. 48).

A standard method of minimizing the effects of this problem is to monitor the volume of the speech during recording with a volume indicator, or so-called VU-meter. Adjustments to the record volume can be made if necessary either at the recording stage itself, or later during editing and copying, such that the VU-meter response bears a stable relationship with defined aspects of the speech pattern (e.g. the intensity "peaks" of the speech). Despite the criticisms which can be levelled against the VU-meter method, it is widely accepted and provides a cheap and reasonably effective method for intensity matching of items (sentences) and complete lists. In the case of the BKB Sentence Lists, the sentences were recorded such that the maximum speech peaks, excluding obvious and rare exceptions, attained the zero mark on the meter.

Notwithstanding the effort taken to balance the BKB Sentence Lists for both linguistic content and speech intensity, it is useful to have observations with which to test the efficacy of these procedures for ensuring list interchangeability. Section II (List Equalization) describes two sets of data, one from hearing-impaired children and the other from normally-hearing children, which indicates that, with certain reservations, the lists have been satisfactorily equalized.

Section IV is concerned with the problem of the calibration of speech tests. Speech audiometry is frequently used to assess some change in the hearing for speech of a particular patient. This change, for example, may be due to fitting the patient with a hearing aid, or may be the result of a period of intensive auditory training, or it may be the result of middle-ear surgery. Whatever the cause of such a change, in these cases the patient acts as his own control. That is, the audiologist will be comparing two or more intelligibility curves, both derived from the same patient but under different conditions, the effects of which the tester wishes to assess. The absolute level of the speech is not important in such cases: what is of primary interest are the relative positions and shapes of the intelligibility curves. However, more often than not the tester will wish to compare the intelligibility curves, and in particular their position on the abscissa (relative speech level) of the audiogram, with those obtained from certain pathological groups, in his own clinic or elsewhere. In addition, he may wish to compare the level of the 50% point on the intelligibility curve (the Speech Intelligibility Threshold, SIT) for a particular patient with the same patient's responses on other audiometric tests, such as the pure tone test, because such comparisons often have diagnostic value. In order to be able to make such comparisons, in order that different testers using different equipment do not test at different absolute speech levels, and in order to ensure that a tester can set up his equipment at different times so that the same readings on the speech audiometer give the same levels of output, it is conventional to record on each tape an acoustically simple signal which can be used as an anchor for calibration. The standard method is to record a 1 kHz pure tone at the start of each tape. It is then a relatively simple task for the tester to measure the sound level of this "calibration tone" for any given set of equipment. Providing he always sets the output volume of his equipment to a defined level (usually deflection to zero on the audiometer VU-meter) with the calibration tone, and providing that the test designers can tell him the relationship between the recorded level of the calibration tone and the recorded level of the speech, then the "speech level" can be given some absolute meaning, and comparisons between patients and between different audiometric tests can be made. In the case of the BKB Sentence Lists, the calibration tone was recorded at deflection to zero of the VU-meter, and thus the maximum speech peaks are at the same level as the calibration tone.

On its own, however, this "electro-acoustic" calibration is not enough. It is little help to a tester who wishes to change to the BKB Sentence Lists for his speech audiometry to know that the calibration tone is at the same intensity level as the maximum speech peaks, whereas in the speech test he used previously the calibration tone was recorded at, say, the level of the *average* of the speech peaks; he needs to know the effect of this difference.

Furthermore, it is useful for the tester to have some idea of the position and shape of the speech intelligibility curve which a normally-hearing listener might be expected to give. Such a curve would not start at zero relative speech level on the audiogram, since the electro-acoustic calibration usually equates this point with zero dB SPL, and speech becomes intelligible only at levels somewhat higher than this. For these reasons, "subjective calibration" is needed in addition to the electro-acoustic calibration. This is best achieved by deriving a speech intelligibility curve for the speech material using a group of normally-hearing subjects; this curve can then be used as a standard for comparison. In Section IV (Calibration) we describe such a "subjective calibration" of the BKB Sentence Lists (ST and PR tests) and of the other speech audiometry tests available in the UK, in addition to giving details of the electro-acoustic calibration.

Finally, in Section V (Scoring Methods), we discuss and compare some of the possible methods of scoring the BKB Sentence Lists. As we saw in Chapter 4, one of the constraints on sentence construction was the number of "key words"—those words which carry the main burden of meaning in a sentence—in each sentence and in each list. There are 50 key words per list in the BKB Sentence Lists, which, if key word scoring is adopted, makes for easy conversion of the raw score for a list into a percentage score. Thus, with 16 sentences per list, there are 14 sentences with three key words and two sentences containing four key words. Key word scoring is not the only method for scoring performance on a sentence-repetition task, however, and in Section V we compare key word scoring with other possible methods. It is up to the user to decide which method best suits his particular aims in speech audiometry, but the comparative data which we present in Section V may help him to make this decision.

II. List equalization

It would take a major project on its own to design and carry out a thorough and independent test of the equality of difficulty of the BKB Sentence Lists, and this we have not been able to undertake as yet. Sometime in the future it may be possible to improve and refine the lists if necessary, but meanwhile we need to be sure that there are no obvious or marked differences in difficulty between the lists as they are now. Following the amendments made to the ST Lists and the PR Lists as a result of the pilot test (see Chapter 4), we feel that the two modest studies on the ST Lists reported in this Section provide a sufficient check on the list equalization processes (i.e. the balancing of linguistic and recording variables across lists) which were described in Chapter 4 and in the Introduction to this Chapter.

Before proceeding, however, it should be pointed out that a recent study by Hood and Poole (1977) *does* attempt a thorough check on the equality of speech audiometry lists, in this case 20 of the 25-word MRC monosyllabic word lists, and the authors report that as a consequence they were able significantly to improve list equalization. Hood and Poole's method was notable in that it allowed the authors to estimate a "speech intelligibility curve" for each list separately. Their normally-hearing subjects listened to a given list at sensation levels of 10, 15, 20, 25, 30 and 35 dB above the "speech detection threshold" which had been estimated previously for each subject. Each list was tested six times at each of the sensation levels (i.e. using six different subjects), the order and level of presentation being systematically varied in order to control the effects of memory that intrude when a subject is tested several times on the same list. Thus, 20 intelligibility curves could be drawn, one for each word list. Hood and Poole argue that each curve represents the "distribution of intrinsic difficulty" for that list, more difficult words only being understood at a level some 30 dB higher than that required for recognition of the easier words. The steepness of this cumulative distribution will depend upon factors such as the number of items in the list, the inherent redundancy of the items (for example, spondee words are more redundant than monosyllabic words which in turn are more redundant than nonsense syllables), and so on, although it is not true to argue, as do Hood and Poole, that if all the items in a list were of identical difficulty, then the curve would rise "steeply". Single items in a list do not exhibit an absolute threshold of perception: they too are subject to a "threshold curve", the steepness of which will depend upon such factors as the redundancy within the word due to sequential constraints. Thus it is only true to say that if all the list items were of identical order of difficulty, the intelligibility curve for that list would be steeper than if the list items were of variable difficulty, but the curve could still be relatively flat if item redundancy was low. However, it is certainly correct to argue that list equalization requires ideally that the distributions of intrinsic difficulties (the curve for each list) should be identical across lists, and it was clear that the MRC word lists differed both in respect of slope and displacement. In order to correct for this, the authors fitted regression lines to the linear portion of each curve, allowing them to measure the departures of the individual curves from the mean curve. From these values, they were able to compute intensity adjustments which would either bring the curves into virtually complete correspondence in the case of curves with the same slope as the mean, or make them cross each other at the 17·5 dB sensation level in the case of those with differing slopes. Correcting in this way for differences in the *mean* difficulty between lists, and eliminating five lists which exhibited *slopes* markedly different from the mean slope, significantly improved the performance of the test by reducing its variability.

The two equalization checks reported below are more limited in their aim than the Hood and Poole study, there being already fairly good grounds for supposing that the BKB Lists are reasonably equal in difficulty. Hood and Poole used normally-hearing adults for their equalization, but since the BKB Tests were designed primarily for children it seems rather more appropriate to carry out our checks on representative samples of hearing-impaired and normally-hearing children. Also, our equalization check has been performed on what we consider to be the more important of our tests, namely the ST (standard) version, although we feel reasonably sure from our own use of the PR (picture-related) Test that its 11 lists contain no major imbalances.

A. List equalization with a group of hearing-impaired children

As part of an ongoing study designed to standardize and validate the BKB Sentence Tests, the ST Lists have been used by us to estimate the speech intelligibility curves of 205 hearing-impaired children, aged from 7–16 years and drawn from residential schools and partial-hearing units in Berkshire and the surrounding counties. Many of these children had never been seen by us before, although some had taken part in the picture-description exercise (see Chapter 3) which provided the linguistic guide-lines for construction of the test sentences. Speech intelligibility curves were estimated using not only the BKB Tests but other speech audiometric material, and in addition other audiometric data and background information were collected from each subject. Since the chief aim of this has been to standardize and validate the BKB Tests against existing tests, both speech and non-speech, the data collection was designed with this aim in mind. The results of this standardization will be reported elsewhere at a later date. However, the data on the ST Test do provide us meanwhile with the raw material for a convenient, if crude, method of checking the equality of difficulty of the lists, although the reader should remember that the study was not primarily designed for this purpose, which creates some problems in the analysis. These are noted where appropriate.

The 21 lists of the ST Test were recorded onto two separate tapes, Lists 1–10 on one and Lists 11–21 on the other. Each of the 205 subjects was allocated a single list, any one of the 21 lists, both as a practice list and to allow the tester to estimate the speech level range over which the intelligibility curve was likely to lie. The subject was then given anything from three to seven further lists, each at a different intensity, from which the whole of his speech intelligibility curve could be estimated. Scoring was by key word. The lists used were those immediately consecutive to the subject's practice list, and on the same tape. Thus a subject allocated to List 2 for his practice list would have had the intelligibility curve estimated from his performance on Lists 3, 4, 5, and so on, using however many points were needed to draw the whole curve with reasonable certainty. Furthermore, the lists which were administered following the final lists on each tape—Lists 10 and 21—were Lists 1 and 11 respectively: thus changing tapes was avoided. Such a design raises some problems for the list equalization analysis. For example, any direct comparisons of list difficulties we may make will apply within Lists 1–10 and within Lists 11–21, but not between these blocks. Furthermore, although practical considerations—in particular, the minimizing of testing time—necessitated a cyclical or non-randomized use of the lists, this does tend to weaken the equalization analysis. On the other hand, a certain degree of randomization has been recovered in the design by changing the speech intensity levels independently of lists, so that where lists come relative to each other on the intelligibility curves is variable.

The design considerations discussed above meant that we had no baseline information with which to compare each set of data, and therefore the data had to supply their own baseline. The method of generating such a baseline was to begin by assuming that there are *no* inter-list differences, thus implying that each subject's set of data points should lie on a speech intelligibility curve of sigmoid properties (Fig. 1). Each curve could be fitted to each set of data by either a cumulative normal distribution (probit analysis) or a cumulative logistic distribution (logit analysis), and then the differences in percentages between the observed and fitted values at each speech intensity level used

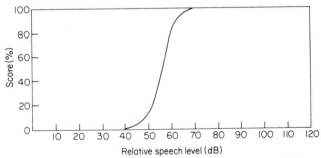

Fig. 1   *An idealized speech intelligibility curve illustrating its sigmoid shape.*

could be analysed. A method simpler to carry out in practice since it used an available computer programme was to take the logistic transformations of the percentages and use these as y-values for an unweighted simple linear regression. This is effectively the same procedure, the only difference being that the full logistic-fitting routine would have attached different weights to the different percentages, on the grounds that a reading near 100% or near 0% would be subject to less error than one nearer 50%. With each fit using a set of, on average, only about five points, the choice of procedure was fairly arbitrary and we feel the one actually used is not detectably different in its application from any of the other possibilities.

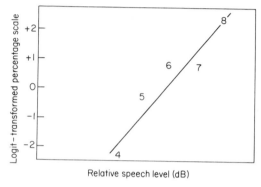

Fig. 2   A typical logit-transformed baseline derived from the data for one subject. Also shown are the actual observed data points. The position of each point is marked by the list number from which the point was obtained. The deviation of each point from the line is a measure of the "residual" for that list, from this particular subject.

The line so fitted provides a baseline for each set of data from which the observed points will depart. Figure 2 shows a typical example of the logit line and the observed data points for one subject. The *residuals* (the amount by which each data point departs from the line) are the "observations" in which we are now interested. Since the residuals result from a line-fitting process they do not act like real observations, each contributing a degree of freedom; instead two degrees of freedom are taken up by the line-fitting, leaving $(n-2)$ degrees of freedom for an individual with n data points. It was for this reason—lack of degrees of freedom—that those individuals with only three data points per intelligibility curve were excluded, and the analysis performed on the remaining 147 subjects who had four points or more per curve.

Readers familiar with speech audiometry will have realized that not all the intelligibility curves of the remaining individuals will have been sigmoid functions: some hearing-impaired patients exhibit intelligibility curves which are clearly non-sigmoid—the so-called "roll-over" curves in which intelligibility begins to decrease at higher speech intensity levels. There is, unfortunately, no independent way of identifying these and no *a priori* reason for excluding them from the analysis. Since, however, the analysis is concerned with identifying systematic trends in the residuals according to list number, and since such speech audiograms can still be fitted to the model to give a series of residuals which (like the residuals derived from truly sigmoid curves) may or may not be systematic departures from the fitted baseline, their inclusion need not concern us overmuch.

We would not expect the residuals to depend upon subjects nor upon speech intensity levels, since the effects of both these have been accounted for in fitting a line for each subject. They may, however, depend upon list number: if it were found that one list systematically gave residuals above

Table I. List residuals for the 21 BKB (ST) Sentence Lists: summary analysis of variance

Source	d.f.	Sum of squares	Mean square	F ratio
Between lists	20	250·185	12·509	1·21 N.S.
Within lists	690	7145·466	10·356	
Total	710	7395·651		

the line, say, then this would indicate that the list in question was always easier than those with which it appeared. The aim of the analysis, then, was to examine the distributions of the residuals for each of the 21 lists across all subjects to see if any list had significantly larger residuals either in the positive direction—above the baselines, indicating an "easy" list—or in the negative direction—below the baselines, indicating a "difficult" list. In the original percentage scale the residuals would have different distributions at different percentage values, but in the transformed logit scale they are rather more homoscedastic. The data have therefore been analysed in this form, using a one-way analysis of variance. The independent-observation assumption of the analysis of variance is clearly violated, but the comparison of variability "between" and "within" lists remains apt as a descriptive measure. The F-ratio quoted should of course be viewed very conservatively. The summary table for the analysis is shown in Table I, and it can be seen that there are no significant differences between the residuals for different lists (F 20, 690 = 1·21, N.S.).

This analysis indicates that there are no differences amongst the mean difficulties of the lists, which are large relative to the within list variability. There is, therefore, no evidence from this somewhat limited analysis for any marked differences in difficulty between lists.

B. List equalization with a group of normally-hearing children

As we have seen, the analysis just described was performed on data which were not entirely suited to a check upon the equality of lists. For this reason, a further small study was conducted using a group of normally-hearing children who, as regards hearing and linguistic ability, could be considered to be a very homogeneous group. Every one of the ST Lists was administered to each child at the same relative speech level, thus permitting examination of the relative difficulty of lists in terms of the percentage correct score. Furthermore, since each child was assessed with all 21 lists, this design allows comparisons between all lists, not just comparisons within Lists 1–10 or within Lists 11–21 as was the case with the previous data from the hearing-impaired children.

Eleven children aged from 10–15 years and with normal hearing (pure tone average between -7 and $+12$ dB ISO, mean $1 \cdot 7$ dB) took part in this exercise. Each child listened to all 21 of the BKB (ST) Lists presented at the same relative speech level. The particular level used for any given child was that level at which the child attained as near as possible 50% correct on sentence repetition scored by key words. This level allows maximum variability and minimizes "ceiling" and "floor" effects. If the 21 lists are of equal difficulty, one would expect no differences between the means of the subjects' scores for each list. If any list were easier or harder than the other lists, however, one would expect this difference to be reflected in a systematic way in the score for that list from each subject.

Each child's testing was completed in one session of about two and a half hours' duration. A pure tone hearing test was administered first. Then, using TDH-39 headphones, two or sometimes three lists were presented for practice to the better ear. The lists used for practice were drawn from the 11 BKB Picture-related Lists, and were presented without the pictures. The tester used these lists to vary the relative speech level and hence determine a level for that child at which he was scoring about 50% correct. Using this level, the 21 ST Lists were presented one at a time in consecutive order, the starting list being varied systematically across subjects. As usual, the task was to repeat back each sentence after presentation. Testing took place in a quiet room, and considerable effort was made by the tester to ensure not only that listening conditions remained constant throughout, but that the subject remained attentive and fully motivated for all the lists. To this end, a short rest was given after each list.

Table II shows the results of an analysis of variance on the percentage correct scores from each subject from each list. That there are highly significant differences between the mean scores by subjects (F 10, $200 = 24.5$, $P < 0.001$) is not surprising, since this simply reflects the fact that the subjects were not all performing at the 50% level: some were performing around the 40% level, others around the 60% level, and so on. Of greater importance is the fact that there are significant differences between the means for each list (F 20, $200 = 4.68$, $P < 0.001$). It seems, then, that there *are* systematic differences in difficulty between lists. These differences are not due to order effects, since presentation order was balanced across subjects. Table III shows

Table II. List equalization with normally-hearing children (N=11): summary analysis of variance

Source	d.f.	Sum of squares	Mean square	F ratio
List	20	11 481·091	574·055	4·68**
Subject	10	30 011·853	3001·185	24·50**
Error	200	24 538·147	122·691	
Total	230	66 031·091		

the mean percentage scores for each of the 21 lists. The overall mean score across lists is 57·89%, and it can be seen that there are four lists whose means deviate from this grand mean by more than 9%. These are Lists 2 (42%), 12 (45%), 17 (68%) and 20 (71%). The remaining list means fall within the range 50–66% and for most practical purposes can be regarded as being of equal difficulty. The overall mean percentage score for Lists 1–10 is 57·83%, and for Lists 11–21 is 57·98%. If the four outlying Lists (2, 12, 17 and 20) are excluded, then these means become 59·56% for the first block of lists, and 56·61% for the second block of lists. We can, therefore, be sure that there are no marked differences between the two list blocks.

The scores for the four outlying lists were examined sentence-by-sentence, across subjects, and it was found that on each list, the scores were not independent of sentence number (for List 2, $\chi^2 = 88.54$, d.f. $= 15$, $P < 0.001$; for List 12, $\chi^2 = 75.06$, d.f. $= 15$, $P < 0.001$; for List 17, $\chi^2 = 31.55$, d.f. $= 15$, $P < 0.01$; and for List 20, $\chi^2 = 54.30$, d.f. $= 15$, $P < 0.001$). Thus, the score on a single sentence item within any of these lists is not a simple reflection of the list score; rather, the list score is the mean of a distribution of different scores, some high, some low, which probably reflect the intrinsic difficulty of the individual sentences themselves. List 2, therefore, has a markedly low mean percentage score because it contains a larger number of "difficult" sentences than the other lists. List 20, on the other hand, has a high mean percentage score because it contains a larger number of "easy" sentences than the other lists. The question arises as to whether the more "average" lists also

Table III. List equalization with normally-hearing children (N=11): mean percentage correct scores for each ST list

List number	Mean score (%)
1	59
2	42
3	55
4	56
5	54
6	55
7	64
8	61
9	66
10	66
11	56
12	45
13	51
14	57
15	64
16	54
17	68
18	52
19	59
20	71
21	60

consist of "easy" and "difficult" sentences, but more evenly balanced than in the four outlying lists, or whether the sentences within each list are of equal difficulty. To answer this, the four lists with mean percentage scores nearest to the grand mean (57·89%) were selected and analysed sentence-by-sentence. It was apparent that for these lists as well, different sentences gave markedly different scores (for List 1, $\chi^2 = 35\cdot05$, d.f. $= 15$, $P < 0\cdot01$; for List 14, $\chi^2 = 30\cdot16$, d.f. $= 15$, $P < 0\cdot05$; for List 19, $\chi^2 = 34\cdot75$, d.f. $= 15$, $P < 0\cdot01$; and for List 21, $\chi^2 = 43\cdot70$, d.f. $= 15$, $P < 0\cdot001$).

Methods and analyses such as these, if they were extended, would provide us with the means of not only adjusting the four outlying lists so as to bring them into greater correspondence with the other lists, but of refining and improving all the lists. For example, we ha·.e noted earlier that if all the items in a list are of equal difficulty, then the intelligibility curve for that list will be steeper than if they are of variable difficulty; furthermore, steeper curves for individual lists will tend to produce steeper speech intelligibility curves derived from the scores from different lists, and large differences in percentage correct for small differences in intensity is generally held to be a desirable feature of speech tests. The foregoing analyses have indicated that such improvements and refinements will not involve the application of complex manipulations to whole lists, but will be possible by simply adjusting or substituting individual sentence items. A further useful by-product of such an approach may be the identification of those features (grammatical, semantic, phonetic, etc.) which tend to be associated with the more difficult or the easier sentences.

But this is for the future. In the meantime, as a result of the checks described in this section we are satisfied that 17 of the BKB ST Lists are for all practical purposes of equal difficulty. The four lists over which there remains some doubt (Lists 2, 12, 17 and 20) have for the moment been left as they stand, and are given along with all the other lists in Appendix I. However, users of the Test are advised to treat these four lists with some caution. One final caveat: the assumption of equality of difficulty of at least 17 of the ST Lists will not necessarily hold for all possible patients to whom the test may be administered in the future. Occasionally a patient with idiosyncratic patterns of syntactical, morphological or vocabulary knowledge may find a certain list easier or more difficult than the others to which he listens. Nevertheless, the rigorous guide-lines which have been applied to the construction and recording of the sentence lists will keep such cases to a minimum.

We can now proceed to consider the test–retest variability of the BKB ST Sentence Lists.

III. Test–retest variability

A. The problem

Speech audiometry involves the interplay of a large number of variables, and even if a person were tested on two separate occasions with the same material under identical listening conditions, one could not expect the "test" and "retest" scores to be identical. That is, there will be some degree of test–retest variability, this variability being that which is not attributable to any known or measured variables. Unless the degree of test–retest variability is reasonably small the value of the test for accurately assessing the degree of hearing loss or the effects of different listening conditions is thereby limited. A test in which the Speech Intelligibility Threshold (the relative speech level at which the patient scores 50% correct) varies by 20 dB or thereabouts when the listener and the testing conditions are identical will be of little clinical value for estimating the effects of, say, different hearing aids, which may produce shifts in thresholds of only 5 or 10 dB.

B. Assessment of test–retest variability: methodological considerations

It is useful for the potential user of a test such as the BKB Sentence Lists to have some estimate of the test–retest variability, and the best method for deriving such an estimate is to administer the test twice to a representative sample of the people for whom the test was designed. The test–retest variability can be estimated from the amount by which each subject's scores differ across the two test sessions. Since the aim is to control as much of the variability as possible, it is important to be sure that the subject's hearing has not improved or deteriorated between the first and second session, because of surgery or because of a cold, for example. Furthermore, the subjects should be given the same lists at the same relative speech levels by the same tester, if possible in the same room under similar acoustic conditions. Good experimental techniques should ensure that the subjects are given the same instructions in both sessions, and are as far as possible equally (fully) motivated and attentive in both sessions. All aspects of the equipment should also be invariant across sessions: the calibration, the type of headset, the pressure of the earphones on the ear, and so on. Finally, the time period between testing sessions should not be so short (e.g. one day) that the subject remembers the test material on the second session, thus contaminating the results with memory factors. One does not, however, want to extend the time period between sessions so much (e.g. a year) that there is a clear possibility of the listener or his hearing ability changing to a significant degree.

C. Assessment of test-retest variability with selected groups of children

1. Method

We selected 15 partially-hearing children from schools in Berkshire to serve as subjects for a test–retest study. They were aged from 8–15 years, with average pure tone hearing loss in the better ear between 35 and 93 dB ISO (mean 67·5 dB), and were thought to be representative of the sort of children for whom the BKB Tests had been designed. That is not to imply that they were in any sense a homogeneous group: homogeneity of groups of hearing-impaired children is difficult to attain without selecting from a huge population. Nonetheless, in their ages, abilities and hearing losses, they covered a large part of the ranges within which most hearing-impaired children would fall, and they therefore provide a reasonably meaningful estimate of test–retest variability.

On the first (the test) session, each child's pure tone hearing loss was assessed. Then, using the better ear, each child's speech intelligibility curve was estimated with the BKB Sentence Lists. Scoring was by key word. Each child was randomly allocated to one of the 21 lists as a practice list, and then the lists immediately consecutive to this were presented at various relative speech levels in order to obtain sufficient points to estimate the curve reliably.

Some three months after the test sessions, the children underwent the retest session in which their pure tone hearing was reassessed and their speech intelligibility curve was re-estimated using the same lists presented at the same relative speech levels as in the test session. The same person acted as tester in both sessions, and care was taken in the retest session to keep all other possible factors (environment, equipment, subject motivation, etc.) as far as possible identical with the test session.

In addition to this group of 15 partially-hearing children, a small group (N=7) of normally-hearing children of similar ages was also tested twice with the BKB (ST) Lists. Their pure tone hearing was checked in the first session, but was not retested in the second session.

Before proceeding to analyse the results in detail, it is convenient to digress here for a short while in order to discuss some general points concerning speech intelligibility curves. These points are neatly illustrated by the test–retest speech intelligibility curves.

2. Intelligibility curves: some general points

Figures 3, 4, 5 and 6 show the test and retest percentage scores plotted as a function of relative speech level for four of the subjects, two hearing-impaired and two normally-hearing. Speech intelligibility curves have been fitted to the points by eye. The degree of disparity between each pair of curves is reasonably typical of the remaining subjects.

Firstly, we wish to draw attention to the fact that there is variability of the individual data points around the intelligibility curve: this is especially evident with the hearing-impaired, the effect of whose impairment is as

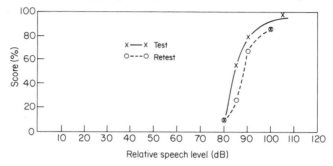

Fig. 3   *Test–retest speech intelligibility curves for a hearing-impaired child using the BKB (ST) Sentence Lists. Average pure tone hearing loss in the better (tested) ear was 65 dB at test and 63 dB at retest.*

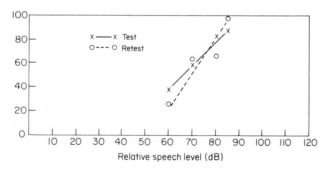

Fig. 4   *Test–retest speech intelligibility curves for a hearing-impaired child using the BKB (ST) Sentence Lists. Average pure tone hearing loss in the better (tested) ear was 53 dB at both test and retest.*

though to increase the amount and variability of the "noise" in the system. Best-fit curves have therefore to be estimated, and since it is impractical to do this in any way other than by eye when speech audiometry is used in the clinic or the school, we have adopted the same procedure here. The assumption must be made, as it is in the clinic or school, that the lines so fitted are indeed the best fit.

Secondly, the possible variability of a curve drawn from four or five data points is considerably less than the possible variability of the points themselves, and this is one of the reasons why we strongly recommend that the clinical implications of speech audiometry be drawn from the speech intelligibility curve, rather than from the observations (list scores) from which the curve itself was estimated, despite the extra time involved. It is unfortunate, for example, that workers in this area are often content to administer one

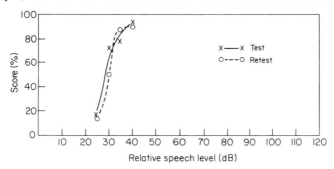

Fig. 5 Test–retest speech intelligiblity curves for a normally-hearing child using the BKB (ST) Sentence Lists.

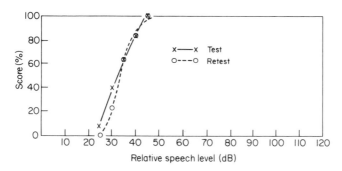

Fig. 6 Test–retest speech intelligibility curves for a normally-hearing child using the BKB (ST) Sentence Lists.

list only at a particular level under certain listening conditions, then change the conditions, and measure the effect of this change in terms of the change in score on another single list given at the same level. The effects of the change in listening conditions will have to be large to emerge above the inherent variability in the score from a single list. If one works from a curve fitted to four or five points, one can identify smaller effects. This argument applies even if one is comparing curves in terms of *single* points such as the speech intelligibility threshold or the optimum intelligibility score: if the measure is derived from the *curve* rather than from a single observation it will be that much more reliable. The test–retest data have been analysed in both these ways (see below) to illustrate the difference.

The third point we wish to make, and again this is illustrated by Figs 3, 4, 5 and 6, is that sentences, being highly redundant (i.e. predictable), produce relatively steep intelligibility curves. Material which is less redundant—monosyllabic words or nonsense syllables, for example—produces flatter curves (e.g. Miller *et al.*, 1951). However, the effect of hearing-impairment

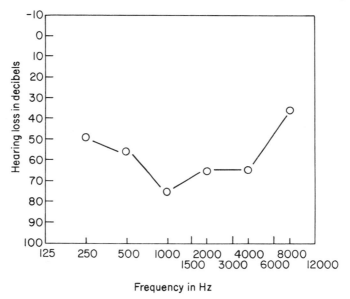

Fig. 7   The pure tone audiogram for the better (tested) ear of the subject whose speech intelligibility curves are shown in Fig. 3.

is very often not only to attenuate the signal, which produces a shift of the curve along the x-axis, but also to distort the signal in various complex ways, and this is evidenced by a tendency for the curve to be somewhat less steep than the typical normally-hearing curve. This is particularly so when the pure tone audiogram is sloping (more loss at the high frequencies than the low) rather than flat: the subject who gave the curves shown in Fig. 3 had a fairly flat pure tone audiogram, at least across the important speech frequencies (Fig. 7), whereas the subject who gave the curves shown in Fig. 4 had a more sloping pure tone audiogram across the speech frequencies (Fig. 8). Notwithstanding the tendency for some impairments to flatten the intelligibility curve, however, the important observation in the present context is the overall tendency towards steep slopes in speech audiometry, particularly when the slopes are derived from sentences.

This brings us to the fourth and final point to be made in general before we proceed to examine our test–retest data in detail: if a speech intelligibility curve rises very steeply, a small change in the abscissa (relative speech level) is accompanied by a large change in the ordinate (percentage correct). That part of the curve in Fig. 3 which is virtually linear (i.e. between 20% and

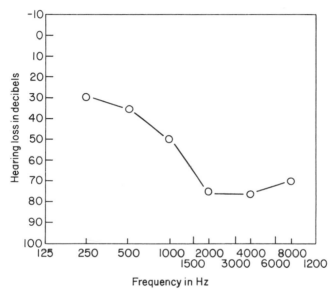

Fig. 8 *The pure tone audiogram for the better (tested) ear of the subject whose speech intelligibility curves are shown in Fig. 4.*

80% on the ordinate) increases at a rate of about 5% per one dB increase in the speech level; in Fig. 5 the slope increases at a rate of about $6\frac{1}{2}$% per one dB increase in speech level. What may appear as a large effect of changed listening conditions (e.g. a new hearing aid) in terms of percentages, therefore, may reflect quite a small change in terms of decibel gain. It can be misleading to the unwary reader to report the effects of changed listening conditions in terms of one or the other measure, without reference to the rate of gain, the slope, of the speech audiogram. Indeed, the slope itself may in certain circumstances be a more important indicator of performance than, say, the speech intelligibility threshold on its own (Bench and Cotter, 1979).

It is for the reasons briefly discussed in this section that, despite the extra time involved, we consider it necessary to draw the implications of speech audiometry from complete performance–intensity functions, rather than from scores on single lists.

3. Results and discussion

We can now turn to a more detailed consideration of the test–retest data. In all cases, the test speech intelligibility curve and the retest speech intelligibility curve were fitted to the observed points by eye, and the curve so fitted is assumed (as it is assumed in the clinic) to be the best fit. The reader should

Table IV. SIT (speech intelligibility thresholds, 50% correct level) and PTA (average pure tone hearing losses in the better (test) ear at 500, 1000, 2000 Hz) at test and retest sessions for 15 partially-hearing children. SIT in dB relative speech level, PTA in dB ISO. Material was the BKB Sentence Lists (ST version), scored by key words

Subject	PTA Test	SIT Test	PTA Retest	SIT Retest
1	65	89	70	85
2	80	87	73	83
3	80	102	83	102
4	90	104	90	104
5	92	113	87	114
6	57	69	62	73
7	57	67	60	70
8	63	85	57	84
9	88	105	92	104
10	93	105	90	103
11	53	67	53	69
12	57	84	58	82
13	35	55	28	58
14	65	87	63	88
15	37	60	38	61

bear this in mind throughout the remainder of this discussion, since it is certainly true that the idiosyncratic nature of curve-fitting by eye will tend to lessen the generality of the results. Table IV shows the test and retest speech intelligibility thresholds derived from these curves, and the average pure tone hearing losses at both sessions, for each of the partially-hearing subjects.

The correlation coefficient (Spearman's rho) between the test and retest speech intelligibility thresholds in Table IV is $+0.98$, which is extremely high, and appears to confirm that if a person's hearing for speech is assessed with the BKB Lists, the assessment is likely to be highly reliable. However, the use of correlation measures in this context is not entirely justified: the partially-hearing children were selected so as to span the range of "partial" pure tone hearing loss, so with only 15 cases the differences between subjects has been made artificially high, and it is not surprising, therefore, that in comparison the within-subject differences (test to retest) are small, giving a high correlation coefficient.

A rather more informative method of comparing test performance with retest performance is to look at the distribution of the differences between SITs at test and retest. If no test–retest variability intruded at any stage from the listening task for the subject to estimating the listener's best-fit curve by the tester, one would expect each subject's SITs to be identical. In fact, the differences between test and retest SITs vary from $+4$ to $-4\,dB$, with a mean of $-0{\cdot}067$ and a standard deviation (SD) of $2{\cdot}351$. If we make the assumption that this SD is the "population" value, then the least significant difference (lsd) between two SITs (comparing, for example, the effect of monaural versus binaural hearing aids) can be approximated by:

$$\text{lsd}\ (P=0{\cdot}05) = 1{\cdot}96\ \text{SD}\sqrt{2}$$
$$= 6{\cdot}5\,dB$$

Although our value for the SD of the distribution of differences and the SD of the "population" are unlikely to be the same, nonetheless our value of the lsd provides a useful rule of thumb. Thus, a difference between two SITs of $7\,dB$ or more can reasonably be regarded as a real effect. On the other hand, any difference between two SITs of less than $7\,dB$ cannot be regarded as constituting evidence of a difference between two listening conditions. Of course, if each of the two SITs is itself a mean of n SITs derived under identical listening conditions, then the expression for the lsd given above has to be divided by $\sqrt{n}$, thus reducing the lsd. However, this is unlikely to occur in the clinic, where SITs are usually measured no more than once for each listening condition.

It could be argued that in calculating the test–retest variability account should be taken of a subject's pure tone hearing loss. If, for example, PTA has increased by $5\,dB$ from test to retest session because of a slight head cold, then this change in the hearing for pure tones might affect the hearing for speech, and this difference should be allowed for in calculating SITs. That is to say, the difference represents not random variability in the test but variability which can be accounted for. The trouble with this argument is that it ignores the fact that pure tone testing has its own test–retest variability, and a difference of $5\,dB$ may be simply a reflection of this. Furthermore, the

John Bamford and Ian Wilson

relationship between pure tone hearing and speech hearing is too unpredict-able to be "allowed for" in the calculation of the test–retest variability for speech-hearing loss. It is a complex relationship, and has been the subject of considerable discussion and research (e.g. Siegenthaler and Strand, 1964; Harris, 1965; Hood and Poole, 1977); we ourselves expect to make a con-tribution to this discussion as a result of ongoing work on the standardization of the BKB Lists. If, for example, one uses a simple subtractive method to allow for PTA change, by comparing the difference between SIT and PTA for the test session with the difference between SIT and PTA for the retest session (difference between test and retest $= (SIT_1 - PTA_1) - (SIT_2 - PTA_2)$),

Table V. SIT (speech intelligibility thresholds, 50% correct level) in dB relative speech level at test and retest sessions for seven normally-hearing children

Subject	SIT test	SIT retest
1	37	36
2	29	34
3	37	39
4	29	30
5	37	37
6	32	33
7	32	33

one is assuming that changes in detection thresholds for pure tones are some-how linearly reflected in the hearing for connected-speech at and above thres-hold. Such is not the case, and the effect may be simply to increase the vari-ability, in so far as SIT and PTA vary independently of each other.

Table V shows the test and retest SITs for the normally-hearing children ($N = 7$). The differences between test and retest SITs vary between $+1$ and -5 dB, with a mean of -1.29 and a standard deviation of 1.75. The lsd ($P = 0.05$) of this distribution is 4.9 dB. Thus our rule of thumb for normally-hearing children indicates that two SITs must be separated by at least 5 dB if the separation is to be taken as significant, and not due simply to test–retest variability.

Another way of comparing test performance with retest performance is in terms of the slopes of the speech intelligibility curves. Table VI shows the slopes of the linear portions of the curves, measured in degrees from the hori-zontal (British Society of Audiology test blank), for the 15 partially-hearing children.

Table VI. The slopes of the linear portions of the speech intelligibility curves at test and retest for the 15 partially-hearing children. Slopes are measured in degrees from the horizontal. Material was the BKB Sentence Lists (ST version), scored by key words

Subject	Test	Retest
1	74	68
2	69	69
3	78	78
4	68	69
5	78	75
6	62	62
7	55	67
8	72	63
9	72	67
10	73	78
11	47	56
12	75	68
13	52	57
14	70	67
15	70	68

The test–retest slope differences vary from $+9$ to -12 degrees, with a mean of $+0.20$ and a standard deviation of 5.71. Applying the same procedure as before, this gives an lsd value between two speech intelligibility slopes of 15.83 degrees ($P = 0.05$).

Table VII shows the test and retest slopes for the seven normally-hearing children. The mean of the differences between test and retest is -1.14 degrees, with a standard deviation of 1.73. This gives an lsd value of 4.80 degrees

Table VII. The slopes of the linear portions of the speech intelligibility curves at test and retest for the seven normally-hearing children

Subject	Test	Retest
1	75	74
2	71	74
3	61	65
4	76	76
5	75	75
6	72	72
7	68	70

($P=0.05$). The normally-hearing slopes thus tend to differ less than the partially-hearing slopes, reflecting, not unexpectedly, that the hearing of the normally-hearing group was rather more invariable than the hearing of the partially-hearing group.

Finally, we argued earlier that to determine the effects of changed listening conditions on the basis of the change in score (per cent correct) between two single lists, one given under each condition, is much less reliable than working from the complete speech intelligibility curves. This is illustrated by Table VIII, which shows the scores (per cent correct) on a single list at test and

Table VIII. The per cent correct on a single BKB sentence list (ST version) at both test and retest for the 15 partially-hearing children. List scored by key words

Subject	Test %	Retest %
1	50	62
2	38	58
3	34	28
4	64	60
5	76	62
6	56	54
7	60	54
8	42	30
9	46	56
10	56	70
11	58	62
12	62	66
13	58	40
14	56	26
15	56	58

at retest for the 15 partially-hearing children. For each subject, the list/speech level combination chosen for this analysis from those lists/speech levels administered to him was that which, on the test session, scored closest to 50%, thus excluding the constraints of "floor" and "ceiling" effects on its freedom to vary from test session to retest session.

It can be seen that in some cases the difference between the two scores is quite large. The differences vary from +30% to −20%, with a mean of +1·73 and a standard deviation of 12·88. Using this SD as before, the approximate lsd between the scores on two lists is 35·7%. Clearly, the effects of changed listening conditions have to be considerable in order to be identified by their effect on the score for a single list, and we can see now the extent of the reduction in variability of the BKB (ST) Lists when inferences are made from speech intelligibility curves rather than from scores on single lists.

IV. Calibration

The need for electro-acoustic calibration of any new speech-hearing test was discussed in the Introduction to this Chapter. In order to facilitate comparisons of a given patient's performance on the speech test with his performance on other audiometric tests, or comparisons of the performances of different subjects on the same speech test, the relative speech level must be given some absolute meaning. This is done by recording an acoustically simple signal (a 1 kHz tone) at the start of each tape, which bears a specified relationship with the complex speech signal, and which can then be used as a calibration anchor. The first part of this section describes the detailed procedure and equipment that we used for the calibration of our lists. In the Introduction we also pointed out the need for subjective calibration with a group of normally-hearing subjects: this provides a "standard" speech intelligibility curve for the test against which comparisons may be made. The second part of this section describes the procedure for and results of this subjective calibration.

A. Electro-acoustic calibration

On all tape-recordings of the PR and ST versions of the BKB Sentence Lists, a 1 kHz pure tone has been recorded at the same level as the maximum speech peaks.

The equipment we use to present the sentence lists to a listener consists of Philips C–90 cassette tapes played from a Sony Stereo Cassette Recorder model TC–520 CS, through an Interacoustics DA 111 5 dB-step attenuator into Telephonics TDH 39 headphones. To carry out the electro-acoustic calibration of this equipment, the headphone was attached to a B. and K. 4152 Artificial Ear (including a 6 cm³ coupler, number DB 0138), and the 1 kHz calibration tone output to a B. and K. 2606 Measuring Amplifier, a B. and K. 1022 Beat Frequency Analyser, a B. and K. 2107 Frequency Analyser, and a B. and K. 2305 Level Recorder. Using this apparatus, the equipment was adjusted so that with the attenuator dial set at 120, and the needle of a VU-meter attached to the attenuator deflecting to zero, the level of the 1 kHz calibration tone was 120 dB SPL. The attenuator was checked by reducing the dial reading stepwise, 5 dB at a time, down to zero, and confirming that this reduced the output by 5 dB SPL throughout the scale (the tolerance which is applied in pure tone audiometer calibration was allowed here i.e. ± 3 dB at each dial setting). Having gone through this procedure (and rechecking the calibration every six months or so) it was a simple matter to adjust the tape-recorder output volume at the start of each test session such that the attenuator VU-meter needle deflected to zero with the attenuator dial set at 120. The calibration thus achieved meant that the attenuator dial readings represented dB SPL for the calibration tone. Although this gives the speech level some absolute meaning, it would be quite wrong (because of the complex and fluctuating nature of speech) to refer to the speech level itself in terms of dB SPL. For this reason it is generally expressed in terms of dB relative speech level.

B. Subjective calibration

The electro-acoustic calibration fixes the zero point on the relative speech level axis of the speech audiogram at zero dB SPL for the calibration tone. Zero dB SPL (which represents an intensity of 10^{-16} W cm^2, equivalent to a pressure of 0·0002 dyn cm^2) is a reference level to which other sound intensities can be related. It is a very low sound level which was chosen to be close to the absolute human threshold for a 1 kHz pure tone under ideal listening conditions (although it now appears that this average threshold is at about 6·5 dB SPL). The important point in the present context, however, is that zero dB SPL is near the threshold for detection of a 1 kHz tone, which is a considerably easier task than identifying spoken words at the same level. Thus one would expect a normally-hearing listener's speech intelligibility curve to be somewhat higher than the zero dB point on the speech audiogram—but by how much such a curve is shifted along the x-axis will depend upon the speech material, the speaker, the electro-acoustic properties of the equipment, the scoring method, and the relationship between the recorded level of the speech and the level of the calibration tone. Some indication of where the "standard" normally-hearing curve lies on speech audiogram for a particular test is useful for comparative purposes in the clinic, so we have attempted here to determine its position for the BKB lists using a group of normally-hearing listeners.

Eleven children aged between 10 and 15 years were paid as subjects for this exercise. Testing took place in a quiet sound-damped room with an ambient noise level varying between 20 and 26 dBA, most of the energy of which occurred at the low frequencies (see Table IX). Each child attended for testing on two consecutive mornings. At the start of the first morning the pure tone hearing in both ears was assessed using a Madsen TD 60 pure tone audiometer with Telephonics TDH 39 headphones. That ear which gave the lower threshold averaged across 500, 1000 and 2000 Hz was chosen as the test ear. A speech audiogram was then obtained from the child for each of the following tests: BKB Sentence Lists (ST and PR), Fry's Sentence Lists, Boothroyd Word Lists (AB(S) recording), and the Manchester Sentence Lists.

The Manchester Lists are only available in printed form, so we recorded them ourselves in the same way as we recorded the BKB Lists, and using

Table IX. The peak ambient noise levels at each octave band in the room in which the normally-hearing calibration took place. The levels were measured with a B. and K. Sound Level Meter type 2203, with 1613 Filter Unit

Frequency in Hz	Peak level in dB SPL
63	40
125	24
250	14
500	16
1000	16
2000	10
4000	10
8000	10

the same speaker. In addition to these five tests, and for comparison purposes, we made a recording of the Fry Sentence Lists using our speaker and the same warning noise prior to each sentence as in the BKB Lists (see Chapter 4 for details of the BKB recording procedure), and a recording of the Boothroyd Word Lists using our speaker. To distinguish these recordings from the originals, we will adopt the following nomenclature:

Original	*Our Recording*
Fry (DBF)	Fry (CNW)
Boothroyd AB(S)	Boothroyd (CNW)

Each child gave a further speech audiogram for each of the two new recordings, giving a total of seven speech audiograms from each child. Testing for each child was spread over the two mornings, with long rest periods (about half an hour) between each test, and short rest periods (about two minutes) between each list. In the long rest periods the children were free to leave the testing room and go for a walk, play, or do whatever they wished. To guard against contamination by memory factors, care was taken to ensure that for each child the lists from which the audiogram for Fry (CNW) was estimated were not the same as the lists from which the audiogram for Fry (DBF) was estimated, and similarly for the two recordings of the Boothroyd Word Lists. Five of the children performed the seven tests in one order, and the six remaining children performed them in the reverse order.

All tests were recorded (or copied) onto Philips C–90 cassette tapes, which were played at $1\frac{7}{8}$ i.p.s. on a Sony Stereo Cassette Recorder model TC–520 CS, through an Interacoustics DA 111 5 dB-step attenuator into Telephonics TDH 39 headphones.

The Boothroyd Word Lists AB(S) and (CNW) were scored by phonemes repeated back correctly (30 phonemes per 10-word list, converted to a percentage score), while the other five tests, all sentence tests, were scored by the "key word (loose)" system (see Section V, this Chapter, for a discussion of scoring methods). Under this system, a key word is scored as correct even if the morphological additions to its root are incorrect: providing that the *root* of the word is reported correctly, the subject scores a mark. Thus "They buy bread" as a response to "They're buying some bread" is scored as three key words correct. In our own tests (ST and PR) each list contains 50 key words which have been defined by us during the design of the tests and which are marked (see Appendixes I and II). The Manchester lists also contain 50 defined key words per list. In the Fry lists, however, key words have not been defined by the test designer, so before the start of this exercise we identified 100 key words in each list which were then used as the basis for scoring.

The children's pure tone thresholds, averaged in the better ear at 500, 1000 and 2000 Hz, ranged from -8.3 to $+3.3$ dB ISO, with a mean of -3.0 dB.

The mean speech intelligibility curves averaged over all subjects for the five sentence tests are shown in Fig. 9. It can be seen that the curves are all quite similar, with the 50% correct thresholds (SITs) centred around the 30 dB relative speech level. The slopes of the middle portions of the curves and the SITs are shown in Table X.

The slopes of the linear portions of the curves are very similar. They are all fairly steep, which is to be expected since sentences exhibit a high degree of redundancy. There are no significant differences between the slopes, and the only remarkable aspect of the slope figures is that the PR Lists give the least-steep slope, when the increased redundancy (or decreased uncertainty) provided by the pictures might have led us to predict especially steep slopes for this test. It has become clear with use, however, that while some subjects

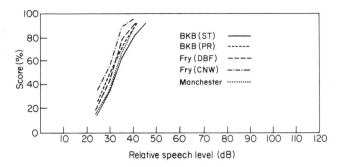

Fig. 9 The mean speech intelligibility curves from N=11 normally-hearing subjects for five different sentence tests: BKB (ST) version; BKB (PR) version; Fry (DBF); Fry (CNW); and Manchester.

may find the pictures helpful there are others who find them confusing or interfering, requiring as they do some degree of visual search in addition to the auditory discrimination task.

The SITs of the five sentence-test curves are also very similar, although a Friedman two-way analysis of variance showed that there are significant differences, albeit small, between the tests ($\chi^2 = 19{\cdot}69$, d.f. $= 4$, $P < 0{\cdot}001$). Generally speaking one would expect differences in the list material (degree of redundancy, linguistic difficulty, etc.) to produce differences in the slopes of the intelligibility curves, and hence differences in intelligibility thresholds. However, differences in thresholds unaccompanied by differences in slopes, as we have here, are more indicative of simple differences in the precise relationship between recorded voice level and the level of the calibration tone. Thus it appears that the BKB ST Lists may have been recorded at a slightly lower level than the other tests.

Table X. Subjective calibration with a group of normally-hearing children (N=11): speech intelligibility thresholds (in dB relative speech level) and slopes (in degrees from horizontal) of the speech intelligibility curves of five sentence tests

Test	SIT (dB)	Slope (degrees)
BKB ST version	33	71
BKB PR version	30	66
Fry (DBF)	31	74
Fry (CNW)	29	74
Manchester	32	71

Table XI. Subjective calibration with a group of normally-hearing children (N=11): speech intelligibility thresholds (in dB relative speech level) and slopes (in degrees from horizontal) of the speech intelligibility curves of two recordings of the Boothroyd Word Lists

Test	SIT (dB)	Slope (degrees)
Boothroyd AB(S)	30	63
Boothroyd (CNW)	38	51

The mean speech intelligibility curves for the two-word list tests—Boothroyd AB(S) and Boothroyd (CNW)—are shown in Fig. 10. The SITs and slopes of these two curves are shown in Table XI.

As expected, several Wilcoxon Signed Ranks Tests indicated that the differences between the slopes for the word lists and the slopes for the sentence lists were all significant ($P < 0.01$). This is a reflection of the relative lack of redundancy in monosyllabic words compared with sentences, there being no

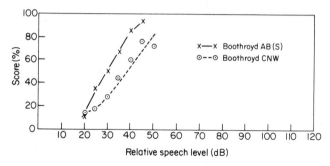

Fig. 10 The mean speech intelligibility curves from N=11 normally-hearing subjects for two recordings of the Boothroyd Word Lists: Boothroyd AB(S) and Boothroyd (CNW).

syntactic (as opposed to morphological) constraints in the former. The slopes shown in Table XI have been derived from the percentage of *phonemes* repeated correctly on each list, and one has to be cautious when comparing these curves with the sentence list curves in Table X, which are derived from correctly repeated *words*. If the word list data is rescored in terms of words repeated correctly, the resulting intelligibility curves would be even flatter. The slope of the Boothroyd (CNW) recording is significantly less than the slope derived from the AB(S) recording, and this is thought to reflect speaker effects—for one thing, the (CNW) recording has the words spoken much more slowly and deliberately than one would find them in normal speech, perhaps making perception more difficult.

As a consequence of the flatter slope of the Boothroyd (CNW) recording, the associated SIT is higher than all of the sentence list SITs (Wilcoxon, $P < 0.01$ in all cases). The Boothroyd AB(S) recording, however, gives an SIT not significantly different from the sentence list SITs. The reason for this apparent anomaly is clear if one compares the speech level at which the word lists begin to be correctly reported: performance on the word lists "takes off from the floor" at slightly lower levels, suggesting that the word lists may have been recorded at slightly higher levels than the sentence lists. This would account for the absence of significant differences between the Boothroyd AB(S) word list SIT and the SITs of the sentence tests despite the steeper slopes of the latter.

All these arguments, however, are concerned with essentially very small differences discernible only over groups of individuals. The important outcome of this Section is that we have now established normally-hearing intelligibility curves for our BKB Tests, as well as for other widely-used speech tests, and these will provide some reference point or standard for users of the tests. The fact that the curves for the BKB Tests are essentially no different from the other Sentence Test curves is not surprising, since *normally*-hearing children of the age tested might be expected to cope reasonably well (in linguistic terms) with all the tests. The advantages of the BKB Tests accrue in the testing of younger or hearing-impaired children. The details of these advantages will be published at a later date when standardization of the Tests has been completed.

V. Scoring methods

The way in which speech audiometry tests are scored affects the displacement and slope of the resulting speech intelligibility curves. Word lists are usually scored by phoneme or by word reported correctly, but there are other possible methods which could be used with sentence lists. As we pointed out in the introduction to this Chapter, the choice of method belongs to the user, but we have arguments and data which may help him to make this choice.

To score sentence lists by phoneme would be so tedious and lengthy a task as to make it very unlikely that it would be considered for use in a clinical setting. Furthermore, phoneme scoring would run counter to the arguments which underpin the use of sentences for speech audiometry: their face validity as samples of everyday speech material, their "naturalness" and the opportunity they afford the listener to take advantage of not only morphological but syntactical constraints. For these reasons we do not regard scoring the BKB Tests by phoneme as a viable alternative in the clinical setting.

Probably the most popular method for scoring sentences is by the percentage of "key words" reported correctly, key words being those words which are thought to carry the burden of the meaning of each sentence. Thus, articles and most (but not all) function words are usually considered to be less important to the fundamental meaning of a sentence than nouns and verbs. The "importance" of adjectives and adverbs is more equivocal and will depend upon the particular sentence. There may, then, be some argument as to which words are to be regarded as "key" and which are not, but it does not really matter as long as the designer defines what he regards as the key words, and all test users stick to his scheme. In the BKB Tests we have identified 50 key words per list, making for easy conversion to a percentage score.

Most users who score sentences by key word require the listener to repeat each key word completely correctly in order to be credited with a score for that word. We have called this scoring method the tight key word (KW(T)) method. However, the logic which argues that, for a realistic measure of speech-hearing ability, it is only the important meaning-carrying words which really matter can also be invoked to argue that it is only the *root* of the key words, not their inflexions, precise word endings, or whatever, that carry the burden of communication between speaker and listener. This gives us a second method of scoring by key word, and we shall refer to it as the loose key word (KW(L)) method. It has the advantage that for use with listeners whose quality of uttered speech is not all it might be, such as the hearing-impaired, errors due to the faulty perception by the tester of what the listener actually said are reduced, since such errors are usually associated with word endings rather than word-roots.

It could be argued that to assess the impairment of a person's hearing for speech by a key word method is to obscure the difference between his speech-hearing ability and that of normally-hearing listeners, since as key words often contain more syllables than non-key words and as they are usually the words which carry most stress in a sentence, they are precisely those words that the impaired *will* tend to hear correctly. Thus it might be more fruitful to measure the percentage of non-key words correctly repeated. This argument emphasizes the use of a speech-hearing test to discriminate between impaired and normally-hearing listeners, rather than its use as a measure of "communication ability". We shall refer to it as the non-key word (NKW) method. There are two further non-key word methods which are refinements of this method. The first argues that articles occur so regularly in our sentences that a subject could obtain a certain percentage score on the NKW method simply by repeating articles for each sentence. This might tend to obscure real effects and it might be useful, therefore, to look at the percentage of non-key words excluding articles (NK(EA)) repeated correctly. The other refinement of the NKW method argues that the percentage correct should be based upon all the non-key words except the initial word in the sentence (if it *is* a non-key word), since factors associated with the temporal uncertainty of the time-of-arrival of this initial word will increase the variability of the listener's performance on this word, thus decreasing the reliability of the NKW score as a measure of hearing ability proper. This method we shall refer to as the non-key word, excluding initial word, method (NKW(EI)).

Finally, an obvious method for scoring sentence lists is in terms of the percentage of sentences correct, a sentence having to be completely correct to score. We have examined a version of this whole-sentence (WS) method which requires the listener to report correctly all the key words (loose) in a sentence in order to obtain a score for it. By this method the maximum raw score per BKB List is therefore 16.

We have thus compared six methods of scoring sentence lists:

(1) Percentage of key words (tight) repeated correctly, KW(T).
(2) Percentage of key words (loose) repeated correctly, KW(L).
(3) Percentage of non-key words repeated correctly, NKW.
(4) Percentage of non-key words excluding articles repeated correctly, NKW(EA).
(5) Percentage of non-key words exluding initial word repeated correctly, NKW(EI).
(6) Percentage of whole sentences repeated correctly, WS.

The reader will, of course, be able to devise scoring methods other than those listed above, but we feel that those above do cover the important aspects. The obvious omission is a method based on scoring at the phonemic level, but as we argued earlier such approaches are generally both inappropriate and impractical for lists of sentences.

In Section II of this Chapter it was noted that at the time of writing, the BKB (ST) Test had been administered as part of a standardization exercise to just over 200 hearing-impaired children. This has provided us with the data we need to compare the various scoring methods. Initially, 20 older children (aged 11–16 years) were selected from the sample so that they covered a wide range of pure tone hearing losses. Their performance on the

BKB (ST) Lists was scored according to the five word-level methods: KW(T), KW(L), NKW, NKW(EA) and NKW(EI). Five speech intelligibility curves were drawn for each subject, according to scoring method. Each subject's curves were then ranked at the 50% intelligibility score (the speech intelligibility threshold, SIT), rank 1 being given to that threshold with the *lowest* relative speech level. The results of this procedure are shown in Table XII.

The first thing to notice is that there is a large degree of agreement across subjects, and there do not appear to be any interactions between scoring methods and level of hearing loss. The suggestion that certain methods (e.g. NKW) are more discriminating, then, is not supported. What is clear, however, is that the different methods do affect the speech intelligibility thresholds in a systematic manner. Not surprisingly, KW(L) scoring gives lower thres-

Table XII. *The ranks of the speech intelligibility thresholds (SITs) from 20 subjects whose performance on the BKB ST Test was scored by five different word-level methods. Rank 1 is given to the lowest threshold. Also shown is each subject's average pure tone hearing loss (PTA) in the test ear*

Subject	PTA (dB ISO)	Scoring method				
		KW(T)	KW(L)	NKW	NKW(EA)	NKW(EI)
1	42	5	4	1	2	3
2	45	3	2	1	5	4
3	45	4	3	1	5	2
4	47	3	2	1	5	4
5	47	5	4	1	2	3
6	52	5	4	1	3	2
7	52	5	4	1	3	2
8	58	4	3	1	5	2
9	67	4	3	1	5	2
10	68	3	2	1	5	4
11	77	3	2	1	5	4
12	77	3	2	1	5	4
13	78	4	2	1	5	3
17	80	5	4	1	2	3
15	83	5	4	1	2	3
16	85	3	2	1	5	4
17	85	3	2	1	5	4
18	92	5	4	1	3	2
19	97	3	2	1	5	4
20	100	2	1	3	5	4
Mean rank		3·8	2·7	1·1	4·1	3·1

holds than KW(T) scoring. NKW scoring produces the lowest thresholds (NKW mean rank = 1·10), but this is largely due to the frequent and regular perception (or reporting) of articles, which if omitted from the scheme, gives a method (NKW(EA)) which produces easily the *highest* thresholds. NKW(EI) is intermediate, with a mean rank of 3·15, and is of less interest.

As a check, the same procedure was then followed for a group of 17 slightly younger children (aged 10–12 years). The results of the ranking analysis on these children is shown in Table XIII, and it can be seen that the picture is essentially the same as for the older children: loose key word scoring gives lower thresholds than tight key word scoring; non-key word scoring gives the lowest thresholds, but this is largely due to the inclusion of articles, which if excluded give intelligibility curves with the highest thresholds.

Interestingly, when the effects of the five word-level scoring methods were compared on data from the Fry Sentence Lists and the Manchester Sentence Lists (which also formed part of the standardization exercise), it was found

Table XIII. The ranks of the speech intelligibility thresholds from 17 younger subjects whose performance on the BKB ST Test was scored by five different word-level methods. Rank 1 is given to the lowest threshold. Also shown is each subject's average pure tone hearing loss (PTA) in the test ear

Subject	PTA (dB ISO)	Scoring method				
		KW(T)	KW(L)	NKW	NKW(EA)	NKW(EI)
1	13	3	1·5	1·5	5	4
2	40	3	2	1	5	4
3	42	4	3	2	5	1
4	45	3	2	1	5	4
5	58	5	3	1	4	2
6	60	3	1	2	5	4
7	63	4	3	1	5	2
8	65	5	4	1	3	2
10	66	3	2	1	5	4
11	68	3	2	1	5	4
12	70	4	3	1	5	2
13	71	5	4	1	3	2
14	78	4	2	1	5	3
15	78	5	4	1	3	2
16	90	4	3	1	5	2
17	93	4	3	1	5	2
Mean rank:		3·9	2·6	1·2	4·6	2·7

that while the Fry Lists gave similar results to those shown in Tables XII and XIII from the BKB (ST) Lists, the Manchester Lists did not. In particular, although as expected KW(L) scoring gave lower thresholds than KW(T) scoring, the NKW method did *not* give the lowest thresholds, and excluding the articles (NKW(EA)) made little difference. A further (parametric) analysis was carried out to check this finding; the performance of three groups of hearing-impaired subjects, 10 subjects in each group, were compared, one group performing on the BKB (ST) Lists, another on the Fry Lists, and the third group on the Manchester Lists. For each subject, two speech intelligibility curves were drawn, one using the KW(T) scoring method, the other using the NKW scoring method. The difference between each pair of curves was measured in terms of the difference between a measure of the area under each curve. Thus there were 10 difference measurements (one for each subject) for each test—BKB, Fry and Manchester. An analysis of variance of these difference measurements showed that there were significant differences between the three groups, i.e. according to the test being used (F 2, 27= 9·52, $P < 0.001$). Uncorrelated t-tests confirmed that there was no difference between the Fry Test and the BKB Test, but that the Manchester Test differed significantly in its scoring method effect from both the other tests ($P < 0.001$ in both cases).

It is clear, then, that although NKW scoring gives lower thresholds for the BKB and the Fry Lists, this is not the case with the Manchester Lists. Furthermore, exclusion of the articles (NKW(EA)) cancels out the method's advantage in the case of BKB and Fry, but has little effect on the Manchester Lists. A plausible explanation for this rather different effect of non-key word scoring on the Manchester Lists is that these lists contain different types of sentence structures—commands and questions, in addition to statements— many of them quite complex, and the predictability of the articles within them is considerably less than the predictability of the articles within our sentences or Fry's sentences, all (or nearly all, in the case of Fry) of which are short statement-type sentences. In each of our BKB (ST) Sentence Lists, for example, nine of the 16 sentences were of the type subject–verb–complement or object, six were of the type subject–verb–adverbial, and one was of the type subject–verb. With such uniformity, articles become rather predictable. This uniformity is not present in the Manchester Lists.

Up to now, no mention has been made in these analyses of the whole sentence (WS) method of scoring, although a little thought makes it clear what effect the WS method would have on a list score, and hence on a speech intelligibility curve: percentage scores on each list would tend to be lower than the percentage scores derived from the five word-level methods, since under a given set of listening conditions the probability of being correct on all three or four key words in a sentence is much less than the probability of being correct on any one or two or three of them; furthermore, with only 16 scoring items per list the variability of the scores will be greater than the score variability of the other methods. The likely effect of the WS method on the intelligibility curve, therefore, is to displace it to the right on the audiogram (i.e. towards higher relative speech levels) and to flatten the slope of its linear portion.

The final analysis of different scoring methods which we will describe in this section looks at all six methods, including WS. Scores on the BKB(ST) Test were obtained from 36 hearing-impaired subjects, and each observation from each subject (i.e. performance at a particular relative speech level) was scored in six different ways, according to the six methods described earlier: KW(T), KW(L), NKW, NKW(EA), NKW(EI) and WS. Each observation and its six scores were treated in this analysis as independent: that is, repeat observations by the same subject at different relative speech levels were not distinguished from those deriving from different subjects. This is not a problem, because the between-subjects variance we might obtain is not relevant to a comparison of scoring methods—and as we shall see, the results of the analysis are so conclusive as to render any treatment by subjects an unnecessary refinement. In this form, then, the data consisted of 163 observations, each associated with six scores derived from the six scoring methods. The correlations between the scores are shown in the matrix in Table XIV. The correlations are very large, approaching unity in all cases. The data were subjected to a principal components analysis. The first component accounted for 92·8% of the trace total variation, while the second and third components accounted for only 4·5% and 1·8% of the total variation respectively. The correlations of the variables with the first principal component are shown in Table XV.

Thus it is quite clear that as only one variable is needed to account for 92·8% of the trace total variation, the six different measurements (scoring methods) almost lie along a line in six-dimensional space: that is, they are measuring virtually the same thing, and all six measures can be regarded as interchangeable. One problem with this analysis is that it ignores "ceiling" and "floor" effects: the variance of a proportion depends upon the proportion itself, and therefore the observations have different variances. A method which, it is argued, gets round this problem is an arc-sin transformation of the data (analyse $\sin^{-1} p$ instead of p), which stabilizes the variance. A principal components analysis of the transformed data gave essentially the same results as the previous analysis, the first component accounting for 93·2%

Table XIV. The correlation coefficients between the six different scoring methods, based on 163 observations derived from the speech intelligibility data of 36 hearing-impaired children

	KW(T)	KW(L)	NKW	NKW(EA)	NKW(EI)	WS
KW(T)	1	0·99	0·93	0·88	0·92	0·95
KW(L)		1	0·93	0·87	0·91	0·95
NKW			1	0·91	0·97	0·84
NKW(EA)				1	0·96	0·84
NKW(EI)					1	0·86
WS						1

of the total variance, the second and third components accounting for only 4·3% and 1·6% of the variance respectively. Again, all six variables (scoring methods) were highly correlated with the first component. Statistically, then, it does not matter which scoring method is used, but only one is necessary. In order to choose a method, therefore, one has to consider only the arguments discussed earlier in this section to see if there are good reasons for using any particular method. In fact, the arguments are fairly marginal, but we are in favour of the loose key word scoring system (KW(L)) for three reasons. Firstly, it is simple. Secondly, it involves less error in the tester's perception of what the testee actually said in response to a sentence item than do all the other methods (except the whole sentence (WS) method, which is not recommended on other grounds, chiefly the high degree of variability associated with it as a result of the relatively few scoring items in each list). And thirdly, we subscribe to the view expressed earlier that the roots of the key words carry the burden of everyday communication, and the method is therefore especially valid as a measure of communication ability. We admit, however, that this is an opinion formed on the basis of argument rather than evidence, and a good case can be made for the empirical investigation of this and other questions about scoring methods which have been begged in

Table XV. The correlations of the variables (scoring methods) with the first principal component

	KW(T)	KW(L)	NKW	NKW(EA)	NKW(EI)	WS
Component 1	0·98	0·98	0·96	0·95	0·97	0·94

this section. Until such investigations are forthcoming, however, we are content to use the KW(L) method for scoring our Tests, and it is for this reason that the normally-hearing calibration curves presented in Section IV are derived from KW(L) scoring of the listeners' responses.

References

BENCH, J. and COTTER, S. (1979). Psycholinguistic abilities and audiometric performance in partially-hearing children. *Brit. J. Disord. Comm.* (In press.)

BRANDY, W. T. (1966). Reliability of voice tests of speech discrimination. *J. Speech Hear. Res.* **9,** 461–465.

HARRIS, J. D. (1965). Pure tone acuity and the intelligibility of everyday speech. *J. Acoust. Soc. Amer.* **37,** 824–830.

HOOD, J. D. and POOLE, J. P. (1977). Improving the reliability of speech audiometry. *Brit. J. Audiol.* **11,** 93–102.

LYREGAARD, P. E. (1973). On the statistics of speech audiometry data. NPL Acoustics Report Ac63, National Physical Laboratory, Teddington, Middlesex, UK.

LYREGAARD, P. E., ROBINSON, D. W. and HINCHCLIFFE, R. (1976). A feasibility study of diagnostic speech audiometry, NPL Acoustics Report Ac73, National Physical Laboratory, Teddington, Middlesex, UK.

MILLER, G. A., HEISE, G. A. and LICHTEN, W. (1951). The intelligibility of speech as a function of the context of the test materials. *J. Exp. Psychol.* **41,** 329–335.

SIEGENTHALER, B. M. and STRAND, R. (1964). Audiogram averages and S.R.T. scores. *J. Acoust. Soc. Amer.* **36,** 589–593.

Part II

The Spoken Language of Hearing-impaired Children

6

The Spoken Language of Hearing-impaired Children: Vocabulary

JOHN BENCH, LÜTGEN MENTZ AND
IAN WILSON

I. The vocabulary lists

This Chapter contains the vocabulary data which was sorted according to the procedures described in Chapter 3. Thus we have presented here, according to each cell of the subject classification matrix, lists of all the words used by the subjects in that cell in each parsing category. Each word is listed with the number of times it was uttered. Following each parsing category is given firstly the total and the mean number of words used, with every occurrence of a word given a count of one (i.e. tokens), and secondly the total and mean number of different words (i.e. types).

Words which are unfamiliar, or were used in a sense unfamiliar, to North American readers (e.g. boot meaning the boot of a car) are indicated with an asterisk. The fact that a word is accompanied by an asterisk does not imply that such a word was used in a sense unfamiliar to North American readers on more than one occasion. Readers in Australasia are likely to have fewer problems of this kind, and we have not therefore made similar indications for them.

Homographs (e.g. "read") occurred very rarely, and have not been recorded separately.

To assist the reader in consulting the vocabulary lists we recapitulate here the essentials of the rules for parsing the vocabulary data, with some additional notes.

1. Each word is parsed into one of eleven categories: Nouns, Verbs, Adjectives, Adverbs, Pronouns, Prepositions, Conjunctions, Contractions, Interjections, Articles and Other (including "yes" and "no". Originally (see Chapter 3) the Articles were classified with "Other", but are reclassified here into a separate category).
2. Word order is used as a guide to the appropriate part of speech—thus "broken eggs" is parsed as Adjective–Noun, whereas "eggs broken" is Noun–Verb.
3. Possessive pronouns (his, her, their, etc.) are classed as pronouns.
4. Nouns used as adjectives (e.g. *picnic* basket) are classed as Nouns. Genetive nouns (e.g. *mummy's* bag) are also classed as Nouns.
5. For infinitives (e.g. "to go"), "to" is classed as a Preposition, "go" is a Verb.
6. Context is used as an aid to parsing, as in "He looked over (=examined) the room", where "over" is v. particle and is classed as an Adverb. In "He looked over (=gazed across) the river", "over" is a Preposition.
7. Certain compound words, such as "someone", "everybody", "nothing", "anyone", etc. are classed with Pronouns, or, in the case of compounds such as "anyhow", "nowhere", etc., as Adverbs.
8. Colloquial nouns (e.g. fridge=refrigerator) are classed as Nouns.
9. The Concise Oxford Dictionary is used as a reference.

Subject Group A

(6 children; age: 8–10 years;
performance I.Q.: ≤90; hearing loss: 40–60 dB)

NOUNS

Word	Count	Word	Count	Word	Count	Word	Count
accident	1	bushes	1	dragon	2	grass	2
all	1	butter	1	drain	3	ground	2
ambulance	13	cabbage	2	drawer	2	hair	2
animals	1	cake	6	drink	9	ham	1
apple	9	calendar	1	drinks	2	hand	8
apple-pie	1	car	38	ears	1	hands	1
apples	4	cat	7	egg	8	handstands	2
arm	3	cat's	1	eggs	6	hat	7
baby	5	cats	1	engine	1	head	5
back	3	chair	5	face	2	hedge	1
badge	1	cheese	4	farm	4	hill	2
bag	5	chicken	2	farmer	1	hole	5
ball	24	children	5	farms	1	holiday	1
banana	5	clock	4	father	4	hospital	2
bananas	2	clothes	8	fence	2	house	6
barrow	1	clown	3	field	1	houses	2
basket	8	coat	4	finger	1	ice	10
bat	7	coin	1	fire	1	ice-cream	1
beef	1	colour	1	fish	5	jam	1
bicycle	1	*cooker	3	floor	4	jelly	3
bike	5	corner	1	flower	6	*jumper	2
blanket	3	cow	9	flowers	2	*kerb	1
book	12	crash	1	food	7	kettle	7
books	1	*cricket	2	football	8	kitchen	5
boot	10	cup	3	fork	3	knife	8
boots	5	cupboard	1	forks	3	knives	2
bowl	2	curtains	1	fright	1	ladder	14
boy	87	daddy	24	fronts	1	ladders	2
boy's	1	danger	2	fruit	2	lady	13
boys	13	dark	1	gate	4	legs	3
bread	4	dinner	8	girl	23	lemon	2
room	2	dog	32	girls	5	lighter	1
rother	1	doggy	1	glove	3	line	2
rush	3	doll	4	gloves	1	lips	1
ucket	3	dolly	3	goal	6	locker	1
uilding	11	door	10	goalkeeper	1	lot	2
ull	11	doors	1	golf	1	lots	4

Word	Count	Word	Count	Word	Count	Word	Count
lunch	1	*pavement	1	saucepans	2	there	8
machine	4	pea	1	scarf	3	thing	3
man	60	pear	1	scissors	4	things	4
man's	1	pepper	2	set	1	tie	1
market	1	persons	1	shave	1	time	2
matches	4	picnic	10	shoes	3	towel	4
map	2	picture	4	shop	2	toy	3
meat	3	pictures	1	shoulder	1	toys	2
men	1	pie	1	side	1	train	5
mess	2	piece	1	sink	2	tree	7
milk	9	pig	1	*sitting-room	1	*trousers	1
milkman	3	plant	1	skate	1	van	3
mirror	1	plate	4	skates	1	wall	1
mixer	1	plates	3	*sledge	3	washing	4
money	11	playground	1	snow	3	water	4
mother	6	police	4	spoon	6	week-end	1
mouse	3	policeman	6	spoons	1	wheelbarrow	1
mummy	15	pond	2	stick	8	while	1
mushroom	1	*postman	3	sticks	3	whistle	1
name	2	pot	1	stone	1	window	11
noise	1	potato	1	story	1	windows	1
number	1	*purse	3	strawberries	1	window-sill	2
numbers	1	road	5	street	1	wire	1
one	4	room	3	stuff	6	woman	1
onion	1	*rounders	1	sweet	1	wood	1
orange	3	salt	2	table	12	woods	1
oranges	1	sandwich	1	table-cloth	2		
paint	1	sandwiches	6	*tap	1		
paper	2	sauce	1	tea	3		

		Total words	1111	Total different words	261		
		Mean words	185·17	Mean different words	43·50		

VERBS

Word	Count	Word	Count	Word	Count	Word	Count
allowed	3	blow	1	busted	1	carry	
are	14	break	1	buy	3	clean	
bang	2	bringing	2	call	1	cleans	
banged	1	broke	2	came	9	clearing	
be	1	bump	1	can	3	climb	
been	1	bust	1	carries	11	climbing	

Word	Count	Word	Count	Word	Count	Word	Count
close	1	gone	5	packing	1	slipped	2
comb	1	got	27	pay	1	smashed	1
combing	1	had	3	paying	2	smiling	1
come	3	has	15	play	14	snowing	1
comes	3	have	5	playing	26	standing	3
coming	8	having	17	pointing	1	start	2
cracking	1	help	5	pretending	1	stir	2
crash	12	hit	1	pull	2	stop	7
crashed	3	hold	5	put	16	stopping	1
crawl	1	hurry	2	puts	1	switch	1
cry	1	hurt	2	putting	1	take	4
crying	1	is	48	ran	3	taking	7
do	3	jump	1	read	2	telling	4
does	1	jumped	1	reading	2	think	6
doing	3	jumping	1	ride	1	thought	1
done	2	jumps	1	riding	1	throw	2
drink	2	keeping	1	rolled	1	tired	1
drinking	5	kicked	2	run	7	told	2
drop	12	kill	3	running	4	touch	1
dropped	7	knocked	1	said	1	try	2
dry	1	know	20	sat	1	trying	3
eat	12	knows	1	saw	1	turn	2
eating	7	left	1	say	1	wait	1
fall	10	let	1	says	8	waiting	1
fallen	4	lift	1	see	4	walking	5
falling	1	like	1	sells	1	warming	1
fell	14	living	1	setting	1	was	11
finished	4	look	6	shopping	2	wash	1
folds	1	looking	11	should	1	washing	2
forget	1	make	1	shouting	1	watch	3
forgot	1	making	1	shouts	1	watching	15
frightened	1	might	4	shutting	2	went	10
get	28	must	1	signing	1	were	1
getting	4	open	3	sitting	4	will	4
give	3	opened	1	skating	1	write	1
go	23	pack	1	slide	2	writing	3
going	19	packed	1				

Total words	715		Total different words	170
Mean words	119·17		Mean different words	28·33

ADJECTIVES

Word	Count	Word	Count	Word	Count	Word	Coun
all	24	dead	1	little	14	second	1
angry	1	different	1	more	5	small	1
another	4	dirty	2	no	3	some	12
back	1	five	2	one	9	that	15
big	3	four	3	open	2	those	1
blue	1	funny	2	other	8	three	3
broken	1	horrible	1	ready	1	twelve	4
dark	1	last	1	red	1	two	14

Total words 143
Mean words 23·83

Total different words 32
Mean different words 5·33

ADVERBS

Word	Count	Word	Count	Word	Count	Word	Cou
about	2	in	5	on	2	there	1
again	1	just	1	open	2	today	
as	2	more	1	out	20	together	
away	5	nearly	2	over	5	up	1
back	2	no	1	properly	1	upside-down	
down	20	not	5	quick	1	well	
fast	1	now	3	round	1	where	
here	2	off	6	so	5	yet	
home	9						

Total words 146
Mean words 24·33

Total different words 33
Mean different words 5·50

PRONOUNS

Word	Count	Word	Count	Word	Count	Word	Count
any	1	it's	1	someone's	1	this	5
he	57	my	4	something	6	those	3
her	13	nothing	1	that	29	what	12
him	21	one	4	their	6	when	5
his	17	she	22	them	10	who	5
I	18	somebody	3	these	2	you	15
it	34	somebody's	1	they	44	your	2

Total words	342	Total different words	28
Mean words	57·00	Mean different words	4·67

PREPOSITIONS

Word	Count	Word	Count	Word	Count	Word	Count
about	1	down	4	next	1	round	3
across	3	for	17	of	22	to	56
after	5	in	55	off	3	towards	1
around	1	inside	1	on	26	under	3
at	13	into	9	out	12	up	2
behind	2	like	6	over	14	with	20
beside	1	near	1	past	2		

Total words	284	Total different words	27
Mean words	47·33	Mean different words	4·50

CONJUNCTIONS

Word	Count	Word	Count	Word	Count	Word	Count
and	177	if	1	or	9	that	1
because	3	nor	1	so	4	then	5
but	1						

Total words	202	Total different words	9
Mean words	33·67	Mean different words	1·50

CONTRACTIONS

Word	Count	Word	Count	Word	Count	Word	Count
boy's	5	he's	6	tea's	1	wasn't	1
can't	6	I've	2	that's	4	we've	1
car's	1	isn't	1	there's	23	what's	3
didn't	1	it's	5	they'll	1	where's	2
dog's	1	mummy's	3	they're	16	who's	4
don't	20	o'clock	2	they've	1	you're	2
girl's	1	she's	3				

Total words	116	Total different words	26
Mean words	19·33	Mean different words	4·33

INTERJECTIONS

Word	Count	Word	Count
ah	2	oh	8

Total words	10	Total different words	2
Mean words	1·67	Mean different words	0·33

ARTICLES

Word	Count	Word	Count	Word	Count
a	209	an	8	the	348

Total words	565	Total different words	3
Mean words	94·17	Mean different words	0·50

OTHER

Word	Count	Word	Count	Word	Count	Word	Count
bang	1	Christmas-tree	1	'cos	1	no	
Christmas	2	Coke	1	icing	1	T-shirt	
				littlest	3	yes	

Total words	24	Total different words	10
Mean words	4·00	Mean different words	1·67

Subject Group B

(7 children; age: 8–10 years;
performance I.Q.: ≤90; hearing loss: 61–80 dB)

NOUNS

Word	Count	Word	Count	Word	Count	Word	Count
air	1	butter	5	drawer	3	hook	1
all	3	cabbage	3	dress	2	hospital	2
ambulance	9	cake	7	drink	7	house	8
animal	1	car	33	egg	7	houses	4
animals	1	cat	6	eggs	2	ice	1
apple	9	chair	4	face	3	ice-cream	4
apples	3	cheese	1	family	2	jelly	1
apron	1	chicken	2	farm	2	jug	1
arrow	1	children	2	farmer	2	*jumper	1
baby	5	*chips	1	father	1	kettle	1
back	2	clock	6	fence	3	keys	1
badge	2	cloth	3	field	2	kitchen	5
bag	15	clothes	4	fish	7	kitten	1
ball	36	cloud	1	fishes	1	knife	9
banana	5	clown	7	fishing	1	ladder	4
basket	9	coat	7	floor	6	lady	16
bat	5	cook	1	flower	4	leaf	1
beard	2	cooking	1	flowers	8	leaves	1
bicycle	2	cow	12	food	4	legs	1
bike	6	cream	1	football	11	letter	2
bin	1	*cricket	7	fork	3	lipstick	1
book	6	cup	3	fridge	2	lot	4
books	1	cupboard	2	friend	1	lots	4
boot	5	curtain	1	fruit	3	lunch	6
boots	6	cushion	1	gate	8	machine	2
bottle	5	daddy	4	girl	15	man	59
bottles	2	danger	1	girls	3	man's	1
bottom	1	date	1	glove	2	marmalade	3
boy	85	dinner	14	gloves	1	mash	1
boys	4	dish	1	goal	2	mat	1
bread	5	dog	41	grass	2	matches	4
broom	1	doggie	4	hand	6	meat	2
brush	4	doll	2	handstand	4	men	1
bucket	2	dolly	2	hat	7	mess	2
bull	10	door	5	head	2	milk	17
bull's	1	doors	2	hole	8	milkman	5
bush	1	dragon	3	home	1	*mince	1

Word	Count	Word	Count	Word	Count	Word	Count
minute	1	pepper	1	sausage	1	tart	1
mirror	1	pet	1	scarf	1	tea	3
money	15	picnic	5	scissors	3	teapot	2
mother	7	picture	6	shirts	1	there	5
mother's	1	piece	1	shock	1	thing	2
mouse	3	*pint	1	shoe	5	things	2
mouth	1	pints	1	shoes	1	three	5
mum	1	pipe	2	shop	2	tie	1
mummy	21	place	2	shoulder	1	*tights	1
neck	1	plaster	1	side	1	time	4
nose	2	plate	5	sign	2	tomatoes	6
numbers	1	plates	1	sink	3	towel	5
one	3	pocket	1	skate	1	toys	5
ones	1	police	1	skates	1	train	5
onion	1	policeman	8	*sledge	1	tree	8
orange	1	post	2	sleep	1	trees	1
ovens	1	*postman	1	smell	1	*trifle	1
pail	1	potato	1	snow	2	*trousers	1
paint	1	pudding	1	spoon	4	walking-stick	1
painter	1	*purse	2	stick	10	wall	2
paper	1	puzzle	2	story	1	washing	2
part	1	road	3	straw	1	water	6
*pavement	4	roof	1	strawberries	1	way	
pear	2	salt	2	street	2	wheel	
pennies	1	sandwich	5	sun	1	window	15
people	11	sandwiches	3	table	15	wire	
people's	1	saucepan	2	*tap	2		

Total words   1087   Total different words   255
Mean words   155·29   Mean different words   36·43

VERBS

Word	Count	Word	Count	Word	Count	Word	Count
are	13	bring	2	carried	1	climb	
argue	1	broke	1	carry	3	climbed	
banged	1	broken	4	carrying	6	climbing	
bash	1	bump	1	catch	4	close	
bashed	1	called	2	chases	1	come	
bat	1	came	1	chasing	5	coming	
be	3	can	4	clean	1	cook	
been	1	cannot	1	cleaning	1	cooking	

Word	Count	Word	Count	Word	Count	Word	Count
crash	2	happen	5	painting	1	smash	1
cry	1	happens	1	pick	1	snowing	3
crying	1	has	1	play	12	spilled	1
cut	4	have	6	playing	14	splash	1
cutting	1	having	3	plays	1	stand	1
do	5	help	5	pointing	3	standing	1
does	1	helping	2	pull	2	stop	7
doing	4	hid	1	put	11	take	7
draw	1	hide	1	putting	5	taking	3
drink	3	hit	1	read	6	talk	1
drinking	10	hold	4	reading	2	talking	2
drive	1	holding	7	reads	1	telling	2
driving	1	hurt	3	rescue	1	think	2
drop	8	is	70	run	5	throw	2
dropped	5	jump	4	running	8	throwing	1
eat	8	keep	1	say	3	tidy	2
eating	14	kick	1	saying	4	told	1
fall	14	knocked	1	says	2	train	1
fallen	2	know	12	see	7	try	1
fell	12	leaning	2	seen	1	trying	5
finished	2	let	1	shave	1	walking	4
fixing	1	lifting	1	shaving	3	want	13
frighten	1	like	2	shop	2	wants	4
frightened	2	listen	1	shouting	3	was	5
gave	1	look	18	shuts	1	wash	2
get	16	looked	1	skating	1	washing	4
getting	4	looking	6	sleep	1	watch	2
give	3	looks	1	sleeping	1	watching	3
giving	5	made	1	sleeps	1	went	12
go	12	make	1	slide	4	were	2
goes	2	mean	1	sliding	1	will	5
going	26	might	2	slip	1	winding	2
gone	1	move	1	slipped	1	would	1
got	20	open	4	slips	1	writing	4
had	3	packing	2	smack	2		

Total words	678	Total different words	171
Mean words	96·86	Mean different words	24·43

ADJECTIVES

Word	Count	Word	Count	Word	Count	Word	Count
all	19	dangerous	3	naughty	1	small	3
angry	2	dirty	1	one	9	some	4
another	1	five	2	open	11	square	1
asleep	1	four	3	other	3	that	46
awful	1	funny	3	pink	1	these	1
big	6	horrible	2	red	3	twelve	2
both	1	hot	1	sad	1	two	9
brown	1	little	18	same	2	wet	1
clean	1	long	2	sharp	1	white	1
cold	1	many	1	short	1		

Total words	171	Total different words	39
Mean words	24·43	Mean different words	5·57

ADVERBS

Word	Count	Word	Count	Word	Count	Word	Count
all	5	how	1	on	5	then	9
around	1	just	1	out	15	there	22
away	6	more	1	outside	1	too	2
as	1	nearly	1	over	20	up	16
back	3	never	1	perhaps	1	very	6
down	8	not	3	quickly	1	when	4
here	3	now	5	right	1	where	1
home	11	off	7	round	1	why	5

Total words	168	Total different words	32
Mean words	24·00	Mean different words	4·57

PRONOUNS

Word	Count	Word	Count	Word	Count	Word	Count
all	6	I	19	something	5	this	8
he	41	it	31	that	61	those	2
her	9	nothing	1	their	2	what	14
herself	1	one	8	them	4	you	4
him	21	others	1	these	1	your	2
his	15	she	14	they	19		

Total words	288	Total different words	23
Mean words	41·14	Mean different words	3·29

PREPOSITIONS

Word	Count	Word	Count	Word	Count	Word	Count
about	1	by	2	like	17	past	2
across	1	down	5	of	20	round	2
after	2	for	4	on	23	to	60
along	2	from	1	out	8	under	7
at	9	in	24	over	11	with	21
but	1	into	3				

Total words	226	Total different words	22
Mean words	32·29	Mean different words	3·14

CONJUNCTIONS

Word	Count	Word	Count	Word	Count	Word	Count
and	154	so	1	that	1	then	1
because	6						

Total words	163	Total different words	5
Mean words	23·29	Mean different words	0·71

CONTRACTIONS

Word	Count	Word	Count	Word	Count	Word	Count
aren't	1	door's	1	lady's	1	there's	16
boy's	9	father's	1	man's	1	they're	4
can't	3	girl's	2	milkman's	1	we've	1
cat's	2	he's	18	mother's	2	what's	5
didn't	2	here's	1	o'clock	5	why's	1
dog's	2	I've	2	one's	1	won't	1
doll's	1	isn't	3	she's	7	wouldn't	1
don't	12	it's	8	that's	20		

Total words	135	Total different words	31
Mean words	19·29	Mean different words	4·43

INTERJECTIONS

Word	Count
oh	10

Total words	10	Total different words	1
Mean words	1·43	Mean different words	0·14

ARTICLES

Word	Count	Word	Count	Word	Count
a	188	an	3	the	368

Total words	559	Total different words	3
Mean words	79·86	Mean different words	0·43

OTHER

Word	Count	Word	Count	Word	Count	Word	Count
bang	1	Christmas-		ice	2	Peter	1
bashing	2	tree	3	*Marmite	1	skating	2
*Bovril	1	Cocacola	3	Monday	1	teddy bear	2
brushing	1	'cos	2	no	6	Tuesday	1
climber	1	crash	2	pork	1	yes	4

Total words	37	Total different words	19
Mean words	5·29	Mean different words	2·71

Subject Group C

(3 children; age: 8–10 years;
performance I.Q.: ⩽90; hearing loss: 81–95 dB)

NOUNS

Word	Count	Word	Count	Word	Count	Word	Count
ambulance	6	daddy's	1	holiday	1	plate	1
apple	3	dish	1	home	5	police	1
apples	1	dog	23	house	7	policeman	2
baby	3	doll	2	houses	1	posts	2
badges	1	dolly	1	ice	3	potato	1
bag	8	door	2	jelly	2	*rounders	3
ball	12	draw	1	kettle	1	salt	1
banana	2	drawer	1	kitchen	2	sandwich	4
bang	1	drink	5	knife	1	saucepan	1
baseball	1	egg	2	ladder	1	scissors	1
bat	4	eggs	1	lady	3	shirts	2
bicycle	2	face	1	lettuce	1	shoes	2
bike	1	farmer	1	machine	1	shoulder	1
book	8	father	1	man	14	sign	1
*boot	4	fence	1	map	1	six	1
boots	2	field	1	marmalade	1	sleep	1
boy	48	fish	6	mask	1	snow	1
boys	4	five	1	match	1	sugar	1
branch	1	floor	4	matches	1	table	11
bread	6	flower	5	meat	1	tea	1
brush	4	flowers	1	men	1	things	1
bucket	2	food	3	meringue	1	three	1
bull	5	football	7	mice	1	time	2
butter	1	fork	1	milk	9	tomato	1
calendar	1	four	1	milkman	4	towel	1
car	12	friend	1	money	5	toy	1
cat	7	gate	2	mouse	1	toys	1
catch	1	girl	6	mum	3	train	3
chair	6	girls	2	mummy	20	tree	13
chicken	1	goal	2	night	1	trees	1
children	3	grandfather	1	notebook	1	vegetables	1
clock	4	grandmother	1	one	1	vests	1
clothes	1	ground	1	onion	1	wall	2
coat	4	hand	2	*pavement	1	washing	1
cook	1	hands	3	pepper	1	water	7
cow	2	hat	3	picnic	3	way	1
cup	1	head	2	picture	1	window	3
dad	1	hedge	2	place	1	wood	1
daddy	12						

Total words	474		Total different words	153	
Mean words	158·00		Mean different words	51·00	

VERBS

Word	Count	Word	Count	Word	Count	Word	Count
are	12	fallen	1	jumping	1	shopping	1
been	2	falling	1	know	1	sleep	1
break	1	fell	11	look	3	sliding	1
broken	1	finish	4	looking	3	stop	3
came	2	finished	1	made	1	take	1
carrying	2	get	3	mashed	1	talk	1
chasing	1	getting	2	opening	1	talking	2
climb	3	go	3	packing	2	think	1
climbing	1	going	8	paying	1	throw	1
coming	4	got	2	play	2	tidy	1
cooking	1	grinding	1	playing	7	trying	2
cracked	1	had	2	pull	2	wash	3
dirty	1	has	2	put	1	washing	1
drink	2	have	2	run	1	watching	3
drinking	2	having	3	running	3	wearing	1
eat	4	help	1	said	2	went	1
eating	2	hold	1	saw	2	were	1
fall	7	is	34	saying	1	writing	3

| | Total words | 194 | | Total different words | 72 |
| | Mean words | 64·67 | | Mean different words | 24·00 |

ADJECTIVES

Word	Count	Word	Count	Word	Count	Word	Coun
all	1	five	3	open	3	some	1
asleep	1	hot	2	other	1	sweet	1
big	2	little	3	ready	2	three	2
blue	2	lovely	2	red	2	twelve	1
cold	2	one	3	round	1	two	6

| | Total words | 39 | | Total different words | 20 |
| | Mean words | 13·00 | | Mean different words | 6·67 |

ADVERBS

Word	Count	Word	Count	Word	Count	Word	Count
afterwards	1	home	4	out	3	then	1
along	2	in	1	over	2	there	10
away	1	now	2	perhaps	1	up	5
down	14	off	1	quick	1	upside-down	2

	Total words	51		Total different words	16
	Mean words	17·00		Mean different words	5·33

PRONOUNS

Word	Count	Word	Count	Word	Count	Word	Count
her	1	it	2	their	2	who	1
his	2	she	1	there	1	you	1
I	1	something	1	they	4		

	Total words	17		Total different words	11
	Mean words	5·67		Mean different words	3·67

PREPOSITIONS

Word	Count	Word	Count	Word	Count	Word	Count
after	3	in	3	on	17	to	10
along	1	into	2	over	4	under	2
at	7	near	1	past	2	with	8
for	2	of	2	round	3	which	1
from	1						

	Total words	69		Total different words	17
	Mean words	23·00		Mean different words	5·67

CONJUNCTIONS

Word	Count	Word	Count	Word	Count	Word	Count
and	44	because	3	or	1	so	1

	Total words	49		Total different words	4
	Mean words	16·33		Mean different words	1·33

CONTRACTIONS

Word	Count	Word	Count	Word	Count	Word	Count
don't	1	she's	1	there's	2	they're	1

Total words	5		Total different words	4	
Mean words	1·66		Mean different words	1·33	

INTERJECTIONS

Word	Count	Word	Count	Word	Count	Word	Count
dear	1	eh	2	hey	1	oh	1

Total words	5		Total different words	4	
Mean words	1·67		Mean different words	1·33	

ARTICLES

Word	Count	Word	Count
a	15	the	103

Total words	118		Total different words	2	
Mean words	39·33		Mean different words	0·67	

OTHER

Word	Count	Word	Count	Word	Count	Word	Count
bump	1	Christmas-tree	1	crash	2	no	
				*Marmite	1	yes	

Total words	9		Total different words	6	
Mean words	3·00		Mean different words	2·00	

Subject Group D

(9 children; age: 8–10 years;
performance I.Q.: 91–110; hearing loss: 40–60 dB)

NOUNS

Word	Count	Word	Count	Word	Count	Word	Count
accident	9	brother	2	cream	1	floor	7
all	1	brush	5	*cricket	6	flower	9
ambulance	21	bucket	9	cup	5	flowerpot	1
apple	10	bull	21	cups	2	flowers	5
apples	8	bushes	3	curtain	4	food	12
atlas	1	butcher	1	cut	1	football	13
baby	4	butter	4	dad	1	fork	3
back	6	cabbage	6	daddy	12	forks	1
badges	1	cabbages	1	date	2	friends	1
bag	10	cake	8	daughter	1	front	1
ball	39	cakes	2	day	4	fruit	2
banana	3	calendar	3	dinner	15	game	4
bananas	6	car	47	dinosaur	1	garden	1
bang	2	cardigan	1	dish	4	gate	9
barrel	1	carrots	1	dog	53	girl	25
baseball	1	cart	1	dog's	1	girls	4
basket	12	case	4	doggie	3	glass	1
bat	4	cat	8	doll	6	glove	2
bed	1	cauliflower	2	dolly	2	gloves	6
bench	1	chair	10	door	8	goal	3
bicycle	2	cherries	1	dragon	1	goal-post	1
bike	4	chicken	7	drain	6	grape	1
biscuits	1	children	7	dress	1	grapes	1
bit	1	*chips	1	drink	6	grass	6
blind	2	cleaner	1	egg	8	ground	2
book	12	clock	7	eggs	8	gym	1
boot	11	cloth	1	eye	1	gymnastics	1
boots	8	clothes	7	face	3	hamster	1
bottle	2	clouds	1	family	2	hand	1
bottles	1	coat	8	farmer	5	handstand	1
bow	1	coats	1	farmer's	1	handstands	1
bowl	1	*cooker	5	father	9	hat	8
boy	125	cooking	1	feet	1	hats	1
boys	11	corner	1	fence	6	head	2
branches	1	cover	1	field	9	headstand	1
bread	10	cow	1	fir	1	hedge	2
room	4	crash	1	fish	10	here	2

Word	Count	Word	Count	Word	Count	Word	Count
hill	3	men	4	piece	1	shorts	1
hills	1	mess	4	place	1	shoulder	1
holiday	1	metal	1	plant	3	side	2
home	2	mice	2	plate	3	sign	2
hook	2	milk	12	plates	6	sink	5
hospital	10	milkman	10	players	1	sister	1
house	12	mirror	2	plug	1	sisters	1
houses	9	mixer	1	plums	1	skate	1
ice	20	mobile	1	police	2	skates	2
ice-cream	2	money	11	policeman	5	skin	1
jam	3	mother	21	post	1	sky	3
jar	2	motor	1	*postman	2	*sledge	9
jelly	4	mouse	4	posts	1	snow	6
jug	1	mouth	1	pot	2	son	1
*jumper	2	mum	1	potato	2	sort	1
kettle	5	mummy	13	potatoes	1	spoon	2
*kit	1	mushroom	2	pound	2	spoons	1
kitchen	3	noise	1	pudding	1	step	1
knife	7	nose	1	*purse	6	stick	12
knives	1	note	1	rain	1	sticks	4
ladder	17	nuts	2	raincoat	2	story	1
lady	50	one	3	rice	1	strawberries	1
lady's	1	onion	3	road	9	stuff	7
leaves	1	onions	1	roof	1	stuffing	1
lemonade	1	orange	4	room	1	sun	1
lettuce	1	oven	2	*rounder	1	sweets	1
liquid	2	*ovenglove	1	*rounders	2	table	16
load	2	paint	1	*rubbish	1	*tap	3
*lorry	4	paints	1	salt	3	*taps	2
lot	2	pair	1	sample	1	tea	4
lots	1	pan	3	sandwich	4	team	2
lunch	2	pastry	1	sandwiches	8	teapot	3
machine	2	*pavement	3	saucepan	4	television	
man	86	peach	1	saucepans	1	there	
map	3	pear	1	scarf	7	thing	
maps	1	peg	1	scissors	3	things	
margarine	1	*pence	1	seat	1	thumb	
mark	1	penny	1	set	1	time	
market	5	people	24	shelf	2	tomatoes	
marmalade	2	pepper	3	shirt	1	toothbrush	
mask	3	person	2	shirts	2	top	
matches	5	picnic	10	shoe	2	towel	
mats	1	picture	5	shoes	4	toy	
meat	8	pictures	3	shop	4	toys	
meats	1	pie	4	shopping	4	train	

Word	Count	Word	Count	Word	Count	Word	Count
tray	2	van	1	washing-up	2	windows	4
tree	14	vegetable	1	water	17	window-sill	2
trees	9	vegetables	1	way	3	wines	1
'trousers	1	wall	1	wheel	1	wire	3
truck	1	washbasin	1	windmill	1	wood	2
turkey	2	washing	4	window	18	work	1
twelve	1						

Total words	1701			Total different words	353		
Mean words	189·00			Mean different words	39·22		

VERBS

Word	Count	Word	Count	Word	Count	Word	Count
allowed	1	chasing	4	drive	1	goes	2
are	39	clean	1	driving	5	going	34
asked	1	cleaning	2	drop	8	gone	1
barking	1	climb	2	dropped	9	got	35
bashed	1	climbed	1	dying	1	grow	1
batting	1	climbing	3	eat	10	had	16
be	5	collected	1	eating	21	hand	1
been	2	colouring	1	fainted	1	hanging	3,
bolting	1	come	14	fall	9	happen	1
bolting	1	coming	13	fallen	1	happened	1
bring	3	cook	2	falling	1	happening	3
bringing	1	cooking	2	fell	31	has	2
broke	2	could	1	fetch	1	have	14
broken	5	cracked	4	find	1	having	4
bump	1	crash	3	finish	1	heard	2
bumped	2	crashed	9	finished	4	help	6
burn	1	cried	1	flying	1	helping	2
burning	1	cuddling	4	fold	1	hiding	1
butt	1	cut	1	freezing	2	hit	3
buying	1	cutting	4	frightened	3	hold	4
called	3	decided	1	fussing	1	holding	5
came	15	did	1	gathered	1	hope	1
carried	1	do	8	get	23	hurt	5
carry	3	doing	5	gets	2	is	72
carrying	8	done	2	getting	2	jump	6
catch	1	dot	1	give	1	jumping	4
catching	1	drinking	16	giving	1	keep	2
ceased	1	dripped	1	go	20	kept	1

Word	Count	Word	Count	Word	Count	Word	Count
kick	1	painting	2	shining	1	throw	4
kicked	5	pay	1	shopping	6	throwing	1
knock	5	paying	5	should	1	tired	1
knocked	5	peddling	1	shout	1	told	1
knocking	2	phone	2	shut	2	took	1
know	10	pick	1	sit	3	trapped	1
knows	2	picked	1	sitting	5	tread	1
laid	1	play	4	skating	6	trip	1
laughed	2	played	1	sleep	1	tripped	4
laughing	1	playing	41	sleeps	1	try	2
lay	2	pull	3	sliding	2	trying	10
laying	1	pulling	2	slip	1	tumbling	1
left	4	push	1	slipped	1	turn	2
licking	1	pushing	1	snowed	1	turned	1
lie	1	put	23	snowing	2	turning	1
look	12	putting	6	standing	4	unload	1
looked	4	ran	2	stared	1	walk	3
looking	17	reach	2	staring	3	walking	2
made	3	read	1	starting	1	want	2
make	3	reading	8	sticking	1	wanted	
making	7	riding	2	stop	12	was	64
mark	1	rocking	1	stopped	1	wash	
mean	2	run	11	stuck	1	washing	
melt	1	running	19	sucking	1	watch	
messing	1	rushing	1	supposed	1	watching	1
might	5	said	20	sweep	1	watering	
mix	1	saw	2	sweeping	1	wave	
mixing	1	say	6	take	4	waving	
must	5	saying	5	taking	7	wearing	
nicked	1	says	1	talking	2	went	1
open	6	scaring	1	teaching	3	were	1
opened	2	see	4	telling	4	will	
opening	4	seeing	1	think	3	wondering	
packing	5	serves	1	thought	1	worried	
packs	1	shaving	5	threw	1	writing	

Total words	1188	Total different words	251
Mean words	132·00	Mean different words	27·89

ADJECTIVES

Word	Count	Word	Count	Word	Count	Word	Count
all	36	dozen	1	many	2	small	1
angry	3	electric	1	messy	1	some	32
another	1	five	6	more	5	sweet	1
asleep	5	four	3	muddy	1	that	29
big	11	freezing	1	nice	1	these	3
black	3	frozen	1	old	1	thin	5
blue	5	funny	1	one	14	third	4
brown	8	good	1	open	3	this	4
careful	1	green	6	orange	2	those	2
clever	1	happy	1	other	9	three	1
cold	4	hard	2	own	3	twelve	4
cross	1	hot	1	poor	1	two	20
dangerous	9	hungry	1	ready	1	unhappy	1
dark	1	ill	1	red	13	white	4
dead	1	little	15	sad	2	yellow	2
dirty	1	mad	1	sharp	3	young	1

Total words 310
Mean words 34·44

Total different words 64
Mean different words 7·11

ADVERBS

Word	Count	Word	Count	Word	Count	Word	Count
about	1	before	1	off	8	suddenly	1
again	2	down	34	on	15	then	15
all	4	fast	2	out	46	there	46
almost	1	home	16	outside	2	too	1
alone	1	how	3	over	13	underneath	1
along	5	in	5	quick	1	up	15
already	1	inside	3	ready	1	very	10
around	2	just	1	right	1	well	1
as	1	later	1	round	2	when	15
away	14	nearly	2	somewhere	1	where	6
back	2	not	9	still	1	why	4
badly	1	now	6				

Total words 324
Mean words 36·00

Total different words 46
Mean different words 5·11

PRONOUNS

Word	Count	Word	Count	Word	Count	Word	Count
anything	1	his	31	our	1	this	2
everybody	1	I	12	she	23	we	7
everything	2	it	50	somebody	1	what	12
he	81	its	1	something	4	whatever	1
her	24	itself	1	that	32	who	6
hers	1	me	1	their	26	you	15
him	37	my	4	them	20	yourself	1
himself	2	one	4	they	78		

Total words	482	Total different words	31
Mean words	53·56	Mean different words	3·44

PREPOSITIONS

Word	Count	Word	Count	Word	Count	Word	Count
after	12	in	65	on	65	round	3
at	26	into	15	onto	1	to	90
by	2	like	12	out	14	under	7
down	12	of	30	over	17	up	2
for	16	off	2	past	3	with	44
from	3						

Total words	441	Total different words	21
Mean words	49·00	Mean different words	2·33

CONJUNCTIONS

Word	Count	Word	Count	Word	Count	Word	Count
and	440	for	1	that	3	till	1
because	24	if	1	then	8	while	3
but	3	or	2				

Total words	486	Total different words	10
Mean words	54·00	Mean different words	1·11

CONTRACTIONS

Word	Count	Word	Count	Word	Count	Word	Count
basket's	1	father's	5	lady's	1	there's	23
boy's	6	food's	1	man's	1	they're	20
bull's	3	girl's	1	milkman's	2	they've	5
can't	2	hasn't	1	mother's	5	wasn't	1
cat's	1	he'll	1	one's	1	water's	1
couldn't	1	he's	33	other''s	1	what's	3
didn't	2	I'm	2	raincoat's	1	who's	2
dog's	3	I've	1	she's	3	won't	1
don't	12	isn't	1	that's	15	you're	3
farmer's	1	it's	15				

Total words 182
Mean words 20·22

Total different words 38
Mean different words 4·22

INTERJECTIONS

Word	Count	Word	Count	Word	Count
goodbye	1	oh	10	well	6

Total words 17
Mean words 1·89

Total different words 3
Mean different words 0·33

ARTICLES

Word	Count	Word	Count	Word	Count
a	262	an	10	the	661

Total words 933
Mean words 103·67

Total different words 3
Mean different words 0·33

OTHER

Word	Count	Word	Count	Word	Count	Word	Count
bang	3	Coke	2	*Marmite	1	they's	1
*Bovril	1	*cor	1	*Meccano	2	*Wellington	1
*Chelsea	1	crash	1	Monday	1	wheee	1
Christmas-		gerbil	1	no	12	woof	2
tree	1	*Liverpool	1	Pepsicola	4	yes	20
Cocacola	2	look	1				

Total words	60		Total different words	21	
Mean words	6·67		Mean different words	2·33	

Subject Group E

(13 children; age: 8–10 years;
performance I.Q.: 91–110; hearing loss: 61–80 dB)

NOUNS

Word	Count	Word	Count	Word	Count	Word	Count
accident	1	bit	1	bunch	1	cover	1
all	10	blouse	1	bush	1	cow	3
ambulance	19	book	8	bushes	2	*cricket	11
apple	7	*boot	10	butter	2	cup	2
apples	7	boots	7	cabbage	1	cups	1
atlas	1	bottle	4	cabbages	3	daddy	22
baby	4	bottles	3	cake	6	danger	1
back	5	bottom	1	calendar	3	daughter	1
bag	8	box	2	car	42	day	4
ball	57	boy	113	cars	1	dinner	6
banana	3	boy's	1	cart	1	dinosaur	1
bananas	3	boys	12	case	2	dishes	1
bang	2	bread	4	cat	6	dog	52
*barrow	1	breads	1	chair	5	doggie	2
basket	14	brick	1	chicken	1	dogs	2
bat	8	broom	1	children	4	doll	1
beard	1	brooms	1	clock	4	door	11
beware	1	brother	1	clothes	5	doors	1
bicycle	3	bucket	2	clown	1	dragon	1
bike	3	bull	18	coat	6	drain	3

Word	Count	Word	Count	Word	Count	Word	Count
drink	2	hole	6	milkman	9	rest	2
egg	6	holes	1	money	15	road	7
eggs	6	holiday	5	mother	21	roof	1
elbow	3	holidays	1	mountain	1	salt	1
engine	1	home	6	mouse	1	sandwich	3
faces	1	hospital	1	mouth	1	sandwiches	5
family	1	house	10	much	3	saucepan	2
farm	1	houses	5	mud	1	scarf	3
farmer	5	ice	21	mum	1	scissors	2
father	4	ice-cream	1	mummy	17	seat	2
fence	9	kettle	1	name	1	seven	1
field	6	kids	2	neck	1	shirt	1
finger	1	kitchen	3	night	1	shoe	5
fish	7	knife	5	notice	1	shoes	5
floor	5	knives	1	one	5	shop	2
flower	8	ladder	10	orange	1	side	2
flowers	2	ladies	1	oven	1	sign	1
food	13	lady	27	pair	1	sink	1
football	15	leaf	1	paper	1	skate	1
fork	1	leaves	1	park	1	skates	3
forks	1	leg	1	part	2	*sledge	4
friend	1	letter	2	*pavement	1	*sledges	1
fright	1	letters	1	people	7	snow	4
fruit	1	light	3	pepper	1	socks	1
game	1	line	1	picnic	27	son	2
games	1	loads	1	picture	3	sort	1
gate	11	*lorry	1	piggy	1	spoons	1
girl	18	lot	1	place	3	sport	1
girls	8	lunch	5	plant	1	stalk	3
gloves	2	machine	1	plants	1	stick	20
goal	5	man	58	plate	2	sticks	1
goals	1	man's	2	plates	1	story	2
grass	1	map	1	police	5	strawberries	1
*greengrocer	2	market	1	policeman	7	summer	1
*greengrocer's	1	mask	4	post	1	sweet	1
ground	1	matches	3	posts	1	table	15
hand	3	*mate	1	pot	3	table-cloth	1
handstand	6	meal	1	potatoes	1	tea	5
hanky	1	meat	3	pound	1	there	13
hat	8	medals	1	*pram	1	thing	5
head	4	men	3	pudding	1	things	8
hedge	1	men's	1	puppy	1	three	1
hedges	1	mess	2	*purse	4	tie	1
hill	1	metal	1	rain	1	time	5
hockey	1	milk	15	raincoat	1	tomatoes	1

Word	Count	Word	Count	Word	Count	Word	Count
towel	1	turkey	1	water	4	wine	1
train	5	twelve	1	wheel	5	wire	1
training	1	two	1	wife	5	wires	1
tree	19	wall	3	window	7	woman	1
trees	2	washing	1	windows	1	wood	1
trolley	3						

Total words	1351	Total different words	281
Mean words	103·92	Mean different words	21·62

VERBS

Word	Count	Word	Count	Word	Count	Word	Count
allowed	1	coming	10	felling	2	housing	1
are	28	cooking	1	felt	1	hurry	1
banged	1	cost	1	fetch	2	hurt	11
barking	1	could	1	finished	6	is	77
be	15	crack	1	flying	1	jump	3
been	3	crash	8	forgot	1	jumped	2
beware	2	crashed	7	frightened	4	keep	4
bounced	1	crashing	2	gave	2	kept	1
bring	1	cry	1	get	36	kicked	2
broke	5	decided	1	getting	7	knock	1
broken	5	delivering	1	give	2	know	13
called	1	did	5	giving	3	leaning	1
came	21	do	6	go	18	left	3
can	4	doing	5	going	39	let	1
carry	6	drank	1	gone	3	lick	1
carrying	11	drink	6	got	30	lift	1
catch	2	drinking	3	had	6	likes	1
change	1	drive	1	hanged	1	listening	3
charged	1	driving	5	happened	2	lives	1
charging	1	drop	4	has	8	look	16
chase	1	dropped	13	have	25	looked	2
chasing	2	dropping	5	having	7	looking	11
chatting	1	eat	9	heard	2	looks	3
cleaning	3	eaten	1	help	5	lying	2
clearing	1	eating	10	helped	1	made	1
climb	2	fall	6	helping	1	make	3
climbing	3	fallen	4	hit	2	making	3
come	18	falling	6	hold	11	mean	1
comes	3	fell	26	holding	16	meant	7

Word	Count	Word	Count	Word	Count	Word	Count
might	20	ride	2	sleeping	2	told	1
mixing	1	riding	2	sliding	3	took	1
move	1	rolled	1	slipped	1	trip	2
must	8	run	7	snowing	3	tripped	1
needs	1	running	14	squash	1	try	1
notice	1	rushed	1	squashed	1	trying	9
open	4	said	13	squeeze	1	used	1
opened	5	sat	2	standing	5	walk	1
packed	2	save	1	stands	1	walked	1
packing	3	saw	1	staring	1	walking	4
painting	1	say	2	start	2	want	4
pay	1	saying	3	started	1	was	69
paying	2	says	3	stay	1	washing	2
play	16	scores	1	stop	16	watch	7
played	1	see	8	supposed	1	watching	13
playing	34	seeing	1	take	3	waving	1
pouring	1	shaving	3	taking	1	wearing	6
pretend	1	shopping	1	talk	4	went	13
pull	4	should	2	talking	4	were	18
pulling	1	shouting	1	tell	2	whip	1
put	13	shut	3	telling	1	whizzing	1
putting	8	sit	2	think	8	will	1
quiet	1	sitting	2	thought	1	worried	2
ran	2	skate	1	threw	1	worry	1
reach	1	skiing	4	throwing	2	would	1
read	1	sleep	1	tired	4	writing	2
reading	11						

Total words	1178	Total different words	221
Mean words	90·62	Mean different words	17·00

ADJECTIVES

Word	Count	Word	Count	Word	Count	Word	Count
all	22	capital	1	four	10	longer	1
alright	1	cold	7	front	1	more	2
another	1	cross	1	full	1	much	1
asleep	3	dangerous	2	funny	1	muddy	1
back	2	dirty	1	furry	1	no	1
big	9	each	1	happy	2	old	1
blue	2	first	1	hot	2	one	13
brown	1	five	5	little	23	open	5

Word	Count	Word	Count	Word	Count	Word	Count
other	2	smaller	1	these	3	two	20
packed	1	snowy	2	thin	10	waterproof	1
ready	6	some	11	this	1	wet	1
red	3	such	1	those	2	white	1
sad	1	sweet	1	three	3	yellow	2
silly	4	that	21	twelve	2		

Total words   331   Total different words   54
Mean words   25·46   Mean different words   4·15

ADVERBS

Word	Count	Word	Count	Word	Count	Word	Count
about	4	ever	1	never	1	so	1
again	3	far	2	not	13	somewhere	2
all	3	fast	2	now	8	suddenly	5
along	10	for	2	off	4	then	17
already	3	here	6	on	6	there	44
alright	1	home	11	once	1	too	1
around	1	how	4	only	2	underneath	1
as	1	in	1	out	41	up	15
asleep	1	inside	1	outside	1	upside-down	3
away	12	instead	3	over	12	very	10
back	9	just	9	properly	1	when	9
backwards	1	longest	1	quickly	3	where	3
down	26	maybe	2	slower	1	why	4
else	1	nearly	1				

Total words   226   Total different words   55
Mean words   17·38   Mean different words   4·23

PRONOUNS

Word	Count	Word	Count	Word	Count	Word	Count
any	1	he	83	I	23	somebody	2
anything	1	her	19	it	42	someone	3
each	1	him	30	my	3	something	1
everybody	1	himself	4	other	1	that	24
everything	2	his	40	she	19	their	21

Word	Count	Word	Count	Word	Count	Word	Count
them	11	this	3	what	12	who	5
these	2	those	2	where	1	you	11
they	107						

Total words	475	Total different words	29
Mean words	36·54	Mean different words	2·23

PREPOSITIONS

Word	Count	Word	Count	Word	Count	Word	Count
about	1	down	1	of	27	to	108
across	1	for	16	off	4	towards	1
after	9	from	6	on	50	under	5
along	1	in	52	onto	2	underneath	1
at	12	into	10	out	5	up	1
before	1	like	4	over	26	upon	1
behind	1	near	1	past	2	with	38
by	4	next	1	through	3		

Total words	395	Total different words	31
Mean words	30·38	Mean different words	2·38

CONJUNCTIONS

Word	Count	Word	Count	Word	Count	Word	Count
and	370	but	4	so	7	then	2
because	15	if	6	that	1	while	5
before	1	or	10				

Total words	421	Total different words	10
Mean words	32·38	Mean different words	0·77

CONTRACTIONS

Word	Count	Word	Count	Word	Count	Word	Count
aren't	3	haven't	1	mustn't	1	they're	13
*bumper's	1	he's	28	o'clock	1	they've	4
can't	2	it's	9	she's	9	what's	2
didn't	7	man's	1	that's	16	who's	1
don't	10	mummy's	1	there's	5	you'll	1
hasn't	1						

Total words	117	Total different words	21
Mean words	9·00	Mean different words	1·62

INTERJECTIONS

Word	Count	Word	Count
oh	1	well	3

Total words	4	Total different words	2
Mean words	0·31	Mean different words	0·15

ARTICLES

Word	Count	Word	Count	Word	Count
a	171	an	7	the	603

Total words	781	Total different words	3
Mean words	60.08	Mean different words	0·23

OTHER

Word	Count	Word	Count	Word	Count	Word	Count
brokes	1	Christmas-tree	1	Cokes	1	India	1
bushin	1	Cocacola	6	*Father Christmas	3	no	8
Christmas	3	Coke	4	holded	1	*Wellington	1
						yes	4

Total words	35	Total different words	13
Mean words	2·69	Mean different words	1·00

Subject Group F

(16 children; age: 8–10 years;
performance I.Q.: 90–110; hearing loss: 81–95 dB)

NOUNS

Word	Count	Word	Count	Word	Count	Word	Count
air	1	branch	1	comics	1	father's	1
all	2	bread	13	*cooker	6	fence	8
ambulance	43	bricks	1	cow	8	field	7
*anoraks	3	broom	2	crash	7	fields	2
apple	17	brother	9	*cricket	11	fire	1
apples	9	brush	13	cup	10	fish	23
baby	8	bucket	16	cupboard	2	five	1
back	3	bull	36	cups	3	floor	7
badge	2	bull's	2	curtain	4	flower	27
badges	1	bulls	1	curtains	1	flowers	4
bag	27	bush	1	daddy	26	food	29
ball	84	bushes	1	danger	2	football	18
banana	16	butcher	1	day	3	fork	7
bananas	1	butter	13	dinner	16	friends	2
*barrow	1	cabbage	13	dinosaur	1	fright	2
basket	22	cake	17	dog	100	front	2
bat	16	calendar	5	doll	6	fruit	2
beard	3	can	1	dolly	4	fruits	1
bed	2	car	71	door	16	games	1
bench	1	carrots	1	doors	1	garage	2
bicycle	6	cat	15	dragon	3	garden	2
bike	7	catch	1	drain	3	gas	1
bill	1	chair	20	drawer	3	gate	11
blanket	1	cheese	1	drawers	1	girl	49
board	1	chicken	4	dress	3	girls	2
body	1	children	2	dresses	1	glove	11
book	37	cleaner	2	drink	10	gloves	2
books	2	climb	1	drinks	3	goal	5
*boot	16	clock	15	driver	1	grass	6
boots	13	cloth	8	egg	11	*greengrocers	1
bottle	2	clothes	14	eggs	12	ground	3
bottles	2	cloud	2	face	11	gymnastics	1
bottoms	1	clouds	2	family	1	hair	3
bowls	1	clown	2	farm	1	hand	5
boy	200	coat	17	farmer	13	hands	1
boy's	1	coffee	3	farmer's	1	handstand	8
boys	15	cold	1	father	12	handstands	1

Word	Count	Word	Count	Word	Count	Word	Count
hat	14	market	4	pans	2	*rounder	2
head	8	marmalade	6	paper	1	*rounders	5
hedge	2	*marrow	1	parcel	1	salt	7
hedgehog	1	mask	6	path	1	sandwich	14
help	3	match	4	*pavement	4	sandwiches	9
here	2	matches	7	paw	1	saucepan	5
hill	1	material	1	peach	2	saucepans	2
hole	2	meals	1	peanut	1	scarf	3
holiday	2	meat	11	pear	3	scissors	10
home	10	melon	1	*pence	1	*seaside	2
hospital	4	member	1	pencil	1	shave	3
house	34	men	5	pennies	2	shirt	3
houses	3	mess	3	penny	1	shirts	1
husband	1	mice	2	people	9	shoe	2
ice	18	milk	26	people's	1	shoes	10
ice-cream	3	milkman	16	pepper	6	shop	2
jam	4	*mince	1	*petrol	1	shopping	1
jar	2	*mincer	1	photograph	1	sign	1
jelly	14	mirror	5	picnic	7	sink	8
journey	2	mitten	1	picture	11	sister	2
jug	4	mixer	2	pie	1	skate	4
*jumper	1	money	33	pipe	2	skates	3
keeper	2	monster	2	plant	2	skirt	1
kettle	8	morning	1	plastic	1	sky	1
kitchen	7	mother	22	plate	17	*sledge	5
knee	1	mountain	2	plates	2	sleep	1
knife	19	mouse	7	players	1	snow	8
lad	1	mouth	1	plenty	1	snowing	1
ladder	20	mummy	31	police	5	sons	1
ladders	1	mummy's	1	policeman	12	spoon	10
lady	62	mushroom	2	popcorn	2	steps	1
lady's	1	night	1	*postman	1	stick	10
leg	1	nine	3	pot	1	sticks	1
letter	1	nose	3	potato	1	story	1
life-jacket	1	once	1	potatoes	1	stove	2
light	2	one	1	pound	2	stuff	3
list	1	onion	1	pudding	1	sugar	1
*lorry	5	onions	3	puppy	3	supper	2
lot	2	orange	7	*purse	2	sweet	1
lots	2	oven	2	raincoat	1	table	34
lunch	1	packet	1	rain	1	table-cloth	1
machine	4	pail	1	road	5	*tap	4
man	98	paint	2	robber	1	*taps	2
man's	1	pair	2	robbers	1	tea	15
map	5	pan	7	room	1	teapot	1

Word	Count	Word	Count	Word	Count	Word	Count
eth	1	tomato	1	*trousers	3	water	24
lephone	1	tomatoes	2	truck	1	wheel	3
levision	2	top	1	twelve	1	wheelbarrow	2
ere	9	towel	6	van	2	wife	1
ing	3	toy	2	walk	1	window	25
ings	6	toys	3	wash	3	windows	2
ree	2	train	7	washing	6	winter	1
e	2	tree	29	washing-up	1	woman	1
ne	6	trees	10	watch	1	wood	4

Total words	2603		Total different words	364
Mean words	162·69		Mean different words	22·75

VERBS

Word	Count	Word	Count	Word	Count	Word	Count
owed	1	chasing	4	drinking	13	gone	6
e	23	clean	3	drive	1	got	46
king	1	cleaning	2	driving	3	had	8
nging	1	cleans	1	drop	8	happened	3
rking	1	clearing	1	dropped	18	has	16
	3	climb	5	dropping	2	have	19
en	1	climbed	1	eat	12	having	5
ongs	1	climbing	3	eating	19	help	11
wling	1	close	2	fall	47	helping	2
ked	1	come	27	falling	1	hit	12
ak	4	coming	9	falls	1	hitting	1
ng	2	cooking	3	fell	37	hold	8
ke	3	could	1	fetch	4	holding	5
np	5	cracked	1	finish	4	holds	1
	1	crash	6	finished	7	hurry	4
ed	4	crashed	5	frighten	1	hurt	2
ie	8	crashing	1	frightened	2	is	63
	4	crossed	1	gave	1	jump	10
e	1	cry	2	get	38	jumps	1
ried	1	crying	2	gets	2	keep	4
ies	1	cut	1	getting	4	keeping	2
y	14	did	3	give	3	kick	5
ying	8	do	6	giving	1	kicked	4
h	1	doing	5	go	40	kicking	3
hing	1	draw	1	goes	2	knock	1
se	1	drink	11	going	45	knocked	1

Word	Count	Word	Count	Word	Count	Word	Cou
knocks	1	played	1	shopping	4	think	
know	29	playing	50	shout	1	throw	1
land	1	plays	1	shouted	1	throwing	1
leave	1	pointing	1	shouting	2	throws	
left	1	pour	1	sit	1	tired	
licking	1	practising	1	sitting	3	tried	
lift	1	pretend	2	skating	2	tries	
like	2	pull	9	slam	2	try	
likes	2	pulling	2	slammed	1	trying	
listening	1	put	46	sleep	4	walk	
lives	1	putting	5	slide	3	walking	
lock	1	ran	4	slides	1	want	
look	18	reach	4	slipped	3	wants	
looked	5	reached	1	slipping	2	was	
looking	11	read	7	sloping	1	wash	
made	2	reading	12	smack	1	washing	
make	6	remember	2	smash	1	watch	
making	4	ride	1	smashed	1	watches	
may	1	riding	4	snowing	5	watching	
mean	1	roll	1	spoke	1	wear	
messing	1	rolling	2	stand	2	wearing	
might	6	run	9	stands	1	went	
milking	1	running	16	start	1	were	
mix	1	said	14	started	1	will	
open	7	save	1	starts	1	winding	
opened	2	saw	4	stirring	1	won	
opening	1	say	4	stop	24	work	
opens	1	saying	4	take	8	working	
packed	1	says	9	talk	3	worried	
pat	1	see	5	talking	7	write	
pay	10	setting	2	teaches	1	writes	
pick	1	shave	1	tell	1	writing	
play	28	shaving	2	telling	1		

Total words	1415	Total different words	235
Mean words	88·44	Mean different words	14·69

ADJECTIVES

Word	Count	Word	Count	Word	Count	Word	C
afraid	2	angry	8	asleep	2	bad	
all	22	another	1	back	1	big	

Word	Count	Word	Count	Word	Count	Word	Count
lack	1	front	1	more	3	small	1
lue	3	funny	2	much	2	some	9
roken	7	good	1	muddy	1	sweet	2
rown	4	green	1	naughty	1	ten	1
areful	1	half	1	no	2	terrible	1
old	6	hard	1	one	27	that	21
ross	3	high	1	open	4	thick	2
angerous	2	horrible	1	other	2	thirty	1
ark	1	hot	5	own	2	this	4
eep	1	hungry	1	pink	1	those	4
irty	5	injured	1	ready	7	three	5
asy	2	late	1	red	7	twelve	4
ght	1	like	2	right	1	two	29
npty	2	little	21	silly	3	white	5
ve	6	lovely	1	six	1	wooden	1
ur	3	many	1	sleepy	1		

Total words	287			Total different words	71		
Mean words	17·94			Mean different words	4·44		

ADVERBS

Word	Count	Word	Count	Word	Count	Word	Count
ually	1	high	1	off	10	somewhere	2
ain	3	home	20	on	8	then	1
	4	how	5	once	1	there	30
und	1	in	3	otherwise	1	too	2
	1	indoors	1	out	24	underneath	1
ay	25	inside	1	outside	2	up	22
k	14	mostly	1	over	33	upside-down	2
	1	much	1	perhaps	4	very	31
ore	1	nearly	1	probably	1	well	1
efully	1	never	1	quickly	3	when	7
vn	28	no	1	right	1	where	5
	2	not	10	round	1	why	3
e	8	now	5				

Total words	337			Total different words	50		
Mean words	21·06			Mean different words	3·13		

PRONOUNS

Word	Count	Word	Count	Word	Count	Word	Cou
anything	1	his	34	something	4	those	
each	2	I	24	that	28	we	
everybody	3	it	41	their	16	what	1
everybody's	1	me	2	them	11	which	
he	67	one	3	these	1	who	
her	12	other	2	they	104	you	
him	26	she	12	this	3	your	
himself	1	somebody	3				

Total words	438	Total different words	30
Mean words	27·38	Mean different words	1·88

PREPOSITIONS

Word	Count	Word	Count	Word	Count	Word	Co
about	2	for	31	on	30	through	
across	1	from	5	onto	1	to	1
after	5	in	70	out	5	under	
along	1	into	8	over	26	up	
at	24	like	2	past	4	upon	
behind	1	of	33	round	2	with	
down	3						

Total words	418	Total different words	25
Mean words	26·13	Mean different words	1·56

CONJUNCTIONS

Word	Count	Word	Count	Word	Count	Word	C
after	3	because	23	if	5	so	
and	307	but	7	or	9	then	

Total words	374	Total different words	8
Mean words	23·38	Mean different words	0·50

CONTRACTIONS

Word	Count	Word	Count	Word	Count	Word	Count
baby's	1	don't	24	lady's	3	they're	7
boy's	1	door's	1	mustn't	1	they've	2
bull's	1	farmer's	2	o'clock	3	wasn't	1
can't	5	haven't	1	she's	5	what's	2
cat's	1	he's	18	that's	12	where's	1
didn't	5	I've	2	there's	19	who's	1
dog's	2	it's	7				

Total words	128	Total different words	26
Mean words	8·00	Mean different words	1·63

INTERJECTIONS

Word	Count	Word	Count	Word	Count	Word	Count
ah	1	hello	1	oh	5	well	1
dear	2						

Total words	10	Total different words	5
Mean words	0·63	Mean different words	0·31

ARTICLES

Word	Count	Word	Count	Word	Count
a	222	an	1	the	740

Total words	963	Total different words	3
Mean words	60·19	Mean different words	0·19

OTHER

Word	Count	Word	Count	Word	Count	Word	Count
daddy	1	bump	5	Coke	1	felling	1
ang	3	Christmas	1	Cola	1	*Marmite	3
ovril	1	Cocacola	11	crash	5	*Meccano	1

Word	Count		Word	Count		Word	Count		Word	Coun
'member	1		posties	2		Terry	1		*Wellington	1
mices	1		Red Cross	1		Terry's	2		yes	11
no	6									

Total words	60		Total different words	21	
Mean words	3·75		Mean different words	1·31	

Subject Group G

(3 children; age: 8–10 years;
performance I.Q.: ⩾111; hearing loss: 40–60 dB)

NOUNS

accident	1	brush	2	cups	1	food	7
adults	1	bucket	3	curtain	1	foot	
all	5	bull	8	daddy	1	football	
ambulance	5	bulls	1	dinner	4	fork	
apple	1	butter	2	dog	18	forks	
apples	3	cabbage	3	doll	2	fruit	
arm	1	cake	1	door	4	game	
baby	2	cakes	3	dragon	1	games	
back	3	calendar	1	drain	3	gas	
bag	2	car	18	drawer	1	gate	
ball	10	cars	1	drink	3	girl	
banana	4	cart	1	drinks	1	girls	
basket	3	case	1	driver	1	gloves	
bat	2	cat	2	eggs	3	goal	
beard	1	chair	2	end	1	hat	
bicycle	2	chicken	2	family	1	head	
bike	1	clock	1	farmer	3	hill	
*bonnet	1	clothes	3	farmers	1	holiday	
book	5	cloths	1	father	6	house	
books	1	coat	2	father's	1	houses	
boots	3	comic	1	fault	1	ice	
boy	37	*cooker	1	fence	4	ice-cream	
boys	5	cotton	1	field	1	jar	
bread	2	course	1	fish	3	jelly	
broom	1	crash	2	floor	1	kettle	
brother	1	*cricket	4	flower	3	kitchen	
brothers	1	cup	1	flowers	1	knife	

Word	Count	Word	Count	Word	Count	Word	Count
ladder	8	night	1	sandwiches	2	stove	1
ladies	3	notice	1	saucepan	1	sugar	1
lady	16	one	2	saucepans	1	supper	1
lorry	1	ones	1	saucer	1	sweets	1
machine	2	onions	1	scarf	1	table	4
man	27	orange	1	scissors	1	*taps	1
map	3	peach	1	sea	1	tea	3
maps	1	pear	1	shelf	1	*tea-cloth	1
market	1	pepper	1	shirt	1	there	1
marmalade	2	person	1	shopkeepers	1	things	2
mask	2	picnic	1	side	1	town	1
matches	2	picture	1	sign	1	toys	1
men	4	pie	1	sink	2	train	1
mice	3	plant	2	sister	1	trees	1
milk	3	plants	1	skates	1	*trifle	1
milkman	5	plates	3	skin	2	two	1
mincemeat	1	police	2	*sledge	1	vase	1
mirror	1	policeman	4	smile	1	voice	1
mixer	1	pot	2	snow	1	washing	1
money	5	pots	1	soap	1	water	4
monster	1	*purse	2	spaniel	1	way	1
mother	4	rice	1	spoon	2	wheelbarrow	2
mouse	1	room	1	stick	5	window	3
mummy	5	salt	1	sticks	2	wood	1
mushroom	1	sandwich	1				

Total words	521	Total different words	206
Mean words	173·67	Mean different words	68·67

VERBS

Word	Count	Word	Count	Word	Count	Word	Count
answer	1	can	1	crack	1	drop	2
are	5	carrying	3	crash	3	dropped	3
be	1	chased	1	crashed	3	drowned	1
barking	1	cleaning	1	crashing	2	eat	2
be	2	clearing	1	crying	1	eating	6
been	3	climbing	1	cut	1	fall	2
bringing	1	come	2	does	1	fell	10
broke	1	coming	3	doing	1	frightened	1
called	1	cooking	2	drinking	3	gave	1
came	19	could	2	driving	3	get	12

Word	Count	Word	Count	Word	Count	Word	Coun
getting	1	know	5	putting	2	tell	1
giving	1	left	1	ran	3	told	5
go	3	look	3	reading	3	took	1
going	4	looked	3	realize	1	touching	1
gone	3	looking	2	running	2	tripped	3
got	11	lying	1	said	3	try	1
had	7	made	1	saw	3	trying	6
hang	2	making	1	saying	1	turned	2
have	1	mean	2	says	1	turning	2
having	1	might	3	screaming	1	wait	
helping	1	opened	1	shaving	3	walked	
hit	4	opening	1	shouting	2	want	
hold	1	packing	1	sit	1	wanted	
holding	1	pay	1	skating	2	was	3
hurt	2	paying	1	skiing	1	watching	
is	16	phoned	2	sliding	1	wearing	
jumped	1	play	2	slipped	1	went	1
keeps	1	playing	17	standing	1	were	
knocked	2	please	1	stop	8	writing	
knocking	1	put	5	take	1		

Total words	356	Total different words	119
Mean words	118·67	Mean different words	39·67

ADJECTIVES

Word	Count	Word	Count	Word	Count	Word	Co
all	7	freezing	1	open	1	that	
asleep	2	great	1	other	4	thin	
big	6	little	9	ready	1	three	
dirty	2	much	1	red	1	twelve	
five	2	muddy	1	silly	1	two	
four	2	one	11	some	22		

Total words	95	Total different words	23
Mean words	31·67	Mean different words	7·67

ADVERBS

Word	Count	Word	Count	Word	Count	Word	Count
about	1	how	1	off	2	suddenly	5
all	1	in	3	on	3	then	1
away	5	instead	1	out	7	there	17
back	1	just	2	over	6	too	1
down	12	nearly	1	right	2	up	4
forward	1	not	3	round	4	upside-down	2
home	3	now	1	so	2	where	1

Total words	93	Total different words	28
Mean words	31·00	Mean different words	9·33

PRONOUNS

Word	Count	Word	Count	Word	Count	Word	Count
ᴴe	20	it	18	that	3	we	1
ᴴer	8	my	1	their	9	what	5
ᴵim	8	nothing	1	them	7	who	1
ᴴis	10	others	1	these	2	you	2
	3	she	4	they	28		

Total words	132	Total different words	19
Mean words	44·00	Mean different words	6·33

PREPOSITIONS

Word	Count	Word	Count	Word	Count	Word	Count
ᶜross	1	down	4	of	20	to	34
ᵗter	3	for	5	off	2	under	1
ᵒound	1	in	14	on	15	underneath	2
	5	into	7	out	3	up	1
ᵇhind	3	near	1	over	5	with	25
	4	next	1	through	2		

Total words	159	Total different words	23
Mean words	53·00	Mean different words	7·67

CONJUNCTIONS

Word	Count	Word	Count	Word	Count	Word	Count
and	170	but	6	so	2	then	6
because	5	if	2	that	2		

Total words 193 Total different words 7
Mean words 64·33 Mean different words 2·33

CONTRACTIONS

Word	Count	Word	Count	Word	Count	Word	Count
boy's	1	dog's	2	he's	7	that's	1
cat's	1	don't	2	it's	2	there's	17
couldn't	3	father's	1	lady's	1	they're	4
daddy's	1	he'd	2	she's	4	they've	3
didn't	2						

Total words 54 Total different words 17
Mean words 18·00 Mean different words 5·67

INTERJECTIONS

Word	Count
—	—

Total words 0 Total different words 0
Mean words 0·00 Mean different words 0·00

ARTICLES

Word	Count	Word	Count	Word	Count
a	73	an	2	the	238

Total words 313 Total different words 3
Mean words 104·33 Mean different words 1·00

OTHER

Word	Count	Word	Count	Word	Count	Word	Count
*Bovril	1	icing	1	*Meccano	1	*Wellington	1
Coke	1	knifes	1	micey	1	yes	1
English	1	*Marmite	2	no	3		

Total words	14	Total different words	11
Mean words	4·67	Mean different words	3·67

Subject Group H

(6 children; age: 8–10 years;
performance I.Q.: ≥111; hearing loss: 61–80 dB)

NOUNS

Word	Count	Word	Count	Word	Count	Word	Count
accident	2	body	1	cabbages	2	cup	1
all	4	book	7	cake	3	cups	3
ambulance	16	books	1	cakes	2	curtain	1
apple	7	*boot	3	calendar	4	curtains	1
apples	6	boots	6	car	29	daddy	3
baby	1	bottle	1	cart	5	danger	1
back	2	bottles	2	cat	7	date	1
badge	1	bottom	1	chair	6	dinner	2
bag	4	bowl	1	chicken	2	dinosaur	1
ball	33	boy	80	children	5	dish	1
banana	1	boys	19	chin	1	dog	33
bananas	4	bread	8	chop	1	doggie	1
arrow	1	broom	2	clock	6	doll	5
basket	15	brush	4	cloth	6	door	7
at	3	bucket	4	clothes	3	doors	2
beard	1	building	1	clown	1	dragon	1
eef	1	bull	13	coat	4	drain	3
icycle	2	bull's	2	coats	1	drawer	1
ke	1	bush	1	*cooker	3	drawers	1
scuits	1	bushes	1	corner	2	dress	2
t	1	butter	3	crash	6	dust	1
ard	1	cabbage	1	*cricket	3	egg	2

Word	Count	Word	Count	Word	Count	Word	Count
eggs	5	hospitals	1	money	10	ring	1
elbow	1	house	2	mop	2	road	6
engine	1	houses	2	mother	18	roof	1
face	1	ice	17	mouse	1	*rounders	3
family	2	ingredients	1	mug	1	ruler	1
farm	4	interest	1	mummy	11	salt	1
farmer	5	jam	1	mushroom	2	sandwiches	6
father	12	jelly	1	nose	1	saucepan	1
fault	1	*jumpers	1	notice	1	saucepans	2
fence	3	keeper	1	one	7	saucers	1
field	9	kettle	6	onion	1	scarf	4
finger	1	key	1	onions	1	scissors	3
fir	3	kitchen	7	orange	1	shadow	1
fish	5	knife	6	oven	3	shave	1
floor	4	ladder	12	packet	1	shirt	1
flower	7	ladders	1	paint	1	shoe	1
flowers	3	lady	11	pan	2	shoes	5
food	11	lady's	2	pans	2	shop	2
football	7	ledge	1	pastry	1	shopkeeper	1
fork	1	lettuce	2	*pavement	2	shoulder	1
forks	1	lid	2	pear	1	shoulders	1
friend	1	loaf	1	people	5	sideboard	1
friends	1	*lorry	1	pepper	1	sign	2
front	2	lots	3	person	1	sink	3
fruit	1	lunch	1	picnic	5	skate	1
gas	1	machine	1	picture	5	skates	2
gate	4	man	28	plant	2	ski	1
*ginger	1	man's	1	plate	2	sleep	
girl	23	map	4	plates	3	*sledge	7
girls	4	market	1	plenty	1	slope	
glasses	2	marmalade	1	police	3	snow	
glove	1	mask	6	policeman	3	son	
gloves	2	mat	1	police-		sons	
goal	6	matches	3	station	1	spoon	
goalie	1	meal	1	pond	1	spoons	
grate	1	meat	4	*postman	1	stick	8
ground	3	men	4	posts	1	sticks	2
gymnastics	2	mess	1	pot	4	street	
hands	1	mice	2	potato	1	sugar	
handstand	3	middle	1	puncture	1	table	1
hat	3	milk	10	*purse	5	table-cloth	
head	3	milkman	9	*pussy	1	tail	
hill	2	minutes	1	rain	1	*tap	
holder	1	mirror	3	raincoat	1	tea	
hole	3	mixer	2	rice	1	tennis	

Word	Count	Word	Count	Word	Count	Word	Count
there	3	towel	1	turkey	1	weather	1
thing	2	toy	2	two	1	wine	1
things	6	toys	3	van	3	window	4
time	1	train	4	vegetable	1	windows	3
tomato	1	tree	5	vegetables	1	window-sill	1
tomatoes	3	trees	4	view	1	wire	1
tongue	1	trouble	1	washing	2	wires	1
top	4	*trousers	1	water	2	woman	4
total	1						

Total words	1074	Total different words	300
Mean words	179·00	Mean different words	50·00

VERBS

Word	Count	Word	Count	Word	Count	Word	Count
are	27	climbing	1	drying	1	hear	1
baked	1	come	9	dusting	1	help	2
barking	1	comes	6	eat	3	helping	2
be	3	coming	4	eating	11	hit	6
been	2	cooking	1	fall	1	hold	2
begins	1	covering	1	fallen	1	holding	12
being	1	cracked	2	falls	2	is	84
brought	5	crash	4	fell	18	jump	1
build	1	crashed	4	fetch	3	keep	1
building	1	cross	1	fetching	3	kick	1
built	1	crossed	1	frightened	2	kicked	3
bump	1	crossing	1	frying	1	knocked	3
bumps	1	crushing	1	gave	1	know	6
buy	1	crying	1	get	25	laid	1
came	13	cutting	1	give	3	leave	1
can	3	damaged	2	giving	1	left	4
carried	1	did	2	go	12	lifting	1
carries	1	do	5	going	21	like	2
carry	1	does	1	gone	1	listen	1
carrying	7	doing	12	got	9	listening	1
charge	1	drink	2	had	11	look	6
charging	1	drinking	7	happen	1	looked	1
chased	1	drive	1	happened	1	looking	12
cleaning	2	driving	1	has	4	looks	1
clearing	1	drop	5	have	2	lost	1
climb	2	dropped	11	having	7	made	1

Word	Count	Word	Count	Word	Count	Word	Count
making	5	ran	4	slide	1	tripped	1
messing	1	reach	1	slipped	1	try	1
might	4	read	2	smashed	1	trying	6
mix	1	reading	5	smiling	1	turn	1
need	2	riding	3	snowing	1	unpack	1
open	3	rolled	1	stand	1	upset	2
opened	1	run	5	standing	6	use	1
opening	2	running	5	started	1	using	1
overhanging	1	rush	1	stop	6	waggling	1
pack	3	said	2	stopped	2	waiting	1
packing	1	sat	1	supposed	3	walk	1
painting	1	saw	2	surprised	1	walking	4
passing	1	say	1	take	1	wanted	1
pay	1	saying	1	takes	1	wants	2
paying	2	says	6	taking	3	was	35
pick	1	see	8	talking	3	washing	2
play	4	seen	1	tear	1	watch	4
playing	31	set	1	tell	2	watching	9
plays	1	shaved	1	telling	2	wearing	1
preparing	1	shaving	3	think	10	went	11
pull	2	shout	1	thinks	1	were	10
pushed	1	shut	1	throwing	1	will	5
put	6	sit	1	told	3	writes	2
putting	7	skiing	4	tried	1	writing	4
puzzled	1						

Total words	777	Total different words	201
Mean words	129·50	Mean different words	33·50

ADJECTIVES

Word	Count	Word	Count	Word	Count	Word	Count
all	12	dirty	4	muddy	1	same	1
angry	2	each	1	next	1	some	21
another	1	five	3	one	7	sweet	1
asleep	1	full	2	other	1	ten	1
big	1	hot	1	open	4	terrible	2
blue	1	like	4	own	1	that	8
careless	1	little	33	quick	1	these	1
clean	1	long	1	ready	1	thin	7
cold	1	many	5	red	3	third	1
dangerous	4	much	2	sad	2	this	5

Word	Count	Word	Count	Word	Count	Word	Count
those	4	tired	1	two	21	white	1
three	1	twelve	2				

Total words	181	Total different words	46
Mean words	30·17	Mean different words	7·67

ADVERBS

Word	Count	Word	Count	Word	Count	Word	Count
along	4	home	11	on	1	still	3
already	2	how	1	only	1	then	2
as	3	in	7	otherwise	1	there	28
away	5	just	7	out	27	too	6
back	3	later	1	over	12	up	6
badly	1	maybe	1	perhaps	1	upside-down	2
carefully	1	more	1	probably	1	very	5
down	10	nearly	3	rather	1	well	3
fast	1	not	8	quickly	2	when	1
first	1	now	2	so	2	where	1
half	1	off	5	sometimes	1	why	3
here	1						

Total words	190	Total different words	45
Mean words	31·67	Mean different words	7·50

PRONOUNS

Word	Count	Word	Count	Word	Count	Word	Count
anything	1	his	33	she	13	this	4
everybody	4	I	20	something	5	those	1
he	38	it	26	that	4	we	1
her	20	itself	1	their	4	what	11
him	20	my	1	them	8	who	1
himself	1	nothing	1	they	35	you	11

Total words	264	Total different words	24
Mean words	44·00	Mean different words	4·00

PREPOSITIONS

Word	Count	Word	Count	Word	Count	Word	Count
about	2	by	6	near	1	round	1
across	1	down	6	of	23	through	2
after	5	for	13	off	3	to	65
along	1	from	2	on	50	towards	2
at	10	in	35	onto	4	under	8
before	2	inside	1	over	13	up	1
behind	3	into	9	past	3	with	35
beside	3						

Total words   310   Total different words   29
Mean words   51·67   Mean different words   4·83

CONJUNCTIONS

Word	Count	Word	Count	Word	Count	Word	Count
and	194	or	4	then	5	while	1
because	14	so	3	when	1	whether	1
but	3	that	5	what	1		

Total words   232   Total different words   11
Mean words   38·67   Mean different words   1·83

CONTRACTIONS

Word	Count	Word	Count	Word	Count	Word	Count
boy's	3	don't	5	it's	9	they're	12
bull's	1	girl's	1	lady's	1	they've	
daddy's	1	hadn't	1	mother's	1	wasn't	
didn't	5	haven't	1	she'll	1	won't	
doesn't	1	he'll	1	she's	2	you're	
dog's	1	he's	18	there's	21		

Total words   91   Total different words   23
Mean words   15·17   Mean different words   3·83

INTERJECTIONS

Word	Count
oh	2

Total words	2	Total different words	1
Mean words	0·33	Mean different words	0·17

ARTICLES

Word	Count	Word	Count	Word	Count
a	146	an	8	the	444

Total words	598	Total different words	3
Mean words	99·67	Mean different words	0·50

OTHER

Word	Count	Word	Count	Word	Count	Word	Count
Cocacola	4	*Marmite	1	of	1	'tatoes	1
Coke	1	*Meccano	1	runned	1	*Wellington	2
Dracula	1	no	4				

Total words	17	Total different words	10
Mean words	2·83	Mean different words	1·67

Subject Group I

(11 children; age: 8–10 years;
performance I.Q.: $\geqslant 111$; hearing loss: 81–95 dB)

NOUNS

Word	Count	Word	Count	Word	Count	Word	Count
accident	2	cakes	1	drawer	9	ground	2
ambulance	30	car	52	dress	4	hair	1
apple	20	card	2	drink	11	hand	3
apples	5	cars	1	driver	1	handkerchief	1
baby	9	cart	2	egg	13	handstand	3
back	3	cat	12	eggs	7	hanky	1
badge	3	chair	17	face	8	hat	14
bag	32	chicken	6	faces	1	head	4
ball	70	children	1	fall	1	hedge	1
banana	9	clock	9	family	2	help	1
bananas	3	cloth	3	farmer	2	hole	5
bang	3	clothes	10	farmer's	1	home	9
baseball	1	clothing	1	father	2	honey	1
basket	9	cloud	1	fence	5	hospital	5
bat	13	coat	12	field	2	house	12
beard	1	cook	1	fish	13	houses	2
bicycle	6	*cooker	3	five	3	ice	12
bike	4	cow	4	floor	5	ice-cream	1
bill	2	crash	4	flour	1	jam	1
board	1	crayon	1	flower	22	jar	2
*bobby	1	*cricket	1	flowers	2	jelly	2
book	28	cup	8	food	10	jug	2
*boot	11	cups	1	football	15	jump	1
boots	7	curtain	3	fork	5	*jumper	1
bottles	1	daddy	37	four	4	kettle	5
bowl	1	danger	2	frame	1	kitchen	4
boy	177	date	2	fruit	4	kitchens	1
boys	4	day	1	game	5	knife	14
branches	1	dinner	6	garden	1	ladder	16
bread	22	dirt	1	gate	8	lady	30
broom	2	dog	78	girl	28	laugh	
brush	10	doll	6	glove	4	leaf	
bucket	9	dolly	3	gloves	4	light	
bull	16	door	8	goal	3	lolly	
butter	10	doors	1	goal-keeper	1	look	
cabbage	4	dragon	2	grapefruit	1	*lorry	
cake	12	drain	4	grass	1	lot	

Word	Count	Word	Count	Word	Count	Word	Count
lunch	3	onions	2	sandwich	6	sweet	2
machine	2	orange	7	sandwiches	4	sweets	2
man	85	oranges	1	sauce	1	table	24
map	2	oven	5	saucer	1	*tap	6
marmalade	4	painter	1	saucers	1	*taps	2
mask	2	pan	4	scarf	8	tea	2
match	4	paper	2	scissors	10	*tea-cloth	1
matches	3	*pavement	1	seven	1	there	2
may	1	pear	5	shave	2	thing	1
meat	7	pencil	1	shoe	10	three	6
melon	1	pennies	2	shoes	7	time	1
men	1	penny	1	shop	1	tomatoes	1
mess	1	pepper	9	shopping	1	towel	3
milk	18	picnic	1	sink	3	town	1
milkman	17	picture	7	sister	1	toy	1
minutes	1	pineapple	1	six	2	toys	1
mirror	1	plate	6	skate	1	train	11
money	14	police	5	*sledge	1	tree	30
monster	1	policeman	12	sleep	2	trees	2
month	1	pot	4	snow	7	*trousers	3
mother	5	potatoes	1	sock	1	turkey	1
mouse	8	pots	1	spoon	11	two	5
mud	1	pound	1	stage	1	van	1
muddy	1	*purse	6	stick	8	walk	1
mummy	58	rain	1	sticks	1	washing	2
mushroom	3	raincoat	1	stop	2	water	18
mushrooms	2	ride	1	strawberries	1	water-hole	1
nose	3	road	2	string	2	water-melon	1
number	1	roof	1	sugar	1	window	19
nuts	1	*rounders	1	sweater	2	wood	3
one	4	salt	11	swede	1	world	1
onion	1						

Total words	1840	Total different words	273
Mean words	167·27	Mean different words	24·82

VERBS

Word	Count	Word	Count	Word	Count	Word	Count
are	5	barking	1	broke	4	bumped	1
bang	2	break	1	brush	1	bumping	1
banging	1	breaking	2	bump	3	buy	1

Word	Count	Word	Count	Word	Count	Word	Count
came	10	gave	1	might	1	stop	14
camping	1	get	6	must	1	stopping	1
can	1	give	3	open	4	stuck	1
carry	4	go	19	packing	2	take	5
carrying	5	going	7	pay	7	talk	1
catch	1	got	4	pick	5	talking	1
catching	1	grow	1	play	25	tell	1
chase	1	happened	1	playing	26	tells	1
cleaning	2	happening	1	pull	7	think	4
climb	5	has	6	pulling	2	throw	8
comb	1	have	7	put	10	throwing	3
come	7	having	5	putting	2	thrown	1
coming	6	hear	1	ran	1	thump	1
cooking	1	heard	1	reach	1	took	4
crash	4	help	10	read	3	trip	1
crashed	3	helping	2	reading	7	tripped	1
cry	1	hit	5	riding	2	try	1
cutting	1	hold	13	run	7	trying	1
doing	1	holding	9	running	15	wake	1
drink	2	hurry	1	said	3	walk	1
drinking	7	is	80	saw	3	walking	3
drop	7	jump	8	say	1	want	1
dropped	6	kick	2	says	8	wanted	1
dropping	4	kicked	5	shaving	3	wants	2
eat	13	knock	2	shopping	1	was	15
eating	12	knocked	1	shouting	1	wash	3
eats	1	know	15	shut	2	washing	11
fall	34	left	1	sit	4	watch	4
falling	3	let	1	skating	3	watching	
fell	24	listening	2	sleep	6	went	
felling	1	look	10	sleeping	4	were	
finish	4	looked	1	slide	2	will	
finished	2	looking	7	slip	3	worried	
forget	1	made	1	snowing	2	would	
frighten	1	make	2	stand	1	write	
frightened	2	making	1	starting	1	writing	

Total words   738   Total different words   156
Mean words   67·09   Mean different words   14·18

ADJECTIVES

Word	Count	Word	Count	Word	Count	Word	Count
all	5	cold	9	funny	3	sleepy	1
angry	6	cross	4	half	1	small	1
any	1	dangerous	1	little	14	some	3
asleep	1	dirty	3	more	1	that	10
bad	2	fast	1	one	5	thin	2
big	6	five	1	open	3	three	2
blue	1	four	1	red	1	twelve	1
broken	10	frozen	1	sad	2	two	7

Total words	110		Total different words	32	
Mean words	10·00		Mean different words	2·91	

ADVERBS

Word	Count	Word	Count	Word	Count	Word	Count
about	1	hard	1	out	26	there	10
afterwards	1	here	1	outside	1	too	4
along	3	home	12	over	30	up	9
away	12	inside	1	quickly	3	very	16
back	3	no	1	ready	1	where	1
down	11	now	1	then	9	when	2
fast	2	off	5				

Total words	167		Total different words	26	
Mean words	15·18		Mean different words	2·36	

PRONOUNS

Word	Count	Word	Count	Word	Count	Word	Count
all	2	his	10	someone	1	they	24
everything	1	I	10	something	2	what	3
he	32	is	1	that	18	you	5
her	6	it	8	their	3	your	1
him	14	she	4				

Total words	145		Total different words	18	
Mean words	13·18		Mean different words	1·64	

John Bench, Lütgen Mentz and Ian Wilson

PREPOSITIONS

Word	Count	Word	Count	Word	Count	Word	Coun
after	1	for	12	off	1	through	3
against	1	from	3	on	16	to	32
at	12	in	23	out	2	under	4
behind	2	into	1	over	12	underneath	1
down	4	of	10	past	2	with	21

Total words	163	Total different words	20
Mean words	14·82	Mean different words	1·82

CONJUNCTIONS

Word	Count	Word	Count	Word	Count
and	111	because	3	then	5

Total words	119	Total different words	3
Mean words	10·82	Mean different words	0·27

CONTRACTIONS

Word	Count	Word	Count	Word	Count	Word	Cou
boy's	1	don't	16	she's	2	there's	
bull's	1	he's	5	that's	3	they're	
doesn't	1	it's	2				

Total words	37	Total different words	10
Mean words	3·36	Mean different words	0·91

INTERJECTIONS

Word	Count	Word	Count
hello	1	oh	1

Total words	2	Total different words	2
Mean words	0·18	Mean different words	0·18

ARTICLES

Word	Count	Word	Count	Word	Count
a	126	an	4	the	382

Total words	512	Total different words	3
Mean words	46·55	Mean different words	0·27

OTHER

Word	Count	Word	Count	Word	Count	Word	Count
Alison	1	Christmas-		*Father		no	3
April	1	tree	1	Christmas	1	*Wellington	1
bang	3	Cocacola	2	July	1	woof	7
*Bovril	1	Coke	3	*Marmite	1	Yvonne	1
bump	2	crash	6	moo	1	yes	2

Total words	37	Total different words	18
Mean words	3·36	Mean different words	1·64

Subject Group J

(7 children; age: 11–13 years;
Performance I.Q.: ⩽90; hearing loss: 40–60 dB)

NOUNS

Word	Count	Word	Count	Word	Count	Word	Count
accident	3	banana	2	bill	2	boys	33
all	2	bananas	7	birthday	2	bread	13
ambulance	17	bang	1	bit	3	broom	5
apple	4	*barrow	1	blind	1	brother	9
apples	9	basket	14	board	3	brothers	6
baby	3	bat	2	book	18	brush	1
back	3	beard	4	books	2	bucket	9
badges	1	bench	4	*boot	8	bull	12
bag	15	bicycle	3	boots	18	bus	2
ball	40	bike	8	boy	96	bush	3

Word	Count	Word	Count	Word	Count	Word	Count
bushes	2	dolly	1	hanger	1	*mince	2
butter	9	door	9	hat	9	*mincemeat	1
cabbage	2	dragon	1	head	6	mirror	5
cabbages	2	drain	4	hill	3	mixer	3
cake	8	drawer	4	hills	2	money	22
cakes	3	dress	2	hole	9	monster	1
calendar	5	drink	7	home	2	mop	3
cap	2	drinks	2	hook	2	morning	1
car	41	egg	1	house	1	mother	17
carrots	1	eggs	15	houses	3	mouse	3
cat	12	engine	3	ice	9	mum	8
cauliflower	1	eye	2	ice-cream	2	mummy	22
chair	8	face	1	ice-skates	2	mummy's	2
chairs	2	family	4	jelly	5	mushrooms	1
change	2	farm	4	jug	2	name	1
cheque	2	farmer	1	kettle	8	newspaper	1
chicken	3	father	6	key	2	noses	2
children	11	fence	4	kind	2	number	1
class-room	1	field	4	kitchen	10	numbers	2
clock	9	fish	11	knife	12	onions	3
cloth	6	fishing	1	knives	4	orange	4
clothes	7	floor	6	ladder	13	oranges	1
coal	2	flower	4	ladders	2	oven	2
coat	10	flowers	9	lady	30	pan	1
coats	2	food	11	lamb	1	paper	2
comics	1	foods	2	lawn	2	park	2
conversation	2	football	13	legs	1	*pavement	2
cook	1	fork	1	liquid	1	pea	
*cooker	6	forks	2	list	2	*pence	
*cookery	2	fruit	5	look	1	people	8
corner	2	gang	2	lots	6	pepper	
cow	4	garden	1	machine	2	picnic	
crash	1	gate	5	man	67	picture	
*cricket	6	girl	27	map	2	pictures	
cup	4	girl-friend	1	market	2	pie	
cupboard	1	girls	4	marmalade	5	place	
cups	4	glasses	2	mask	2	plant	
curtains	2	gloves	1	matches	5	plate	
dad	3	goal	8	meat	8	plates	
daddy	16	grass	3	melon	1	police	
day	2	ground	2	men	6	policeman	
dinner	9	hair	10	mess	2	*postman	
disaster	2	hand	5	mice	3	posts	
dog	48	hands	2	milk	16	pot	
doll	4	handstand	5	milkman	12	potatoes	

Word	Count	Word	Count	Word	Count	Word	Count
*purse	5	shopping	3	stuff	4	toys	2
rag	1	side	2	suit	2	train	5
rice	3	sign	2	sweets	1	tree	2
road	6	sink	6	table	14	trees	3
room	1	sister	2	table-cloth	1	trouble	2
*rounders	1	skates	2	*tap	1	*trousers	2
salt	5	skin	1	*taps	2	van	1
sandwich	1	*sledge	3	tea	9	vegetables	5
sandwiches	12	slide	1	*tea-cloths	2	wall	1
saucepan	6	snow	4	there	16	washing	2
saucepans	1	son	1	thing	3	washing-up	1
saucers	4	spoon	6	things	8	water	6
scarf	4	step	2	tie	2	way	3
scissors	11	stick	11	time	2	week	1
seat	2	sticks	1	tomatoes	3	wife	1
shave	1	stop	2	top	2	window	25
shirt	2	strainer	1	towel	7	windows	3
shoes	2	street	4	town	4	wood	3
shop	3						

Total words	1623	Total different words	293
Mean words	231·86	Mean different words	41·86

VERBS

Word	Count	Word	Count	Word	Count	Word	Count
are	30	climbing	2	done	1	fell	20
back	1	come	21	drink	3	fighting	1
be	1	comes	2	drinking	10	fill	2
bounced	2	comfort	2	drive	2	finish	3
break	1	coming	6	driving	3	finished	3
broke	1	concentrating	2	drink	1	forgotten	1
brought	2	cook	2	drop	3	frighten	1
buying	1	crash	6	dropped	15	frightened	4
called	2	crashed	6	drove	2	get	38
came	3	crashing	2	dry	1	give	4
can	1	cry	1	eat	11	gives	1
carry	1	crying	1	eating	12	giving	1
carrying	15	damage	2	expect	2	go	32
catch	2	do	1	fall	12	goes	8
chasing	6	does	4	fallen	4	going	16
cleaning	1	doing	9	falls	3	gone	1

Word	Count	Word	Count	Word	Count	Word	Count
got	36	look	11	read	2	take	1
had	5	looked	2	reading	9	takes	2
handing	2	looking	11	riding	7	taking	6
hanging	4	looks	4	run	3	talk	1
happen	1	make	3	running	5	talking	2
happened	2	making	6	said	4	tell	4
happening	2	mean	5	sat	2	telling	1
has	14	messing	2	saw	3	think	3
have	22	might	4	say	4	throw	9
having	8	money	1	says	8	tidy	1
help	11	open	6	see	4	tired	4
hit	4	opened	2	seen	1	took	1
hold	4	pack	3	shave	2	tried	2
holding	4	packing	2	shaving	4	try	2
hurt	4	paid	2	shout	1	trying	9
is	132	pay	3	shut	6	waiting	1
jump	1	paying	1	sit	1	walk	2
jumped	2	pays	2	sitting	2	walking	4
jumping	1	pinch	2	skating	2	wants	3
keep	3	play	15	snowing	2	was	32
kick	2	played	2	soaked	2	watch	4
kicked	3	playing	30	speeding	2	watched	2
kicking	1	plays	2	standing	2	watching	1
knock	2	poking	2	start	3	waving	4
knocked	1	pull	2	started	3	wearing	3
know	21	pulling	2	stop	6	went	10
knows	1	push	2	stretch	1	were	3
laugh	1	put	16	sucking	2	will	2
laughing	1	putting	2	suppose	1	worried	2
laying	2	puzzled	2	supposed	1	worrying	1
left	3	reaching	2	sweeping	2	writing	8
like	4						

Total words   1042   Total different words   189
Mean words   148·86   Mean different words   27·00

ADJECTIVES

Word	Count	Word	Count	Word	Count	Word	Count
all	26	asleep	3	brown	4	cold	3
angry	4	big	9	busy	2	cross	3
another	2	blue	4	clean	1	curly	2

Word	Count	Word	Count	Word	Count	Word	Count
dangerous	8	funny	2	orange	6	striped	2
different	1	green	6	other	17	such	2
dirty	1	hungry	1	purple	2	that	37
easy	1	icy	2	ready	3	thin	3
electric	1	little	11	real	2	this	6
empty	1	messy	2	red	12	those	2
every	1	more	1	sad	1	three	6
fast	1	most	2	same	1	twelve	2
few	1	much	1	sleepy	1	two	25
five	7	muddy	2	small	3	wet	2
four	2	one	19	snowy	2	what	2
full	2	open	6	some	6	white	2

Total words	292		Total different words	60	
Mean words	41·71		Mean different words	8·57	

ADVERBS

Word	Count	Word	Count	Word	Count	Word	Count
about	8	here	3	on	8	today	1
again	1	home	7	out	29	too	1
all	4	how	1	outside	3	underneath	1
along	1	in	2	over	11	up	14
any	1	inside	4	past	2	upside-down	2
anyway	1	maybe	1	probably	4	very	11
as	10	nearly	1	right	3	well	10
away	4	now	5	so	2	when	6
back	2	off	2	somewhere	2	where	6
down	28	often	1	there	19	why	2
fast	5						

Total words	229		Total different words	41	
Mean words	32·71		Mean different words	5·86	

PRONOUNS

Word	Count	Word	Count	Word	Count	Word	Count
all	13	everything	1	her	32	his	53
anything	1	he	69	him	39	I	19

Word	Count	Word	Count	Word	Count	Word	Count
it	36	someone	2	them	10	we	1
my	3	something	3	they	44	what	9
one	11	that	38	this	3	which	1
she	8	their	18	those	1	you	7
somebody	1						

Total words	423	Total different words	25
Mean words	60·43	Mean different words	3·57

PREPOSITIONS

Word	Count	Word	Count	Word	Count	Word	Count
after	10	for	24	next	1	past	1
against	1	from	1	of	53	through	1
at	17	in	63	off	3	to	64
before	1	inside	3	on	48	underneath	1
beside	2	into	4	out	25	up	8
down	15	like	8	outside	2	with	43
except	2	near	1	over	21		

Total words	423	Total different words	27
Mean words	60·43	Mean different words	3·86

CONJUNCTIONS

Word	Count	Word	Count	Word	Count	Word	Count
and	222	because	10	so	2	then	2
as	1	or	8				

Total words	245	Total different words	6
Mean words	35·00	Mean different words	0·86

CONTRACTIONS

Word	Count	Word	Count	Word	Count	Word	Count
ambulance's	2	don't	22	people's	1	they're	7
boy's	3	he's	27	she's	12	they've	1
can't	4	I've	3	someone's	2	wasn't	3
daddy's	1	it's	14	that's	29	what's	6
didn't	3	lady's	3	there's	15	who's	2
doesn't	4	mother's	1	they'll	2	you're	1

Total words	168	
Mean words	24·00	
Total different words	24	
Mean different words	3·43	

INTERJECTIONS

Word	Count	Word	Count
oh	5	well	6

Total words	11
Mean words	1·57
Total different words	2
Mean different words	0·29

ARTICLES

Word	Count	Word	Count	Word	Count
a	155	an	11	the	588

Total words	754
Mean words	107·71
Total different words	3
Mean different words	0·43

OTHER

Word	Count	Word	Count	Word	Count	Word	Count
Cocacola	3	icing	2	no	11	*Wellingtons	1
Coke	3	knocken	2	thinked	1	yes	4
falled	2	*Marmite	4	*Vim	1		

Total words	34
Mean words	4·86
Total different words	11
Mean different words	1·57

John Bench, Lütgen Mentz and Ian Wilson

Subject Group K

(14 children; age: 11–13 years;
performance I.Q.: ≤90; hearing loss: 61–80 dB)

NOUNS

Word	Count	Word	Count	Word	Count	Word	Count
accident	4	*boot	12	cleaner	1	door	22
afternoon	1	boots	9	clock	13	doors	1
all	9	bottle	4	cloth	6	dragon	1
ambulance	31	bowl	1	clothes	8	drain	6
animal	4	box	2	cloud	2	drawer	3
animals	1	boy	150	cloves	1	drawers	1
apple	15	boys	18	clown	3	dress	3
apples	6	bread	8	coat	13	dresses	1
army	1	broom	7	comic	1	drink	13
baby	7	brooms	1	cook	1	drinks	2
back	7	brother	2	*cooker	7	driver	1
badges	1	brush	5	country	2	egg	14
bag	21	brucket	13	cow	9	eggs	8
bags	2	bull	11	cows	1	end	1
ball	57	bun	1	crack	1	engine	2
banana	9	bushes	1	crash	4	face	8
bananas	3	butter	12	cream	1	family	2
barrel	1	cabbage	7	*cricket	13	farm	3
basket	22	cabbages	1	cross	1	farmer	9
bat	15	cake	14	cup	5	father	16
beard	1	cakes	2	cupboard	1	fence	8
bed	6	calendar	4	cups	4	field	6
beer	1	can	1	currant	1	fish	16
belt	1	candy	1	curtain	4	five	2
bicycle	6	candy-floss	1	curtains	1	flat	1
bike	6	car	71	daddy	14	floor	4
*bin	1	cards	1	danger	2	floss	1
birthday	1	cars	2	date	1	flower	12
*biscuit	1	cart	1	day	3	flowerpot	2
*biscuits	1	case	2	dinner	11	flowers	13
bit	2	cat	16	dinosaur	1	food	23
bits	1	cauliflower	2	dish	1	football	15
blanket	1	chair	14	dog	74	fork	2
blind	1	chairs	1	doll	8	forks	3
board	2	cheese	2	dolls	1	frame	1
*bonnet	2	chicken	7	dolly	3	front	2
book	22	children	13	dolly's	1	fruit	4

Word	Count	Word	Count	Word	Count	Word	Count
fruits	2	knife	17	money	26	plates	2
frying-pan	1	knives	1	monsters	1	play	1
game	1	knock	1	mop	2	police	1
games	2	label	1	morning	1	policeman	18
gate	9	ladder	27	mother	13	police-	
girl	35	ladies	1	mouse	9	station	1
girls	2	lady	45	mouth	1	pond	1
glass	1	lady's	2	mud	3	post	2
glove	3	lead	1	mum	1	*postman	1
gloves	3	leaves	1	mummy	32	pot	4
goal	3	leg	1	mushroom	6	potato	2
goal-posts	1	lemon	1	name	1	pots	1
goals	1	lemonade	1	noise	1	pound	1
grapefruit	3	lettuce	1	nose	2	pudding	2
grass	2	list	1	notice	2	*purse	8
ground	9	look	1	number	1	rabbit	1
gymnastics	1	*lorry	1	one	6	rack	1
hair	1	lot	4	onion	4	raincoat	1
hand	3	lots	2	onions	1	rice	2
hands	2	lunch	3	orange	3	ring	1
handstand	6	*mac	1	orders	1	rings	1
hanger	1	macaroni	1	oven	7	road	5
hat	11	machine	11	packet	1	roof	2
head	10	make-up	2	painter	1	room	1
hedge	3	man	100	painting	1	*rounder	1
here	2	man's	1	pan	2	*rounders	5
hill	1	map	6	pans	1	salt	6
hole	8	margarine	1	paper	5	sandwich	8
holiday	10	market	2	papers	1	sandwiches	12
home	5	marmalade	1	park	2	saucepan	6
hospital	5	mask	4	pear	3	saucer	4
house	24	match	1	peas	1	saucers	2
houses	1	matchbox	1	pencil	1	scarf	3
ice	23	matches	7	people	16	scissors	7
ice-cream	3	meat	10	pepper	6	screens	1
jam	5	medal	1	person	2	seat	4
jar	1	men	3	picnic	8	shame	1
jelly	9	mess	4	picture	14	shirt	1
jug	2	mice	1	pictures	1	shocks	1
keeper	2	middle	1	pieces	1	shoe	1
ketchup	1	milk	24	pig	3	shoes	3
kettle	11	milkman	18	*pint	1	shop	5
key	1	minutes	1	place	1	shopping	5
kitchen	10	mirror	5	plant	3	sink	7
kitten	1	mixer	1	plate	8	sister	1

John Bench, Lütgen Mentz and Ian Wilson

Word	Count	Word	Count	Word	Count	Word	Count
skate	3	string	1	tin	1	vegetables	1
skates	6	stuff	1	tomato	4	walk	1
ski	1	sunshine	1	tomatoes	5	wall	3
sky	1	supper	3	tooth	1	washing	10
*sledge	5	sweets	1	top	1	washing-up	1
sleep	2	table	21	towel	5	watch	2
slide	2	table-cloth	1	toy	4	water	11
snow	12	tack	1	toys	2	way	2
soap	1	*tap	3	train	10	wheel	2
son	3	*taps	2	tray	1	window	27
sort	3	tea	7	tree	20	windows	2
spoon	6	*tea-cloth	1	trees	5	winter	1
stamp	1	there	19	*trousers	1	wire	2
stick	15	thing	4	turkey	2	woman	1
sticks	3	things	8	twelve	1	wood	1
stove	1	three	1	two	1	words	1
strain	1	tie	1	uniform	1	work	1
street	4	time	2				

Total words	2344	Total different words	397
Mean words	167·43	Mean different words	28·36

VERBS

Word	Count	Word	Count	Word	Count	Word	Count
allowed	5	called	4	climbing	7	decorating	1
are	23	came	20	come	17	dreaming	1
arguing	2	can	3	coming	15	did	1
bake	1	carried	1	cook	1	do	4
banged	1	carry	1	cooking	6	doing	8
barking	1	carrying	17	could	7	done	1
be	13	cash	1	crack	2	dressing	1
been	3	catch	3	cracked	1	drink	7
break	4	catching	1	crash	5	drinking	8
bring	2	chased	1	crashed	10	drive	2
broke	3	chasing	3	crashing	1	driving	6
broken	1	chop	1	cross	2	drop	13
bump	2	chopping	1	cry	1	dropped	14
bumped	1	clean	2	cut	2	drove	2
burn	1	clear	2	cutting	3	dry	1
buy	2	climb	2	damaged	1	eat	13
call	1	climbed	1	dancing	1	eating	30

Word	Count	Word	Count	Word	Count	Word	Count
fall	14	landed	1	reach	3	take	16
fallen	7	laughing	3	read	4	taking	6
falling	4	lay	2	reading	9	talking	3
falls	1	lean	1	rescue	1	tap	1
feed	2	left	3	ride	2	telling	2
fell	29	licking	4	riding	4	thank	1
finish	5	like	2	run	12	think	13
finished	1	listen	1	running	16	thinking	1
fixing	1	listening	1	rushing	1	thought	1
frightened	1	look	25	said	5	throw	5
gave	1	looked	4	saw	5	throwing	3
get	36	looking	20	say	10	tidy	1
getting	5	looks	1	saying	3	tired	3
give	6	made	2	says	5	told	3
go	39	make	5	scared	1	took	3
goes	1	making	2	see	5	touch	1
going	37	may	1	seen	1	trapped	1
gone	3	mean	5	shaving	4	tripped	2
got	35	mend	1	shopping	4	try	9
had	4	might	21	shout	1	trying	14
hanging	1	mixes	1	shouting	4	use	1
happen	2	mixing	4	show	1	wait	1
happened	4	moving	1	shut	14	waiting	2
happening	1	*mucking	1	sit	4	walk	5
has	15	notice	1	sitting	3	walked	1
have	19	one	1	skating	3	walking	6
having	10	open	9	ski	1	want	7
heard	1	opened	2	sleeping	1	wants	2
help	11	opening	14	slide	2	was	55
helping	4	packing	5	sliding	1	wash	1
hit	4	painting	2	slipped	2	washing	3
hold	12	pay	4	smashed	2	wasted	1
holding	10	paying	1	snowed	1	watch	4
hurt	3	pick	1	snowing	2	watched	1
is	139	picking	2	spilt	1	watching	16
jump	5	play	37	stand	6	wearing	1
jumped	1	playing	44	standing	3	went	14
jumping	2	pretend	1	start	2	were	10
keep	7	pull	8	stay	1	will	3
kick	3	pulls	1	stick	1	winding	2
kicked	4	push	4	stink	1	wiping	1
kicking	1	pushing	2	stop	11	would	1
kill	3	put	28	stopping	3	write	4
knocked	3	putting	5	stuck	2	writing	6
know	12	ran	4	sweep	1		

Total words	1528			Total different words	247		
Mean words	109·14			Mean different words	17·64		

ADJECTIVES

Word	Count	Word	Count	Word	Count	Word	Coun
able	1	dirty	2	much	3	sure	2
all	24	easy	1	naughty	8	that	54
angry	5	electric	1	next	1	thin	3
another	1	fast	1	one	15	this	9
any	1	first	2	open	5	those	2
asleep	6	five	4	other	11	three	3
big	11	four	1	own	1	tidy	2
black	1	funny	6	pink	1	tiny	2
both	2	good	2	pretty	1	twelve	3
broken	1	high	1	ready	3	two	18
careful	2	hot	2	red	2	untidy	1
clean	1	ill	1	round	1	upset	1
cold	2	little	35	sharp	1	wet	1
cross	1	lovely	1	shopping	1	what	1
dangerous	8	many	1	some	12	white	2
dead	2	more	2	stupid	1	yellow	

Total words	304	Total different words	64
Mean words	21·71	Mean different words	4·57

ADVERBS

Word	Count	Word	Count	Word	Count	Word	Cou
about	3	hard	1	on	4	somewhere	
again	3	here	5	only	2	suddenly	
all	2	home	13	out	46	then	
along	9	how	4	over	25	there	3
already	1	in	6	perhaps	4	too	
although	1	indoors	5	probably	2	up	2
as	1	inside	1	quick	1	upside-down	
away	23	just	2	quickly	3	very	
back	12	nearly	4	really	2	when	
before	1	not	18	right	3	where	
down	46	now	9	round	3	why	
fast	1	off	10	so	1		

Total words	391	Total different words	47
Mean words	27·93	Mean different words	3·36

PRONOUNS

Word	Count	Word	Count	Word	Count	Word	Count
all	4	her	28	one	3	they	97
anybody	1	him	39	our	1	this	2
anybody's	1	himself	1	she	38	we	1
anyone	2	his	35	something	11	what	22
anything	2	I	29	that	35	which	1
everybody	2	it	59	their	10	who	6
everything	2	me	1	them	13	you	16
he	84	my	2	these	1	your	5

Total words	554	Total different words	32
Mean words	39·57	Mean different words	2·29

PREPOSITIONS

Word	Count	Word	Count	Word	Count	Word	Count
about	1	down	11	near	1	over	35
across	1	for	18	of	31	past	4
after	8	from	3	off	4	to	92
along	2	in	89	on	59	under	5
at	18	inside	1	onto	1	up	6
before	1	into	5	out	15	with	41
by	2	like	5				

Total words	459	Total different words	26
Mean words	32·79	Mean different words	1·86

CONJUNCTIONS

Word	Count	Word	Count	Word	Count	Word	Count
and	299	but	1	or	11	then	22
because	13	if	2	that	1	while	1

Total words	350	Total different words	8
Mean words	25·00	Mean different words	0·57

CONTRACTIONS

Word	Count	Word	Count	Word	Count	Word	Count
baby's	1	don't	16	it's	21	table's	1
basket's	1	egg's	1	lady's	5	that's	12
boy's	9	farmer's	1	man's	4	there's	11
brother's	1	father's	1	men's	1	they'll	1
bull's	1	girl's	1	o'clock	1	they're	18
can't	9	he's	29	one's	1	they've	6
cat's	1	I'd	1	she'll	1	wasn't	1
didn't	3	I've	1	she's	15	what's	1
dog's	2	it'll	1	shouldn't	1		

Total words	181	Total different words	35
Mean words	12·93	Mean different words	2·50

INTERJECTIONS

Word	Count	Word	Count	Word	Count
dear	1	oh	9	well	1

Total words	11	Total different words	3
Mean words	0·79	Mean different words	0·21

ARTICLES

Word	Count	Word	Count	Word	Count
a	239	an	15	the	791

Total words	1045	Total different words	3
Mean words	74·64	Mean different words	0·21

OTHER

Word	Count	Word	Count	Word	Count	Word	Count
bootsies	1	Cocacola	3	*Marmite	3	*Wellington	2
*Bovril	1	Cola	2	nana	1	woof	2
Christmas	1	*Father		no	5	yes	6
Christmas-		Christmas	1	sticked	2		
tree	1						

Total words	31		Total different words	14	
Mean words	2·21		Mean different words	1·00	

Subject Group L

(7 children; age: 11–13 years;
performance I.Q.: ≤90; hearing loss: 81–95 dB)

NOUNS

Word	Count	Word	Count	Word	Count	Word	Count
aeroplane	3	bill	1	car	25	curtain	2
all	4	blazer	1	cars	1	daddy	13
ambulance	12	board	1	cat	5	daisies	1
apple	7	book	11	cauliflower	1	dinner	3
apples	3	*boot	1	chair	7	dinner-time	2
apron	1	boots	6	cheese	1	dish	1
arm	2	bottles	1	chicken	3	dog	32
baby	4	boy	67	child	1	doll	4
badge	1	boy's	1	children	1	dolly	1
bag	8	boys	2	clock	6	door	1
ball	28	bread	5	clot	1	dragon	1
balls	1	broom	4	cloth	3	drawer	1
banana	7	brother	1	clothes	2	dress	1
basket	9	brothers	1	coat	4	drink	1
basket-ball	1	brush	3	cook	1	egg	3
cat	6	bucket	6	*cooker	3	eggs	5
bath-room	1	bull	4	corner	1	face	3
beef	1	butter	4	cow	3	family	1
bell	1	cabbage	2	crash	1	farmer	2
bicycle	2	cake	7	*cricket	1	father	3
bike	4	calendar	1	cup	3	fence	3

Word	Count	Word	Count	Word	Count	Word	Count
field	2	kettle	7	park	2	sisters	1
fish	6	kitchen	5	pear	1	skates	1
floor	1	knife	8	pears	1	*sledge	2
flower	9	ladder	14	*pence	1	sleep	1
flowers	6	lady	16	people	9	slide	2
food	12	lemon	1	pepper	1	snow	6
football	7	letter	2	picnic	6	soap	1
fork	1	lot	3	picture	4	son	4
friends	2	machine	1	pie	1	sons	1
fruit	4	man	21	pineapple	1	spoon	3
gas	1	map	2	plate	1	stick	5
gate	3	market	1	plates	3	sticks	1
girl	12	marmalade	1	police	2	table	7
girls	2	mask	2	policeman	3	table-cloth	2
glove	1	match	2	post	1	*tap	2
goal	1	matches	4	*postman	3	tea	2
goals	1	mats	1	pot	2	team	1
grass	2	men	1	pudding	1	thing	1
ground	2	milk	10	*purse	2	tie	1
half	1	milkman	5	puzzle	1	time	2
handbag	2	*mince	1	road	1	tin	1
hands	1	minutes	1	room	1	tomatoes	2
handstand	1	mirror	4	rubber	1	towel	4
hat	3	money	8	salt	2	toys	
head	2	mother	11	sandwich	4	train	
hedge	1	mouse	2	sandwiches	1	tree	
hole	3	mummy	16	saucepan	5	trees	
holidays	1	mushroom	1	saucer	1	van	
home	3	mushrooms	2	scarf	1	wall	
horn	1	mustard	1	school	1	wallpaper	
hospital	1	one	2	scissor	1	washing	
house	10	onion	2	scissors	4	water	
husband	1	orange	1	shoe	1	wheelbarrow	
ice	4	oven	2	shoes	2	wife	
ice-cream	1	paint	1	shopping	4	window	
jam	1	paper	1	sink	1	windows	
jelly	6	parcel	1	sister	1	wood	
jug	2						

Total words	843		Total different words	233	
Mean words	120·43		Mean different words	33·29	

VERBS

Word	Count	Word	Count	Word	Count	Word	Count
add	1	eating	2	know	7	skate	1
am	2	fall	20	look	5	sleep	3
are	2	fallen	1	looking	6	sleeping	1
bought	1	fell	8	looks	1	slide	4
break	3	finish	2	make	1	stop	4
breathe	1	finished	6	move	1	surprised	1
buy	1	freeze	1	open	1	sweep	1
called	1	frighten	1	park	1	swings	1
came	1	frightened	2	paying	1	take	7
carries	1	gave	1	pick	1	takes	1
carry	9	get	3	play	26	taking	1
carrying	2	go	10	played	1	talking	2
catch	1	goes	1	playing	9	think	4
change	1	going	8	pull	4	throw	6
chuck	1	gone	1	pushed	1	throwing	1
clean	2	had	2	put	8	throws	1
cleans	1	have	5	puts	1	tired	1
climbs	2	having	2	putting	1	tried	1
come	4	help	9	reach	3	try	2
coming	3	hide	1	read	2	walking	1
cooking	2	hit	2	reading	4	want	1
crash	3	hold	1	ride	2	was	10
crashed	2	holding	1	riding	1	wash	2
crashing	1	holds	1	ring	1	watch	4
cry	2	hurry	1	run	5	went	3
drink	2	hurt	1	running	4	were	1
drinking	6	is	16	say	4	will	10
drive	2	jump	1	says	11	worried	1
drop	9	jumping	1	shave	2	write	1
dropped	3	keep	2	shopping	5	writing	4
eat	10	kicked	1	shout	1		

Total words	398	Total different words	123
Mean words	56·86.	Mean different words	17·57

ADJECTIVES

Word	Count	Word	Count	Word	Count	Word	Count
...raid	1	asleep	2	fifteen	1	funny	2
...l	9	dangerous	5	five	1	hard	1

Word	Count	Word	Count	Word	Count	Word	Coun
like	1	one	1	smaller	2	three	1
lovely	2	quick	1	some	4	twelve	1
more	2	sad	1	sorry	1	two	4
much	1	six	1	such	1	white	1
naughty	1	small	1	that	6		

Total words 55
Mean words 7·86

Total different words 27
Mean different words 3·86

ADVERBS

Word	Count	Word	Count	Word	Count	Word	Coun
away	7	how	1	on	1	there	2
back	1	in	1	out	4	too	1
down	4	just	1	over	11	up	3
fast	1	not	1	perhaps	1	very	11
home	6	off	2	than	1		

Total words 60
Mean words 8·57

Total different words 19
Mean different words 2·71

PRONOUNS

Word	Count	Word	Count	Word	Count	Word	Cou
each	1	his	3	she	7	they	28
everybody	1	I	12	something	2	those	
he	14	it	11	that	4	we	
her	13	me	1	them	1	what	
him	2	my	4	themselves	1	you	

Total words 110
Mean words 15·71

Total different words 20
Mean different words 2·86

PREPOSITIONS

Word	Count	Word	Count	Word	Count	Word	Count
about	1	in	21	out	1	to	15
at	7	of	4	over	4	under	1
down	3	off	1	past	1	with	11
for	4	on	11	round	2		

Total words	87	Total different words	15
Mean words	12·43	Mean different words	2·14

CONJUNCTIONS

Word	Count	Word	Count	Word	Count	Word	Count
and	68	because	3	or	2	then	1

Total words	74	Total different words	4
Mean words	10·57	Mean different words	0·57

CONTRACTIONS

Word	Count	Word	Count	Word	Count	Word	Count
brother's	1	cat's	1	he's	2	man's	1
can't	3	cow's	1	I'm	1	that's	1
car's	1	don't	8	it's	1	they're	3

Total words	24	Total different words	12
Mean words	3·43	Mean different words	1·71

INTERJECTIONS

Word	Count
oh	1

Total words	1	Total different words	1
Mean words	0·14	Mean different words	0·14

ARTICLES

Word	Count	Word	Count	Word	Count
a	40	an	2	the	289

Total words	331		Total different words	3
Mean words	47·29		Mean different words	0·43

OTHER

Word	Count	Word	Count	Word	Count	Word	Count
*Bovril	1	Cola	4	monies	1	skaties	1
Cocacola	2	*Marmite	1	no	5	yes	4

Total words	19		Total different words	8
Mean words	2·71		Mean different words	1·14

Subject Group M

(10 children; age: 11–13 years;
performance I.Q.: 90–110; hearing loss 40–60 dB)

NOUNS

Word	Count	Word	Count	Word	Count	Word	Count
accident	2	barrel	2	book	10	bush	
all	10	baseball	3	*boot	9	butter	
ambulance	14	basket	16	boots	3	cabbages	
apple	1	bat	5	bottle	2	cake	
apples	6	beard	1	bottles	1	calendar	
arms	2	bed	1	boy	69	car	4
atlas	1	bench	2	boys	19	cart	
baby	2	bicycle	2	brakes	1	cartoon	
back	3	bike	3	bread	3	cat	
bag	8	bill	2	broom	2	cauliflowers	
ball	36	bit	5	brother	11	chair	
banana	2	blame	1	bucket	4	cheese	
bananas	3	*bonnet	1	bull	18	chicken	

Word	Count	Word	Count	Word	Count	Word	Count
child	2	fireman	1	jelly	2	onions	1
children	3	fish	3	*jersey	1	oranges	1
cleaner	1	fishes	1	jug	1	oven	2
clock	4	floor	2	kettle	3	owner	1
cloth	4	flower	2	kitchen	4	pan	1
clothes	3	flowerpot	4	kitten	1	paper	1
coat	4	flowers	3	knife	4	papers	1
*cooker	1	food	9	knives	1	park	2
copper	1	foot	1	ladder	19	part	1
corn	1	football	6	lady	30	party	1
couple	1	footballers	2	lady's	1	*pavement	1
course	1	forks	2	lettuce	1	piece	1
*cricket	4	fridge	1	lot	2	pennies	1
cups	1	friend	3	lots	1	people	14
curry	1	fright	2	lunch	4	pepper	2
curtain	2	front	1	make-up	1	picnic	11
dad	4	fruit	1	man	44	picture	4
daddy	2	fruits	2	man's	1	pictures	1
damage	1	gas	1	map	3	pie	1
dinner	5	gate	3	market	2	piece	2
direction	1	girl	15	marmalade	1	*pints	1
dish	3	girls	2	mask	4	pitch	1
dog	36	gloves	2	matches	2	place	1
doll	1	goal	2	material	1	plant	2
door	8	goal-posts	1	mats	1	plates	3
doors	1	grass	1	meat	1	police	1
dragon	1	*greengrocer	2	medals	1	policeman	7
drain	4	ground	3	men	6	pond	3
drawer	1	hand	1	mess	3	post	2
dress	2	hands	1	middle	2	posts	1
drier	2	handstand	6	milk	9	puppy	2
drink	5	hat	3	milkman	7	*purse	3
drinks	2	head	6	*mincemeat	2	rice	1
driver	3	help	1	mirror	1	road	18
egg	2	hill	1	mixer	2	roast	1
eggs	7	hold	3	money	6	*rounders	1
elbow	1	hole	7	mop	2	salt	1
eye	2	hood	1	mother	14	sandwich	4
face	2	hospital	1	mum	6	sandwiches	4
family	6	house	4	mushrooms	1	saucepan	2
farmer	4	houses	3	noise	1	saucepans	2
father	13	hurry	1	note	1	scarf	3
fence	8	husband	1	notice	4	scissors	1
field	10	ice	21	number	3	seat	1
fire	1	jar	1	one	6	shadows	1

Word	Count	Word	Count	Word	Count	Word	Count
shelf	1	son	2	*tap	1	van	1
shirt	1	sort	1	tea	1	voice	1
shoes	1	spin	1	*tea-cloth	1	walk	1
shopping	5	spoon	1	there	7	way	1
shoulder	1	stall	1	things	4	week-end	1
sign	1	stick	5	toboggan	1	well	1
signpost	2	story	2	tomato	1	wheelbarrow	2
sink	2	stove	1	train	3	wife	3
skates	1	street	5	tree	5	window	8
*sledge	7	string	1	trees	3	windows	1
sleep	1	stuff	3	trifle	1	woman	2
sleigh	1	sweets	1	truck	1	women	1
slots	1	table	11	tulip	1	words	2
snow	4	table-cloth	2	two	1		

	Total words	1114		Total different words	287
	Mean words	111·40		Mean different words	28·70

VERBS

Word	Count	Word	Count	Word	Count	Word	Count
answered	1	carrying	11	do	3	frightened	1
are	10	catch	2	doing	9	gave	1
asking	1	chasing	10	drink	2	get	28
bang	1	cleaning	4	drinking	7	gets	2
barking	1	clearing	2	drive	2	give	1
bashed	2	climb	4	drives	2	giving	1
be	11	climbing	6	driving	3	go	10
been	9	come	6	drop	2	goes	2
being	1	comes	1	dropped	11	going	15
bouncing	2	coming	8	dropping	1	gone	1
broke	1	cooking	2	drove	2	got	22
bumped	2	could	9	eat	6	grab	
burst	1	crack	1	eating	11	had	11
buying	1	cracked	1	fall	4	happened	
call	1	crash	1	fallen	4	happening	
calling	2	crashing	1	falling	3	has	8
calls	1	crying	1	falls	1	have	
came	19	cut	2	fell	18	having	1
can	7	cutting	2	felt	1	help	
carries	1	cycling	1	fetch	1	helping	
carry	5	dashing	1	finished	2	hit	

Word	Count	Word	Count	Word	Count	Word	Count
hold	2	opened	3	selling	1	teaching	1
holding	7	opening	1	setting	1	telling	3
hurried	1	packing	3	shave	1	tells	1
hurt	1	pay	2	shaving	3	think	7
injured	2	paying	2	shocked	2	thought	1
is	56	pick	1	should	3	threw	1
jump	2	playing	32	shout	2	tired	2
keep	1	plunging	2	shouted	1	told	1
keeping	1	pull	3	shouting	2	tried	1
kick	1	put	10	showing	1	tries	3
kicked	3	putting	6	shutting	2	tripped	2
kicking	1	ran	2	signalling	1	try	2
knock	1	reach	2	sit	2	trying	13
knocked	4	reaching	1	sitting	2	tumbling	1
know	4	read	3	skating	7	visiting	1
laid	1	reading	7	ski	1	waiting	1
land	1	realize	1	skid	1	walk	2
lays	1	rescue	3	skidding	1	walked	1
left	2	riding	5	sliding	2	walking	9
licking	1	rolled	1	slipped	2	wanted	2
listening	2	rounding	1	slow	1	warning	1
look	2	roving	1	smack	1	was	58
looked	1	running	6	smashed	1	watch	1
looking	10	said	2	snowing	1	watching	8
looks	2	saw	1	standing	4	waving	4
lost	1	saying	2	staring	2	wearing	1
make	2	says	1	start	3	went	15
making	1	screaming	1	starting	3	were	7
mean	1	see	8	stop	9	wheeling	1
might	3	seeing	1	stopping	1	worried	1
moving	1	seem	2	suppose	2	would	1
must	3	seems	4	take	6	wrap	1
notice	1	seen	1	taking	1	writing	1
open	3	sees	1	talking	2	zooming	1

Total words	869	Total different words	220
Mean words	86·90	Mean different words	22·00

ADJECTIVES

Word	Count	Word	Count	Word	Count	Word	Count
all	13	eldest	1	lucky	1	small	1
angry	3	electric	1	mad	1	some	12
another	3	empty	1	most	1	sure	1
any	2	fast	3	naughty	2	that	26
asleep	2	first	5	no	1	these	1
back	1	five	1	one	25	thin	7
big	13	foolish	1	open	8	this	13
broken	2	four	6	other	7	those	5
busy	1	full	3	own	2	three	1
careless	3	funny	1	red	4	two	23
clear	1	little	29	sensible	1	warm	1
cold	1	loud	1	silly	2	youngest	3

Total words	247	Total different words	48
Mean words	24·70	Mean different words	4·80

ADVERBS

Word	Count	Word	Count	Word	Count	Word	Cour
about	1	first	3	off	6	so	2
accidentally	1	here	1	on	6	straight	2
across	1	home	6	only	1	suddenly	5
all	2	how	1	otherwise	1	sure	2
along	9	in	8	out	27	then	2
also	2	instead	1	outside	1	there	31
around	2	just	9	over	13	too	1
as	6	maybe	2	probably	4	up	11
away	7	more	1	quickly	4	very	6
back	6	nearly	1	rather	1	well	6
before	2	not	5	really	1	when	7
down	18	now	1	right	1	where	4
enough	4						

Total words	245	Total different words	49
Mean words	24·50	Mean different words	4·90

PRONOUNS

Word	Count	Word	Count	Word	Count	Word	Count
everybody	1	I	13	she	11	this	1
everyone	1	it	31	somebody	1	those	1
everything	3	me	2	something	1	what	9
he	59	my	1	that	18	which	1
her	23	nobody	1	their	17	who	1
him	35	no-one	1	them	20	you	3
his	75	nothing	1	they	36		

	Total words	367		Total different words	27		
	Mean words	36·70		Mean different words	2·70		

PREPOSITIONS

Word	Count	Word	Count	Word	Count	Word	Count
about	2	behind	3	into	19	out	9
across	3	by	3	like	1	over	18
after	10	down	9	near	1	through	4
along	2	except	1	of	46	to	94
around	1	for	17	off	3	under	3
at	14	from	4	on	47	up	4
before	2	in	36	onto	1	with	50

	Total words	407		Total different words	28		
	Mean words	40·70		Mean different words	2·80		

CONJUNCTIONS

Word	Count	Word	Count	Word	Count	Word	Count
and	301	but	3	so	9	though	1
because	18	if	4	that	5	while	3
before	2	or	4	then	4		

	Total words	354		Total different words	11		
	Mean words	35·40		Mean different words	1·10		

CONTRACTIONS

Word	Count	Word	Count	Word	Count	Word	Count
*bonnet's	1	flowerpot's	1	it's	11	they'd	1
boy's	3	girl's	1	lady's	3	they're	16
car's	1	he'd	1	man's	3	they've	5
cat's	1	he's	49	money's	1	tree's	1
couldn't	3	here's	1	mum's	1	wasn't	2
didn't	6	I'm	1	player's	1	what's	3
dog's	1	I've	1	she's	9	woman's	1
don't	2	isn't	1	that's	4	you'll	1
farmer's	2	it'll	1	there's	20		

Total words	160	Total different words	35
Mean words	16·00	Mean different words	3·50

INTERJECTIONS

Word	Count	Word	Count	Word	Count
oh	2	well	13	hello	1

Total words	16	Total different words	3
Mean words	1·60	Mean different words	0·30

ARTICLES

Word	Count	Word	Count	Word	Count
a	191	an	9	the	432

Total words	632	Total different words	3
Mean words	63·20	Mean different words	0·30

OTHER

Word	Count	Word	Count	Word	Count	Word	Cou
Christmas	2	Cocacola	2	*Marmite	1	*Wellington	
Christmas-tree	1	'cos	1	no	10	yes	
		disco	1	'tato	1		

Total words	22	Total different words	10
Mean words	2·20	Mean different words	1·00

Subject Group N

(14 Children; age: 11–13 years;
performance I.Q.: 90–110; hearing loss: 61–80 dB)

NOUNS

Word	Count	Word	Count	Word	Count	Word	Count
accident	10	bottles	1	clothes	8	elbow	3
air	1	bowl	1	coat	14	face	9
all	6	boy	149	*cooker	2	faces	1
ambulance	25	boy's	2	corner	2	family	10
apple	10	boys	28	counter	1	farm	1
apples	8	bracelet	1	country	1	farmer	11
apron	1	bracelets	1	cow	4	father	41
area	1	bread	8	crash	1	fence	20
baby	1	broom	4	cream	1	field	9
back	6	brother	1	*cricket	7	fish	10
badge	1	brothers	1	crowd	1	fishes	1
badges	1	brush	7	cup	4	floor	10
bag	11	bucket	8	cupboard	2	flower	6
ball	64	bull	26	cups	2	flowerpot	6
balls	2	bush	3	curtain	3	flowers	7
banana	5	bushes	3	dad	4	food	13
bananas	6	butter	9	date	2	foot	1
bang	1	cabbage	5	daughter	1	football	22
bank	1	cabbages	2	day	4	footballers	1
baseball	2	cake	11	death	1	*footpath	1
basket	27	cakes	3	dinner	5	forest	2
bat	10	calendar	3	dog	79	fork	2
beard	1	car	70	dogs	1	forks	1
bed	2	cars	1	doll	3	friends	1
bell	1	cart	7	door	14	fright	1
bench	3	cartoon	1	doors	1	front	3
bicycle	4	case	3	dragon	2	fruit	9
bike	5	cat	9	drain	3	fruits	1
bill	2	chair	11	drawer	2	frying-pan	1
bin	1	chairs	2	drawers	1	game	2
biscuits	3	cheese	1	dress	3	garage	1
bit	1	cherries	1	drink	6	gate	9
board	3	chicken	3	drinks	3	girl	28
book	15	children	9	driver	1	girl's	1
boot	18	cleaner	1	egg	5	girls	9
boots	11	clock	8	eggs	10	glove	2
bottle	3	cloth	11	egg-shell	1	gloves	3

Word	Count	Word	Count	Word	Count	Word	Count
goal	15	lettuce	1	oranges	2	salt	3
goal-post	1	lip	1	oven	3	sandwich	9
goal-posts	1	loads	1	ovens	1	sandwiches	13
grandad	1	*lorry	4	pail	1	saucepan	3
grass	4	lot	1	paint	1	saucepans	2
grid	1	luggage	2	pair	2	saucers	2
grocer	1	lunch	4	paper	1	scarf	7
ground	1	machine	5	park	4	scissors	7
gymnastics	1	make	1	part	1	seat	1
hand	3	man	106	path	4	seven	2
hands	2	man's	1	*pavement	1	sewage	1
handstand	7	map	4	pear	1	sewing	1
handstands	1	market	3	people	13	shapes	1
hat	15	marmalade	3	pepper	3	shave	3
head	7	mask	6	picnic	14	shirt	3
headache	1	match	2	picture	9	shirts	1
hedge	2	matches	6	pictures	3	shoes	7
help	2	material	1	pipes	2	shopkeeper	1
hill	1	meat	5	place	2	shopping	5
hold	1	medal	1	plant	2	shorts	1
hole	3	men	10	plants	1	shoulder	2
holes	1	mice	1	plate	5	side	
home	2	middle	1	plates	2	sign	
hospital	10	milk	15	play	2	sink	
house	17	milkman	9	playtime	1	skates	
houses	2	*mince	1	pocket	2	ski	
husband	2	mirror	4	police	2	*sledge	1
husband's	1	mixer	1	policeman	12	slide	
ice	35	money	21	pond	5	slope	
jam	1	mother	47	post	5	snow	
jelly	7	mouse	4	posts	4	soap	
*jersey	1	mum	4	pot	5	socks	
jug	1	mummy	3	potato	1	son	
*jumper	2	mushroom	1	pots	1	sort	
keeper	1	mushrooms	1	prison	1	spoon	
kettle	6	name	7	*purse	13	squash	
kitchen	6	noise	1	rain	1	stall	
knife	9	nose	1	rat	1	step	
knives	1	note	1	rent	2	stick	2
ladder	18	notice	11	rescue	2	sticks	
ladies	3	number	6	rice	1	store	
lady	49	office	2	ring	1	story	
leg	1	one	5	road	6	street	
lemon	3	onion	2	roof	2	stuff	
letter	1	orange	1	*rounders	4	suit	

Word	Count	Word	Count	Word	Count	Word	Count
table	24	top	4	*trousers	5	water	16
table-cloth	1	towel	4	turban	2	way	2
tables	3	towels	1	turkey	1	week	1
tap	3	toy	1	two	1	whistle	1
taps	1	toys	2	van	1	window	27
tea	5	train	8	vase	1	windows	4
there	8	tray	1	vegetable	1	winter	1
thing	2	tree	8	village	1	wire	3
things	5	trees	12	wall	1	woman	3
time	1	*trifle	1	warning	2	wood	2
tomato	1	trolley	2	washing	4	works	1
tomatoes	3						

Total words	2224	Total different words	373
Mean words	158·86	Mean different words	26·64

VERBS

Word	Count	Word	Count	Word	Count	Word	Count
add	1	came	29	cool	2	drink	2
answer	1	can	6	cooking	1	drinking	8
are	52	carry	2	cover	1	drive	1
back	1	carrying	23	covered	2	driving	4
bang	2	catch	10	crash	7	drop	7
barbed	1	catching	1	crashed	7	dropped	27
bark	1	changed	1	crashes	1	dropping	2
barking	1	charging	1	crashing	5	eat	11
be	4	chase	1	crawl	1	eating	29
been	5	chased	2	creep	1	eats	2
belong	1	chasing	10	crossing	2	enjoyed	1
bending	1	checked	1	crushed	1	excited	1
blowing	1	clean	2	cry	1	fall	32
break	1	cleaning	4	crying	2	fallen	8
breaking	2	clearing	1	cut	3	falling	1
bringing	2	climb	3	cutting	2	falls	2
broken	1	climbed	2	decided	1	fell	28
brought	1	climbing	14	do	7	fetch	4
bumped	1	closed	1	doing	7	fetching	2
buy	1	coloured	1	done	1	finish	4
call	2	come	10	drag	1	finished	2
called	7	comes	6	dress	1	fit	1
calling	1	coming	22	dressed	1	fixing	1

Word	Count	Word	Count	Word	Count	Word	Coun
flying	2	knock	3	pulled	1	smashed	3
freeze	1	knocked	9	pulling	1	smile	1
freezing	2	knocks	3	put	28	smiling	1
frightened	9	know	22	puts	1	snowing	3
gave	1	laid	1	putting	9	squashed	2
get	27	leave	2	reach	2	staring	1
gets	2	left	2	reaching	2	start	1
getting	5	licked	1	read	5	stop	15
give	2	licking	1	reading	8	stopped	1
gives	1	lie	1	remember	6	stuck	3
giving	1	listen	1	rescue	2	suppose	1
go	35	listening	1	riding	7	take	15
goes	4	look	13	ring	1	taking	4
going	28	looked	3	run	7	talk	1
gone	5	looking	42	running	18	talking	5
got	37	looks	9	said	15	tearing	1
grab	1	loosing	1	save	1	tell	1
had	6	lying	1	saw	10	telling	5
happen	1	made	1	say	3	think	15
happened	6	make	5	saying	4	throwing	1
happening	1	making	2	says	20	throws	
has	19	mending	1	scared	3	ticking	
have	27	might	11	screaming	2	tired	
having	9	mind	1	see	16	told	
heard	2	miss	1	set	1	took	
help	7	missed	1	setting	1	tossed	
helping	6	must	4	shave	1	tried	
hit	6	open	6	shaving	7	tripped	
hold	2	opened	2	shocked	3	try	
holding	16	opening	2	should	1	trying	1
holds	1	pack	1	shout	1	turn	
hurry	3	packing	3	shouting	4	turned	
hurt	7	paid	1	showing	1	used	
including	1	painting	1	shut	2	waiting	
injured	1	pay	2	signing	1	walk	
is	194	paying	2	sit	2	walking	1
jump	2	phoned	1	sitting	3	want	
jumped	1	picked	1	skated	1	wanted	
jumping	1	play	19	skating	6	wants	
keep	3	played	2	sleep	1	was	9
kept	1	playing	54	sliding	3	wash	
kick	1	please	1	slipped	1	washing	
kicked	11	pointing	1	slips	1	watch	
kicking	1	pour	1	smack	2	watching	
kill	2	pull	16	smash	2	waving	

Word	Count	Word	Count	Word	Count	Word	Count
went	17	winding	1	write	1	wrote	2
were	15	wipe	1	writing	4	yelling	1
will	12	wondering	1				

Total words	1779	Total different words	282
Mean words	127·07	Mean different words	20·14

ADJECTIVES

Word	Count	Word	Count	Word	Count	Word	Count
afraid	1	fearful	1	nice	1	smelly	1
all	40	fierce	1	old	1	soft	1
angry	3	five	5	older	2	some	29
another	4	flat	1	one	19	sorry	1
any	4	full	2	open	12	stiff	1
asleep	5	funny	1	ordinary	1	that	23
back	1	good	1	other	15	these	1
bad	1	green	1	own	1	thin	5
big	9	happy	2	past	1	this	8
blind	1	hot	1	poor	2	three	3
blue	5	icy	1	ready	5	twelve	3
clever	2	ill	1	red	9	two	37
cold	8	injured	2	same	1	upset	1
cross	1	little	42	second	1	white	3
dangerous	9	long	3	sharp	2	whole	1
dirty	4	mad	2	short	1	wide	1
each	2	messy	1	silly	1	woolly	1
elder	1	much	1	sleepy	1	younger	2
very	3	muddy	1				

Total words	372	Total different words	74
Mean words	26·57	Mean different words	5·29

ADVERBS

Word	Count	Word	Count	Word	Count	Word	Count
about	1	actually	3	along	11	as	8
accidentally	1	again	1	also	1	away	31
cross	1	all	4	around	1	back	5

Word	Count	Word	Count	Word	Count	Word	Coun
badly	1	like	1	over	47	suddenly	1
down	22	maybe	3	perhaps	1	then	1
else	1	more	1	probably	3	there	56
everywhere	1	nearer	1	quick	1	together	1
fast	5	nearly	3	quickly	6	too	6
first	1	no	2	really	2	up	21
here	7	not	2	right	2	upside-down	1
home	25	now	6	round	2	very	27
how	3	off	14	so	39	well	9
in	4	on	4	somewhere	1	when	7
indoors	2	out	43	still	3	where	8
inside	1	outside	1	straight	1	why	3
just	11						

Total words	482	Total different words	61
Mean words	34·43	Mean different words	4·36

PRONOUNS

Word	Count	Word	Count	Word	Count	Word	Cou
all	1	I	34	somebody	4	this	
everyone	2	it	58	someone	6	those	
everything	2	its	1	something	13	we	
he	106	my	1	that	34	what	18
her	48	nothing	1	their	18	which	
him	42	one	5	them	7	who	
himself	2	other	2	these	2	you	2.
his	51	she	38	they	84		

Total words	620	Total different words	31
Mean words	44·29	Mean different words	2·21

PREPOSITIONS

Word	Count	Word	Count	Word	Count	Word	Co
about	3	along	3	beside	1	from	
across	1	at	21	by	1	in	7
after	10	before	1	down	11	into	3
against	1	behind	1	for	30	like	

Word	Count	Word	Count	Word	Count	Word	Count
near	1	onto	1	through	4	up	5
of	51	out	19	to	160	with	67
off	3	over	37	under	7	without	5
on	55	past	2				

Total words	614	Total different words	30
Mean words	43·86	Mean different words	2·14

CONJUNCTIONS

Word	Count	Word	Count	Word	Count	Word	Count
and	433	but	3	so	6	then	7
as	2	if	2	that	7	though	1
because	37	or	6				

Total words	504	Total different words	10
Mean words	36·00	Mean different words	0·71

CONTRACTIONS

Word	Count	Word	Count	Word	Count	Word	Count
ball's	2	farmer's	2	it's	17	there's	10
boy's	9	food's	1	lady's	5	they'll	2
bull's	3	fruit's	1	man's	8	they're	20
can't	5	girl's	4	mummy's	1	they've	19
cat's	1	haven't	1	mustn't	1	wasn't	3
didn't	13	he'll	3	policeman's	1	what's	2
dog's	2	he's	19	she's	8	where's	1
doggie's	1	I'm	1	shouldn't	1	who's	2
don't	11	I've	1	that's	9		

Total words	190	Total different words	35
Mean words	13·57	Mean different words	2·50

INTERJECTIONS

Word	Count	Word	Count	Word	Count	Word	Count
dear	1	hullo	1	oh	14	well	3

Total words	19		Total different words	4	
Mean words	1·36		Mean different words	0·29	

ARTICLES

Word	Count	Word	Count	Word	Count
a	221	an	12	the	952

Total words	1185		Total different words	3	
Mean words	84·64		Mean different words	0·21	

OTHER

Word	Count	Word	Count	Word	Count	Word	Count
bump	1	Coke	2	Indian	1	'tatoes	1
Christmas	1	Cokes	1	*Marmite	4	they's	1
Christmas-tree	1	Cola	1	no	13	tooked	1
Cocacola	5	'cos	3	O.K.	3	woof	1
cocoa	1	crash	2	pavestones	1	yes	12
		dangered	1				

Total words	57		Total different words	21	
Mean words	4·07		Mean different words	1·50	

Subject Group O

(9 children; age: 11–13 years;
performance I.Q.: 90–110; hearing loss: 81–95 dB)

NOUNS

Word	Count	Word	Count	Word	Count	Word	Count
accident	1	bread	9	cup	3	flu	1
all	4	brother	1	cups	1	food	33
ambulance	20	brush	10	curtain	4	football	12
apple	9	bucket	7	daddy	12	fork	2
apples	5	bull	20	date	1	friend	1
argument	1	bump	1	day	1	fruit	3
baby	5	bushes	1	dinner	1	fun	1
back	3	butter	4	dish	1	game	1
bag	22	cabbage	5	dishes	1	games	2
ball	47	cabbages	1	dog	47	gate	7
banana	2	cake	5	doggie	4	girl	23
bananas	5	calendar	1	doll	2	girls	7
bar	1	cap	1	doll's	1	glass	2
bargain	1	car	42	door	8	glove	1
barrel	5	cart	1	doors	1	gloves	4
*barrow	2	case	1	dragon	1	goal	5
baseball	1	cat	11	drain	1	government	1
basket	9	chair	6	drawer	3	grass	1
bat	5	chairs	2	drawers	1	ground	4
beard	1	cheese	2	drink	6	hair	1
beer	1	chicken	2	egg	5	hand	1
bicycle	6	children	5	eggs	5	handbag	1
bike	2	chin	1	face	3	handstand	2
bill	1	cleaner	1	family	5	handstands	3
bit	1	clock	5	farm	1	hat	6
*blancmange	1	cloth	2	farmer	11	head	8
board	2	clothes	6	farmer's	1	hedges	1
book	16	cloud	1	farmhouse	1	helicopter	1
*boot	7	clouds	1	father	14	hell	1
boots	6	clown	3	fence	9	hole	3
bottle	2	coat	4	field	15	holes	1
bottles	3	coins	1	fir	2	holiday	2
bowl	3	*cooker	3	fish	12	home	11
boy	127	cooking	1	floor	7	hospital	1
boy's	1	corner	3	flour	1	house	11
boys	13	cow	2	flower	10	houses	2
branch	1	*cricket	3	flowers	6	housewife	1

Word	Count	Word	Count	Word	Count	Word	Count
husband	5	mint	1	potatoes	1	story	2
ice	23	mirror	1	pots	1	street	1
jam	2	mixer	6	pudding	1	stuff	4
jar	3	money	12	*purse	4	suit	1
jelly	2	monster	2	rain	2	sun	1
journey	1	mother	20	raincoat	4	sweet	1
keeper	1	mouse	5	road	9	sweets	1
kettle	4	mouth	1	rope	1	table	20
kitchen	8	mug	1	*rounder	1	table-cloth	1
knife	7	mummy	28	*rounders	4	*tap	3
lad	1	mushroom	1	salad	1	*taps	1
ladder	15	mushrooms	1	salt	1	tea	3
lady	33	nail	1	sandwich	12	there	1
lady's	1	nose	2	sandwiches	3	things	5
lamps	1	noses	1	saucepan	2	time	1
leaf	2	notice	1	scar	1	tomatoes	1
leg	1	number	1	scarf	2	towel	8
lettuce	2	one	1	scissors	3	town	1
life	1	onion	1	seven	1	toy	3
light	1	onions	1	shadow	1	toys	2
*lorry	1	orange	2	shelf	2	train	3
lot	3	oranges	1	shell	1	tree	10
lunch	1	oven	2	shoes	3	trees	6
machine	5	pan	2	shop	4	*trifle	1
man	68	pans	2	shops	1	truck	1
man's	3	park	2	shorts	1	two	1
map	2	*pavement	2	side	2	utensils	1
market	1	people	7	sign	5	vase	1
marmalade	2	pepper	1	sink	6	walk	1
mask	2	picnic	3	sister	2	washing	6
match	2	picture	4	sisters	1	water	3
matches	2	pictures	2	skate	1	weed	1
mats	1	piece	1	skates	1	wheel	1
meal	1	plant	1	*sledge	6	wheelbarrow	2
meat	5	plate	6	slide	1	wheels	1
men	1	plates	3	snow	4	whiskers	1
mess	1	play	1	son	13	window	12
mice	1	police	1	sort	3	windows	2
middle	1	policeman	5	spoon	2	wine	1
milk	13	post	3	stick	9	wire	2
milkman	14	*postman	1	sticks	1	woman	4
miller	1	pot	2	stop	1	wood	1
*mincer	2						

Total words	1527	Total different words	317
Mean words	169·67	Mean different words	35·22

VERBS

Word	Count	Word	Count	Word	Count	Word	Count
are	15	dressing	1	is	83	pretending	1
back	1	drink	7	jump	4	pull	9
be	14	drinking	3	jumped	2	pulled	1
been	4	drive	2	jumping	1	push	1
being	1	driving	2	keep	3	put	10
break	3	drop	2	kick	3	putting	1
bring	1	dropped	7	kicked	2	ran	3
broke	1	drown	1	kill	1	reach	1
broken	3	eat	17	knock	3	read	3
bump	2	eating	8	knocked	2	reading	5
bumped	1	fall	26	knocking	1	realizing	1
bumping	1	fallen	6	know	5	rescue	3
call	2	falling	1	knowing	1	returned	2
called	3	fell	19	knows	1	ride	2
came	12	finish	1	laid	1	riding	1
carried	1	finished	2	land	1	rode	1
carry	8	found	1	left	1	run	7
carrying	10	frighten	1	lick	1	running	7
catch	4	frightened	1	licking	3	said	1
charging	1	gave	1	look	22	sat	1
chase	1	get	11	looked	1	save	2
chased	1	gets	1	looking	5	saw	6
chasing	3	getting	2	looks	2	say	4
chuck	1	give	2	lying	1	saying	4
clean	1	giving	1	made	2	says	5
cleaning	1	go	10	make	1	scratching	1
climb	2	goes	2	makes	2	screaming	1
climbing	1	going	19	making	3	see	9
come	11	gone	2	messing	1	seen	1
comes	2	got	25	might	8	sees	1
coming	11	grab	2	move	1	shave	5
cooking	2	had	4	open	3	shaving	3
could	11	happened	2	opened	1	shops	1
crash	5	has	21	packed	2	should	1
crashed	4	have	13	packing	2	shouting	3
crawl	1	having	4	painting	2	shut	1
crawling	1	help	9	pay	5	signing	1
cry	2	hit	4	paying	1	sitting	3
crying	1	hits	1	play	22	skating	2
cut	1	hold	8	played	1	sleep	1
depends	1	holding	6	playing	28	sleeping	1
do	1	hurry	1	pointing	1	slide	3
doing	2	hurt	1	pretend	1	slides	1

Word	Count	Word	Count	Word	Count	Word	Count
smashed	1	telling	2	turn	1	watch	2
smell	2	think	12	waiting	1	watching	11
spread	1	threw	1	walk	5	wear	1
standing	2	throw	9	walked	2	wearing	3
steering	1	throws	1	walking	5	wears	1
stop	12	tired	2	walks	1	went	8
stops	1	told	1	want	1	were	12
suppose	1	took	1	wanting	1	wheeling	1
take	3	tried	2	wants	2	will	1
taking	1	tripped	1	was	44	worried	4
talked	1	try	13	wash	1	write	3
talking	3	trying	5	washing	4	writing	2

Total words	969	Total different words	220
Mean words	107·67	Mean different words	24·44

ADJECTIVES

Word	Count	Word	Count	Word	Count	Word	Count
all	6	five	4	one	18	thin	8
angry	7	four	1	open	6	third	1
another	6	friendly	1	orange	1	this	6
any	1	full	3	other	5	those	3
asleep	2	good	1	ready	2	three	1
big	7	happy	1	red	7	twelve	2
bloody	1	heavy	1	round	1	two	15
both	1	high	1	safe	1	warm	1
careful	1	hot	1	second	1	white	1
cold	3	little	17	silly	2	worth	1
eldest	2	lovely	1	soft	2	yellow	1
electric	1	muddy	1	some	27	younger	3
few	1	old	1	that	15	youngest	2
fierce	2	oldest	1	thick	2		

Total words	211	Total different words	55
Mean words	23·44	Mean different words	6·11

ADVERBS

Word	Count	Word	Count	Word	Count	Word	Count
about	1	easily	1	now	5	round	1
accidentally	1	first	1	off	9	safely	1
across	2	flat	1	on	2	so	1
again	2	here	1	out	15	straight	1
all	3	high	1	over	18	there	37
along	3	home	6	perhaps	1	too	3
around	1	how	2	probably	13	up	8
as	6	in	7	quickly	2	upside-down	2
away	8	just	1	quite	2	very	10
back	6	maybe	2	rather	1	well	6
before	1	never	1	really	4	when	2
down	14	not	5	right	2	where	2

Total words	225	Total different words	48
Mean words	25·00	Mean different words	5·33

PRONOUNS

Word	Count	Word	Count	Word	Count	Word	Count
anything	1	himself	4	something	5	this	3
everybody	3	his	20	that	6	what	4
everything	5	I	19	their	5	who	4
he	33	it	33	them	5	you	4
her	35	she	12	they	32	we	2
him	32						

Total words	267	Total different words	21
Mean words	29·67	Mean different words	2·33

PREPOSITIONS

Word	Count	Word	Count	Word	Count	Word	Count
about	2	by	9	inside	2	of	35
across	1	down	8	into	10	off	4
after	6	for	14	like	4	on	44
at	11	from	3	near	2	onto	1
beside	1	in	34	next	2	out	9

Word	Count	Word	Count	Word	Count	Word	Count
outside	1	round	5	under	5	with	48
over	16	through	4	underneath	1	without	2
past	2	to	78	up	1		

Total words	365	Total different words	31
Mean words	40·56	Mean different words	3·44

CONJUNCTIONS

Word	Count	Word	Count	Word	Count	Word	Count
and	189	but	8	so	2	though	2
as	2	if	5	that	4	while	2
because	12	or	4				

Total words	230	Total different words	10
Mean words	25·56	Mean different words	1·11

CONTRACTIONS

Word	Count	Word	Count	Word	Count	Word	Count
boy's	3	farmer's	1	mustn't	1	they're	8
couldn't	1	he'll	2	people's	1	they've	4
didn't	1	he's	12	she's	11	who's	3
doesn't	1	husband's	1	shouldn't	1	wouldn't	1
dog's	1	I'll	1	that's	5	you'll	1
don't	8	it's	5	there's	13		

Total words	86	Total different words	23
Mean words	9·56	Mean different words	2·56

INTERJECTIONS

Word	Count	Word	Count	Word	Count	Word	Count
hell	1	hello	1	oh	1	well	1

Total words	4	Total different words	4
Mean words	0·44	Mean different words	0·44

ARTICLES

Word	Count	Word	Count	Word	Count
a	179	an	11	the	533

Total words	723	Total different words	3
Mean words	80·33	Mean different words	0·33

OTHER

Word	Count	Word	Count	Word	Count	Word	Count
bang	2	gymnick	1	*sweetie	1	*Wellington	2
Cocacola	3	Indian	3	Tom	1	woof	2
Coke	3	*Marmite	3	*wellies	1	yes	2
Fred	2	no	1				

Total words	27	Total different words	14
Mean words	3·00	Mean different words	1·56

Subject Group P

(6 children; age: 11–13 years;
performance I.Q.: ⩾ 111; hearing loss: 40–60 dB)

NOUNS

Word	Count	Word	Count	Word	Count	Word	Count
accident	14	back	2	beard	1	*boot	17
accidents	1	background	2	bedroom	1	boots	4
afternoon	2	bag	7	bench	2	bottle	1
air	1	baker	1	bicycle	2	bottles	6
all	1	ball	41	bike	2	bowl	3
ambulance	17	bananas	7	bill	3	box	2
amount	1	barrel	1	bit	2	boxes	1
anger	1	*barrow	1	blind	3	boy	79
apple	2	baseball	3	board	3	boys	21
apples	6	basket	12	book	9	brake	1
atlas	3	bat	7	books	2	brakes	2

Word	Count	Word	Count	Word	Count	Word	Count
bread	4	crockery	1	foam	1	ice	22
broom	4	cup	2	foil	1	jar	3
brush	3	cupboards	1	food	15	jelly	6
bucket	4	cups	3	football	10	jug	2
bull	17	cutlery	1	fork	3	kettle	4
bun	1	daddy	2	forks	2	kids	1
bushes	1	dairy	1	front	3	kind	1
butter	6	danger	1	fruit	3	kitchen	7
cabbage	1	date	1	fruits	1	knife	7
cabbages	5	day	2	fun	1	knives	2
cake	7	decoration	1	game	3	ladder	16
cakes	4	delivery	1	gamekeeper	1	lady	24
calendar	4	dinner	2	games	1	lady's	1
cap	1	distance	2	gate	6	land	1
car	35	dog	36	girl	14	leg	1
car's	1	doll	7	girls	3	legs	1
cart	2	door	11	glass	1	lids	1
case	2	doors	1	gloves	4	life	2
casserole	1	dragon	2	goal	4	*lorry	2
cat	7	drain	6	goal-posts	3	lot	2
cauliflower	1	drawer	2	grass	1	lots	2
ceiling	1	drawers	2	grating	1	lovers	1
chair	5	drawings	1	grinder	1	machine	4
chairs	1	drink	7	groceries	1	*mackintosh	1
change	1	driver	2	grocers	1	man	43
chicken	3	egg	2	grocery	1	man's	3
child	5	eggs	9	ground	3	map	2
children	11	end	4	hand	1	market	1
cleaner	3	engine	1	handbag	1	marmalade	2
clock	7	face	1	hands	1	*marrow	2
clockwork	2	family	5	handstand	1	marshmallow	1
cloth	2	farm	1	handstands	4	mask	5
clothes	1	farmer	6	hanger	1	masks	1
clothing	1	farmer's	1	hat	3	matches	3
cloths	1	father	13	head	2	material	3
coat	9	father's	2	headlamp	1	mats	4
coats	1	fence	8	hedge	5	meal	1
coin	1	field	10	hedges	2	measure	1
comics	1	fields	3	here	1	meat	2
*cooker	6	finger	3	hill	3	medals	3
cook's	1	fish	6	hole	2	men	5
corner	4	floor	6	hook	3	mess	2
couple	1	flower	5	house	6	mice	4
crash	1	flowerpot	4	houses	6	middle	3
*cricket	2	flowers	2	husband	2	milk	11

Word	Count	Word	Count	Word	Count	Word	Count
milkman	6	picture	8	shopkeeper	1	sun	1
mince	2	piece	1	shopping	5	sweets	1
mincer	2	place	3	shorts	2	table	25
mirror	1	plant	2	shoulder	3	*taps	2
mittens	1	plate	5	side	4	tea	1
mixer	6	plates	9	sides	1	team	1
money	9	police	1	sign	6	there	4
mop	3	policeman	6	silver	1	thing	3
morning	1	pond	8	sink	6	things	6
mother	23	posts	3	sister	1	three	1
motorbike	1	pot	5	sisters	1	time	4
mouse	1	pots	3	skates	3	tin	1
moustache	1	*prawn	1	ski	1	tomato	1
mouth	3	*purse	6	*sledge	9	tomatoes	1
mud	1	raincoat	1	*sledges	1	top	3
mugs	1	rice	5	slopes	1	towel	1
mummy	2	right	1	snow	4	town	3
mushroom	1	road	16	son	3	toy	5
mushrooms	4	*rounders	2	sons	1	toys	1
mustard	2	*rubbish	1	sort	3	train	6
name	1	salt	5	sponge	1	tree	4
notice	2	sandwich	2	spoon	2	trees	3
number	1	sandwiches	7	spoons	2	*trousers	2
one	2	saucepan	2	sports	1	turban	1
onions	4	saucepans	1	spreads	1	vase	3
onlookers	2	saucer	1	spring	1	wall	5
ornaments	1	saucers	1	stall	2	washing	5
oven	2	scarf	4	stick	4	water	5
owner	2	scene	1	sticks	4	wheelbarrow	3
paper	1	scissors	2	store	1	wife	2
party	1	seller	1	strawberries	1	window	19
pavement	1	shave	2	street	5	windows	2
peanut	1	shelf	1	string	2	window-sill	1
pears	2	shirt	2	*studs	1	winter	1
pedestrian	1	shirts	3	stuff	2	woman	5
people	14	shock	1	sugar	3	woods	1
pepper	4	shoes	7	suit	1	world	1
picnic	11	shop	3	summer	2		

Total words	1506			Total different words	375	
Mean words	251·00			Mean different words	62·50	

VERBS

Word	Count	Word	Count	Word	Count	Word	Count
allowed	2	cutting	3	hit	1	pulling	1
are	60	died	1	hold	2	push	1
arrive	1	doing	6	holding	8	pushing	1
astonished	1	drink	1	hurry	1	put	5
ate	1	drinking	7	hurt	4	putting	4
attending	1	driving	4	is	117	racing	1
barking	1	dropped	14	kicked	6	raging	1
be	4	drove	1	knock	4	ran	4
belongs	1	eat	1	knocked	4	reach	1
bite	1	eating	10	knocks	1	reached	
bring	1	enjoying	2	know	6	reaching	
brought	1	excited	1	land	1	read	
bumped	1	exhausted	1	lapping	1	reading	
buying	2	expect	3	lay	1	returned	
calling	1	failing	1	laying	1	rid	
came	14	fall	4	leaning	3	riding	
can	2	fallen	5	left	3	rolled	
carry	1	falling	4	licking	1	rolling	
carrying	13	fell	12	like	1	run	
charge	1	fetch	1	look	3	running	
charging	1	flying	1	looked	3	rushing	
chased	1	gaping	1	looking	19	said	
chasing	1	gathering	1	looks	11	save	
chopping	2	get	25	lying	1	saw	
cleaning	2	getting	4	made	1	saying	
clearing	1	giving	1	making	2	says	
climb	2	go	5	mean	2	scraping	
climbing	1	going	18	mending	1	screaming	
close	2	gone	2	might	3	screeching	
come	10	got	29	miss	1	see	
comes	2	had	1	moving	1	seemed	
comforting	1	handing	1	must	4	set	
coming	12	hang	1	notice	1	shaving	
control	1	hanging	6	open	2	shining	
could	4	happened	6	opening	3	should	
covered	2	happening	3	packing	4	shouting	
crash	6	has	17	pay	1	skating	
crashed	2	have	7	paying	5	*sledged	
crashes	1	having	5	phoned	2	*sledging	
crawl	1	heading	1	play	2	sleeping	
crawling	1	heard	1	playing	34	slide	
crying	2	help	4	pointing	1	sliding	
cut	1	helping	3	pull	2	slipped	

Word	Count	Word	Count	Word	Count	Word	Count
smashed	3	swerve	1	tripped	4	washing	1
smiling	1	swerved	1	try	2	watch	1
snorting	1	taking	5	trying	15	watching	7
snowing	1	talking	1	unloading	1	waving	1
sort	1	tell	2	used	1	went	16
squashed	1	telling	3	using	1	were	25
standing	7	think	4	wait	2	will	5
starting	2	tied	1	waiting	3	wondering	1
stop	6	tipped	3	walking	3	work	1
stopped	3	took	1	wanting	1	working	1
stopping	1	trailing	1	warn	1	worried	2
stuck	3	tried	1	warning	3	would	1
support	1	trip	1	was	44	writing	4

Total words	962	Total different words	224
Mean words	160·33	Mean different words	37·33

ADJECTIVES

Word	Count	Word	Count	Word	Count	Word	Count
aged	1	five	4	older	5	such	1
all	11	four	10	oldest	1	sunny	1
another	5	full	1	one	17	sweet	1
anxious	1	furious	1	open	7	ten	1
asleep	4	green	2	other	7	that	5
big	6	little	36	own	1	thin	5
blue	1	main	1	pretty	1	third	1
bushy	1	many	4	ready	1	this	11
busy	3	middle	1	red	12	those	1
cold	1	much	2	same	2	three	8
dirty	1	muddy	2	six	1	twelve	2
eldest	1	next	2	smaller	1	two	46
empty	2	nine	1	snowy	1	white	1
far	1	no	1	some	38	wooden	1
few	3	old	1	sorry	1	youngest	1
first	1						

Total words	294	Total different words	61
Mean words	49·00	Mean different words	10·17

ADVERBS

Word	Count	Word	Count	Word	Count	Word	Count
about	3	easier	1	nearby	2	safely	1
accidentally	1	else	1	nearer	1	still	1
across	1	everywhere	2	nearly	1	straight	1
all	1	fast	3	not	13	then	7
along	14	half	1	now	5	there	72
also	2	here	11	off	2	through	1
angrily	1	home	7	on	2	too	2
apparently	1	how	2	out	22	toward	2
around	4	in	5	over	15	towards	5
as	7	just	24	perhaps	1	up	7
away	9	like	6	probably	5	very	1
back	1	maybe	1	quite	1	well	5
by	1	meanwhile	1	really	2	where	4
down	11	near	1	round	2		

Total words	306	Total different words	55
Mean words	51·00	Mean different words	9·17

PRONOUNS

Word	Count	Word	Count	Word	Count	Word	Count
all	1	it	32	that	3	we	
everybody	2	its	2	their	14	what	
he	33	one	1	them	23	whatever	
her	24	she	11	themselves	1	which	
him	24	somebody	1	they	49	who	1
his	41	someone	1	this	1	you	
I	16	something	3	those	2	your	

Total words	309	Total different words	28
Mean words	51·50	Mean different words	4·67

PREPOSITIONS

Word	Count	Word	Count	Word	Count	Word	Count
about	3	after	3	along	4	at	3
across	6	against	1	around	3	behind	

Word	Count	Word	Count	Word	Count	Word	Count
below	2	in	68	onto	3	to	85
beside	2	into	17	out	19	towards	4
by	11	like	2	over	16	under	4
down	14	near	1	past	4	underneath	2
except	1	of	61	round	4	up	7
for	25	off	10	through	7	with	68
from	5	on	87				

Total words	582	Total different words	34
Mean words	97·00	Mean different words	5·67

CONJUNCTIONS

Word	Count	Word	Count	Word	Count	Word	Count
and	338	but	3	so	3	when	2
as	4	for	1	that	2	while	6
because	8	if	3	then	4	whilst	1
before	1	or	10	through	4		

Total words	390	Total different words	15
Mean words	65·00	Mean different words	2·50

CONTRACTIONS

Word	Count	Word	Count	Word	Count	Word	Count
boy's	3	family's	1	lady's	1	there's	55
lock's	1	farmer's	1	man's	2	they'll	1
cross	1	father's	2	mum's	1	they're	11
didn't	3	fruit's	1	o'clock	1	they've	8
doesn't	1	he'll	1	someone's	1	tree's	1
dog's	1	he's	16	son's	1	where's	1
don't	7	it's	17	that's	3	who's	1

Total words	144	Total different words	28
Mean words	24·00	Mean different words	4·67

INTERJECTIONS

Word	Count	Word	Count
oh	9	well	1

Total words	10	Total different words	2
Mean words	1·67	Mean different words	0·33

ARTICLES

Word	Count	Word	Count	Word	Count
a	335	an	14	the	551

Total words	900	Total different words	3
Mean words	150·00	Mean different words	0·50

OTHER

Word	Count	Word	Count	Word	Count	Word	Cou...
Coke	2	icing	1	mices	1	*rugby	
Dachshund	1	June	1	O.K.	1	Saturday	
gonna	1	Market Street	2	pneumonia	1	*Wellington	
*High Street	1	*Marmite	2	raining-coat	1	yes	
iced	1	*Meccano	1				

Total words	24	Total different words	18
Mean words	4·00	Mean different words	3·00

Subject Group Q

(17 children; age: 11–13 years;
performance I.Q.: ⩾111; hearing loss: 61–80 dB)

NOUNS

Word	Count	Word	Count	Word	Count	Word	Count
accident	8	book	14	cheese	1	dad	10
accidents	1	books	1	cherries	1	daddy	6
address	1	*boot	23	chicken	3	danger	4
all	21	boots	10	child	3	date	1
ambulance	46	bottle	1	children	24	day	4
ambulances	1	bottles	5	chin	1	dinner	8
anoraks	1	bottom	1	chunk	1	dinosaur	1
apple	4	bowl	2	cleaner	4	dish-cloth	4
apples	16	box	3	cloak	1	dog	93
apron	1	boy	152	clock	7	dogs	1
area	1	boys	49	cloth	4	doll	10
argument	1	brakes	1	clothes	11	dolly	1
arm	2	bread	4	cloths	1	door	15
atlas	2	broom	4	clown	1	doors	2
baby	1	brother	8	coat	7	drain	14
back	2	brush	3	coins	2	drawer	1
background	5	bucket	8	cold	6	dress	2
badge	1	buildings	2	colour	2	drink	7
bag	7	bull	46	coloured	1	duty	1
ball	107	bull's	3	concentration	1	egg	1
banana	6	bulls	1	*cooker	4	eggs	13
bananas	11	bushes	1	*cookers	1	elbow	1
bank	3	butter	7	corner	1	escape	1
baseball	13	cabbage	4	course	1	excitement	1
basin	1	cabbages	3	cover	3	exercise	1
basket	34	cake	5	crack	1	face	4
basket-ball	1	calendar	6	crash	9	fact	1
bat	14	cane	1	cream	2	family	10
beard	1	car	85	*cricket	11	farm	2
bench	5	cart	3	crocodile	1	farmer	25
bicycle	1	case	6	cross	2	father	17
bike	2	cat	12	cup	4	feet	2
bit	8	cauliflower	7	cupboard	1	fence	14
bits	2	cauliflowers	2	curtain	1	field	33
blanket	2	chair	7	customer	1	fields	1
board	1	character	2	cycle	1	fire	1
bones	1	cheeks	1	cyclist	3	fish	8

Word	Count	Word	Count	Word	Count	Word	Count
flats	1	help	2	mask	9	package	1
floor	5	helpers	1	masks	1	pail	4
flower	6	hill	6	mat	1	pan	2
flowerpot	8	hockey	1	match	2	pans	3
flowers	6	hole	4	matches	4	paper	1
foam	1	holes	1	material	2	part	2
food	22	home	4	meal	5	path	1
football	23	horns	1	meanwhile	1	*pavement	1
fork	1	hospital	5	meat	7	pear	1
forks	5	house	16	medal	1	people	18
fridge	1	houses	3	medals	1	pepper	2
front	4	husband	4	men	12	permission	1
fruit	8	ice	67	mice	1	person	2
fruits	1	ice-cream	2	middle	8	picnic	44
fun	1	idea	1	milk	15	picture	11
game	7	incident	3	milkman	6	pictures	1
garden	1	jacket	1	minute	1	pin	1
gas	1	jackets	1	mirror	4	place	6
gate	6	jelly	11	mixer	5	plant	3
gentleman's	1	jug	2	model	2	plate	4
girl	39	*jumper	1	moment	1	plateful	1
girls	3	kettle	6	money	23	plates	6
glass	1	kind	2	mother	28	police	1
glove	2	kitchen	9	mouse	2	policeman	14
goal	13	knife	8	mud	1	pond	3
goalkeeper	2	knives	5	mum	2	pop	2
goal-posts	1	ladder	40	mummy	4	post	6
goals	4	lady	39	mushroom	2	posts	7
grate	1	leg	2	mushrooms	1	pot	1
*greengrocer	1	light	1	napkin	1	potato	2
grocer's	3	list	1	net	1	pressure	2
groceries	2	look	4	netball	1	pudding	1
ground	4	loop	1	noise	12	*purse	14
group	1	lot	3	nose	5	*pussy	
hair	4	lots	2	noses	1	raincoat	
hand	8	lunch	10	note	4	religion	
handhold	1	*mac	1	notice	26	rent	
handstand	12	machine	5	office	1	ride	
handstands	3	man	105	one	24	ring	
hat	12	man's	3	ones	1	rink	
*hawker	1	map	4	onion	1	road	1
head	20	maps	1	onions	2	*rounders	
headstand	1	market	5	orange	2	rubber	
hedge	6	marmalade	1	others	1	run	
hedges	1	*marrow	1	oven	5	salt	

Word	Count	Word	Count	Word	Count	Word	Count
sandwich	7	sisters	1	stump	1	trap	1
sandwiches	22	site	1	surface	1	tree	3
saucepans	3	skate	2	surprise	1	trees	2
saucer	2	skates	9	sweets	1	*trousers	2
sausage	1	skating	1	table	42	turban	12
scarf	10	*sledge	28	table-cloth	7	tweed	1
scene	1	sleigh	1	table-mat	1	twigs	1
school	10	slope	3	tail	1	two	12
scissors	6	snow	7	*tap	1	van	3
seats	1	son	16	*taps	1	vegetables	2
second	1	sons	2	tea	2	village	1
sets	1	sort	9	team	2	washing	5
shadows	1	sorts	1	there	3	water	6
shave	5	spoon	2	thing	5	way	11
shirt	3	square	1	things	20	weather	1
shirts	6	stall	8	time	17	weight	6
shock	1	star	1	toboggan	1	wheelbarrow	2
shoe	1	stick	31	tomato	1	wheels	2
shoes	4	sticks	2	tomatoes	9	whisk	1
shop	4	story	1	top	7	wife	1
shopkeeper	3	stove	2	towel	2	window	27
shopper	2	strawberries	4	towels	1	windows	1
shopping	1	street	13	toy	2	wire	2
side	9	streets	1	toys	4	woman	18
sign	7	string	2	train	7	world	1
sink	6						

Total words	2898	Total different words	429
Mean words	170·47	Mean different words	25·24

VERBS

Word	Count	Word	Count	Word	Count	Word	Count
ble	2	asking	4	belonging	1	broken	2
iming	1	attracted	1	bother	1	bump	1
llowed	1	avoid	1	bounced	1	bumped	2
m	2	barking	1	bouncing	1	bumps	1
nswering	1	be	42	break	5	call	7
re	79	been	31	breaks	1	called	10
rranged	1	being	5	bring	1	calling	1
rrived	10	believe	3	bringing	3	came	18
sked	5	bellow	1	broke	1	can	19

Word	Count	Word	Count	Word	Count	Word	Count
care	1	dodges	1	going	61	lifting	1
carried	1	does	1	gone	13	light	1
carry	9	doing	19	got	65	lightened	1
carrying	30	drink	5	grab	4	like	3
catch	2	drinking	22	grabs	1	likes	1
caught	1	drive	2	grinding	1	listening	2
charges	1	driven	1	grip	2	living	1
charging	9	driving	11	gripping	1	look	28
chase	2	drop	3	had	25	looked	1
chased	1	dropped	29	hanging	2	looking	34
chasing	4	dropping	1	happened	27	looks	24
chatting	1	drops	1	happening	6	losing	1
check	2	drowned	1	happens	1	made	8
*clambering	1	eat	8	has	56	make	14
cleaner	1	eating	30	have	76	making	5
cleaning	1	eats	2	having	24	may	2
clearing	1	edging	1	heard	1	mean	7
climb	5	end	1	heaving	1	measure	1
climbed	5	excuse	1	heed	1	mending	1
climbing	3	expect	1	help	14	might	34
collect	2	explain	1	helping	4	mixing	1
coloured	1	fall	14	helps	1	must	9
come	21	fallen	24	hiding	1	need	1
comes	6	falling	3	hit	14	needs	1
coming	38	fell	30	hold	14	notice	1
concentrating	2	fetch	3	holding	10	noticed	1
control	1	finish	1	holds	1	noticing	1
could	7	finished	4	hoping	1	open	2
cracked	2	flashing	1	hurry	1	opened	1
cracks	1	flying	1	hurt	7	opening	6
crash	5	folded	1	is	246	pack	1
crashed	12	follow	1	jump	4	packed	2
crashes	1	following	1	jumped	3	packing	13
crashing	1	forgot	1	keep	4	packs	1
crawl	3	frighten	1	kicked	16	paid	2
creep	1	frightened	6	kicking	1	parked	1
cut	3	full	1	kicks	1	pay	1
cutting	2	get	81	knew	2	paying	7
cycling	1	gets	1	knocked	20	pick	2
decide	1	getting	12	know	31	picked	1
delivering	1	give	1	knowing	2	picking	2
depends	1	given	1	laid	5	pinch	1
did	1	gliding	2	land	2	plans	2
do	19	go	40	landed	1	play	1
dodge	1	goes	1	lie	1	played	1

Word	Count	Word	Count	Word	Count	Word	Count
playing	112	sat	1	smashed	1	trapped	1
plays	2	save	1	snowing	2	travelling	1
pointing	1	saw	15	spread	2	tried	6
positions	1	say	5	spreads	4	tripped	12
practising	1	saying	7	stand	2	tripping	1
prepared	1	says	4	standing	5	try	13
presume	1	scattered	1	stands	4	trying	46
pretend	1	see	28	staring	1	turn	1
pull	13	seeing	1	start	6	turned	6
pulling	1	seem	1	started	6	unpack	1
pushed	1	seen	10	stayed	1	unpacking	1
pushing	1	sell	1	stop	33	used	2
put	34	selling	1	stopped	5	wait	1
puts	1	set	4	stuck	1	waiting	1
putting	12	shall	2	suffering	1	walk	2
racing	1	shave	1	suppose	11	walking	8
ran	9	shaving	6	supposed	1	want	6
reach	4	shocked	2	swerve	1	wanted	1
reaches	1	shopping	1	swerved	1	wants	2
reaching	4	should	6	swerving	1	warmed	2
read	8	shouting	4	take	12	warn	1
reading	18	show	1	taking	11	warned	2
realized	1	showing	1	talk	1	warning	3
release	1	shows	2	talking	3	was	58
remember	2	shut	1	telephoned	1	washing	1
rescue	4	sit	2	tell	14	watching	23
resting	1	sitting	6	telling	15	wear	2
returned	1	skated	1	thin	1	wearing	6
riding	4	skating	7	think	27	wears	1
risked	1	skidded	1	threatening	1	went	36
roll	1	*sledging	5	threw	2	were	25
rolling	3	sleighing	1	throwing	1	will	23
run	2	slide	1	tidy	1	wondering	1
running	21	sliding	11	tired	8	worried	4
rush	1	slip	1	told	7	would	11
rushing	1	slipped	3	took	2	writing	3
said	4	smash	1				

Total words   2806   Total different words   362
Mean words   165·06   Mean different words   21·29

ADJECTIVES

Word	Count	Word	Count	Word	Count	Word	Count
able	4	different	1	mean	2	silly	2
all	27	drunken	1	more	5	small	6
angry	16	easier	3	most	3	smaller	1
annoyed	1	either	1	much	2	some	44
another	4	eldest	2	naughty	1	still	1
any	9	electric	2	near	2	striped	1
asleep	6	far	1	nearer	2	sure	2
bad	2	fast	2	nice	2	that	107
best	1	first	3	no	2	these	2
big	18	five	4	old	1	thick	2
bigger	3	foreign	1	older	3	thin	18
biggest	1	four	4	one	26	this	26
blue	7	funny	3	only	1	those	11
both	1	good	2	open	14	twelve	2
bright	1	great	1	opposite	1	two	46
broken	1	green	3	other	21	unconscious	1
bronchial	1	hard	1	own	1	upset	1
brown	2	high	1	pink	1	white	1
busy	2	huge	1	previous	1	wild	1
careful	2	important	1	proper	4	wooden	2
check	1	last	1	rainy	1	worse	1
close	1	late	1	ready	11	wrong	1
cold	7	left	6	red	23	yellow	5
cooking	1	less	1	right	7	yellowy	1
cross	1	like	32	safe	2	young	1
curly	1	little	46	same	1	younger	5
dangerous	2	long	2	several	2	youngest	3
dark	1	main	1				

Total words   688   Total different words   110
Mean words   40·47   Mean different words   6·47

ADVERBS

Word	Count	Word	Count	Word	Count	Word	Count
about	7	again	5	around	5	badly	1
accidentally	1	all	2	as	28	before	2
across	10	along	16	away	24	below	1
after	3	also	9	awfully	1	by	3
afterwards	2	anyway	3	back	27	carefully	2

Word	Count	Word	Count	Word	Count	Word	Count
down	73	likely	2	outside	2	then	14
else	1	maybe	17	over	41	there	81
even	1	meanwhile	5	past	1	though	10
evenly	1	most	1	perhaps	19	too	11
ever	1	much	2	presumably	6	under	1
fearlessly	1	near	4	probably	45	underneath	1
foolishly	1	nearby	1	quite	2	up	38
forward	1	never	5	rather	7	upside-down	2
forwards	1	not	16	ready	1	very	10
happily	1	now	18	really	5	weekly	1
here	9	nowhere	1	right	4	well	16
home	13	obviously	4	round	5	when	10
how	4	off	26	sideways	1	where	22
in	19	on	20	so	19	whereas	1
inside	1	other	1	sometimes	1	why	3
instead	4	otherwise	2	somewhere	2	yet	1
just	42	out	106	straight	5		

Total words	945	Total different words	87
Mean words	55·59	Mean different words	5·12

PRONOUNS

Word	Count	Word	Count	Word	Count	Word	Count
anything	2	I	88	someone	1	those	1
everybody	4	it	144	something	43	we	4
everything	6	its	1	that	23	what	39
he	155	me	8	their	32	whatever	3
her	67	my	1	them	71	which	8
him	110	one	5	these	2	who	11
himself	3	she	52	they	186	you	50
his	77	somebody	3	this	6	your	2

Total words	1208	Total different words	32
Mean words	71·06	Mean different words	1·88

PREPOSITIONS

Word	Count	Word	Count	Word	Count	Word	Count
about	8	down	14	next	1	round	4
above	1	for	61	of	138	through	2
across	10	from	13	off	8	to	286
after	12	in	143	on	132	towards	8
along	5	inside	1	onto	2	under	16
at	49	into	52	out	13	up	6
behind	4	like	15	over	39	with	137
beside	5	near	2	past	2	without	1
by	30						

Total words	1220	Total different words	33
Mean words	71·76	Mean different words	1·94

CONJUNCTIONS

Word	Count	Word	Count	Word	Count	Word	Count
and	643	but	22	that	13	until	1
as	5	if	22	then	8	when	26
because	48	or	55	though	1	while	10
before	1	so	22	unless	3	whilst	9

Total words	889	Total different words	16
Mean words	52·29	Mean different words	0·94

CONTRACTIONS

Word	Count	Word	Count	Word	Count	Word	Count
*boot's	1	door's	1	isn't	1	person's	1
boy's	29	farmer's	2	it'll	1	she's	32
brother's	4	father's	10	it's	36	shopkeeper's	1
bull's	2	hasn't	1	lady's	6	shouldn't	3
can't	11	haven't	1	man's	12	somebody's	3
couldn't	1	he'd	2	milkman's	1	table's	1
didn't	29	he'll	7	money's	1	that's	16
doesn't	3	he's	52	mother's	13	there'd	1
dog's	204	here's	1	mummy's	1	there's	67
don't	20	I'm	1	mustn't	1	they'd	1

Word	Count		Word	Count		Word	Count		Word	Count
they'll	2		they've	25		what's	9		won't	2
they're	45		wasn't	4		who's	3		wouldn't	4

Total words	675		Total different words	48
Mean words	39·71		Mean different words	2·82

INTERJECTIONS

Word	Count		Word	Count		Word	Count		Word	Count
dear	1		strange	1		well	68		why	1
oh	21									

Total words	92		Total different words	5
Mean words	5·41		Mean different words	0·29

ARTICLES

Word	Count		Word	Count		Word	Count
a	436		an	25		the	1363

Total words	1824		Total different words	3
Mean words	107·29		Mean different words	0·18

OTHER

Word	Count		Word	Count		Word	Count		Word	Count
American	1		danger	1		India	2		*poom	1
bang	1		England	1		Indian	1		*Sikh	1
Bangladesh	1		English	1		Market Street	3		spaniel	1
chopboard	1		et cetera	1		*Marmite	2		them's	1
Cocacola	6		felled	1		Mr.	7		thirteens	1
Coke	3		*Hamish	1		no	30		*T-junction	1
Cola	3		handstanding	1		O.K.	2		T-shirt	2
cos	1		*High Street	1		*plonk	1		*winger	1
crash	1		*Horley	1		pneumonia	3		yes	166
Croydon	1									

Total words	254		Total different words	37
Mean words	14·94		Mean different words	2·18

Subject Group R

(14 children; age: 11–13 years;
performance I.Q.: ⩾ 111; hearing loss: 81–95 dB)

NOUNS

Word	Count	Word	Count	Word	Count	Word	Count
accident	6	broom	4	*cooker	2	family	2
all	11	brother	1	corner	2	farm	2
ambulance	22	brush	2	country	1	farmer	8
amount	1	bubble	1	court	1	father	13
angle	1	bucket	3	courts	1	fence	9
apple	2	bull	29	crash	4	field	9
apples	13	bunch	1	cream	3	fish	5
area	1	bushes	1	*cricket	4	floor	7
atlas	2	butter	4	cup	1	flower	4
avenue	1	cabbage	4	cutlery	1	flowerpot	8
baby	5	cabbages	2	dad	1	flowers	3
back	7	cake	1	danger	1	food	12
bag	4	cakes	1	day	1	football	18
ball	54	calendar	3	dinner	7	fork	2
banana	2	car	49	dinosaur	1	forks	1
bananas	7	cars	2	dish	1	four	1
*barrow	2	cart	1	dog	41	fright	1
baseball	4	carton	1	doggy	1	front	2
basket	19	cartoon	1	doll	4	fruit	6
bat	8	cartoons	1	dolls	2	fruits	1
beard	1	case	1	door	8	game	1
bicycle	5	cat	5	dragon	1	gate	3
bike	3	cauliflowers	2	drain	3	girl	16
*bin	1	chair	4	drain-pipe	1	girls	2
bit	2	chairs	1	drawer	2	glove	1
blankets	1	chicken	2	drawers	1	gloves	2
board	1	children	14	dresses	1	goal	7
book	9	class	2	drier	1	goals	2
books	4	clean	1	drink	1	grass	1
*boot	13	clock	5	drive	1	grocer	3
boots	12	cloth	5	driver	1	groceries	1
bottle	1	clothes	3	egg	2	ground	4
bottom	1	coat	6	eggs	6	hair	1
bowl	2	coats	1	elbow	1	half	1
boy	84	coconut	1	exams	1	hamper	2
boys	19	comic	2	excitement	1	hand	9
bread	4	comics	1	face	1	hands	1

Word	Count	Word	Count	Word	Count	Word	Count
handstand	3	mask	5	path	1	shirts	8
handstands	1	master	1	*pavement	2	shock	2
hat	10	mat	1	penny	1	shoes	3
hats	1	match	4	people	8	shopkeeper	1
head	4	matches	1	pepper	1	shops	1
hedge	6	material	2	picnic	15	shorts	3
hill	4	mats	2	picture	4	side	2
hole	4	meal	1	pictures	1	sight	1
home	9	meat	4	plates	5	sign	5
hook	1	medals	2	pole	2	sink	4
hospital	4	men	5	police	1	siren	1
house	6	meringues	2	policeman	7	sister	2
houses	2	mice	3	pond	1	six	1
ice	35	middle	1	post	3	skates	6
ice-cream	1	milk	13	posts	5	*sledge	11
intelligence	1	milkman	6	pot	1	slope	1
jam	1	*mince	1	potato	1	snow	5
jar	3	*mincemeat	1	potatoes	1	socks	3
jelly	4	mirror	1	pots	2	son	3
jerseys	1	mixer	4	pressure	1	spoon	4
jug	2	model	3	pudding	2	stall	3
jump	1	money	6	pumpkin	1	stick	14
jumper	1	month	2	*purse	5	sticks	2
kettle	3	mop	2	raincoat	1	stock	1
kind	1	mother	15	remains	1	strawberries	2
kit	2	mountain	1	ribs	1	street	1
kitchen	4	mouse	1	ring	1	stuff	6
knife	5	mud	1	road	23	sugar	1
knives	2	netball	3	roller	1	surprise	1
lad	1	nine	2	roofs	1	sweeper	1
ladder	23	noise	1	room	1	sweet	1
lady	26	nose	1	running	1	table	19
leaves	1	notice	3	salt	1	table-cloth	1
lorry	1	number	1	sandwich	1	*tap	1
lot	1	numbers	2	sandwiches	10	tea	5
lunch	1	one	17	saucepans	2	team	1
machine	3	onion	2	saucer	2	teeth	1
magazines	1	orange	2	scarf	3	ten	2
man	57	oranges	1	scarves	1	tennis	1
man's	1	outing	2	school	5	there	3
map	2	oven	1	scissors	5	thing	2
market	1	pair	3	seven	1	things	5
marmalade	1	pairs	1	shadow	2	thirteen	1
marrow	1	pans	2	shave	2	three	1
marshmallows	1	park	6	shirt	3	time	8

Word	Count	Word	Count	Word	Count	Word	Coun
towel	1	turban	3	wash	2	wheelbarrow	3
toy	1	two	1	washing	3	*wicket	1
toys	2	unit	1	water	4	wife	2
train	3	van	1	way	2	window	11
tree	2	vase	1	weather	1	windows	5
trees	2	vegetables	1	weeks	1	woman	2
trouble	1	warning	1	wheel	1	year	1

Total words	1523	Total different words	356
Mean words	108·79	Mean different words	25·43

VERBS

Word	Count	Word	Count	Word	Count	Word	Cou
allowed	2	chasing	3	driving	2	happen	2
are	18	cleaning	4	drop	1	happened	
argue	1	clear	1	dropped	11	happening	2
asked	1	clearing	1	eat	2	has	1(
attacking	1	climb	5	eating	10	have	19
avoid	3	climbed	2	eats	1	having	8
barking	1	climbing	2	fall	13	hearing	2
bash	1	come	16	fallen	12	help	
be	7	comes	3	falling	6	helps	
been	15	coming	17	fell	12	hit	
being	3	cooking	2	find	1	hold	
bite	1	could	1	finished	1	holding	1(
brake	1	cover	1	float	1	hurt	
break	2	crack	2	frightened	7	is	4
breaks	1	cracked	1	gave	2	jerk	
bring	1	crash	6	get	32	jump	
bringing	5	crashed	6	gets	1	keep	
broken	1	crawl	1	getting	2	kick	
brought	2	cross	1	give	2	kicked	
bump	1	cut	3	gives	1	kill	
call	1	cutting	3	giving	2	kneels	
called	3	cycling	1	go	23	knock	
came	15	dining	1	goes	1	knocked	
can	10	disgust	1	going	30	knocks	
carry	4	do	5	gone	6	know	1
carrying	11	dodge	1	got	29	laid	
caused	3	doing	5	grab	1	land	
chase	1	drinking	11	had	3	lay	

Word	Count	Word	Count	Word	Count	Word	Count
leaning	1	pulled	1	sleeps	1	tired	1
leave	1	put	12	sleeping	1	toboganning	1
let	1	puts	1	slide	2	told	1
licking	1	putting	4	sliding	4	took	1
lie	1	raining	2	slip	2	tried	2
like	1	ran	2	slipped	1	tries	2
listen	1	reach	6	smack	1	tripped	4
live	1	read	4	smashed	1	trips	1
look	5	reading	4	sort	1	try	9
looking	8	rescue	6	speaking	1	trying	7
looks	5	ride	1	stand	1	turn	1
lost	1	riding	3	standing	11	turns	1
made	1	rings	1	staring	1	twists	3
make	4	run	7	started	2	upset	1
making	5	running	12	stayed	2	use	1
night	10	runs	3	steps	1	using	1
miss	1	rush	2	sticks	1	walk	1
moved	1	said	2	stood	1	walking	6
moving	1	saw	3	stop	11	walks	1
open	8	saying	1	stopped	2	want	1
opened	1	says	3	stuck	2	wants	1
opening	3	score	1	surprised	2	warmed	1
opens	1	see	5	swearing	1	warning	1
owns	1	seem	1	swerved	1	was	20
packed	1	seen	1	switch	1	washing	3
packing	3	sees	2	take	5	watched	2
packs	1	served	1	taken	1	watching	10
aid	1	shave	1	taking	5	wearing	6
assing	1	shaving	6	talking	1	went	11
ay	2	shining	1	teaching	1	were	4
aying	3	shocked	1	tell	3	will	6
icks	1	shot	1	telling	5	won	2
lay	9	should	5	tells	1	wondering	1
laying	45	shouting	1	think	25	work	1
lays	1	sits	1	throw	4	worried	1
ointing	1	sitting	6	throwing	2	would	2
refer	1	skating	5	throws	1	writing	3
ull	6	skids	2				

Total words	1110	Total different words	262
Mean words	79·29	Mean different words	18·71

ADJECTIVES

Word	Count	Word	Count	Word	Count	Word	Count
all	16	four	1	muddy	3	temporary	1
angry	4	funny	1	naughty	2	terrible	1
another	5	glad	1	next	1	that	33
any	1	good	1	one	21	these	2
asleep	3	green	5	open	5	thick	1
big	7	grey	1	orange	1	thin	5
blue	5	heavy	1	other	6	third	2
brown	1	hot	2	pink	1	this	18
careful	1	late	2	ready	4	those	4
cold	6	left	1	red	6	three	4
cool	1	like	5	right	1	twelve	2
dangerous	1	little	30	safest	1	two	2
dirty	1	many	2	same	1	what	
easy	1	messy	1	sharp	1	whole	
fast	2	more	2	six	1	yellow	
first	1	most	1	some	25	younger	
five	4	much	2	striped	1		

	Total words	304			Total different words	67	
	Mean words	21·71			Mean different words	4·79	

ADVERBS

Word	Count	Word	Count	Word	Count	Word	Count
about	1	everywhere	1	onto	1	sometimes	
accidentally	2	fast	1	otherwise	2	somewhere	
across	5	forward	2	out	28	soon	
again	2	here	2	over	26	still	
along	14	home	2	partially	1	then	1
already	1	how	2	past	1	there	2
also	1	in	6	probably	15	through	
anyway	1	just	6	quickly	4	together	
around	1	maybe	4	quite	3	too	
as	15	next	1	ready	1	up	2
away	11	not	10	really	1	upside-down	
back	7	now	2	right	3	very	
by	3	obviously	5	round	6	well	
down	27	off	2	so	18	when	
else	2	on	12	sometime	1	why	
ever	1	only	3				

	Total words	372			Total different words	62	
	Mean words	26·57			Mean different words	4·43	

PRONOUNS

Word	Count	Word	Count	Word	Count	Word	Count
anything	1	himself	2	she	14	those	1
each	1	his	33	some	1	we	7
everybody	1	I	43	somebody	2	what	8
everyone	1	it	53	something	2	whatever	1
everything	1	me	3	that	10	which	1
he	65	my	3	their	8	who	2
her	19	nothing	1	them	19	you	7
him	35	other	1	they	62	your	1

Total words	409	Total different words	32
Mean words	29·21	Mean different words	2·29

PREPOSITIONS

Word	Count	Word	Count	Word	Count	Word	Count
about	1	for	20	onto	3	through	4
across	5	from	5	opposite	1	to	113
after	9	in	68	out	3	towards	1
against	1	inside	2	outside	1	under	7
at	19	into	20	over	21	underneath	1
behind	1	of	42	past	2	up	4
by	6	off	6	round	2	with	49
down	20	on	58	than	1		

Total words	496	Total different words	31
Mean words	35·43	Mean different words	2·21

CONJUNCTIONS

Word	Count	Word	Count	Word	Count	Word	Count
and	323	but	7	so	2	though	1
because	20	if	7	that	2	till	1
before	1	or	7	then	1	unless	2

Total words	374	Total different words	12
Mean words	26·71	Mean different words	0·86

CONTRACTIONS

Word	Count	Word	Count	Word	Count	Word	Cou
*boot's	1	door's	3	lady's	11	someone's	1
boy's	17	family's	3	man's	10	sun's	1
brother's	1	farmer's	3	milkman's	1	that's	12
bull's	1	father's	2	money's	3	there's	40
can't	4	girl's	7	mother's	6	they'll	3
car's	2	haven't	1	mustn't	1	they're	30
cat's	3	he'll	1	o'clock	2	they've	13
cleaner's	2	he's	35	picnic's	1	we're	
clock's	1	I'd	2	policeman's	1	we've	
didn't	4	I'm	1	she's	6	what's	
doesn't	3	I've	1	shouldn't	2	won't	
dog's	14	it's	16	sister's	1	wouldn't	
don't	18						

Total words	301	Total different words	49
Mean words	21·50	Mean different words	3·50

INTERJECTIONS

Word	Count	Word	Count	Word	Count
oh	5	well	10	why	1

Total words	16	Total different words	3
Mean words	1·14	Mean different words	0·21

ARTICLES

Word	Count	Word	Count	Word	Count
a	203	an	11	the	676

Total words	890	Total different words	3
Mean words	63·57	Mean different words	0·21

OTHER

Word	Count	Word	Count	Word	Count	Word	Count
Africa	1	icing	1	*Meccano	2	*shooters	1
aftershave	1	Indian	3	Negro	2	Simon	1
Cocacola	5	Indians	1	no	12	*Wellington	1
Coke	4	*Kenwood	1	runned	1	*Wellingtons	1
'cos	2	Market Street	1	Saturday	1	yes	29
High Street	2	*Marmite	2				

Total words	75			Total different words	22	
Mean words	5·36			Mean different words	1·57	

Subject Group S

(3 children; age: 14–15 years;
performance I.Q.: ⩽90; hearing loss: 40–60 dB)

NOUNS

Word	Count	Word	Count	Word	Count	Word	Count
ambulance	6	board	1	cabbage	1	corner	1
apple	2	book	4	cabbages	1	cow	3
apples	3	books	1	cake	4	crash	1
back	2	*boot	4	cakes	1	*cricket	3
badges	1	boots	2	calendar	1	cup	1
bag	9	bottle	3	car	14	cups	2
ball	14	bottles	1	cat	2	curtain	1
banana	2	bowl	2	chair	3	dad	4
bananas	1	boy	29	cheeks	1	dad's	1
basket	1	boys	6	cheese	2	daddy	3
bat	3	bread	3	chicken	3	danger	2
bath	1	broom	2	children	3	date	2
beard	1	brother	1	cleaner	1	dinner	1
bed	3	bucket	2	cleaning	1	dog	10
bike	3	buckets	1	clock	1	doll	3
bill	1	building	1	cloth	1	doll's	1
biscuit	1	bull	2	clothes	3	dolly	2
blancmange	1	bunch	1	clown	2	door	2
blinds	1	bushes	1	coat	4	drain	1
bloke	1	butter	3	*cooker	1	drawer	1

Word	Count	Word	Count	Word	Count	Word	Count
dresses	1	jar	1	mushrooms	2	sandwiches	4
drink	1	jelly	2	name	1	sauce	1
egg	3	jug	1	nose	2	saucepan	1
eggs	2	kettle	3	notice	1	saucepans	1
face	4	*kit	1	number	2	scarf	2
farmer	2	kitchen	2	onion	1	scissors	3
father	4	knife	4	onions	1	*seaside	1
fence	2	ladder	6	oven	2	set	1
field	1	lady	10	paintings	1	shelf	2
fish	4	leaves	2	pan	1	shoes	4
fishing	1	leg	1	pans	1	shopkeeper	1
floor	6	line	1	paper	1	shoulder	1
flower	3	lemonade	1	park	1	sign	1
flowerpot	1	lot	2	party	1	sink	3
flowers	3	machine	4	path	2	skates	2
food	3	man	16	*pavement	1	*sledge	4
football	6	man's	2	pear	1	snow	2
fork	1	map	2	people	1	socks	1
fruit	2	marmalade	1	pepper	2	son	2
garden	1	marshmallows	1	picnic	8	spoon	2
gate	2	mask	2	picture	3	stick	1
girl	5	matches	2	pictures	1	sticks	2
girl's	1	medal	1	piece	1	table	4
girls	2	medals	1	plate	2	*tap	2
gloves	2	melon	1	plates	1	*taps	
goal	2	middle	1	policeman	2	tea	
goalkeeper	1	milk	7	pond	1	time	
hair	1	milkman	4	posts	1	tomato	
hand	1	*mince	1	potatoes	1	toothbrush	
hands	1	mirror	2	*purse	2	towel	
handstand	4	mixer	1	rag	1	town	
hat	3	money	4	rain	1	toy	
head	2	monsters	1	raincoat	1	train	
hole	5	mother	12	road	3	trees	
hospital	1	mouse	2	*rounders	1	*trousers	
houses	1	mum	1	rubber	1	washing	
ice	7	mummy	1	salt	2	window	
ice-cream	1	mushroom	1	sandwich	2	wire	

Total words	558		Total different words	232	
Mean words	186·00		Mean different words	77·33	

VERBS

Word	Count	Word	Count	Word	Count	Word	Count
adding	1	finish	2	play	4	smashed	1
are	8	fixing	1	playing	11	squashed	1
arrived	1	get	10	pointing	1	standing	5
ask	3	gets	1	pull	1	stop	3
barking	2	getting	3	put	13	sweeping	1
bash	1	give	4	putting	3	switch	1
be	3	go	8	reach	1	take	3
boiling	1	going	7	read	1	taking	3
broke	1	got	44	reading	2	talk	1
brought	1	has	5	riding	1	talking	1
bumped	1	having	3	run	1	telling	1
buy	1	help	7	running	6	threw	1
carrying	2	hit	1	rushed	1	throw	1
chasing	2	holding	3	saying	1	tidy	1
chopping	1	is	44	says	1	tired	1
clear	1	keep	2	scare	1	trapped	1
climb	1	keeps	1	scared	1	tripped	1
come	3	kicked	3	see	5	try	4
coming	5	knocked	3	seen	1	trying	12
crash	1	know	2	shaving	2	unpacking	1
cut	1	land	1	shouting	1	walk	1
dare	1	like	4	shut	2	want	1
doing	4	look	2	shutting	1	wash	2
dressed	1	looking	9	sit	2	washing	2
drinking	4	looks	2	sitting	1	watching	1
driving	1	measuring	1	skating	1	wearing	1
drop	2	moaning	2	skip	1	went	1
dropped	7	*mucking	1	sleep	1	were	2
eat	3	opening	1	slide	2	will	1
eating	5	packing	2	sliding	1	winding	2
fall	3	paying	1	slipped	1	worried	1
fell	8	pick	3	smash	1		

Total words	395			Total different words	127
Mean words	131·67			Mean different words	42·33

ADJECTIVES

Word	Count	Word	Count	Word	Count	Word	Count
all	9	every	1	much	1	sharp	1
angry	2	fast	1	muddy	1	some	10
another	1	first	2	no	1	that	9
asleep	1	five	5	old	2	this	2
back	2	four	3	one	7	three	2
brown	1	funny	1	open	1	twelve	4
careful	2	*ginger	1	other	2	two	11
dangerous	3	hot	1	ready	1	untidy	1
each	1	little	13	red	4	white	3

Total words	113	Total different words	36
Mean words	37·67	Mean different words	12·00

ADVERBS

Word	Count	Word	Count	Word	Count	Word	Count
about	1	how	2	off	1	tight	1
as	2	inside	1	on	3	too	3
away	4	just	4	out	8	up	12
back	2	maybe	1	over	7	very	9
down	5	never	1	round	3	well	1
harder	1	not	2	then	8	when	1
here	1	now	2	there	14	where	2
home	2						

Total words	104	Total different words	29
Mean words	34·67	Mean different words	9·67

PRONOUNS

Word	Count	Word	Count	Word	Count	Word	Count
all	2	his	17	somebody	3	they	16
everybody	1	I	1	something	10	we	3
everything	2	it	10	that	5	what	1
he	31	its	1	their	7	you	19
her	7	me	1	them	3	your	1
him	12	she	2				

Total words	155	Total different words	22
Mean words	51·67	Mean different words	7·33

PREPOSITIONS

Word	Count	Word	Count	Word	Count	Word	Count
after	1	for	3	off	3	round	1
against	1	from	1	on	21	to	39
along	1	in	22	onto	1	under	1
at	5	into	3	out	4	up	5
behind	1	like	1	over	4	with	16
down	7	of	10	past	4	without	2

Total words 157 Total different words 24
Mean words 52·33 Mean different words 8·00

CONJUNCTIONS

Word	Count	Word	Count	Word	Count	Word	Count
and	76	but	1	or	7	though	1
because	6	if	1	then	3		

Total words 95 Total different words 7
Mean words 31·67 Mean different words 2·33

CONTRACTIONS

Word	Count	Word	Count	Word	Count	Word	Count
boy's	6	he's	13	mother's	1	they've	2
cat's	2	it's	4	she's	1	wasn't	1
dog's	6	kettle's	1	that's	5	we've	5
don't	2	men's	1	there's	3	what's	1
everybody's	1	money's	1	they're	5	you've	3
girl's	1						

Total words 65 Total different words 21
Mean words 21·67 Mean different words 7·00

INTERJECTIONS

Word	Count
oh	1

Total words	1	Total different words	1
Mean words	0·33	Mean different words	0·33

ARTICLES

Word	Count	Word	Count	Word	Count
a	66	an	4	the	180

Total words	250	Total different words	3
Mean words	83·33	Mean different words	1·00

OTHER

Word	Count	Word	Count	Word	Count	Word	Count
*Ajax	1	Coca cola	2	*Kenwood	1	Pakistani	1
Christmas-		Coke	1	*Marmite	2	T-shirt	1
tree	1	'cos	1	*Meccano	1	yes	1

Total words	13	Total different words	11
Mean words	4·33	Mean different words	3·67

Subject Group T

(9 children; age: 14–15;
performance I.Q.: ≤90; hearing loss 61–80 dB)

NOUNS

Word	Count	Word	Count	Word	Count	Word	Count
accident	4	bottles	2	clown	2	farmer	7
account	2	bowl	5	coat	10	father	24
address	1	box	2	cold	1	fault	1
air	1	boy	108	*cooker	2	fence	3
all	2	boys	21	corner	1	fences	2
ambulance	27	bread	11	cover	1	field	10
animal	1	brick	1	cow	3	fields	1
anything	1	broom	5	crash	1	fire	1
apple	11	brother	2	cream	1	fireman	1
apples	6	brush	3	*cricket	6	fish	9
apron	1	bucket	7	cup	4	flap	1
arm	2	bull	17	cupboard	1	flat	1
baby	2	bush	2	cups	2	floor	9
back	7	bushes	1	curtain	4	flower	9
badges	1	butter	8	danger	5	flowerpot	3
bag	13	button	1	date	2	flowers	2
ball	40	cabbage	2	day	1	food	12
banana	8	cabbages	1	dinner	5	football	14
bananas	3	cake	6	dinosaur	2	*foot-path	2
bank	2	cakes	1	dog	45	fork	5
*barrow	3	calendar	6	dog's	1	forks	2
baseball	2	candy-floss	1	dogcart	1	frame	1
basket	11	car	45	doggie	1	fridge	2
bat	7	carrots	1	doll	6	friend	2
bath	1	cart	2	doll's	1	front	1
beach	2	cat	9	dolly	1	fruit	5
beard	1	cauliflower	5	door	10	game	1
bed	1	chair	9	doors	3	games	2
bicycle	4	cheese	1	drain	3	garage	1
bike	2	chicken	6	drawer	2	gardener	1
blind	1	child	2	dresses	2	gas	1
board	3	children	7	drink	3	gate	10
*bonnet	1	cleaner	4	egg	8	girl	22
book	13	clock	8	eggs	4	girls	2
*boot	15	clockwork	1	engine	1	glove	3
boots	6	cloth	4	face	5	gloves	3
bottle	2	clothes	7	family	8	goal	7

Word	Count	Word	Count	Word	Count	Word	Count
goal-posts	2	man	75	pan	3	shoe	1
grapefruit	1	man's	2	park	2	shoes	5
grocer	1	map	5	path	1	shop	1
ground	1	margarine	1	*pavement	4	shopping	2
hand	3	market	4	peanut	1	shorts	2
handbag	1	marmalade	4	pear	1	shoulder	2
handstand	1	mask	5	*pence	1	side	4
handstands	1	match	1	people	16	sign	3
hat	9	matches	4	pepper	5	sink	5
haven	1	*mates	1	picnic	13	skate	1
head	9	meadow	1	picture	7	skates	3
hedge	5	meal	1	pictures	3	sky	1
here	1	means	2	piece	2	*sledge	5
hill	2	meat	5	pieces	2	snow	9
hold	1	medal	1	*pints	1	son	1
hole	4	medals	1	plate	6	spoon	6
holiday	1	melon	2	plates	1	stair	1
home	2	men	3	police	4	stairs	1
hospital	1	mess	3	policeman	5	stall	2
house	15	metal	1	pond	3	station's	1
houses	4	mice	2	posts	2	stick	8
husband	1	middle	2	pot	6	sticks	1
ice	20	milk	15	potato	3	straw	1
interest	2	milkman	11	puppy	1	street	1
jar	1	mirror	4	*purse	4	stretcher	1
jellies	1	model	1	*pussy	1	string	2
jelly	6	money	15	railway	1	stuff	2
jug	1	mop	2	raincoat	1	sugar	1
*jumper	2	mops	1	rhubarb	1	supper	1
*jumpers	1	mother	29	rice	2	sweet	1
kettle	7	mouse	3	road	8	table	19
kitchen	9	mummy	4	*rounder	1	*tap	4
knife	13	mushroom	4	*rounders	1	tea	2
knives	1	mushrooms	1	rug	1	teacher	1
knock	1	name	1	salt	6	teapot	1
ladder	21	noise	4	sandwich	5	there	3
lady	51	noon	2	sandwiches	7	thing	6
lady's	1	notice	2	sauce	2	things	7
lead	1	object	4	saucepan	4	time	2
leg	4	onion	4	saucer	1	tomato	2
*lorry	2	orange	4	scar	1	tomatoes	3
lot	1	oranges	1	scarf	10	top	1
lump	2	oven	2	scene	6	towel	4
lunch	1	pair	1	scissors	6	toy	2
machine	11	palette	1	seating	1	toys	7

Word	Count	Word	Count	Word	Count	Word	Count
train	5	vegetable	2	water	11	window-sill	1
tree	6	vegetables	1	way	3	winter	5
trees	3	village	1	wheel	1	wire	2
*trouser	1	wallet	2	wheelbarrow	1	woman	3
*trousers	4	washing	5	window	24	wood	2
van	1						

Total words	1731	Total different words	349
Mean words	192·33	Mean different words	38·78

VERBS

Word	Count	Word	Count	Word	Count	Word	Count
allowed	1	climbing	4	fell	15	hurry	1
are	49	come	13	fetch	1	hurt	6
asked	2	comes	2	finished	4	is	111
bang	1	coming	10	fix	1	jump	4
barbed	1	cook	1	framed	2	jumped	1
be	15	cooking	5	frighten	2	jumping	3
been	1	could	3	frightened	2	keep	1
bending	2	cover	1	frying	1	kick	6
bothered	2	covered	1	get	28	kicked	3
bounce	1	crash	8	give	2	kill	1
break	2	crashed	3	giving	1	knocked	7
bringing	1	crashes	1	go	15	know	9
broke	2	cross	1	goes	1	knowing	2
broken	2	crying	2	going	34	laid	3
bumped	1	cycling	2	got	25	laugh	1
buying	1	die	1	grab	2	laying	2
call	3	do	1	had	4	left	3
came	14	doing	7	happen	2	like	1
can	6	drink	3	happened	6	look	12
carry	3	drinking	12	happening	1	looks	1
carrying	17	drive	3	has	15	looked	1
change	1	driving	5	have	6	looking	21
charge	2	drop	8	having	6	lure	2
chase	1	dropped	11	heard	3	made	1
chasing	3	drowned	1	hearing	2	make	4
clean	2	eat	7	help	10	making	7
cleaning	5	eating	16	helping	3	mashed	1
clearing	1	fall	4	hit	1	may	3
climb	3	fallen	6	hold	3	mean	3
climbed	2	falling	3	holding	2	might	7

Word	Count	Word	Count	Word	Count	Word	Count
missing	1	rolling	2	slipped	1	waiting	1
moaning	1	run	6	smashed	1	walk	1
must	7	running	10	standing	7	walked	1
open	1	rushing	1	stands	1	walking	11
opened	2	said	2	staring	1	want	2
opening	1	saw	2	start	1	wanted	1
pack	2	say	5	starting	1	wants	3
packing	4	saying	6	stop	7	was	30
pass	1	says	7	suppose	2	wash	2
pay	4	scared	1	swerved	1	washed	1
paying	1	scattered	2	taking	2	watch	3
pick	1	scream	1	talk	1	watching	10
picking	3	see	9	talked	1	wave	2
play	10	seems	2	talking	5	waving	1
playing	48	shave	1	telling	3	wearing	5
pointing	2	shaving	5	terrified	1	went	4
pretend	1	shocked	3	think	16	were	10
pull	3	shout	2	thought	1	whipped	1
pulling	1	shouting	3	throwing	3	will	3
push	2	shove	1	throws	1	wind	1
put	20	shut	4	tied	2	wondering	1
putting	8	sit	1	tired	3	work	1
ran	1	sitting	5	trip	2	worried	2
reach	1	skating	3	tripped	6	worry	1
read	6	slaughter	1	try	9	would	1
reading	9	sleeping	2	trying	13	write	4
realize	2	slide	1	upset	1	writing	2
riding	3	sliding	1				

Total words	1153	Total different words	230
Mean words	128·11	Mean different words	25·56

ADJECTIVES

Word	Count	Word	Count	Word	Count	Word	Count
all	16	both	1	dirty	1	good	2
angry	5	big	2	dreadful	1	green	1
another	3	bright	1	fifty-six	1	happy	1
any	2	brown	1	five	6	hungry	2
asleep	5	cold	2	four	6	hurt	3
awful	1	dangerous	6	funny	2	icy	1
back	1	different	1	gentle	1	late	1

Word	Count	Word	Count	Word	Count	Word	Count
little	18	one	31	selfish	1	thin	8
long	1	open	8	slight	2	thirsty	1
middle	1	other	15	small	3	this	3
much	1	own	3	some	15	three	5
muddy	2	past	1	stupid	2	tidy	1
next	2	ready	1	sweet	1	tiny	1
nice	3	red	4	terrible	1	twelve	3
noisy	1	sad	1	that	37	two	20
odd	2	same	1				

Total words	276	Total different words	62
Mean words	30·67	Mean different words	6·89

ADVERBS

Word	Count	Word	Count	Word	Count	Word	Count
about	5	gently	1	on	4	straight	1
all	4	here	2	out	31	that	1
along	12	high	1	outside	3	then	4
around	1	home	8	over	24	there	28
as	6	how	1	perhaps	1	together	2
away	12	in	5	properly	1	too	2
back	4	inside	1	quick	1	under	1
before	1	just	29	rather	1	up	12
below	1	maybe	5	ready	1	upside-down	2
down	19	nearly	1	really	3	very	13
easier	1	never	2	sideways	1	well	6
else	1	not	10	so	2	when	4
far	1	now	5	somewhere	1	where	10
fast	1	off	5	still	4		

Total words	309	Total different words	55
Mean words	34·33	Mean different words	6·11

PRONOUNS

Word	Count	Word	Count	Word	Count	Word	Count
I	3	her	18	his	38	it	45
e	69	him	47	I	26	me	2

Word	Count	Word	Count	Word	Count	Word	Coun
one	7	their	7	those	1	which	6
others	1	them	16	us	1	who	3
she	21	these	2	we	1	you	8
something	8	they	64	what	11	your	2
that	8	this	2				

Total words	417	Total different words	26
Mean words	46·33	Mean different words	2·89

PREPOSITIONS

Word	Count	Word	Count	Word	Count	Word	Cou
about	3	between	1	near	1	to	89
across	2	by	4	of	46	toward	
after	13	down	3	off	4	towards	9
along	2	for	14	on	63	under	8
around	3	from	5	onto	1	underneath	
at	27	in	61	out	6	up	
back	1	inside	2	over	20	with	5.
behind	3	into	14	past	2	without	
below	1	like	4	through	2		

Total words	479	Total different words	35
Mean words	53·22	Mean different words	3·89

CONJUNCTIONS

Word	Count	Word	Count	Word	Count	Word	Cou
and	254	either	2	so	2	though	
because	18	if	1	that	4	while	
but	1	or	6	then	2		

Total words	298	Total different words	11
Mean words	33·11	Mean different words	1·22

CONTRACTIONS

Word	Count	Word	Count	Word	Count	Word	Count
anybody's	1	don't	10	it's	8	room's	2
*boot's	2	everybody's	1	lady's	3	she's	11
boy's	9	farmer's	2	man's	1	that's	2
bull's	4	father's	4	mother's	5	there's	30
can't	4	girl's	1	o'clock	1	they're	12
didn't	3	haven't	1	picnic's	2	they've	9
dog's	4	he's	32	policeman's	1	you're	1

Total words	166	Total different words	28
Mean words	18·44	Mean different words	3·11

INTERJECTIONS

Word	Count	Word	Count
oh	5	well	8

Total words	13	Total different words	2
Mean words	1·44	Mean different words	0·22

ARTICLES

Word	Count	Word	Count	Word	Count
a	213	an	15	the	631

Total words	859	Total different words	3
Mean words	95·44	Mean different words	0·33

OTHER

Word	Count	Word	Count	Word	Count	Word	Count
jump	1	'cos	1	no	16	sweep	1
christmas-		English	1	Pepsi	1	*Wellington	2
tree	2	India	2	scissor	2	yes	5
oke	6	*Marmite	2	Scotland	1		

Total words	43	Total different words	14
Mean words	4·78	Mean different words	1·56

Subject Group U

(4 children; age: 14–15 years;
performance I.Q.: ≤90; hearing loss: 81–95 dB)

NOUNS

Word	Count	Word	Count	Word	Count	Word	Count
aid	1	bread	5	dish	2	fruit	3
all	2	brother	2	dish-cloth	1	gas	1
ambulance	9	bucket	1	dog	23	gate	3
apple	6	bull	11	doll	5	gates	2
apples	2	bushes	1	dolls	1	girl	10
argument	2	butter	5	dolly	2	girls	4
arm	2	cabbage	2	door	4	gloves	6
baby	1	cake	10	dragon	1	goal	3
back	1	calendar	2	drain	2	goalkeeper	1
background	1	car	29	drawer	1	goal-post	1
badge	1	cat	5	dress	1	grass	2
bag	5	cauliflower	1	dresses	2	hand	3
ball	29	chair	4	drink	3	handstand	1
banana	1	cheese	1	egg	7	handstands	1
bananas	1	chicken	1	eggs	1	hat	4
barns	1	children	7	face	1	head	5
barrel	2	clock	5	faces	2	hedge	1
basket	10	cloth	6	family	6	here	2
bat	6	clothes	5	farm	2	hill	
beard	2	clown	1	farmer	5	hole	
bench	2	coat	5	farmhouse	1	home	2
bicycle	2	cocoa	1	father	10	honey	
bill	1	coin	1	fellow	1	house	
*biscuits	2	comics	2	fence	1	houses	
*blancmange	1	*cooker	1	field	10	ice	14
blanket	1	cooking	1	finger	1	jacket	
blind	2	country	1	fish	4	jam	
board	2	couple	1	floor	1	kettle	
book	8	crack	1	flower	3	kitchen	
*boot	8	crash	1	flowerpot	5	knife	1
boots	4	cup	1	flowers	2	ladder	1
bottle	2	cupboard	2	food	6	lady	2
bottles	1	cups	4	fool	1	look	
bottom	1	curtain	2	football	5	*lorry	
bowl	1	curtains	1	fork	6	lot	
boy	47	dad	2	friend	2	lunch	
boys	8	dinner	5	front	2	machine	

Word	Count	Word	Count	Word	Count	Word	Count
make-up	1	notice	4	sandwiches	5	teapot	1
man	35	onion	2	sauce	1	there	6
map	5	onions	1	saucepan	5	thing	1
marmalade	4	oven	5	saucer	4	things	7
marrow	3	paint	2	scarf	4	time	2
mask	2	paper	1	scissors	7	times	1
matches	2	path	1	shelf	1	toboggan	1
material	1	pattern	1	shirts	1	top	1
matter	1	pear	1	shoe	2	towel	2
meal	3	people	6	shoes	1	town	2
meat	7	pepper	5	shopping	2	toy	5
melon	1	picnic	2	sink	2	toys	1
men	3	picture	5	skate	2	train	5
ness	5	plate	2	sky	1	tree	3
nice	1	plates	1	slide	2	trees	4
milk	7	play	2	snow	4	*trousers	2
milkman	9	plums	1	son	1	uniform	1
mirror	2	police	1	spoon	7	vase	1
mixer	1	policeman	4	stall	3	vegetables	2
money	7	pond	1	stick	9	wall	1
monster	1	pork	1	stove	1	washing	2
mop	1	pudding	1	straw	1	washing-up	2
mother	9	puppy	1	stuff	1	water	3
house	4	*purse	4	sugar	1	way	1
mud	2	rain	1	sweets	1	wheelbarrow	1
mummy	3	raincoat	1	table	8	whisk	1
mushroom	1	rhubarb	1	table-cloth	1	window	13
mushrooms	2	road	4	*tap	4	wires	1
mustard	2	sack	2	*taps	1	woman	3
noise	1	salt	5	tea	2	wood	1
noises	1						

Total words	949	Total different words	269
Mean words	237·25	Mean different words	67·25

VERBS

Word	Count	Word	Count	Word	Count	Word	Count
e	15	bringing	1	bumping	3	can	3
rived	1	broke	1	buy	1	carries	2
	1	bump	2	call	1	carry	9
ckoned	1	bumped	1	came	7	carrying	4

Word	Count	Word	Count	Word	Count	Word	Count
chopping	1	grab	1	packing	2	stay	1
cleaning	2	had	2	painting	1	stick	1
climbing	2	happen	2	park	2	stop	7
close	1	happened	1	paying	3	stopping	1
come	11	happening	1	pick	3	suck	1
comes	1	has	3	play	20	supposed	1
coming	2	have	6	playing	14	sweeping	1
cook	1	having	2	prepare	1	take	2
could	1	heard	2	pretend	1	talk	2
counting	1	help	4	pull	3	talking	7
cracking	1	hit	8	put	7	telephoned	1
crash	5	hold	3	putting	3	telling	1
crashed	3	holding	4	rampage	1	terrified	3
crashing	1	hurry	2	ran	1	think	13
crushed	1	hurt	2	reach	4	thinking	
do	1	is	46	reaching	2	throw	2
doing	2	jump	3	reading	5	throwing	
drink	1	jumped	2	remember	1	tidy	
drinking	8	jumping	1	run	1	tired	
driving	4	keep	1	running	4	tripped	
drop	6	kicked	2	save	2	trying	8
dropped	4	knocked	3	saw	10	turned	
dropping	2	know	1	say	2	walk	
eating	7	land	1	says	1	walking	
fall	2	leaving	1	see	7	want	
fell	20	let	1	shaving	6	wanted	
fighting	2	lift	2	shouting	2	was	1
finished	1	like	1	sit	2	washing	
forget	1	look	5	sitting	3	watch	
forgot	1	looked	3	skating	4	watching	
get	6	looking	9	*sledging	1	wearing	
getting	1	make	1	stand	1	went	
give	4	making	1	standing	7	will	
go	8	might	2	start	2	worried	
going	4	open	6	started	1	writing	
got	12						

Total words	567		Total different words	157	
Mean words	141·75		Mean different words	39·25	

ADJECTIVES

Word	Count	Word	Count	Word	Count	Word	Count
all	9	dirty	2	older	1	thin	4
angry	4	electric	1	one	3	three	1
asleep	1	first	1	other	2	tidy	2
awful	1	five	5	own	1	twelve	5
big	1	four	1	red	1	two	14
blue	1	like	2	sad	1	warm	1
busy	2	little	12	some	9	white	1
cross	2	many	1	that	7	whole	1
dangerous	1	next	2	these	1	wooden	1

Total words 105   Total different words 36
Mean words 26·25   Mean different words 9·00

ADVERBS

Word	Count	Word	Count	Word	Count	Word	Count
about	7	fast	1	on	2	there	31
long	5	home	2	out	17	to	1
also	1	how	1	over	8	too	1
anywhere	2	in	1	perhaps	5	up	12
round	1	just	2	quickly	2	upside-down	1
s	3	like	2	ready	1	very	6
sleep	1	near	1	right	2	well	2
way	4	next	1	sometimes	1	when	5
ack	4	not	3	suddenly	4	where	1
own	6	off	9				

Total words 159   Total different words 38
Mean words 39·75   Mean different words 9·50

PRONOUNS

Word	Count	Word	Count	Word	Count	Word	Count
erything	2	his	25	somebody	3	they	23
e	50	I	26	something	6	this	3
er	5	it	16	that	4	what	3
m	13	me	1	their	5	who	3
mself	2	she	8	them	5	you	3

Total words 206   Total different words 20
Mean words 51·50   Mean different words 5·00

PREPOSITIONS

Word	Count	Word	Count	Word	Count	Word	Count
across	2	for	3	off	3	to	44
after	6	from	2	on	23	under	2
along	2	in	23	out	5	underneath	1
at	9	into	5	over	14	up	1
behind	1	near	1	past	5	upon	2
by	3	of	13	through	6	with	36
down	4						

Total words	216		Total different words	25	
Mean words	54·00		Mean different words	6·25	

CONJUNCTIONS

Word	Count	Word	Count	Word	Count	Word	Count
and	154	but	1	if	2	so	
because	4	for	2	or	17		

Total words	183		Total different words	7	
Mean words	45·75		Mean different words	1·75	

CONTRACTIONS

Word	Count	Word	Count	Word	Count	Word	Count
didn't	3	hasn't	1	isn't	2	that's	
doesn't	1	he'll	1	it's	4	wasn't	
don't	1	he's	4	man's	1	what's	

Total words	23		Total different words	12	
Mean words	5·75		Mean different words	3·00	

INTERJECTIONS

Word	Count		
—	—		

| Total words | 0 | Total different words | 0 |
| Mean words | 0·00 | Mean different words | 0·00 |

ARTICLES

Word	Count	Word	Count	Word	Count
a	181	an	6	the	318

| Total words | 505 | Total different words | 3 |
| Mean words | 126·25 | Mean different words | 0·75 |

OTHER

Word	Count	Word	Count	Word	Count	Word	Count
Coke	1	*Marmite	2	themself	2	*Wellington	1
crash	1	no	1				

| Total words | 8 | Total different words | 6 |
| Mean words | 2·00 | Mean different words | 1·50 |

Subject Group V

(9 children; age: 14–15 years;
performance I.Q.: 91–110; hearing loss: 40–60 dB)

NOUNS

Word	Count	Word	Count	Word	Count	Word	Count
accident	6	all	15	anger	1	apple	3
afternoon	2	ambulance	17	animal	1	apples	8

Word	Count	Word	Count	Word	Count	Word	Count
argument	1	cabbages	1	door	11	goalie	1
atlas	1	cake	2	dragon	1	go-cart	1
baby	1	cakes	1	drain	5	grape-fruit	1
back	2	calendar	6	drawer	2	grapefruits	1
badges	1	cap	8	dress	1	grating	1
bag	10	car	27	drink	2	grocers	1
ball	45	cart	2	egg	4	grocery	1
banana	4	cat	6	eggs	6	ground	1
bananas	3	cauliflower	2	end	1	hand	3
barrel	1	chain	1	engine	1	hands	3
baseball	3	chair	4	equipment	1	handstand	6
basket	12	chairs	1	face	2	handstands	1
bat	8	change	1	family	2	hat	5
beef	1	cheese	1	farm	2	head	7
behind	1	chicken	2	farmer	7	hedge	2
bicycle	1	child	2	father	16	hedges	1
bike	5	children	10	fence	8	helmet	1
bill	3	cleaner	1	field	11	here	2
*bin	1	clock	5	fields	3	hill	1
*blancmange	2	cloth	5	fire	1	hold	1
*bloke	6	clothes	6	fireman	1	hole	3
*blokes	1	clown	1	fish	7	holiday	1
board	3	coat	6	floor	8	home	1
book	14	coats	1	flower	3	hospital	1
books	3	coffee	1	flowerpot	3	hours	1
*boot	6	*cooker	3	flowers	4	house	3
boots	11	corner	1	food	9	houses	2
bottle	2	cow	1	football	9	ice	18
bottles	2	crash	1	fork	3	ice-cream	2
bowl	4	cup	3	forks	1	jacket	1
box	1	cupboard	1	front	1	jam	1
boy	67	cups	2	fruit	6	jar	3
boys	7	curtain	1	games	1	jelly	4
brake	1	curtains	1	gas	1	jug	2
branch	1	dad	5	gate	6	*kerb	2
bread	6	danger	3	girl	15	kettle	6
broom	3	day	5	girls	2	kids	2
brother	6	death	2	glass	1	kitchen	6
brothers	2	decoration	1	glasses	4	knife	9
brush	4	dinner	7	glove	2	ladder	17
bucket	6	dinosaur	1	gloves	3	lady	24
bull	11	dog	45	goal	1	land	1
bushes	2	dog's	2	goal-post	1	leg	2
butter	5	doll	3	goal-posts	3	legs	1
cabbage	3	dolly	1	goals	1	lemon	1

Word	Count	Word	Count	Word	Count	Word	Count
loads	1	mouth	1	racquet	1	sound	1
loaf	1	mum	1	referee	1	spoon	3
look	1	mummy	1	rink	2	sports	1
*lorry	2	mushroom	2	road	18	stick	10
lots	2	mushrooms	1	*rounders	6	sticks	3
lunch	4	mustard	1	salt	1	strawberries	1
machine	2	*neckerchief	1	sandwich	6	street	4
maggot	1	noise	1	sandwiches	6	stuff	8
man	52	one	4	saucepan	1	suit	2
man's	2	onion	1	saucepans	2	summer	1
map	2	onions	2	saucer	3	sun	1
maps	2	onlookers	2	scarf	5	table	19
market	2	oranges	1	scissors	7	table-cloth	6
marmalade	2	order	1	scouts	1	*tap	1
mask	4	oven	5	set	2	*taps	1
matches	5	pair	1	shadows	2	tea	1
meal	2	pans	1	shave	3	*tea-cloth	2
meanwhile	1	*pavement	1	shirt	1	there	3
meat	6	pears	1	shirts	1	thing	3
mechanic	4	people	16	shoes	5	things	3
mechanics	1	pepper	2	shop	1	time	5
medal	1	person	1	shopping	1	tomato	1
men	4	picnic	10	side	1	tomatoes	6
mess	2	picture	6	sides	1	toy	4
mice	1	pictures	1	sign	5	toys	1
middle	3	pie	1	signpost	1	train	9
milk	8	place	9	sink	6	tree	6
milkman	7	plant	2	sister	2	trees	1
milkman's	1	plate	4	skates	2	trouble	1
*mince	1	plates	5	ski	2	*trousers	1
*mincer	1	plums	1	skirt	2	two	4
mirror	2	police	5	*sledge	8	wagon	2
mixer	3	policeman	5	*sledges	1	washing	2
models	1	pond	3	slide	2	water	3
money	12	post	1	slopes	1	way	2
month	1	posts	1	snack	2	while	1
mop	2	pot	6	snow	2	window	20
morning	1	potato	1	soldier	1	winter	1
mother	12	pots	2	son	3	woman	10
motor-car	1	pudding	1	sort	1	wood	1
mouse	2	*purse	7				

Total words	1424	Total different words	350
Mean words	158·22	Mean different words	38·89

VERBS

Word	Count	Word	Count	Word	Count	Word	Count
allowed	1	crawls	1	got	15	making	3
answering	1	crying	2	had	2	mark	1
are	23	cutting	1	happened	3	marks	1
arrive	3	cycling	1	happening	1	mean	1
arrived	1	did	1	has	6	mending	1
astonished	1	die	1	have	7	might	7
bang	1	dives	1	having	17	mixing	1
be	11	do	4	heard	1	moving	2
been	3	doing	11	help	8	notice	1
break	1	done	1	helping	5	open	7
bring	1	dress	1	hiding	1	opening	3
bringing	1	dressing	1	hit	9	pack	1
broke	1	drinking	9	hitting	1	packing	6
build	1	driving	1	hits	1	paid	1
building	1	drop	1	hold	1	painting	1
bump	1	dropped	13	holding	1	pay	2
call	1	drops	3	holds	1	paying	3
calling	1	drove	1	injure	3	phoned	2
came	5	drowning	1	is	83	play	5
can	5	eat	1	jump	2	playing	36
carry	2	eating	12	jumped	2	point	2
carrying	23	empty	3	jumping	1	pointing	3
charges	1	exhausted	1	keep	1	pull	1
charging	1	facing	1	kick	1	pulling	2
chase	1	fall	9	kicked	5	pushed	1
chasing	2	fallen	3	kill	1	put	6
chatting	2	falling	3	knock	1	putting	3
chucked	1	falls	1	knocked	5	raging	1
cleaning	3	fell	15	know	4	ran	1
climb	3	fetch	2	knows	1	reach	2
climbing	1	finished	1	laid	3	read	3
closing	1	flying	2	land	2	reading	9
come	11	forgot	1	lay	3	rescue	3
comes	6	frightened	1	leave	1	riding	5
comforting	1	frozen	2	listen	1	run	2
coming	7	get	34	listening	2	running	14
corned	1	getting	3	look	6	rushing	2
could	6	give	1	looked	2	said	2
covered	2	giving	1	looking	7	save	1
cracked	1	go	10	looks	15	saying	3
crash	4	goes	4	lost	1	says	4
crashed	4	going	23	made	1	scared	1
crashes	1	gone	2	make	2	screaming	1

Word	Count	Word	Count	Word	Count	Word	Count
screeching	1	smash	1	taking	5	turned	1
see	4	smashed	3	talking	5	using	1
seeing	3	snorting	1	tell	2	walking	9
seems	2	snowing	2	telling	3	warn	1
set	2	spread	1	tells	1	warning	1
shall	2	squashed	1	think	2	was	19
shave	3	stand	3	throwing	3	wash	2
shaving	2	standing	4	tired	1	washing	2
shining	1	staring	2	told	1	watch	2
shot	1	start	3	took	1	watching	17
shouting	1	started	4	trapped	1	wearing	4
sitting	2	stirs	1	tried	1	went	11
skating	6	stood	1	trip	1	were	2
skiing	2	stop	6	tripped	2	will	2
sleep	3	stopped	1	trips	1	work	7
sleeping	1	stopping	2	trying	26	worried	2
sliding	1	suppose	1	tumbled	1	writing	2
slipped	1	surprised	1	turn	1		

Total words 952
Mean words 105·78

Total different words 243
Mean different words 27·00

ADJECTIVES

Word	Count	Word	Count	Word	Count	Word	Count
aged	1	first	1	nine	1	sure	5
all	29	five	7	old	1	ten	1
angry	2	four	8	older	3	that	3
another	4	front	3	oldest	3	these	4
asleep	2	full	4	one	16	thin	4
big	5	furious	1	open	2	third	2
bigger	1	green	6	other	3	this	6
blue	3	half	3	ready	2	three	3
both	3	hurt	1	red	10	twelve	4
brown	2	left	2	sharp	1	two	21
bushy	1	like	8	six	1	unconscious	1
busy	3	little	33	slippery	1	vicious	1
clumsy	1	many	4	small	2	whole	1
cross	1	middle	1	snowy	1	wrong	1
dangerous	1	most	1	some	23	young	2
different	1	muddy	2	such	1	youngest	1
few	1	nice	2	sunny	3		

Total words 282
Mean words 31·33

Total different words 67
Mean different words 7·44

ADVERBS

Word	Count	Word	Count	Word	Count	Word	Count
about	4	fast	1	off	8	safely	1
accidentally	1	here	2	on	5	somewhere	1
across	4	home	6	only	1	still	3
again	1	how	1	out	44	straight	1
all	5	in	4	outside	1	suddenly	1
along	10	instead	1	over	14	then	2
around	5	just	11	past	1	there	37
as	4	maybe	3	probably	19	up	12
away	10	nearby	2	quickly	1	very	3
back	6	nearly	1	quite	2	well	1
down	15	not	6	round	1	when	3
everywhere	1	now	5				

Total words	271	Total different words	46
Mean words	30.11	Mean different words	5·11

PRONOUNS

Word	Count	Word	Count	Word	Count	Word	Count
everything	1	his	43	somebody	1	these	2
he	50	I	12	someone	4	they	29
her	13	it	55	something	10	what	8
herself	1	its	1	that	17	which	3
him	37	other	1	their	15	you	8
himself	1	she	7	them	20		

Total words	339	Total different words	23
Mean words	37·67	Mean different words	2·56

PREPOSITIONS

Word	Count	Word	Count	Word	Count	Word	Count
about	6	down	10	next	1	past	5
across	8	for	10	of	36	to	79
after	5	from	8	off	33	too	2
against	1	in	58	on	70	towards	6
along	1	into	16	onto	2	under	4
at	13	like	6	out	4	up	4
beside	1	near	3	over	15	with	57
by	4						

Total words	468	Total different words	29
Mean words	52·00	Mean different words	3·22

CONJUNCTIONS

Word	Count	Word	Count	Word	Count	Word	Count
and	209	but	5	so	2	though	2
as	6	if	6	that	1	when	1
because	13	or	17	then	1	while	7

Total words	270		Total different words	12	
Mean words	30·00		Mean different words	1·33	

CONTRACTIONS

Word	Count	Word	Count	Word	Count	Word	Count
bloke's	2	didn't	2	isn't	6	shouldn't	1
boot's	1	dinner's	1	it's	28	someone's	1
boy's	12	dog's	5	lady's	5	stuff's	1
brother's	3	don't	5	man's	4	table's	1
bull's	3	family's	1	mother's	6	that's	4
can't	1	farmer's	1	mum's	4	there's	75
car's	2	father's	1	one's	1	they're	23
cat's	2	girl's	2	person's	1	they've	2
child's	2	he'll	1	picnic's	1	tree's	1
couldn't	1	he's	43	pot'll	1	wasn't	2
dad's	5	I've	1	she's	5	what's	1

Total words	271		Total different words	44	
Mean words	30·11		Mean different words	4·89	

INTERJECTIONS

Word	Count
well	14

Total words	14		Total different words	1	
Mean words	1·56		Mean different words	0·11	

ARTICLES

Word	Count		Word	Count		Word	Count
a	323		an	16		the	533

	Total words	872	Total different words	3
	Mean words	96·89	Mean different words	0·33

OTHER

Word	Count		Word	Count		Word	Count		Word	Count
*Ajax	1		Coke	16		*Fairy-liquid	1		themself	2
American	4		comed	1		June	1		them's	1
*Bovril	1		'cos	3		*Marmite	2		*Wellington	1
camed	1		Dachshund	1		no	3		*Wellingtons	1
Christmas-tree	4		Egypt	1		Saturday	1		yes	3
Cocacola	2									

	Total words	51	Total different words	21
	Mean words	5·67	Mean different words	2·33

Subject Group W

(9 children; age: 14–15 years;
performance I.Q.: 91–110; hearing loss: 61–80 dB)

NOUNS

Word	Count		Word	Count		Word	Count		Word	Count
accident	3		back	7		bat	9		books	2
ambulance	21		badge	1		bench	1		*boot	12
ankle	1		badges	1		bicycle	4		boots	
apple	6		bag	14		bike	3		bottle	
apples	5		balcony	1		*bin	1		bottles	
apron	1		ball	50		*biscuit	1		bowl	
argument	2		banana	5		*bloke	1		boy	9
atlas	1		bananas	3		board	2		boys	1
baby	5		basket	17		book	17		bread	

Word	Count	Word	Count	Word	Count	Word	Count
broom	7	door	16	grass	1	match	2
brother	3	down	1	grocers	1	matches	5
brush	1	dragon	2	ground	3	material	1
bucket	9	drain	5	guard	1	meal	1
bull	16	drawer	2	hair	1	meat	12
bushes	2	drink	1	hand	7	medal	4
butter	9	drinks	1	handstand	2	men	1
cabbage	5	driver	1	handstands	1	mess	4
cabbages	2	egg	4	hat	8	mice	1
cake	11	eggs	7	head	9	middle	1
cakes	1	end	1	headstands	1	milk	13
calendar	3	engine	1	hedge	2	milkman	10
car	42	face	3	help	1	*mince	1
carts	1	family	4	hill	3	mirror	4
case	2	farm	2	hole	4	mixer	1
cat	9	farmer	8	holiday	2	mixture	1
cauliflower	1	farmer's	1	home	2	model	4
chair	9	father	14	house	4	money	15
chicken	2	fence	11	houses	5	monster	2
children	9	field	15	husband	2	month	2
clock	9	fire	1	ice	28	mop	1
cloth	8	fish	9	jam	1	mother	21
clothes	5	floor	10	jar	4	mountain	1
coat	10	flower	6	jelly	6	mouse	5
cooker	2	flowerpot	2	jug	1	mud	1
corner	4	flowerpots	1	*jumper	1	mum	6
cow	1	flowers	7	kettle	10	mummy	3
crash	4	food	16	kid	3	mushroom	4
cream	1	football	13	kids	2	mushrooms	1
cricket	6	forest	1	kitchen	7	name	1
cucumber	2	fork	5	knife	17	night-time	1
cup	5	forks	2	ladder	19	noise	1
cups	2	frame	1	lady	41	notice	1
curtain	6	front	1	lemon	1	notices	1
lad	4	fruit	7	loaf	2	numbers	1
lad's	1	game	1	*lorry	2	onion	5
langer	4	games	1	lot	9	orange	2
date	3	gate	9	lunch	1	oranges	1
daughter	1	girl	22	machine	7	oven	7
day	1	girls	3	man	78	packet	1
dinner	3	glove	5	map	7	pair	1
dog	39	gloves	3	market	1	pan	2
doll	6	goal	1	marmalade	4	paper	2
dolls	1	goalkeeper	3	mask	7	park	4
dolly	2	goal-posts	1	mat	1	part	2

Word	Count	Word	Count	Word	Count	Word	Count
path	2	pots	1	shoulder	1	top	2
pattern	1	pudding	2	side	1	towel	2
patterns	1	pumpkin	1	sign	1	toy	5
*pavement	1	puncture	1	signpost	1	toys	6
pear	2	*purse	7	sink	6	train	7
*pence	1	rags	1	skates	2	tray	1
people	11	rain	1	skin	1	tree	6
pepper	6	raincoat	2	*sledge	4	trees	5
person	4	rest	1	snow	8	trolley	2
picnic	15	rice	4	son	11	trouble	2
picture	6	road	5	sort	3	*trousers	3
pictures	1	room	3	spoon	9	van	1
pie	2	*rounders	3	spoons	1	vegetable	3
piece	2	row	1	stall	3	vegetables	1
pieces	1	rubber	1	stick	7	wall	2
place	1	*rubbish	1	sticks	2	washing	3
plant	2	salt	6	story	2	washing-up	1
plate	4	sandwich	4	strawberries	1	water	8
plates	2	sandwiches	7	string	1	way	3
plums	1	saucepan	5	sweeper	1	week	1
point	1	saucer	1	table	21	week-end	1
pole	1	saucers	2	table-cloth	1	wheelbarrow	3
policeman	10	scarf	3	*tap	5	wife	2
pond	4	scissors	9	*taps	2	window	22
pop	1	shave	6	*tea-cloth	1	windows	4
posters	2	sheet	1	thing	2	window-sill	1
*postman	1	shirts	2	things	8	wire	1
posts	1	shoe	1	tomato	1	wood	1
pot	3	shoes	4	tomatoes	1	world	1
potato	5	shopping	1				

Total words   1702   Total different words   334
Mean words   189·11   Mean different words   37·11

VERBS

Word	Count	Word	Count	Word	Count	Word	Count
allowed	1	banged	1	being	1	bring	
are	24	barking	1	boil	1	broke	
argue	1	be	5	bounce	1	broken	
arrived	1	been	4	break	1	bump	
ask	1	begin	1	breaking	1	called	

Word	Count	Word	Count	Word	Count	Word	Count
calls	1	fell	18	knocking	1	pulling	1
came	10	finish	2	knocks	1	pulls	2
can	3	finished	2	know	7	put	12
carries	1	flew	1	knows	1	puts	2
carry	4	follow	1	laid	2	putting	7
carrying	13	forgot	1	land	1	ran	7
catching	1	freezing	1	laughing	1	reach	6
chase	2	frightened	1	left	4	reaching	1
chasing	1	gave	3	licking	1	read	2
clean	1	get	21	lift	1	reading	9
cleaning	5	getting	3	like	2	riding	3
climb	1	giving	2	look	6	rolled	1
climbed	1	go	12	looked	2	run	6
climbing	4	goes	2	looking	18	running	8
climbs	1	going	21	looks	1	said	2
close	1	gone	3	lost	1	saw	5
collapsed	1	got	21	made	4	say	5
colouring	1	had	3	make	3	saying	1
come	19	happen	2	making	2	says	3
coming	14	happened	2	managed	1	screams	1
ooking	1	happens	1	mashed	1	see	6
osts	1	has	3	meet	1	shaving	3
rack	2	have	16	might	2	shocked	1
racking	1	having	13	mixing	2	shopping	1
rash	10	hear	1	moved	1	shot	1
rashed	4	heard	1	must	5	shout	1
rashing	4	help	8	noticing	1	shouting	3
rawled	1	helped	1	open	5	shut	2
utting	2	helping	2	opening	4	shuts	1
o	6	helps	1	opens	1	signing	1
oing	12	hit	3	pack	2	sit	1
rinking	13	hold	5	packed	1	skating	3
riving	3	holding	15	packing	2	sleep	3
rop	6	hurt	4	paid	2	slide	3
ropped	11	is	84	painting	1	sliding	1
ropping	2	jump	4	pay	1	smash	2
rops	2	jumped	1	peddling	1	smashed	1
rove	2	jumping	2	picks	1	snowing	2
t	5	keep	5	pinch	1	speeding	2
ten	1	kick	2	play	14	spill	1
ting	10	kicked	7	played	1	standing	5
ll	10	kicking	1	playing	35	start	2
llen	1	kicks	1	plays	1	started	2
lling	1	knock	4	pointing	1	starting	2
lls	2	knocked	1	pull	2	stop	10

Word	Count	Word	Count	Word	Count	Word	Count
sunk	1	think	9	turning	1	watching	14
suppose	3	throw	3	use	1	wear	1
sweep	1	throwing	3	walk	2	went	19
swimming	1	tidy	1	walked	1	were	8
take	9	tired	5	walking	9	will	1
taking	2	told	1	want	4	working	1
talking	5	took	1	wants	1	worried	1
talks	1	tried	3	was	31	would	2
tell	2	try	1	wash	1	write	3
telling	3	trying	7	washing	1	writes	1
tells	1			watch	6	writing	2

Total words 1024
Mean words 113·78
Total different words 244
Mean different words 27·11

ADJECTIVES

Word	Count	Word	Count	Word	Count	Word	Count
all	28	fast	4	nice	1	that	2
angry	7	fat	1	old	2	these	
another	4	first	1	old-fashioned	1	thin	
asleep	4	five	5	one	28	this	
back	1	four	2	open	3	those	
bad	1	front	1	other	12	three	
big	4	full	2	plastic	1	tiny	
broken	1	funny	1	ready	2	top	
brown	1	happy	1	real	1	twelve	
busy	1	high	1	right	1	two	1
careful	1	hot	1	sad	1	untidy	
cold	1	little	30	silly	1	upside-down	
dangerous	3	mad	2	slippery	1	very	
deaf	1	messy	1	small	1	weak	
dirty	1	much	2	some	16	wet	
each	3	muddy	3	ten	1	white	
evergreen	1	next	2	terrible	1		

Total words 268
Mean words 29·78
Total different words 67
Mean different words 7·44

ADVERBS

Word	Count	Word	Count	Word	Count	Word	Count
about	7	fast	1	next	1	then	21
after	5	here	2	not	4	there	35
again	1	home	11	now	8	too	4
along	8	how	2	off	9	underneath	1
already	1	in	2	on	4	up	12
around	2	indoors	1	out	22	upside-down	2
as	1	instead	1	over	22	upstairs	2
away	14	just	4	perhaps	1	very	11
back	4	like	2	quickly	2	well	2
by	1	longer	1	quite	1	when	6
down	17	maybe	6	round	3	where	5
everywhere	1	much	2	somewhere	1	without	1
far	1	never	1	suddenly	3	yet	1

Total words 283
Mean words 31·44
Total different words 52
Mean different words 5·78

PRONOUNS

Word	Count	Word	Count	Word	Count	Word	Count
	1	I	13	something	9	those	1
everybody	4	it	46	that	19	we	6
	42	one	1	their	9	what	7
	15	she	12	them	14	which	1
	27	somebody	3	they	61	who	4
	29	someone	3	this	2	you	13
	2						

Total words 344
Mean words 38·22
Total different words 25
Mean different words 2·78

PREPOSITIONS

Word	Count	Word	Count	Word	Count	Word	Count
across	3	be	6	down	7	in	47
	15	behind	1	for	13	into	9
	10	beside	1	from	7	near	1

Word	Count	Word	Count	Word	Count	Word	Cou...
of	47	over	24	through	2	up	4
off	9	past	4	to	75	with	55
on	59	round	2	under	7	without	1
out	10						

Total words	419	Total different words	25
Mean words	46·56	Mean different words	2·78

CONJUNCTIONS

Word	Count	Word	Count	Word	Count	Word	Cou...
and	288	but	4	or	14	then	
because	8	if	2	so	5		

Total words	328	Total different words	7
Mean words	36·44	Mean different words	0·78

CONTRACTIONS

Word	Count	Word	Count	Word	Count	Word	Co...
ambulance's	1	didn't	3	he'll	2	she's	
baby's	1	dinner's	1	he's	18	somebody's	
boot's	1	dog's	3	it's	8	that's	
boy's	3	don't	4	lady's	1	there's	
can't	3	father's	1	man's	1	they're	
car's	1	haven't	1	mother's	1	they've	
couldn't	1						

Total words	92	Total different words	25
Mean words	10·22	Mean different words	2·78

INTERJECTIONS

Word	Count	Word	Count
oh	1	well	3

Total words	4	Total different words	2
Mean words	0·44	Mean different words	0·22

ARTICLES

Word	Count	Word	Count	Word	Count
a	204	an	11	the	662

Total words	877	Total different words	3
Mean words	97·44	Mean different words	0·33

OTHER

Word	Count	Word	Count	Word	Count	Word	Count
Cocacola	2	danger	1	ready	1	there	1
Coke	2	*Marmite	1	runned	1	*Wellington	2
orung	1	no	5	T-shirts	1		

Total words	18	Total different words	11
Mean words	2·00	Mean different words	1·22

Subject Group X

(6 children; age 14–15 years;
performance I.Q.: 91–110; hearing loss: 81–95 dB)

NOUNS

Word	Count	Word	Count	Word	Count	Word	Count
ccident	4	banana	3	bill	1	broom	4
ccidents	1	bananas	3	board	1	brooms	1
dults	1	*barrow	3	book	9	brother	4
ir	1	basin	1	books	1	bucket	6
l	4	basket	10	*boot	12	bull	12
nbulance	15	basketball	1	boots	5	bull's	1
nimal	1	bat	5	bottle	1	bushes	3
ople	1	beard	2	bowl	2	butter	4
oples	7	bed	2	box	1	cabbage	5
adges	2	*beetroot	1	boy	61	cake	7
ag	4	bicycle	2	boys	14	calendar	2
all	29	bike	4	bread	5	car	22

Word	Count	Word	Count	Word	Count	Word	Coun
cars	1	field	6	jug	1	onion	3
cat	5	fish	6	keeper	1	orange	2
cauliflower	1	fishknife	1	kettle	5	oranges	1
ceiling	1	floor	2	*kerb	1	oven	2
chair	5	flower	3	*kit	2	pan	2
cheese	1	flowerpot	4	kitchen	5	park	3
cherries	1	flowers	2	knife	7	*pavement	3
chicken	2	flu	1	ladder	15	pay	1
children	7	food	9	lady	21	pear	3
cleaner	1	football	11	lemonade	1	people	5
clock	4	fork	4	lettuce	1	pepper	3
cloth	4	fruit	4	load	1	picnic	12
clothes	6	gas	1	lot	2	picture	2
clothing	1	gate	4	lots	1	pictures	1
coat	4	girl	18	*mac	2	plant	
cold	1	girls	4	machine	3	plate	
colour	2	glove	1	man	40	police	
*cooker	3	gloves	1	man's	2	policeman	
countries	1	goal	3	map	5	pond	
crash	1	goal-posts	1	marmalade	1	posts	
*cricket	1	grass	1	mask	3	potato	
cucumber	1	grocer	1	match	1	potatoes	
cup	3	ground	3	matches	1	pound	
cupboard	3	handbag	1	meat	4	*purse	
cups	1	handkerchief	1	medal	1	quarter	
curtain	4	handstand	2	men	4	rice	
dinner	3	handstands	2	mess	1	road	
dog	33	hat	4	milk	7	*rounders	
doggie	1	head	4	milkman	6	salt	
doll	4	hedge	1	mirror	4	sandwich	
door	10	hill	2	mixer	3	sandwiches	
dragon	1	hole	2	money	9	saucepan	
drain	2	holiday	2	mop	2	saucepans	
drawer	1	home	2	mother	21	saucer	
dress	1	horns	1	mouse	4	scarf	
dresses	1	hospital	2	moustache	1	scissors	
drink	4	house	5	mud	2	shirts	
egg	5	houses	1	mum	1	shoe	
eggs	5	husband	1	mushroom	3	shoes	
exercise	1	ice	15	mushrooms	1	shopping	
face	4	jacket	1	names	1	shoulder	
family	1	jackets	1	neighbours	1	sign	
farmer	5	jam	3	noise	1	sink	
father	18	jar	1	number	1	sisters	
fence	10	jelly	2	one	1	skates	

Word	Count	Word	Count	Word	Count	Word	Count
*sledge	4	suitcase	1	toy	6	washing	3
snow	3	supper	2	toys	1	water	3
son	2	table	7	train	3	way	2
spoon	5	table-cloth	1	tree	1	week	1
stall	1	*tap	3	trees	3	while	1
stick	5	*taps	1	*trousers	2	wife	1
sticks	3	thing	2	trucks	1	wind	1
story	1	time	3	turban	1	window	14
strawberries	1	today	1	vegetable	1	wire	1
street	1	top	2	vegetables	2	woman	3
stuff	2	towel	1	wall	1		

Total words	1039	Total different words	271
Mean words	173·17	Mean different words	45·17

VERBS

Word	Count	Word	Count	Word	Count	Word	Count
are	12	cleared	1	eat	3	have	8
asked	2	clears	1	eating	6	having	3
bash	1	climb	5	eats	1	heard	1
be	7	come	2	fall	2	help	11
been	4	coming	6	fallen	1	helping	2
bet	2	cooking	3	feels	1	hit	11
bouncing	1	cost	1	fell	11	hold	2
bringing	1	could	4	finished	1	holding	3
brings	1	crash	3	frying	1	is	42
broken	2	crawl	1	gathered	1	jump	2
brushing	1	cut	1	get	12	jumped	1
bump	1	cutting	1	getting	2	keep	2
bumped	3	do	3	give	1	kicked	3
call	1	doing	3	giving	1	knocked	6
came	13	drag	2	go	7	knocking	2
carry	10	drink	3	goes	2	know	4
carrying	7	drinking	3	going	13	lay	1
catches	1	drive	1	got	21	laying	1
change	1	driving	1	grown	1	left	2
chase	2	drop	1	hang	1	let	2
clean	2	dropped	11	happen	1	licking	2
cleaning	1	dropping	3	happened	1	lift	1
clear	3	drown	1	has	5	live	2

Word	Count	Word	Count	Word	Count	Word	Count
look	3	related	1	standing	2	trod	1
looked	1	ride	1	start	1	try	5
looking	9	riding	1	started	1	trying	11
making	6	run	1	stop	5	upset	1
mashed	1	running	3	stuck	1	walk	2
*mucking	1	said	1	stuffed	1	walked	1
must	2	saw	8	supposed	1	walking	2
notice	1	saying	1	surprised	1	wanted	2
open	8	says	3	sweeping	1	was	58
opened	1	see	2	take	7	wash	2
opening	1	seem	1	taking	1	washing	1
packing	4	seems	3	talking	1	watch	1
pay	1	shaving	4	tell	2	watching	8
paying	1	should	1	telling	2	waving	1
play	11	shouting	1	terrified	1	went	9
playing	26	sit	1	think	6	were	12
pull	4	sitting	1	thought	1	will	6
put	12	skate	1	throw	2	winding	1
putting	4	skating	5	tired	1	wondering	1
ran	1	*sledging	1	told	1	working	1
reach	1	sleep	1	tried	2	worried	1
reaching	1	slide	3	trip	1	would	2
read	3	sliding	2	tripped	1	writing	2
reading	2	smashed	1				

Total words   677   Total different words   186
Mean words   112·83   Mean different words   31·00

ADJECTIVES

Word	Count	Word	Count	Word	Count	Word	Count
all	9	empty	1	much	1	some	6
angry	4	every	1	old	1	that	5
another	3	five	3	one	7	thin	5
asleep	1	four	2	open	2	third	1
bad	1	funny	2	other	3	this	1
bare	1	hot	1	own	1	three	2
big	7	left	2	ready	6	twelve	3
broken	1	like	2	red	3	two	18
dangerous	3	little	19	sharp	1	untidy	1
dirty	3	lovely	1	sleepy	1	yellow	1
electric	2						

Total words   138   Total different words   41
Mean words   23·00   Mean different words   6·83

ADVERBS

Word	Count	Word	Count	Word	Count	Word	Count
about	4	better	1	now	4	somewhere	1
across	1	by	2	off	6	then	7
actually	1	down	10	on	2	there	11
again	1	first	1	out	15	to	1
all	1	home	6	over	12	up	14
almost	1	how	2	probably	2	upside-down	2
along	6	in	3	quickly	1	very	7
around	1	just	7	ready	1	when	3
away	6	later	2	round	2	where	1
back	3	not	1				

Total words	152	Total different words	38
Mean words	25·33	Mean different words	6·33

PRONOUNS

Word	Count	Word	Count	Word	Count	Word	Count
everybody	1	his	26	someone	1	they	47
everything	1	I	8	something	5	this	1
he	23	it	17	that	4	what	1
her	8	my	1	their	13	who	4
him	29	she	4	them	11	you	1
himself	1						

Total words	207	Total different words	21
Mean words	34·50	Mean different words	3·50

PREPOSITIONS

Word	Count	Word	Count	Word	Count	Word	Count
about	1	down	8	off	4	round	1
after	1	for	7	on	40	to	77
at	12	from	3	out	6	under	1
before	1	in	20	over	11	up	2
behind	1	into	6	past	3	with	30
by	3	of	15				

Total words	253	Total different words	22
Mean words	42·17	Mean different words	3·67

CONJUNCTIONS

Word	Count	Word	Count	Word	Count	Word	Count
and	191	before	1	or	5	then	3
because	11	if	1	so	2		

Total words	214		Total different words	7
Mean words	35·67		Mean different words	1·17

CONTRACTIONS

Word	Count	Word	Count	Word	Count	Word	Count
boy's	1	father's	1	lady's	1	they'll	3
bull's	1	he's	16	penny's	1	they're	15
didn't	1	here's	1	she's	2	they've	5
dog's	2	isn't	1	that's	2	wasn't	1
don't	2	it's	6	there's	12	what's	2

Total words	76		Total different words	20
Mean words	12·67		Mean different words	3·33

INTERJECTIONS

Word	Count
well	6

Total words	6		Total different words	1
Mean words	1·00		Mean different words	0·17

ARTICLES

Word	Count	Word	Count	Word	Count
a	144	an	7	the	386

Total words	537		Total different words	3
Mean words	89·50		Mean different words	0·50

OTHER

Word	Count	Word	Count	Word	Count	Word	Count
Christmas-tree	1	Coke	2	no	3	teddy bear	1
		hello	1	November	2	T-shirt	2
Cocacola	1	*Marmite	2	slurping	1	*Wellingtons	2

Total words	18	Total different words	11
Mean words	3·00	Mean different words	1·83

Subject Group Y

(2 children; age: 14–15 years;
performance I.Q.: ⩾111; hearing loss: 40–60 dB)

NOUNS

Word	Count	Word	Count	Word	Count	Word	Count
accident	2	bread	2	crash	1	front	1
ambulance	5	broom	1	cup	1	gate	1
apples	3	brother	2	cups	1	girl	4
arms	1	brush	1	dinner	1	goal	1
baby	1	bucket	2	dog	9	goalkeeper	1
back	2	bull	7	door	3	grass	1
bag	2	butter	1	drain	2	handbag	1
ball	7	cake	1	drink	1	handstand	1
bananas	2	calendar	2	driver	1	hat	2
baseball	1	can	1	eggs	3	head	1
basket	1	car	6	elbow	1	hill	2
bat	1	carrots	1	family	5	hole	1
bicycle	1	case	1	farmer	1	holiday	1
bike	1	cat	1	father	8	hood	1
birds	1	chair	2	fence	1	house	1
board	2	child	4	field	3	ice	3
book	5	children	5	fish	2	jelly	2
*boot	5	chin	1	floor	1	journey	1
bottle	1	clock	2	flower	1	kids	1
bottom	1	cloth	1	flowerpot	2	kitchen	2
box	1	clothes	1	flowers	2	knife	2
boy	16	coat	1	food	3	ladder	5
boys	2	cotton	1	football	2	lady	8

Word	Count	Word	Count	Word	Count	Word	Coun
lives	1	mother	8	raincoat	1	stick	2
*lorry	1	noise	1	road	2	stones	1
lunch	1	notice	2	*rounders	1	street	1
machine	1	opposition	1	sandwiches	2	table	5
man	11	pan	1	scarf	2	tea	1
map	1	pans	2	school	1	team	1
maps	1	people	1	scissors	1	tea-towel	1
margarine	1	pieces	1	shirts	1	tomatoes	1
mask	1	picnic	4	shopping	1	top	1
matches	1	picture	1	side	1	toy	2
meat	1	*pint	1	sink	2	tree	1
melons	1	plates	1	skates	1	vegetables	2
men	3	policeman	1	*sledge	1	washing	1
message	1	posts	1	slide	2	water	1
milk	4	pot	1	snow	1	week	1
milkman	2	pots	1	son	1	wheelbarrow	1
mirror	1	puppy	1	spoon	1	window	2
mixer	1	*purse	1	stall	1	windows	1
money	2						

Total words	325			Total different words	165		
Mean words	162·50			Mean different words	82·50		

VERBS

Word	Count	Word	Count	Word	Count	Word	Coun
are	7	comes	1	fell	5	hurt	2
arrived	1	coming	5	forgot	1	is	16
be	2	cooking	2	frightened	2	kicked	3
been	1	covering	1	get	6	knocked	2
beginning	1	cracked	1	go	2	know	1
being	1	crash	1	going	7	knows	1
brought	1	crashed	2	gone	2	laying	1
called	1	crying	1	got	4	left	1
calling	1	do	1	had	2	lie	2
came	5	doing	1	happened	1	like	1
can	2	drinking	3	has	3	listening	1
carrying	4	dropped	3	have	6	look	1
chased	1	drops	1	having	5	looked	1
chasing	1	eating	5	help	1	looking	2
cleaning	1	enjoyed	1	hit	3	looks	7
climbing	3	falls	1	hold	1	may	2

Word	Count	Word	Count	Word	Count	Word	Count
moaning	1	riding	1	smashed	1	tripped	1
must	5	running	4	standing	5	trying	9
pack	1	runs	2	stands	2	turn	1
packing	1	rushed	1	stolen	1	turned	2
paid	3	said	1	stop	2	used	1
paying	1	saw	1	stopped	1	walk	1
playing	12	say	1	streak	1	walks	1
pull	2	saying	1	suppose	3	was	2
put	1	see	2	take	1	watch	1
putting	1	seen	1	tell	3	watching	7
ran	5	sell	1	telling	1	went	1
read	3	shaving	2	ticking	1	winding	1
reading	2	shopping	2	tired	1	writing	1
ride	1						

Total words	269	Total different words	117
Mean words	134·50	Mean different words	58·50

ADJECTIVES

Word	Count	Word	Count	Word	Count	Word	Count
all	7	both	1	long	1	red	1
angry	1	electric	1	much	1	some	10
any	1	enough	1	nice	1	that	1
bad	1	frozen	1	old	1	these	1
bald	1	full	1	one	2	this	1
big	4	happy	1	open	3	two	4
blue	1	little	10	other	3	weekly	1

Total words	63	Total different words	28
Mean words	31·50	Mean different words	14·00

ADVERBS

Word	Count	Word	Count	Word	Count	Word	Count
about	2	as	4	even	1	how	1
across	1	away	1	fast	1	in	1
along	1	back	3	here	6	just	2
around	1	down	8	home	1	like	7

Word	Count	Word	Count	Word	Count	Word	Count
maybe	6	on	1	round	2	up	7
near	1	out	7	so	1	upside-down	1
nearly	1	over	2	somewhere	1	well	4
not	1	past	1	there	6	where	2
now	1	probably	8	too	1	yet	1
off	2						

Total words	98	Total different words	37
Mean words	49.00	Mean different words	18.50

PRONOUNS

Word	Count	Word	Count	Word	Count	Word	Count
everything	1	I	4	something	6	themselves	1
he	16	it	21	that	1	they	8
her	6	she	3	their	3	what	2
him	14	someone	6	them	13	you	1
his	5						

Total words	111	Total different words	17
Mean words	55·50	Mean different words	8·50

PREPOSITIONS

Word	Count	Word	Count	Word	Count	Word	Count
about	1	from	2	on	13	toward	1
after	4	in	6	out	1	under	2
at	2	into	7	over	6	up	2
behind	2	of	18	till	1	with	11
down	1	off	2	to	23	within	1
for	4						

Total words	110	Total different words	21
Mean words	55·00	Mean different words	10·50

CONJUNCTIONS

Word	Count	Word	Count	Word	Count	Word	Count
and	56	but	2	or	4	that	3
because	4	if	1	so	5		

Total words	75		Total different words	7	
Mean words	37·50		Mean different words	3·50	

CONTRACTIONS

Word	Count	Word	Count	Word	Count	Word	Count
boy's	3	dog's	3	lady's	2	she's	1
bull's	1	farmer's	1	man's	1	there're	1
cat's	1	father's	5	mother's	4	there's	23
didn't	4	he's	4	policeman's	1	they're	3
doesn't	1	it's	1				

Total words	60		Total different words	18	
Mean words	30·00		Mean different words	9·00	

INTERJECTIONS

Word	Count
—	—

Total words	0		Total different words	0	
Mean words	0·00		Mean different words	0·00	

ARTICLES

Word	Count	Word	Count	Word	Count
	50	an	2	the	150

Total words	202		Total different words	3	
Mean words	101·00		Mean different words	1·50	

OTHER

Word	Count	Word	Count	Word	Count	Word	Cour
Coke	2	T-shirts	1	*Wellington	2	yes	1
India	1						

Total words	7	Total different words	5	
Mean words	3·50	Mean different words	2·50	

Subject Group Z

(11 children; age 14–15 years;
performance I.Q.: $\geqslant 111$; hearing loss 61–80 dB)

NOUNS

Word	Count	Word	Count	Word	Count	Word	Cou
accident	14	bill	3	buttons	2	colander	
acrobatics	2	bit	11	cabbage	5	cold	
all	4	bits	2	cabbages	2	cook	
alley	2	*blancmange	2	cake	5	*cooker	
ambulance	26	blind	1	cakes	6	cooking	
apple	1	*bloke	1	calendar	6	corner	
apples	12	board	2	car	55	country	
area	2	book	11	cars	2	countryside	
atlas	3	*boot	11	cart	3	couple	
back	7	boots	7	cat	10	crash	
background	1	bottle	2	cauliflower	5	cravat	
badges	2	bottles	2	chair	3	cream	
bag	8	bowl	3	chalk	2	*cricket	
ball	55	box	4	chaos	2	cup	
balls	2	boy	67	chicken	7	cupboard	
banana	2	boys	20	child	2	curtain	
bananas	7	bread	8	children	20	customer	
barrel	1	broom	3	*chutney	2	cutlery	
*barrow	2	brother	1	cleaner	4	cutter	
baseball	10	brush	2	clock	4	day	
basket	17	bucket	5	cloth	4	dinner	
bat	7	building	2	clothes	4	dog	
bicycle	6	bull	29	coat	2	dog's	
bike	3	butter	6	coin	2	doll	

Word	Count	Word	Count	Word	Count	Word	Count
doll's	1	goal	4	lady	17	mud	1
dolls	1	goal-post	2	ledge	2	mug	1
door	12	goal-posts	6	leg	2	mum	1
doors	2	*greengrocer	2	legs	2	mummy	1
drain	8	grid	2	lemonade	1	mushroom	2
drawer	1	groceries	1	lemons	2	mushrooms	2
drink	5	ground	3	liquid	1	mustard	1
egg	2	group	1	load	2	napkin	1
eggs	15	hair	2	loaf	4	*neckerchief	1
elbow	2	hamper	1	look	16	noise	1
end	2	hand	4	*lorry	2	notice	10
exercise	1	handstand	3	lot	4	novice	2
exposure	2	handstands	1	lots	2	nuisance	2
face	2	hat	4	lunch	3	one	16
family	9	head	12	machine	6	onion	1
arm	2	headlamp	4	man	59	ornament	1
armer	13	headgear	2	man's	3	outfit	2
ather	21	hedge	8	map	2	oven	5
ence	12	hedges	2	market	2	packet	1
ield	24	help	2	marmalade	1	pair	1
ish	8	hill	6	mask	9	pan	2
ishes	1	hills	2	matches	6	pans	2
at	4	hole	3	material	2	park	3
oor	5	holiday	1	meal	6	parsley	1
ower	2	home	6	meat	1	part	2
owerpot	8	hospital	3	medals	5	*pavement	1
owers	10	house	9	melon	1	people	16
oam	3	husband	8	melons	2	pepper	2
ood	9	hypothermia	1	men	4	permission	2
ootball	15	ice	51	mess	3	person	1
oreground	1	insects	2	mice	2	picnic	26
oreigner	2	jackets	1	middle	1	picture	3
ork	2	jar	4	milk	12	piece	1
orks	2	jellies	1	milkman	7	pieces	2
ours	2	jelly	3	*mincemeat	2	place	5
ont	3	*jersey	1	mirror	3	plant	1
uit	11	jug	2	mixer	9	plate	6
ame	4	*jumper	1	moment	4	plates	2
ames	2	kettle	6	money	10	plus	2
ate	7	kitchen	5	month	2	point	2
rms	2	knife	11	mop	2	policeman	9
rl	18	knives	2	mother	21	pork	2
rls	3	knock	1	motor-car	2	posts	3
ove	1	ladder	27	mouse	2	pot	1
oves	2	ladies	2	mouth	1	potato	1

Word	Count	Word	Count	Word	Count	Word	Cou...
potatoes	2	set	2	stick	12	train	1
pots	2	shave	4	sticks	3	tree	6
pressure	6	shaving	1	story	1	*trifle	2
pumpkin	1	shelf	3	stove	2	trip	1
*purse	7	shock	1	strawberries	1	*trousers	2
rain	2	shoe	1	street	7	turban	3
raincoat	6	shoes	1	stuff	5	tweed	2
rest	2	shop	1	style	2	two	6
rice	1	shopkeeper	2	sudden	2	unit	2
road	18	shopping	4	table	36	vegetable	2
roads	2	shoulder	3	*tap	1	vegetables	5
roast	2	sign	6	*taps	1	wall	
*rounders	1	sink	8	tea	2	washing	6
run	1	skates	3	teaspoon	1	washing-up	
salt	2	skirt	1	there	1	water	
sandwich	2	*sledge	20	thing	2	way	
sandwiches	7	sleep	1	things	14	weight	
saucepan	3	snow	6	time	5	wheelbarrow	
saucepans	2	son	27	tomatoes	3	wife	1
scar	1	sons	4	toothbrush	1	window	2
scarf	5	sort	6	top	2	windows	
scene	4	spoon	5	towel	2	window-sill	
school	2	stall	9	toy	9	wire	
scissors	3	step	1	toys	2	woman	
seat	1						

Total words	1994		Total different words	373
Mean words	181·27		Mean different words	33·91

VERBS

Word	Count	Word	Count	Word	Count	Word	Co...
admiring	2	being	2	came	3	climb	
allowed	1	belong	1	can	10	climbing	
are	45	broke	2	carry	1	collect	
arrive	2	broken	3	carrying	27	collected	
arrived	5	bump	1	catch	2	come	
arriving	2	bumped	1	charging	4	coming	
avoid	2	bumping	1	chasing	5	cooking	
banged	2	buying	2	clean	1	could	
be	34	call	4	cleaning	7	counting	
been	15	calls	1	clearing	1	covered	

Word	Count	Word	Count	Word	Count	Word	Count
cracked	2	had	7	open	2	shaving	12
crash	2	hanging	1	opening	5	shocked	3
crashed	4	happened	8	owes	1	shopping	3
crawl	3	happening	9	owns	2	should	6
crawling	1	has	34	pack	1	shouting	8
cross	4	have	26	packing	3	shut	2
cut	2	having	19	paid	1	shutting	1
cutting	4	heading	6	park	2	sipping	2
describe	2	heard	3	pay	1	sitting	5
do	5	help	3	paying	6	skate	2
dodge	2	hit	12	pinch	1	skating	2
doing	14	hold	2	play	13	skid	2
drag	2	hurry	2	playing	64	*sledging	1
drink	2	hurrying	1	pointing	2	sleeping	1
drinking	10	hurt	6	practising	2	slide	1
drive	1	including	1	preparing	2	slow	2
driving	3	interested	4	prevent	2	smash	3
drop	5	is	143	pull	8	snowing	1
dropped	11	jumping	1	pulled	2	spread	4
dropping	6	keep	3	put	5	spreads	2
drops	2	kick	3	putting	10	standing	6
ying	2	kicked	7	ran	2	staring	1
at	4	kneeling	2	reach	11	start	1
aten	1	knock	2	reaching	1	started	1
ating	13	knocked	8	read	2	stop	9
ll	2	knocking	1	reading	10	stopped	4
allen	17	knocks	2	realizing	1	stopping	3
alling	4	know	11	rescue	2	stretch	2
scinated	2	knowing	1	riding	2	stretching	2
ashioned	2	known	2	rolling	2	suffering	2
ll	5	laid	4	run	6	suppose	2
tch	3	laying	4	running	11	supposed	2
nish	2	leaning	2	sat	2	surprised	4
nished	2	listening	2	saw	2	swerve	2
ying	1	lock	2	saying	4	swerved	4
ightened	5	look	8	says	2	take	5
ve	2	looking	40	scattered	1	taken	2
t	33	looks	10	see	18	taking	6
tting	2	loosing	1	seeing	3	talking	7
ve	2	lying	2	seem	7	tell	2
	31	making	9	seems	10	telling	10
es	1	messing	1	selling	1	think	7
ing	35	might	5	serving	1	throw	1
ne	19	move	2	set	2	throwing	2
t	17	must	4	shaking	1	tidying	2

Word	Count	Word	Count	Word	Count	Word	Cour
tired	6	used	1	warning	4	went	14
told	2	using	4	was	28	were	2
tried	4	venture	1	watch	6	will	3
tripped	9	waiting	2	watched	2	worn	1
trips	1	walked	1	watching	13	worried	2
try	13	walking	6	waving	2	would	10
trying	26	want	1	wear	2	writing	
use	4	wanting	1	wearing	2		

Total words	1532	Total different words 251
Mean words	139·27	Mean different words 22·82

ADJECTIVES

Word	Count	Word	Count	Word	Count	Word	Cou
able	2	few	2	much	2	set	
actual	1	first	2	muddy	2	several	
all	40	five	5	narrow	2	sharp	
angry	3	flat	3	near	2	six	
another	12	four	4	nearby	4	sixty	
any	2	full	1	next	4	small	
asleep	4	funny	2	nineteen	2	some	3
big	3	further	1	obvious	2	that	2
blue	1	green	1	old	3	these	
busy	2	half	4	one	21	thin	1
careless	2	hard	2	open	6	thinner	
chocolate	1	high	3	other	14	third	
cold	6	last	2	own	1	this	
cross	2	left	1	parallel	2	those	
dangerous	4	less	1	pet	2	three	
deep	2	like	1	pretty	4	twelve	
dirty	2	little	21	proper	4	two	
easier	2	low	2	quick	4	whole	
eldest	8	main	2	ready	10	young	
empty	3	middle	2	red	5	younger	
enough	2	more	3	same	4	youngest	
fast	4	most	2	sensible	2		

Total words	425	Total different words 87
Mean words	38·64	Mean different words 7·91

ADVERBS

Word	Count	Word	Count	Word	Count	Word	Count
about	13	between	2	not	19	really	9
above	2	by	2	now	16	so	22
again	5	down	33	obviously	8	somewhere	2
ahead	2	easily	2	off	8	soon	2
almost	2	else	10	on	5	straight	4
along	5	even	1	only	2	suddenly	2
already	1	everywhere	1	out	55	there	67
also	21	further	1	outside	2	through	9
any	2	here	4	over	21	too	9
around	1	home	5	perhaps	5	up	23
as	23	in	4	possibly	2	very	8
away	33	just	24	probably	31	well	12
back	6	likely	2	quickly	4	when	7
below	3	maybe	5	quite	4	where	9

| Total words | 582 | | | Total different words | 56 | | |
| Mean words | 52·91 | | | Mean different words | 5·09 | | |

PRONOUNS

Word	Count	Word	Count	Word	Count	Word	Count
anyone	2	himself	1	someone	1	they	61
anything	6	his	51	something	9	this	2
everybody	4	I	16	that	7	what	21
everything	2	it	94	their	12	whatever	1
he	62	me	2	them	31	which	9
her	30	she	15	themselves	2	who	5
him	52	somebody	19	these	1	you	2

| Total words | 520 | | | Total different words | 28 | | |
| Mean words | 47·27 | | | Mean different words | 2·55 | | |

PREPOSITIONS

Word	Count	Word	Count	Word	Count	Word	Count
about	2	after	7	around	2	before	2
across	6	against	2	at	43	behind	6

Word	Count	Word	Count	Word	Count	Word	Cou
below	2	into	27	out	4	towards	5
by	31	like	8	over	35	under	16
down	15	of	121	past	7	underneath	4
for	26	off	10	since	2	up	1
from	21	on	91	through	9	with	7.
in	61	onto	9	to	158	without	3

Total words	803
Mean words	73·00

Total different words	32
Mean different words	2·91

CONJUNCTIONS

Word	Count	Word	Count	Word	Count	Word	Cou
and	266	but	17	so	3	whether	
as	2	if	11	that	11	while	
because	38	or	16	though	5	whilst	

Total words	376
Mean words	34·18

Total different words	12
Mean different words	1·09

CONTRACTIONS

Word	Count	Word	Count	Word	Count	Word	Co
anybody's	2	don't	17	man's	6	there's	
baby's	2	else's	2	milkman's	2	they'll	
basket's	1	farmer's	4	money's	3	they're	
boy's	9	father's	8	mother's	15	they've	
bull's	2	flowerpot'll	2	one's	3	what's	
can't	7	food's	2	policeman's	2	where's	
car's	1	he'll	8	she's	14	who's	
children's	2	he's	42	should've	2	who've	
couldn't	2	I'll	1	shouldn't	7	woman's	
didn't	3	isn't	2	somebody's	6	you'll	
doesn't	10	it's	19	son's	8	you're	
dog's	11	lady's	2	that's	8		

Total words	352
Mean words	32·00

Total different words	47
Mean different words	4·27

INTERJECTIONS

Word	Count
well	11

Total words	11	Total different words	1
Mean words	1·00	Mean different words	0·09

ARTICLES

Word	Count	Word	Count	Word	Count
a	328	an	25	the	827

Total words	1180	Total different words	3
Mean words	107·27	Mean different words	0·27

OTHER

Word	Count	Word	Count	Word	Count	Word	Count
Afrostyle	2	handstanding	2	*Marmite	1	*Wellington	4
Cocacola	1	icing	1	no	8	*wellyboots	1
Cola	1	India	4	Pakistan	2	yes	8
crash	1	*Kenwood	2				

Total words	38	Total different words	14
Mean words	3·45	Mean different words	1·27

Subject Group Å

(10 children; age: 14–15 years;
performance I.Q.: ⩾ 111; hearing loss: 81–95 dB)

NOUNS

Word	Count	Word	Count	Word	Count	Word	Count
accident	8	boots	5	child	1	dinosaurs	1
all	11	bottle	3	children	14	dirt	1
alley	1	bottles	1	chopper	1	dish	1
ambulance	25	bowl	1	cleaner	1	dog	58
animal	1	box	4	clock	9	doll	9
*anorak	1	boy	86	cloth	5	door	12
apple	4	boy-friend	1	clothes	9	doors	2
apples	8	boys	26	clothing	1	dozen	1
area	2	branch	1	cloths	1	dragon	3
arm	1	bread	7	club	1	drain	7
atlas	4	broom	5	coat	7	drawer	5
baby	4	brother	1	coffee	1	dress	3
back	3	brush	3	coins	1	dresses	1
bag	11	bucket	7	comics	2	dressmaking	1
ball	61	bull	22	common	3	drink	1
balls	1	bush	1	*cooker	5	drinks	1
banana	3	butcher	1	cookie	1	east	1
bananas	6	butter	9	corn	1	edge	1
bang	1	cabbage	3	corner	4	egg	7
baseball	11	cabbages	2	country	1	eggs	14
basin	1	cake	4	countryside	1	end	2
basket	17	cakes	3	couple	3	engine	1
bat	5	calendar	8	crash	1	equipment	2
beach	1	cap	1	cream	2	evening	2
beard	1	car	47	*cricket	4	face	6
bench	3	carrot	2	cup	3	family	10
bicycle	6	cart	1	cups	2	farm	1
bike	2	casserole	1	curtain	2	farmer	12
bill	8	cat	10	cutlery	1	father	23
bit	5	cauliflower	2	dad	1	father's	1
*blancmange	2	cauliflowers	2	danger	2	fault	1
blind	3	chair	7	date	2	feet	2
board	7	chance	3	dawn	2	fence	14
*bonnet	1	chat	1	day	4	field	10
book	11	cheese	2	days	1	fields	2
books	2	cherries	1	dinner	8	finger	1
*boot	17	chicken	5	dinosaur	1	fish	8

Word	Count	Word	Count	Word	Count	Word	Count
fishes	1	hole	5	material	3	opposite	1
flat	1	holes	1	meal	6	oranges	1
floor	11	home	2	meat	4	order	1
flower	3	hook	1	medal	2	outing	1
flowerpot	6	hospital	1	medals	4	outside	1
flowers	7	hours	1	melon	2	oven	5
foam	1	house	2	men	5	packet	1
food	26	houses	3	meringue	1	pair	1
football	8	housewife	2	meringues	1	pal	1
forest	1	hurry	1	mess	4	pan	1
fork	2	husband	4	metal	1	pans	1
forks	2	ice	37	mice	1	paper	1
frost-bite	1	jam	1	middle	3	park	1
fruit	4	jelly	6	milk	13	part	1
fudge	1	journey	1	milkman	13	path	1
fun	1	jug	4	*mince	2	pattern	1
game	3	keeper	1	*mincemeat	1	*pavement	7
games	1	kettle	8	minds	1	people	19
garlic	1	kind	3	minute	1	pepper	3
gate	7	kitchen	8	minutes	1	person	4
girl	29	knife	12	mirror	3	pet	1
girl's	1	ladder	23	mistake	2	picnic	21
girls	4	ladders	1	mixer	7	picture	4
glove	2	lady	45	model	1	pictures	1
gloves	1	lady's	1	money	8	pie	1
goal	7	lids	1	monster	1	piece	1
goal-posts	3	light	1	mop	3	pieces	2
grinder	1	lightening	1	mother	32	*pint	1
ground	7	liquid	2	mouse	8	place	4
group	1	loaf	1	mouth	1	places	1
gymnastics	1	*lorry	1	mug	3	plant	2
hamper	1	lot	5	mum	2	plate	3
hand	1	lunch	3	mushroom	4	plates	3
handbag	1	machine	5	mushrooms	1	play	2
handle	1	*mackintosh	1	mustard	1	police	5
hands	1	man	81	name	2	policeman	8
handstand	1	man's	3	names	1	pool	2
handstands	3	map	5	neighbour	1	post	4
hare	1	market	3	noise	2	*postman	1
hat	7	marmalade	4	notice	8	posts	2
head	6	*marrow	3	number	1	pot	5
hedge	4	mask	9	numbers	1	potatoes	4
help	3	mat	2	one	5	pressure	2
hill	2	match	3	onion	4	pumpkin	2
hold	1	matches	3	onions	1	*purse	10

Word	Count	Word	Count	Word	Count	Word	Count
radio	1	shoes	2	suit	1	van	2
rag	1	shopping	2	surface	1	vase	1
rain	2	shops	1	sweeper	1	vegetable	3
raincoat	3	shoulder	1	sweets	4	vegetables	1
rear	1	shoulders	1	table	24	village	1
religion	1	side	3	table-cloth	1	walk	1
rice	5	sign	4	*tap	1	wall	2
ride	1	signpost	2	*taps	5	washing	5
road	10	sill	1	tea	4	water	4
roll	1	sink	9	*tea-cloth	1	waterproof	1
room	1	sister	1	test	1	way	9
*rounder	1	site	1	there	4	weather	1
*rounders	1	skates	2	thing	5	week	1
rubber	2	*sledge	10	things	7	weight	2
salt	3	*sledges	1	time	12	west	1
sandwich	4	sleep	1	tomato	1	wheelbarrow	5
sandwiches	5	snow	4	tomatoes	1	while	1
saucepan	8	softball	1	top	3	wife	1
saucepans	3	son	29	towel	4	window	26
saucer	1	sort	2	towels	1	windows	4
saucers	3	sponge-cakes	1	toy	12	wing	1
scarf	5	spoon	6	toys	7	winter	2
scissors	7	stall	6	train	7	wire	1
seat	2	station	1	tree	3	woman	3
service	1	step	1	trees	4	wood	1
shadow	1	stick	14	*trifle	2	woods	1
shave	1	sticks	2	trip	1	word	1
shelf	4	story	1	*trouser	1	work	2
shirt	1	strawberries	1	*trousers	2	writing	1
shock	7	street	3	turban	4	year	1
shoe	1	stuff	3				

Total words	2107	Total different words	450
Mean words	210·70	Mean different words	45·00

VERBS

Word	Count	Word	Count	Word	Count	Word	Count
annoyed	1	arrive	1	avoid	2	been	8
appears	1	arrived	2	bang	1	beginning	1
are	35	ask	1	be	14	belongs	1
arranged	1	asked	2	beat	1	bending	1

Word	Count	Word	Count	Word	Count	Word	Count
bought	1	crash	4	gored	1	let	2
bounced	1	crashed	8	got	35	licking	1
break	2	crawl	2	grab	1	lifting	1
breaks	1	crawled	1	guess	1	like	2
bringing	2	crossing	1	had	11	listen	1
broke	2	crying	2	hanging	4	listening	1
broken	1	cut	3	happen	3	live	1
bump	3	cutting	2	happened	5	living	2
bumped	4	dialled	2	happening	2	look	8
bumping	1	disobey	1	happens	1	looked	2
bunging	1	disobeyed	1	has	21	looking	22
buy	1	do	7	have	26	looks	6
buying	1	doing	8	having	14	lose	1
call	1	dressing	1	heard	5	lying	1
called	5	drinking	4	help	12	made	4
came	25	driving	2	helps	1	make	5
can	21	drop	3	hit	5	makes	1
care	1	dropped	21	hold	3	making	2
carried	1	dropping	3	holding	2	mashed	1
carries	1	drops	3	holds	1	may	1
carry	8	drove	2	hurry	1	mean	6
carrying	19	eat	2	hurt	2	might	10
caused	1	eating	17	is	107	mincing	1
changed	1	enjoyed	1	joining	1	move	1
chase	1	enjoying	3	judge	1	must	9
chases	1	fall	3	jugged	2	nagging	1
chasing	6	fallen	7	jump	4	need	1
check	1	falling	3	jumped	1	notice	2
checking	1	feel	1	jumping	2	noticed	2
clean	1	fell	21	keep	2	open	3
cleaning	6	find	1	kick	1	opened	2
clear	2	finish	2	kicked	9	opening	4
cleared	1	finished	4	knock	2	ordering	1
clearing	1	foaming	1	knocked	10	packed	1
climb	2	follow	1	knocking	2	packing	3
climbed	2	forgetting	1	knocks	2	pay	4
climbing	1	frightened	3	know	11	paying	4
close	2	get	28	laid	4	phoned	1
come	7	gets	2	land	1	picked	1
comes	1	getting	4	lapping	1	play	12
coming	16	give	3	laying	1	played	1
confused	1	giving	1	leaning	1	playing	59
could	5	go	17	leave	1	plays	1
counting	1	going	34	leaving	1	pointing	1
cracked	1	gone	3	left	11	pull	3

Word	Count	Word	Count	Word	Count	Word	Count
pulling	2	seen	1	staring	2	trying	23
pushing	1	sell	1	start	3	turned	3
put	21	selling	1	started	4	unlay	1
putting	4	serving	1	step	1	use	1
ran	2	shaving	9	stop	5	used	3
reach	4	shining	1	stopping	1	walking	10
reaching	1	shopping	1	suppose	2	want	1
read	3	should	4	supposed	1	wanted	1
reading	8	shouted	2	surprised	6	wants	1
relieves	1	shouting	9	surround	1	warming	1
rescue	4	showed	1	take	3	warned	2
riding	4	shutting	1	taking	3	warning	1
rolling	1	sitting	1	talking	4	was	99
rolls	1	skating	8	teaching	2	wash	1
run	4	skidded	1	tell	2	washing	3
running	9	sleeping	3	telling	3	watch	1
runs	1	slide	1	think	34	watching	9
rush	1	sliding	2	thought	1	waving	1
said	2	slow	1	throwing	1	wearing	4
save	3	smashed	1	tired	7	went	21
saves	1	smiling	1	told	3	were	29
saw	6	sold	1	took	1	will	8
saying	5	spell	1	tossed	1	winding	1
says	2	spilled	1	tried	1	work	2
see	27	spoiled	1	trip	4	worried	4
seeing	1	spread	2	tripped	3	would	4
seem	1	stand	1	trips	1	writing	4
seems	1	standing	2	try	4		

Total words   1540   Total different words   307

Mean words   154·00   Mean different words   30·70

ADJECTIVES

Word	Count	Word	Count	Word	Count	Word	Count
all	17	black	3	comfortable	1	eldest	1
alright	1	blue	2	cross	1	electric	2
angry	7	busy	1	dangerous	4	expensive	1
another	12	careful	1	dead	1	fancy	1
any	1	careless	1	disappointing	1	few	1
asleep	3	clumsy	1	each	1	first	1
big	2	cold	4	easier	1	five	9

Word	Count	Word	Count	Word	Count	Word	Count
flat	2	like	6	other	19	terrible	1
fluffy	1	little	38	own	2	that	27
four	1	long	1	plastic	1	these	9
freezing	1	loud	1	ready	1	thick	1
full	3	lovely	1	real	1	thin	8
funny	2	mad	1	red	10	this	17
good	2	more	11	sane	1	three	1
greenish	1	most	1	sensible	1	twelve	7
guilty	1	much	1	seven	1	two	32
half	1	muddy	1	silly	2	ugly	1
happy	1	new	1	small	1	untidy	1
hard	1	next	5	smallest	2	weekly	1
hot	1	nice	1	some	39	wooden	2
hurt	2	nine	3	sorry	1	wrong	1
injured	1	old	5	stupid	1	yellow	1
last	1	older	7	sure	1	young	8
late	1	oldest	5	sweet	1	younger	2
left	2	one	24	taller	1	youngest	7
less	1	open	10	ten	1		

Total words	445	Total different words	103
Mean words	44·50	Mean different words	10·30

ADVERBS

Word	Count	Word	Count	Word	Count	Word	Count
about	10	badly	1	less	1	quickly	5
above	1	before	3	like	4	quite	3
across	1	by	1	likely	10	rather	2
again	5	carefully	2	maybe	1	ready	2
all	4	down	15	more	1	really	6
almost	1	easily	2	much	2	right	1
along	8	else	3	never	3	round	2
alright	1	even	2	not	15	so	7
also	2	everywhere	1	now	14	sometimes	1
always	1	fast	2	off	7	somewhere	4
anyhow	1	here	1	on	1	still	5
anyway	1	home	13	out	32	straight	1
around	6	how	2	outside	2	suddenly	3
as	12	in	6	over	22	then	2
away	12	instead	1	past	2	there	33
back	10	just	19	perhaps	10	through	2

Word	Count	Word	Count	Word	Count	Word	Count
tidily	1	up	14	very	21	when	17
together	3	upside-down	2	well	10	where	11
too	2						

Total words	437	Total different words	73
Mean words	43·70	Mean different words	7·30

PRONOUNS

Word	Count	Word	Count	Word	Count	Word	Count
each	2	himself	2	she	22	they	75
everybody	2	his	64	somebody	3	this	3
everyone	1	I	71	someone	4	those	2
everything	3	it	59	something	7	what	17
he	70	nobody	1	that	15	which	3
her	40	nothing	1	their	15	who	11
herself	1	one	2	them	31	you	20
him	57	other	2	these	1	your	1

Total words	608	Total different words	32
Mean words	60·80	Mean different words	3·20

PREPOSITIONS

Word	Count	Word	Count	Word	Count	Word	Count
about	13	below	1	near	2	round	
above	1	beside	2	of	80	through	
across	4	by	19	off	6	to	15
after	13	down	9	on	118	towards	
along	1	for	35	onto	2	under	
around	1	from	14	out	13	underneath	
at	19	in	66	outside	2	up	
back	1	inside	1	over	29	with	9
before	3	into	24	past	8	without	
behind	4	like	6				

Total words	764	Total different words	38
Mean words	76·40	Mean different words	3·80

CONJUNCTIONS

Word	Count	Word	Count	Word	Count	Word	Count
and	358	but	17	so	12	then	5
as	3	if	10	than	1	though	4
because	28	or	20	that	1	while	11
before	1						

Total words 471 Total different words 13
Mean words 47·10 Mean different words 1·30

CONTRACTIONS

Word	Count	Word	Count	Word	Count	Word	Count
boy's	1	football's	1	o'clock	2	they're	16
can't	3	he'll	3	one's	1	they've	9
clock's	1	he's	25	she's	8	tree's	2
couldn't	1	here's	1	shopkeeper's	1	wasn't	1
didn't	6	I'm	1	shouldn't	4	water's	1
doesn't	3	I've	1	somebody's	2	weren't	1
dog's	2	it's	19	that's	8	what's	5
don't	15	lady's	3	there's	40	who's	5
farmer's	1	mother's	5	they'll	2	won't	2
father's	1						

Total words 203 Total different words 37
Mean words 20·30 Mean different words 3·70

INTERJECTIONS

Word	Count	Word	Count	Word	Count
dear	2	oh	20	well	14

Total words 36 Total different words 3
Mean words 3·60 Mean different words 0·30

ARTICLES

Word	Count		Word	Count		Word	Count
a	334		an	20		the	879

Total words	1233		Total different words	3
Mean words	123·30		Mean different words	0·30

OTHER

Word	Count		Word	Count		Word	Count		Word	Coun
Christmas-tree	1		Indian	2		Pepsi	1		*Wellington	2
Cocacola	1		*Kenwood	1		Pepsis	1		*Wellingtons	1
Coke	5		*Marmite	5		pop	1		*winger	1
icing	1		no	7		rabies	1		yes	3?
India	1									

Total words	65		Total different words	17
Mean words	6·50		Mean different words	1·70

II. Analysis of the vocabulary data

A. Introduction

Having presented the vocabulary lists, with counts of words according to Subject Group (cell) and to parsing category, we may now attempt a statistical analysis of the counts. The reader will have noted that the word counts were made in terms of the number of words used with each occurrence of a word counted separately (tokens), and of the number of different words used (types). We may thus consider an analysis of the counts of tokens and of types, and we shall include some comment on the analysis of the ratio of types to tokens. By the design of our study, the data have been grouped in 27 cells defined by age, non-verbal I.Q. and hearing loss, and the analysis thus applies only to the cells of the matrix and not to individual subjects. Because the numbers of subjects differed from cell to cell, the mean counts for each cell are used as the data in the ensuing analyses, which are concerned mainly with the effects of differences in age, non-verbal I.Q. and hearing loss.

Non-verbal I.Q. will be referred to in the remainder of this Chapter as IQ, but it should be remembered that it designates *non-verbal* I.Q.

B. Overall analysis

Our first analysis is concerned with the overall pattern of the data and ignores the partitions of the data into different parsing categories. It is thus concerned with the overall mean words for each cell. Analyses for tokens, types and type/token ratio are considered separately.

1. Tokens

The overall results for tokens are shown graphically in Fig. 1, in which the mean number of tokens per child (ordinate) is shown for the three levels (designated low, medium, high on the abscissa) each of age, IQ and hearing loss. To show the effects of any one variable (e.g. age) the data have been summed over the remaining two variables (IQ and hearing loss). The trends suggested in Fig. 1 are as might be expected from Chapter 2, with the mean

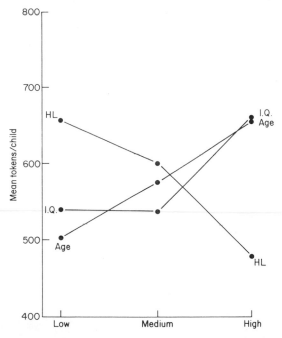

Fig. 1 Mean number of tokens/child according to age, non-verbal I.Q. and hearing loss.

Table I. Analysis of variance for tokens according to age, non-verbal I.Q. and hearing loss

Source	d.f.	MS	F	P
Age	2	472397·0	4·49	< 0·05
Hearing loss	2	431430·0	4·09	NS
Age × Hearing loss	4	224583·5	2·32	NS
IQ	2	339533·5	3·22	NS
IQ × Hearing loss	4	125514·5	1·19	NS
Age × IQ	4	47233·6	0·45	NS
Residual	8	105313·7	—	—

number of tokens per child decreasing with increasing hearing loss and increasing with increasing age and IQ. As the next step, the data were subjected to an analysis of variance (Table I). Since the numbers of subjects differed in the different cells, the design is unbalanced and a weighted analysis was performed using the GLIM programme. Changing the order of fitting the model terms therefore changes the calculated effects, as in a typical regression fit. The rows in our analysis of variance tables represent attributions to the sources, conditional on the fitting of terms higher up the Table. The results of the analysis broadly confirmed the results shown in Fig. 1, but the only significant differences (P< 0·05) were those attributable to age. Moreover none of the three interactions (age × hearing loss, IQ × hearing loss, and age × IQ) reached statistical significance.

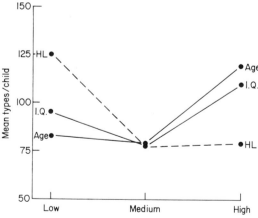

Fig. 2   Mean number of types/child according to age, non-verbal I.Q. and hearing loss.

2. Types

The procedures adopted for the overall analyses of tokens may next be applied to the data for types. Thus Fig. 2 shows graphically the effects of different levels of age, IQ and hearing loss on the mean number of types per child. Once again, the trends are generally as expected, with the mean number of types tending to decrease with increasing hearing loss and to increase with age and IQ. A similar analysis of variance (Table II) showed that there were statistically significant differences for age ($P < 0.05$) and for hearing loss ($P < 0.01$) but not for IQ. None of the three interactions was statistically significant.

Table II. *Analysis of variance for types according to age, non-verbal I.Q. and hearing loss*

Source	d.f.	MS	F	P
Age	2	19177·00	7·60	< 0·05
Hearing loss	2	21621·35	8·57	< 0·01
Age × Hearing loss	4	3790·21	1·50	NS
IQ	2	8096·63	3·21	NS
IQ × Hearing loss	4	9254·68	3·67	NS
Age × IQ	4	2155·23	0·85	NS
Residual	8	2523·25	—	—

3. Type/token ratio

As a third step in the overall analyses, the procedures used for tokens and for types may be used to assess differences in the type/token ratio. The effects of age, IQ and hearing loss on the mean type/token ratio are shown in graphical form in Fig. 3. On the hypothesis that higher type/token ratios seem likely to be associated with higher levels of linguistic advancement, we might have expected the type/token ratio to decrease with increasing hearing loss and if anything to increase with increasing age and IQ. The results shown in Fig. 3 are difficult to explain on this basis, as age, IQ and hearing loss show similar trends across their three levels, with the medium level associated with the lowest type/token ratio in each case. However, the range of values of the type/token ratio is rather small, and hence the results shown in Fig. 3 may be too unreliable to support further hypothesizing. This is shown in the analysis of variance in Table III where only one effect, that for hearing loss, just reaches significance at 5%.

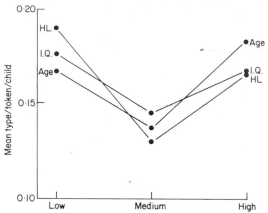

Fig. 3   Mean type/token ratio/child according to age, non-verbal I.Q. and hearing loss.

Table III. Analysis of variance for type/token ratio according to age, non-verbal I.Q. and hearing loss

Source	d.f.	MS	F	P
Age	2	0·009979	1·301	NS
Hearing loss	2	0·037299	4·864	< 0·05
Age × Hearing loss	4	0·016828	2·195	NS
IQ	2	0·020214	2·636	NS
IQ × Hearing loss	4	0·016714	2·180	NS
Age × IQ	4	0·008487	1·107	NS
Residual	8	0·007668	—	—

C. Analyses according to parsing category

The analyses described in Section B above show that when considering the overall data summed over parsing categories, there are statistically significant differences for some main effects (age and hearing loss) but not for any of the interactions tested. The levels of statistical significance obtained are low to moderate ($P < 0.05$ to < 0.01). It remains to consider the effects of different levels of age, hearing loss and IQ on the data for the separate parsing categories. Accordingly, the word counts were further analysed to assess the effects on each parsing category in turn for tokens, types, and type/token ratios (Figs 4–12). Figures 4–6 show the percentage of tokens for each parsing category, excluding "Other", according to age (Fig. 4), IQ (Fig. 5) and hearing loss (Fig. 6). Figures 7–9 show the same information for types, and Figs 10–12 for the type/token ratios. These figures show clearly for tokens and

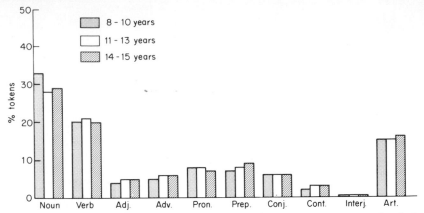

Fig. 4 The relative proportions of tokens according to parsing category (excluding "Other") for the three age levels.

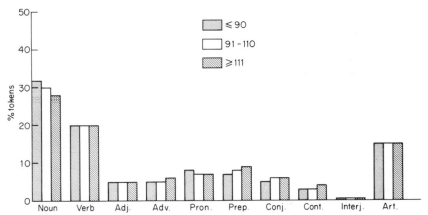

Fig. 5 The relative proportions of tokens according to parsing category (excluding "Other") for the three non-verbal I.Q. levels.

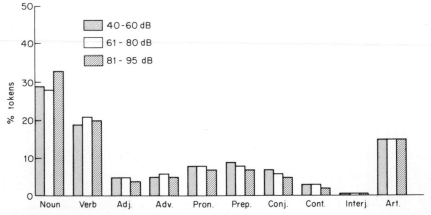

Fig. 6 The relative proportions of tokens according to parsing category (excluding "Other") for the three hearing loss levels.

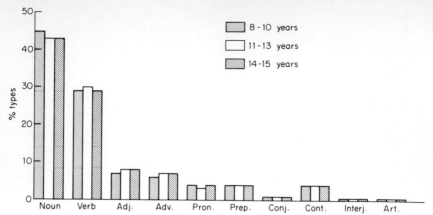

Fig. 7 *The relative proportions of types according to parsing category (excluding "Other") for the three age levels.*

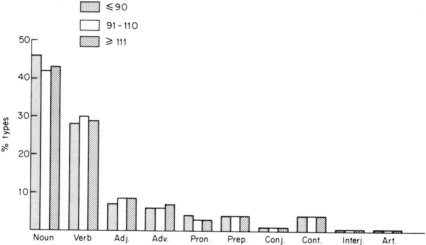

Fig. 8 *The relative proportions of types according to parsing category (excluding "Other") for the three non-verbal I.Q. levels.*

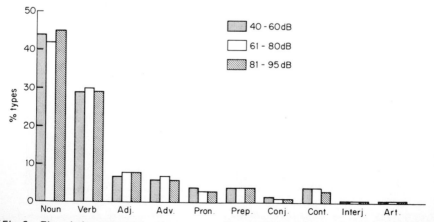

Fig. 9 *The relative proportions of types according to parsing category (excluding "Other") for the three hearing loss levels.*

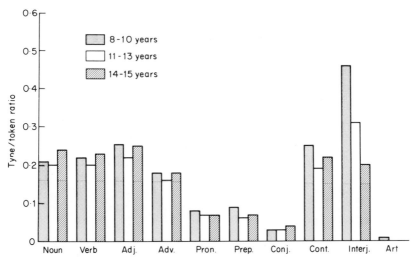

Fig. 10 The type/token ratio according to parsing category (excluding "Other") for the three age levels.

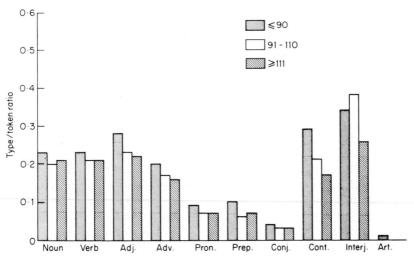

Fig. 11 The type/token ratio according to parsing category (excluding "Other") for the three non-verbal I.Q. levels.

for types, and to a lesser extent for type/token ratios, that differences attributable to differences in the variable concerned, namely different levels of age, IQ and hearing loss, and differences between the three main variables, are relatively small. This is particularly so when the differences are compared with the underlying similarities in the proportions of the different parsing categories. Further statistical analyses produced few significant differences in any consistent direction and we believe that Figs 4–12 effectively summarize the important features of the data. The only clear outcome relates to contractions, where significant differences in the expected direction are

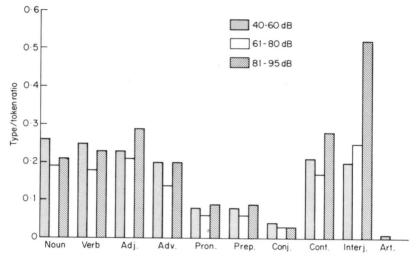

Fig. 12 *The type/token ratio according to parsing category (excluding "Other") for the three hearing loss levels.*

found for both tokens ($P < 0.01$) and for types ($P < 0.05$). In this case, high levels of hearing loss are associated with less frequent proportions of both tokens (Fig. 6) and of types (Fig. 9), probably because of difficulty with morphological items.

The data were subjected to a Principal Components (PC) analysis with the parsing categories treated as variables. When this was done, using the covariance matrix, two PCs were found to account for over 92% of the variation for tokens (PC1 accounted for *c.* 75% and PC2 for *c.* 20%); two PCs accounted for *c.* 99% of the variation for types (PC1 accounted for *c.* 96% and PC2 for *c.* 3%); and two PCs accounted for *c.* 90% of the variation in type/token ratio (PC1 accounted for *c.* 65% and PC2 for *c.* 25%). Moreover, on inspecting the table of coefficients from the PC analysis, it is possible to explain the dimensions attributable to the PCs in a mean-ingful way—thus PC1 for tokens is a dimension which emphasizes nouns, articles and verbs (action words?) vs. the remaining categories. Unfortun-ately, however, it proves impossible to relate the positions of the 27 individual cells of the subject classification matrix along the dimensions of the PCs in a clear and unequivocal way. Such results as do emerge are very open to interpretation, and hence are not described here.

D. Conclusion

In view of the work reviewed in Chapter 2, and the considerable effort which we have expended on statistical evaluation, the outcomes of the analyses de-scribed in Sections B and C above are rather surprising and perhaps dis-appointing. Large and significant differences are generally not found for the overall analyses nor for the analyses of the parsing data according to different levels of age, IQ and hearing loss, and the implications of the Principal Com-ponents analysis are unclear. However, sufficient differences are found to warrant the presentation of the lists of words in their given form, namely, according to the cells of the subject classification matrix and according to different parsing categories. In this form, they are convenient as a reference for the therapist or teacher.

The main reasons for the scarcity of significant differences seem fairly clear. Firstly, the level of linguistic analysis through adoption of the Oxford Dic-tionary for parsing is an arbitrary and somewhat limited procedure. Secondly, as regards hearing loss, we studied differences in losses over the range of partial hearing only, excluding profoundly deaf children, and thirdly, and perhaps most importantly, our method of analysing the vocabu-lary data according to cell, without taking note of individual subjects within cells, means that we are unable to take into account the probable large dif-ferences between the subjects within the cells. Such differences would reflect factors such as different home environments, schooling, ages at assessment of the impairment, and so on. Yet the fact that we recorded our data for this analysis in a form (i.e. by cell only) which makes such a thorough analysis impossible has its advantages. For since it would seem that the differences between individual subjects within cells are large compared with the variables of age, IQ and hearing loss, we are warned against accepting the latter vari-ables as sufficient to account for the variations in the language ability of hear-ing-impaired children. They are certainly important (Chapter 7), but they leave a large proportion of the variation concerning the overall vocabulary and parsing analyses unexplained.

7

The Spoken Language of Hearing-impaired Children: Grammar

JOHN BAMFORD AND LÜTGEN MENTZ

I. Introduction

This Chapter is concerned with an analysis and discussion of the grammatical data from the 263 hearing-impaired children described in Chapter 3. This sample includes not only the 241 partially-hearing children, but also 22 additional children with an average pure tone hearing loss in the better ear of more than 95 db (ISO). Such children are usually called "profoundly deaf" to distinguish them from the partially-hearing; for this reason we shall refer to the full sample of 263 children as "hearing-impaired" rather than partially-hearing.

In Chapter 3 we saw how each sample of spoken language, elicited by a set of pictures, was transcribed and then analysed onto a LARSP profile (Crystal *et al.*, 1976) which records the number of occurrences of various syntactical and morphological structures in each subject's sample of speech. (Following Crystal *et al.*, a distinction has been made between word structure (morphology) and the way in which sequences of words constitute patterns (syntax). "Grammar" is made up of both these two subfields, and is concerned with all matters of structural organization other than pronunciation and semantics.) This Chapter takes the LARSP profiles as the starting point of the analysis, and attempts to extract some generalizations about the development of grammatical performance in hearing-impaired children. To what extent this grammatical performance reflects grammatical knowledge is uncertain, but the two are probably closely related. The distinction between linguistic performance and linguistic competence was stressed by Chomsky (e.g. 1967): a native speaker of English is said to "know" all the "rules" of English grammar perfectly, and competence describes this ideal model and its functioning. However, for various reasons the structural model will be violated in the actual performance of speaking, writing or comprehending a sentence. Linguistic theory is concerned with identifying the internalized set of rules of the ideal speaker/listener—i.e. competence; the psycholinguist, on the other hand, is concerned not only with the underlying competence, but with assessing individual and variable performance, and with determining the factors which might account for the deviations of performance from competence. A completed LARSP profile provides an assessment of aspects of linguistic—or grammatical—performance, and this Chapter is firmly anchored, therefore, at the performance end of the distinction. If performance turns out to be disordered in any way we cannot be sure to what extent this is a reflection of limitations in competence itself or whether the rules are in fact known but for some reason not used. We tend to assume that in the case of the prelingually hearing-impaired child, poor performance reflects limited competence, and this seems a reasonable assumption to make. However, it should be remembered throughout this Chapter that this *is* an assumption, and that what we are measuring are aspects of linguistic performance. The relationship between performance and competence in the hearing-impaired child is an area for future research.

In Section II we examine the mean profile (i.e. all 263 profiles are grouped and averaged onto a single mean profile), and compare it with the mean profile from a small number of normally-hearing children. Section III examines the profiles grouped and averaged according to hearing loss, age and non-verbal I.Q. The limitations of these analyses are discussed and in Section IV a rather different approach is adopted, in which the profiles are subjected to a factor analysis procedure. In Section V the grammatical performance of the children is further examined as a function of hearing loss, age and non-verbal I.Q., and in addition an attempt is made to assess the effects of other variables such as age at onset of hearing impairment, social class, educational background, and so on. The work is summarized in Section VI.

II. The overall mean LARSP profile

Initially, the 263 LARSP profiles were grouped together and the mean number of entries for each profile structure was calculated (Fig. 1).

The interpretation of Fig. 1 must depend to a large extent upon what a "normal" profile looks like. With this in mind, a small homogeneous group (N = 11) of normally-hearing children with no known language problems, of average or above average intelligence and aged between 10 and 15 years, performed the same picture-description task under the same conditions as the hearing-impaired children. Figure 2 shows the mean number of entries for each profile structure for these normally-hearing subjects. It might be objected that our normally-hearing children were "super-normals", since they came from advantaged social backgrounds and were in most cases of above average non-verbal intelligence. As a check, therefore, we analysed the picture-description speech samples from a group of 10 normally-hearing 14- to 15-year-olds of below average non-verbal I.Q. There were no marked differences between the two mean profiles from these normally-hearing groups. Thus, we are satisfied to regard Fig. 2 as a valid comparison.

To further aid the interpretation of Fig. 1 we may refer to Crystal *et al.* who show profiles for a normally-hearing $3\frac{1}{2}$-year-old and for a normally-hearing adult (although Auckland, 1979, has raised some doubts about the internal consistency of these particular profiles). In addition, Crystal *et al.* review the rather limited literature available on the development of grammar, and (pp. 113–117) they tentatively distinguish 11 different patterns or types of profile. Finally, it should be remembered that the profile itself is laid out in such a way as to reflect "normal" grammatical advancement: that is, a normally-developing child will advance through the profile Stages, without obvious imbalance or gaps, on the three levels of clause, phrase and word. By the age of five or so his language will be fluent and mature, consisting largely of Stage 3 and 4 entries, with some Stage 2 entries, and with a fair proportion of recursiveness, sentence connectivity, and complex sentence patterns (Stages 5, 6 and 7).

Armed with these comparators, we can begin to make sense of the mean profile in Fig. 1. At first glance both profiles (Figs 1 and 2) look reasonably similar and complete, without obvious imbalances or gaps. However, the hearing-impaired children do not constitute a homogeneous group, and it may well be that the mean profile hides important features of the individual profiles. This point will be examined later.

ANALYSED:

Deviant	Ambiguous	Analyser's Comments:
X	1·39	

ANALYSED

Minor "Sentences": Social 0·98	Stereotypes 0·26	Problems

Major "Sentences"

	Excl.	Comm.	Quest.	Statement			
		'V'	'Q'	'V'	'N'	Other	Problems
0.9–1.6	0·28	0·61	X	2·05	12·08	0·37	

			Conn.	Clause		Phrase		Word
1.6–2.0	X	VX 0·22	QX 0·10		SV 9·10 VC/O 3·98 S C/O 1·00 AX 2·44 Neg X X Other X		DN 42·08 vv 3·56 Adj N 4·03 v part 11·91 NN 0·66 int x 1·20 Pr N 2·70 other X	Inf. 4·25 -ing 21·05 pl. 9·91 fut. 0·92

		Clause				Phrase			Word
2.0–2.6	VXY X let XY VS doXY X	QXY X	X+S:NP 4·72	X+V:VP 7·08	X+C/O:NP 2·53	X+A:AP 1·51			-ed 12·63 -en 2·10 3s 7·67

2.0–2.6 Clause:
SVC/O 23·35   VC/OA 1·19
SVA 8·83   V Od Oi 0·10
Neg XY X   Other 0·24

2.0–2.6 Phrase:
D Adj N 5·10   Cop 6·64 Aux 17·27
Adj Adj N 0·37   Pron 20·87
Pr DN 12·22   Pr Pron 1·23
N Adj X   Other 0·29

	Conn.	Clause				Phrase			Word
2.6–3.0	QXYZ X +S QVS X	XY+S:NP 15·13	XY+V:VP 14·80	XY+C/O:NP 14·17	XY+A:AP 6·94				gen 4·72 n't 1·20 'cop 3·01 'aux 5·37

2.6–3.0 Clause:
SVC/OA 5·87   AAXY 1·44
SVO$_d$O$_i$ 0·44   Other 0·37

2.6–3.0 Phrase:
N Pr NP X   Neg V 1·45
Pr D Adj N 1·18   Neg X 0·22
c X 0·48   2 aux 0·51
X c X 4·57   Other 0·32

		Conn.	Clause	Phrase	Word
3–3.6	how X what	tag X	and 13·15 c 1·17 s 3·57 other X	Coord. 1 9·48 1+ 2·13 Subord. 1 3·54 1+ X Clause: S X Clause: C/O 3·21 Comparative X Clause: A 2·39	Postmod. 1 1·03 1+ X clause Postmod. 1+ X phrase	-est 0·19 -er 0·22 -ly 0·75

+			–		
NP	VP	Clause	NP	VP	Clause
Initiator 1·19	Complex X	Passive X	Pron. 0·22 Adj. Seq. X	Modal X	Concord 0·29
Coord. 0·15		Complement X	Det. 0·29 N irreg. 0·10	Tense 0·51	A Position X
				V irreg. X	W Order 0·21

Other:			Other: 11·70		

4.0+				
A connectivity: 1·22	Emphatic order: X		it: 1·37
Comment clause: 0·37	Other:		there: 2·48

NUMBER OF WORDS IN EACH SENTENCE*

MEAN SENTENCE LENGTH : 7·21 WORDS
MEAN MINIMUM " " : 2·54 "
MEAN MAXIMUM " " : 17·37 "

MEAN NUMBER OF SENTENCES ANALYSED: 45·42

sentence means: Any utterance which is neither deviant nor ambiguous, but excluding all Stage 1 utterances.

Fig. 1   The mean LARSP profile for the hearing-impaired group of children (N=263). An "X" is entered if the mean was less than 0·10. Where a structure was never used it is left blank.

Deviant	Ambiguous
	X

Analyser's Comments:

ANALYSED

Minor "Sentences":	Social		Stereotypes		Problems	

				Major	"Sentences"			

	Excl.	Comm.	Quest.		Statement			

STAGE I (0.9 – 1.6)

	'V'	'Q'	'V'		'N'	Other	Problems
			0·36				

STAGE 2 (1.6 – 2.0)

	VX	QX	Conn.		Clause		Phrase		Word
				SV 6·91	VC/O 5·73	DN 52·55	vv 6·00	Inf. 6·64
								-ing 31·1?
				S C/O X	AX 4·09	Adj N 5·73	v part 14·73	
						NN X	int x 1·55	pl. 23·36
				Neg X X	Other	Pr N 3·00	other	
								fut. 0·73

STAGE 3 (2.0 – 2.6)

	VXY	QXY	X+S:NP 3·73	X+V:VP 10·00	X+C/O:NP 4·09	X+A:AP 3·09	-ed 5·45
	let XY	VS	SVC/O 24·18	VC/OA 1·18	D Adj N 7·91	Cop 12·00	-en 12·0?
	doXY		SVA 13·18	V Od Oi 0·36	Adj Adj N 0·45	Aux 38·73 Pron 18·91	3s 20·8?
			Neg XY	Other 0·64	Pr DN 24·73 N Adj N	Pr Pron 1·82 Other 1·36	gen 8·36

STAGE 4 (2.6 – 3.0)

		QXYZ	XY+S:NP 20·18	XY+V:VP 24·54	XY+C/O:NP 18·18	XY+A:AP 9·72	n't 1·00
	+S	QVS	SVC/OA 11·09	AAXY 3·09	N Pr NP 1·00	Neg V 1·36	'cop 5·9
			SVOdOi 0·18	Other 1·64	Pr D Adj N 2·64 c X 0·36 X c X 6·27	Neg X X 2 aux 1·45 Other 1·00	'aux 15·3

STAGE 5 (3 – 3.6)

	how		and 25·27	Coord. 1 11·27 1+ 5·64	Postmod. 17·45 1+ 0·18 clause	-est 1·0?
		tag	c 1·18	Subord. 1 7·45 1+ Clause: S		-er 0·6?
	what		s 7·45	Clause: C/O 2·91 Comparative	Postmod. 1+ 0·45 phrase	-ly 1·8?
			other 1·18	Clause: A 4·00		

STAGE 6 (3.6 – 4.6)

	+			—		
	NP	VP	Clause	NP	VP	Clause
	Initiator 3·95	Complex	Passive 0·36	Pron. Adj. Seq.	Modal Tense X	Concord ?· A Position
	Coord. X		Complement 0·27	Det. N irreg. 0·27	V irreg.	W Order
	Other:			Other: 3·27		

STAGE 7 (4.6+)

A connectivity: 1·45	Emphatic order:	it: 2·00
Comment clause: 0·27	Other:	there: 6·82

NUMBER OF WORDS IN EACH SENTENCE* MEAN SENTENCE LENGTH: 15·92 WORDS

MEAN MINIMUM " : 9·73 "
MEAN MAXIMUM " : 43·00 "

MEAN NUMB? OF SENTENC? ANALYSE): ?

*Here sentence means: Any utterance which is neither deviant nor ambiguous, but excluding all Stage 1 utterances.

Fig. 2 The mean LARSP profile for the normally-hearing group of children (N=11). An "X" is entered if the mean was less than 0·10. Where a structure was never used it is left blank.

A. Clause level analysis

Looking at the clause level of analysis in Figs 1 and 2, it can be seen that the hearing-impaired group are retarded with reference to the normally-hearing group. The mean number of clause level entries totalled at each Stage is shown in Table I for each group. The hearing-impaired use less of the advanced clause structures, at Stages 3 and 4, but rather more of the least advanced structures, at Stage 1. They exhibit less recursiveness (Stage 5) and consequently fewer connecting devices (*and*, etc.). Stage 5 structures are characteristic of the creative aspects of language, and this Stage is accordingly of great significance in normal development, since it increases enormously

Table I. Clause level analysis: mean number of entries totalled within Stages for the hearing-impaired and the normally-hearing groups ("expansion" entries have not been included in the Stage 3 and Stage 4 figures)

Structure	Group	
	Hearing-impaired	Normally-hearing
Stage 1 "clauses"	14·50	0·36
Stage 2 clauses	16·65	16·73
Stage 3 clauses	33·71	39·54
Stage 4 clauses	8·12	16·00
Stage 5 clauses	20·83	31·27
Connecting devices	17·89	35·08

the range of expression available to the child. The hearing-impaired group used Stage 5 structures much less than did the normally-hearing group, although it is interesting to note that the hearing-impaired group's biggest shortfall in the advanced Stages (Stages 3, 4 and 5) is at Stage 4, rather than at Stage 5. A Chi squared test on the raw frequencies from which the means, totalled within Stages, in Table I were derived showed the differences between the two groups to be highly significant ($\chi^2 = 318\cdot18$, d.f. $= 5$, $P < 0\cdot001$).

Note that for the purposes of this and subsequent analyses, Stage 1 entries are included in the clause level of analysis. There is considerable controversy in the literature as to whether one-element utterances can be called clauses or sentences at all (McNeill, 1970; Bloom, 1973). This theoretical dispute need not concern us here: from our point of view, it is important that the one-element entries be included in the analysis somewhere, and it makes more sense to contrast them with the clause level analysis at other Stages than the phrase level analysis. The use of quotation marks, both by Crystal *et al.* (p. 63) for Stage 1 entries and by us for Stage 1 "clauses", is intended to show that we regard the question as unresolved. Note also that the figures for Stage 3 clauses and Stage 4 clauses in Table I do not include "expansion" entries (e.g. X + S : NP, XY + S : NP). We will consider these separately.

Table II compares the hearing-impaired group's mean expansion entries with those of the normally-hearing group. The figures in Table II are the sums of the subject, verb, object, and adverbial mean expansion entries at each Stage for each group from Figs 1 and 2. Thus the entry in Table II for the hearing-impaired group's two-element expansions, for example, is 15·84, which is the sum of 4·72, 7·08, 2·53 and 1·51 from Fig. 1. The expansion entries are not exclusive of the clause level entries proper: an entry in either

Table II. Mean number of two- and three-element expansion entries totalled for both groups of subjects. (The number of clause entries in the previous Stage to that from which these entries are drawn is given in parentheses for each figure)

	Group	
	Hearing-impaired	Normally-hearing
Two-element expansions (e.g. X + S : NP)	15·84 (16·65)	20·91 (16·73)
Three-element expansions (e.g. XY + S : NP)	51·04 (33·71)	72·62 (39·54)

Stage 2 or Stage 3 clauses may also give one or more entries in the appropriate expansion boxes in Stages 3 and 4 respectively. Thus the number of expansion entries at Stages 3 and 4 depends partly upon the number of clauses available for expansion: that is, the number of clause entries in the preceding Stages (2 and 3 respectively). For this reason, Table II shows in parentheses with each expansion figure the sum of the means of the clause level entries in the previous Stage. Note that since one clause level entry may give more than one expansion entry (i.e. if more than one of its elements is expanded) any of the expansion numbers in Table II may exceed the number of clauses (in parentheses) associated with it. But since a clause level entry may give no expansion entries (i.e. if none of its elements is expanded), it is also possible for the number of expansions to be exceeded by the corresponding number of clauses.

Chi squared tests on the raw frequencies from which the figures in Table

II were calculated show that the differences between the expansions of the hearing-impaired group and the expansions of the normally-hearing group are significant ($\chi^2 = 18\cdot47$, d.f. $= 3$, $P < 0\cdot001$ for the two-element expansions; $\chi^2 = 10\cdot43$, d.f. $= 3$, $P < 0\cdot05$ for the three-element expansions). Thus, although each group produced a similar number of Stage 2 clauses (16·65 and 16·73), less of these entries were expanded by the hearing-impaired than by the normally-hearing, which is a clear indication of lack of advancement (e.g. "boy eat" as opposed to "The boy is eating"). Similarly, the hearing-impaired group expanded a smaller number of Stage 3 clauses into Stage 4 expansions: 51·04 as opposed to 72·62. Even if these figures are corrected for differences in the number of Stage 3 clauses, of which the normally-hearing had more, the outcome is the same: the hearing-impaired children expanded proportionately less of their Stage 3 clauses (e.g. "Boy eat dinner" as opposed to "The boy is eating his dinner") than did the normally-hearing.

The interpretation of the relative degree of subject, verb, object and adverbial expansion at a given Stage for either group depends upon whether one examines the mean entries in Figs 1 and 2 as they stand or corrects each one for the number of clauses in the previous Stage which contain the appropriate element. For example, the mean number of three-element adverbial expansions of the hearing-impaired in Fig. 1, 6·94, is considerably smaller than the mean number of corresponding subject, verb or object expansions, and is therefore an apparent imbalance. If, however, one takes into account the number of Stage 3 clauses available for expansion—that is, all those Stage 3 clauses containing an adverbial element (8·83 SVAs + 1·19 VC/OAs)—then in fact 69·26% of the adverbial elements were expanded, which is a higher percentage than for the corrected subject, verb or object expansions. These percentages for each group, for each type of expansion, are shown in Table III.

Considering first the three-element expansions, there are no glaring imbalances in either group. Depending upon which method one chooses, the adverbial expansions ("The boys are playing *under the table*") occur either more (percentage in Table III) or less (means in Figs 1 and 2) than the other three-element expansions for both groups. This simply means that if an adverbial element is used by either group in a three-element clause, which is not very often in comparison with the use of S, V and C/O elements, then it will tend to be an expanded adverbial element: "He ran *from the house*", for example, rather than "He ran *out*". These two sentences are both, of course, grammatically acceptable in adult language, which illustrates the point that unexpanded elements are not always "immature". "Baby sleeping pram" rather than "The baby is sleeping in the pram", on the other hand, is an example of lack of expansion suggesting lack of development of certain structures. The other three-element expansions (S, V and C/O) are similar across the two groups, although there is a tendency for the percentage of verb expansions to be rather low for the hearing-impaired group—only 44% as opposed to the normally-hearing group's figure of 63%.

Table III. The expansion entries for each group taken from Figs 1 and 2 and expressed as a percentage of the number of clauses in the preceding Stage available for that particular type of expansion

	Group	
	Hearing-impaired	Normally-hearing
Two-element expansions		
X+S:NP	47	54
X+V:VP	54	79
X+C/O:NP	51	71
X+A:AP	62	76
Three-element expansions		
XY+S:NP	47	54
XY+V:VP	44	63
XY+C/O:NP	58	70
XY+A:AP	69	68

For the two-element clauses the picture as regards adverbial expansion is similar. Adverbial elements tend to be used less often (Figs 1 and 2), but when they are used, they tend to be expanded. As far as the other elements are concerned, Figs 1 and 2 indicate that most expansion takes place in the verb element, but as the percentages in Table III show, that is true only for the normally-hearing group. For the hearing-impaired group, S, V, and C/O expansion is similar in degree, while the normally-hearing children show more expansion of the V and C/O elements than of the S element. The development of structure in object rather than in subject position is a regular feature of normal language development, and the fact that it is not so apparrant for the hearing-impaired group may be important. The most significant features of Table III, then, are the lack of verb and object expansion by the hearing-impaired relative to the normally-hearing group.

B. Phrase level analysis

At the phrase level of analysis the hearing-impaired profile (Fig. 1) shows a relative lack of verb auxiliaries (Aux), which are especially low in comparison with the normally-hearing (Fig. 2). This is one reflection of the lack of verb element expansion just noted, and is in agreement with previous research, which has identified a similar lack of auxiliaries and other "function" words in deaf and partially-hearing language (Goda, 1964; Myklebust, 1964; Brannon, 1966). Otherwise, at the phrase level, the hearing-impaired children exhibit a somewhat lower level of advancement and a generally depressed level of entries, largely as a consequence of the relative lack of expansion of the clause level elements. Thus, in almost every case, the number of entries for each phrase structure is less for the hearing-impaired children, despite the fact that both groups gave almost exactly the same mean number of clauses *in toto* across Stages 1–4 (excluding expansions): 72·83 for the hearing-impaired, 72·63 for the normally-hearing group (cf. Table I). The interesting exception is the entry under pronouns (Pron), and it may be relevant to note that the development of the use of pronouns is one of the few advances in syntax which tends to decrease rather than increase the number of words per sentence. One might be tempted to speculate that the rules governing the use of pronouns are for this reason more easily mastered by the hearing-impaired child than rules involving expansion. However, not only did the profoundly deaf children in the sample use markedly fewer pronouns (see below, Fig. 4) than the normally-hearing group, a finding which is in agreement with results from Wilbur *et al.* (1975), but when the LARSP profiles are put into rather more homogeneous sub-groups according to age, hearing loss and non-verbal I.Q. (see below, Section III and Appendix III), it is clear that for the younger age groups at least pronoun use decreases with increased hearing loss.

The figures for the phrase level entries at different Stages are compared in Table IV, and it can be seen that the number of entries given by the hearing-impaired group is smaller than that given by the normally-hearing group at

Table IV. *Phrase level analysis: mean number of entries totalled within Stages for the hearing-impaired and the normally-hearing groups*

Structures	Group	
	Hearing-impaired	Normally-hearing
Stage 2 phrases	66·14	83·56
Stage 3 phrases	63·99	105·91
Stage 4 phrases	8·73	14·08
Stage 5 phrases	1·03	8·08
Total	139·89	211·63

every Stage. Furthermore, in moving from Stage 2 to Stage 5 (less to more advanced) the separation of the two groups increases. A Chi squared test on the raw frequencies from which the totalled means in Table IV were derived showed the differences between the two groups to be highly significant ($\chi^2 = 271 \cdot 69$, d.f. $= 3$, $P < 0 \cdot 001$).

C. Word level analysis

At the word level of analysis, only the entries under -ed, fut. and n't are larger for the hearing-impaired group than the normally-hearing group (Figs 1 and 2). Fut. and n't were used rarely by either group, probably because the nature of the task (picture-description) was such as to offer few opportunities for either the future tense or negated verbs. Picture-description tends to elicit statements about what *is* happening *now* (or what *has* happened), rather than statements about what will happen, or about what is not happening. Furthermore, the difference between the two groups on fut. and n't were small, and these particular structures can therefore be dismissed as of little interest in the present context. The entries for past tense (-ed), which was the only other word level structure used more by the hearing-impaired group, look more important. This structure was used moderately frequently by both groups, but considerably more by the hearing-impaired than by the normally-hearing children: 12·63 as opposed to 5·45. On the other hand, the entries for the past participle (-en) are 12·09 for the normally-hearing group as opposed to only 2·10 for the hearing-impaired group. It may be that the hearing-impaired child finds the rules governing the use of the past participle form more difficult to grasp than the rules governing the past tense form of verbs, which he therefore tends to use instead. When the LARSP profiles are organized into subgroups according to the ages, hearing losses and non-verbal I.Q.s of the subjects (see below, Section III and Appendix III), every group, in contrast to our group of normally-hearing children, used the -ed structure more frequently than the -en structure. This is in agreement with Pressnell (1973), who found that hearing-impaired children had less difficulty with the simple past tense than with the past participle form. However, we also have some LARSP profiles from 10 normally-hearing children of below average non-verbal I.Q. who performed the same picture-description task under the same conditions as the present study, and it seems that these children too use more -ed forms than -en forms. Whether there is some truth in the possibility that both hearing-impaired and low I.Q. children tend to substitute the past tense for the past participle form can only be determined from further research with more specific material and more homogeneous groups of subjects.

At the word level, then, -ed is the only frequently-occurring structure which is used more by the hearing-impaired group. On the other hand, for all the remaining word level structures the hearing-impaired children gave fewer entries. Of those items which were used relatively frequently, plurals (pl.), contracted auxiliaries ('aux), third person singular inflexions (3s) and, as noted above, past participles (-en) are particularly depressed. Of the less frequently used structures, superlative (-est) and comparative (-er) exhibit large proportionate differences between the two groups, again in favour of the normally-hearing. The total number of mean word level entries is 74·10 for the hearing-impaired and 134·36 for the normally-hearing children, which is a larger shortfall than at the phrase level. Such a result is not unexpected (see, for example, Cooper, 1967), since we might suspect that hearing-impaired children face special problems with morphological items which, because of their generally short duration, are particularly difficult to hear. In this connection, Schultz and Kraat (1971) studied a group of 10- to 13-year-old children with moderate to severe bilateral hearing losses, who wore hearing aids and communicated primarily via the auditory modality, and argued from their data that for these children the syllable, not the phoneme, is the minimum perceptual unit. If this applies to the children in the present study it would adversely affect the entries at the word level, some of the structures of which consist of single phonemes (e.g. 3s) rather than single syllables.

D. Stages 6 and 7

The entries at Stages 6 and 7 are as expected: the hearing-impaired group generally show more errors and fewer positive features in Stage 6 (especially Initiator), but the numbers are rather small. There was virtually no use of passive clauses by the 263 hearing-impaired children: the passive voice was used on a total of only two occasions, as opposed to a total of four occasions by the normally-hearing group, who were only 11 in number. This agrees with previous findings and is thought to relate to sequencing problems in the hearing-impaired. Tervoort (1970), for example, argued that the hearing-impaired tend to understand language by the recognition of semantic content words, often failing to appreciate the implications of grammatical rules. This tendency to extract meaning by going from content word to content word works to the detriment of the perception of passive sentences, since while the active sentence identifies real actor with grammatical subject, usually in the first position, and real acted-upon with grammatical object, usually in the second position, the passive sentence removes this identification and reverses the sequence. In other words, the passive sentence tends to be interpreted in terms of its surface Subject–Verb–Object order. In fact, this is done by young, normally-hearing children (Turner and Rommetveit, 1967) who also find the passive voice relatively difficult, but they have usually mastered the correct processing rules by eight or nine years, which is earlier than hearing-impaired children. The process of comprehension and production of passive voice sentences by deaf children parallels that in hearing children, but appears to be much delayed (Power and Quigley, 1973).

E. Sentence length

Mean sentence length, and the means of the sentence length minima and maxima, are considerably smaller for the hearing-impaired group. Note that the one-element Stage 1 "clauses" were excluded from this exercise; had they been included the hearing-impaired figures would have been depressed further. Again, this agrees with previous observations and, of course, will tend to follow as a consequence of the lack of recursiveness and the lack of clause-element expansion by the hearing-impaired children. Indeed, Brown (1973) has pointed out that almost every new kind of grammatical knowledge increases sentence length. Brannon and Murry (1966) compared the number of words per sentence spoken by a group of 12- to 13-year-old normally-hearing children with the number of words per sentence spoken by a group of hearing-impaired children aged between 8 and 18 years (mean 12·6 years). The hearing-impaired children were divided into two groups, one partially-hearing (pure tone hearing loss in the better ear of 27–66 dB ASA), the other deaf (pure tone hearing loss in the better ear > 75 dB ASA). The mean number of words per sentence differed significantly between groups at 7·9 (normally-hearing), 6·9 (partially-hearing), and 6·0 (deaf).

F. The concept of deviancy

It is popularly supposed that much of the language of the hearing-impaired is deviant or ambiguous, but such was not the case with our sample of children (Fig. 1). The reasons for this apparent disagreement are equivocal. Firstly, our sample consists largely of partially-hearing rather than profoundly deaf children, and the lack of deviant or ambiguous sentences may therefore be a genuine reflection of the quality of the language of the partially-hearing about which rather little published work is available. It is also possible that those who work with the hearing-impaired have been misled into expecting a large number of deviant utterances, since many published examples of such are in fact written rather than spoken examples (e.g. Lenneberg, 1967, p. 321), and the deviancies and ambiguities may in some way be a function of the processes involved in writing, processes that are not necessarily the same as those involved in speaking. Thus, for example, the recent publication by Russell *et al.* (1976) is concerned entirely with deaf children, and to a large extent with their written language. Finally, the lack of deviant sentences in our study is at least partly due to the problem of definition and a lack of information as to what exactly is "inadmissible in the adult grammar, and not part of the expected grammatical development of normal children (insofar as this can be established by reference to the language acquisition literature)". This is the narrow sense of "deviant" which Crystal *et al.* favour, and which is the criterion for an entry in the "deviant" box on the profile. They admit that gaps in the literature on language acquisition often make it difficult to identify deviant sentences with sufficient reliability, but argue nonetheless that this definition of the term is operationally useful.

The use of the concept of deviancy is fundamental to any approach such as that of Crystal *et al.* which analyses grammar in terms of a comparison with the normal developmental sequence, and it is essential therefore, that we make our use of the term quite clear, particularly since it is used in different ways by different workers in the field. In one sense it is used to describe language in which the range of structures used is comparable to an earlier stage in normal development, but the frequency of use of specific structures falls outside normal development; but in another, narrower, sense it is used by such as Crystal *et al.* to describe sentences which do not conform to the grammatical rules of adult language, and as they point out, considerations of frequency of use are not, therefore, critical. The narrow definition also excludes instances of delay: although some sentences are deviant from the point of view of the rules of adult grammar, they are nonetheless admissible in terms of normal child development. Crystal *et al.* regard the latter as instances of delay, and therefore retain the notion of deviancy in its narrow sense: structures (or sentences) which are part of neither the normal adult language nor the language of the normally-developing child.

Since we have chosen to use the LARSP profile produced by Crystal *et al.*, then clearly we have to adopt their definitions when it comes to analysing a language sample onto the profile. Thus, we have used the narrow definition of deviancy as the criterion for an entry in the deviancy box on the profile. The problem with this definition, however, is that since all profile entries which are non-deviant are by definition either normal or delayed, it follows that a sample of "non-normal" language which contains no deviant sentences is simply delayed. Yet it is quite possible for such a sample of language to be unlike anything that a younger normal speaker would produce, and it seems to us that the notion of "delay", which is in a sense complementary to that of "deviance", should be reserved for instances of simple retardation. Crystal *et al*., however, argue that there are several types of delayed language, and that delay need not be simple, in the sense of the speech being a replica of that expected from juniors, but can also be manifested in terms of abnormal frequencies of use. Thus it seems that one can either adopt a narrow definition of deviancy with a broader definition of delay, or a narrow definition of delay with a broader definition of deviancy.

There are those who argue for the narrow definition of deviancy on the grounds that the term should be reserved for those occasions when there is clear evidence that different grammatical rules (different from the rules used by normal adults or by children with normal language development) are being used, and that what constitutes such evidence are deviant sentences in the narrow sense (e.g. "cat angry are"), not abnormal frequencies of acceptable structures. Whether a single instance of a deviant sentence provides sufficient evidence to infer a "rule" is another question, and one that relates to the distinction between performance and competence. It seems to us that single instances of deviant sentences are manifestations of deviant performance, which may or may not reflect deviant competence. The LARSP profile is essentially concerned with linguistic performance, so the notion of deviancy applied to single instances is entirely in accord with the aims of the analysis onto the profile. Linguistic rules, on the other hand, which reflect aspects of linguistic competence, are used with some degree of consistency, and it has been argued that the use of deviant rules can be inferred from frequency data. Thus, Moran and Byrne (1977) compared a group of learning-disabled children with a group of normally-achieving children and were able to argue from their pattern of responses that the learning-disabled consistently used different rules to formulate the past tense from those used by the normal children. It is noteworthy that this was taken as evidence of linguistic deviancy, even though instances of their deviant rules (e.g. "they did climb" for "they climbed") would not have qualified for an entry in the deviant box on the LARSP profile under the definition of Crystal *et al*. The latter "only ask the question whether, regardless of frequency, the structures used are possible adult or expected normal child sentences. If the answer is no, then this is a deviant sentence for us. If the answer is yes, it is nondeviant ..." (p. 29).

It seems to us, however, to be inadequate to describe abnormal frequencies of usage of different structures merely as "delay", and in this we are in agreement with some other workers in the field, although admittedly not all of them regard it necessary to show that different linguistic rules are being applied in order to infer deviancy. Menyuk (1964), for example, argued that the term delayed language was not sufficient to describe the verbal behaviour of a group of children whose structures were not only late in appearing but were being expressed in ways that probably would not lead to Standard English without special instruction. Leonard (1972) used omission of verb forms to distinguish deviant from normal language users, and Morehead and Ingram (1973) concluded that uneven mastery of inflexions characterized the language of a group of children considered linguistically deviant. Wiig *et al.* (1973, reported by Moran and Byrne, 1977) compared a group of learning-disabled children with a group of normal children of the same age and concluded that unlike mentally-retarded children the learning-disabled did not exhibit overall delay in morphological development but a scattered development of inflexions.

Part of the confusion surrounding the concept of deviancy in this context arises from a logical error. It is not the case that the two definitions of the term which we have discussed—its narrow sense and its somewhat broader sense—are necessarily mutually exclusive. If one chooses to use one definition, one does not have to discard the other, since they are definitions which apply to different levels of analysis. Thus, when considering single instances of structures or sentences (i.e. when entering items onto the profile) we use the term in the narrow sense formulated by Crystal *et al.* and in order to be entered on the profile as an example of a "deviant" item a structure must meet their criteria. However, at a different level, when we are examining a completed profile, either that from a single child or the mean profile from a group of children, we consider it to be quite legitimate and in no way inconsistent to talk about the deviant patterning of such a profile—if the pattern is such as to be unlike any that might be expected from a normal adult or a child with normally-developing language. (Patterns similar to those expected from younger children with normally-developing language are, for us, examples of delayed or retarded profiles.) Thus, for example, we would consider a profile pattern which exhibited clause and phrase structures developed up to Stage 4 but little or no development of word level (morphological) structures, as deviant. Again, a profile displaying strong word level development with correspondingly weak clause and phrase structure (a pattern which has been reported in some educationally subnormal children) would be an example of deviant patterning. Whether such deviant patterning of complete profiles can ever be taken as evidence for the use of linguistic rules which are different from those in use by normally-developing children and by adults is a rather different question, although we can conceive of certain relative proportions of profile entries which could be considered as good evidence for the use of deviant rules. It should be pointed out, however, that the LARSP profile does not necessarily provide the most useful tool for obtaining such evidence. Detailed error analyses of the use of single specific rules would probably be better. Evidence for deviant linguistic rules is less likely to be manifested in the overall patterning of profiles (since this patterning reflects the interplay of a complex array of linguistic rules), than in specific aspects of the profiles, aspects which can be related to the use of single rules. For example, a profile which exhibited regular development of structure at all levels up to and including Stage 5, but which contained a large number of Aux entries (Stage 2, phrase level) without any -ing, fut. or -en entries (word level) would provide strong evidence for the use of a simple rule which generated the uninflected root of verbs for use as present participle, past participle and so on. Such a single simple rule might be used instead of the series of more complex rules which govern verb inflexions in normal language. Furthermore, although on the level of analysis of single structures or sentences examples of this rule (e.g. "he is run") would not be regarded as deviant by the criteria in force at this level, in conjunction with an otherwise normal profile advanced to Stage 5 it does represent deviant patterning, as far as we are aware. The last clause is meant to draw attention to a dimension of ambiguity which runs through and clouds the whole of this discussion, namely the lack of certainty at all levels and most ages as to what is to be considered as part of normal language development and what is not. It is abundantly clear from the literature and from our own work that normative data are badly needed if we are to make any inferences about the performance of children whose development may be deviant. When such data are available in reliable detail, then many of the problems concerned with the identification of deviancy will be resolved, and examples of deviancy at the two levels of single sentences and profile patterns will come into greater correspondence than is the case at present. Meanwhile, we are content to examine individual or grouped profiles for what we call deviant patterning, and in the next section we do just this with the overall mean profile.

G. The pattern of the mean profile

The overall pattern of the mean hearing-impaired profile does not seem to match any one of the patterns suggested by Crystal *et al.* It is probably best approximated by their Type 3 pattern (general delay overlaid with weak phrase structure), but it is not unlike their Type 4 (clause and phrase structure to Stages 3 and 4 with little or no word-level development), nor their Type

6 (lack of recursiveness, complex sentence patterns and sentence connectivity). The pattern in Fig. 1 is one of delay on all fronts overlaid with weak phrase structure and even weaker word structure. Wilcox and Tobin (1974) studied the performance of 11 partially-hearing children on a sentence repetition task with particular regard to their use of different forms of verb and verb phrases. The authors argued that the lower level of performance exhibited by the partially-hearing group represented a difference in degree rather than kind, "as the experimental group displayed linguistic performance similar to the (normally-hearing) control group, but showed a general delay in language development". However, it is arguable whether such a conclusion can be inferred from only six measures (the proportion of correct responses for six types of verb construction), including two which did, in fact, indicate a "marked divergence in performance" between the two groups. The profile pattern in Fig. 1 seems to indicate not simply general delay but a deviant patterning as well. Normative data are urgently required in order to test such conclusions more rigorously, but until such data are forthcoming we have to rely on what little is available. The ratio of clause (in Stages 1–4, excluding expansions) to phrase to word structures for the normally-hearing group profile (Fig. 2) is 1 : 3 : 2. This is similar to the ratios from a normally-hearing adult profile (Crystal *et al.*, p. 107), which are 1 : 2·5 : 1·5. The hearing-impaired group profile (Fig. 1), however, gives ratios of 1 : 2 : 1. These ratios are not only unlike those from the normally-hearing adult profile and the normally-hearing mean profile in Fig. 2, they are unlike those from the profile of a normally-hearing 3½-year-old (Crystal *et al.*, p. 106), which are 1 : 1 : 1. Crystal *et al.* state that a profile presenting a case of "pure" delayed language would have an even distribution of structures across the page, as in the 3½-year-old's profile. How the "normal" adult ratios of clause to phrase to word of something like 1 : 3 : 2 develop from the "normal" 3½-year-old ratios of 1 : 1 : 1 is uncertain, and will remain so until we have more normative studies. However, the possibility that the normally-hearing child develops phrase structure before he develops his word (i.e. morphological) structure is unlikely. Such a pattern of development would make the ratios for our hearing-impaired children 1 : 2 : 1 look like a fairly normal stage in the development from child ratios of 1 : 1 : 1 to adult ratios of 1 : 3 : 2, and would imply that the mean profile for our hearing-impaired children is a reflection of simple delayed development. Crystal *et al.* suggest, albeit tentatively, that phrase and word structure both begin to emerge at Stage II. It may be, therefore, that the hearing-impaired ratios of 1 : 2 : 1 from Fig. 1 reflect not only delayed but deviant patterning.

Figure 3 expresses the patterning of the hearing-impaired profile (Fig. 1) in diagrammatic form, and is based on the assumption that we can regard the normally-hearing profile in Fig. 2 as a standard (i.e. a baseline). The totals of the mean entries for various parts of the hearing-impaired profile in Fig. 1 are therefore calculated as a percentage of the totalled mean entries of the same parts of the normally-hearing profile.

Comparisons should be related to the clause analysis in Stages 1–4, since every clause, whether part of a complex (multiple clause) sentence or not, is analysed into these Stages as a single entry under one structure. In terms

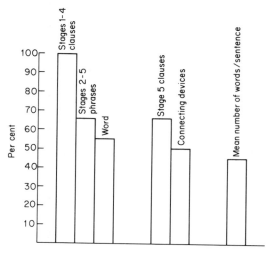

Fig. 3   *The total of the mean entries at the three analysis levels of clause, phrase and word for the hearing-impaired group expressed as a percentage of the same totalled mean entries for the normally-hearing group. Also shown is the mean number of words per sentence expressed as a percentage of the normally-hearing group's mean.*

of clauses, the hearing-impaired said as much as the normally-hearing children, but they tended to use no more than one clause per sentence: hence there are less Stage 5 clause entries (recursiveness), and fewer connecting devices. Furthermore, the elements in the hearing-impaired children's clauses were expanded into noun, verb or adverbial phrases on significantly fewer occasions than were the normally-hearing children's clause elements (Tables II and III), giving a shortfall at the phrase level. All these trends produce fewer words per sentence: it can be seen from Fig. 3 that the mean sentence length of the hearing-impaired group is only 45% of the normally-hearing group's mean sentence length. Finally, we have already suggested that the special difficulties associated with hearing short-duration morphological structures accounts for the hearing-impaired group producing only 55% (Fig. 3) of the number of morphological entries given by the normally-hearing group.

H. The mean profile excluding the profoundly deaf children

Although some of the differences between the two grouped profiles in Figs 1 and 2 will be due to the inclusion of the 22 profoundly deaf children in the hearing-impaired sample, it can by no means be argued that the poorer advancement of the hearing-impaired as a group is a result of their inclusion. For one thing, 22 out of 263 is a small proportion. For another, later analyses show (see below, Section V) that hearing loss on its own is not a perfect predictor of grammatical ability, and that there are many other factors involved. The mean profile for the 22 profoundly deaf children is shown in Fig. 4, and for comparison purposes the mean profile for the sample *excluding* these children (i.e. for $N=241$) is shown in Fig. 5. We do not propose to discuss these profiles in depth, since the analysis of groups of non-homogeneous children has been taken far enough. Suffice it to say that inspection of the profiles in Figs 1, 2, 4 and 5 clearly indicates that although, as expected, the

Table V. The mean profile entries totalled across various parts of the profile for each group

	Group			
	Hearing-impaired (all) $N=263$	Profoundly deaf $N=22$	Partially-hearing (i.e. excluding profoundly deaf) $N=241$	Normally-hearing $N=11$
Stages 1–4 clauses	72·98	103·91	69·99	72·63
Stages 2–5 phrases	139·89	61·12	147·09	211·63
Word	74·10	33·37	77·70	134·36
Stage 5 clauses	20·83	5·51	22·41	31·27
Connecting devices	17·89	4·73	19·09	35·08
Mean number words per sentence	7·21	3·87	7·52	15·92

UNANALYSED:

Deviant	Ambiguous	Analyser's Comments:
0·14	**1·68**	

ANALYSED

		Minor "Sentences": Social **0·77**			Stereotypes **0·32**		Problems	
				Major "Sentences"				

STAGE 1 0.9 – 1.6		Excl.	Comm.	Quest.		Statement		
			'V' **0·41**	'Q' X	'V' **9·05**	'N' **56·68**	Other **1·18**	Problems

STAGE 2 1.6 – 2.0			VX X	QX X	Conn.	Clause		Phrase		Word
						SV **11·23**	VC/O **3·55**	DN **19·95**	vv **1·45**	Inf. **1·46**
						S C/O **2·27**	AX **2·14**	Adj N **1·77**	v part **6·86**	-ing **11·0⁹**
								NN **0·68**	int x **1·00**	pl. **5·73**
						Neg X	Other	Pr N **1·73**	other	fut. **0·27**

STAGE 3 2.0 – 2.6			VXY	QXY	X+S:NP **3·50**	X+V:VP **4·46**	X+C/O:NP **1·41**	X+A:AP **0·96**	-ed **6·23**
			let XY	QXY					
				VS	SVC/O **11·09**	VC/OA **0·36**	D Adj N **2·00**	Cop **3·18**	-en **1·05**
			doXY	X				Aux **6·95**	
					SVA **4·18**	V Od Oi	Adj Adj N X	Pron **7·41**	3s **3·14**
							Pr DN **4·32**	Pr Pron **0·27**	
					Neg XY X	Other	N Adj N	Other **0·14**	

STAGE 4 2.6 – 3.0				QXYZ X	XY+S:NP **6·64**	XY+V:VP **5·55**	XY+C/O:NP **5·50**	XY+A:AP **2·36**	gen **1·18**
			+S	QVS X			N Pr NP	Neg V **0·77**	n't **0·86**
					SVC/OA **1·27**	AAXY **0·68**	Pr D Adj N **0·36**	Neg X **0·14**	'cop **0·8**
					SVOdOi **0·23**	Other X	c X	2 aux **0·23**	'aux **1·2**
							X c X **1·64**	Other	

STAGE 5 3 – 3.6		how X		tag X	and **3·05**	Coord. 1 **2·14** 1+ **0·55**		Postmod. 1 **0·27** 1+ clause	-est
					c **0·41**	Subord. 1 **1·27** 1+			
					s **1·27**	Clause: S		Postmod. 1+ phrase	-er X
		what			other	Clause: C/O **0·91** Comparative			
						Clause: A **0·64**			-ly **0·2**

STAGE 6 3.6 – 4.6		+				—			
		NP	VP	Clause		NP	VP	Clause	
		Initiator X	Complex	Passive		Pron. X	Modal	Concord X	
						Adj. Seq.	Tense **0·14**	A Position	
		Coord. **0·25**		Complement		Det.	V irreg.	W Order	
						N irreg. X			

	Other:				Other: **7·32**		

STAGE 7 4.6+	A connectivity: **0·27**		Emphatic order:	it: **0·55**
	Comment clause: **0·18**		Other:	there: **0·55**

NUMBER OF WORDS IN EACH SENTENCE* **MEAN SENTENCE LENGTH: 3·87 WORDS**
     MEAN MAXIMUM " " : 8·59 "
     MEAN MINIMUM " " : 2·14 "

*Here sentence means: Any utterance which is neither deviant nor ambiguous, but excluding all Stage 1 utterances.

Fig. 4 The mean LARSP profile for those 22 of the hearing-impaired children who were labelled as profoundly deaf on the basis of their pure tone hearing loss (i.e. PTA >95 dB).

eviant	Ambiguous
X	1·36

Analyser's Comments:

ALYSED

	Minor "Sentences": Social			Stereotypes		Problems	
	Major "Sentences"						
	Excl.	Comm.	Quest.	Statement			
0.9 – 1.6		'V' 0·63	'Q' X	'V' 1·41	'N' 8·01	Other 0·30	Problems

			Conn.	Clause		Phrase		Word
1.6 – 2.0		VX	QX	SV 8·91	VC/O 4·02	DN 44·10	vv 3·75	Inf. 4·51
			X	S C/O 0·88	AX 2·47	Adj N 4·24	v part 12·37	-ing 21·96
						NN 0·66	int x 1·22	pl. 10·29
				Neg X X	Other	Pr N 2·79	other X	fut. 0·98

2.0 – 2.6		VXY X	QXY X	X+S:NP 4·83	X+V:VP 7·32	X+C/O:NP 2·63	X+A:AP 1·56	-ed 13·21
		let XY	VS	SVC/O 24·47	VC/OA 1·27	D Adj N 5·38	Cop 6·96	-en 2·20
		doXY	X	SVA 9·25	V Od Oi 0·11	Adj Adj N 0·40	Aux 18·21 Pron 22·10	3s 8·08
				Neg XY X	Other 0·26	Pr DN 12·94 N Adj N X	Pr Pron 1·32 Other 0·30	

2.6 – 3.0		+S	QXYZ X	XY+S:NP 15·90	XY+V:VP 15·64	XY+C/O:NP 14·96	XY+A:AP 7·36	gen 5·04
			QVS X	SVC/OA 6·29	AAXY 1·51	N Pr NP X Pr D Adj N 1·26	Neg V 1·51 Neg X 0·23	n't 1·23
				SVOdOi 0·46	Other 0·37	c X 0·52 X c X 4·84	2 aux 0·54 Other 0·35	'cop 3·21 'aux 5·75

3 – 3.6		how X		and 14·07	Coord. 1 10·15 1+ 2·27	Postmod. 1 1·10	1+ X	-est 0·21
			tag X	c 1·24	Subord. 1 3·75 1+ X Clause: S X	clause		-er 0·24
		what		s 3·78	Clause: C/O 3·42 Comparative X	Postmod. 1+ X		-ly 0·79
				other X	Clause: A 2·55	phrase		

	+			–		
	NP	VP	Clause	NP	VP	Clause
3.6 – 4.6	Initiator 1·30	Complex X	Passive X	Pron. Adj. Seq. X 0·24	Modal X	Concord 0·32
	Coord. 0·14		Complement X	Det. N irreg. 0·32 0·11	Tense 0·54 V irreg. X	A Position X W Order 0·23
	Other:			Other: 12·10		

4.6+	A connectivity: 1·31	Emphatic order: X	it: 1·44
	Comment clause: 0·19	Other:	there: 2·66

MEAN SENTENCE LENGTH: 7·52 WORDS

MEAN MINIMUM " " : 2·58 "

MEAN MAXIMUM " " : 18·17 "

sentence means: Any utterance which is neither deviant nor ambiguous, but excluding all Stage 1 utterances.

Fig. 5 The mean LARSP profile for the 241 partially-hearing children: i.e. excluding the 22 profoundly deaf.

profoundly deaf children (Fig. 4) exhibit very poor grammatical advancement, if their data are removed from the mean profile in Fig. 1 the remaining profile for the partially-hearing children (Fig. 5) is still markedly less advanced than the mean normally-hearing profile in Fig. 2. These relationships between the four mean profiles (Figs 1, 2, 4 and 5) are summarized in Table V (p. 401), which shows the mean number of words per sentence for each group and the mean number of entries totalled across various parts of the profile (e.g. the total of the means of the clause entries in Stages 1–4) for each group. The inclusion of the profoundly deaf children has only a small effect on the data from the whole sample (N=263) when compared with the difference between the profiles of the partially-hearing (N=241) and the normally-hearing children. Nonetheless, as a group the profoundly deaf children exhibit very poor grammatical advancement, the clause:phrase: word ratio as calculated from Fig. 4 being 1:0·6:0·3. Note (Table V) that in itself the fact that the profoundly deaf group gave more clause level entries at Stages 1–4 (due mainly to a large number of Stage 1 "clauses") is of little importance. It does mean, however, that if their other entries were "corrected" for this difference between the groups, the entries for the profoundly deaf (e.g. Stages 2–5 phrases) would be depressed even further relative to the entries for the other groups.

III. The LARSP profiles grouped and analysed by hearing loss, age and non-verbal I.Q.

The kind of analyses of the mean profile in Fig. 1 which we have described in Section II can provide useful indications of some of the important differences between the grammatical advancement of our group of hearing-impaired children and that of a normally-hearing comparison group. However, in understanding the effects of hearing loss and other "background" variables upon grammatical advancement, the overall mean profile is of limited value since the group consists of a very heterogeneous collection of subjects. The mean profile may well hide trends which would be more in evidence if the profiles for smaller, more homogeneous groups of subjects were examined. For this reason, the 263 hearing-impaired children were classified into the 27 groups of the subject classification matrix, described in Chapter 3, defined by three levels each of age, pure tone hearing loss in the better ear (average loss at 500, 1000 and 2000 Hz), and non-verbal I.Q. The three levels of age were: 8–10 years, 11–13 years, and 14–15 years. The three levels of pure tone hearing loss were: 40–60 dB (ISO), 61–80 dB and

81 dB or above. The three levels of non-verbal I.Q. (assessed with the WISC performance scales) were: 64–90, 91–110, and 111 or above. We shall refer to the three levels of hearing loss as mild, moderate and severe, and to the three levels of non-verbal I.Q. as below average, average and above average.

The mean number of entries for each LARSP profile structure for each of the groups of hearing-impaired children has been calculated, and the 27 resulting mean profiles (one for each group) are presented in Appendix III. The definition of each group in terms of age, hearing loss, and non-verbal I.Q. is shown at the top of each profile (under "Analyser's Comments"). Also shown is the number of subjects in each group. Care must be taken when interpreting the data from groups containing few subjects: note that groups A, G, H, J, L, P, S, U, X and Y have fewer than nine members.

The reader should not assume that hearing-impaired children of similar ages, with similar pure tone hearing losses and similar non-verbal I.Q.s constitute homogeneous groups. Numerous other factors, particularly with regard to the hearing-impairment (e.g. the slope of the pure tone audiogram, the age at onset of the impairment), are likely to relate differentially to the grammatical ability of the children within the groups, and the mean profiles in Appendix III may still, therefore, conceal important information. However, classifying the subjects into groups according to the three major variables of hearing loss, age and non-verbal I.Q. will account for some of the between-subject variability and help us to assess the effects of these factors.

Unfortunately, to present the 27 mean profiles in this way gives the reader something of an assimilation problem, and at this stage a full-scale analysis of every entry from the 27 profiles is clearly not what is needed. What is required is an analysis which helps us to extract the important trends, and which allows us to assess reliably the main effects of hearing loss, age and non-verbal I.Q. or grammatical advancement. For this reason, we performed a factorial analysis of variance to assess the effects of the levels of hearing loss, age and non-verbal I.Q. on selected blocks of profile entries, choosing those aspects of the profiles which our previous analyses of the overall mean profile (Section II) had shown to be important. These were: at the clause level of analysis, the sums of the mean number of entries in Stage 1, in Stage 2, in Stage 3, in Stage 4 and in Stage 5; at the phrase level of analysis, the sums of the mean number of entries in Stage 2, in Stage 3, in Stage 4 and in Stage 5, as well as the sum of these sums (i.e. the sum of all the mean phrase level entries); at the word level of analysis, the sum of all the mean word level entries. Although we include the total of the mean phrase level entries (i.e. summed across Stages 2–5) in the analysis, this is not done for the clause level entries, which remain defined according to Stage, since we

Table VI. The effects in the analysis of variance and their degrees of freedom (N=263)

Source	d.f.
Hearing loss	2
Age	2
Non-verbal I.Q.	2
Age × Hearing loss	4
Age × Non-verbal I.Q.	4
Hearing loss × Non-verbal I.Q.	4
Age × Hearing loss × Non-verbal I.Q.	8
Error: within groups	236
Total	262

Table VII. Analysis of variance of entries in blocks of profile structures for N=263 children grouped by hearing loss (HL), age, and non-verbal I.Q. (IQ): the significance of the main effects and the interactions[a]

Variable	Main effects			Interactions			
	HL	Age	IQ	Age × HL	Age × IQ	HL × IQ	Age × HL × IQ
Stage 1 "clauses"	SS	SS	S	S			
Stage 2 clauses		SS	S				
Stage 3 clauses	SS	SS	SS	SS			
Stage 4 clauses	SS	SS	SS				
Stage 5 clauses	SS	SS	SS	SS			
Connecting devices	SS	SS	SS	SS			
Stage 2 phrases	SS	SS		SS			
Stage 3 phrases	SS	SS	SS	SS	SS		
Stage 4 phrase	SS	SS	SS		SS		
Stage 5 phrases		SS	SS				
Total phrase level	SS	SS	SS	SS		S	
Total word level	SS	SS	SS	S			
MSL (Mean sentence length)	SS	SS	SS	SS			

[a] "S" indicates significance of $P < 0.05$ and "SS" of $P < 0.01$.

know that the inclusion of Stage 1 "clauses" gives a cross-over effect. That is, while poor grammatical advancement is manifested at phrase level by fewer entries across all the phrase level Stages, at the clause level it is manifested not simply by the use of fewer entries in the more advanced Stages (Stages 3, 4 and 5), but by the use of *more* entries in Stage 1. The totalling of entries across Stages at the clause level would therefore not be appropriate. In addition to the above profile measures we included the mean sentence length (MSL) in the analysis, since we have seen that many of the grammatical advances on the profile (increasing the elements in clauses, expansion of elements, use of recursive clauses, etc.) will be reflected in increased sentence length. Thus the analysis has been performed on 13 derived variables.

The structure of the analysis of variance is shown in Table VI, and the results of the analysis are summarized in Table VII. It can be seen from Table VII that hearing loss, age and non-verbal I.Q. all have significant effects on most or all of the 13 profile variables. Of the interactions, that of age and hearing loss gives significant effects for nine of the profile variables; age and non-verbal I.Q. affects only three of the variables; and neither the interaction between hearing loss and non-verbal I.Q. nor the three-way interaction has any significant effects.

A. Hearing loss

Considering first the main effects, Table VIII shows the summed means for each profile variable for each level of hearing loss. Remember that for any given group of children (e.g. mild hearing loss) and any given block of profile structures (e.g. Stage 2 clauses), the figure shown is the sum of the mean number of entries for those profile structures within the block given by those children. Note also that since the variables are highly correlated with each other, the results are by no means independent. The main effects of hearing loss are as we might expect from our analyses of the grouped profile in Section II. Thus, Stage 1 "clauses" (i.e. one-word utterances, usually either a verb or a noun) are used significantly more by those with a severe hearing loss than by those with a moderate or a mild loss. The figure for those children with a mild loss (3·6) is still higher than the mean number of Stage 1 "clauses" used by the normally-hearing comparison group, which was 0·36 (see Fig. 2), but this difference is not significant. Of the 12 variables other than Stage 1 "clauses", 10 show a significant effect of hearing loss, but in the reverse direction. That is, all the other variables except Stage 2 clauses and Stage 5 phrases (no significant effects of hearing loss) were used less as the level of hearing loss increased. Thus the greater the hearing-impairment, the

Table VIII. Summed mean entries for blocks of profile structures showing the effect of the three levels of hearing loss (N=263)

Variable	Level of hearing loss		
	Mild	Moderate	Severe
Stage 1 "clauses"	3·6	7·1	25·4
ªStage 2 clauses	15·2	16·5	16·9
Stage 3 clauses	38·8	35·6	29·4
Stage 4 clauses	9·6	9·0	6·4
Stage 5 clauses	26·1	22·1	15·2
Connecting devices	22·4	19·0	13·6
Stage 2 phrases	73·7	70·7	60·1
Stage 3 phrases	74·5	69·9	48·8
Stage 4 phrases	10·1	9·0	7·3
ªStage 5 phrases	1·3	1·1	1·1
Total phrase level	159·5	150·7	117·2
Total word level	91·1	77·3	59·3
MSL (Mean sentence length)	8·3	7·6	6·4
Number of subjects in group:	59	103	101
Mean hearing loss of group (dB ISO):	49	71	90

[a] No significant differences

larger was the number of simple Stage 1 "clauses" in the speech samples, but the smaller was the number of clause level entries at Stage 3 and beyond, the smaller was the number of phrase level entries at each Stage except Stage 5 (used rarely by any group), the smaller was the number of word level entries, and the fewer were the number of words per sentence. The clause level cross-over which has been referred to previously occurred at the two-element clause level (Stage 2), which showed no effect of degree of hearing loss. The effect of hearing loss on the 11 variables which did show significant effects is not symmetrical, however, in that the differences between moderate and severe losses are more marked than the differences between mild and moderate losses. Thus (for those variables which showed an effect) all the differences between the moderate hearing loss means and the severe hearing loss means in Table VIII are significant beyond $P=0.01$; while only Stage 3 clauses, Stage 5 clauses, connecting devices, total word level, and mean sentence length show a significant difference ($P < 0.05$) between the means for mild and moderate hearing loss, the remaining differences being non-significant although in the expected direction. The contrast between those derived variables which show an effect of moderate hearing loss and those which show an effect of severe hearing loss is interesting, and indicates a kind of "two-stage" effect of hearing loss level: the effects of moderate levels of hearing loss are to be found at the clause and word level but not the phrase level, while the effects of severe levels of loss are to be found at all three levels. The data suggest that moderate levels of loss may affect the degree of recursion (Stage 5 clauses, connecting devices, and hence MSL), while leaving the phrase structure fairly complete. Severe levels of loss, however, seem to affect the phrase level as well as recursions and other clause level entries. Word level entries are affected by both moderate and severe levels of hearing loss.

B. Age

The main effects of age on the 13 blocks of profile variables are shown in Table IX. As age level increases, the number of Stage 1 "clauses" decreases,

Table IX. Summed mean entries for blocks of profile structures showing the effect of the three levels of age (N=263)

Variable	Age in years		
	8–10	11–13	14–15
Stage 1 "clauses"	24·0	8·8	3·3
Stage 2 clauses	18·5	15·2	14·9
Stage 3 clauses	30·4	35·8	37·5
Stage 4 clauses	6·0	8·6	10·4
Stage 5 clauses	18·0	21·4	24·1
Connecting devices	16·2	18·5	20·3
Stage 2 phrases	61·0	67·6	76·0
Stage 3 phrases	52·7	69·1	71·3
Stage 4 phrases	7·5	9·8	9·1
Stage 5 phrases	0·6	1·4	1·4
Total phrase level	121·9	147·8	157·8
Total word level	65·1	77·9	84·8
MSL (Mean sentence length)	6·1	7·5	8·7
Number of subjects in group	92	106	65
Mean age of group: (years and months)	9·6	12·6	15·0

while the number of all other variables used tends to increase. The differences between the 8- to 10-year-old and the 11- to 13-year-old children are more marked than the differences between the 11- to 13-year-olds and the 14- to 15-year-olds. All the former differences except that for connecting devices are significant ($P < 0.05$), while only four of the latter differences (Stage 1 "clauses", Stage 4 clauses, Stage 2 phrases, MSL) are significant ($P < 0.05$). Finally, it should be noted that there are significant differences between the means for Stage 2 clauses, in the same direction as Stage 1 "clauses" (i.e. used more frequently by the younger group), and therefore the clause level cross-over for the effect of age occurs not at Stage 2 but "between" Stages 2 and 3, the latter showing effects in the reverse direction (i.e. used less frequently by the younger group).

C. Non-verbal I.Q.

The main effects of non-verbal I.Q. on the 13 blocks of profile variables are shown in Table X. The effects are similar to those of age level. Thus, as non-verbal I.Q. level increases the numbers of Stage 1 "clauses" and Stage 2 clauses decrease, while all other variables tend to increase in number. All the differences between the "below average" means and the "average" means are significant ($P < 0.05$) except for Stage 1 "clauses", Stage 2 clauses, and Stage 5 phrases (none of the differences between the means of Stage 2 phrases are significant). The differences between the "average" means and the "above average" means are significant ($P < 0.05$), excepting Stage 3 clauses, Stage 5 clauses, connecting devices, Stage 4 phrases and total phrase level, which are not significant. That there is a relationship between non-verbal I.Q. and frequencies of entries on the LARSP profile, which is essentially a reflection of aspects of verbal ability, is not particularly surprising, since even in the hearing-impaired child there is a relationship between verbal and non-verbal I.Q. (Hine, 1970), both of which to some extent tap a common general ability (see also Section V C, below).

D. Age/non-verbal I.Q. interactions

The significant interactions from the analysis of variance are shown in Figs 6–17. Figures 6, 7 and 8 show the three age/non-verbal I.Q. interactions, and these are not easy to interpret. The striking feature is that in the above average non-verbal I.Q. 11-13 age group the frequency of use of Stage 3 phrases, Stage 4 phrases, and hence total phrases, is very high. Further analyses of variance not reported here were carried out on each individual profile

Table X. Summed mean entries for blocks of profile structures showing the effect of the three levels of non-verbal I.Q. (N=263)

Variable	Level of non-verbal I.Q.		
	Below average	Average	Above average
Stage 1 "clauses"	17·2	12·5	6·4
Stage 2 clauses	17·3	17·1	14·3
Stage 3 clauses	32·1	35·3	36·3
Stage 4 clauses	6·2	8·6	10·2
Stage 5 clauses	14·0	24·5	25·0
Connecting devices	13·2	21·2	20·6
[a]Stage 2 phrases	65·3	70·1	69·2
Stage 3 phrases	54·0	65·9	73·3
Stage 4 phrases	6·6	9·5	10·3
Stage 5 phrases	0·8	1·1	1·6
Total phrase level	126·5	146·5	154·4
Total word level	63·1	77·6	87·1
MSL (Mean sentence length	6·5	7·6	8·2
Number of subjects in group:	68	106	89
Mean non-verbal I.Q. of group:	82	101	122

[a] No significant differences.

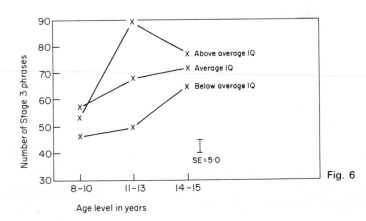

Fig. 6

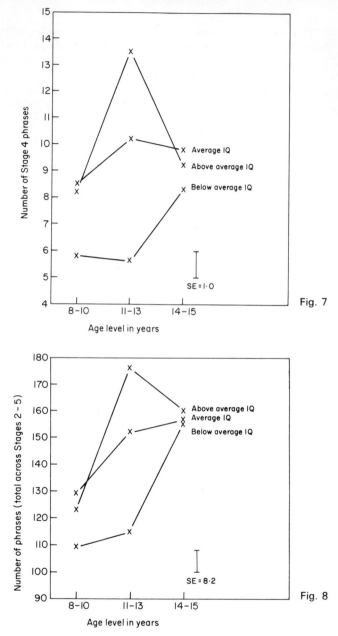

Figs 6–8 The age/non-verbal I.Q. (IQ) interactions (N=263) for those derived profile variables which showed significant effects.

structure to assess the effects of the levels of hearing loss, age and non-verbal I.Q. on the entries for these structures. The analyses showed that the interaction in Fig. 6 largely results from the high I.Q. 11- to 13-year olds who used many PrDN structures (e.g. "in the garden") and copulas (Cop: e.g. "he *is* happy"). The interaction in Fig. 7 is largely due to the high frequency of usage by the above average 11- to 13-year-olds of XcX structures (e.g. "the boy and the girl"). The interaction in Fig 8 (total phrase level) is a reflection of the relationships shown in Figs 6 and 7. Exactly why this group alone should exhibit these significantly different frequencies is not clear.

Before proceeding to discuss the significant age/hearing loss interactions, which are of much more interest to us, we should mention briefly the standard error (SE) figures given on each graph. The SE shown is an average based upon the assumption that each point represents results derived from $N = 30$ children. However, there were different numbers of subjects in each cell of the $(3 \times 3 \times 3)$ subject classification matrix, and the interaction points are therefore based on differing numbers. The actual frequencies with which the subjects fell in the groups defined by the age and hearing loss and the age and non-verbal I.Q. cross-classifications are shown in Tables XI and XII. The average standard errors shown in Figs 6–17 give a good approximation, since for a point based on only 15 observations, rather than 30, the average SE would be increased by a factor of only $\sqrt{2}$, i.e., about 1·5. Table XIII

Table XI. Distribution of subjects by age and hearing loss $(N=263)$

Age	Hearing loss		
	Mild	Moderate	Severe
8–10	22	28	42
11–13	23	45	38
14–15	14	30	21

Table XII. Distribution of subjects by age and non-verbal I.Q. $(N=263)$

Age	Non-verbal I.Q.		
	Below average	Average	Above average
8–10	24	45	23
11–13	28	36	42
14–15	16	25	24

Table XIII. The error mean square (EMS) (from the analysis of variance)
for each variable (N=263)

Variable	EMS
Stage 1 "clauses"	670·0
Stage 2 clauses	47·6
Stage 3 clauses	116·0
Stage 4 clauses	24·4
Stage 5 clauses	154·6
Connecting devices	147·7
Stage 2 phrases	391·3
Stage 3 phrases	736·5
Stage 4 phrases	27·4
Stage 5 phrases	2·7
Total phrase level	2028·3
Total word level	879·4
MSL (Mean sentence length)	5·5

shows the error mean squares (EMS) for each variable, and these can be used to calculate exact confidence intervals for the interaction points (or for the means in Tables VIII, IX and X) according to:

$$95\% \text{ confidence intervals} = \pm(1\cdot96 \times \text{SE}) \quad \text{where the SE} = \sqrt{\frac{\text{EMS}}{N}}$$

E. Age/hearing loss interactions

The significant age/hearing loss interactions are shown in Figs 9–17. For comparison, each graph also shows the number of entries (again, the sums of the means) for that block of profile structures from ten normally-hearing children, aged 14–15 years, of below average non-verbal I.Q., whose speech samples from the same picture-description task were analysed onto a mean LARSP profile in the usual manner. We noted at the beginning of this Chapter that the data from this group of normally-hearing children were obtained in order to confirm the validity of the data in Fig. 2. We have used their data to supply the comparison points in Figs 9–17, rather than the data from Fig. 2, since they represent one age group (14–15), and since we can be sure that non-verbal I.Q. is not confounded (in the sense that the 10 subjects were selected on the basis of below average non-verbal I.Q.).

Figures 9–17 present a striking and very uniform picture, although again it must be pointed out that the reader should not be too impressed with the

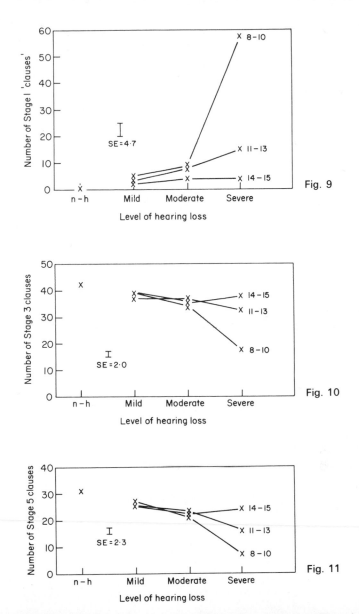

Figs 9–17   The age/hearing loss interactions (N=263) for those derived profile variables
which showed significant effects. The parameter is age level in years. Each figure also shows
the number of corresponding structures used by the normally-hearing comparison group
(n–h).

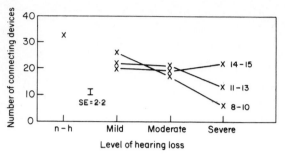

Fig. 12

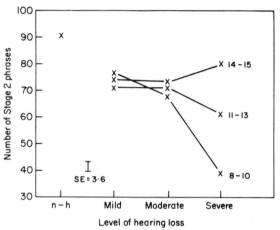

Fig. 13

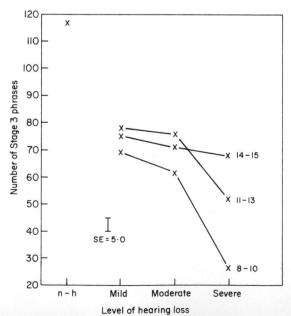

Fig. 14

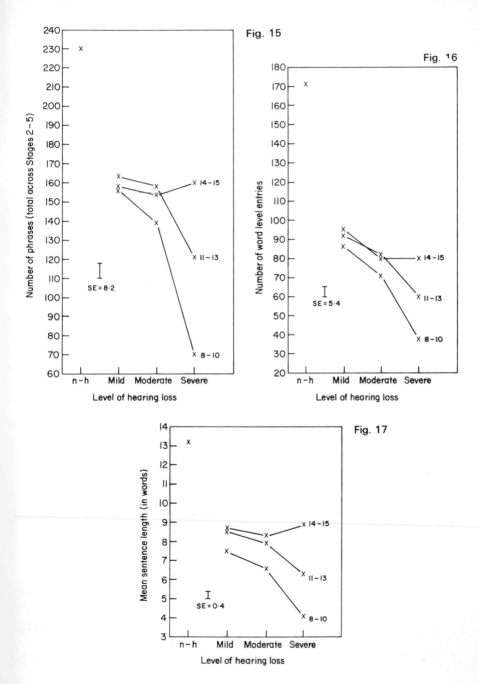

Fig. 15

Fig. 16

Fig. 17

uniformity of the data, since the profile structures are not independent and to a large extent are all measuring the same thing. Figures 9–17 show that the disadvantageous effects of hearing loss, and severe hearing loss in particular, are more marked for the 8- to 10-year-olds than for the 11- to 13-year-olds, and for the 11- to 13-year-olds than the 14- to 15-year-olds. Indeed, for the latter group the level of hearing loss has no effect and the graphs for this age group attain a "plateau". Furthermore, the graphs for the 11- to 13-year-olds show no significant differences between mild and moderate levels of hearing loss, indicating that the effects of moderate losses on aspects of grammatical expression tend to disappear by 11–13 years. The effects of severe hearing loss are apparent in the 11- to 13-year-olds, however, and tend to disappear only in the 14- to 15-year-olds. That is, they tend to disappear when compared with the performance levels of the mild-hearing-loss group. But if we compare the levels achieved by the 14- to 15-year-olds' plateaux with the data points from the normally-hearing group of children (who were also aged 14–15 years), only Stage 1 "clauses" and Stage 3 clauses (Figs 9 and 10) show no significant differences between the 14- to 15-year-old hearing-impaired data points and the normally-hearing datum. The 14- to 15-year-olds' plateaux are significantly lower than the normally-hearing comparison point for Stage 5 clauses (recursions), connecting devices, Stage 2 phrases, Stage 3 phrases, total phrase level, total word level, and mean sentence length (Figs 11–17 respectively). As we might expect from our discussion in Section II of the overall mean profiles, the differences between the performance levels of the 14- to 15-year-olds and the normally-hearing group are particularly marked for Stage 3 phrases (which includes auxiliaries), total phrase level entries, total word level entries, and mean sentence length. Thus the plateaux of the 14- to 15-year-old hearing-impaired children are in many cases well below the performance levels of the normally-hearing comparison group.

This important and somewhat unexpected finding of an age/hearing loss interaction such that hearing loss has a pronounced effect on the grammar from the younger groups of children, but no effect on the grammar from the 14- to 15-year-olds, may surprise some readers. Certainly, much previous research (see Chapter 2) has dealt with young deaf children, and the effect of hearing loss on the spoken grammar of older, partially-hearing children has been studied or reported less often. However, people in regular contact with such children, teachers for example, would probably have expected some sort of effect of hearing loss—albeit a smaller effect, perhaps, than for young children. Before we can accept these results, and discuss their implications, we must be reasonably sure, therefore, that they are not artificial. In particular, we must satisfy ourselves that the results have not come about through errors in sampling.

This study is not "longitudinal" in its design, and the 14- to 15-year-olds in the sample are not the same children as our 8- to 10-year-olds. We cannot be certain, therefore, that our 8- to 10-year-olds are going to exhibit similar grammatical advancements as they grow into their early teens. Changes in educational practices, for example, may have made our 14- to 15-year-olds unrepresentative of what our 8- to 10-year-olds will be like in five years' time (the optimist would argue, of course, that any such changes will have been for the better, so the improvement with age found here would be the minimum expected; but that is another argument). In other words, short of conducting a separate longitudinal study (and there are good grounds for so doing), we must be reasonably certain that we have not confounded age with any other factor which could account for the improvement in the performance levels of the severely-impaired children. The possibility that was mentioned above—that there has been some major change in educational technique over the past five or so years which applies uniformly to all the children—seems unlikely. Such a change would have had to be fairly major and universal, since our subjects were selected widely, and represent different social classes, educational backgrounds, etc. The other possibility is that the children in each group (in particular, the three age groups of the severe-hearing-loss children) are not matched on one or more of the "background variables". Thus, for example, if all the children in the 14- to 15-year-old severe hearing-loss group were impaired at a late age (i.e. the onset age was postlingual), in contrast to the 8- to 10-year-old severe-hearing-loss group, then one might expect the grammatical ability of these 14- to 15-year-olds to be much better than that of the 8- to 10-year-olds. As another example of this kind of explanation, it could have been that all the 14- to 15-year-old severe-hearing-loss group came from one school, and all the 8- to 10-year-old severe-hearing-loss group from another. Differences between the performance of the two groups might then be a result simply of differences between these particular schools. In order to discount such confounding factors, the background data of the children in the nine age/hearing loss sub-groups were examined. The background variables which could plausibly contribute to the age/hearing loss interaction if the sub-groups were unmatched or biased in particular ways are: hearing loss, non-verbal I.Q., age at onset of impairment, age at diagnosis of impairment (given age at onset), Social Class, and school. As far as the latter five variables are concerned—that is, non-verbal I.Q., onset age, diagnosis age, Social Class and school—there are no differences between the sub-groups which could contribute to the interaction effect.

However, the remaining variable—hearing loss—is not perfectly matched across the sub-groups. In particular, the mean hearing loss values for the three severe-hearing-loss categories are not the same, being 92·5 dB for the youngest age group, 89·1 dB for the 11- to 13-year-olds, and 87·3 dB for the oldest age group. This is due to the fact that there are more profoundly deaf children in the 8- to 10-year-old group than in the 11- to 13-year-old group, and more in the 11- to 13-year-old group than in the 14- to 15-year-old group. This could have exaggerated the pronounced effects of hearing loss in the younger children and could account in part, therefore, for the results. For this reason, the analysis of variance was rerun on N = 241 children, grouped by hearing loss, age and non-verbal I.Q., excluding the 22 children with an average hearing loss of greater than 95 dB. The exclusion of these children resulted in mean hearing loss values (for those in the severe category) of 87·1, 87·6 and 86·8 dB for the 8–10, 11–13 and 14- to 15-year-olds respectively.

F. The analysis of variance excluding the profoundly deaf children

The results of the analysis of variance on the 241 partially-hearing children are summarized in Table XIV. A comparison of these results with those from the full sample of 263 (Table VII) shows that the two outcomes are virtually identical: having discarded the profoundly deaf children from the sample, we are still left with significant main effects of hearing loss, age, and non-verbal I.Q., and with the same significant age/hearing loss interactions.

Considering the main effect of hearing loss, the means for the severe-hearing-loss group are shown in Table XV. The means for the mild- and moderate-hearing-loss groups remain, of course, unchanged by the exclusion of the profoundly deaf subjects, and these means will be found in Table VIII, along with the severe-hearing-loss means including the profoundly deaf. The effect of excluding the profoundly deaf has been to reduce slightly the difference between the moderate- and severe-hearing-loss means, but in nearly all cases the differences between these means are still significant ($P < 0.01$), and are still asymmetrical in the sense that they are larger than the differences between the mild- and moderate-hearing-loss means. As far as Stage 4 phrases are concerned, the change has rendered the differences non-significant.

The significant age/hearing loss interactions for N = 241 are shown in Figs 18–26. The standard error term (SE) is, again, an average value, this time based upon N = 27. For the reader who wishes to calculate exact confidence intervals for each point, the error mean square (EMS) values from the analysis of variance are shown in Table XVI. Of the severe-hearing-loss group

Table XIV. Analysis of variance of entries in blocks of profile structures for N=241 children (i.e. excluding the "profoundly deaf" subjects), grouped by hearing loss (HL), age and non-verbal I.Q. (IQ): the significance of the main effects and the interactions[a]

	Main effects			Interactions			
Variable	HL	Age	IQ	Age × HL	Age × IQ	HL × IQ	Age × HL × IQ
Stage 1 "clauses"	S	SS	S	S			
Stage 2 clauses		SS	SS				
Stage 3 clauses	SS	SS	S	SS			
Stage 4 clauses	S	SS	SS				
Stage 5 clauses	SS	S	SS	SS			
Connecting devices	SS		SS	S			
Stage 2 phrases	S	SS		S			
Stage 3 phrases	SS	SS	SS	S	SS		
Stage 4 phrases		SS	SS		SS		
Stage 5 phrases		SS	SS				
Total phrase level	SS	SS	SS	SS	SS		
Total word level	SS	SS	SS	S			
MSL (Mean sentence length)	SS	SS	SS	S			

[a] "S" indicates significance of $P < 0.05$ and "SS" of $P < 0.01$.

excluding the profoundly deaf, there were 26 children aged 8–10 years, 33 aged 11–13 years, and 20 aged 14–15 years.

Again, comparing Figs 18–26 with Figs 9–17, it can be seen that removing the data of the 22 profoundly deaf children had little effect on the overall pattern of the results. The same grammatical measures as before—that is, nine of the thirteen derived profile variables—show a significant interaction effect. The interaction pattern remains virtually unchanged, and cannot be explained by the confounding of age and hearing loss.

G. Discussion

There is an inverse relationship between level of hearing loss and the level of advancement of the expressed grammar in the 8- to 10-year-old children on our picture description task. This relationship begins to disappear in the 11- to 13-year-olds, such that there are no differences between the grammatical performance of those with mild and moderate losses, although those

Table XV. Summed mean entries for blocks of profile structures for the children with severe hearing losses, excluding the 22 profoundly deaf children cf. Table VIII

Variable	Level of Hearing loss severe
Stage 1 "clauses"	21·0
Stage 2 clauses	16·8
Stage 3 clauses	30·8
Stage 4 clauses	7·0
Stage 5 clauses	16·4
Connecting devices	14·8
Stage 3 phrases	63·6
Stage 3 phrases	51·9
Stage 4 phrases	7·9
Stage 5 phrases	1·1
Total phrase level	124·5
Total word level	60·9
MSL (Mean sentence length)	6·7
Number of subjects in group:	79
Mean hearing loss of group (dB ISO):	87

Table XVI. The error mean square (EMS) (from the N=241 analysis of variance) for each variable

Variable	EMS
Stage 1 "clauses"	476·9
Stage 2 clauses	45·3
Stage 3 clauses	101·5
Stage 4 clauses	25·0
Stage 5 clauses	159·5
Connecting devices	152·4
Stage 2 phrases	338·0
Stage 3 phrases	691·6
Stage 4 phrases	27·2
Stage 5 phrases	2·9
Total phrase level	1790·9
Total word level	808·1
MSL (Mean sentence length)	5·5

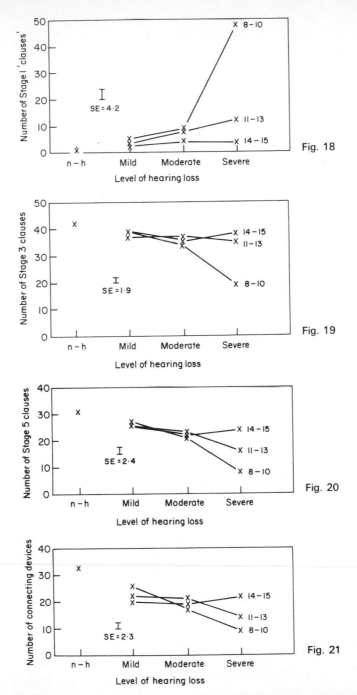

Figs 18–26   The age/hearing loss interactions for those derived profile variables which showed significant effects, for N=241 subjects—i.e. excluding 22 profoundly deaf subjects. The parameter is age level in years. Each figure also shows the number of corresponding structures used by the normally-hearing comparison group (n–h).

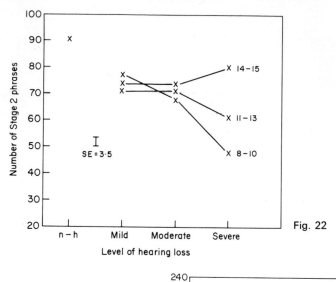

Fig. 22

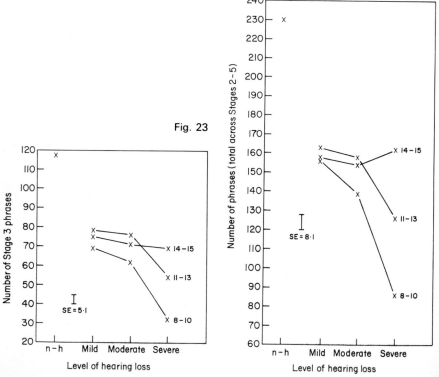

Fig. 23

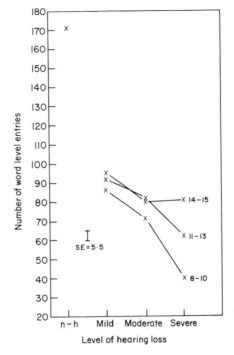

Fig. 25

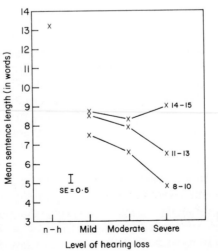

Fig. 26

11- to 13-year-olds with severe losses exhibit lower performance levels. In the 14- to 15-year-olds the performance of those with severe losses is improved such that the relationship disappears completely, with no significant differences between the mild-, the moderate- and the severe-hearing-loss performance levels. However, for seven out of the nine measures of grammatical performance which showed a significant interaction effect, the level of the 14- to 15-year-old's plateau was significantly lower than the datum obtained from a group of normally-hearing 14- to 15-year-olds of below average non-verbal I.Q. The seven measures are: number of Stage 5 clauses and number of connecting devices (i.e. clause co-ordination and subordination); Stage 2 phrases, Stage 3 phrases (i.e. the important phrase level entries concerned with the expansion of clausal elements into verb and noun phrases in particular) and, therefore, total phrases; word level entries (morphological structures); and finally, and to a large extent as a consequence of the preceding shortfalls, mean sentence length.

The nature of the hearing loss/age interaction is made clearer, perhaps, by considering it in terms of the relationship between grammatical performance and age, with hearing loss as the parameter. If the interaction points from Figs 9–17 or Figs 18–26 are replotted in this way, the severe-hearing-loss group shows significant improvements in grammatical performance with increasing age across the three age levels; the moderate-hearing-loss group shows an improvement with age between the 8–10 and the 11- to 13-year-old groups, but not between the 11–13 and the 14- to 15-year-old groups; and the mild-hearing-loss group shows no significant improvements with age. We do not intend to present all the appropriate graphs in this manner, since this would be unnecessary duplication. However, it may help the reader to be aware of the form of the interaction when it is plotted in this way, and to this end Fig. 27 shows the relationship between age and the total number of phrase level entries (see Fig. 24) for the three different hearing loss groups. Notice that the level of performance of the mild hearing loss group is below that of the normally-hearing comparison group (aged 14–15). Thus, although extrapolation of the severe-hearing-loss function in Fig. 27 suggests that, given a year or two more (e.g. up to 17 years), these children would attain normally-hearing performance levels, the functions for the mild- and moderate-hearing-loss groups suggest that this is not the case. If these lines are extrapolated, they show no improvement with age. Since it would be implausible to suggest that the severe-hearing-loss group improve beyond the levels attained by the mild-hearing-loss group, it seems that the performance levels of the mild group may represent some upper limit or "ceiling" to grammatical advancement. In a study of the written language of severely hearing-impaired children (aged 7–17 years), Myklebust (1964) found such a ceiling effect in the development of syntax, the "plateau" being well below the levels attained by comparison groups of normally-hearing children. However, it should be noted that some of Myklebust's other measures of written language did not show this ceiling effect.

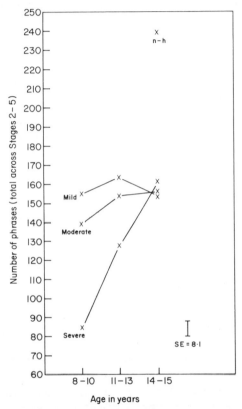

Fig. 27   *Total number of phrase level entries plotted against age for different hearing loss groups (n–h=normally-hearing datum).*

Since hearing loss is the variable in which we are particularly interested, we will now return to a consideration of the hearing loss/age interaction in its original form: that is, hearing loss on the horizontal axis, age as the parameter. Although from one point of view the lack of an inverse relationship between the grammatical measures and hearing loss in the 14- to 15-year-olds (Figs 18–26) is encouraging, it should not be concluded that the disadvantageous effects of hearing loss are fully mitigated with age. If the

14- to 15-year-old children's plateaux represent genuine ceiling effects then the differences between the levels of most of these plateaux and the normally-hearing data points indicate that the ceiling effects represent relatively low upper limits. It is of course encouraging (and perhaps surprising) to observe the lack of any marked differences between the effects of mild and severe levels of hearing loss in the older children, since it suggests that a large degree of the deficit in grammatical ability associated with severe hearing loss is made good with age. Whether this is a spontaneous process or, more likely, a result of education and rehabilitation cannot be determined here. On the other hand, the failure of those children in our sample with only mild levels of hearing loss to make good the smaller but significant deficits in their grammatical ability with reference to that of the normally-hearing children is disappointing. It suggests that the "making good" process for children with mild (and, to some extent, moderate) hearing losses is not successful. There is no improvement with age. This may be due in part to certain cognitive mechanisms (productive short-term memory, for example) being to a degree underdeveloped, perhaps permanently, as a result of the hearing-impairment and years of relatively impoverished language input and relatively retarded language production. It may also be due in part to "social" factors, in the sense that children with mild hearing losses may function like partially-hearing children precisely because that is what is expected of them. This is likely to affect their own expectations for and of themselves, and this raises important questions concerning the nature of the self-concept of the hearing-impaired person. Furthermore, if mildly-impaired children can "get by" with the performance levels associated with mild hearing losses, or if children with more severe losses can get by with the performance levels attained at 14–15 years, they may lack the motivation required to improve their spoken language. John *et al.* (1976) have argued similarly that school environment, including the expectations of teachers, can have marked effects upon linguistic achievement. A combination of "social" and "perceptual" factors may account, therefore, not only for the failure of those with mild hearing losses to improve with age, but also for the differences between the normally-hearing performance levels and the hearing-impaired 14- to 15-year-olds' performance levels. Without wishing to underestimate in any way the needs of those children with severe levels of hearing loss, it may be that we should devote more thought to the less obvious needs of those with milder levels of hearing loss. In so doing, it may be possible to raise the ceiling of the age/hearing loss interaction, such that the 14- to 15-year-old children, whatever their hearing loss, more nearly approximate the normally-hearing performance levels.

The major points which emerge from Figs 18–26, therefore, are as follows: the grammatical ability (assessed in terms of produced grammar for a straightforward picture-description task) of children with moderate and severe levels of hearing loss improves with age, but only up to the level of ability of children with mild hearing losses, who show no improvement with age. On most of the measures of produced grammar which we used, this level of ability is significantly lower than that demonstrated by a comparison group of normally-hearing children. Since there is some improvement with age in the severe and moderate groups, one could justifiably argue that the education of partially-hearing children is to an extent successful. Whether it is successful enough is not for us to judge. Any such judgement will depend upon what criteria are deemed to be appropriate, and upon what interpretation is put on the size of the gaps between the 14- to 15-year-old children's plateaux and the normally-hearing data points. Criteria for estimating success are hard enough to agree upon in the education of normally-hearing children, who despite their differences are a far more homogeneous population than are the hearing-impaired, and the topic will always be difficult and controversial.

Whether one regards the improvement with age of the grammatical ability of the children with moderate and severe hearing losses as an encouraging or a disappointing degree of success, one thing that should be pointed out is that it is not relevant to the famous controversy between "oralism" (speech, lip-reading and writing) and "manualism" (signing and finger-spelling). It is not relevant because this controversy (see for example RNID, 1976) is about the methods of communication which should be used in the education of deaf, rather than partially-hearing, children. Indeed, in educational matters the terms partially-hearing and deaf are defined not in terms of pure tone hearing loss, but operationally, in terms of "educability by particular methods". Thus, Ministry of Education Circular 10/62 (1962) gives the following definitions:

(1) Deaf pupils: those with impaired hearing who require education by methods suitable for pupils with little or no naturally acquired speech or language.

(2) Partially-hearing pupils: those with impaired hearing whose development of speech and language, even if retarded, is following a normal pattern, and who require for their education special arrangements or facilities though not necessarily all the educational methods used for deaf pupils.

The circular points out that the distinction is not necessarily directly related to degree of pure tone hearing loss, although the latter will usually be one of the major factors in determining speech and language competence. Although the definitions above do not make the distinction explicit with regard to oralism, the Lewis Report on the place of finger-spelling and signing in the education of the deaf (H.M.S.O. 1968) does. Thus (para. 283): "It follows from the nature of this distinction, relating as it does to speech and language development, that partially-hearing pupils by definition are children who are more closely approaching an attainment of the aims set out above than are children who are classified as deaf. We have received no evidence which would suggest that a full attainment would be more likely if fingerspelling or signing were added to the oral media through which these children are at present taught."

It seems widely accepted, then, that by definition partially-hearing children (with no additional handicaps) are educated using oral methods of communication (see also Morris, 1978). There may be occasions when supplementary methods prove useful for some partially-hearing children, but in general the oral/manual debate concerns the education of the deaf. The age/hearing loss interactions in Figs 18–26 provide the data for a partial assessment, based on picture-description, of the success of one aspect (produced grammar) of the education of our sample of partially-hearing children. We know of no other studies which have concerned themselves in comparable detail with the spoken grammar of 14- to 15-year-old partially-hearing children.

There have, however, been studies which give an indication of the performance levels achieved by partially-hearing children approaching school-leaving age with regard to other aspects of speech and language. Thus Kyle (1977) examined the relationships between various measures of pure tone hearing loss and the intelligibility of produced speech in prelingually impaired 15- to 16-year-olds. He did not find, as we did with children of this age or slightly less, that the performance of those children other than the profoundly deaf was similar across different levels of hearing loss. Specifically, he found that those with losses of less than 65 dB exhibited more intelligible speech than those with hearing losses greater than 65 dB. One might expect the intelligibility of speech to be more closely linked to level of pure tone hearing loss than the advancement of spoken grammar, and it is not obvious how the two types of behaviour are related (although see John *et al.*, 1976). Kyle's results and ours are not contradictory; rather, they both provide data which might be useful is assessing the efficacy of the education of samples of partially-hearing children. Again, how one interprets these results depends upon what one thinks should be the aims of this education, and upon what criteria one employs.

Conrad (1977a) has reported on the reading ability of hearing-impaired school-leavers (i.e. aged 15–16½). He found that there was no significant relationship between pure tone hearing loss and reading age for those children with hearing losses up to 85 dB. This aspect of his data may relate to the plateaux of our 14- to 15-year-old children. His data also indicate that these children performed well below the comparative levels for normally-hearing children, as indicated by the reading ability norms: only 8% of the children with losses up to 85 dB had a reading age commensurate with their chronological age, and about 50% of them had a reading age of below 10 years. Again, both our data and Conrad's show a normally-hearing/partially-hearing performance gap. Thus, his results seem to agree with those from our 14- to 15-year-olds, although it must be noted that the hearing loss categories varied across the studies: we placed the boundary between "partial" and "profound" losses at 95 dB, so that our sample includes children with losses of between 86 and 95 dB (see Table III, Chapter 3), and Conrad found a significant lowering of the reading age in his 86–95 dB group compared to the children with losses of 85 dB or less. We will return later to the question of the grouping of pure tone hearing losses.

Clearly, one would expect linguistic ability and reading ability to be closely related in the hearing-impaired. Indeed, one might have speculated that the improvement in the performance of our severely-impaired children with age was a result of the improvement of reading skills (which provide a much-needed linguistically unequivocal input to the hearing-impaired child). The amount by which Conrad's partially-hearing children fall short of the normally-hearing mean reading ages makes such a speculation doubtful. Either reading skills and grammatical ability proceed together or, and our data make this look more likely, reading ability lags behind grammatical ability (which, of course, is the sequence in normally-hearing children). If so, it suggests that reading deficiency in the hearing-impaired is not necessarily to be accounted for wholly by linguistic incompetence, and that other cognitive deficits are limiting performance. For the moment, these notions are speculative. It is not clear to what extent we can compare our children with Conrad's. One point which may be important is that Conrad's partially-hearing children were all from schools for the partially-hearing and profoundly deaf, and not from partial-hearing units (PHUs) attached to ordinary schools. There may be constraints which come into play in the placement of partially-hearing children into schools rather than PHUs, and which may have affected the results. Specifically, it might be argued that children in units perform better, for a variety of possible reasons, than children in schools, and Conrad's data may therefore present an exaggerated picture with regard to the gap in performance between the partially-hearing and the normally-hearing child. In fact, Conrad (personal communication) has comparative data from children in PHUs which are as yet unpublished, but which indicate that this is not the case: considering the children in the sample (the majority) who had hearing losses of between 41–80 dB, those who were in schools had a mean reading age only seven months below those who were in units.

As regards the question of the performance levels of 14- to 15-year-old profoundly deaf children, which *is* relevant to the oral/manual controversy, we have an insufficient number of profoundly deaf 14- to 15-year-olds in our sample to be able to estimate a meaningful performance level for produced grammar. Thus, we cannot say whether the profoundly deaf improve with age like our severe partials, such that their performance matches that of children with mild levels of loss, or whether their performance is still well below this at school-leaving age. Other data, using other measures of speech and language, suggest that their performance levels are in fact well down (see Morris, 1978). Of Conrad's (1977a) children with losses of 86 dB or more (and he tested almost the entire population of such school-leavers in England and Wales), almost 50% had a reading age of below seven years. Kyle (1977) found that the intelligibility of the speech of children with pure tone losses of 85 dB or more was very poor, while at less than this hearing loss it was considerably better. In an investigation of the use of morphological rules, Cooper (1967) found that 19-year-old profoundly deaf students performed at lower levels than 9- to 10-year-old normally-hearing children. Russell *et al.* (1976) review a number of American studies concerned with the grammatical competence of deaf children, and although these studies do not allow comparison between performance levels of the partially-hearing and the profoundly deaf (because data are reported only for the latter), the general picture is of fairly severe retardation along with a degree of deviancy. For example, the authors conclude that as many as 30–40% of deaf children leave school not having gained control of the use of the determiner and auxiliary systems in Standard English. Quigley *et al.* (1974) found that profoundly deaf students aged 18 years understood aspects of relative clauses slightly less well than 8- to 10-year-old hearing children. In an attempt to assess lip-reading ability, Conrad (1977b) reports data which show that deaf school-leavers lip-read no better than a group of normally-hearing children of similar age and (presumed) similar non-verbal I.Q., who were "deafened" by white noise. However, since another measure suggested that the linguistic ability of the deaf children was significantly worse than that of hearing children, Conrad's interpretation of these data as indicating that the deaf children's lip-reading ability was "relatively poor" is in some doubt. In any case, this particular study is a good example of the difficulty in choosing one's criteria: it could be argued that the normally-hearing are quite proficient at lip-reading (it certainly plays a role in speech perception: see McGurk, 1976; Haggard and Summerfield, 1978), and therefore that if the deaf perform at similar levels then they are doing reasonably well.

Kyle's suggestion (1977) that an average pure tone hearing loss of 85 dB tends to separate the profoundly deaf from the partially-hearing highlights a point to which we have drawn attention previously. Namely, even though such pure tone boundaries are to an extent arbitrary and the subject of some disagreement, the boundaries that we have chosen are higher than those generally used. Thus, for example, our boundary separating "profounds" from "severe partials" is at 95 dB. Green (1972) gives a "scale of terms commonly used to describe the severity of hearing impairment" and relates each term to a hearing threshold level, which is the average of the thresholds at 500, 1000 and 2000 Hz. Green's scale describes thresholds of 27–40 dB (ISO) as mild, 41–55 dB as moderate, 56–70 dB as moderately severe, 71–90 dB as severe and 91 or above as profound. These are, of course, only labels used for the sake of convenience, but the reader should remember that the children whom we have characterized as having a mild hearing loss (40–60 dB) would be regarded by many as having a moderate hearing loss. Just as our data do not allow us to estimate where 14- to 15-year-old children with profound hearing losses would lie on the age/hearing loss interaction graphs, so we also have no data from those children whom many would label as having a mild loss (27–40 dB). We do not know therefore whether the difference between the plateaux of the hearing-impaired 14- to 15-year-old children and the normally-hearing datum points is bridged by such children, and this question needs investigating. It is also possible that the nature of the age/hearing loss interactions has to some extent been dictated by the boundaries chosen for the three levels of hearing loss. We are unable to rerun the current analysis with different boundaries. However, in Section IV of this Chapter we describe a factor analysis procedure which allows us to reduce the data on each LARSP profile to a single index of grammatical advancement. This measure is then used (Section V) to examine further the relationships between grammatical ability and age and hearing loss, this time treating hearing loss as a continuum.

IV. Multivariate analysis of the LARSP profiles

A. Introduction

In the previous Section we investigated the effects of hearing loss, age and non-verbal I.Q. on some single LARSP profile structures and on some combinations of profile structures which reflect aspects of grammatical advancement. In order to simplify interpretation and to examine the interactions between the three factors, we used a $3 \times 3 \times 3$ factorial structure. However, such an approach ignores the somewhat arbitrary nature of the three different age groups, of the three different hearing loss groups, and of the three different non-verbal I.Q. groups. There is little reason to suppose that the subjects within each group will be necessarily very similar. The difference between an average pure tone hearing loss of 40–60 dB, for example, is probably of greater import for language development than the difference between 60–61 dB, yet the former would be in the same hearing loss group ("mild"), and the latter in different groups ("mild" and "moderate" respectively). There is in any case some disagreement as to how pure tone hearing threshold levels relate to the severity of the hearing-impairment measured in terms of the loss of hearing for speech or in terms of its effect upon produced speech. A number of considerations, which need not be listed here, led us to label 40–60 dB pure tone losses as "mild", 61–80 dB pure tone losses as "moderate", and above 80 dB pure tone losses as "severe" (or "profound" if above 95 dB), but as we have seen, various other workers have suggested various other divisions (Goodman, 1965; Montgomery, 1967; Green, 1972; Newby, 1972; O'Neill and Oyer, 1973; Vernon, 1976; Kyle, 1977; Morris, 1978).

As we remarked earlier, variables associated with the hearing-impairment other than the degree of loss (e.g. age at onset of hearing-impairment, age at diagnosis of hearing-impairment, the diagnosis itself) may also affect grammatical development, thus further reducing the likelihood of our groups being homogeneous. Still other variables, not directly associated with the hearing loss, could interact with the impairment in ways important for the grammatical development of the child: social class, for example.

What is required is an analysis which can be used to investigate the effects of age, hearing loss, non-verbal I.Q. and the other background variables, in a less arbitrary manner. In this Section we attempt such an analysis: a factor analysis procedure is used to summarize the LARSP profiles by extracting from the data a combination of LARSP items which retains the variation between subjects and reflects the underlying attributes which are measured by the profile. The relationships between these attributes and the background variables can then be examined without relying on arbitrary definitions of subject groups (see Section V). We have previously given an account of this approach (Bamford and Bench, 1979).

Factor analysis has two objectives: firstly to determine how many distinct attributes underlie or generate the observed data; secondly, to find the relationship between these underlying "factors" and the observed data. Starting with the covariance matrix of the data, the procedure extracts independent linear combinations of the variables and, associated with each combination or "factor", a quantity called the eigenvalue or latent root. The eigenvalue indicates how much of the total variation in the data may be attributed to its corresponding linear combination. The relationship between each variable and a particular factor is expressed by the "communality" between the variable and the factor. The communality is the proportion of the variable's variance which is held "in common" with the factor. The model thus states that each observed variable value is the "result" of an underlying factor or factors, and if a factor can be expressed in terms of the variables, then the observed variable values can be replaced by factor values, resulting in a large reduction in the amount of information under consideration. Thus:

Factor value (score)$= a_1 x_1 + a_2 x_2 + \ldots a_n x_n$ where a_i are "factor loadings" and x_i are the individual mean difference variable scores.

The factor score expresses the degree to which a particular case (in the present context a "case" is the LARSP profile data from one child) possesses the quality or property that the factor describes. The scaling of factor scores is arbitrary, and they are generally scaled to have a mean of zero and standard deviation of one. Factor scores can be used in later analyses, replacing the original observed variable values, and under certain circumstances the factor scores have less error, and are therefore more reliable measures, than the original variables.

For a non-mathematical description of factor analysis the interested reader is referred to Child (1970), while Maxwell (1977) presents a more advanced treatment.

B. Results of the factor analysis

There are 107 items on our modification of the LARSP profile, and initially all these 107 profile variables for all 263 hearing-impaired subjects were included in a preliminary analysis. The aim of the analysis was to reduce the set of profile variables included in the factor analysis, in order to aid convergence and to reduce the problem to one which could be more easily handled by the computing facilities available. The possibility of a reduction in the set of variables arises because not all the variables will be reliable discriminators between different subjects. As Crystal *et al.* (1976, p. 105) point out: "We do ... appreciate the need to establish better presentations of the data, but do not think this will be useful until the number of linguistic variables is somewhat reduced. At the moment, we count everything, and while in principle any structure could be of diagnostic significance and a focus of remediation, it is likely that a fairly small range of patterns will emerge regularly as being particularly important. If this is so, it will be possible to take from a sample only the most salient structural characteristics, and perform statistical analyses on them which have some predictive value for groups."

Fifty-one of the 107 LARSP items were deleted as a result of this preliminary analysis, the criteria for deletion being:

(1) very infrequent occurrence, giving small mean and variance (see also (3) below);

(2) small total communality (the total communality of a variable is the proportion of its variance which is common to it and to the factor structure; a variable with low communal variance has a large proportion of error variance or variance unique to itself);

(3) no apparent difference in occurrence between the *a priori* groups of subjects (the 27 groups, defined according to hearing loss, age and non-verbal I.Q.). In applying this criterion we were helped by the results of a $(3 \times 3 \times 3)$ factorial analysis of variance which was carried out on all 107 profile variables (this lengthy analysis is not reported here).

The remaining 56 profile variables were then subjected to the full factor analysis. This was performed on the covariance matrix rather than the correlation matrix, since it was felt that the natural scaling would be more meaningful than the assumption that all variables had equal weight. The results of the analysis are shown in Table XVII, where the factor loadings of the first two factors onto each of the 56 variables are tabulated. Note that because the analysis was performed on the covariance matrix, the factor loadings are non-standardized. Also shown in Table XVII are the communalities between each factor and each variable: that is, the proportion of the variance of each variable that is held in common with a particular factor. This quantity may also be thought of as the square of the correlation coefficient between the variable and the factor (i.e. $C = r^2$). In an analysis which factors the correlation matrix, and which derives standardized factor loadings, the loading is the same as this correlation coefficient. The sum of squares of the factor loadings for each factor is known as the eigenvalue. Again, because the analysis was performed on the covariance matrix, giving non-standardized loadings, the eigenvalues in Table XVII are not immediately meaningful to the reader, since their interpretation depends upon the total variance. (With standardized factor loadings, the maximum possible loading of a variable on a factor is 1·0, and thus the maximum possible eigenvalue of any factor is equal to the number of variables.) For this reason, the eigenvalue associated with each factor has been converted into a percentage of the total possible variance.

It can now be seen that the first factor (Factor 1 or F_1) accounts for about 54% of the total variance, while the second factor extracted (F_2) accounts for only 8·86% of the total variance. Subsequent factors, not shown in Table XVII, account for ever decreasing proportions of the variance. A Scree Test (Cattell, 1952) indicated that of the first 10 factors extracted only F_1 is significant in summarizing the data. Hence, the analysis shows that the data can be reduced from over 100 variables to one derived variable (F_1) and yet still account for over half the variance.

C. Interpretation of factor one

F_1 has both positive and negative loadings. Ambiguous, Stage 1 "clause" "V" and "N", SV, SC/O and VC/O have negative loadings, while the remainder are all positive. Thus entries in Stages 1 and 2 at the clause level count particularly "against" the subject, while entries at other levels tend to reflect positive advancement in varying degrees. In a sense, the factor plays off the occurrence of positively-loaded structures against the occurrence of the negatively-loaded structures. The reader might wonder what is so especially important about, for example, the DN (determiner-noun) structure, which has a high positive loading. The DN structure has a large mean value and partly in consequence of this it is a highly reliable discriminator. The "jump" from using nouns without determiners to using them with determiners is, the analysis shows, a very important and indicative progression for our subjects.

There is, then, only one factor of any importance in determining the results. On reflection this is not surprising: Crystal *et al.* did not pick the 100-odd variables which go to make up the LARSP profile out of a hat containing a wide variety of behavioural skills; they picked their variables from a restricted and specific set of grammatical structures which, according to the

Table XVII. The results of the factor analysis on the restricted set of 56 LARSP variables. The table shows the loadings of each variable onto Factors 1 and 2, the first two factors extracted by the analysis, and the communalities between each variable and Factors 1 and 2. The table also shows the mean ($\bar{x}$) and standard deviation (S^2) for each variable.
Data from all ($N=263$) subjects

Variable				Factor 1		Factor 2	
Number	Name	$\bar{x}$	S^2	Factor loading	Communality	Factor loading	Communality
1	Ambiguous	1·39	2·31	−1·04	20	0·10	00
2	Stage 1 "V"	2·05	4·35	−2·84	43	−1·63	14
3	Stage 1 "N"	12·08	26·79	−18·93	50	−10·88	16
4	SV	9·10	4·48	−1·26	08	0·05	00
5	SC/O	1·00	1·66	−0·94	32	−0·12	01
6	VC/O	3·98	3·08	−0·47	02	−0·39	02
7	X+S:NP	4·72	3·35	0·21	00	1·02	09
8	X+V:VP	7·08	3·83	1·19	10	0·12	01
9	X+C/O:NP	2·53	2·29	0·07	00	0·27	01
10	X+A:AP	1·51	1·60	0·08	00	0·02	00
11	SVC/O	23·35	9·79	6·39	43	6·29	41
12	SVA	8·83	4·42	2·83	41	0·96	05
13	XY+S:NP	15·13	8·32	4·71	32	4·34	27
14	XY+V:VP	14·80	8·38	6·89	68	1·45	03
15	XY+C/O:NP	14·17	7·19	4·53	40	4·83	45
16	XY+A:AP	6·94	3·70	2·49	45	1·00	07
17	SVC/OA	5·87	4·30	3·36	61	−0·09	00
18	AAXY	1·44	1·69	1·04	38	−0·36	05
19	and	13·15	10·90	7·80	51	0·62	00
20	s	3·57	3·58	2·56	51	−0·58	03
21	Coord. 1	9·48	7·87	4·74	36	1·36	03
22	Coord. 1+	2·13	2·86	1·64	33	−0·33	01
23	Subord. 1	3·54	3·54	2·52	51	−0·58	05
24	Clause:C/O	3·21	2·91	1·80	38	0·15	00
25	Clause:A	2·39	2·65	1·78	45	−0·47	03
26	DN	42·08	17·56	10·03	33	11·45	43
27	AdjN	4·03	3·79	1·02	07	0·23	00
28	vv	3·56	2·92	1·44	24	−0·10	00
29	v part	11·91	5·02	2·54	26	0·55	01
30	DAdjN	5·10	4·24	2·73	41	0·32	01
31	PrDN	12·22	7·47	5·86	62	0·74	00
32	Cop	6·64	5·23	3·63	43	0·48	00
33	Aux	17·27	11·29	8·84	61	−0·51	00
34	Pron	20·87	13·18	8·05	37	1·78	02
35	PrPron	1·23	1·68	0·76	21	−0·27	03

Table XVII cont.

Variable				Factor 1		Factor 2	
				Factor loading	Com-mun-ality	Factor loading	Com-mun-ality
Number	Name	$\bar{x}$	S^2				
36	PrDAdjN	1·18	1·47	0·86	34	−0·22	02
37	XcX	4·57	3·69	1·79	23	0·61	03
38	NegV	1·45	1·73	0·58	11	0·01	00
39	2 aux	0·51	1·27	0·31	06	−0·06	00
40	Postmod. clause 1	1·03	1·59	0·80	25	−0·10	00
41	Inf.	4·25	3·79	1·40	40	−0·50	02
42	-ing	21·05	9·90	6·54	44	0·38	00
43	pl.	9·91	6·79	2·55	14	−0·75	00
44	-ed	12·63	9·91	4·57	21	0·43	00
45	-en	2·10	2·96	1·17	16	−0·30	00
46	3s	7·67	7·13	3·73	27	−0·23	00
47	gen	4·72	4·03	2·81	49	0·11	00
48	n't	1·20	1·54	0·41	07	0·00	00
49	'cop	3·01	3·05	1·80	26	0·16	00
50	'aux	5·37	6·18	3·07	25	−1·16	04
51	Initiator	1·19	1·43	0·58	16	0·12	01
52	it	1·37	1·66	0·74	20	−0·14	01
53	there	2·48	3·46	1·86	29	−0·01	00
54	mean words per sentence	7·21	2·82	2·65	88	−0·06	00
55	maximum words per sentence	17·37	8·33	6·87	68	−0·10	00
56	total number of sentences analysed	45·42	9·79	2·28	05	5·67	34
Eigenvalues				1479·58		242·63	
Percentage of total variance				53·97		8·86	

literature, reflect grammatical advancement. We would expect the main determiner of a person's performance on the profile to be his grammatical advancement, since that is precisely what the profile was designed to reflect. Thus, we are satisfied to regard F_1 as a measure of grammatical advancement.

This interpretation of F_1 is supported by an examination of the communalities between the profile variables and F_1. Remember that the communality represents the proportion of an item's variance held in common with the factor, and may also be thought of as the square of the correlation coefficient between the item and the factor. In the present case the communalities are more meaningful than the unstandardized factor loadings produced from the analysis of the covariance matrix. However, those variables which exhibit negative loadings with F_1 must be considered to impart a negative sign to the correlation coefficient, if one is thinking of the communalities as the squares of the correlations between variable and factor. The advantages of analysing the non-standardized covariance matrix accrue during the procedures which aim to identify the optimum factor structure. Once this structure has been defined it is as well to consider its interpretation in terms of some standardized quantity such as communality. In a very general sense, the larger the communality between an item and a factor, the more important is the item's contribution to the factor. However, one must be careful to remember that the calculation of factor score coefficients and hence the factor score for a particular subject's profile will, because of our approach, depend also upon the absolute value of each variable: that is, upon the number of times it occurs on the profile. But for the straightforward interpretation and naming of a factor, the communality values serve very well.

Thus, recalling that we have suggested that F_1 reflects grammatical advancement, it is noteworthy that the item with the largest communality with F_1 is variable 54, the mean number of words per sentence. The correlation between this and F_1 is $+0.94$. We have already noted that Brown (1973) has argued that practically all advances in grammatical ability are reflected in increased sentence length. In recent years his Mean Length of Utterance (MLU) measure has been used as an independent indicator of grammatical advancement (e.g. Linares-Orama and Sanders, 1977), and although two sentences may be of the same length but quite different in terms of complexity, it can be a useful measure for grouping subjects prior to grammatical analysis proper, or it can be used with measures of complexity to produce a combined evaluation. The use to which a length measure may be put depends upon one's aims. Certainly, length measures by themselves do not generate useful procedures for the teacher: knowing that utterances are unduly short is one thing, doing something about it is another. However, our analysis does show that it is a good overall indicator of grammatical advancement, despite its drawbacks, and as a preliminary easy-to-use measure, it may be very valuable.

In point of fact, MLU is measured in terms of morphemes, and Brown's statement that "almost every new kind of (grammatical) knowledge increases (utterance) length" applies to the number of morphemes in each utterance. The picture is not very different, however, for utterance (or sentence) length measured in terms of words. Advancement at clause or phrase level almost always involves an increase in the number of words used, and with few exceptions it is only advances within the word level of analysis which remain unaccompanied by an increased number of words: pl., -ed, -est, for example, are grammatical advances marked only by extra morphemes. Even some of the word level items, however, may still reflect, albeit indirectly, increased number of words: 'aux and 'cop, for example.

Other items which have more than half their variance in common with F_1 (i.e. have correlation coefficients with F_1 of more than 0·7) are XY + V : VP (variable 14), which indicates the expansion of verb elements into verb phrases at the level of three-element clauses; SVC/OA (variable 17), one of the four-element clauses; "and" (variable 19), the use of "and" as a connector of separate clauses within a single sentence; s (variable 20), the use of devices to introduce subordinate clauses; PrDN (variable 31), the use of prepositional phrases such as "in the garden"; Aux (variable 33), the use of auxiliary verbs; the maximum number of words per sentence (variable 55)—an important but understandably less reliable indicator than the mean number of words per sentence, which is less susceptible to errors in the difficult initial task for grammatical analysis of demarcation of sentences; and finally, the Stage 1 "N" "clauses", which, being a negatively-loaded variable, correlates negatively with F_1.

Bearing in mind the arrangement of the LARSP profile from least to most advanced structures, our notion of F_1 as reflecting grammatical advancement is further supported by the negative loadings associated with the least advanced structures (variables 1–6). Clearly, the over-use of some of these, particularly "V", "N" and SC/O, indicates real lack of development.

That certain of the more advanced structures of Crystal *et al.* (e.g. 2 aux, variable 31—the use of two auxiliary verbs in a verb phrase, such as "he *has been* running", "you *might have* said") do not correlate highly with F_1 is no reason to question our interpretation of F_1. The communality in such cases is small, presumably because their means are small (and standard deviations relatively large), and their measurement errors are high. It should be recalled that our analysis took account of the natural scaling of items, and it is clear that 2 aux, for example, was used too rarely to be of much discriminative value along the dimension of grammatical advancement, at least amongst the subjects in our sample.

Figure 28 shows the communalities between LARSP items and F_1, for those variables with a communality of 10% or more. (It is common practice to consider only those variables with loadings greater than $\pm 0·3$—i.e. with communalities of about 10% or more—when it comes to interpreting factors. There *are* more mathematical methods for deciding which factor loadings

Deviant	Ambiguous
	20 (–)

Analyser's Comments:

ANALYSED

	Minor "Sentences": Social	Stereotypes	Problems

				Major "Sentences"	

| | | Excl. | Comm. | Quest. | Statement | |

STAGE 1 0.9 – 1.6

	'V'	'Q'	'V' **43 (–)**	'N' **50 (–)**	Other	Problems

STAGE 2 1.6 – 2.0

				Conn.	Clause		Phrase		Word
	VX	QX		SV	VC/O	DN **33**	vv **24**	Inf. **40**
				S C/O **32(–)**	AX	Adj N	v part **26**	-ing **44**
						NN	int x	pl. **14**
				Neg X	Other	Pr N	other	
								fut.

STAGE 3 2.0 – 2.6

	VXY	QXY	X+S:NP	X+V:VP **10**	X+C/O :NP	X+A:AP	-ed **21**
	let XY	VS	SVC/O **43**	VC/O A	D Adj N **41**	Cop **43** / Aux **61**	-en **16**
	doXY		SVA **41**	V O_d O_i	Adj Adj N / Pr DN **62**	Pron **37** / Pr Pron **21**	3s **27**
			Neg XY	Other	N Adj N	Other	

STAGE 4 2.6 – 3.0

		QXYZ	XY+S:NP **32**	XY+V:VP **68**	XY+ C/O:NP **40**	XY+A:AP **45**	gen **49**
	+S	QVS	SVC/OA **61**	AAXY **38**	N Pr NP / Pr D Adj N **34**	Neg V **11** / Neg X	n't
			SVO_dO_i	Other	c X / X c X **23**	2 aux / Other	'cop **26**
							'aux **25**

STAGE 5 3 – 3.6

	how		and **51**	Coord. 1 **36** 1+ **33**	Postmod. 1 **25** 1+ clause	-est
		tag	c	Subord. 1 **51** 1+		
	what		s **51**	Clause: S	Postmod. 1+ phrase	-er
				Clause: C/O **38** Comparative		
			other	Clause: A **45**		-ly

STAGE 6 3.6 – 4.6

	+			–		
	NP	VP	Clause	NP	VP	Clause
	Initiator **16**	Complex	Passive	Pron. Adj. Seq.	Modal Tense	Concord A Position
	Coord.		Complement	Det. N irreg.	V irreg.	W Order

Other: | | | | Other: | | |

STAGE 7 4.6+

A connectivity:	Emphatic order:	it: **20**
Comment clause:	Other:	there: **29**

NUMBER OF WORDS IN EACH SENTENCE*

MEAN WORDS PER SENTENCE : **88**

MAXIMUM " " " **68**

*Here sentence means: Any utterance which is neither deviant nor ambiguous, but excluding all Stage 1 utterances.

Fig. 28 The structure of F_1: the communalities between LARSP variables and F_1. Only communalities of 10% or more are marked.

are worth considering, but none are as free from ambiguity as this simple rule of thumb.) The numbers in Fig. 28 are taken directly from Table XVII, and illustrated in this manner (i.e. on a profile) they may help the reader to appreciate the structure of F_1.

Four profile items, PrPron, Inf., fut., and Clause : A, are not contained in the original LARSP profile (Crystal *et al.*, 1976), but were added as part of the present project for the reasons outlined in Chapter 3. We discarded fut. from the factor analysis as a result of the preliminary analysis which isolated and removed those variables of little significance. The unimportance of fut. probably results from the particular method used to obtain the speech samples: picture-description is unlikely to elicit the future tense very frequently, and future auxiliaries are, therefore, understandably rare. The other three additions, PrPron, Inf., and Clause : A were included in the factor analysis proper, and have turned out to be reasonable predictors of grammatical advancement, having communalities with F_1 of 21 (PrPron), 40 (Inf.) and 45 (Clause : A). However, they are not structures which occur particularly frequently (see Fig. 1).

Lee (1974) has devised a Developmental Sentence Scoring procedure (DSS), which she has described as "a method for making a detailed, readily quantified and scored evaluation of a child's use of Standard English grammatical rules ... (which) provides a way of measuring a child's growth and progress throughout the period of clinical teaching". Lee's approach is in many ways very similar to that of Crystal *et al.*, but the DSS has been developed to provide a method of scoring which presumably has predictive power for groups, and some standardization of the measure has been undertaken. If our interpretation of F_1 as reflecting grammatical advancement has been correct, we would expect some correspondence between the components of DSS and of our F_1, and this does indeed seem to be the case. Lee selected eight syntactic features which appear early in children's production of sentences, and which show a particular progression of development. They are:

(a) indefinite pronouns or noun modifiers (e.g. this, some);
(b) personal pronouns (e.g. she, my);
(c) main verbs (e.g. is, have, see);
(d) secondary verbs (e.g. she is *sleeping*, I want *to go*);
(e) negatives (e.g. not, isn't);
(f) conjunctions (e.g. and, because);
(g) interrogative reversals (e.g. is it?);
(h) wh- questions (e.g. what?).

The last two categories and the negatives are not included in our grammatical analysis, since the picture-description task did not elicit questions and negatives. The other five categories, however, correspond to various profile entries such as: determiners + noun (DN), pronouns (Pron), copula (Cop), auxiliaries (Aux), infinitives (Inf.), and conjunctions (and, s), all of which are highly correlated with F_1. The chief criticism of Lee's measure is that it concentrates unduly on the phrase level of grammatical development, and the verb phrase at that, to the exclusion of clause level structures, noun-phrase structure, and morphological items. Following Crystal *et al.*, the approach adopted in the present project makes no initial assumptions about which areas or levels of grammatical analysis are more important than others. Whether because of this it will produce a more valid measure than DSS remains to be seen, and in the end is an empirical question awaiting the outcome of future research.

It should be pointed out, however, that before a comparison of F_1 with DSS or any other measure of grammatical development can be made, F_1 itself will have to be standardized—or restructured—for groups of normally-hearing children. The factor structure presented here is the optimum structure for assessing the grammatical advancement of the hearing-impaired individuals who constituted our sample. The sample is assumed to be representative of hearing-impaired children, and the factor structure will not necessarily, therefore, be as meaningful for groups of normally-hearing children. For example, there may be normally-hearing children who vary significantly and reliably on some of the structures found in Stages 6 and 7, and such a group would probably give a slightly different factor structure and weighting. We would not expect a grammatical advancement factor derived from groups of normally-hearing children to differ fundamentally from the structure derived here from the spoken language of the hearing-impaired; but the differences, although small, might be important.

D. Interpretation of factor two

As we noted earlier, it is possible to derive a score on F_1 for each subject by calculating a weighted sum of his observed variable values, the weights being proportional to the factor loadings. These grammatical advancement scores are scaled to have zero mean and unit variance. Similarly, it is possible to compute each subject's scores on Factor Two (or any other subsequent factor), although it is clear from the analysis that Factor Two (F_2) and all succeeding factors were relatively unimportant. We have seen how F_2 accounts for only 8·9% of the total variance, and the Scree Test indicates that it is of little significance. There are other criteria, however, for deciding how many factors to extract in a factor analysis. One of these, Kaiser's criterion, indicates that F_2 should be considered as well as F_1, although as Cattell (1952) has argued, this method tends to extract too many factors when the number of variables exceeds 50. It may, however, be worth pausing for a moment to consider F_2 and its possible interpretation.

Few of the 56 variables have any significant communality with F_2 (Table

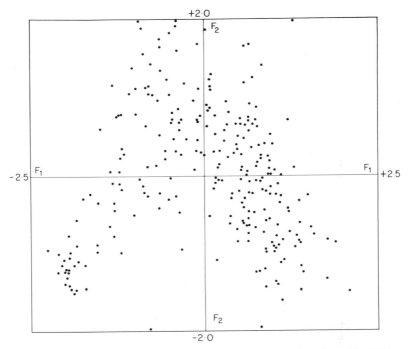

Fig. 29   Score on F_1 plotted against score on F_2 for all subjects (N=263).

XVII). There are six variables having a communality with F_2 of 0·16 or greater, which represents a correlation coefficient between item and factor of 0·4 or greater. The six variables are: Stage 1 "N" "clauses" (variable 3); SVC/O (variable 11); XY+S:NP (variable 13); XY+O:NP (variable 15); DN (variable 26); and total number of sentences analysed (variable 56). The correlation of these items with F_2 (and bearing in mind that variable 3, Stage 1 "N", is negatively loaded) suggests that F_2 has something to do with the expansion of nouns into noun phrases with a determiner, and with the overall size (i.e. length) of the analysed speech sample. In Fig. 29 each subject is plotted with his score on F_1 against his score on F_2, and examination of the individual profiles of some of the outliers tends to confirm the view that F_2 is closely associated with the amount of material analysed. In most cases, this amount depended upon variables associated with the analyser, not with the subject: in particular, it had been left to the analyser to decide when enough of the language sample had been analysed to provide a reasonably stable profile. This indicates the probably trivial characteristics of F_2. Figure 29 should, however, be regarded with some caution: the apparent quadratic relationship between F_1 and F_2 could be an artefact of the mathematical constraints (orthogonality) in the analysis. It seems clear that we need consider F_2 no further.

We can now proceed to examine the relationships between grammatical advancement, i.e. F_1 score, and the background variables, some of which are directly associated with the hearing-impairment (e.g. pure tone hearing loss, age at onset of impairment), others of which are not (e.g. sex, social class).

V. The relationships between grammatical advancement and the background variables

The calculated F_1 scores, which reflect, we have argued, grammatical advancement, ranged from $-2 \cdot 12$ (least advanced) to $+1 \cdot 88$ (most advanced). In this Section we examine the relationships between the F_1 scores and the background variables. These variables are either interval variables (e.g. degree of pure tone hearing loss), ordinal variables (e.g. social class) or categorical variables (e.g. sex). It is possible to compute correlation coefficients between F_1 and the interval or ordinal variables (Pearson's r in all cases), whereas the relationships, if any, between F_1 and the categorical variables are determined by examination of the differences between the mean F_1 scores for each category. We will discuss the effects of each background variable in turn before examining the relationships between combinations of the background variables and F_1 scores in Section V K (Multiple Correlations).

A. Pure tone hearing loss

As expected, pure tone hearing loss in the better ear (averaged over 500, 1000, 2000 Hz) correlates negatively with F_1 score ($r = -0 \cdot 42$; $N = 263$; $P < 0 \cdot 001$). Thus, the greater the impairment measured in terms of detection ability for pure tones, the less advanced the subject's grammatical ability is likely to be. The coefficient, although very significant, is not especially large, and this points to the fact that degree of pure tone loss alone is by no means the only determinant of grammatical advancement. Much of the unexplained variability in the relationship will be due to the other background variables which show a significant correlation with F_1 score. One of these is age (see below), and, as we saw in Section III, the relationship between many of the LARSP profile measures and hearing loss interacted with age to a significant degree. That is, there were marked differences (in the expected direction) between the mean performance levels of the mild-, moderate- and severe-hearing-loss groups for the 8- to 10-year-olds, but these differences were not apparent for the 14- to 15-year-olds. For this reason, in Fig. 30, which shows F_1 score plotted against average pure tone hearing loss, best fit regression lines are shown for each age group separately. It can be seen that the now familiar age/hearing loss interaction is still apparent, the 14- to 15-year-old children with more severe losses tending to have higher F_1 scores than the 8- to 10-year-old children

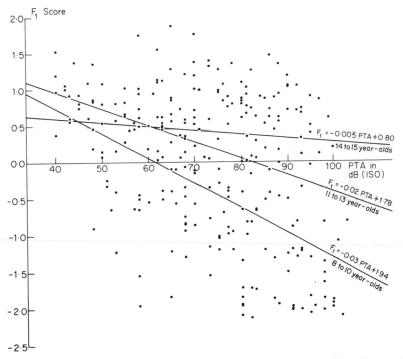

Fig. 30 F_1 score plotted against average pure tone hearing loss (PTA). Best fit regression lines are shown for each age group.

with similar levels of hearing loss, while these differences in F_1 scores are not apparent for those with milder hearing losses. Figure 30 shows that the variability of F_1 increases as pure tone hearing loss increases. With relatively mild degrees of loss F_1 scores tend to be reasonably good (although not as good as one might expect from normally-hearing children: the F_1 scores from the 11 normally-hearing children aged from 10–15 years whose mean LARSP profile is shown in Fig. 2 ranged from $+1\cdot10$ to $+4\cdot26$ with a mean of $2\cdot47$ and a standard deviation of $0\cdot82$). However, as the degree of impairment increases, the F_1 scores vary more, presumably because the greater the impairment, the more the other background variables (e.g. age, non-verbal I.Q.) can have a counteracting effect. Thus it seems that although the effects of moderate to high degrees of hearing loss may be severe (at least in terms of grammatical advancement), this is not necessarily so, and depending upon certain other factors the effects need not be irreversible.

In a small study of twenty prelingually partially-hearing children (mean pure tone hearing loss 64 dB ISO) aged from 8–9 years, Owrid (1972) compared their performance on the Reception Scale of the Northwestern Syntax Screening Test (Lee, 1969) with that of 20 normally-hearing children aged from 3–4 years. As we might expect from our own data on the 8- to 10-year-olds, Owrid found a close association between syntax score and hearing level, and this association was much closer than that between syntax score and chronological age. He commented that for the hearing-impaired children the level of access to the data of experience is a crucial determinant of the development of grammatical knowledge. Our data suggest that although this is the case for the 8- to 10-year-olds, as the children grow older the "level of access" becomes less important.

One final point concerning Fig. 30 is that hearing loss is plotted here as a continuum, whereas the factorial analyses in Section III treated it at the three levels of mild, moderate and severe. There is little evidence in Fig. 30 for any "steps" or "boundaries" in the level of hearing loss which might separate such categories of hearing loss in terms of F_1 scores. The categorization of hearing loss into three levels was, therefore, rather arbitrary, and it is comforting to know that the age/hearing loss interaction discussed in Section III was not an artefact of this categorization. Indeed, we have calculated the correlations between F_1 score and hearing for each age group separately, and these correlations are shown in Table XVIII. They further confirm the interaction of hearing loss with age in its effect on grammatical advancement, since the negative coefficient is relatively high and significant for the 8- to 10-year-olds, intermediate for the 11- to 13-year-olds, and is not significant for the 14- to 15-year-olds.

Table XVIII. The correlation coefficients (r) *between average pure tone hearing loss (PTA) and F₁ score for each of the three age groups*

Age group	r	N	Significance level
8, 9, 10 years	−0·544	92	P<0·001
11, 12, 13 years	−0·366	106	P<0·001
14, 15 years	−0·108	65	P=0·196

There are many ways of characterizing the pure tone audiogram of a hearing-impaired person. We have chosen what is probably the most commonly used measure, namely the detection threshold in dB ISO averaged across 500, 1000, 2000 Hz. These are known to be the important frequencies for speech perception, so it makes good sense to use this measure or something like it for predicting grammatical advancement. It is certainly true, however, that pure tone audiograms of quite different shapes can result in the same mean loss by this method. Thus, the question is whether different pure tone audiogram shapes are related to different degrees of the handicap—ability to hear speech, quality of produced speech, linguistic advancement or whatever— or whether the handicap is best predicted simply by the average loss at three frequencies, whatever the pattern of the audiogram. There have been many attempts to answer this question (e.g. Fowler, 1942; Harris, 1965; Montgomery, 1967; Risberg and Martony, 1970; Erber, 1974). Kyle (1977) recently concluded that a simple mean of five frequencies (250, 500, 1000, 2000 and 4000 Hz) was the best predictor of the intelligibility of the produced speech of hearing-impaired 15- to 16-year-olds. He pointed out, however, that any combination which has the threshold at 1000 Hz as a major component will provide a valid measure. One problem is that because of the magnitude of the variability apparent in Fig. 30, no pure tone measure can hope to predict aspects of speech production or spoken language particularly well, and the search for better pure tone predictors than simple mean loss measures will be subject to the law of diminishing returns.

Risberg and Martony (1970) have described a system of classifying pure tone audiogram patterns which takes four factors into consideration: the information-carrying elements in the speech signal; the boundary between hearing and vibration in the low frequencies; the intensity of a speaker's own speech in his ears; and the level of loudness discomfort. They divided the frequencies below 1000 Hz into four areas labelled A, B, C and D, and the frequencies above 1500 Hz into five areas labelled 1, 2, 3, 4 and 5 (Fig. 31). Using this system, any pure tone audiogram can be classified according to the areas in which the low and high parts of the audiogram mainly lie. Thus a flat audiogram of uniform 30 dB loss would be classified A1, while a steep high-frequency loss audiogram with fairly good low-frequency hearing might be classified A3.

The correlation coefficients between F_1 score and the low-frequency Risberg and Martony classification is -0.38, while that between F_1 and the high-

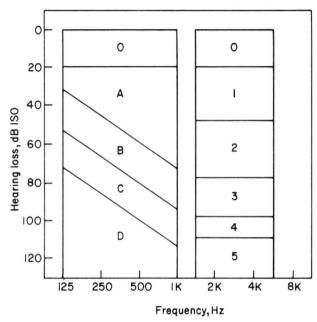

Fig. 31   *The Risberg and Martony (1970) system for classifying pure-tone audiograms (by permission of the Alexander Graham Bell Association for the Deaf, Inc.)*

frequency classification is -0.28. Both are statistically significant ($N = 263$, $P < 0.001$), and although neither correlation on its own is as large as the simple mean-of-three-frequencies correlation (-0.42), the low-frequency classification accounts for more of the variability than the high-frequency classification. Kyle's analyses (1977) suggest that this is because the low-frequency classification includes the threshold at 1000 Hz. When the two classifications are taken together, the multiple correlation coefficient (R) between F_1 score and the combined low- and high-frequency classifications is 0.40. (The square of a multiple correlation coefficient (R^2) indicates how much of the total variability is accounted for by the combined variables; multiple correlations are not given a sign, since some of the variables may be negatively related to the measure under consideration, others positively. However, in the present example, both components are negatively related to F_1, so the multiple coefficient can be considered as -0.40.) The multiple correlation is not markedly higher than either of the two classifications correlated alone with F_1 score. This is not surprising, because the two classifications are themselves positively correlated ($r = 0.38$, $N = 263$, $P < 0.001$). Furthermore, the multiple correlation of the two classifications with F_1 is not significantly different from the simple correlation between F_1 and pure tone loss averaged at 500, 1000 and 2000 Hz. There is, therefore, no extra explanatory advantage to be gained by using the Risberg and Martony classifications in this manner.

However, since the Risberg and Martony classification gives the pure tone audiogram from each subject both a low- and high-frequency coding, more properly the two classifications should be combined into a single measure for each subject. But whereas each classification considered independently is clearly ordinal in nature (A–D; 1–5), it is not so clear how to order the classifications when they are combined. Classifications A1 to A5 can be ordered, but there are no *a priori* grounds for placing A5 and B1, for example, in any particular order. Thus, if the classifications are to be combined, correlational techniques are inappropriate. Instead, the mean F_1 scores for each of the classifications (A3, B4, etc.) have been calculated, and these are shown in Table XIX. There are significant differences between these means (F13, $249 = 5.55$, $P < 0.001$). The effect of the low-frequency classifications (A, B, C or D) is significant (F3, $249 = 10.13$, $P < 0.001$), and there is also a significant effect of the high-frequency classifications (1, 2, 3, 4 or 5) upon F_1 score (F4, $249 = 2.90$, $P = 0.023$). The mean F_1 scores and their 95% confidence limits for each audiogram classification are shown in Fig. 32. Those points which are derived from only one observation are largely responsible for the significant effect of the high-frequency classification upon F_1. Thus, if the analysis of variance is rerun excluding the four classifications which contain only one subject, the differences between the ten remaining means are still highly significant (F9, $249 = 6.98$, $P < 0.001$), as is the main effect of the low-frequency classification (F2, $249 = 15.8$, $P < 0.001$). However, the statistical significance of the main effect of the high-frequency classification falls below $P = 0.05$ (F3, $253 = 2.41$, $P = 0.068$). Ignoring, then, the four points in Fig. 32 which are derived from $N = 1$, it is clear that the important classification is that determined by the lower frequencies, that is, up to an including 1000 Hz. Certainly, if the hearing loss in these lower frequencies is mild (i.e. category A), then the degree of loss in the higher frequencies bears little rela-

Table XIX. The means and standard deviations of the F_1 scores by Risberg and Martony's pure tone audiogram classification

Audiogram classification	Mean F_1 score	Standard deviation	N
A1	0·65	0·28	4
A2	0·39	0·78	59
A3	0·36	0·59	17
A4	0·41	1·17	7
A5	—	—	0
Total A	0·40	0·76	87
B1	—	—	0
B2	0·08	0·93	51
B3	0·32	0·76	36
B4	−0·38	1·13	15
B5	—	—	0
Total B	0·10	0·92	102
C1	1·28	0·00	1
C2	−0·11	1·01	23
C3	−0·73	0·99	23
C4	−0·85	1·03	24
C5	−1·63	0·00	1
Total C	−0·56	1·06	72
D1	—	—	0
D2	—	—	0
D3	0·13	0·00	1
D4	−1·74	0·00	1
D5	—	—	0
Total D	−0·80	1·32	2
Grand total	0·01	0·99	263

tionship to F_1 score. As the degree of loss in the lower frequencies increases (categories B and C), F_1 score tends to decrease. There is a suggestion of an interaction effect, such that the higher frequency categories (1–5) begin to show an inverse relationship with F_1 score as the lower frequency hearing loss worsens. Thus, although there are no differences between the mean F_1 scores for A1, A2, A3 and A4, the mean F_1 score for C2 is significantly higher than that for C3 and C4. Excluding the N=1 cells, this interaction just fails to reach significance at $P=0·05$ (F4, $249=2·21$, $P=0·069$). Such an inter-action effect seems quite plausible: the frequencies above 1500 Hz may become particularly important only if the hearing for low frequencies is badly impaired. However, more data are required in the empty cells in order to confirm this effect. One point that should be made is that we are assessing here the relationship between pure tone hearing and a score which reflects the advancement of produced grammar. That the relationship between this and the hearing for the higher frequencies seems to be rather weak does not

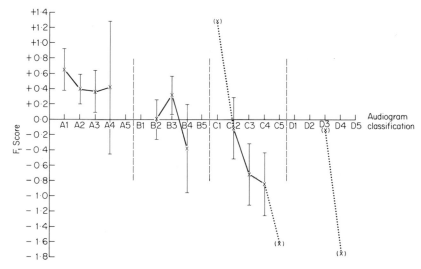

Fig. 32 The mean F_1 scores of the subjects according to the Risberg and Martony audio-gram classification. The 95% confidence intervals are shown for each point. Four of the points are derived from only $N=1$, and these are marked: (x).

mean that the higher frequencies are not more closely related to other speech and language skills. It is likely, for example, that the higher frequencies will be implicated more in the quality of speech production. Or again, if we were to assess morphological skills alone it might be that they would be more strongly related to high-frequency hearing loss than are the all-round gram-matical skills (syntax and morphology) reflected by F_1 scores.

Concerning the question posed earlier as to whether different pure tone audiogram patterns—which may reflect identical mean hearing losses averaged at 500, 1000 and 2000 Hz—are associated with differences in gram-matical advancement, the answer seems to be a cautious affirmative. That is, the simple mean-of-three-frequencies summary of the pure tone audiogram may hide differences in grammatical advancement which are associated with the pattern of the audiogram. The audiogram pattern has an effect on F_1 score (Fig. 32), and it is unlikely that different mean hearing loss values are uniquely associated with different audiogram patterns. In fact, Table XX shows the mean pure tone average hearing loss (PTA) for the subjects in our sample according to audiogram classification. Although there is, not surprisingly, a fairly close association between PTA and the Risberg and Martony classification (indeed, the correlations between PTA and the low- and

Table XX. The means and standard deviations of the pure tone average hearing losses at 500, 1000 and 2000 Hz of the subjects according to Risberg and Martony's pure tone audiogram classification

Audiogram classification	Mean hearing loss (dB ISO)	Standard deviation	N
A1	43	4·0	4
A2	56	7·8	59
A3	58	9·0	17
A4	70	14·2	7
A5	—	—	—
Total A	57	9·7	87
B1	—	—	—
B2	71	8·0	51
B3	81	8·0	36
B4	87	8·1	15
B5	—	—	—
Total B	77	10·0	102
C1	75	0·0	1
C2	82	6·6	23
C3	91	6·4	23
C4	96	6·8	24
C5	98	0·0	1
Total C	90	9·0	72
D1	—	—	—
D2	—	—	—
D3	97	0·0	1
D4	83	0·0	1
D5	—	—	—
Total D	90	9·9	2

high-frequency classifications are $+0.77$ and $+0.61$ respectively), nonetheless the variability associated with each of the means in Table XX makes it clear that identical PTA values from different individuals are to be found across different audiogram pattern classifications.

B. Age

There is a significant positive correlation of 0.36 between F_1 score and chronological age $(N = 263; P < 0.001)$. This is as we would expect from our discussion of the age/hearing loss interaction, there being a significant effect of age upon grammatical advancement for the severe-hearing-loss group, but not for the moderate- or mild-hearing-loss groups. This interaction accounts for some of the variability in Fig. 33, where F_1 is plotted against age. Best fit regression lines are fitted for each hearing loss category separately. Pressnell (1973) studied a group of prelingually hearing-impaired children aged from 5–13 years, with pure tone hearing losses ranging from 50 to over 100 dB

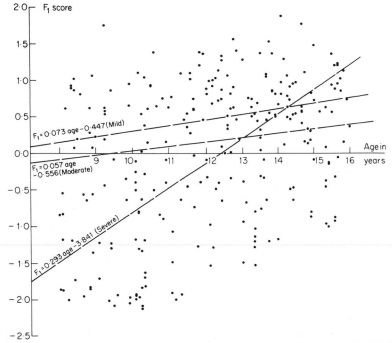

Fig. 33 F_1 score plotted against age. Best fit regression lines are shown for each hearing loss category.

ISO. She found a positive relationship between chronological age and scores on the Northwestern Syntax Screening Test, although there was a great deal of variability and the precise nature of the relationship is somewhat equivocal (see Bench's comments in Chapter 2). Pressnell failed to find a relationship between the Developmental Sentence Score (Lee, 1974) and age, but as we noted previously DSS is largely phrase level based, and we suggested in Section III A that it is only when the degree of hearing loss is severe that phrase level structures are markedly affected. If so, the children with more moderate hearing losses in Pressnell's study may have provided scores which gave an overall non-significant relationship between DSS and age. Pressnell also found a significant multiple correlation relating three measures of linguistic performance to age and degree of hearing impairment ($R = 0.72$, $P < 0.003$). Again, the precise nature of this relationship was not discussed, and it is not clear whether an interaction effect similar to our own was found between age and hearing loss.

C. Non-verbal I.Q.

The correlation coefficient between non-verbal I.Q. and F_1 score is $+0.24$ ($N = 263$; $P < 0.001$). In Fig. 34 F_1 is plotted against non-verbal I.Q., and it can be seen that as non-verbal I.Q. increases so there is a tendency for F_1 score to increase. The direction and size of this relationship is not unexpected, since non-verbal I.Q. is in part a measure of general ability, and it seems reasonable to suggest that this general ability has some effect on a hearing-impaired child's ability to develop the grammatical aspects of his language. Prelingually-impaired children are usually taught normal adult language in a rather more overt and structured manner than occurs in the natural language acquisition of normally-hearing children, who of course develop grammatical structure with little formal tuition. General ability as measured by I.Q. tests is related (almost by definition) to the type of learning ability required in the classroom (though perhaps less so to other types of learning). Thus we might expect non-verbal I.Q. to be related to grammatical advancement in the hearing-impaired, many of whom have to be instructed formally, but not in normally-hearing children, who have usually advanced the length of the LARSP profile by five or six years of age.

This is not to suggest that non-verbal I.Q. and verbal I.Q. are unrelated in the normally-hearing. Verbal I.Q. is not the same as grammatical advancement, although language development in general will influence achievement on a verbal test such as the WISC verbal I.Q. test, partly because the test is presented in linguistic form, and partly because the information required to answer the questions correctly is acquired through spoken or written language. Weschler (1949) gives correlation coefficients of about $+0.6$ between WISC verbal and non-verbal I.Q.s for different groups of normally-hearing children. We might expect the correlation between verbal and non-verbal I.Q.s for hearing-impaired children to be less than this because of the variability introduced by the hearing loss. Hine (1970) studied a group of 8- to 16-year-old partially-hearing children and found a correlation between

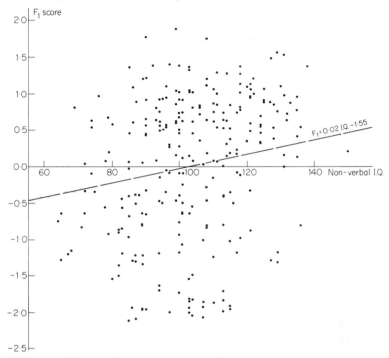

Fig. 34 *F₁ score plotted against non-verbal I.Q. showing the best fit regression line.*

verbal and non-verbal I.Q. of $+0.38$, which increased to 0.51 if hearing loss was allowed for by computing the multiple correlation between verbal I.Q. and non-verbal I.Q. combined with mean pure tone hearing loss. Hine also found a correlation of -0.31 between average pure tone hearing loss and verbal I.Q. for his sample, and it is interesting to compare this figure with our correlation of -0.42 between hearing loss and F_1 score. Our figure for the multiple correlation between F_1 score and non-verbal I.Q. combined with hearing loss is $R = 0.56$ ($N = 263$, $P < 0.001$), which is remarkably close to Hine's figure of $R = 0.51$.

D. Age at onset of hearing-impairment

The F_1 score correlates positively with age at onset of the hearing-impairment ($r = 0.17$; $N = 188$; $P < 0.05$). The correlation is in the expected direction, since the older the child when his hearing is first impaired, the more time he has had to acquire linguistic skills under normal conditions. Although significant, the correlation is low, and this is probably a reflection of at least three factors. Firstly, inaccuracies in the subjects' educational and medical records, from where the data were obtained. Secondly, of the 188 children for whom the data were available, there were no less than 158 cases of onset age at seven months or earlier, and only 17 cases of onset age later than two years (see Table V, Chapter 3). With such a skewed distribution we are fortunate to find a correlation at all. And thirdly, F_1 score might be affected not only by the age at onset of the impairment, but by the amount of time which elapses between the onset and the diagnosis of the impairment, the latter being a reflection of the point at which formal remedial measures can begin. The longer the delay in taking such measures the more likely it is that aspects of linguistic performance will be affected detrimentally. However, if this time between onset of the hearing-impairment and its diagnosis is calculated for each subject for whom both age at onset and age at diagnosis were recorded ($N = 159$), and if F_1 score is then regressed against onset age and the delay in diagnosis, the multiple correlation coefficient is $R = 0.19$ (F2, $156 = 3.03$, $P = 0.051$). This represents a negligible increase on the simple correlation between F_1 and onset ($r = 0.17$).

E. Age at diagnosis of hearing-impairment

The correlation between F_1 score and the age at which the hearing-impairment was diagnosed is $+0.21$ ($N = 213$, $P < 0.01$). At first sight the direction of this correlation is unexpeected, but since this simple correlation confounds onset age with diagnosis age (late onsets are bound to give late diagnoses when the measure is time from birth), it is more meaningful to consider, as above, the delay between onset and diagnosis of the impairment and the relationship between this delay and grammatical advancement. One might expect that the greater the delay in diagnosis, the greater is the delay in taking appropriate remedial measures, and therefore the greater the detrimental effect upon grammatical advancement or F_1 score. However, the correlation between F_1 score and the amount of the "diagnostic delay" is not only small, but positive rather than negative ($r = 0.12$, $N = 159$, $P = 0.062$). A possible explanation for this anomalous result, which implies a tendency for longer diagnostic delays to be associated with higher F_1 scores, is that it is often the *milder* hearing losses which are more difficult to diagnose (and which are associated, therefore, with greater diagnostic delays), and yet precisely because such losses are milder, they tend to go with higher F_1 scores. In fact, there is a highly significant negative correlation between PTA and diagnostic delay ($r = 0.35$, $N = 159$, $P < 0.001$), which tends to confirm this explanation.

F. Social class

For 185 of our subjects, we were able to record the occupation of the family "bread-winner" (see Table IX, Chapter 3). As we described in Chapter 3, this occupation was classified into one of the five Social Classes distinguished by the Office of Population Censuses and Surveys (Classification of Occupations, 1970). It seems reasonable to regard the five Classes (I–V) as being in some sense ordinal, so F_1 score was correlated against Social Class. However, the correlation coefficient is small ($r = -0.1$; $N = 185$; $P = 0.08$). An analysis of variance of the F_1 scores by Social Class revealed that there were significant differences (F4, $180 = 3.69$, $P = 0.0065$). Table XXI shows the appropriate means and standard deviations. However, there is no obvious

Table XXI. *Means and standard deviations of the F_1 scores according to the Social Class of the "bread-winning parent"*

Social class	Mean F_1 score	Standard deviation	N
I	0·20	0·94	29
II	0·53	0·73	35
III	−0·18	0·99	71
IV	0·08	0·91	43
V	0·25	0·92	7

explanation for these differences between the mean F_1 scores. If the mean F_1 score of Classes I and II combined (0·37) is compared with the mean F_1 score for Classes III and IV combined (−0·05), and Class V is ignored because of the small number of observations, the difference between Classes (I+II) and Classes (III+IV) is fairly large and in the expected direction. However, it is not statistically significant at $P = 0.05$ ($t = 1.48$, d.f. $= 174$).

G. Sex

The mean F_1 score for the boys (N = 140) in our sample was -0.06 (SD = 1.0), and the mean F_1 score for the girls (N = 123) was 0.10 (SD = 1.0). This difference is in the expected direction but is small and non-significant (F1, 261 = 1.67, NS).

H. Cause of hearing-impairment

Six categories of "cause of hearing-impairment" (aetiology) were defined (see Table IV, Chapter 3). They were: hereditary (N = 29), pre-natal (N = 57), peri-natal complications (N = 52), post-natal accidental (N = 4), post-natal clinical (N = 25), and "multiple" (N = 5). A one-way analysis of variance of the F_1 scores according to cause category showed that there were no significant differences between the categories (F5, 166 = 1.80, NS). Using the same arguments that were used to explain the effects of onset age on language ability, we might have predicted that the post-natal categories would give higher F_1 scores than the other categories. However, in one post-natal category there were too few subjects (post-natal accidental), and in the other (post-natal clinical) most of the subjects were affected within the first year of birth. If our sample had included more cases of children diagnosed as suffering from conductive hearing-impairment only, the causes of which would probably be classified as post-natal clinical, then F_1 scores for this group might have been significantly elevated. This is because onset of this type of impairment often occurs later than the first two years of life, and because conductive losses are generally argued to produce simple linear attenuation of the auditory signal, without the added frequency distortions which tend to occur with sensori-neural impairments. Our sample contained primarily sensori-neural diagnoses, with some cases of conductive overlay. The absence of pure conductive losses is probably due to the age range under consideration (8–15 years): conductive impairments are more frequent in younger (and older) patients. However, in the context of the present discussion, it should be noted that Hamilton and Owrid (1974) found no evidence for language differences between children with conductive hearing-impairments and children with sensori-neural hearing impairments.

I. Type of school

There were significant differences between the F_1 scores according to the particular school attended (F36, 226 = 10.60, $P < 0.001$). By itself such a finding is of little interest, since it merely reflects the fact that children are placed in particular schools not only by age but also according to their degree of handicap. However, Table XXII shows the mean F_1 scores of the subjects categorized according to type of schooling: residential deaf, residential partially-hearing, PHU (partial-hearing unit) attached to an ordinary school (with or without some integration into normally-hearing classes), and fully integrated into an ordinary school. Some of the schools were difficult to classify unequivocally, and the subjects attending such schools were in consequence not included in the analysis. This accounts for the number of subjects ($N=$ 198) being less than the full sample (cf. Table VIII, Chapter 3).

The differences between the mean F_1 scores in Table XXII are statistically significant ($P<0.01$ for all comparisons except 2 vs. 3, which is $P<0.05$). The 1% significant differences are in the expected direction, and are most probably a reflection of differences in the degree of hearing loss. The residential partially-hearing children gave a higher mean F_1 score than the children in PHUs ($P<0.05$), and this difference does not seem to be accounted for by differences in degree of hearing loss, since the mean pure tone hearing loss of the former group was slightly worse than that of the children in PHUs ($P<0.05$). However, one possibility is that the difference in F_1 scores is related to differences in the mean ages of the two groups, the residential partially-hearing being on average about two and a half years older than the children in PHUs. Presumably this difference in age is in turn a result of the fact that there are PHUs at both secondary and primary age levels, whereas most residential partially-hearing schools are for secondary age groups only.

Table XXII. Means and standard deviations (SD) of F_1 score, PTA and age according to type of school

Type of school	F_1 score		PTA (dB ISO)		Age (decimal years)		N
	Mean	SD	Mean	SD	Mean	SD	
1. Residential deaf	-0.97	0.50	93.2	8.8	11.3	1.77	39
2. Residential partially-hearing	0.29	0.79	75.0	13.5	13.69	2.12	43
3. PHU	0.09	0.53	69.8	15.2	11.05	2.09	101
4. Fully integrated	0.76	0.48	60.0	12.9	13.26	1.85	15

J. Type of hearing aid

The type of hearing aid worn by the subject was classified as follows: bone conduction, one post-aural, two post-aural, one body-worn, two body-worn, and body-worn with Y-cord. It was decided to note the type of aid sometime after the start of the project, so data are not available for the whole sample. A one-way analysis of variance showed that there were significant differences between the F_1 scores according to hearing-aid category (F5, $180 = 5 \cdot 18$, $P < 0 \cdot 001$). Table XXIII shows the mean F_1 score for each hearing-aid category. Also shown are the mean hearing losses and mean ages for each category.

Table XXIII. Mean F_1 score, mean PTA and mean age according to hearing aid category

Type of hearing aid	Mean F_1 score	Mean PTA (dB ISO)	Mean age (decimal years)	N
Bone conduction	0·68	65·0	14·0	1
One post-aural	0·43	63·5	13·3	52
Two post-aural	0·30	66·5	12·1	21
One body-worn	−0·36	75·2	12·0	51
Two body-worn	−0·47	83·4	11·1	57
Body-worn Y-lead	−0·45	88·0	9·5	4
Error mean square	0·97	230·05	4·47	186

The differences between scores in the first three categories are not significant, and the differences between scores in the last three categories are not significant, but all the differences between the scores in the first three categories and the scores in the last three categories are significant ($P < 0 \cdot 01$). Thus there is a distinct split between post-aural and body-worn aids according to F_1 scores, the body-worn aids being associated with poorer grammatical advancement (with N of only one, the score for the bone-conduction aid is very unreliable). This seems to be a reflection of the effects of degree of hearing loss and age, the tendency having been to fit younger and more severely impaired children with the generally more powerful body-worn aids. Thus, there are significant differences between the mean hearing losses (F5, $180 = 8 \cdot 17$, $P < 0 \cdot 001$) and the mean ages (F5, $180 = 5 \cdot 5$, $P < 0 \cdot 001$) in Table XXIII. There were no significant differences between mean non-verbal I.Q. scores according to hearing-aid category.

K. Multiple correlations

We have now examined the relationships between grammatical advancement, reflected by F_1 score, and the background variables, both interval or ordinal (mean hearing loss, age, non-verbal I.Q., age at onset of impairment, age at diagnosis of impairment, Social Class) and categorical (audiogram pattern, Social Class, sex, aetiology, school, type of school and type of hearing aid). The relationships between the interval or ordinal variables and grammatical advancement are each summarized by a correlation coefficient. These coefficients have not been large, and it has been apparent that taken individually none of the variables is a particularly good predictor of F_1 score. It remains to be seen how much of the variability of the F_1 scores can be accounted for if we regress combinations of the interval variables onto the F_1 scores, and in this subsection we present these multiple correlations. One point that should be noted is that all the multiple correlation coefficients are based on the data from only those 117 subjects for whom complete observations were available. This means that we can examine the effects of adding in each variable one at a time in order to obtain a clear indication of the relative importance of each in explaining the variability in F_1 scores. It also means that the individual correlation coefficients between each variable and F_1 score are not the same as those presented previously, since they are based upon $N = 117$ instead of $N = 263$. However, such differences as there are can be ascribed to sampling error, and there is no reason to believe that the smaller sample is any different from the full sample.

Considering first the three measures of the pure tone audiogram—i.e. average threshold at 500, 1000 and 2000 Hz (PTA); the Risberg and Martony low-frequency audiogram classification (LFAC); and the Risberg and Martony high-frequency audiogram classification (HFAC)—Table XXIV shows the correlations between these, individually and combined, and F_1 score. Individual correlations are represented by r, multiple correlations by R, and R^2 (or r^2) is a measure of the proportion of the total variability accounted for by the variables in the regression. For example, regressing PTA and LFAC onto F_1 gives a multiple correlation (R) or 0·352, and thus these two variables together account for 0·124 ($= R^2$) or about 12% of the total variability of F_1.

It is clear from the figures in Table XXIV that, not unexpectedly, any one of the three measures accounts for nearly as much of the variability in F_1 scores as any other of the measures or as any combination of the measures. To a large extent they are all measuring the same thing, and they are highly or moderately intercorrelated (the correlation between PTA and LFAC is 0·77; between PTA and HFAC is 0·61; between LFAC and HFAC is 0·30). These variables are, therefore, largely overlapping, and the F_1 variability for which any one of them accounts is the same variability that is accounted for by the other variables. Combining LFAC and HFAC gives a significantly

Table XXIV. Individual (r) *and multiple* (R) *correlations between three measures of pure tone hearing loss* (see text) *and* F_1 *score*

Variable(s)	r	r^2	R	R^2
PTA	−0·345	0·119		
LFAC	−0·311	0·096		
HFAC	−0·306	0·094		
PTA+LFAC			0·352	0·124
PTA+HFAC			0·365	0·133
LFAC+HFAC			0·383	0·147
PTA+LFAC+HFAC			0·384	0·148

higher correlation than either of the two measures correlated individually with F_1 ($R=0·383$ as opposed to $r=0·311$ and $r=0·306$). If PTA is included, the addition of either LFAC or HFAC or both gives higher correlations ($R=0·352$, $R=0·365$, $R=0·384$) than PTA alone ($r=0·345$), but none of the increases is significant at $P=0·05$. These figures indicate that there is little advantage to be gained by using the Risberg and Martony classifications of pure tone audiogram rather than simple mean threshold, although as we saw earlier it is perhaps inappropriate to consider LFAC and HFAC separately. If they are not separated, the resulting single variable is categorical rather than ordinal, and we have seen that as such there may be aspects of its relationship with F_1 score which would not be predicted by simple PTA.

Table XXV shows the correlations between PTA, age and non-verbal I.Q., individually and combined, and F_1 score. Each of these variables is strongly associated with F_1 and they are not overlapping. That is, the inclusion of any one of the variables with any other in a multiple regression onto F_1 significantly increases the value of the correlation and the proportion of the total variance accounted for. PTA regressed with non-verbal I.Q. on F_1 gives the largest correlation (0·562), closely followed by PTA with age (0·548). If all three variables are included in the equation, R is increased significantly to a value of 0·668, which accounts for some 45% of the total variance. If all the interval or ordinal variables are included in the regression, R is raised to 0·696 (48% of the total variance), but this is not significantly greater than the coefficient derived from PTA+age+I.Q. (0·668). Clearly, these three variables are the important ones, although as we have noted previously, the apparent unimportance of, for example, age at onset of impairment is due partly to the lack of reliable information about these aspects of the medical history of many of the subjects in our sample, and partly to sampling bias (the age at onset for most subjects was two years or earlier). Nonetheless,

Table XXV. Individual (r) *and multiple* (R) *correlations of PTA, age, and non-verbal I.Q.* (IQ) *with F_1 score, and the multiple correlation when PTA, Age, IQ, LFAC, HFAC, age at onset of hearing impairment, age at diagnosis of hearing impairment and Social Class are regressed with F_1 score*

Variable(s)	r	r^2	R	R^2
PTA	−0·345	0·119		
Age	0·431	0·186		
IQ	0·314	0·099		
PTA + Age			0·548	0·301
PTA + IQ			0·562	0·316
Age + IQ			0·500	0·250
PTA + Age + IQ			0·668	0·447
PTA + Age + IQ + LFAC + HFAC + onset age + diagnosis age + Social Class			0·696	0·484

hearing loss, age, and non-verbal I.Q. appear to be the main determining variables. A recent review by Morris (1978) of the receptive oral language skills of hearing-impaired children reaches similar conclusions, and identifies these three variables as the primary factors influencing the development of the children's receptive language.

In Section V we found, as might be expected, that hearing loss, age and non-verbal I.Q. are all correlated with grammatical advancement in the expected directions. However, in causal terms they by no means uniquely determine the F_1 scores. Other variables which might be expected to influence F_1 scores are shown to do so in a rather weak manner. Thus, age at onset of the hearing-impairment, the delay between onset and diagnosis of the impairment, and Social Class have low correlations with F_1 score, and account for little more of the variability of F_1 scores than can be explained by hearing loss, age and non-verbal I.Q. It is clear that F_1 score is determined by a larger set of variables than those we have explored, even allowing for sampling errors and imprecision in the measures (the Lewis Report (H.M.S.O., 1968) presents and discusses a list of 22 variables which might be expected to affect the linguistic development of hearing-impaired children). Nevertheless, the analyses in this Section of the ordinal and interval variables have enabled us to assess the relative importance of some of the more obvious determinants of grammatical ability in the hearing-impaired child, despite the degree of unexplained variability. Furthermore, the analyses of the relationships between F_1 scores and the categorical variables, many of which are clearly not directly causal, generally show differences in F_1 scores in the expected directions. Despite the "noisy" data, this encourages us to regard F_1 score as a reasonably valid measure of grammatical ability.

VI. Summary

Samples of spoken language were elicited from 263 hearing-impaired children aged from 8–15 years using a picture-description method. Each of these samples was analysed onto a LARSP profile (Crystal *et al.*, 1976), which is essentially a record of the frequencies of occurrence of certain grammatical structures at clause, phrase and word level. These structures are arranged on the profile in such a way as to reflect normal grammatical development, the structures becoming more advanced with age as one moves down the profile. The patterns of the entries on a profile, therefore, can be used as an indication of the degree to which the analysed language sample approaches that expected from a sample of normal language.

In Section II we examined the pattern of the overall profile in which all subjects were grouped onto one profile. Although such an approach conceals important differences between more homogeneous sub-groups of children, it nevertheless provided a useful and informative method for assessing the important differences between the grammatical advancement of the hearing-impaired group and what might be expected from normally-hearing children. To aid this comparison, we administered the picture-description task to a small group of normally-hearing children, and analysed their spoken language samples onto another grouped profile. In contrast to the latter profile, the hearing-impaired profile showed a marked lack of entries at the word level; a lack of entries at the phrase level, the shortfall becoming larger the more advanced the structures; and a shortfall in the more advanced clause level entries, balanced by an increase in the least advanced clause level entries. The hearing-impaired profile reflected not unexpectedly a lack of clause recursion, a lack of clause expansion, and in consequence a lack of development at phrase level. These effects combined to produce much shorter sentences than those used by the normally-hearing children. The overall pattern of the grouped hearing-impaired profile was argued to be deviant, rather than simply retarded, although this is to use the terms in a way rather different from their use by Crystal *et al.* (1976), and is in any case a difficult distinction to make in the face of a dearth of detailed normative data on the grammatical development of the normally-hearing child. In the last part of Section II the grouped profile for the profoundly deaf children ($N = 22$) was separated from that for the partially-hearing children ($N = 241$). It was shown that the overall trends discussed above could not be due simply to the inclusion of the profoundly deaf in the total sample.

In Section III the effects on the LARSP entries of hearing loss, age and non-verbal I.Q., *a priori* the most important determiners of linguistic advancement, were analysed by an analysis of variance. Since there are some 100-odd structures on a profile, the analysis and its interpretation was conducted not on each individual structure but on groups of structures which were summed to give several derived structures (e.g. Stage 2 clauses; Stage 4 phrases). Mean sentence length was also included in this analysis. There were significant effects of the three variables in the expected directions: that is, the more advanced grammatical structures were used less often as hearing loss increased, more often as age increased, and more often as non-verbal I.Q. increased. The only interaction of any importance was that between hearing loss and age, and this provides perhaps the most interesting result in the Chapter. The data showed that for the youngest group of children the use of all but the least advanced of the grammatical structures on the profile decreased with increased hearing loss, whereas for the oldest group of children the performance of those with severe or moderate impairments was no different from the performance of those with mild hearing losses. The 11- to 13-year-old group of children showed an intermediate position. However, the performance levels achieved by the 14- to 15-year-old children were, for many of the derived grammatical structures, well below those achieved by a group of 14- to 15-year-old normally-hearing children of below average non-verbal I.Q.

In Section IV we attempted to reduce the number of linguistic variables on the profile, since it was clear that in practice many of the profile structures were used rarely. It seemed likely that there were only a few structures of importance for regular use, and it might be possible to isolate these. This would simplify analyses at all levels. We were able to reduce the profile variables (structures) from 107 in number to 56. A factor analysis of these 56 variables revealed a single major factor (F_1), which we called grammatical advancement, and which accounted for just over half the total variability of the LARSP data. One important finding from the factor analysis was that further data reductions may be possible, since only a small number of the reduced set (56) of profile structures appeared to discriminate consistently between individuals. These structures were those that possessed high (F_1) factor loadings (and hence large communalities with F_1). It was also noteworthy that mean sentence length (in words) had a correlation of > 0.95 with

F_1, suggesting that this variable may be used in place of or as a summary for F_1 score when, for instance, there is insufficient time available for a full grammatical analysis.

In Section V the relationships between grammatical advancement and the background variables of hearing loss, age and non-verbal I.Q. were further examined, this time treating the three variables as continua rather than using the somewhat arbitrary levels adopted for the analysis in Section III, and using F_1 score as the measure of grammatical advancement. Correlation techniques showed that the three variables were related to F_1 in the expected directions, and, in combination, accounted for some 45% of the variability of F_1 scores. Other variables which might be thought to influence grammatical advancement in important ways (onset age, diagnostic delay, Social Class) were shown to do so only weakly, and when included in a multiple regression with the three major variables accounted for only a further 3% of the inter-subject variability of F_1 score. It appears that a maximum of some 48% of F_1 variability can be accounted for by the ranges of the background variables studied—a figure which may seem disappointingly low for some readers. Indeed, when it is considered that F_1 contains about 54% of the total LARSP variability, we can deduce that the background variables "explain" (account for) only about 26% of the total LARSP variability.

The sometimes rough and ready statistical treatment employed in this Chapter may not always have done justice to the data. However, the grammatical aspects of spoken language are not easy to define or to measure, and it is therefore not surprising that any attempt at such should produce a fair proportion of "random noise" as well as useful information. Some of the results in this Chapter help to answer familiar questions, while others point to useful directions that might be taken by future research. For example, confirmation of the age/hearing loss interaction is needed, including a convincing explanation of the apparent ceiling effect. More normative data on grammatical development are required, and more rigorous attempts to account for the unexplained variability of F_1 scores would be valuable. Chapter 8 discusses these and other possibilities for future research.

References

AUCKLAND, M. (1979). The Audiology Unit, Reading: a pre-school group. *In* "Working with LARSP: Methods and Applications" (D. Crystal, ed.). Edward Arnold, London, UK. (In press.)

BAMFORD, J. M. and BENCH, J. (1979). A grammatical analysis of the speech of partially-hearing children. *In* "Working with LARSP: Methods and Applications" (D. Crystal, ed.). Edward Arnold, London, UK. (In press.)

BLOOM, L. M. (1973). "One Word at a Time: The Use of Single Word Utterances Before Syntax". Mouton, The Hague, Netherlands.

BRANNON, J. B. (1966). The speech production and spoken language of the deaf. *Lang. Speech* **9,** 127–136.

BRANNON, J. B. and MURRY, T. (1966). The spoken syntax of normal, hard-of-hearing and deaf children. *J. Speech Hear. Res.* **9,** 604–610.

BROWN, R. (1973). "A First Language". Harvard University Press, Cambridge, Mass., USA.

CATTELL, R. B. (1952). "Factor Analysis". Harper, New York, USA.

CHILD, D. (1970). "The Essentials of Factor Analysis". Holt, Rinehart and Winston, London, UK.

CHOMSKY, N. (1967). The formal nature of language. *In* "Biological Foundations of Language" (E. H. Lenneberg, ed.), pp. 387–442. John Wiley and Sons, New York and London.

CONRAD, R. (1977a). The reading ability of deaf school-leavers. *Brit. J. Educ. Psychol.* **47,** 138–148.

CONRAD, R. (1977b). Lip-reading by deaf and hearing children. *Brit. J. Educ. Psychol.* **47,** 60–65.

COOPER, R. (1967). The ability of deaf and hearing children to apply morphological rules. *J. Speech Hear. Res.* **10,** 77–86.

CRYSTAL, D., FLETCHER, P. and GARMAN, M. (1976). "The Grammatical Analysis of Language Disability". Edward Arnold, London, UK.

ERBER, N. P. (1974). Pure tone thresholds and word recognition abilities of hearing impaired children. *J. Speech Hear. Res.* **17,** 194–202.

FOWLER, E. F. (1942). A simple method of measuring percentage of capacity for hearing speech. *Arch. Otolarlyng.* **36,** 874–890.

GODA, S. (1964). Spoken syntax of normal, deaf and retarded adolescents. *J. Verb. Learn. Verb. Behav.* **3,** 401–405.

GOODMAN, A. (1965). Reference zero levels for pure-tone audiometer. *ASHA,* **7,** 262–263.

GREEN, D. S. (1972). Pure tone air conduction thresholds. *In* "Handbook of Clinical Audiology" (J. Katz, ed.), pp. 67–86. Williams and Wilkins, Baltimore, USA.

HAGGARD, M. and SUMMERFIELD, Q. (1978). On realizing the multiple possibilities in speech audiometry. Paper presented to meeting of the British Society of Audiology, London, UK.

HAMILTON, P. and OWRID, H. L. (1974). Comparisons of hearing impairment and socio-cultural disadvantage in relation to verbal retardation. *Brit. J. Audiol.* **8,** 27–32.

HARRIS, J. D. (1965). Pure tone acuity and the intelligibility of everyday speech. *J. Acoust. Soc. Amer.* **37,** 824–830.

HINE, W. D. (1970). Verbal ability and partial hearing loss. *Teacher of the Deaf* **75,** 90–100.

H.M.S.O. (1968). "The Education of Deaf Children: The Possible Place of Finger Spelling and Signing". H.M.S.O., London, UK.

JOHN, J. E. J., GEMMILL, J., HOWARTH, N. N., KITZINGER, M., and SYKES, M. (1976). Some factors affecting the intelligibility of deaf children's speech. *In* "Disorders of

Auditory Function, II" (S. D. G. Stephens, ed.), pp. 187–196. Academic Press, London and New York.

KYLE, J. G. (1977). Audiometric analysis as a predictor of speech intelligibility. *Brit. J. Audiol.* **11**, 51–58.

LEE, L. L. (1969). "The Northwestern Syntax Screening Test". Northwestern University Press, Evanston, Illinois, USA.

LEE, L. L. (1974). "Developmental Sentence Analysis: a Grammatical Assessment Procedure for Speech and Language Disorders". Northwestern University Press, Evanston, Illinois, USA.

LENNEBURG, E. H. (1967). "Biological Foundations of Language". John Wiley and Sons, New York and London.

LEONARD, L. B. (1972). What is deviant language? *J. Speech Hear. Disord.* **37**, 427–446.

LINARES-ORAMA, N. and SANDERS, L. J. (1977). Evaluation of syntax in three-year-old Spanish-speaking Puerto Rican children. *J. Speech Hear. Res.* **20**, 350–357.

MAXWELL, A. E. (1977). "Multivariate Analysis in Behavioural Research". Chapman and Hall, London, UK.

McGURK, H. (1976). Hearing lips and seeing voices. *Nature* **264**, No. 5588, 746–748.

McNEILL, D. (1970). "The Acquisition of Language". Harper and Row, New York, USA.

MENYUK, P. (1964). Comparison of grammar of children with functionally deviant and normal speech. *J. Speech Hear. Res.* **7**, 109–121.

MINISTRY OF EDUCATION (1962). Children with impaired hearing. (Circular 10/62) Ministry of Ed., London.

MONTGOMERY, G. W. G. (1967). Analysis of pure tone audiometric responses in relation to speech development in the profoundly deaf. *J. Acoust. Soc. Amer.* **41**, 53–59.

MORAN, M. R. and BYRNE, M. C. (1977). Mastery of verb tense markers by normal and learning-disabled children. *J. Speech Hear. Res.* **20**, 529–542.

MOREHEAD, D. M. and INGRAM, D. (1973). The development of base syntax in normal and linguistically deviant children. *J. Speech Hear. Res.* **16**, 330–352.

MORRIS, T. (1978). Some observations on the part played by oral teaching methods in perpetrating low standards of language achievement in severely and profoundly deaf pupils. *J. Brit. Assn. Teachers of the Deaf* **2**, 130–135.

MYKLEBUST, H. R. (1964). "The Psychology of Deafness". Grune and Stratton, New York and London.

NEWBY, H. A. (1972). "Audiology". Appleton, Century, Crofts, New York, USA.

O'NEILL, J. J. and OYER, H. J. (1973). Aural rehabilitation. *In* "Modern Developments in Audiology" (J. Jerger, ed.), pp. 212–252. Academic Press, London and New York.

OWRID, H. L. (1972). Impaired hearing and knowledge of grammar. Paper presented to XIth International Congress of Audiology, Budapest.

POWER, D. J. and QUIGLEY, S. P. (1973). Deaf children's acquisition of the passive voice. *J. Speech Hear. Res.* **16**, 5–11.

PRESSNELL, L. M. (1973). Hearing-impaired children's comprehension and production of syntax in oral language. *J. Speech Hear. Res.* **16**, 12–21.

QUIGLEY, S. P., SMITH, N. L. and WILBUR, R. B. (1974). Comprehension of relativized sentences by deaf students. *J. Speech Hear. Res.* **17**, 325–341.

RISBERG, A. and MARTONY, J. (1970). A method for the classification of audiograms.

In "International Symposium on Speech Communication Ability and Profound Deafness" (G. Fant, ed.), pp. 135–139. Alexander Graham Bell, Washington, USA.

RNID (1976). "The Harrogate Papers". R.N.I.D., London, UK.

RUSSELL, W. K., QUIGLEY, S. P. and POWER, D. J. (1976). "Linguistics and Deaf Children". Alexander Graham Bell, Washington, USA.

SCHULTZ, M. C. and KRAAT, A. W. (1971). Lack of perceptual reality of the phoneme for hearing handicapped children. *Lang. Speech* **9**, 127–136.

TERVOORT, B. TH. (1970). The understanding of passive sentences by normal and hearing impaired children. *In* "International Symposium on Speech Communication Ability and Profound Deafness" (G. Fant, ed.), pp. 203–208. Alexander Graham Bell, Washington, USA.

TURNER, E. and ROMMETVEIT, R. (1967). The acquisition of sentence voice and reversibility. *Child Develop.* **38**, 649–660.

VERNON, MCKAY (1976). Communication and education of deaf and hard-of-hearing children. *In* "Methods of Communication Currently Used in the Education of Deaf Children", pp. 99–109. R.N.I.D., London, UK.

WESCHLER, D. (1949). "Weschler Intelligence Scale for Children: Manual". Psychol. Corp., New York, USA.

WILBUR, R. G., MONTANELLI, D. S. and QUIGLEY, S. P. (1975). Pronominalization in the language of deaf students. Unpublished manuscript, Institute for Research on Exceptional Children, University of Illinois at Urbana-Champaign. Quoted by Russell *et al.* (1976).

WILCOX, J. and TOBIN, H. (1974). Linguistic performance of hard-of-hearing and normal hearing children. *J. Speech Hear. Res.* **17**, 288–293.

8

Future Work

JOHN BENCH AND JOHN BAMFORD

I. Introduction

This book is concerned, in Part I, with the design, construction and pilot testing of lists of sentences suitable for use in speech audiometry with partially-hearing children, and, in Part II, with a description of the spoken vocabulary and grammar of such children. Although it is complete within its own frame of reference and as such is, we feel, of use to a large number of those who work with hearing-impaired children, the research which we have discussed is by no means complete. Firstly, it remains for us to show by extensive validation and standardization trials that the BKB Sentence Lists for Children meet the aims described in the early chapters of this book. Secondly, it remains for us to consider whether the vocabulary and grammatical data first described in Part II might be of use in preparing further sentences for speech audiometry with children; in particular, it might be possible to construct simple non-declarative sentences for specialist requirements. Thirdly, we need to consider how far the information in Part II of this book has amplified the areas reviewed in Chapters 1 and 2, with a view to considering aspects of future work on the spoken language of hearing-impaired children. These topics are now discussed in turn.

II. Validation and standardization of the BKB Sentence Lists for Children

The pilot test of our BKB Sentence Lists described in Chapter 4 shows that, generally, the lists seem to be of the right order of difficulty, and the work reported in Chapter 5 suggests *inter alia* that the lists are reasonably reliable and that they are for the most part interchangeable. Thus we already have a fair indication that the BKB Sentence Lists meet the criteria for sentence lists suitable for use in speech audiometry as discussed in Chapter 1. However, we feel that such a "fair indication" is not enough, and that in particular we need more evidence to define the range of application and to clarify the role of the BKB Sentence Lists. To obtain this evidence a programme of validation and standardization is required. At the time of writing, we have begun to analyse a large body of data which bear directly on the issues of validation and standardization, and the results of this analysis will be published in the near future. This Chapter is not the place for us to describe in detail the rationale and the procedures which are appropriate for conducting the validation and standardization, nor to give in detail the results of the analysis. However, it does seem appropriate to give the reader the gist of our approach and to indicate the nature of the preliminary results.

Drever (1964) defines the validity of a test as the extent to which it measures what it is intended or purports to measure, which is determined by the correlation between its results and some other criterion of what it was devised to measure. The problem with validation is the choice of the appropriate validating standard against which to compare the test results. In the context of the present study, the question is what other indicator of speech-hearing ability can we use to confirm that scores on the BKB Tests reflect just that? There is, in the final analysis, no completely satisfactory solution to this problem. For example, parents' or teachers' ratings of the children's ability to hear speech are unlikely to provide much more than a very broad categorization into one of, say, five levels of speech-hearing ability. However, on an operational level we would argue that the appropriate validating standards are the existing published sentence lists for speech audiometry, despite our misgivings about them (see Chapter 1), and possibly also one or more of the published word lists (although for reasons discussed in Chapter 1 word lists can only be regarded as a quasi-standard for sentence lists). Thus, using a large number of appropriate listeners (i.e. partially-hearing children), we are in the process of comparing the speech intelligibility curves obtained from the BKB lists with the curves obtained from other published sentence and word lists, and with the curves obtained from other published sentence and word lists when they are rerecorded and spoken by our own speaker. This design will enable us to approach the problem of validation with controls for the effects of different speakers and of diffferent materials. Such features, however, can give only partial control, since in practice it is all but impossible to match for intonation, pausing, etc., in rerecording a given set of speech materials. Additionally, factors such as overall recording level differences will need to be taken into account in the validation work. These aspects have already been discussed in Chapter 5 (Section IV).

A standardized test is one which has a high degree of reliability (see Chapter 5, Section III). The procedures for its administration and scoring should be clearly and unambiguously laid down, its performance norms should be made available, and the user should be given a clear idea of the range of its application. Most of these requirements for standardization have or will be met for the BKB Tests. Performance norms from a group of normally-hearing children have been obtained (see Chapter 5, Section IV), and it remains to analyse the data resulting from the administration of the Standard and Picture-related BKB Tests in several hundred child test sessions. The children who have taken part in this exercise are defined in terms of age, non-verbal I.Q., pure tone hearing loss, educational background, hearing-aid use, parental occupation, medical history and so on. The relationships between these variables and performance on the BKB Tests will be defined.

To date, preliminary analyses of our data suggest rather clearly that the BKB Sentence Lists offer significant advantages over other published sentence lists for testing the hearing ability of hearing-impaired children. These advantages may be expressed in terms of increased sensitivity as shown by lower SIT levels and steeper slopes measured at SIT. They do not seem to be artefacts of speaker or recording level differences. However, these encouraging preliminary findings have yet to be confirmed by an exhaustive analysis of the data.

III. Additional speech audiometric tests

As the reader will be well aware, our main aim in devising the BKB Sentence Lists for Children has been to design interchangeable lists of relatively simple declarative sentences based on the natural vocabulary and grammar of partially-hearing children. Such simple declarative sentences are, we would claim, good examples of naturally-occurring declarative sentences of a type which will be familiar to most hearing-impaired children. However, such children commonly hear not only declarative sentences but other sentence types as well. They are familiar, for example, with questions and commands. Questions and commands are probably unsuitable for tests in which the task is to repeat back, rather than to answer or obey. However, for the child who for various reasons has problems in repeating back a sentence it may be that speech audiometric tests containing only questions and/or commands would provide a viable alternative. Examples might be: "Is that a dog or a cat?"; "Point to the car"; "Draw a circle in the square"; etc. In such cases the type of response required would be a short utterance (the answer), a non-verbal gesture (e.g. pointing), or a simple visual-motor task. The large number of words listed in the vocabularies of Chapter 6 would be more than sufficient for preparing material of this kind. As regards grammar, only a few hints are available from the material described in Chapter 7, since almost all of this material was obtained from descriptive utterances. However, for many purposes only the simpler forms of questions and commands would be required, and since every hearing-impaired child is used to the simpler forms, it should be possible to devise at least simple question and command items from the material which we have collected.

The vocabulary and grammatical data in Chapters 6 and 7 would also provide material suitable for the construction of lists of declarative sentences simpler than the BKB Lists. These might be appropriate for those children whose linguistic skills are such that they find the BKB Lists too advanced. Another obvious possibility would be to use the vocabulary lists in Chapter 6 to construct phonemically-balanced word lists for speech audiometry. The design of the existing word lists leaves something to be desired (e.g. on the grounds of familiarity), and a new set of lists for children might be a valuable addition to existing tests.

The visual dimension of speech perception has yet to find a place in speech audiometry, and it has been suggested to us that there is a need for both word lists and sentence lists which are not only linguistically balanced but balanced for "speech-readability" (lip-readability). Such lists would be appropriate for assessing the speech communication of severely-impaired children who rely to some extent on speech-reading and who cannot cope with the auditory input alone, as in conventional speech audiometric tests. Live-voice presentation might be used for such balanced word or sentence lists, although we would prefer the controlled presentation provided, for example, by video-tape. With this future possibility in mind, some of the BKB Lists were recorded on video-tape as well as on audio-tape in the original recording session.

Finally, a further type of speech audiometric test which might be developed from the data which we have collected involves assessment of the child's ability to demonstrate his knowledge and use of grammar and semantics. Thus, if it were possible to test the child with two kinds of speech audiometric material—one being the BKB Sentences and the second being the key words from these sentences—then any differences in speech audiometric functions arising from the two kinds of material should reflect mainly the child's ability to take advantage of the contextual aspects of the material. Some preliminary work in this area is already being undertaken by our colleague Åse Kowal, using hearing-impaired children attending schools in the Midlands and South-east England. Briefly, the appproach is to assess hearing-impaired children with a wide and known range of psycholinguistic abilities by means of selected BKB Sentence Lists and lists of randomly-ordered key words derived from the same lists. To date the provisional results look promising, and we await the outcome of the project with interest.

IV. Future work on the spoken language of hearing-impaired children

Chapters 6 and 7 have gone some considerable way to providing a full description of the development of the spoken language of hearing-impaired children in their middle- and secondary-school years. Nonetheless, many questions remain to be answered by further controlled research. One point about these Chapters which has not previously been commented upon is the difference between their findings. That is, while it was found in Chapter 7 that hearing loss, age and non-verbal I.Q. showed significant relationships with spoken grammar, and indeed, of the variables studied, appeared to be its major determinants, the effects of these variables on spoken vocabulary were found in Chapter 6 to be more tantalizing than compelling. The explanation for this difference is probably to be found in the differences between the organization and analyses of the data in the two Chapters, rather than in real differences between the factors affecting spoken grammar and spoken vocabulary. In particular, the traditional parts of speech categories which were used in Chapter 6 are too broad and ill-defined in comparison with the finer LARSP profile categories used in Chapter 7. Also, the analyses in Chapter 7, Section III, allowed the removal of individual variation within sub-groups (i.e. cells) of the subject classification matrix. In Chapter 6, on the other hand, the data were available only by whole cell, and not by individual. Hence individual variation within cells could not be estimated, rendering the analysis considerably less sensitive. It is appropriate for us to consider ways in which the data could be organized in order to make the application of relevant statistical techniques more efficient. This is a particular topic for ourselves, since we retain the transcripts of the original utterances, and it is a matter of time and application, therefore, for us to realize a more thorough analysis. This is not to say, of course, that the organization of the vocabulary data as presented in Chapter 6 was inappropriate for our main task—namely, the provision of a pool of vocabulary suited to the construction of lists of test sentences for hearing-impaired children.

As far as the data and analyses in Chapter 7 (grammar) are concerned, there are several pathways that future research might take. The hearing loss/ age interaction needs confirming and elucidating. The underlying reasons for what we have called the ceiling effect—that is, an improvement of grammatical ability only up to a point apparently often well below the performance levels of normally-hearing children—need to be discovered. There is a good case to be made for undertaking longitudinal studies for such research, for as we noted in Chapter 7 we cannot be certain that some of the apparent changes with age are not artificial. Further research on groups we have not tested would provide interesting comparative data—for example, profoundly deaf 14- to 15-year-olds, and 14- to 15-year-olds with only very mild hearing losses (25–40 dB ISO). The factor analysis in Chapter 7 was useful in that it succeeded in reducing the number of variables to be considered, although as it turned out not all the 56 LARSP variables which contribute to Factor One are important. Further simplification may well be possible, while still retaining the predictive power of LARSP for groups of children, and such improvements will be welcomed by those (e.g. speech therapists and teachers) who use the procedure in the clinic or school and who are constrained by the amount of time available for testing. Finally, two areas for future effort can be expected to produce important results. One is the systematic collection of normative data on grammatical development, in particular with regard to the LARSP profile. The other is the recording of "background data" on individuals. In Section V of Chapter 7 we saw that much of the variability of F_1 score (grammatical advancement) remained unexplained, even when all the background variables were included in the regression equation. An important task for future research will be to explain that residual variability, and in all probability a significant portion of it will be due to less than complete medical and educational notes.

To argue that aspects of spoken language (vocabulary or grammar for example) are retarded or deviant then poses the question as to why this should be the case. In the hearing-impaired, the answer need not be as obvious as it first seems. It may not simply be due to the handicap *per se*. Thus it has been argued that over-formal methods of instruction are also contributory, at least at the level of syntax and morphology. This grammatical formalism was commented upon by van Uden (1968), who characterized traditional approaches as "constructivist", in that they take words ("parts of speech") as ingredients, put them together and "bake" them into rote-learned sentences. This results, he feels, in a restricted and inflexible set of internalized linguistic rules, which are manifested in the deviant or retarded performance which we have seen. A more flexible, less structured approach to language teaching is favoured by van Uden, although it is beyond the scope of this book to comment on educational methods. What should be stressed in closing, however, is that the somewhat rigorous structuralist approach to the recording and analysis of the spoken language samples adopted in this book should be interpreted as neither supporting, nor for that matter challenging, particular educational approaches. We know that the language of hearing-impaired children is retarded and also (depending upon one's definition) to some extent deviant. The precise reasons for this, and the degree of its irreversibility, remain to be clearly established.

References

DREVER, J. (1964). "A Dictionary of Psychology". Penguin, Harmondsworth, UK.
VAN UDEN, A. (1968). "A World of Language for Deaf Children. Part I, Basic Principles". Institute for the Deaf, St Michielsgestel, Netherlands.

Appendix 1

The Bamford–Kowal–Bench (BKB) Standard Sentence Lists

ST Sentence List 1

The clown had a funny face.
The car engine's running.
She cut with her knife.
Children like strawberries.
The house had nine rooms.
They're buying some bread.
The green tomatoes are small.
He played with his train.
The postman shut the gate.
They're looking at the clock.
The bag bumps on the ground.
The boy did a handstand.
A cat sits on the bed.
The lorry carried fruit.
The rain came down.
The ice cream was pink.

ST Sentence List 2

The ladder's near the door.
They had a lovely day.
The ball went into the goal.
The old gloves are dirty.
He cut his finger.
The thin dog was hungry.
The boy knew the game.
Snow falls at Christmas.
She's taking her coat.
The police chased the car.
A mouse ran down the hole.
The lady's making a toy.
Some sticks were under the tree.
The little baby sleeps.
They're watching the train.
The school finished early.

ST Sentence List 3

The glass bowl broke.
The dog played with a stick.
The kettle's quite hot.
The farmer keeps a bull.
They say some silly things.
The lady wore a coat.
The children are walking home.
He needed his holiday.
The milk came in a bottle.
The man cleaned his shoes.
They ate the lemon jelly.
The boy's running away.
Father looked at the book.
She drinks from her cup.
The room's getting cold.
A girl kicked the table.

ST Sentence List 4

The wife helped her husband.
The machine was quite noisy.
The old man worries.
A boy ran down the path.
The house had a nice garden.
She spoke to her son.
They're crossing the street.
Lemons grow on trees.
He found his brother.
Some animals sleep on straw.
The jam jar was full.
They're kneeling down.
The girl lost her doll.
The cook's making a cake.
The child grabs the toy.
The mud stuck on his shoe.

ST Sentence List 5

The bath towel was wet.
The matches lie on the shelf.
They're running past the house.
The train had a bad crash.
The kitchen sink's empty.
A boy fell from the window.
She used her spoon.
The park's near the road.
The cook cut some onions.
The dog made an angry noise.
He's washing his face.
Somebody took the money.
The light went out.
They wanted some potatoes.
The naughty girl's shouting.
The cold milk's in a jug.

ST Sentence List 6

The paint dripped on the ground.
The mother stirs the tea.
They laughed at his story.
Men wear long trousers.
The small boy was asleep.
The lady goes to the shop.
The sun melted the snow.
The father's coming home.
She had her pocket money.
The lorry drove up the road.
He's bringing his raincoat.
A sharp knife's dangerous.
They took some food.
The clever girls are reading.
The broom stood in the corner.
The woman tidied her house.

ST Sentence List 7

The children dropped the bag.
The dog came back.
The floor looked clean.
She found her purse.
The fruit lies on the ground.
Mother fetches a saucepan.
They washed in cold water.
The young people are dancing.
The bus went early.
They had two empty bottles.
A ball's bouncing along.
The father forgot the bread.
The girl has a picture book.
The orange was quite sweet.
He's holding his nose.
The new road's on the map.

ST Sentence List 8

The boy forgot his book.
A friend came for lunch.
The match boxes are empty.
He climbed his ladder.
The family bought a house.
The jug stood on the shelf.
The ball broke the window.
They're shopping for cheese.
The pond water's dirty.
They heard a funny noise.
Police are clearing the road.
The bus stopped suddenly.
She writes to her brother.
The footballer lost a boot.
The three girls are listening.
The coat lies on a chair.

ST Sentence List 9

The book tells a story.
The young boy left home.
They're climbing the tree.
She stood near her window.
The table has three legs.
A letter fell on the mat.
The five men are working.
He listens to his father.
The shoes were very dirty.
They went on holiday.
Baby broke his mug.
The lady packed her bag.
The dinner plate's hot.
The train's moving fast.
The child drank some milk.
The car hit a wall.

ST Sentence List 10

A tea towel's by the sink.
The cleaner used a broom.
She looked in her mirror.
The good boy's helping.
They followed the path.
The kitchen clock was wrong.
The dog jumped on the chair.
Someone's crossing the road.
The postman brings a letter.
They're cycling along.
He broke his leg.
The milk was by the front door.
The shirts hang in the cupboard.
The ground was too hard.
The buckets hold water.
The chicken laid some eggs.

ST Sentence List 11

The sweet shop was empty.
The dogs go for a walk.
She's washing her dress.
The lady stayed for tea.
The driver waits by the corner.
They finished the dinner.
The policeman knows the way.
The little girl was happy.
He wore his yellow shirt.
They're coming for Christmas.
The cow gave some milk.
The boy got into bed.
The two farmers are talking.
Mother picked some flowers.
A fish lay on the plate.
The father writes a letter.

ST Sentence List 12

The food cost a lot.
The girl's washing her hair.
The front garden was pretty.
He lost his hat.
The taps are above the sink.
Father paid at the gate.
She's waiting for her bus.
The bread van's coming.
They had some cold meat.
The football game's over.
They carry some shopping bags.
The children help the milkman.
The picture came from a book.
The rice pudding was ready.
The boy had a toy dragon.
A tree fell on the house.

ST Sentence List 13

The fruit came in a box.
The husband brings some flowers.
They're playing in the park.
She argued with her sister.
A man told the police.
Potatoes grow in the ground.
He's cleaning his car.
The mouse found the cheese.
They waited for one hour.
The big dog was dangerous.
The strawberry jam was sweet.
The plant hangs above the door.
The children are all eating.
The boy has black hair.
The mother heard her baby.
The lorry climbed the hill.

ST Sentence List 14

The angry man shouted.
The dog sleeps in a basket.
They're drinking tea.
Mother opens the drawer.
An old woman was at home.
He dropped his money.
They broke all the eggs.
The kitchen window was clean.
The girl plays with the baby.
The big fish got away.
She's helping her friend.
The children washed the plates.
The postman comes early.
The sign showed the way.
The grass is getting long.
The match fell on the floor.

ST Sentence List 15

A man's turning the tap.
The fire was very hot.
He's sucking his thumb.
The shop closed for lunch.
The driver starts the engine.
The boy hurried to school.
Some nice people are coming.
She bumped her head.
They met some friends.
Flowers grow in the garden.
The tiny baby was pretty.
The daughter laid the table.
They walked across the grass.
The mother tied the string.
The train stops at the station.
The puppy plays with a ball.

ST Sentence List 16

The children wave at the train.
Mother cut the Christmas cake.
He closed his eyes.
The raincoat's very wet.
A lady buys some butter.
They called an ambulance.
She's paying for her bread.
The policeman found a dog.
Some men shave in the morning.
The driver lost his way.
They stared at the picture.
The cat drank from a saucer.
The oven door was open.
The car's going too fast.
The silly boy's hiding.
The painter used a brush.

ST Sentence List 17

The apple pie's cooking.
He drinks from his mug.
The sky was very blue.
They knocked on the window.
The big boy kicked the ball.
People are going home.
The baby wants his bottle.
The lady sat on her chair.
They had some jam pudding.
The scissors are quite sharp.
She's calling her daughter.
Some brown leaves fell off the tree.
The milkman carried the cream.
A girl ran along.
The mother reads a paper.
The dog chased the cat.

ST Sentence List 18

The cake shop's opening.
They like orange marmalade.
The mother shut the window.
He's skating with his friend.
The cheese pie was good.
Rain falls from clouds.
She talked to her doll.
They painted the wall.
The towel dropped on the floor.
The dog's eating some meat.
A boy broke the fence.
The yellow pears were lovely.
The police help the driver.
The snow lay on the roof.
The lady washed the shirt.
The cup hangs on a hook.

ST Sentence List 19

The family like fish.
Sugar's very sweet.
The baby lay on a rug.
The washing machine broke.
They're clearing the table.
The cleaner swept the floor.
A grocer sells butter.
The bath water was warm.
He's reaching for his spoon.
She hurt her hand.
The milkman drives a small van.
The boy slipped on the stairs.
They're staying for supper.
The girl held a mirror.
The cup stood on a saucer.
The cows went to market.

ST Sentence List 20

The boy got into trouble.
They're going out.
The football hit the goalpost.
He paid his bill.
The teacloth's quite wet.
A cat jumped off the fence.
The baby has blue eyes.
They sat on a wooden bench.
Mother made some curtains.
The oven's too hot.
The girl caught a cold.
The raincoat's hanging up.
She brushed her hair.
The two children are laughing.
The man tied his scarf.
The flower stands in a pot.

ST Sentence List 21

The pepper pot was empty.
The dog drank from a bowl.
A girl came into the room.
They're pushing an old car.
The cat caught a mouse.
The road goes up a hill.
She made her bed.
Bananas are yellow fruit.
The cow lies on the grass.
The egg cups are on the table.
He frightened his sister.
The cricket team's playing.
The father picked some pears.
The kettle boiled quickly.
The man's painting a sign.
They lost some money.

Appendix 2

The Bamford–Kowal–Bench (BKB) Picture-related Sentence Lists

PR Sentence List 1

Ice

The lady waves her hand.
The big dog's watching.
She wore her coat.

Crash

The girl ran into the road.
The man looks at the ball.
Some fruit fell on the ground.
He has his toy train.

Football

They're by the gate.
A boy's climbing the fence.
The farm's near some trees.

Kitchen

The children made a mess.
The kitchen chair's red.
The woman pays the money.

PR Sentence List 2

Ice

The boy's helping his friend.
They broke the ice.
Men are fetching a ladder.

Crash

He rides his bicycle.
The window cleaner fell.
She's dropping her money.

Football

The sign's near the gate.
The children played football.
The farmer came quickly.

Kitchen

The baby girl's hungry.
A doll sits by the chair.
The shopping bag's green.

PR Sentence List 1—(*Cont.*)

Picnic

Father opened the boot.
The table cloth's yellow.
They're drinking from bottles.

PR Sentence List 3

Ice

The boy fell in the water.
The small girl's cold.
He's wearing his gloves.

Crash

A man came off the ladder.
The brown dog's running.
They're looking down the road.
Some apples lie on the ground.

Football

They stopped the game.
The bull chases the children.
The farmer waves a stick.

Kitchen

The coat hangs on a hook.
Mummy cooked the meat.
The milkman holds a book.

Picnic

The lady brings some food.
The car window was open.
She sits with her son.

PR Sentence List 5

Ice

The two girls are watching.
Snow stopped the ambulance.
They skated on the pond.

PR Sentence List 2—(*Cont.*)

Picnic

The mother walks to the car.
Some plates lie on the table.
They were under a tree.
The woman brings the basket.

PR Sentence List 4

Ice

The child fell into a hole.
The girl's wearing a scarf.
They slide down the hill.

Crash

The car came round the corner.
The man dropped some eggs.
The ladder stands by the wall.

Football

He fetched his ball.
The big bull's dangerous.
They run away.

Kitchen

She's paying her milkman.
A hot dinner's waiting.
The kitchen knife is sharp.

Picnic

Mother holds her basket.
The son has a cricket bat.
The family eats the food.
The boy walked on his hands.

PR Sentence List 6

Ice

The young girls are friends.
The dog stands on the ice.
They're bringing a ladder.

Crash

The people heard the crash.
Some eggs fell on the road.
A lady talks to her friend.

Football

The ball went over the fence.
The big gate's shut.
The boy sees the bull.

Kitchen

He holds his toy.
The sweet jar's full.
She's wearing her mask.
The milkman's on the step.

Picnic

They're playing a game.
The father eats a sandwich.
The family comes home.

Crash

The lady dropped her purse.
People watch the accident.
She shouts from her window.

Football

The fence goes round the field.
The bull is running fast.
The farmer got angry.

Kitchen

The milkman came to the door.
The child wanted some jelly.
A small cat's drinking.
The doll has yellow hair.

Picnic

The car waits by the tree.
They had a nice meal.
He carries his son.

PR Sentence List 7

Ice

The water's very cold.
They called an ambulance.
He crawls towards his friend.
The men run across the snow.

Crash

She played with her ball.
A policeman saw the crash.
The woman wanted some eggs.

Football

The bull's getting near.
The three boys are safe.
The farmer wears a jacket.

Kitchen

The lady fed the cat.
They're in the kitchen.
The broom's behind the door.

PR Sentence List 8

Ice

The thin ice cracked.
The boy's getting wet.
A man brought an ambulance.
The girls stand by the notice.

Crash

He sucks his thumb.
The driver had a bad crash.
The cleaner drops his bucket.

Football

The brown bull was angry.
The farmer shouts at the child.
The blue coats are on the grass.

Kitchen

They have a little cat.
The scissors lie near the chair.
Mother talks to the milkman.

PR Sentence List 7—(*Cont.*)

Picnic

Daddy's driving a car.
The child looks at his book.
The small son's eating.

PR Sentence List 9

Ice

The girl holds her skates.
They're rescuing the child.
The boy has a red nose.

Crash

The dog's getting away.
A flowerpot fell down.
The crash frightened the man.

Football

They climbed into the field.
The three friends are shouting.
The football boots are white.

Kitchen

She played with her doll.
Mother opened the door.
The mask looks very funny.
The clock tells the time.

Picnic

The family goes by car.
He reads from his book.
The father throws a ball.

PR Sentence List 8—(*Cont.*)

Picnic

The father watched his son.
She's taking her basket.
They're walking to the house.

PR Sentence List 10

Ice

The boy's holding a stick.
She watches with her friend.
Some children ride on a sledge.

Crash

The young lady's shopping.
A man's shaving his face.
The car crashes in the street.
The corner shop was open.

Football

They jumped over the fence.
He found his football.
The bull was in the next field.

Kitchen

Mother made some cakes.
They sit on the floor.
The pet cat has some milk.

Picnic

The father wears brown trousers.
The little dog's hungry.
The son reads a story.

PR Sentence List 11

Ice

The boy went through the ice.
Somebody stops the sledge.
The girls look sad.

Crash

She's buying her eggs.
They're watching the crash.
A man cycles along.

Football

The football shirts have numbers.
He turned his head.
The fierce bull's coming.

Kitchen

The kitchen got in a mess.
The toys lie on the floor.
The water bucket's green.
The clock hangs on the wall.

Picnic

The dog sat in the car.
They finished the picnic.
The mother clears the table.

Appendix 3

Mean LARSP Profiles for Children grouped by Hearing Loss, Age and Non-verbal I.Q.

UNANALYSED:

Deviant	Ambiguous
	3.33

Analyser's Comments:
CELL A. N= 6. AGE:= 8-10
HEARING LOSS: 40 - 60 dB
NON-VERBAL I.Q: 90 and below

ANALYSED

Minor "Sentences": Social 1.00	Stereotypes 1.83	Problems

Major "Sentences"

Excl.	Comm.	Quest.	Statement			

0.9 – 1.6

	'V'	'Q'	'V'	'N'	Other	Problems
0.50	0.83	0.17	1.50	4.83		

1.6 – 2.0

	Conn.	Clause		Phrase		Word
VX 0.33	QX 0.33	SV 12.00	VC/O 5.00	DN 53.17	vv 3.33	Inf. 3.33
		S C/O	AX 1.50	Adj N 4.50	v part 12.50	-ing 21.50
				NN 0.50	int x	
		Neg X 0.17	Other	Pr N 2.50	other 0.50	pl. 11.00
						fut. 0.83

2.0 – 2.6

VXY	QXY	X+S:NP 5.33	X+V:VP 7.33	X+C/O:NP 3.00	X+A:AP 0.83	-ed 12.00
let XY	VS	SVC/O 31.33	VC/OA 1.50	D Adj N 3.67	Cop 8.83	-en 1.67
doXY		SVA 9.33	V O$_d$ O$_i$ 0.17	Adj Adj N 0.17	Aux 14.67	3s 9.60
		Neg XY	Other	Pr DN 12.83	Pron 28.67	
				N Adj N	Pr Pron 1.00	
					Other	

2.6 – 3.0

	QXYZ 0.33	XY+S:NP 16.17	XY+V:VP 14.67	XY+C/O:NP 20.83	XY+A:AP 8.33	gen 4.67
+S	QVS 0.50	SVC/OA 6.00	AAXY 1.17	N Pr NP	Neg V 1.00	n't 0.83
		SVO$_d$O$_i$ 0.17	Other	Pr D Adj N 0.83	Neg X 0.17	'cop 4.00
				c X 0.50	2 aux	'aux 5.17
				X c X 5.00	Other 0.17	

3 – 3.6

how	and 16.67	Coord. 1 9.67 1+ 3.67	Postmod. 1 1.17 1+ clause	-est 0.50
		Subord. 1 2.33 1+		-er
what	tag 0.17	c 0.83 Clause: S	Postmod. 1+ phrase	
		s 2.33 Clause: C/O 3.00 Comparative		-ly 0.33
	other	Clause: A 1.17		

3.6 – 4.6

+				–		
NP	VP	Clause		NP	VP	Clause
Initiator 1.50	Complex	Passive		Pron. 17.00 Adj. Seq.	Modal	Concord 1.00
Coord. 0.33		Complement		Det. 1.00 N irreg. 0.17	Tense 0.50	A Position
					V irreg. 0.17	W Order
Other:				Other:		

4.6+

A connectivity: 1.00	Emphatic order:	it: 1.00
Comment clause: 0.17	Other:	there: 3.67

NUMBER OF WORDS IN EACH SENTENCE* $\bar{X} = 6.65$

re sentence means: Any utterance which is neither deviant nor ambiguous, but excluding all Stage 1 utterances.

UNANALYSED:

Deviant	Ambiguous
	2.89

Analyser's Comments:

CELL B. N = 9. AGE := 8 - 10
HEARING LOSS : 61 - 80 dB
NON - VERBAL I.Q = 90 and below

ANALYSED

	Minor "Sentences": Social	1.33		Stereotypes	8.33		Problems	

Major "Sentences"

	Excl.	Comm.	Quest.		Statement				

STAGE 1 (0.9 – 1.6)

		'V'	'Q'	'V'	'N'	Other	Problems
Excl. 0.44	Comm. 0.11	0.22		1.89	9.67	0.78	

STAGE 2 (1.6 – 2.0)

			Conn.	Clause		Phrase		Word
	VX 0.22	QX 0.22		SV 10.56 VC/O 5.22		DN 44.56 vv 4.44		Inf. 3.44
				S C/O 1.11 AX 2.78		Adj N 2.67 v part 10.89		-ing 21.56
				Neg X Other		NN 0.33 int x 0.78		pl. 8.67
						Pr N 3.56 other		fut. 1.33

STAGE 3 (2.0 – 2.6)

		VXY	QXY 1.11	X+S:NP 5.22	X+V:VP 8.33	X+C/O:NP 3.11	X+A:AP 1.56	-ed 3.56
		let XY	VS 0.22	SVC/O 20.78 VC/O A 1.33		D Adj N 3.22 Cop 7.00		-en 1.00
		doXY		SVA 7.78 V O_d O_i		Aux 13.89		3s 9.67
				Neg XY Other 0.11		Adj Adj N 0.67 Pron 21.67		
						Pr DN 8.11 Pr Pron 1.11		gen 2.89
						N Adj N Other 0.11		

STAGE 4 (2.6 – 3.0)

			QXYZ 0.11	XY+S:NP 9.89	XY+V:VP 11.56	XY+C/O:NP 13.00	XY+A:AP 6.22	n't 1.44
		+S	QVS 0.33	SVC/OA 3.78	AAXY 0.67	N Pr NP 0.11 Neg V 1.44		'cop 3.11
				SVO_dO_i 0.33	Other 0.11	Pr D Adj N 0.67 Neg X 0.11		'aux 6.33
						c X 0.67 2 aux 0.11		
						X c X 3.89 Other 0.33		

STAGE 5 (3 – 3.6)

	how			and 9.22	Coord. 1 7.44 1+ 1.00	Postmod. 1 0.33 1+	-est
			tag 0.11	Subord. 1 1.22 1+	clause	
				Clause: S	
	what			c 0.33	Clause: C/O 1.56 Comparative	Postmod. 1+	-er
			s 1.22	phrase	
				other	Clause: A 0.11		-ly 0.22

STAGE 6 (3.6 – 4.6)

	+			−		
	NP	VP	Clause	NP	VP	Clause
	Initiator 0.89	Complex	Passive	Pron. 0.11 Adj. Seq.	Modal 0.11 Tense	Concord A Position
	Coord.		Complement	Det. 0.11 N irreg.	V irreg. 0.22	W Order 0.11
	Other:			Other: 24.78		

STAGE 7 (4.6+)

A connectivity: 0.89		Emphatic order:		it: 0.89
Comment clause: 0.44		Other:		there: 1.89

NUMBER OF WORDS IN EACH SENTENCE* $\overline{X} = 5.35$

*Here sentence means: Any utterance which is neither deviant nor ambiguous, but excluding all Stage 1 utterances.

UNANALYSED:			Analyser's Comments:
Deviant	Ambiguous **2·33**		CELL C N=9 AGE : 8-10 HEARING LOSS: 81 dB AND ABOVE NON-VERBAL I·Q: 90 AND BELOW

ANALYSED

	Minor "Sentences": Social **0·44**				Stereotypes **0·56**			Problems	

				Major	"Sentences"				

	Excl.	Comm.	Quest.		Statement				
0.9 – 1.6		'V'	'Q'	'V'		'N'	Other	Problems	
	0·22	**0·11**	**0·33**	**8·56**		**70·22**	**1·56**		

			Conn.	Clause		Phrase		Word	
1.6 – 2.0		VX	QX		SV **9·89** VC/O **2·89**		DN **13·89** vv **1·11**	Inf. **0·78**	
			0·11		S C/O **3·33** AX		Adj N **1·67** v part **5·67** NN **0·33** int x **0·22**	-ing **8·22**	
					Neg X Other		Pr N **2·11** other	pl. **4·78**	
								fut. **0·44**	

2.0 – 2.6		VXY	QXY	X+S:NP **3·78**	X+V:VP **3·78**	X+C/O :NP **0·78**	X+A:AP **1·22**	-ed **4·44**	
		let XY	VS	SVC/O **6·11**	VC/OA **0·22**	D Adj N **1·44** Cop **3·11** Aux **5·67**		-en **0·44**	
		doXY		SVA **3·33**	V O$_d$ O$_i$	Adj Adj N **1·67** Pron **1·67** Pr DN **3·11** Pr Pron		3s **0·67**	
				Neg XY	Other	N Adj N Other **0·11**			

2.6 – 3.0			QXYZ	XY+S:NP **5·11**	XY+V:VP **3·11**	XY+ C/O:NP **2·67**	XY+A:AP **1·78**	gen **1·00**	
		+S		SVC/OA **1·00**	AAXY	N Pr NP Neg V **0·56** Pr D Adj N **0·11** Neg X **0·11**		n't **0·56**	
			QVS	SVO$_d$O$_i$ **0·11**	Other	c X **0·11** 2 aux **0·22** X c X **1·56** Other		'cop **0·33**	
								'aux **0·22**	

3 – 3.6	how		and **2·33**	Coord. 1 **1·22** 1+ **0·44**		Postmod. 1 **0·11** 1+	clause		
		tag	c **0·11**	Subord. 1 **0·11** 1+				-est	
			s **0·11**	Clause: S		Postmod. 1+	phrase		
	what		other	Clause: C/O **0·33** Comparative				-er	
				Clause: A				-ly	

	+			**—**			
	NP	VP	Clause	NP		VP	Clause
3.6 – 4.6	Initiator	Complex	Passive	Pron.	Adj. Seq.	Modal Tense V irreg.	Concord A Position W Order
	Coord.		Complement	Det.	N irreg. **0·11**		

	Other:			Other: **9**		
4.6+ 7	A connectivity:		Emphatic order:		it:	
	Comment clause:		Other:		there:	

NUMBER OF WORDS IN EACH SENTENCE* $\overline{x}$ = **3·58**

where sentence means: Any utterance which is neither deviant nor ambiguous, but excluding all Stage 1 utterances.

UNANALYSED:

Deviant	Ambiguous
	0·54

Analyser's Comments:

AGE: **8-10**
CELL D N=13 HEARING LOSS: **40-60 dB**
NON-VERBAL I.Q: **91-110**

ANALYSED

Minor "Sentences": Social **0·92**	Stereotypes **0·46**	Problems

Major "Sentences"

		Excl.	Comm.	Quest.	Statement			
STAGE 1 0.9 – 1.6			'V' **0·62**	'Q'	'V' **1·38**	'N' **7·15**	Other	Problems

				Conn.	Clause		Phrase		Word
STAGE 2 1.6 – 2.0		VX **0·54**	QX **0·15**		SV **11·08** VC/O **3·54** S C/O **1·92** AX **3·85** Neg X **0·08** Other		DN **46·38** vv **3·69** Adj N **5·77** v part **12·00** NN **0·85** int x **0·54** Pr N **1·92** other		Inf. **4·77** -ing **25·00** pl. **10·54** fut. **0·69**
STAGE 3 2.0 – 2.6		VXY **0·08** let XY doXY	QXY VS **0·08**		X+S:NP **5·77** X+V:VP **7·77** SVC/O **25·38** VC/OA **0·85** SVA **10·23** V O$_d$O$_i$ **0·15** Neg XY **0·15** Other **0·62**		X+C/O:NP **2·62** X+A:AP **2·15** D Adj N **5·08** Cop **8·15** Aux **18·77** Adj Adj N **0·15** Pron **23·85** Pr DN **12·69** Pr Pron N Adj N Other **0·15**		-ed **14·31** -en **1·31** 3s **9·15** gen **5·15**
STAGE 4 2.6 – 3.0		+S	QXYZ **0·08** QVS		XY+S:NP **15·08** XY+V:VP **14·15** SVC/OA **6·00** SVO$_d$O$_i$ **0·54** Other AAXY **1·46**		XY+C/O:NP **15·08** XY+A:AP **7·54** N Pr NP Neg V **0·85** Pr D Adj N **1·38** Neg X **0·23** c X 2 aux **0·15** X c X **5·62** Other **0·08**		n't **0·69** 'cop **4·92** 'aux **6·77**
STAGE 5 3 – 3.6		how what		tag	and **17·62** c **2·08** s **5·00** other	Coord. 1 **15·62** 1+ **1·77** Subord. 1 **5·00** 1+ Clause: S Clause: C/O **4·62** Comparative Clause: A **3·46**	Postmod. 1 **1·15** 1+ clause Postmod. 1+ phrase		-est -er -ly **0·38**

		+			—		
		NP	VP	Clause	NP	VP	Clause
STAGE 6 3.6 – 4.6		Initiator **1·54** Coord.	Complex	Passive Complement	Pron. **0·62** Adj. Seq. Det. **0·23** N irreg.	Modal **0·08** Tense **1·08** V irreg.	Concord **0·08** A Position **0·08** W Order
		Other:			Other: **11·92**		

STAGE 7 4.6+	A connectivity: **0·77** Comment clause: **0·46**	Emphatic order: Other:	it: **0·62** there: **4·85**

NUMBER OF WORDS IN EACH SENTENCE*

$$\overline{X} = 7·28$$

*Here sentence means: Any utterance which is neither deviant nor ambiguous, but excluding all Stage 1 utterances.

ANALYSED:		Analyser's Comments:
...viant	Ambiguous 0·77	AGE: 8-10 CELL E N=13 HEARING LOSS: 61-80 dB NON-VERBAL I.Q: 91-110

...ALYSED

Minor "Sentences": Social 0·85	Stereotypes 0·15	Problems

Major "Sentences"

	Excl.	Comm.	Quest.	Statement			
0.9 – 1.6	'V' 0·69	'V' 1·69	'Q' 3·15	'V'	'N' 12·15	Other 0·85	Problems

		Conn.	Clause		Phrase		Word
1.6 – 2.0	VX 0·15	QX 0·31	SV 9·92 VC/O 5·85 S C/O 1·85 AX 4·08 Neg X 0·08 Other		DN 42·62 vv 3·31 Adj N 3·77 v part 12·23 NN 0·15 int x 1·77 Pr N 2·23 other 0·08		Inf. 5·08 -ing 21·38 pl. 7·00 fut. 0·38
2.0 – 2.6	VXY 0·08 let XY doXY	QXY 0·15 VS	X+S:NP 5·77 X+V:VP 7·85 X+C/O:NP 2·54 X+A:AP 2·00 SVC/O 24·62 VC/OA 0·69 SVA 9·46 V O$_d$O$_i$ 0·15 Neg XY Other 0·15		D Adj N 5·23 Cop 5·92 Aux 18·77 Adj Adj N Pron 26·00 Pr DN 11·46 Pr Pron 0·85 N Adj N Other		-ed 14·69 -en 1·54 3s 5·00
2.6 – 3.0	+S	QXYZ 0·23 QVS 0·31	XY+S:NP 14·46 XY+V:VP 14·62 XY+C/O:NP 13·54 XY+A:AP 6·15 SVC/OA 4·62 AAXY 1·62 SVO$_d$O$_i$ 0·15 Other 0·31		N Pr NP 0·08 Neg V 2·23 Pr D Adj N 0·69 Neg X 0·38 c X 0·15 2 aux 0·31 X c X 6·38 Other 0·23		gen 5·77 n't 1·46 'cop 2·00 'aux 4·38
3 – 3.6	how what	tag 0·08	and 17·00 c 1·15 s 4·38 other	Coord. 1 13·46 1+ 2·46 Subord. 1 4·31 1+ Clause: S Clause: C/O 4·23 Comparative Clause: A 3·23	Postmod. 1 0·38 1+ 0·08 clause Postmod. 1+ 0·08 phrase		-est 0·08 -er 0·08 -ly 1·0

	+			.	—		
	NP	VP	Clause		NP	VP	Clause
3.6 – 4.6	Initiator 1·54 Coord. 0·23	Complex 0·15	Passive Complement 0·08		Pron. 0·46 Adj. Seq. Det. 0·31 N irreg.	Modal 0·15 Tense 1·54 V irreg.	Concord 0·31 A Position W Order 0·31
	Other:				Other: 19·77		

4.6+	A connectivity: 1·31	Emphatic order:	it: 2·31
	Comment clause: 0·31	Other:	there: 1·08

...MBER OF WORDS IN EACH SENTENCE*

$$\overline{X} = 6·96$$

...e sentence means: Any utterance which is neither deviant nor ambiguous, but excluding all Stage 1 utterances.

UNANALYSED:

Deviant	Ambiguous
	1·53

Analyser's Comments:

AGE: 8–10
CELL F   N = 19   HEARING LOSS: 81 dB and ABOVE
NON-VERBAL I.Q: 91–110

ANALYSED

Minor "Sentences": Social **0·58**   Stereotypes **0·74**   Problems

Major   "Sentences"

	Excl.	Comm.	Quest.	Statement			

STAGE 1 (0.9 – 1.6)

Excl.	Comm. 'V'	Quest. 'Q'	'V'	'N'	Other	Problems
0·63	1·05	0·05	6·42	45·89	1·05	

STAGE 2 (1.6 – 2.0)

	Comm.	Quest.	Conn.	Clause		Phrase		Word
0·05	VX 0·16	QX 0·11		SV 8·42 VC/O 6·21		DN 28·32 vv 3·26		Inf. 2·89
				S C/O 2·00 AX 2·84		Adj N 3·32 v part 8·68		-ing 13·47
						NN 1·95 int x 1·26		pl. 6·37
				Neg X 0·16 Other		Pr N 2·37 other		fut. 1·05

STAGE 3 (2.0 – 2.6)

	Comm.	Quest.		Clause		Phrase		Word
	VXY 0·05	QXY 0·05		X+S:NP 3·53	X+V:VP 4·95	X+C/O:NP 3·21	X+A:AP 1·63	-ed 8·68
	let XY	VS 0·11		SVC/O 14·37 VC/O A 0·58		D Adj N 2·37	Cop 4·54 Aux 7·32	-en 1·05
	doXY			SVA 4·11	V O_d O_i	Adj Adj N 0·05	Pron 12·05	3s 3·84
						Pr DN 6·47	Pr Pron 0·26	
				Neg XY 0·11 Other 0·11		N Adj N	Other 0·26	

STAGE 4 (2.6 – 3.0)

	Comm.	Quest.		Clause		Phrase		Word
		QXYZ		XY+S:NP 7·84	XY+V:VP 6·37	XY+C/O:NP 7·74	XY+A:AP 3·26	gen 3·11
	+S	QVS 0·11		SVC/OA 3·16 AAXY 0·58		N Pr NP	Neg V 1·32	n't 0·95
				SVOd Oi 0·32 Other 0·26		Pr D Adj N 0·42	Neg X	'cop 1·74
						c X 0·21	2 aux 0·05	'aux 1·74
						X c X 2·74	Other 0·26	

STAGE 5 (3 – 3.6)

	Comm.	Quest.	Conn.	Clause		Phrase		Word
	how		and 6·21	Coord. 1 3·68 1+ 1·42		Postmod. 1 1+		
			c 0·53	Subord. 1 1·74 1+		clause 0·53		-est
		tag		Clause: S				
	what		s 2·05	Clause: C/O 1·26 Comparative		Postmod. 1+		-er
			other	Clause: A 1·32		phrase		-ly 0·26

STAGE 6 (3.6 – 4.6)

	+			–			
	NP	VP	Clause	NP		VP	Clause
	Initiator 0·63	Complex	Passive	Pron. 0·05	Adj. Seq.	Modal	Concord 0·5
						Tense 0·01	A Position
	Coord.		Complement	Det. 0·11	N irreg. 0·05	V irreg.	W Order 0·3
	Other:			Other:			

STAGE 7 (4.6+)

A connectivity: 0·53	Emphatic order:	it: 0·74
Comment clause: 0·05	Other:	there: 1·05

NUMBER OF WORDS IN EACH SENTENCE*

$$\overline{X} = 4·09$$

*Here sentence means: Any utterance which is neither deviant nor ambiguous, but excluding all Stage 1 utterances.

NANALYSED:		
eviant	Ambiguous 0·33	

Analyser's Comments:

AGE: 8-10   CELL G   N=3   HEARING LOSS: 40-60 dB
NON-VERBAL I.Q: 111 and ABOVE

NALYSED

	Minor "Sentences": Social 0·33				Stereotypes 0·33		Problems	
			Major "Sentences"					
	Excl.	Comm.	Quest.		Statement			
0.9 – 1.6		'V' 0·33	'Q'	'V' 0·33	'N'	Other		Problems

			Conn.	Clause		Phrase		Word
1.6 – 2.0		VX 0·66	QX	SV 8·67 VC/O 4·33 S C/O 0·33 AX 2·00 Neg X 0·33 Other		DN 56·33 vv 3·67 Adj N 3·33 v part 13·67 NN int x 1·0 Pr N 2·33 other		Inf. 5·00 -ing 22·67 pl. 13·00 fut. 0·33
2.0 – 2.6		VXY 0·33 let XY doXY	QXY VS	X+S:NP 6·67 X+V:VP 9·00 SVC/O 26·00 VC/OA 0·67 SVA 11·67 V O$_d$ O$_i$ Neg XY Other		X+C/O :NP 3·00 X+A:AP 1·67 D Adj N 6·67 Cop 8·33 Aux 16·00 Adj Adj N 1·00 Pron 19·00 Pr DN 16·67 Pr Pron 1·33 N Adj N Other		-ed 30·67 -en 1·67 3s 7·67
2.6 – 3.0		 +S	QXYZ QVS	XY+S:NP 23·00 XY+V:VP 16·00 SVC/OA 5·33 AAXY 2·67 SVO$_d$O$_i$ 1·67 Other		XY+C/O:NP 16·67 XY+A:AP 10·00 N Pr NP Neg V 1·67 Pr D Adj N 2·67 Neg X 0·33 c X 0·67 2 aux X c X 8·00 Other		gen 7·00 n't 1·00 'cop 4·33 'aux 4·67
3 – 3.6	how what		tag	and 26·67 c 2·00 s 8·33 other	Coord. 1 16·00 1+ 6·00 Subord. 1 3·33 1+ Clause: S Clause: C/O 4·33 Comparative Clause: A 2·00	Postmod. 1 0·33 1+ clause Postmod. 1+ phrase 0·33		-est -er -ly 1·33

	+			—		
	NP	VP	Clause	NP	VP	Clause
3.6 – 4.6	Initiator 2·33 Coord.	Complex 0·33	Passive Complement	Pron. Adj. Seq. Det. N irreg. 0·67	Modal Tense V irreg.	Concord A Position W Order
	Other:			Other: 8·67		

4.6+ 7	A connectivity: 2·33	Emphatic order:	it: 1·33
	Comment clause: 0·33	Other:	there: 4·67

NUMBER OF WORDS IN EACH SENTENCE*

$$\overline{X} = 8·57$$

re sentence means: Any utterance which is neither deviant nor ambiguous, but excluding all Stage 1 utterances.

UNANALYSED:

Deviant	Ambiguous 0·17

Analyser's Comments:

CELL H. N=6 AGE: 8-10 HEARING LOSS: 61-80dB
NON·VERBAL I.Q: 111 and ABOVE

ANALYSED

		Minor "Sentences": Social 0·17			Stereotypes		Problems	
		Major	"Sentences"					
	Excl.	Comm.	Quest.			Statement		
STAGE 1 0.9 – 1.6		'V' 1·67	'Q'	'V' 0·17		'N' 0·17	Other 0·17	Problems

			Conn.	Clause		Phrase		Word
STAGE 2 1.6 – 2.0		VX	QX	SV 9·33 S C/O Neg X	VC/O 0·50 AX 2·00 Other	DN 45·67 Adj N 4·33 NN 0·67 Pr N 1·50	vv 3·17 v part 12·17 int x 0·67 other	Inf. 4·50 -ing 25·00 pl. 11·67 fut. 1·00
STAGE 3 2.0 – 2.6		VXY let XY doXY	QXY VS 0·17	X+S:NP 5·17 SVC/O 27·67 SVA 9·67 Neg XY	X+V:VP 6·50 VC/OA 1·17 V O$_d$ O$_i$ Other	X+C/O:NP 1·67 D Adj N 6·00 Adj Adj N 0·17 Pr DN 11·83 N Adj N	X+A:AP 1·67 Cop 5·83 Aux 19·50 Pron 19·17 Pr Pron 1·50 Other 0·33	-ed 14·33 -en 1·00 3s 4·83
STAGE 4 2.6 – 3.0		+S 0·17	QXYZ 0·17 QVS 0·17	XY+S:NP 17·33 SVC/OA 6·83 SVO$_d$O$_i$ 0·67	XY+V:VP 19·17 AAXY 1·50 Other	XY+C/O:NP 15·83 N Pr NP Pr D Adj N 1·50 c X X c X 4·50	XY+A:AP 7·17 Neg V 1·17 Neg X 0·17 2 aux 0·17 Other 0·50	gen 5·17 n't 0·83 'cop 2·50 'aux 4·50
STAGE 5 3 – 3.6		how what		tag	and 4·50 c 1·17 s 2·33 other	Coord. 1 12·67 1+ 1·33 Subord. 1 2·33 1+ 0·83 Clause: S Clause: C/O 4·00 Comparative Clause: A 1·67	Postmod. 1 1+ clause Postmod. 1+ phrase	-est -er 0·17 -ly 0·67

		+			—			
	NP	VP	Clause	NP		VP		Clause
STAGE 6 3.6 – 4.6	Initiator 1·50 Coord.	Complex	Passive Complement	Pron. 0·17 Det.	Adj. Seq. 0·17 N irreg.	Modal 0·17 Tense 0·17 V irreg. 0·17		Concord 0·33 A Position W Order 0·17
	Other:			Other: 9·33				

STAGE 7 4.6+	A connectivity: 1·50 Comment clause:		Emphatic order: Other:	it: 1·50 there: 2·50

NUMBER OF WORDS IN EACH SENTENCE*

$$\bar{X} = 7·36$$

*Here sentence means: Any utterance which is neither deviant nor ambiguous, but excluding all Stage 1 utterances.

UNANALYSED:

Deviant	Ambiguous 2·21

Analyser's Comments:

AGE: 8 - 10
CELL I N=14 HEARING LOSS: 81 dB and ABOVE
NON-VERBAL I.Q: 111 and ABOVE

ANALYSED

Minor "Sentences": Social		Stereotypes 1·21		Problems	
Major "Sentences"					
Excl.	Comm.	Quest.	Statement		

0.9 – 1.6	'V' 0·07	'Q' 0·71	'V' 4·64	'N' 32·36	Other 1·36	Problems

1.6 – 2.0		Conn.	Clause	Phrase	Word
	VX 0·14	QX 0·14	SV 9·29 VC/O 3·43	DN 30·86 vv 1·21	Inf. 1·00
			S C/O 2·50 AX 2·86	Adj N 1·69 v part 7·07	-ing 14·57
			Neg X 0·07 Other	NN 0·14 int x 0·93	pl. 5·50
				Pr N 1·71 other	fut. 0·14

2.0 – 2.6	VXY let XY doXY	QXY VS 0·14	X+S:NP 3·36 X+V:VP 3·14	X+C/O:NP 2·07 X+A:AP 1·64	-ed 5·86
			SVC/O 16·50 VC/OA 0·64	D Adj N 2·86 Cop 3·21 Aux 8·00	-en 1·00
			SVA 4·93 V O_d O_i	Adj Adj N Pron 10·71	3s 2·57
			Neg XY Other 0·14	Pr DN 7·21 Pr Pron 0·43 N Adj N Other	

2.6 – 3.0	+S	QXYZ QVS	XY+S:NP 11·00 XY+V:VP 8·71	XY+C/O:NP 9·29 XY+A:AP 3·07	gen 1·14 n't 0·43
			SVC/OA 1·79 AAXY 0·43	N Pr NP Neg V 0·36	'cop 1·21
			SVO_dO_i 0·43 Other 0·14	Pr D Adj N 0·29 Neg X 0·07 c X 0·07 2 aux X c X 2·57 Other 0·07	'aux 1·43

3 – 3.6	how what	tag 0·14	and 5·93 Coord. 1 3·57 1+ 1·29	Postmod. 1 0·21 1+ clause	-est
		^c 0·43 ^s 0·17 other	Subord. 1 0·71 1+ Clause: S Clause: C/O 1·07 Comparative Clause: A 0·36	Postmod. 1+ phrase	-er 0·07 -ly 0·21

	+			—		
	NP	VP	Clause	NP	VP	Clause
3.6 – 4.6	Initiator 0·07 Coord. 0·29	Complex	Passive Complement	Pron. 0·07 Adj. Seq. Det. 0·21 N irreg. 0·07	Modal Tense 0·07 V irreg.	Concord 0·21 A Position W Order
	Other:			Other: 6·50		

4.6+	A connectivity: 0·43 Comment clause: 0·21	Emphatic order: Other:	it: 0·21 there: 0·50

NUMBER OF WORDS IN EACH SENTENCE*

$$\bar{x} = 4·37$$

*where sentence means: Any utterance which is neither deviant nor ambiguous, but excluding all Stage 1 utterances.

UNANALYSED:

Deviant	Ambiguous
	1·71

Analyser's Comments:

AGE: 11-13
CELL J. N=7 HEARING LOSS: 40·60 dB
NON·VERBAL I.Q: 91 and BELOW

ANALYSED

Minor "Sentences": Social 0·86				Stereotypes 0·43				Problems

				Major "Sentences"					

	Excl.	Comm.	Quest.		Statement				

STAGE 1 (0.9 – 1.6)

Excl. 'V'	Comm. 'V'	Quest. 'Q'	'V'	'N'	Other	Problems
0·43	1·00	0·14	0·14	8·43	0·14	

STAGE 2 (1.6 – 2.0)

		Conn.	Clause		Phrase		Word
VX 0·14	QX 0·14		SV 11·86	VC/O 4·71	DN 38·43	vv 2·86	Inf. 3·43
			S C/O 2·57	AX 2·00	Adj N 2·57	v part 11·00	-ing 17·57
					NN 0·29	int x 1·00	
			Neg X 0·29	Other	Pr N 3·57	other	pl. 10·57
							fut. 0·57

STAGE 3 (2.0 – 2.6)

		Conn.	Clause		Phrase		Word
VXY	QXY		X+S:NP 3·57	X+V:VP 7·57	X+C/O:NP 3·57	X+A:AP 1·43	-ed 12·14
let XY	VS		SVC/O 22·57	VC/OA 2·00	D Adj N 3·57	Cop 5·86	-en 2·14
						Aux 16·14	
do XY			SVA 7·29	V O$_d$ O$_i$ 0·29	Adj Adj N	Pron 23·29	3s 10·00
					Pr DN 9·57	Pr Pron 0·86	
			Neg XY	Other 0·71	N Adj N	Other 1·0	

STAGE 4 (2.6 – 3.0)

		Conn.	Clause		Phrase		Word
	QXYZ		XY+S:NP 15·14	XY+V:VP 1·43	XY+C/O:NP 15·14	XY+A:AP 6·86	gen 5·71
							n't 1·71
+S	QVS		SVC/OA 4·86	AAXY 1·14	N Pr NP	Neg V 1·43	
					Pr D Adj N 1·14	Neg X	'cop 3·86
			SVO$_d$O$_i$ 0·14	Other 0·57	c X 0·29	2 aux 0·14	
					X c X 3·57	Other 0·29	'aux 5·57

STAGE 5 (3 – 3.6)

how		tag	and 9·14	Coord. 1 5·29 1+ 1·57	Postmod. 1 0·71 1+ clause	-est
			c	Subord. 1 2·43 1+		
				Clause: S		-er
what			s 2·43	Clause: C/O 1·86 Comparative	Postmod. 1+ phrase	
			other	Clause: A 2·14		-ly 0·43

STAGE 6 (3.6 – 4.6)

	+			–			
NP	VP	Clause		NP		VP	Clause
Initiator 2·57	Complex	Passive		Pron. 0·14	Adj. Seq. 0·14	Modal	Concord
						Tense 1·00	A Position
Coord. 0·14		Complement		Det. 0·29	N irreg. 0·29	V irreg. 0·29	W Order
Other:				Other: 13·00			

STAGE 7 (4.6+)

A connectivity: 0·43	Emphatic order:	it: 1·57
Comment clause: 0·14	Other:	there: 1·29

NUMBER OF WORDS IN EACH SENTENCE*

$$\overline{X} = 6.84$$

*Here sentence means: Any utterance which is neither deviant nor ambiguous, but excluding all Stage 1 utterances.

ANALYSED:

viant	Ambiguous
	2·43

Analyser's Comments:

AGE: 11-13
CELL K.N=14. HEARING LOSS: 61-80 dB
NON-VERBAL I.Q: 90 and BELOW

ALYSED

| Minor "Sentences": Social **0·21** | | Stereotypes **0·14** | | | Problems | |

| Major | | | "Sentences" | | | |

| Excl. | Comm. | Quest. | Statement | | | |

0.9 – 1.6

	'V'	'Q'	'V'	'N'	Other	Problems
0·43	**0·50**	**0·14**	**1·93**	**10·00**	**0·21**	

1.6 – 2.0

	Conn.	Clause		Phrase		Word
VX **0·50**	QX **0·07**	SV **9·71**	VC/O **3·93**	DN **43·71**	vv **3·64**	Inf. **3·29**
		S C/O **1·29**	AX **2·07**	Adj N **0·14**	v part **12·43**	-ing **22·14**
				NN **0·43**	int x **0·93**	pl. **7·36**
		Neg X **0·07**	Other	Pr N **3·64**	other	fut. **0·79**

2.0 – 2.6

	VXY **0·07**	QXY **0·07**	X+S:NP **5·36**	X+V:VP **8·14**	X+C/O:NP **3·14**	X+A:AP **1·86**	-ed **12·14**
	let XY	VS **0·07**	SVC/O **22·43**	VC/OA **1·71**	D Adj N **4·64**	Cop **5·36**	-en **1·71**
	doXY		SVA **8·71**	V O$_d$ O$_i$ **0·07**	Aux **16·79**		3s **5·79**
					Adj Adj N **0·07**	Pron **21·93**	
					Pr DN **8·57**	Pr Pron **1·07**	
		Neg XY **0·07**	Other **0·21**	N Adj N	Other **0·07**	gen **3·21**

2.6 – 3.0

		QXYZ **0·07**	XY+S:NP **14·14**	XY+V:VP **14·86**	XY+C/O:NP **12·71**	XY+A:AP **7·00**	n't **0·71**
	+S	QVS **0·21**	SVC/OA **1·57**	AAXY **0·86**	N Pr NP **0·07**	Neg V **1·36**	'cop **2·29**
			SVO$_d$O$_i$ **0·36**	Other	Pr D Adj N **0·29**	Neg X	'aux **5·14**
					c X **0·64**	2 aux **0·36**	
					X c X **3·43**	Other **0·07**	

3 – 3.6

	how		and **9·71**	Coord. 1 **6·64** 1+ **1·36**	Postmod. 1 **0·43** 1+ clause	-est
		tag	c **0·29**	Subord. 1 **1·79** 1+		-er
	what		s **1·93**	Clause: S	Postmod. 1+ phrase	-ly **0·43**
			other	Clause: C/O **1·86** Comparative		
				Clause: A **1·36**		

+			—		
NP	VP	Clause	NP	VP	Clause

3.6 – 4.6

NP	VP	Clause	NP	VP	Clause
Initiator **1·36**	Complex	Passive	Pron. **0·29** Adj. Seq.	Modal **0·07**	Concord
				Tense **0·57**	A Position
Coord.		Complement	Det. **0·36** N irreg. **0·29**	V irreg.	W Order

| Other: | | | Other: **24·93** | | |

4.6+

A connectivity: **1·64**	Emphatic order:	it: **1·07**
Comment clause: **0·14**	Other:	there: **0·79**

MBER OF WORDS IN EACH SENTENCE*

$$\overline{X} = 6·01$$

re sentence means: Any utterance which is neither deviant nor ambiguous, but excluding all Stage 1 utterances.

UNANALYSED:

Deviant	Ambiguous
0·14	2·00

Analyser's Comments:

AGE: 11-13
CELL L. N=7. HEARING LOSS: 81 dB and ABOVE
NON-VERBAL I.Q: 90 and BELOW

ANALYSED

Minor "Sentences": Social **0·71**   Stereotypes **0·43**   Problems

Major "Sentences"

	Excl.	Comm.	Quest.	Statement			
STAGE 1 0.9 – 1.6	0·29	'V'	'Q' 0·29	'V' 4·00	'N' 20·00	Other 0·43	Problems

STAGE 2 (1.6 – 2.0)

	Conn.	Clause		Phrase		Word
VX 1·14	QX 0·14		SV **8·29** VC/O **3·71**	DN **38·57** vv **1·00**		Inf. 0·71
			S C/O 1·29 AX **2·14**	Adj N 1·57 v part **5·71**		-ing **9·14**
			Neg X 0·29 Other	NN 1·29 int x 1·71		pl. **8·29**
				Pr N 2·29 other		fut. 1·57

STAGE 3 (2.0 – 2.6)

		Clause		Phrase		Word
VXY	QXY	X+S:NP **2·43**	X+V:VP **4·86**	X+C/O:NP **3·14**	X+A:AP 1·29	-ed 6·14
let XY		SVC/O **17·86** VC/OA 0·86	D Adj N 1·29	Cop **2·14** Aux **6·57**		-en 0·71
doXY	VS 0·29	SVA **7·86** V O_d O_i 0·14	Adj Adj N	Pron **12·43**		3s **5·14**
		Neg XY 0·14 Other	Pr DN **5·86** Pr Pron 0·29			
			N Adj N Other 0·14			

STAGE 4 (2.6 – 3.0)

		Clause		Phrase		Word
	QXYZ	XY+S:NP **12·71**	XY+V:VP **5·14**	XY+C/O:NP **11·00**	XY+A:AP **6·14**	gen 1·57
+S		SVC/OA 1·00 AAXY 0·29	N Pr NP	Neg V 0·43		n't 0·43
	QVS	SVO_dO_i Other 0·29	Pr D Adj N 0·43 Neg X			'cop 0·57
			c X 0·43 2 aux			'aux 1·00
			X c X **2·14** Other			

STAGE 5 (3 – 3.6)

			Conn.	Clause	Phrase	Word
how			and **5·43**	Coord. 1 **3·71** 1+ **0·71**	Postmod. 1 **0·14** 1+ clause	
		tag	c	Subord. 1 0·86 1+		-est
			s 0·86	Clause: S	Postmod. 1+ phrase	-er 0 29
what			other	Clause: C/O 1·86 Comparative		-ly
				Clause: A 0·29 0·14		

STAGE 6 (3.6 – 4.6)

	+			–		
	NP	VP	Clause	NP	VP	Clause
	Initiator **1·43**	Complex	Passive	Pron. Adj. Seq.	Modal Tense	Concord 0·14 A Position 0·14
	Coord.		Complement	Det. N irreg. **1·00**	V irreg.	W Order 0·7
	Other:			Other: **27·00**		

STAGE 7 (4.6+)

A connectivity: 0·29	Emphatic order:	it: 0·57
Comment clause: 0·14	Other:	there:

NUMBER OF WORDS IN EACH SENTENCE*

$$\overline{X} = 4·82$$

*Here sentence means: Any utterance which is neither deviant nor ambiguous, but excluding all Stage 1 utterances.

UNANALYSED:

Deviant	Ambiguous 0·4

Analyser's Comments:

AGE: 11-13
CELL M. N=10. HEARING LOSS: 40-60 dB
NON-VERBAL I.Q: 91-110

ANALYSED

Minor "Sentences": Social **1·00**	Stereotypes **0·10**	Problems

		Major	"Sentences"		

Excl.	Comm.	Quest.	Statement		

STAGE I 0.9 – 1.6

Excl.	Comm. 'V'	Quest. 'Q'	'V'	'N'	Other	Problems
0·10	0·60		0·20	0·60		

STAGE 2 1.6 – 2.0

		Conn.	Clause		Phrase		Word
	VX	QX	SV **8·0** VC/O **3·8**		DN **50·80** vv **5·00**		Inf. **6·10**
			S C/O **0·20** AX **2·30**		Adj N **5·50** v part **15·70**		-ing **28·30**
			Neg X Other		NN **0·90** int x **1·30**		pl. **11·80**
					Pr N **3·00** other **0·10**		fut. **0·80**

STAGE 3 2.0 – 2.6

	VXY	QXY	X+S:NP **5·30**	X+V:VP **8·20**	X+C/O:NP **3·10**	X+A:AP **1·80**	-ed **17·50**
	let XY	VS	SVC/O **29·50** VC/OA **1·70**		D Adj N **7·40**	Cop **8·80** Aux **22·80**	-en **2·60**
	doXY		SVA **9·40** V O_d O_i **0·30**		Adj Adj N **0·70** Pr DN **14·20**	Pr Pron **27·90** Pr Pron **2·10**	3s **12·30**
			Neg XY Other **0·70**		N Adj N	Other **0·20**	

STAGE 4 2.6 – 3.0

		QXYZ	XY+S:NP **19·30**	XY+V:VP **21·40**	XY+C/O:NP **19·90**	XY+A:AP **8·20**	gen **11·30**
	+S	QVS	SVC/OA **7·50**	AAXY **2·00**	N Pr NP **0·10** Neg V **1·60**		n't **1·30**
			SVO_dO_i **0·90**	Other **0·70**	Pr D Adj N **2·40** Neg X **0·60**		'cop **3·40**
					c X **0·80** 2 aux **1·10**		
					X c X **6·20** Other **0·60**		'aux **9·80**

STAGE 5 3 – 3.6

	how		and **24·10**	Coord. 1 **17·00** 1+ **3·70**	Postmod. 1 **1·60** 1+ clause		-est **0·70**
		tag	c **0·50**	Subord. 1 **6·20** 1+			
	what		s **6·20**	Clause: S **0·10**	Postmod. 1+ phrase		-er
			other	Clause: C/O **3·80** Comparative			-ly **1·40**
				Clause: A **4·10**			

STAGE 6 3.6 – 4.6

	+			—		
NP	VP	Clause	NP		VP	Clause
Initiator **1·40**	Complex **0·20**	Passive	Pron. **1·10** Adj. Seq. **0·10**		Modal Tense **0·70**	Concord **0·30** A Position
Coord. **0·10**		Complement	Det. **0·50** N irreg.		V irreg.	W Order
Other:			Other: **10·70**			

STAGE 7 4.6+

A connectivity: **1·20**	Emphatic order:	it: **1·80**
Comment clause: **0·50**	Other:	there: **3·10**

NUMBER OF WORDS IN EACH SENTENCE*

$$\overline{X} = 9·27$$

*Here sentence means: Any utterance which is neither deviant nor ambiguous, but excluding all Stage 1 utterances.

UNANALYSED:

Deviant	Ambiguous
	2·57

Analyser's Comments:

CELL N. N=14.　AGE: 11-13
　　　　　　　HEARING LOSS: 61-80 dB
　　　　　　　NON-VERBAL I.Q: 91-110

ANALYSED

| Minor "Sentences": Social 1·00 | | Stereotypes 0·21 | | Problems | |

Major "Sentences"

	Excl.	Comm.	Quest.	Statement			

STAGE 1 (0.9 – 1.6)

	Excl.	Comm. 'V'	Quest. 'Q'	'V'	'N'	Other	Problems
	0·71	1·14	0·14	1·86	6·79	0·43	

STAGE 2 (1.6 – 2.0)

		Conn.	Clause		Phrase		Word
VX 0·43	QX		SV 8·79	VC/O 3·00	DN 43·28	vv 3·07	Inf. 4·36
			S C/O 0·64	AX 2·36	Adj N 4·21	v part 13·50	-ing 22·50
			Neg X 0·07	Other	NN 0·93	int x 1·93	pl. 11·21
					Pr N 2·43	other 0·07	fut. 0·79

STAGE 3 (2.0 – 2.6)

VXY	QXY	X+S:NP 5·14	X+V:VP 8·07	X+C/O:NP 2·07	X+A:AP 1·07	-ed 12·79
let XY	VS 0·07	SVC/O 25·64	VC/OA 1·36	D Adj N 5·86 / Cop 5·86		-en 2·86
doXY		SVA 9·86	V Od Oi	Adj Adj N 0·71 / Aux 23·00		3s 7·07
		Neg XY	Other 0·14	Pr DN 15·07 / Pron 21·86	Pr Pron 1·00	
				N Adj N	Other 0·21	gen 5·21

STAGE 4 (2.6 – 3.0)

	QXYZ	XY+S:NP 17·29	XY+V:VP 16·29	XY+C/O:NP 17·36	XY+A:AP 7·93	n't 1·36
+S	QVS 0·21	SVC/OA 6·71	AAXY 1·64	N Pr NP / Pr D Adj N 1·07	Neg V 1·29 / Neg X 0·21	'cop 2·14
		SVOdOi 0·50	Other 0·14	c X 0·29 / X c X 4·93	2 aux 0·29 / Other 0·36	'aux 5·14

STAGE 5 (3 – 3.6)

how		and 16·29	Coord. 1 12·00 1+ 2·86	Postmod. 1 11·29 1+ 0·07 clause	-est 0·29
	tag	c 2·00	Subord. 1 4·00 1+		
		s 4·43	Clause: S 0·07	Postmod. 1+ 0·14 phrase	-er 0·29
what		other	Clause: C/O 4·29 Comparative		-ly 0·71
			Clause: A 2·93		

	+			—		

STAGE 6 (3.6 – 4.6)

	NP	VP	Clause	NP	VP	Clause
	Initiator 1·00	Complex	Passive	Pron. 0·43　Adj. Seq.	Modal	Concord 0·29
	Coord.				Tense 0·71	A Position
			Complement	Det. 0·43　N irreg. 0·07	V irreg. 0·21	W Order 0·21
	Other:			Other: 12·00		

STAGE 7 (4.6+)

A connectivity: 0·93	Emphatic order:	it: 1·79
Comment clause:	Other:	there: 2·36

NUMBER OF WORDS IN EACH SENTENCE*

$$\overline{X} = 7·92$$

*Here sentence means: Any utterance which is neither deviant nor ambiguous, but excluding all Stage 1 utterances.

UNANALYSED:

Deviant	Ambiguous
	1·00

Analyser's Comments:

AGE: 11-13
CELL O. N=12 HEARING LOSS: 81 dB and ABOVE
NON-VERBAL I.Q: 91-110

ANALYSED

		Minor "Sentences": Social		Stereotypes		Problems	
		Major		"Sentences"			
		Excl.	Comm.	Quest.		Statement	

Stage 1 (0.9 – 1.6)

	'V'	'Q'	'V'	'N'	Other	Problems
	0·67		3·25	12·50	0·58	

Stage 2 (1.6 – 2.0)

	VX	QX	Conn.	Clause		Phrase		Word
0·08	0·42			SV 9·17 VC/O 3·00		DN 40·00 vv 2·00		Inf. 2·67
				S C/O 1·00 AX 2·33		Adj N 5·50 v part 8·58		-ing 13·33
						NN 0·92 int x 1·17		pl. 8·58
				Neg X 0·08 Other 0·08		Pr N 2·17 other		fut. 1·83

Stage 3 (2.0 – 2.6)

	VXY	QXY	X+S:NP	X+V:VP	X+C/O :NP	X+A:AP	
			5·50	4·58	2·50	1·67	-ed 12·75
	let XY	QXY / VS	SVC/O 22·83 VC/O A 0·42		D Adj N 4·42 Cop 3·08 Aux 13·42		-en 2·17
	doXY		SVA 7·33 V O_d O_i		Adj Adj N 0·17 Pron 14·25 Pr DN 10·17 Pr Pron 0·75		3s 5·00
			Neg XY	Other 0·25	N Adj N	Other 0·58	

Stage 4 (2.6 – 3.0)

		QXYZ	XY+S:NP	XY+V:VP	XY+ C/O:NP	XY+A:AP	gen 3·42
			16·17	11·33	12·67	5·33	n't 1·42
	+S	QVS	SVC/OA 5·33	AAXY 0·58	N Pr NP 0·17 Neg V 1·67 Pr D Adj N 0·92 Neg X 0·08		'cop 1·33
			SVO_dO_i 0·50	Other 0·17	c X 0·33 2 aux 0·33 X c X 4·92 Other 0·17		'aux 2·92

Stage 5 (3 – 3.6)

	how		and 11·25	Coord. 1 8·92 1+ 1·58	Postmod. 10·92 1+ clause		-est 0·17
		tag	c 0·92	Subord. 1 1·83 1+			-er 0·08
	what		s 1·58	Clause: S 0·08 Clause: C/O 2·50 Comparative	Postmod. 1+ phrase 0·25		-ly 0·42
			other 0·25	Clause: A 0·67			

Stage 6 (3.6 – 4.6)

	+			—			
NP	VP	Clause		NP	VP	Clause	
Initiator 0·83	Complex 0·08	Passive		Pron. 0·08 Adj. Seq. 0·08	Modal Tense 0·50	Concord 0·17 A Position	
Coord.		Complement 0·17		Det. 0·25 N irreg. 0·17	V irreg.	W Order 0·33	
Other:				Other: 11·50			

Stage 7 (4.6+)

A connectivity: 1·08	Emphatic order:	it: 1·00
Comment clause:	Other:	there: 1·75

NUMBER OF WORDS IN EACH SENTENCE*

$$\bar{X} = 6·56$$

*Here sentence means: Any utterance which is neither deviant nor ambiguous, but excluding all Stage 1 utterances.

UNANALYSED:

Deviant	Ambiguous

Analyser's Comments:

CELL P. N=6 AGE: 11-13   HEARING LOSS: 40-60 dB
NON-VERBAL I.Q: 111 and ABOVE

ANALYSED

				Minor "Sentences": Social **0·50**		Stereotypes		Problems	

Major "Sentences"

		Excl.	Comm.	Quest.		Statement			
STAGE 1 0.9 – 1.6		**0·33**	'V' **0·67**	'Q'	'V' **0·33**		'N'	Other	Problems

				Conn.	Clause		Phrase		Word
STAGE 2 1.6 – 2.0		VX	QX		SV **7·00** VC/O **3·00**		DN **45·17** vv **8·67**		Inf. **6·00**
					S C/O AX **1·17**		Adj N **5·33** v part **13·83**		-ing **27·6**
							NN int x **0·33**		pl. **35·33**
					Neg X **0·17** Other		Pr N **2·33** other		
									fut. **11·33**

			VXY	QXY **0·17**	X+S:NP **5·67** X+V:VP **7·00**		X+C/O:NP X+A:AP		-ed **10·67**
STAGE 3 2.0 – 2.6			let XY VS		SVC/O **21·67** VC/OA **1·50**		D Adj N **9·83** Cop **14·17**		-en **5·83**
			doXY		SVA **9·00** V O$_d$ O$_i$ **0·17**		Adj Adj N **0·33** Aux **24·17**		3s **4·33**
							Pr DN **22·67** Pron **19·67**		
					Neg XY Other		N Adj N Pr Pron **0·83**		
							Other **0·50**		

				QXYZ	XY+S:NP **18·00** XY+V:VP **19·00**		XY+C/O:NP **15·17** XY+A:AP **9·17**		gen **8·67**
STAGE 4 2.6 – 3.0			+S	QVS	SVC/OA **9·50** AAXY **3·33**		N Pr NP Neg V **1·50**		n't **4·83**
							Pr D Adj N **3·00** Neg X **0·33**		'cop **1·67**
					SVO$_d$O$_i$ **0·17** Other **0·83**		c X **0·50** 2 aux **0·17**		
							X c X **8·17** Other **0·83**		'aux **4·33**

		how		and **16·5**	Coord. 1 **13·83** 1+ **1·83**		Postmod. 1 **3·33** 1+		
STAGE 5 3 – 3.6			tag	c **1·50**	Subord. 1 **5·33** 1+		clause		-est **3·50**
		what		s **5·33**	Clause: S **0·17**		Postmod. 1+		-er **0·83**
				other	Clause: C/O **4·00** Comparative		phrase		-ly **0·83**
					Clause: A **3·00**				

			+			—			
		NP	VP	Clause	NP		VP		Clause
STAGE 6 3.6 – 4.6		Initiator **0·50**	Complex	Passive	Pron.	Adj. Seq.	Modal Tense **0·33**		Concord A Position
		Coord.		Complement	Det. **0·33**	N irreg.	V irreg.		W Order **0·17**
		Other:			Other: **7·67**				

STAGE 7 4.6+	A connectivity: **0·33**		Emphatic order:		it: **0·83**
	Comment clause: **0·83**		Other:		there: **7·83**

NUMBER OF WORDS IN EACH SENTENCE*

$$\overline{X} = 9·50$$

*Here sentence means: Any utterance which is neither deviant nor ambiguous, but excluding all Stage 1 utterances.

UNANALYSED:

Deviant	Ambiguous 0·35

Analyser's Comments:

CELL Q. N=17 AGE: 11-13 HEARING LOSS: 61-80 dB NON-VERBAL I.Q: 111 and ABOVE

ANALYSED

Minor "Sentences": Social **5·96**	Stereotypes	Problems

Major "Sentences"

	Excl.	Comm.	Quest.	Statement			

0.9 – 1.6

	Excl.	Comm.	Quest.	'V'	'N'	Other	Problems
	0·12	'V' 0·06	'Q' 0·12	0·71	1·24		

1.6 – 2.0

		Conn.	Clause		Phrase		Word
	VX 0·06	QX 0·24	SV **8·82** S C/O 0·29 Neg X 0·06	VC/O **3·59** AX 2·06 Other	DN **42·35** Adj N **4·24** NN 0·76 Pr N **4·65**	vv **7·71** v part **13·18** int x **1·88** other	Inf. 6·53 -ing **24·47** pl. 10·65 fut. 1·53

2.0 – 2.6

| | VXY let XY doXY | QXY VS 0·24 | X+S:NP **3·82** SVC/O **25·76** SVA **10·53** Neg XY | X+V:VP **8·24** VC/OA 2·29 V O$_d$O$_i$ 0·18 Other 0·29 | X+C/O:NP 2·29 D Adj N **7·47** Adj Adj N 0·12 Pr DN **18·41** N Adj N | X+A:AP **1·71** Cop 10·06 Aux **26·24** Pron **33·47** Pr Pron 2·00 Other 0·41 | -ed **13·47** -en **4·82** 3s 10·24 |

2.6 – 3.0

| | +S | QXYZ 0·35 QVS 0·29 | XY+S:NP **15·41** SVC/OA **10·24** SVO$_d$O$_i$ **0·53** | XY+V:VP **19·41** AAXY 2·29 Other 0·29 | XY+C/O:NP **15·0** N Pr NP 0·18 Pr D Adj N **1·94** c X 0·35 X c X **5·94** | XY+A:AP **8·29** Neg V 2·88 Neg X 0·53 2 aux 2·06 Other 0·59 | gen **5·88** n't 2·59 'cop 4·88 'aux 9·06 |

3 – 3.6

| | how what | and **15·76** tag 0·06 other | c **3·35** s **7·12** | Coord. 1 **10·65** 1+ **3·53** Subord. 1 **7·82** 1+ Clause: S 0·12 Clause: C/O **4·4** Clause: A **4·88** | | Comparative | Postmod. 1 **11·82** 1+ 0·06 clause Postmod. 1+ 0·18 phrase | -est 0·41 -er 1·00 -ly **1·47** |

+			—		
NP	VP	Clause	NP	VP	Clause

3.6 – 4.6

NP	VP	Clause	NP	VP	Clause
Initiator **1·12** Coord. **0·47**	Complex	Passive Complement 0·06	Pron. 0·06 Adj. Seq. 0·06 Det. 0·12 N irreg.	Modal 0·06 Tense 0·29 V irreg. 0·06	Concord 0·35 A Position W Order 0·18
Other:			Other: **8·06**		

4.6+ / 7

A connectivity: 1·82	Emphatic order:	it: 2·06
Comment clause: 0·82	Other:	there: 3·06

NUMBER OF WORDS IN EACH SENTENCE*

$$\overline{X} = 9.44$$

*where sentence means: Any utterance which is neither deviant nor ambiguous, but excluding all Stage 1 utterances.

UNANALYSED:

Deviant	Ambiguous
	1·00

Analyser's Comments:

CELL R N=19   AGE: 11-13   HEARING LOSS: 81 dB and ABOVE
NON-VERBAL I.Q: 111 and ABOVE

ANALYSED

				Minor "Sentences": Social 2·24			Stereotypes 0·35		Problems		

						Major "Sentences"					

		Excl.	Comm.	Quest.			Statement				

STAGE 1 (0.9 – 1.6)

	Excl.	Comm.	Quest.	'V'	'N'	Other	Problems
	0·41	0·35	0·06	1·18	3·94	0·06	

STAGE 2 (1.6 – 2.0)

			Conn.	Clause		Phrase		Word
	VX	QX		SV 12·06	VC/O 2·53	DN 48·35	vv 3·71	Inf. 5·65
	0·12	0·06		S C/O 0·41	AX 1·65	Adj N 5·29	v part 15·82	-ing 23·53
				Neg X 0·06	Other	NN 0·76	int x 2·41	pl. 12·88
						Pr N 2·71	other	
								fut. 1·53

STAGE 3 (2.0 – 2.6)

	VXY	QXY 0·06	X+S:NP 5·35	X+V:VP 9·65	X+C/O :NP 2·00	X+A:AP 1·18	-ed 16·88
	let XY	VS	SVC/O 32·41	VC/OA 0·71	D Adj N 8·65	Cop 10·29	-en 9·94
	doXY	0·06	SVA 12·35	V O_d O_i 0·06	Adj Adj N 1·06	Aux 24·53 Pron 27·29	3s 11·47
			Neg XY 0·06	Other 0·02	Pr DN 7·47 N Adj N	Pr Pron 2·53 Other 0·53	

STAGE 4 (2.6 – 3.0)

		QXYZ 0·06	XY+S:NP 18·88	XY+V:VP 20·41	XY+ C/O:NP 18·53	XY+A:AP 9·59	gen 4·82
	+S	QVS	SVC/OA 7·53	AAXY 2·06	N Pr NP 0·41	Neg V 2·41	n't 1·88
		0·06	SVO_dO_i 0·41	Other 0·18	Pr D Adj N 2·00 c X 0·35 X c X 6·18	Neg X 0·24 2 aux 1·00 Other 0·06	'cop 5·59

STAGE 5 (3 – 3.6)

	how 0·12	and 15·59	Coord. 1 10·88 1+ 2·29	Postmod. 1 1·47 1+ clause	-est 0·06
		tag	Subord. 1 4·82 1+ 0·12		-er 0·24
	what	c 1·29	Clause: S	Postmod. 1+ phrase 0·06	
		s 5·06	Clause: C/O 4·24 Comparative		-ly 1·47
		other	Clause: A 3·06		

STAGE 6 (3.6 – 4.6)

	+			—		
	NP	VP	Clause	NP	VP	Clause
	Initiator 1·06	Complex	Passive	Pron. 0·18 Adj. Seq.	Modal 0·18	Concord 0·57
	Coord. 0·47		Complement	Det. 0·06 N irreg.	Tense 0·53 V irreg. 0·06	A Position W Order 0·12
	Other:			Other: 23·08		

STAGE 7 (4.6+)

A connectivity: 2·00	Emphatic order:	it: 1·59
Comment clause: 0·94	Other:	there: 3·29

NUMBER OF WORDS IN EACH SENTENCE*

$$\overline{X} = 7·58$$

*Here sentence means: Any utterance which is neither deviant nor ambiguous, but excluding all Stage 1 utterances.

UNANALYSED:

Deviant	Ambiguous
	1·67

Analyser's Comments:

AGE : 14-15
CELL S. N=3   HEARING LOSS : 40-60 dB
NON-VERBAL I.Q.: 90 and BELOW

ANALYSED

	Minor "Sentences": Social		Stereotypes	Problems

Major "Sentences"

	Excl.	Comm.	Quest.	Statement			

STAGE 1 (0.9 – 1.6)

	Excl.	Comm.	Quest.	'V'	'N'	Other	Problems
'V' / 'Q'	0·33	0·67	'Q' 0·33	'V' 0·33			

STAGE 2 (1.6 – 2.0)

	Conn.	Clause		Phrase		Word
VX / QX		SV 5·67 VC/O 4·33		DN 43·33 vv 4·33		Inf. 3·67
		S C/O 0·33 AX 3·33		Adj N 8·67 v part 13·00		-ing 25·00
				NN 2·00 int x 1·67		pl. 10·67
		Neg X Other		Pr N 4·00 other		fut.

STAGE 3 (2.0 – 2.6)

	VXY / QXY	X+S:NP 1·67	X+V:VP 5·33	X+C/O:NP 2·00	X+A:AP 2·67	-ed 10·67
let XY / VS / doXY		SVC/O 28·67 VC/OA 2·67		D Adj N 4·67 Cop 5·33 / Aux 20·67		-en 2·33
		SVA 8·00 V O$_d$ O$_i$		Adj Adj N 0·33 Pron 26·67		3s 10·00
		Neg XY Other 0·33		Pr DN 11·67 Pr Pron 1·33 / N Adj N Other 0·67		

STAGE 4 (2.6 – 3.0)

	QXYZ / +S / QVS / 0·33	XY+S:NP 16·33	XY+V:VP 17·33	XY+C/O:NP 17·67	XY+A:AP 8·00	gen 7·33
		SVC/OA 7·67 AAXY 2·00		N Pr NP Neg V 1·00		n't 0·33
		SVO$_d$O$_i$ 0·33 Other		Pr D Adj N 1·00 Neg X		'cop 3·00
				c X 0·67 2 aux		'aux 8·00
				X c X 5·00 Other		

STAGE 5 (3 – 3.6)

	how / what	tag	and 14·33 / c 0·67 / s 3·33 / other	Coord. 1 10·33 1+ 2·00	Postmod. 1 0·67 1+ clause	-est
				Subord. 1 3·33 1+		-er 0·33
				Clause: S	Postmod. 1+ phrase	-ly
				Clause: C/O 3·00 Comparative		
				Clause: A 2·00		

STAGE 6 (3.6 – 4.6)

	+			−		
	NP	VP	Clause	NP	VP	Clause
	Initiator 1·33	Complex	Passive	Pron. 0·33 Adj. Seq.	Modal	Concord 0·33
	Coord.		Complement	Det. 0·33 N irreg. 0·33	Tense / V irreg. 1·00	A Position / W Order
Other:				Other: 20·67		

STAGE 7 (4.6+)

A connectivity: 2·33	Emphatic order:	it: 2·33
Comment clause:	Other:	there: 0·67

NUMBER OF WORDS IN EACH SENTENCE*

$$\overline{X} = 8·16$$

*Here sentence means: Any utterance which is neither deviant nor ambiguous, but excluding all Stage 1 utterances.

UNANALYSED:

Deviant	Ambiguous 2·33

Analyser's Comments:

CELL T. N = 9   AGE: 14-15   HEARING LOSS: 61-80dB   NON-VERBAL I.Q: 90 and BELOW

ANALYSED

Minor "Sentences": Social **0·56**   Stereotypes **0·11**   Problems

Major "Sentences"

		Excl.	Comm.	Quest.	Statement				

STAGE 1 (0.9 – 1.6)

	'V'	'Q'	'V'	'N'	Other	Problems
Excl. 0·22	Comm. 0·78		0·33	3·22	0·11	

STAGE 2 (1.6 – 2.0)

		Conn.	Clause		Phrase		Word
VX	QX		SV 9·00	VC/O 3·56	DN 47·33	vv 5·11	Inf. 3·89
0·11			S C/O 0·67	AX 1·33	Adj N 5·00	v part 11·22	-ing 25·56
			Neg X 0·11	Other	NN 0·56	int x 1·11	pl. 10·11
					Pr N 2·78	other	fut. 0·56

STAGE 3 (2.0 – 2.6)

			Clause		Phrase		Word
VXY 0·22	QXY		X+S:NP 5·67	X+V:VP 7·67	X+C/O:NP 2·22	X+A:AP 1·00	-ed 8·89
let XY	VS		SVC/O 24·67	VC/OA 1·44	D Adj N 4·33	Cop 7·56 / Aux 20·78	-en 2·56
doXY			SVA 10·22	V O$_d$ O$_i$	Adj Adj N 0·11	Pron 19·44	3s 8·78
			Neg XY	Other 0·22	Pr DN 13·44	Pr Pron 2·22	
					N Adj N	Other 0·89	

STAGE 4 (2.6 – 3.0)

			Clause		Phrase		Word
	QXYZ		XY+S:NP 18·89	XY+V:VP 17·33	XY+C/O:NP 14·78	XY+A:AP 8·22	gen 4·33
+S	QVS		SVC/OA 6·89	AAXY 1·44	N Pr NP	Neg V 1·33	n't 0·89
	0·11		SVO$_d$O$_i$ 0·44	Other 0·89	Pr D Adj N 1·22	Neg X 0·11	'cop 2·89
					c X 0·33	2 aux 0·11	'aux 7·00
					X c X 4·44	Other 0·44	

STAGE 5 (3 – 3.6)

		Conn.	Clause	Phrase	Word
how		and 13·89	Coord. 1 8·56 1+ 2·56	Postmod. 1 11·11 1+ clause	
	tag	c 0·11	Subord. 1 3·78 1+		-est
what		s 3·78	Clause: S Clause: C/O 3·56 Comparative	Postmod. 1+ 0·11 phrase	-er 0·11
		other	Clause: A 2·56		-ly 0·33

STAGE 6 (3.6 – 4.6)

	+			–		
NP	VP	Clause	NP	VP	Clause	
Initiator 1·67	Complex	Passive	Pron. Adj. Seq.	Modal Tense 0·56	Concord 0·11	
Coord.		Complement	Det. N irreg. 0·78	V irreg.	A Position W Order	

Other: Other: 20·11

STAGE 7 (4.6+)

A connectivity: 0·89	Emphatic order:	it: 1·67
Comment clause: 0·33	Other:	there: 2·11

NUMBER OF WORDS IN EACH SENTENCE*

$$\overline{X} = 8.12.$$

*Here sentence means: Any utterance which is neither deviant nor ambiguous, but excluding all Stage 1 utterances.

ANALYSED:

eviant

Ambiguous
2·25

Analyser's Comments:

AGE: 14-15   HEARING LOSS: 81 dB and ABOVE
CELL U. N=4   NON-VERBAL I.Q: 90 and BELOW

ALYSED

	Minor "Sentences": Social		Stereotypes			Problems	

			Major	"Sentences"			

	Excl.	Comm.	Quest.			Statement	

| 0.9 – 1.6 | | 'V' | 'Q' | 'V' | 'N' | Other | Problems |
| | 0·25 | 0·75 | | 1·75 | 4·00 | 0·25 | |

| 1.6 – 2.0 | | VX
1·00 | QX | Conn. | Clause
SV **8·00**   VC/O 6·50
S C/O 0·50   AX 4·00
Neg X 0·25   Other | Phrase
DN **56·25**   vv 3·50
Adj N **3·00**   v part 18·00
NN 1·75   int x 1·50
Pr N 4·75   other 0·25 | Word
Inf. 4·75
-ing 22·5
pl. 12·50
fut. 0·25 |

| 2.0 – 2.6 | | VXY
let XY
doXY | QXY
VS | X+S:NP **5·50**   X+V:VP 8·75
SVC/O 25·5   VC/OA 1·00
SVA 10·25   V O_d O_i 0·50
Neg XY   Other 0·25 | X+C/O:NP **5·25**   X+A:AP 2·75
D Adj N **2·50**   Cop 6·25 / Aux 7·75
Adj Adj N 0·75   Pron 20·75
Pr DN 12·50   Pr Pron 0·75
N Adj N   Other 0·25 | -ed 16·75
-en 0·25
3s 2·00 |

| 2.6 – 3.0 | | +S | QXYZ
QVS | XY+S:NP **24·5**   XY+V:VP 12·25
SVC/OA 6·50   AAXY 1·00
SVO_dO_i 0·25   Other 0·50 | XY+C/O:NP **17·00**   XY+A:AP 8·75
N Pr NP   Neg V 1·50
Pr D Adj N 1·50   Neg X
c X 0·75   2 aux
X c X 4·50   Other 0·75 | gen 5·75
n't 1·25
'cop 1·25
'aux 0·25 |

| 3 – 3.6 | how
what | | tag | and 17·25
c 0·75
s 2·00
other | Coord. 1 **4·00** 1+ 5·25
Subord. 1 2·00 1+
Clause: S
Clause: C/O 3·75   Comparative
Clause: A 1·25 | Postmod. 1 2·00 1+ clause
Postmod. 1+ phrase | -est
-er 0·25
-ly 1·25 |

				+			

	NP	VP	Clause	NP	VP	Clause	
3.6 – 4.6	Initiator 0·25 Coord.	Complex	Passive Complement	Pron. Adj. Seq. Det. N irreg. 0·75	Modal 0·25 Tense 0·50 V irreg.	Concord 0·50 A Position W Order 0·25	

	Other:			Other: 15·75			

| 4.6+ | A connectivity: 0·75 | | | Emphatic order: | | it: 0·75 | |
| | Comment clause: 1·25 | | | Other: | | there: 3·75 | |

IBER OF WORDS IN EACH SENTENCE*

$$\overline{X} = 9·24.$$

sentence means: Any utterance which is neither deviant nor ambiguous, but excluding all Stage 1 utterances.

UNANALYSED:

Deviant	Ambiguous
	0·78

Analyser's Comments:

AGE: 14-15
CELL V. N=9   HEARING LOSS: 40-60 dB
NON-VERBAL I.Q: 91 - 110

ANALYSED

		Minor "Sentences": Social **0·33**			Stereotypes		Problems
				Major	"Sentences"		
	Excl.	Comm.	Quest.		Statement		

STAGE 1 (0.9 – 1.6)

	'V'	'Q'	'V'	'N'	Other	Problems
	0·22	0·22		0·44		

STAGE 2 (1.6 – 2.0)

		Conn.	Clause		Phrase		Word
	VX	QX	SV 6·78	VC/O 4·44	DN 43·78	vv 4·56	Inf. 6·22
			S C/O 0·33	AX 2·00	Adj N 4·89	v part 13·89	-ing 28·1
			Neg X	Other	NN 1·33	int x 0·56	pl. 10·78
					Pr N 2·22	other	fut. 0·67

STAGE 3 (2.0 – 2.6)

	VXY	QXY	X+S:NP 3·44	X+V:VP 6·56	X+C/O :NP 3·11	X+A:AP 1·67	-ed 9·7
	let XY	VS	SVC/O 25·78	VC/OA 1·22	D Adj N 7·33	Cop 13·56 / Aux 22·44	-en 1·78
	doXY		SVA 10·78	V O$_d$ O$_i$	Adj Adj N 0·11	Pron 19·78	3s 16·00
			Neg XY	Other	Pr DN 15·00 / N Adj N	Pr Pron 2·22 / Other 0·33	

STAGE 4 (2.6 – 3.0)

		QXYZ	XY+S:NP 16·89	XY+V:VP 19·78	XY+ C/O:NP 16·11	XY+A:AP 8·56	gen 5·22
	+S	QVS	SVC/OA 6·89	AAXY 2·00	N Pr NP 0·11 / Pr D Adj N 1·44	Neg V 1·44 / Neg X 0·33	n't 1·56
			SVO$_d$O$_i$ 0·56	Other 1·11	c X 0·89 / X c X 5·78	2 aux 0·44 / Other 0·11	'cop 6·67
							'aux 11·3

STAGE 5 (3 – 3.6)

	how		and 17·56	Coord. 1 14·11 1+ 2·11		Postmod. 1 1·00 1+ 0·11 clause	-est 0·5
		tag	c 1·22	Subord. 1 3·89 1+			-er 0·4
	what		s 3·33	Clause: S		Postmod. 1+ phrase	-ly 0·5
			other	Clause: C/O 4·00 Comparative / Clause: A 3·22			

+			−		

STAGE 6 (3.6 – 4.6)

NP	VP	Clause	NP		VP	Clause
Initiator 2·33	Complex	Passive	Pron. 0·11	Adj. Seq.	Modal	Concord
Coord. 0·11		Complement	Det. 0·33	N irreg.	Tense 0·56	A Position
					V irreg. 0·11	W Order 0·22
Other:			Other: 10·00			

STAGE 7 (4.6+)

A connectivity: 0·89	Emphatic order: 0·11	it: 3·44
Comment clause: 0·44	Other:	there: 6·00

NUMBER OF WORDS IN EACH SENTENCE*

$$\overline{X} = 8·85$$

*Here sentence means: Any utterance which is neither deviant nor ambiguous, but excluding all Stage 1 utterances.

NANALYSED:				Analyser's Comments:		
eviant		Ambiguous **1·9**		CELL W N·I O	AGE: 14-15 HEARING LOSS: 61-80 dB NON-VERBAL I.Q: 91-110	

NALYSED

Minor "Sentences": Social **0·70**	Stereotypes	Problems

Major   "Sentences"

	Excl.	Comm.	Quest.	Statement			
0.9 – 1.6		'V'	'Q'	'V'	'N'	Other	Problems
	0·40	**0·60**		**0·50**	**4·70**		

	Conn.	Clause		Phrase		Word
1.6 – 2.0 VX QX **0·10** **0·10**		SV **10·30** · VC/O **4·60** S C/O **1·20** · AX **1·70** Neg X **0·10** · Other		DN **48·3** · vv **4·5** Adj N **6·20** · v part **15·20** NN **0·50** · int x **1·70** Pr N **2·50** · other		Inf. **4·10** -ing **21·90** pl. **9·90** fut. **1·00**

| | VXY QXY let XY VS doXY | | X+S:NP **6·60** · X+V:VP **7·70** SVC/O **24·90** · VC/OA **1·90** SVA **11·10** · V O_d O_i **0·20** Neg XY **0·10** · Other **0·30** | X+C/O:NP **3·90** · X+A:AP **1·40** Cop **5·30** Aux **14·10** Adj Adj N **0·30** · Pron **23·20** Pr DN **15·90** · Pr Pron **1·70** N Adj N · Other **0·10** | D Adj N **4·00** | -ed **15·30** -en **2·50** 3s **5·90** |

| **2.6 – 3.0** | QXYZ +S QVS | XY+S:NP **18·80** · XY+V:VP **15·80** SVC/OA **6·40** · AAXY **1·90** SVO_dO_i **0·70** · Other **0·50** | XY+ C/O:NP **15·10** · XY+A:AP **8·00** N Pr NP **0·10** · Neg V **1·00** Pr D Adj N **0·90** · Neg X **0·10** c X **0·60** · 2 aux **0·80** X c X **4·50** · Other **0·20** | | | gen **3·60** n't **0·80** 'cop **1·90** 'aux **5·50** |

| **3 – 3.6** | how what | | tag | and **17·60** c **1·70** s **3·50** other | Coord. 1 **10·90** 1+ **3·50** Subord. 1 **3·50** 1+ Clause: S Clause: C/O **3·50** Comparative Clause: A **2·40** | Postmod. 1 **0·80** 1+ clause Postmod. 1+ phrase | -est -er -ly **0·50** |

	+			–		
	NP	VP	Clause	NP	VP	Clause
3.6 – 4.6	Initiator **1·60** Coord. **0·20**	Complex	Passive Complement	Pron. **0·20** Adj. Seq. Det. **0·30** N irreg. **0·50**	Modal Tense **0·30** V irreg. **0·20**	Concord **0·20** A Position W Order **0·20**
	Other:			Other: **23·9**		

4.6+	A connectivity: **3·10**	Emphatic order:	it: **1·60**
	Comment clause: **0·80**	Other:	there: **1·80**

MBER OF WORDS IN EACH SENTENCE*

$$\overline{X} = 8·44$$

re sentence means: Any utterance which is neither deviant nor ambiguous, but excluding all Stage 1 utterances.

UNANALYSED:

Deviant	Ambiguous
	0·50

Analyser's Comments:

CELL ✗ N°6. AGE: 14-15 HEARING LOSS: 81 dB and ABOVE NON-VERBAL I.Q: 91-110

ANALYSED

	Minor "Sentences": Social 0·17		Stereotypes		Problems

| | Major "Sentences" | | | | |

	Excl.	Comm.	Quest.	Statement			
STAGE 1 0.9 – 1.6	'V' 0·17	'V' 0·50	'Q'	'V'	'N' 2·00	Other 0·17	Problems

				Conn.	Clause		Phrase		Word
STAGE 2 1.6 – 2.0		VX 0·17	QX		SV 9·83 S C/O 0·50 Neg X 0·17	VC/O 2·67 AX 1·67 Other	DN 51·17 Adj N 4·17 NN 0·83 Pr N 2·83	vv 5·67 v part 12·67 int x 1·00 other	Inf. 12·33 -ing 19·17 pl. 11·00 fut. 1·83
STAGE 3 2.0 – 2.6		VXY let XY doXY	QXY VS		X+S:NP 5·50 SVC/O 26·67 SVA 10·67 Neg XY	X+V:VP 8·83 VC/OA 1·33 V O$_d$ O$_i$ Other	X+C/O:NP 2·00 D Adj N 6·67 Adj Adj N 0·33 Pr DN 15·17 N Adj N 0·17	X+A:AP 1·17 Cop 5·00 Aux 20·00 Pron 22·33 Pr Pron 0·83 Other	-ed 21·83 -en 1·00 3s 6·00
STAGE 4 2.6 – 3.0		+S	QXYZ QVS		XY+S:NP 21·67 SVC/OA 8·50 SVO$_d$O$_i$ 0·50	XY+V:VP 20·33 AAXY 1·83 Other 0·33	XY+C/O:NP 19·00 N Pr NP 0·17 Pr D Adj N 1·83 c X 1·00 X c X 5·67	XY+A:AP 9·50 Neg V 0·50 Neg X 2 aux 0·33 Other 0·67	gen 5·17 n't 0·33 'cop 2·17 'aux 5·17
STAGE 5 3 – 3.6	how what		tag	and 19·17 c 0·83 s 2·17 other	Coord. 1 14·67 1+ 2·67 Subord. 1 2·17 1+ Clause: S Clause: C/O 3·00 Comparative Clause: A 2·17		Postmod. 1 1·00 1+ clause Postmod. 1+ phrase		-est -er -ly 0·17

		+			–		
	NP	VP	Clause	NP	VP	Clause
STAGE 6 3.6 – 4.6	Initiator 0·83 Coord.	Complex	Passive Complement 0·17	Pron. 0·50 Det. 0·33 Adj. Seq. N irreg.	Modal Tense 0·83 V irreg. 0·33	Concord 0·33 A Position W Order 0·33
	Other:			Other: 17·67		

STAGE 7 4.6+	A connectivity: 2·00 Comment clause:		Emphatic order: Other:		it: 1·00 there: 1·83

NUMBER OF WORDS IN EACH SENTENCE*

$$\overline{X} = 8·44$$

*Here sentence means: Any utterance which is neither deviant nor ambiguous, but excluding all Stage 1 utterances.

UNANALYSED:		Analyser's Comments:
Deviant	Ambiguous	AGE: 14-15
		CELL Y. N=2 HEARING LOSS: 40-60 dB
		NON-VERBAL I.Q: 111 and ABOVE

ANALYSED

	Minor "Sentences": Social		Stereotypes		Problems	

Major   "Sentences"

	Excl.	Comm.	Quest.		Statement		
0.9 – 1.6		'V'	'Q'	'V'	'N' **6·00**	Other	Problems

			Conn.	Clause		Phrase		Word
1.6 – 2.0		VX	QX		SV **5·00** VC/O **4·00**	DN **45·50** vv **5·00**		Inf. **4·50** -ing **32·50**
					S C/O **0·50** AX **3·00**	Adj N **3·50** v part **17·0**		pl. **10·00**
					Neg X Other	NN **0·50** int x **0·50**		
						Pr N **2·00** other		fut. **0·50**

		VXY	QXY		X+S:NP **2·50** X+V:VP **6·00**	X+C/O :NP **1·50** X+A:AP **1·00**	-ed **9·50**
2.0 – 2.6		let XY	VS	SVC/O **26·00** VC/O A	D Adj N **7·00** Cop **6·50**	-en **2·50**
		doXY		SVA **11·00** V O_d O_i	Aux **25·00**	3s **19·00**
				Neg XY Other **0·50**	Adj Adj N **0·50** Pron **9·00**	
					Pr DN **12·00** Pr Pron **4·50**	gen **3·50**
					N Adj N Other	

			QXYZ	XY+S:NP **23·50** XY+V:VP **24·00**	XY+C/O:NP **15·00** XY+A:AP **7·00**	n't **1·50**
2.6 – 3.0		+S	QVS	SVC/OA **5·50** AAXY **2·00**	N Pr NP Neg V **1·50**	'cop **4·50**
				SVO_d O_i **0·50** Other **1·00**	Pr D Adj N **1·00** Neg X	'aux **12·50**
					c X **1·00** 2 aux **1·50**	
					X c X **2·50** Other	

	how		and **10·00**	Coord. 1 **13·00** 1+	Postmod. 1 **1·00** 1+ clause	-est
3 – 3.6		tag		Subord. 1 **5·00** 1+		-er
	what		c **3·00**	Clause: S	Postmod. 1+ phrase	-ly **2·50**
			s **5·00**	Clause: C/O **4·50** Comparative		
			other	Clause: A **5·00**		

	+			—		
	NP	VP	Clause	NP	VP	Clause
3.6 – 4.6	Initiator **2·00**	Complex	Passive	Pron. Adj. Seq.	Modal Tense **1·00**	Concord **1·50** A Position
	Coord.		Complement	Det. N irreg. **0·50**	V irreg.	W Order
	Other:			Other: **5·00**		

4.6+ / 7	A connectivity: **2·50**	Emphatic order:	it: **1·00**
	Comment clause: **0·50**	Other:	there: **4·50**

NUMBER OF WORDS IN EACH SENTENCE*

$$\overline{X} = 9\cdot13$$

*re sentence means: Any utterance which is neither deviant nor ambiguous, but excluding all Stage 1 utterances.

UNANALYSED:

Deviant	Ambiguous 0·73

Analyser's Comments:

CELL 2 N=11   AGE: 14-15   HEARING LOSS: 61-80 dB   NON-VERBAL I.Q: 111 and ABOVE

ANALYSED

	Minor "Sentences": Social 0·27		Stereotypes		Problems	

Major "Sentences"

	Excl.	Comm.	Quest.	Statement			

STAGE 1 (0.9 – 1.6)

'V' 0·09	'Q'	'V' 0·64	'N' 2·09	Other	Problems

Comm.: 0·27

STAGE 2 (1.6 – 2.0)

	Conn.	Clause	Phrase	Word
VX QX	0·09	SV 7·09 VC/O 3·45	DN 41·55 vv 5·09	Inf. 5·91 -ing 21·18
		S C/O 0·27 AX 2·27	Adj N 4·73 v part 12·55 NN 0·09 int x 1·09 Pr N 3·18 other	pl. 10·00
		Neg X Other		fut. 0·82

STAGE 3 (2.0 – 2.6)

VXY QXY 0·09	Conn.	X+S:NP 4·64 X+V:VP 7·09	X+C/O:NP 1·55 X+A:AP 1·45	-ed 7·36
let XY VS doXY		SVC/O 21·91 VC/OA 1·18 SVA 9·27 V O_d O_i Neg XY 0·09 Other 0·64	D Adj N 5·45 Cop 8·55 Aux 20·64 Adj Adj N 0·64 Pron 21·91 Pr DN 24·27 Pr Pron 2·18 N Adj N Other 0·27	-en 2·27 3s 9·45

STAGE 4 (2.6 – 3.0)

QXYZ		XY+S:NP 15·27 XY+V:VP 14·73	XY+C/O:NP 13·00 XY+A:AP 7·64	gen 4·91
+S QVS 0·09		SVC/OA 9·27 AAXY 2·27 SVO_dO_i 0·78 Other 0·36	N Pr NP 0·36 Neg V 1·85 Pr D Adj N 1·82 Neg X 0·55 c X 0·09 2 aux 1·27 X c X 3·82 Other 0·27	n't 1·55 'cop 4·64 'aux 7·82

STAGE 5 (3 – 3.6)

how what	tag	and 10·45 c 2·82 s 4·73 other	Coord. 1 9·00 1+ 1·64 Subord. 1 4·73 1+ Clause: S Clause: C/O 3·36 Comparative Clause: A 3·36 0·09	Postmod. 1 1·91 1+ clause Postmod. 1+ phrase 0·18	-est 1·00 -er 0·55 -ly 1·27

STAGE 6 (3.6 – 4.6)

+			−		
NP	VP	Clause	NP	VP	Clause
Initiator 1·55	Complex	Passive 0·18	Pron. Adj. Seq.	Modal Tense 0·18 V irreg.	Concord 0·27 A Position W Order 0·27
Coord. 0·27		Complement 0·09	Det. N irreg. 0·18		

Other: Other:

STAGE 7 (4.6+)

A connectivity: 1·55	Emphatic order:	it: 1·73
Comment clause: 0·27	Other:	there: 4·09

NUMBER OF WORDS IN EACH SENTENCE*

$$\overline{X} = 8.53$$

*Here sentence means: Any utterance which is neither deviant nor ambiguous, but excluding all Stage 1 utterances.

ANALYSED:

eviant	Ambiguous 0·36

Analyser's Comments:

AGE: 14·15
CELL A. N°11. HEARING LOSS: 81 dB and ABOVE
NON-VERBAL I.Q.: 111 and ABOVE

ALYSED

	Minor "Sentences": Social **1·82**		Stereotypes **0·09**		Problems	

				Major	"Sentences"		

	Excl.	Comm.	Quest.		Statement		
0·9 – 1·6		'V'	'Q'	'V'	'N'	Other	Problems
	0·18	**0·09**		**0·27**	**2·55**	**0·09**	

			Conn.	Clause		Phrase		Word
1·6 – 2·0		VX	QX	SV **6·45** / VC/O **4·73** / S C/O / AX **2·55** / Neg X **0·18** Other		DN **48·00** vv **4·09** / Adj N **3·91** v part **13·00** / NN **0·55** int x **1·64** / Pr N **2·91** other **0·45**		Inf. **5·73** / -ing **22·36** / pl. **10·45** / fut. **1·36**
2·0 – 2·6		VXY / let XY / doXY	QXY / VS	X+S:NP **3·64** / X+V:VP **7·55** / SVC/O **26·91** VC/OA **1·73** / SVA **8·64** V O_d O_i **0·36** / Neg XY Other **0·27**	X+C/O:NP **2·64** / X+A:AP **1·55**	D Adj N **7·64** Cop **7·27** / Adj Adj N **0·64** Aux **21·36** / Pr DN **17·73** Pron **24·73** / N Adj N Other **0·64**		-ed **19·00** / -en **1·73** / 3s **9·18**
2·6 – 3·0		+S	QXYZ / QVS	XY+S:NP **17·73** / XY+V:VP **19·09** / SVC/OA **8·36** AAXY **2·27** / SVO_dO_i **0·55** Other **1·73**	XY+C/O:NP **17·45** / XY+A:AP **7·64**	N Pr NP Neg V **2·09** / Pr D Adj N **1·64** Neg X **0·45** / c X **0·55** 2 aux **1·36** / X c X **3·64** Other **0·45**		gen **7·00** / n't **1·73** / 'cop **3·55** / 'aux **3·55**
3 – 3·6		how / what	tag	and **13·45** / c **0·82** / s **7·73** / other	Coord. 1 **11·73** 1+ **1·64** / Subord. 1 **7·55** 1+ / Clause: S **0·36** / Clause: C/O **5·36** Comparative **0·09** / Clause: A **4·91**		Postmod. 1 1+ / clause **2·55** / Postmod. 1+ / phrase **0·18**		-est **1·09** / -er **0·73** / -ly **1·64**

		+			—		
	NP	VP	Clause	NP	VP	Clause	
3·6 – 4·6	Initiator **1·64** / Coord. **0·18**	Complex **0·18**	Passive / Complement	Pron. **0·18** Adj. Seq. / Det. **0·09** N irreg. **0·27**	Modal / Tense **0·36** / V irreg. **0·09**	Concord **0·36** / A Position / W Order	
	Other:			Other:			
4·6+	A connectivity: **1·27** / Comment clause: **0·82**			Emphatic order: / Other:	it: **1·64** / there: **3·36**		

MBER OF WORDS IN EACH SENTENCE*

$$\overline{X} = 9·08$$

e sentence means: Any utterance which is neither deviant nor ambiguous, but excluding all Stage 1 utterances.

Appendix 4

List of Schools Visited

(A) = Residential schools for deaf and/or partially-hearing children.
(B) = Other special schools.
(C) = Schools for normally-hearing children with a partial-hearing unit (PHU) or tutorial unit attached.
(D) = Schools for normally-hearing children without an attached PHU or tutorial unit.

(C) Auriol Middle School, Vale Road, Stoneleigh, Ewell, Surrey.
(C) Bannister First School, Bannister Gardens, Southampton.
(C) Bedgrove School, Ingram Avenue, Bedgrove Estate, Aylesbury, Buckinghamshire.
(C) Broadmere Middle School, Devonshire Avenue, Sheerwater, Surrey.
(A) Burwood Park School, Walton-on-Thames, Surrey.
(C) Cheney School, Cheney Lane, Headington, Oxford.
(D) Cliffdale Junior School, Battenburg Avenue, Portsmouth.
(C) Coley Park Junior School, Wensley Road, Reading, Berkshire.
(C) Cove Manor Junior School, Fernhill Road, Cove, Farnborough, Hampshire.
(D) Cove Secondary School, St John's Road, Cove, Farnborough, Hampshire.
(B) Crofton Day Special School, Stubbington, Fareham, Hampshire.
(C) Emmbrook Secondary School, Emmbrook Road, Wokingham, Berkshire.
(C) Ewell County Secondary School, Ruxley Lane, West Ewell, Surrey.
(D) Fitzharrys Secondary School, Northcourt Road, Abingdon, Oxfordshire.
(D) Foundry Lane Middle School, Foundry Lane, Southampton.
(D) Foxbury School, Perth Road, Gosport, Hampshire.
(D) Gillots Comprehensive School, Gillots Lane, Henley-on-Thames, Oxfordshire.
(C) Hightown Comprehensive School, Burgoyne Road, Southampton.
(A) Larchmoor School, Gerrards Cross Road, Stoke Poges, Slough, Berkshire.
(B) Maple Ridge School, Maple Crescent, Basingstoke, Hampshire.
(A) Mary Hare Grammar School, Arlington Manor, Snelsmore Common, Newbury, Berkshire.

(D) Moor Hill Secondary School, West End Minstead Avenue, Southampton.

(B) Netley Court School, Victoria Road, Netley Abbey, Southampton.

(C) New Marston Junior School, Copse Lane, Headington, Oxford.

(C) Northway School, Maltfield Road, Oxford.

(A) Nutfield Priory Boarding Secondary School for the Deaf, Blatchingley Road, Redhill, Surrey.

(A) Ovingdean Hall School for Partially-Hearing Children, Greenways, Brighton, Sussex.

(C) Penhale Middle School, Penhale Road, Portsmouth, Hampshire.

(A) Portley House School for Deaf Children, Whyteleafe Road, Caterham, Surrey.

(A) Rayners School, Penn, High Wycombe, Buckinghamshire.

(C) Rush Common County Primary School, Hendred Way, Abingdon, Oxfordshire.

(D) Scholing Girls School, Middle Road, Southampton.

(A) Sir Winston Churchill Secondary School for the Deaf, 37 Churchfields, South Woodford, London, E.18.

(C) South Oxford Middle School, 60 St Aldates, Oxford (PHU now moved to Northway School, Oxford).

(A) St Thomas's School for Deaf Children, Darlington Road, Basingstoke, Hampshire.

(D) Swaythling Primary School, Mayfield Road, Southampton.

(C) Tanners Brook Middle School, Elmes Drive, Southampton.

(C) Terriers First School, Potteridge Lane, High Wycombe, Buckinghamshire.

(C) Terriers Middle School, Highworth Close, Potteridge Lane, High Wycombe, Buckinghamshire.

(A) Tewin Water School, Digswell, Welwyn, Hertfordshire.

(D) Theale Green School, Theale, Reading, Berkshire.

(C) Wallisdean Junior School, Wallisdean Avenue, Fareham, Hampshire.

(C) Wellsbourne Secondary School, Kingshill Road, High Wycombe, Buckinghamshire.

(D) Weston Park Middle School, Weston Lane, Southampton.

(D) Weston Park Secondary Girls School, Winchfield Close, Weston Lane Estate, Southampton.

(A) Woodford School for Deaf Children, 12–14 Churchfields, South Woodford, London, E.18.

Subject Index